# ADVANCED ENGINE PERFORMANCE DIAGNOSIS

## FIFTH EDITION

## James D. Halderman

**Prentice Hall**

Boston   Columbus   Indianapolis   New York   San Francisco   Upper Saddle River
Amsterdam   Cape Town   Dubai   London   Madrid   Milan   Munich   Paris   Montréal   Toronto
Delhi   Mexico City   São Paulo   Sydney   Hong Kong   Seoul   Singapore   Taipei   Tokyo

**Editorial Director:** Vernon Anthony
**Acquisitions Editor:** Wyatt Morris
**Editorial Assistant:** Yvette Schlarman
**Director of Marketing:** David Gesell
**Marketing Manager:** Harper Coles
**Senior Marketing Coordinator:** Alicia
  Wozniak
**Marketing Assistant:** Les Roberts
**Senior Managing Editor:** JoEllen Gohr
**Project Manager:** Jessica H. Sykes
**Senior Operations Supervisor:** Pat
  Tonneman
**Operations Specialist:** Laura Weaver

**Senior Art Director:** Diane Ernsberger
**Text and Cover Designer:** Anne DeMarinis
**Cover Art:** Shutterstock
**Media Editor:** Michelle Churma
**Lead Media Project Manager:** Karen Bretz
**Full-Service Project Management:** Kelli Jauron
**Composition:** S4Carlisle Publishing Services
**Printer/Binder:** Courier/Kendallville
**Cover Printer:** Lehigh-Phoenix Color/Hagerstown
**Text Font:** Helvetica Neue

10 9 8 7 6 5 4 3 2 1

**Prentice Hall**
is an imprint of

www.pearsonhighered.com

ISBN 10:    0-13-254009-6
ISBN 13: 978-0-13-254009-4

# PREFACE

## PROFESSIONAL TECHNICIAN SERIES
Part of Pearson Automotive's Professional Technician Series, the fifth edition of *Advanced Engine Performance Diagnosis* represents the future of automotive textbooks. The series is a full-color, media-integrated solution for today's students and instructors. The series includes textbooks that cover all 8 areas of ASE certification, plus additional titles covering common courses.

Current revisions are written by a team of very experienced writers and teachers. The series is also peer reviewed for technical accuracy.

## UPDATES TO THE FIFTH EDITION

- All content is correlated to the latest NATEF tasks.
- A dramatic, new full-color design enhances the subject material.
- Three new chapters including:
  **Wide Band Oxygen Sensors** (Chapter 16)
  **Gasoline Direct Injection** (Chapter 20)
  **Electronic Throttle Control Systems** (Chapter 21)
- Over 80 new color photos and line drawings have been added to this edition.
- Content has been streamlined for easier reading and comprehension.
- This text is fully integrated with MyAutomotiveKit, an online supplement for homework, quizzing, testing, multimedia activities, and videos.
- Unlike other textbooks, this book is written so that the theory, construction, diagnosis, and service of a particular component or system is presented in one location. There is no need to search through the entire book for other references to the same topic.

## ASE AND NATEF CORRELATED
NATEF certified programs need to demonstrate that they use course material that covers NATEF and ASE tasks. All Professional Technician textbooks have been correlated to the appropriate ASE and NATEF task lists. These correlations can be found in an appendix to each book.

## A COMPLETE INSTRUCTOR AND STUDENT SUPPLEMENTS PACKAGE
All Professional Technician textbooks are accompanied by a full set of instructor and student supplements. Please see page vi for a detailed list of supplements.

## A FOCUS ON DIAGNOSIS AND PROBLEM SOLVING
The Professional Technician Series has been developed to satisfy the need for a greater emphasis on problem diagnosis. Automotive instructors and service managers agree that students and beginning technicians need more training in diagnostic procedures and skill development. To meet this need and demonstrate how real-world problems are solved, "Real World Fix" features are included throughout and highlight how real-life problems are diagnosed and repaired.

The following pages highlight the unique core features that set the Professional Technician Series book apart from other automotive textbooks.

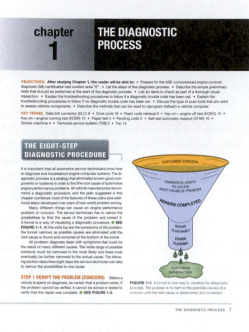

**chapter 1** — THE DIAGNOSTIC PROCESS

THE EIGHT-STEP DIAGNOSTIC PROCEDURE

FIGURE 1–1 A funnel is one way to visualize the diagnostic process. The purpose is to narrow the possible causes of a concern until the root cause is determined and corrected.

THE DIAGNOSTIC PROCESS 1

## OBJECTIVES AND KEY TERMS
appear at the beginning of each chapter to help students and instructors focus on the most important material in each chapter. The chapter objectives are based on specific ASE and NATEF tasks.

## SAFETY TIP

### Never Disconnect a Spark Plug Wire When the Engine Is Running!

Ignition systems produce a high-voltage pulse necessary to ignite a lean air-fuel mixture. If you disconnect a spark plug wire when the engine is running, this high-voltage spark could cause personal injury or damage to the ignition coil and/or ignition module.

## SAFETY TIPS
alert students to possible hazards on the job and how to avoid them.

## REAL WORLD FIX

### Negative Fuel Trim Bank #1; Positive Fuel Trim Bank #2

If one bank of a V-6 or V-8 engine has a restricted exhaust on one bank, the fuel trim numbers will be negative on the bank that is restricted and positive on the bank that is not restricted. ● SEE FIGURES 17–5 THROUGH 17–8.

## REAL WORLD FIXES
present students with actual automotive service scenarios and show how these common (and sometimes uncommon) problems were diagnosed and repaired.

## TECH TIP

### Smoke Machine Testing

Vacuum (air) leaks can cause a variety of driveability problems and are often difficult to locate. One good method is to use a machine that generates a stream of smoke. Connecting the outlet of the **smoke machine** to the hose that was removed from the vacuum brake booster allows smoke to enter the intake manifold. Any vacuum leaks will be spotted by observing smoke coming out of the leak. ● SEE FIGURE 1–5.

## TECH TIPS
feature real-world advice and "tricks of the trade" from ASE-certified master technicians.

## FREQUENTLY ASKED QUESTION

### What Is a BUS?

A **BUS** is a term used to describe a communications network. Therefore, there are *connections to the BUS* and *BUS communications*, both of which refer to digital messages being transmitted among electronic modules or computers.

## FREQUENTLY ASKED QUESTIONS
are based on the author's own experience and provide answers to many of the most common questions asked by students and beginning service technicians.

**NOTE: Gasoline in the oil will cause the engine to run rich by drawing fuel through the positive crankcase ventilation (PCV) system.**

**NOTES** provide students with additional technical information to give them a greater understanding of a task or procedure.

**CAUTION: By disconnecting the battery, the radio presets and clock information will be lost. They should be reset before returning the vehicle to the customer. If the radio has a security code, the code must be entered before the radio will function. Before disconnecting the battery, always check with the vehicle owner to be sure that the code is available.**

**CAUTIONS** alert students about potential to the vehicle that can occur during a specific task or service procedure.

**WARNING**

The spark from an ignition coil is strong enough to cause physical injury. Always follow the exact service procedure and avoid placing hands near the secondary ignition components when the engine is running.

**WARNINGS** alert students to potential dangers to themselves during a specific task or service procedure.

**THE SUMMARY, REVIEW QUESTIONS, AND CHAPTER QUIZ** at the end of each chapter help students review the material presented in the chapter and test themselves to see how much they've learned.

**STEP-BY-STEP** photo sequences show in detail the steps involved in performing a specific task or service procedure.

## SUPPLEMENTS

**INSTRUCTOR SUPPLEMENTS** The instructor supplement package has been completely revamped to reflect the needs of today's instructors. The all new **Online Instructor's Manual (ISBN: 0-13-255156-X)** is the cornerstone of the package.

To access supplementary materials online, instructors need to request an instructor access code. Go to **www.pearsonhighered.com/irc,** where you can register for an instructor access code. Within 48 hours after registering, you will receive a confirming e-mail, including an instructor access code. Once you have received your code, go to the site and log on for full instructions on downloading the materials you wish to use.

Here you will find:

- PowerPoint presentations*
- Image Library containing every image in the book for use in class or customized PowerPoints*
- My Test*
- Chapter Quizzes
- Chapter Review Questions
- English and Spanish Glossary*

- NATEF Correlated task Sheets* (also available as a printed supplement [ISBN: 0-13-254516-0])
- NATEF/ASE Correlation Charts

* All of these are available for download from www.pearson highered.com

**STUDENT SUPPLEMENTS** NO MORE CDs!!
As a result of extensive student input, Pearson is no longer binding CDs into automotive students' textbooks. Today's student has more access to the Internet than ever, so all supplemental materials are downloadable at the following site for no additional charge:

## www.pearsoned.com/autostudent

On the site, students will find:

- PowerPoint presentations
- Chapter review questions and quizzes
- English and Spanish Glossary
- A full Spanish translation of the text

# ACKNOWLEDGMENTS

The author wishes to express sincere thanks to the following individuals for their special contributions:

ASE
Bill Fulton, Ohio Automotive Technology
Dan Marinucci, Communique'
Dave Scaler, Mechanic's Education Association
Dr. Norman Nall
Jim Linder, Linder Technical Services, Inc.
John Thornton, Autotrain
Mark Warren
Randy Dillman
Rick Escalambre, Skyline College
Jim Morton, Automotive Training center (ATC)
Scot Manna

## TECHNICAL AND CONTENT REVIEWERS

The following people reviewed the manuscript before production and checked it for technical accuracy and clarity of presentation. Their suggestions and recommendations were included in the final draft of the manuscript. Their input helped make this textbook clear and technically accurate while maintaining the easy-to-read style that has made other books from the same author so popular.

**Jim Anderson**
Greenville High School

**Victor Bridges**
Umpqua Community College

**Matt Dixon**
Southern Illinois University

**Dr. Roger Donovan**
Illinois Central College

**A. C. Durdin**
Moraine Park Technical College

**Herbert Ellinger**
Western Michigan University

**Al Engledahl**
College of Dupage

**Larry Hagelberger**
Upper Valley Joint Vocational School

**Oldrick Hajzler**
Red River College

**Betsy Hoffman**
Vermont Technical College

**Steven T. Lee**
Lincoln Technical Institute

**Richard Krieger**
Michigan Institute of Technology

**Carlton H. Mabe, Sr.**
Virginia Western Community College

**Roy Marks**
Owens Community College

**Tony Martin**
University of Alaska Southeast

**Kerry Meier**
San Juan College

**Fritz Peacock**
Indiana Vocational Technical College

**Dennis Peter**
NAIT (Canada)

**Jeff Rehkopf**
Florida State College

**Kenneth Redick**
Hudson Valley Community College

**Omar Trinidad**
Southern Illinois University

**Mitchell Walker**
St. Louis Community College at Forest Park

**Jennifer Wise**
Sinclair Community College

Special thanks to instructional designer **Alexis I. Skriloff James.**

## PHOTO SEQUENCES

The author wishes to thank Blaine Heeter, Mike Garblik, and Chuck Taylor of Sinclair Community College in Dayton, Ohio, and James (Mike) Watson who helped with many of the photos. A special thanks to Dick Krieger for his detailed and thorough reviews of the manuscript before publication.

Most of all, I wish to thank Michelle Halderman for her assistance in all phases of manuscript preparation.

—James D. Halderman

**JIM HALDERMAN** brings a world of experience, knowledge, and talent to his work. His automotive service experience includes working as a flat-rate technician, a business owner, and a professor of automotive technology at a leading U.S. community college for more than 20 years.

He has a Bachelor of Science Degree from Ohio Northern University and a Masters Degree in Education from Miami University in Oxford, Ohio. Jim also holds a U.S. Patent for an electronic transmission control device. He is an ASE certified Master Automotive Technician and Advanced Engine Performance (L1) ASE certified.

Jim is the author of many automotive textbooks all published by Prentice Hall.

Jim has presented numerous technical seminars to national audiences including the California Automotive Teachers (CAT) and the Illinois College Automotive Instructor Association (ICAIA). He is also a member and presenter at the North American Council of Automotive Teachers (NACAT). Jim was also named Regional Teacher of the Year by General Motors Corporation and an outstanding alumnus of Ohio Northern University.

Jim and his wife, Michelle, live in Dayton, Ohio. They have two children. You can reach Jim at

jim@jameshalderman.com

# BRIEF CONTENTS

# CONTENTS

## chapter 26

## IN-VEHICLE ENGINE SERVICE  362

## chapter 27

## SYMPTOM-BASED DIAGNOSIS  372

# THE DIAGNOSTIC PROCESS

**OBJECTIVES:** **After studying Chapter 1, the reader will be able to:** • Prepare for the ASE computerized engine controls diagnosis (A8) certification test content area "E". • List the steps of the diagnostic process. • Describe the simple preliminary tests that should be performed at the start of the diagnostic process. • List six items to check as part of a thorough visual inspection. • Explain the troubleshooting procedures to follow if a diagnostic trouble code has been set. • Explain the troubleshooting procedures to follow if no diagnostic trouble code has been set. • Discuss the type of scan tools that are used to assess vehicle components. • Describe the methods that can be used to reprogram (reflash) a vehicle computer.

**KEY TERMS:** Data link connector (DLC) 6 • Drive cycle 18 • Flash code retrieval 9 • Key-on—engine off test (KOEO) 10 • Key-on—engine running test (KOER) 10 • Paper test 4 • Pending code 5 • Self-test automatic readout (STAR) 10 • Smoke machine 4 • Technical service bulletin (TSB) 5 • Trip 14

## THE EIGHT-STEP DIAGNOSTIC PROCEDURE

It is important that all automotive service technicians know how to diagnose and troubleshoot engine computer systems. The diagnostic process is a strategy that eliminates known-good components or systems in order to find the root cause of automotive engine performance problems. All vehicle manufacturers recommend a diagnostic procedure, and the plan suggested in this chapter combines most of the features of these plans plus additional steps developed over years of real-world problem solving.

Many different things can cause an engine performance problem or concern. The service technician has to narrow the possibilities to find the cause of the problem and correct it. A funnel is a way of visualizing a diagnostic procedure. ● **SEE FIGURE 1–1.** At the wide top are the symptoms of the problem; the funnel narrows as possible causes are eliminated until the root cause is found and corrected at the bottom of the funnel.

All problem diagnosis deals with symptoms that could be the result of many different causes. The wide range of possible solutions must be narrowed to the most likely and these must eventually be further narrowed to the actual cause. The following section describes eight steps the service technician can take to narrow the possibilities to one cause.

**STEP 1 VERIFY THE PROBLEM (CONCERN)** Before a minute is spent on diagnosis, be certain that a problem exists. If the problem cannot be verified, it cannot be solved or tested to verify that the repair was complete. ● **SEE FIGURE 1–2.**

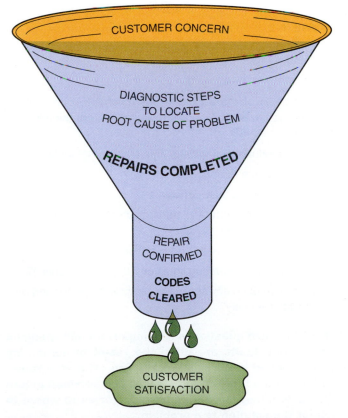

**FIGURE 1–1** A funnel is one way to visualize the diagnostic process. The purpose is to narrow the possible causes of a concern until the root cause is determined and corrected.

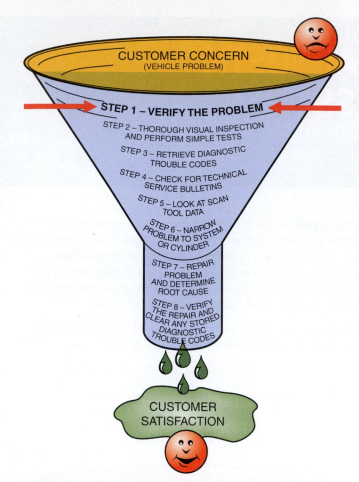

CUSTOMER CONCERN
(VEHICLE PROBLEM)

STEP 1 – VERIFY THE PROBLEM

STEP 2 – THOROUGH VISUAL INSPECTION AND PERFORM SIMPLE TESTS

STEP 3 – RETRIEVE DIAGNOSTIC TROUBLE CODES

STEP 4 – CHECK FOR TECHNICAL SERVICE BULLETINS

STEP 5 – LOOK AT SCAN TOOL DATA

STEP 6 – NARROW PROBLEM TO SYSTEM OR CYLINDER

STEP 7 – REPAIR PROBLEM AND DETERMINE ROOT CAUSE

STEP 8 – VERIFY THE REPAIR AND CLEAR ANY STORED DIAGNOSTIC TROUBLE CODES

CUSTOMER SATISFACTION

**FIGURE 1–2** Step #1 is to verify the customer concern or problem. If the problem cannot be verified, then the repair cannot be verified.

The driver of the vehicle knows much about the vehicle and how it is driven. *Before* diagnosis, always ask the following questions:

- Is the malfunction indicator light (check engine) on?
- What was the temperature outside?
- Was the engine warm or cold?
- Was the problem during starting, acceleration, cruise, or some other condition?
- How far had the vehicle been driven?
- Were any dash warning lights on? If so, which one(s)?
- Has there been any service or repair work performed on the vehicle lately?

**NOTE: This last question is very important. Many engine performance faults are often the result of something being knocked loose or a hose falling off during repair work. Knowing that the vehicle was just serviced before the problem began may be an indicator as to where to look for the solution to a problem.**

After the nature and scope of the problem are determined, the complaint should be verified before further diagnostic tests

**"Original Equipment" Is Not a Four-Letter Word**

To many service technicians, an original-equipment part is considered to be only marginal and to get the really "good stuff" an aftermarket (renewal market) part has to be purchased. However, many problems can be traced to the use of an aftermarket part that has failed early in its service life. Technicians who work at dealerships usually begin their diagnosis with an aftermarket part identified during a visual inspection. It has been their experience that simply replacing the aftermarket part with the factory original-equipment (OE) part often solves the problem.

Original equipment parts are *required* to pass quality and durability standards and tests at a level not required of aftermarket parts. The technician should be aware that the presence of a new part does not necessarily mean that the part is good.

are performed. A sample form that customers could fill out with details of the problem is shown in ● **FIGURE 1–3.**

**NOTE: Because drivers differ, it is sometimes the best policy to take the customer on the test drive to verify the concern.**

## STEP 2 PERFORM A THOROUGH VISUAL INSPECTION AND BASIC TESTS
The visual inspection is the most important aspect of diagnosis! Most experts agree that between 10% and 30% of all engine performance problems can be found simply by performing a *thorough* visual inspection. The inspection should include the following:

- **Check for obvious problems (basics, basics, basics).**
  Fuel leaks
  Vacuum hoses that are disconnected or split
  Corroded connectors
  Unusual noises, smoke, or smell
  Check the air cleaner and air duct (squirrels and other small animals can build nests or store dog food in them). ● **SEE FIGURE 1–4.**

- **Check everything that does and does not work.** This step involves turning things on and observing that everything is working properly.

- **Look for evidence of previous repairs.** Any time work is performed on a vehicle, there is always a risk that something will be disturbed, knocked off, or left disconnected.

- **Check oil level and condition.** Another area for visual inspection is oil level and condition.
  **Oil level.** Oil should be to the proper level.
  **Oil condition.** Using a match or lighter, try to light the oil on the dipstick; if the oil flames up, gasoline is present

# ENGINE PERFORMANCE DIAGNOSIS WORKSHEET

(To Be Filled Out By the Vehicle Owner)

Name: _____  Mileage: _____  Date: _____

Make: _____  Model: _____  Year: _____  Engine: _____

| (Please Circle All That Apply in All Categories) | |
|---|---|
| **Describe Problem:** | |
| **When Did the Problem First Occur?** | • Just Started   • Last Week   • Last Month<br>• Other _____ |
| **List Previous Repairs in the Last 6 Months:** | |
| **Starting Problems** | • Will Not Crank   • Cranks, but Will Not Start   • Starts, but Takes a Long Time |
| **Engine Quits or Stalls** | • Right after Starting   • When Put into Gear   • During Steady Speed Driving<br>• Right after Vehicle Comes to a Stop   • While Idling   • During Acceleration<br>• When Parking |
| **Poor Idling Conditions** | • Is Too Slow at All Times   • Is Too Fast   • Intermittently Too Fast or Too Slow<br>• Is Rough or Uneven   • Fluctuates Up and Down |
| **Poor Running Conditions** | • Runs Rough   • Lacks Power   • Bucks and Jerks   • Poor Fuel Economy<br>• Hesitates or Stumbles on Acceleration   • Backfires   • Misfires or Cuts Out<br>• Engine Knocks, Pings, Rattles   • Surges   • Dieseling or Run-On |
| **Auto. Transmission Problems** | • Improper Shifting (Early/Late)   • Changes Gear Incorrectly<br>• Vehicle Does Not Move when in Gear   • Jerks or Bucks |
| **Usually Occurs** | • Morning   • Afternoon   • Anytime |
| **Engine Temperature** | • Cold   • Warm   • Hot |
| **Driving Conditions During Occurrence** | • Short—Less Than 2 Miles   • 2–10 Miles   • Long—More Than 10 Miles<br>• Stop and Go   • While Turning   • While Braking   • At Gear Engagement<br>• With A/C Operating   • With Headlights On   • During Acceleration<br>• During Deceleration   • Mostly Downhill   • Mostly Uphill   • Mostly Level<br>• Mostly Curvy   • Rough Road |
| **Driving Habits** | • Mostly City Driving   • Highway   • Park Vehicle Inside   • Park Vehicle Outside<br>**Drive Per Day:** • Less Than 10 Miles   • 10–50   • More Than 50 |
| **Gasoline Used** | **Fuel Octane:** • 87   • 89   • 91   • More Than 91<br>**Brand:** _____ |
| **Temperature when Problem Occurs** | • 32–55° F   • Below Freezing (32° F)   • Above 55° F |
| **Check Engine Light/ Dash Warning Light** | • Light on Sometimes   • Light on Always   • Light Never On |
| **Smells** | • "Hot"   • Gasoline   • Oil Burning   • Electrical |
| **Noises** | • Rattle   • Knock   • Squeak   • Other |

**FIGURE 1–3** A form that the customer should fill out if there is a driveablilty concern to help the service technician more quickly find the root cause.

FIGURE 1–4 This is what was found when removing an air filter from a vehicle that had a lack-of-power concern. Obviously the nuts were deposited by squirrels or some other animal, blocking a lot of the airflow into the engine.

LEAK AT GASKET

YELLOW PLASTIC CAP

FIGURE 1–5 Using a bright light makes seeing where the smoke is coming from easier. In this case, smoke was added to the intake manifold with the inlet blocked with a yellow plastic cap and smoke was seen escaping past a gasket at the idle air control.

### TECH TIP

**Smoke Machine Testing**

Vacuum (air) leaks can cause a variety of driveability problems and are often difficult to locate. One good method is to use a machine that generates a stream of smoke. Connecting the outlet of the **smoke machine** to the hose that was removed from the vacuum brake booster allows smoke to enter the intake manifold. Any vacuum leaks will be spotted by observing smoke coming out of the leak. ● **SEE FIGURE 1–5.**

running. For the paper test, hold a piece of paper (even a dollar bill works) or a 3-by-5-inch card within 1 inch (2.5 centimeters) of the tailpipe with the engine running at idle. The paper should blow evenly away from the end of the tailpipe without "puffing" or being drawn inward toward the end of the tailpipe. If the paper is at times drawn *toward* the tailpipe, the valves in one or more cylinders could be burned. Other reasons why the paper might be drawn toward the tailpipe include the following:

1. The engine could be misfiring because of a lean condition that could occur normally when the engine is cold.

2. Pulsing of the paper toward the tailpipe could also be caused by a hole in the exhaust system. If exhaust escapes through a hole in the exhaust system, air could be drawn—in the intervals between the exhaust puffs—from the tailpipe to the hole in the exhaust, causing the paper to be drawn toward the tailpipe.

■ **Ensure adequate fuel level.** Make certain that the fuel tank is at least one-fourth to one-half full; if the fuel level is low it is possible that any water or alcohol at the bottom of the fuel tank is more concentrated and can be drawn into the fuel system.

■ **Check the battery voltage.** The voltage of the battery should be at least 12.4 volts and the charging voltage (engine running) should be 13.5 to 15.0 volts at 2,000 RPM. Low battery voltage can cause a variety of problems including reduced fuel economy and incorrect (usually too high) idle speed. Higher-than-normal battery voltage can also cause the PCM problems and could cause damage to electronic modules.

■ **Check the spark using a spark tester.** Remove one spark plug wire and attach the removed plug wire to the spark tester. Attach the grounding clip of the spark tester to a good clean engine ground, start or crank the engine,

in the engine oil. Drip some engine oil from the dipstick onto the hot exhaust manifold. If the oil bubbles or boils, coolant (water) is present in the oil. Check for grittiness by rubbing the oil between your fingers.

**NOTE: Gasoline in the oil will cause the engine to run rich by drawing fuel through the positive crankcase ventilation (PCV) system.**

■ **Check coolant level and condition.** Many mechanical engine problems are caused by overheating. The proper operation of the cooling system is critical to the life of any engine.

**NOTE: Check the coolant level in the radiator only if the radiator is cool. If the radiator is hot and the radiator cap is removed, the drop in pressure above the coolant will cause the coolant to boil immediately, which can cause severe burns because the coolant expands explosively upward and outward from the radiator opening.**

■ **Use the paper test.** A sound engine should produce even and steady exhaust flow at the tailpipe when

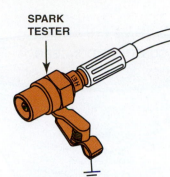

SPARK
TESTER

**FIGURE 1–6** A spark tester connected to a spark plug wire or coil output. A typical spark tester will only fire if at least 25,000 volts is available from the coil, making a spark tester a very useful tool. Do not use one that just lights when a spark is present, because they do not require more than about 2,000 volts to light.

and observe the spark tester. ● **SEE FIGURE 1–6.** The spark at the spark tester should be steady and consistent. If an intermittent spark occurs, then this condition should be treated as a no-spark condition. If this test does not show satisfactory spark, carefully inspect and test all components of the primary and secondary ignition systems.

**NOTE: Do not use a standard spark plug to check for proper ignition system voltage. An electronic ignition spark tester is designed to force the spark to jump about 0.75 inch (19 mm). This amount of gap requires between 25,000 and 30,000 volts (25 to 30 kV) at atmospheric pressure, which is enough voltage to ensure that a spark can occur under compression inside an engine.**

■ **Check the fuel-pump pressure.** Checking the fuel-pump pressure is relatively easy on many port-fuel-injected engines. Often the cause of intermittent engine performance is due to a weak electric fuel pump or clogged fuel filter. Checking fuel pump pressure early in the diagnostic process eliminates low fuel pressure as a possibility.

## STEP 3 RETRIEVE THE DIAGNOSTIC TROUBLE CODES (DTCs)
If a diagnostic trouble code (DTC) is present in the computer memory, it may be signaled by illuminating a malfunction indicator lamp (MIL), commonly labeled "check engine" or "service engine soon." ● **SEE FIGURE 1–7.** Any code(s) that is displayed on a scan tool when the MIL is *not* on is called a **pending code**. Because the MIL is not on, this indicates that the fault has not repeated to cause the PCM to turn on the MIL. Although this pending code is helpful to the technician to know that a fault has, in the past, been detected, further testing will be needed to find the root cause of the problem.

## STEP 4 CHECK FOR TECHNICAL SERVICE BULLETINS (TSBs)
Check for corrections or repair procedures in **technical service bulletins (TSBs)** that match the symptoms. ● **SEE FIGURE 1–8.** According to studies performed by automobile manufacturers, as many as 30% of vehicles can be repaired

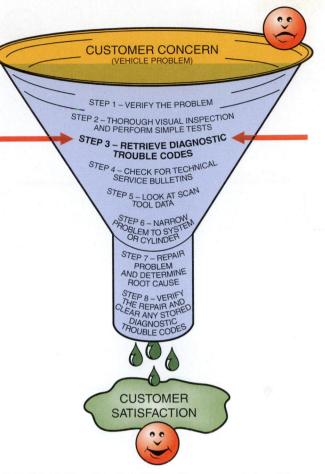

CUSTOMER CONCERN
(VEHICLE PROBLEM)

STEP 1 – VERIFY THE PROBLEM

STEP 2 – THOROUGH VISUAL INSPECTION AND PERFORM SIMPLE TESTS

STEP 3 – RETRIEVE DIAGNOSTIC TROUBLE CODES

STEP 4 – CHECK FOR TECHNICAL SERVICE BULLETINS

STEP 5 – LOOK AT SCAN TOOL DATA

STEP 6 – NARROW PROBLEM TO SYSTEM OR CYLINDER

STEP 7 – REPAIR PROBLEM AND DETERMINE ROOT CAUSE

STEP 8 – VERIFY THE REPAIR AND CLEAR ANY STORED DIAGNOSTIC TROUBLE CODES

CUSTOMER SATISFACTION

**FIGURE 1–7** Step 3 in the diagnostic process is to retrieve any stored diagnostic trouble codes.

**FIGURE 1–8** After checking for stored diagnostic trouble codes (DTCs), the wise technician checks service information for any technical service bulletins that may relate to the vehicle being serviced.

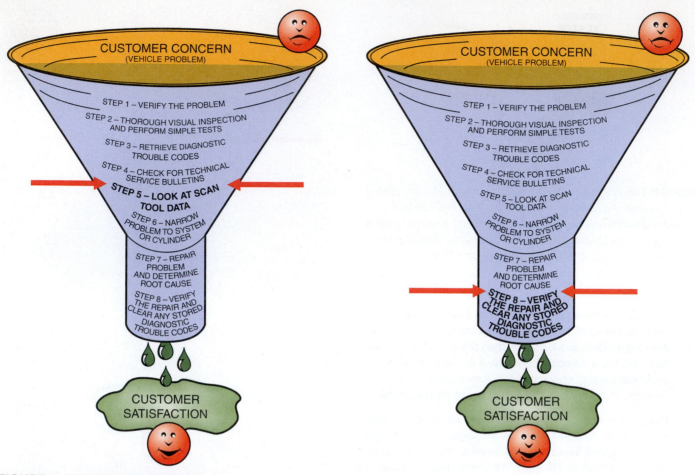

FIGURE 1–9 Looking carefully at the scan tool data is very helpful in locating the source of a problem.

FIGURE 1–10 Step 8 is very important. Be sure that the customer's concern has been corrected.

following the information, suggestions, or replacement parts found in a service bulletin. DTCs must be known before searching for service bulletins, because bulletins often include information on solving problems that involve a stored diagnostic trouble code.

### STEP 5 LOOK CAREFULLY AT SCAN TOOL DATA

Vehicle manufacturers have been giving the technician more and more data on a scan tool connected to the **data link connector (DLC).** ● SEE FIGURE 1–9. Beginning technicians are often observed scrolling through scan data without a real clue about what they are looking for. When asked, they usually reply that they are looking for something unusual, as if the screen will flash a big message "LOOK HERE—THIS IS NOT CORRECT." That statement does not appear on scan tool displays. The best way to look at scan data is in a definite sequence and with specific, selected bits of data that can tell the most about the operation of the engine, such as the following:

- Engine coolant temperature (ECT) is the same as intake air temperature (IAT) after the vehicle sits for several hours.
- Idle air control (IAC) valve is being commanded to an acceptable range.
- Oxygen sensor ($O_2S$) is operating properly:
  1. Readings below 200 mV at times
  2. Readings above 800 mV at times
  3. Rapid transitions between rich and lean

### STEP 6 NARROW THE PROBLEM TO A SYSTEM OR CYLINDER
Narrowing the focus to a system or individual cylinder is the hardest part of the entire diagnostic process.

- Perform a cylinder power balance test.
- If a weak cylinder is detected, perform a compression and a cylinder leakage test to determine the probable cause.

### STEP 7 REPAIR THE PROBLEM AND DETERMINE THE ROOT CAUSE
The repair or part replacement must be performed following vehicle manufacturer's recommendations and be certain that the root cause of the problem has been found. Also follow the manufacturer's recommended repair procedures and methods.

### STEP 8 VERIFY THE REPAIR AND CLEAR ANY STORED DTCS
● SEE FIGURE 1–10.

- Test drive to verify that the original problem (concern) is fixed.
- Verify that no additional problems have occurred during the repair process.
- Check for and then clear all diagnostic trouble codes. (This step ensures that the computer will not make any changes based on a stored DTC, but should not be performed if the

**TECH TIP**

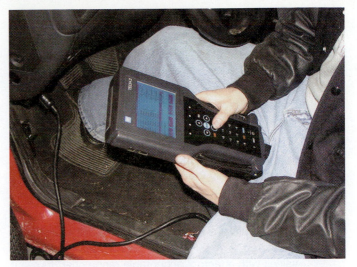

**FIGURE 1–11** A TECH 2 scan tool is the factory scan tool used on General Motors vehicles.

vehicle is going to be tested for emissions because all of the monitors will need to be run and pass.)

- Return the vehicle to the customer and double-check the following:

1. The vehicle is clean.
2. The radio is turned off.
3. The clock is set to the right time and the radio stations have been restored if the battery was disconnected during the repair procedure.

## SCAN TOOLS

Scan tools are the workhorse for any diagnostic work on all vehicles. Scan tools can be divided into two basic groups:

1. **Factory scan tools.** These are the scan tools required by all dealers that sell and service the brand of vehicle. Examples of factory scan tools include:

    - **General Motors**—Tech 2. ● **SEE FIGURE 1–11.**
    - **Ford**—New Generation Star (NGS) and IDS (Integrated Diagnostic Software).
    - **Chrysler**—DRB-III or Star Scan (CAN-equipped vehicles)
    - **Honda**—HDS or Master Tech
    - **Toyota**—Master Tech

All factory scan tools are designed to provide bidirectional capability which allows the service technician the opportunity to operate components using the scan tool thereby confirming that the component is able to work when commanded. Also all factory scan tools are capable of displaying all factory parameters.

2. **Aftermarket scan tools.** These scan tools are designed to function on more than one brand of vehicle. Examples of aftermarket scan tools include:

    - **Snap-on** (various models including the MT2500 and Modis)

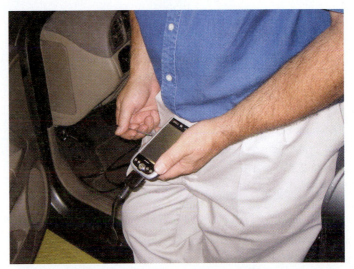

**FIGURE 1–12** Some scan tools use pocket PCs which make it very convenient to use.

- **OTC** (various models including Pegasus, Genisys and Task Master)
- **AutoEnginuity** and other programs that use a laptop or handheld computer for the display

While many aftermarket scan tools can display most if not all of the parameters of the factory scan tool, there can be a difference when trying to troubleshoot some faults. ● **SEE FIGURE 1–12.**

## RETRIEVAL OF DIAGNOSTIC INFORMATION

To retrieve diagnostic information from the Powertrain Control Module (PCM), a scan tool is needed. If a factory or factory-level scan tool is used, then all of the data can be retrieved. If a global (generic) only type scan tool is used, only the emissions-related data can be retrieved. To retrieve diagnostic information from the PCM, use the following steps:

**STEP 1**  Locate and gain access to the data link connector (DLC).

**STEP 2**  Connect the scan tool to the DLC and establish communication.

**NOTE: If no communication is established, follow the vehicle manufacturer's specified instructions.**

**STEP 3**  Follow the on-screen instructions of the scan tool to correctly identify the vehicle.

**STEP 4**  Observe the scan data, as well as any diagnostic trouble codes.

**STEP 5**  Follow vehicle manufacturer's instructions if any DTCs are stored. If no DTCs are stored, compare all sensor values with a factory acceptable range chart to see if any sensor values are out-of-range.

### Parameter Identification (PID)

| Scan Tool Parameter | Units Displayed | Typical Data Value |
|---|---|---|
| Engine Idling/Radiator Hose Hot/Closed Throttle/ Park or Neutral/Closed Loop/Accessories Off/ Brake Pedal Released | | |
| 3X Crank Sensor | RPM | Varies |
| 24X Crank Sensor | RPM | Varies |
| Actual EGR Position | Percent | 0 |
| BARO | kPa/Volts | 65–110 kPa/ 3.5–4.5 Volts |
| CMP Sensor Signal Present | Yes/No | Yes |
| Commanded Fuel Pump | On/Off | On |
| Cycles of Misfire Data | Counts | 0–99 |
| Desired EGR Position | Percent | 0 |
| ECT | °C/°F | Varies |
| EGR Duty Cycle | Percent | 0 |
| Engine Run Time | Hr: Min: Sec | Varies |
| EVAP Canister Purge | Percent | Low and Varying |
| EVAP Fault History | No Fault/ Excess Vacuum/ Purge Valve Leak/ Small Leak/ Weak Vacuum | No Fault |
| Fuel Tank Pressure | Inches of $H_2O$/ Volts | Varies |
| HO$_2$S Sensor 1 | Ready/Not Ready | Ready |
| HO$_2$S Sensor 1 | Millivolts | 0–1,000 and Varying |

| Scan Tool Parameter | Units Displayed | Typical Data Value |
|---|---|---|
| HO$_2$S Sensor 2 | Millivolts | 0–1,000 and Varying |
| HO$_2$S X Counts | Counts | Varies |
| IAC Position | Counts | 15–25 preferred |
| IAT | °C/°F | Varies |
| Knock Retard | Degrees | 0 |
| Long Term FT | Percent | 0–10 |
| MAF | Grams per second | 3–7 |
| MAF Frequency | Hz | 1,200–3,000 (depends on altitude and engine load) |
| MAP | kPa/Volts | 20–48 kPa/ 0.75–2 Volts (depends on altitude) |
| Misfire Current Cyl. 1–10 | Counts | 0 |
| Misfire History Cyl. 1–10 | Counts | 0 |
| Short Term FT | Percent | 0–10 |
| Start Up ECT | °C/°F | Varies |
| Start Up IAT | °C/°F | Varies |
| Total Misfire Current Count | Counts | 0 |
| Total Misfire Failures | Counts | 0 |
| Total Misfire Passes | Counts | 0 |
| TP Angle | Percent | 0 |
| TP Sensor | Volts | 0.20–0.74 |
| Vehicle Speed | MPH/Km/h | 0 |

**Note:** Viewing the PID screen on the scanner is useful in determining if a problem is occurring at the present time

## TROUBLESHOOTING USING DIAGNOSTIC TROUBLE CODES

Pinning down causes of the actual problem can be accomplished by trying to set the opposite code. For example, if a code indicates an open throttle position (TP) sensor (high resistance), clear the code and create a shorted (low-resistance) condition. This can be accomplished by using a jumper wire and connecting the signal terminal to the 5-volt reference terminal. This should set a diagnostic trouble code.

- **If the opposite code sets,** this indicates that the wiring and connector for the sensor is okay and the sensor itself is defective (open).

- **If the same code sets,** this indicates that the wiring or electrical connection is open (has high resistance) and is the cause of the setting of the DTC.

## METHODS FOR CLEARING DIAGNOSTIC TROUBLE CODES
Clearing diagnostic trouble codes from a vehicle computer sometimes needs to be performed. There are three methods that can be used to clear stored diagnostic trouble codes.

**CAUTION: Clearing diagnostic trouble codes (DTCs) also will clear all of the noncontinuous monitors.**

- **Clearing codes—Method 1.** The preferred method of clearing codes is by using a scan tool. This is the method recommended by most vehicle manufacturers if the procedure can be performed on the vehicle. The computer of some vehicles cannot be cleared with a scan tool.

- **Clearing codes—Method 2.** If a scan tool is not available or a scan tool cannot be used on the vehicle being serviced, the power to the computer can be disconnected.

  1. Disconnect the fusible link (if so equipped) that feeds the computer.
  2. Disconnect the fuse or fuses that feed the computer.

**NOTE: The fuse may not be labeled as a computer fuse. For example, many Toyotas can be cleared by disconnecting the fuel-injection fuse. Some vehicles require that two fuses be disconnected to clear any stored codes.**

- **Clearing codes—Method 3.** If the other two methods cannot be used, the negative battery cable can be disconnected to clear stored diagnostic trouble codes.

**NOTE: Because of the adaptive learning capacity of the computer, a vehicle may fail an exhaust emissions test if the vehicle is not driven enough to allow the computer to run all of the monitors.**

**CAUTION: By disconnecting the battery, the radio presets and clock information will be lost. They should be reset before returning the vehicle to the customer. If the radio has a security code, the code must be entered before the radio will function. Before disconnecting the battery, always check with the vehicle owner to be sure that the code is available.**

## FLASH CODE RETRIEVAL ON OBD-I GENERAL MOTORS VEHICLES

The GM system uses a "check engine" or "check engine soon" MIL to notify the driver of possible system failure. Under the dash (on most GM vehicles) is a data link connector (DLC) previously called an assembly line communications link (ALCL) or assembly line diagnostic link (ALDL).

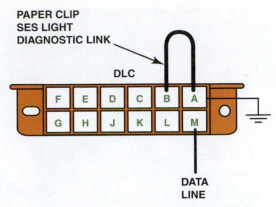

**FIGURE 1–13** To retrieve flash codes from an OBD-I General Motors vehicle, without a scan tool, connect terminals A and B with the ignition on–engine off. The M terminal is used to retrieve data from the sensors to a scan tool.

  TECH TIP

**Do Not Lie to a Scan Tool!**
Because computer calibration may vary from year to year, using the incorrect year for the vehicle while using a scan tool can cause the data retrieved to be incorrect or inaccurate.

Most General Motors diagnostic trouble codes can be retrieved by using a metal tool and contacting terminals A and B of the 12-pin DLC. ● **SEE FIGURE 1–13.** This method is called **flash code retrieval** because the MIL will flash to indicate diagnostic trouble codes. The steps are as follows:

1. Turn the ignition switch to on (engine off). The "check engine" light or "service engine soon" light should be on. If the amber malfunction indicator light (MIL) is not on, a problem exists within the light circuit.

2. Connect terminals A and B at the DLC.

3. Observe the MIL. A code 12 (one flash, then a pause, then two flashes) reveals that there is no engine speed indication to the computer. Because the engine is not running, this simply indicates that the computer diagnostic system is working correctly.

**NOTE: Refer to service manual diagnostic procedures if the MIL is on and does not flash a code 12 when terminals A and B are connected.**

4. After code 12 is displayed three times, the MIL will flash any other stored DTCs in numeric order starting with the lowest-number code. If only code 12 is displayed another three times, the computer has not detected any other faults.

**NOTE: Trouble codes can vary according to year, make, model, and engine. Always consult the service literature or service manual for the exact vehicle being serviced. Check service information for the meaning and recommended steps to follow if a diagnostic trouble code is retrieved.**

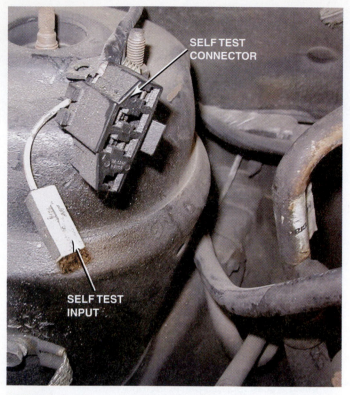

**FIGURE 1–14** A Ford OBD-I self-test connector. The location of this connector can vary with model and year of vehicle.

**Put a Wire in the Attic and a Light in the Basement!**

Retrieving DTCs from a Ford using low-cost test equipment is easier when you remember the following: *"Put a wire in the attic and a light in the basement."*

After warming the engine to operating temperature, perform these simple steps:

1. Locate the data link connector (DLC) under the hood. Connect a jumper wire from the single-wire pigtail called the self-test input to terminal #2 at the top (attic) of the connector.
2. To read DTCs, connect a standard 12-volt test light (not a self-powered continuity light) to the positive battery terminal and the lower (basement) terminal (#4) of the DLC. ● SEE FIGURE 1–15. Turn the ignition to on (engine off). The DTCs will be displayed by means of the flashes of the test light.

To clear stored Ford DTCs, simply disconnect the jumper wire from the self-test input while the codes are being flashed. This interruption is the signal to the computer to clear any stored DTCs.

# RETRIEVING FORD DIAGNOSTIC CODES

The best tool to use during troubleshooting of a Ford vehicle is a **self-test automatic readout (STAR)** tester, new generation STAR (NGS), WDS (Worldwide Diagnostic System), or another scan tool with Ford capabilities. If a STAR tester or scan tool is not available, a needle (analog) type of voltmeter can be used for all OBD-I (prior to 1996) systems. See the Tech Tip "Put a Wire in the Attic and a Light in the Basement!" to obtain flash codes. The test connector is usually located under the hood on the driver's side. ● SEE FIGURE 1–14.

### KEY ON–ENGINE OFF TEST (ON-DEMAND CODES OR HARD FAULTS)
With the ignition key on (engine off), watch the voltmeter pulses, which should appear within 5 to 30 seconds. (Ignore any initial surge of voltage when the ignition is turned on.)

The computer will send a two-digit code that will cause the voltmeter to pulse or move from left to right. For example, if the voltmeter needle pulses two times, then pauses for 2 seconds, and then pulses three times, the code is 23. There is normally a 4-second pause between codes.

**SEPARATOR PULSE.** After all the codes have been reported, the computer will pause for about 6 to 9 seconds, then cause the voltmeter needle to pulse once, and then pause for another 6 to 9 seconds. This is the normal separation between current trouble codes and continuous memory codes (for intermittent problems). Code 11 is the normal pass code, which means that no fault has been stored in memory. Therefore, normal operation of the diagnostic procedure using a voltmeter should indicate the following if no codes are set: 1 pulse (2-second pause), 1 pulse (6- to 9-second pause), 1 pulse (6- to 9-second pause), 1 pulse (2-second pause), and finally, 1 pulse. These last two pulses that are separated by a 2-second interval represent a code 11, which is the code used between current and intermittent trouble codes.

### CONTINUOUS MEMORY CODES (SOFT CODES)
Continuous memory codes are set based on information stored while the vehicle was in normal operation. These codes represent an intermittent problem and should only be used for diagnosis if the **KOEO** test results in code 11 (no faults detected). Therefore, any codes displayed after the separation pulse represent failures that have been detected but may no longer be present.

### KEY ON–ENGINE RUNNING (KOER) TEST
During the **KOER** self-test, the sensors are checked by the computer under actual operating conditions and the output devices (actuators) are operated and checked for expected results. Start the engine and raise the speed to 2500 to 3000 RPM to warm the oxygen sensor within 20 seconds of starting. Hold a steady high engine

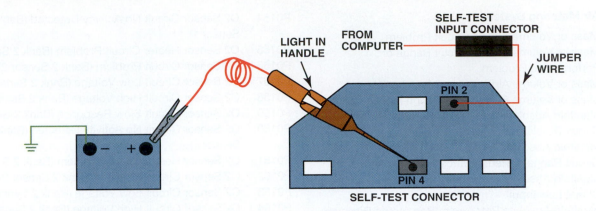

**FIGURE 1–15** To retrieve Ford DTCs using a test light and a jumper wire, turn the ignition switch on (engine off) and make the connections shown. The test light will blink out the diagnostic trouble codes.

speed until the initial pulses appear (2 pulses for a four-cylinder engine, 3 pulses for a six-cylinder, and 4 pulses for an eight-cylinder). These codes are used to verify the proper processor (computer) is in the vehicle and that the self-test has been entered. Continue to hold a high engine speed until the code pulses begin (10 to 14 seconds).

### STEERING, BRAKE, AND OVERDRIVE SWITCH TEST

To test the power steering pressure switch, the technician must turn the steering wheel one-half turn after the ID code has been displayed. The brake pedal and the overdrive cancel switch must also be cycled after the ID code to allow the system to detect a change of state of these switches.

**DYNAMIC RESPONSE CHECK.** The dynamic response test checks the throttle position (TP) mass air flow (MAF) and manifold absolute pressure (MAP) sensors during a brief wide-open throttle (WOT) test performed by the technician. The signal for the technician to depress the throttle briefly to wide open is a single pulse or a code 10 on a STAR tester.

If any hard (on-demand) faults appear, these should be repaired first and then any soft (continuous) codes next. Use the factory "pinpoint tests" to trace the problem. Refer to service information for a description of Ford-specific alpha-numeric DTCs.

## FLASH CODE RETRIEVAL ON CHRYSLER VEHICLES

To put the computer into the self-diagnostic mode, the ignition switch must be turned on and off three times within a 5-second period (on-off-on-off-on). The computer will flash a series of fault codes. Older Chrysler brand products flash the "check engine" lamp on the dash.

**FIGURE 1–16** A typical OBD-II data link connector (DLC). The location varies with make and model and may even be covered, but a tool is not needed to gain access. Check service information for the exact location if needed.

**NOTE: Unlike other manufacturers, most Chrysler brand vehicles equipped with OBD II will display the P-codes on the odometer display by cycling the ignition key as previously performed on older vehicles.**

## OBD-II DIAGNOSIS

Starting with the 1996 model year, all vehicles sold in the United States must use the same type of 16-pin data link connector (DLC) and must monitor emission-related components. ● **SEE FIGURE 1–16.**

### RETRIEVING OBD-II CODES

A scan tool is required to retrieve diagnostic trouble codes from most OBD-II vehicles. Every OBD-II scan tool will be able to read all generic Society of Automotive Engineers (SAE) DTCs from any vehicle.

## Fuel and Air Metering System

P0100 Mass or Volume Airflow Circuit Problem
P0101 Mass or Volume Airflow Circuit Range or Performance Problem
P0102 Mass or Volume Airflow Circuit Low Input
P0103 Mass or Volume Airflow Circuit High Input
P0105 Manifold Absolute Pressure or Barometric Pressure Circuit Problem
P0106 Manifold Absolute Pressure or Barometric Pressure Circuit Range or Performance Problem
P0107 Manifold Absolute Pressure or Barometric Pressure Circuit Low Input
P0108 Manifold Absolute Pressure or Barometric Pressure Circuit High Input
P0110 Intake Air Temperature Circuit Problem
P0111 Intake Air Temperature Circuit Range or Performance Problem
P0112 Intake Air Temperature Circuit Low Input
P0113 Intake Air Temperature Circuit High Input
P0115 Engine Coolant Temperature Circuit Problem
P0116 Engine Coolant Temperature Circuit Range or Performance Problem
P0117 Engine Coolant Temperature Circuit Low Input
P0118 Engine Coolant Temperature Circuit High Input
P0120 Throttle Position Circuit Problem
P0121 Throttle Position Circuit Range or Performance Problem
P0122 Throttle Position Circuit Low Input
P0123 Throttle Position Circuit High Input
P0125 Excessive Time to Enter Closed-Loop Fuel Control
P0128 Coolant Temperature Below Thermostat Regulating Temperature
P0130 O2 Sensor Circuit Problem (Bank 1* Sensor 1)
P0131 O2 Sensor Circuit Low Voltage (Bank 1* Sensor 1)
P0132 O2 Sensor Circuit High Voltage (Bank 1* Sensor 1)
P0133 O2 Sensor Circuit Slow Response (Bank 1* Sensor 1)
P0134 O2 Sensor Circuit No Activity Detected (Bank 1* Sensor 1)
P0135 O2 Sensor Heater Circuit Problem (Bank 1* Sensor 1)
P0136 O2 Sensor Circuit Problem (Bank 1* Sensor 2)
P0137 O2 Sensor Circuit Low Voltage (Bank 1* Sensor 2)
P0138 O2 Sensor Circuit High Voltage (Bank 1* Sensor 2)
P0139 O2 Sensor Circuit Slow Response (Bank 1* Sensor 2)
P0140 O2 Sensor Circuit No Activity Detected (Bank 1* Sensor 2)
P0141 O2 Sensor Heater Circuit Problem (Bank 1* Sensor 2)
P0142 O2 Sensor Circuit Problem (Bank 1* Sensor 3)
P0143 O2 Sensor Circuit Low Voltage (Bank 1* Sensor 3)
P0144 O2 Sensor Circuit High Voltage (Bank 1* Sensor 3)
P0145 O2 Sensor Circuit Slow Response (Bank 1* Sensor 3)
P0146 O2 Sensor Circuit No Activity Detected (Bank 1* Sensor 3)
P0147 O2 Sensor Heater Circuit Problem (Bank 1* Sensor 3)
P0150 O2 Sensor Circuit Problem (Bank 2 Sensor 1)
P0151 O2 Sensor Circuit Low Voltage (Bank 2 Sensor 1)
P0152 O2 Sensor Circuit High Voltage (Bank 2 Sensor 1)
P0153 O2 Sensor Circuit Slow Response (Bank 2 Sensor 1)
P0154 O2 Sensor Circuit No Activity Detected (Bank 2 Sensor 1)
P0155 O2 Sensor Heater Circuit Problem (Bank 2 Sensor 1)
P0156 O2 Sensor Circuit Problem (Bank 2 Sensor 2)
P0157 O2 Sensor Circuit Low Voltage (Bank 2 Sensor 2)
P0158 O2 Sensor Circuit High Voltage (Bank 2 Sensor 2)
P0159 O2 Sensor Circuit Slow Response (Bank 2 Sensor 2)
P0160 O2 Sensor Circuit No Activity Detected (Bank 2 Sensor 2)
P0161 O2 Sensor Heater Circuit Problem (Bank 2 Sensor 2)
P0162 O2 Sensor Circuit Problem (Bank 2 Sensor 3)
P0163 O2 Sensor Circuit Low Voltage (Bank 2 Sensor 3)
P0164 O2 Sensor Circuit High Voltage (Bank 2 Sensor 3)
P0165 O2 Sensor Circuit Slow Response (Bank 2 Sensor 3)
P0166 O2 Sensor Circuit No Activity Detected (Bank 2 Sensor 3)
P0167 O2 Sensor Heater Circuit Problem (Bank 2 Sensor 3)
P0170 Fuel Trim Problem (Bank 1*)
P0171 System Too Lean (Bank 1*)
P0172 System Too Rich (Bank 1*)
P0173 Fuel Trim Problem (Bank 2)
P0174 System Too Lean (Bank 2)
P0175 System Too Rich (Bank 2)
P0176 Fuel Composition Sensor Circuit Problem
P0177 Fuel Composition Sensor Circuit Range or Performance
P0178 Fuel Composition Sensor Circuit Low Input
P0179 Fuel Composition Sensor Circuit High Input
P0180 Fuel Temperature Sensor Problem
P0181 Fuel Temperature Sensor Circuit Range or Performance
P0182 Fuel Temperature Sensor Circuit Low Input
P0183 Fuel Temperature Sensor Circuit High Input

## Fuel and Air Metering (Injector Circuit)

P0201 Injector Circuit Problem—Cylinder 1
P0202 Injector Circuit Problem—Cylinder 2
P0203 Injector Circuit Problem—Cylinder 3
P0204 Injector Circuit Problem—Cylinder 4
P0205 Injector Circuit Problem—Cylinder 5
P0206 Injector Circuit Problem—Cylinder 6
P0207 Injector Circuit Problem—Cylinder 7
P0208 Injector Circuit Problem—Cylinder 8
P0209 Injector Circuit Problem—Cylinder 9
P0210 Injector Circuit Problem—Cylinder 10
P0211 Injector Circuit Problem—Cylinder 11
P0212 Injector Circuit Problem—Cylinder 12
P0213 Cold Start Injector 1 Problem
P0214 Cold Start Injector 2 Problem

## Ignition System or Misfire

P0300 Random Misfire Detected
P0301 Cylinder 1 Misfire Detected
P0302 Cylinder 2 Misfire Detected
P0303 Cylinder 3 Misfire Detected
P0304 Cylinder 4 Misfire Detected
P0305 Cylinder 5 Misfire Detected
P0306 Cylinder 6 Misfire Detected

| P0307 | Cylinder 7 Misfire Detected |
|---|---|
| P0308 | Cylinder 8 Misfire Detected |
| P0309 | Cylinder 9 Misfire Detected |
| P0310 | Cylinder 10 Misfire Detected |
| P0311 | Cylinder 11 Misfire Detected |
| P0312 | Cylinder 12 Misfire Detected |
| P0320 | Ignition or Distributor Engine Speed Input Circuit Problem |
| P0321 | Ignition or Distributor Engine Speed Input Circuit Range or Performance |
| P0322 | Ignition or Distributor Engine Speed Input Circuit No Signal |
| P0325 | Knock Sensor 1 Circuit Problem |
| P0326 | Knock Sensor 1 Circuit Range or Performance |
| P0327 | Knock Sensor 1 Circuit Low Input |
| P0328 | Knock Sensor 1 Circuit High Input |
| P0330 | Knock Sensor 2 Circuit Problem |
| P0331 | Knock Sensor 2 Circuit Range or Performance |
| P0332 | Knock Sensor 2 Circuit Low Input |
| P0333 | Knock Sensor 2 Circuit High Input |
| P0335 | Crankshaft Position Sensor Circuit Problem |
| P0336 | Crankshaft Position Sensor Circuit Range or Performance |
| P0337 | Crankshaft Position Sensor Circuit Low Input |
| P0338 | Crankshaft Position Sensor Circuit High Input |

**Auxiliary Emission Controls**

| P0400 | Exhaust Gas Recirculation Flow Problem |
|---|---|
| P0401 | Exhaust Gas Recirculation Flow Insufficient Detected |
| P0402 | Exhaust Gas Recirculation Flow Excessive Detected |
| P0405 | Air Conditioner Refrigerant Charge Loss |
| P0410 | Secondary Air Injection System Problem |
| P0411 | Secondary Air Injection System Insufficient Flow Detected |
| P0412 | Secondary Air Injection System Switching Valve or Circuit Problem |
| P0413 | Secondary Air Injection System Switching Valve or Circuit Open |
| P0414 | Secondary Air Injection System Switching Valve or Circuit Shorted |
| P0420 | Catalyst System Efficiency below Threshold (Bank 1*) |
| P0421 | Warm Up Catalyst Efficiency below Threshold (Bank 1*) |
| P0422 | Main Catalyst Efficiency below Threshold (Bank 1*) |
| P0423 | Heated Catalyst Efficiency below Threshold (Bank 1*) |
| P0424 | Heated Catalyst Temperature below Threshold (Bank 1*) |
| P0430 | Catalyst System Efficiency below Threshold (Bank 2) |
| P0431 | Warm Up Catalyst Efficiency below Threshold (Bank 2) |
| P0432 | Main Catalyst Efficiency below Threshold (Bank 2) |
| P0433 | Heated Catalyst Efficiency below Threshold (Bank 2) |
| P0434 | Heated Catalyst Temperature below Threshold (Bank 2) |
| P0440 | Evaporative Emission Control System Problem |
| P0441 | Evaporative Emission Control System Insufficient Purge Flow |
| P0442 | Evaporative Emission Control System Leak Detected |

| P0443 | Evaporative Emission Control System Purge Control Valve Circuit Problem |
|---|---|
| P0444 | Evaporative Emission Control System Purge Control Valve Circuit Open |
| P0445 | Evaporative Emission Control System Purge Control Valve Circuit Shorted |
| P0446 | Evaporative Emission Control System Vent Control Problem |
| P0447 | Evaporative Emission Control System Vent Control Open |
| P0448 | Evaporative Emission Control System Vent Control Shorted |
| P0450 | Evaporative Emission Control System Pressure Sensor Problem |
| P0451 | Evaporative Emission Control System Pressure Sensor Range or Performance |
| P0452 | Evaporative Emission Control System Pressure Sensor Low Input |
| P0453 | Evaporative Emission Control System Pressure Sensor High Input |

**Vehicle Speed Control and Idle Control**

| P0500 | Vehicle Speed Sensor Problem |
|---|---|
| P0501 | Vehicle Speed Sensor Range or Performance |
| P0502 | Vehicle Speed Sensor Low Input |
| P0505 | Idle Control System Problem |
| P0506 | Idle Control System RPM Lower Than Expected |
| P0507 | Idle Control System RPM Higher Than Expected |
| P0510 | Closed Throttle Position Switch Problem |

**Computer Output Circuit**

| P0600 | Serial Communication Link Problem |
|---|---|
| P0605 | Internal Control Module (Module Identification Defined by J1979) |

**Transmission**

| P0703 | Brake Switch Input Problem |
|---|---|
| P0705 | Transmission Range Sensor Circuit Problem (PRNDL Input) |
| P0706 | Transmission Range Sensor Circuit Range or Performance |
| P0707 | Transmission Range Sensor Circuit Low Input |
| P0708 | Transmission Range Sensor Circuit High Input |
| P0710 | Transmission Fluid Temperature Sensor Problem |
| P0711 | Transmission Fluid Temperature Sensor Range or Performance |
| P0712 | Transmission Fluid Temperature Sensor Low Input |
| P0713 | Transmission Fluid Temperature Sensor High Input |
| P0715 | Input or Turbine Speed Sensor Circuit Problem |
| P0716 | Input or Turbine Speed Sensor Circuit Range or Performance |
| P0717 | Input or Turbine Speed Sensor Circuit No Signal |
| P0720 | Output Speed Sensor Circuit Problem |
| P0721 | Output Speed Sensor Circuit Range or Performance |
| P0722 | Output Speed Sensor Circuit No Signal |
| P0725 | Engine Speed Input Circuit Problem |
| P0726 | Engine Speed Input Circuit Range or Performance |

*(continued)*

| P0727 | Engine Speed Input Circuit No Signal |
| P0730 | Incorrect Gear Ratio |
| P0731 | Gear 1 Incorrect Ratio |
| P0732 | Gear 2 Incorrect Ratio |
| P0733 | Gear 3 Incorrect Ratio |
| P0734 | Gear 4 Incorrect Ratio |
| P0735 | Gear 5 Incorrect Ratio |
| P0736 | Reverse Incorrect Ratio |
| P0740 | Torque Converter Clutch System Problem |
| P0741 | Torque Converter Clutch System Performance or Stuck Off |
| P0742 | Torque Converter Clutch System Stuck On |
| P0743 | Torque Converter Clutch System Electrical |
| P0745 | Pressure Control Solenoid Problem |
| P0746 | Pressure Control Solenoid Performance or Stuck Off |
| P0747 | Pressure Control Solenoid Stuck On |
| P0748 | Pressure Control Solenoid Electrical |
| P0750 | Shift Solenoid A Problem |
| P0751 | Shift Solenoid A Performance or Stuck Off |
| P0752 | Shift Solenoid A Stuck On |
| P0753 | Shift Solenoid A Electrical |
| P0755 | Shift Solenoid B Problem |
| P0756 | Shift Solenoid B Performance or Stuck Off |
| P0757 | Shift Solenoid B Stuck On |
| P0758 | Shift Solenoid B Electrical |
| P0760 | Shift Solenoid C Problem |
| P0761 | Shift Solenoid C Performance or Stuck Off |
| P0762 | Shift Solenoid C Stuck On |
| P0763 | Shift Solenoid C Electrical |
| P0765 | Shift Solenoid D Problem |
| P0766 | Shift Solenoid D Performance or Stuck Off |
| P0767 | Shift Solenoid D Stuck On |
| P0768 | Shift Solenoid D Electrical |
| P0770 | Shift Solenoid E Problem |
| P0771 | Shift Solenoid E Performance or Stuck Off |
| P0772 | Shift Solenoid E Stuck On |
| P0773 | Shift Solenoid E Electrical |

* The side of the engine where number one cylinder is located.

## OBD-II ACTIVE TESTS

The vehicle computer must run tests on the various emission-related components and turn on the malfunction indicator lamp (MIL) if faults are detected. OBD II is an *active* computer analysis system because it actually tests the operation of the oxygen sensors, exhaust gas recirculation system, and so forth whenever conditions permit. It is the purpose and function of the Powertrain Control Module (PCM) to monitor these components and perform these active tests.

For example, the PCM may open the EGR valve momentarily to check its operation while the vehicle is decelerating. A change in the manifold absolute pressure (MAP) sensor signal will indicate to the computer that the exhaust gas is, in fact, being introduced into the engine. Because these tests are active and certain conditions must be present before

these tests can be run, the computer uses its internal diagnostic program to keep track of all the various conditions and to schedule active tests so that they will not interfere with each other.

### OBD-II DRIVE CYCLE
The vehicle must be driven under a variety of operating conditions for all active tests to be performed. A **trip** is defined as an engine-operating drive cycle that contains the necessary conditions for a particular test to be performed. For example, for the EGR test to be performed, the engine has to be at normal operating temperature and decelerating for a minimum amount of time. Some tests are performed when the engine is cold, whereas others require that the vehicle be cruising at a steady highway speed.

### TYPES OF OBD-II CODES
Not all OBD-II diagnostic trouble codes are of the same importance for exhaust emissions. Each type of DTC has different requirements for it to set, and the computer will only turn on the MIL for emissions-related DTCs.

**TYPE A CODES.** A type A diagnostic trouble code is emission related and will cause the MIL to be turned on at the *first trip* if the computer has detected a problem. Engine misfire or a very rich or lean air–fuel ratio, for example, would cause a type A diagnostic trouble code. These codes alert the driver to an emissions problem that may cause damage to the catalytic converter.

**TYPE B CODES.** A type B code will be stored as a pending code in the PCM and the MIL will be turned on only after the second consecutive trip, alerting the driver to the fact that a diagnostic test was performed and failed.

**NOTE: Type A and Type B codes are emission related and will cause the lighting of the malfunction indicator lamp, usually labeled "check engine" or "service engine soon."**

**TYPE C AND D CODES.** Type C and type D codes are for use with non-emission-related diagnostic tests. They will cause the lighting of a "service" lamp (if the vehicle is so equipped).

### OBD-II FREEZE-FRAME
To assist the service technician, OBD II requires the computer to take a "snapshot" or freeze-frame of all data at the instant an emission-related DTC is set. A scan tool is required to retrieve this data. CARB and EPA regulations require that the controller store specific freeze-frame (engine-related) data when the first emission related fault is detected. The data stored in freeze-frame can only be replaced by data from a trouble code with a higher priority such as a trouble related to a fuel system or misfire monitor fault.

**NOTE: Although OBD II requires that just one freeze-frame of data be stored, the instant an emission-related DTC is set, vehicle manufacturers usually provide expanded data about the DTC beyond that required. However, retrieving enhanced data usually requires the use of an enhanced or factory level scan tool.**

The freeze-frame has to contain data values that occurred at the time the code was set (these values are provided in standard units of measurement). Freeze-frame data is recorded during the first trip on a two-trip fault. As a result, OBD-II systems record the data present at the time an emission-related code is recorded and the MIL activated. This data can be accessed and displayed on a scan tool. Freeze-frame data is one frame or one instant in time. Freeze-frame data is not updated (refreshed) if the same monitor test fails a second time.

### REQUIRED FREEZE-FRAME DATA ITEMS.

- Code that triggered the freeze-frame
- A/F ratio, airflow rate, and calculated engine load
- Base fuel injector pulse width
- ECT, IAT, MAF, MAP, TP, and VS sensor data
- Engine speed and amount of ignition spark advance
- Open- or closed-loop status
- Short-term and long-term fuel trim values
- For misfire codes—identify the cylinder that misfired

**NOTE: All freeze-frame data will be lost if the battery is disconnected, power to the PCM is removed, or the scan tool is used to erase or clear trouble codes.**

**DIAGNOSING INTERMITTENT MALFUNCTIONS** Of all the different types of conditions that you will see, the hardest to accurately diagnose and repair are intermittent malfunctions. These conditions may be temperature related (only occur when the vehicle is hot or cold), or humidity related (only occur when it is raining). Regardless of the conditions that will cause the malfunction to occur, you must diagnose and correct the condition.

When dealing with an intermittent concern, you should determine the conditions when the malfunction occurs, and then try to duplicate those conditions. If a cause is not readily apparent to you, ask the customer when the symptom occurs. Ask if there are any conditions that seem to be related to, or cause the concern.

Another consideration when working on an OBD-II-equipped vehicle is whether a concern is intermittent, or if it only occurs when a specific diagnostic test is performed by the PCM. Since OBD-II systems conduct diagnostic tests only under very precise conditions, some tests may only be run once during an ignition cycle. Additionally, if the requirements needed to perform the test are not met, the test will not run during an ignition cycle. This type of onboard diagnostics could be mistaken as "intermittent" when, in fact, the tests are only infrequent (depending on how the vehicle is driven). Examples of this type of diagnostic test are $HO_2S$ heaters, evaporative canister purge, catalyst efficiency, and EGR flow. When diagnosing intermittent concerns on an OBD-II-equipped vehicle, a logical diagnostic strategy is essential. The use of stored freeze-frame information can also be very useful when diagnosing an intermittent malfunction if a code has been stored.

# SERVICE/FLASH PROGRAMMING

Designing a program that allows an engine to meet strict air quality and fuel economy standards while providing excellent performance is no small feat. However, this is only part of the challenge facing engineers assigned with the task of developing OBD-II software. The reason for this is the countless variables involved with running the diagnostic monitors. Although programmers do their best to factor in any and all operating conditions when writing this complex code, periodic revisions are often required.

Reprogramming consists of downloading new calibration files from a scan tool, personal computer, or modem into the PCM's electronically erasable programmable read-only memory (EEPROM). This can be done on or off the vehicle using the appropriate equipment. Since reprogramming is not an OBD-II requirement however, many vehicles will need a new PCM in the event software changes become necessary. Physically removing and replacing the PROM chip is no longer possible.

The following are three industry-standard methods used to reprogram the EEPROM:

- Remote programming
- Direct programming
- Off-board programming

**REMOTE PROGRAMMING.** Remote programming uses the scan tool to transfer data from the manufacturer's shop PC to the vehicle's PCM. This is accomplished by performing the following steps:

- Connect the scan tool to the vehicle's DLC. ● **SEE FIGURE 1–17.**
- Enter the vehicle information into the scan tool through the programming application software incorporated in the scan tool. ● **SEE FIGURE 1–18.**
- Download VIN and current EEPROM calibration using a scan tool.
- Disconnect the scan tool from the DLC and connect the tool to the shop PC.
- Download the new calibration from the PC to the scan tool. ● **SEE FIGURE 1–19.**
- Reconnect the scan tool to the vehicle's DLC and download the new calibration into the PCM.

**CAUTION: Before programming, the vehicle's battery must be between 11 and 14 volts. Do not attempt to program while charging the battery unless using a special battery charger which does not produce excessive ripple voltage such as the Midtronics PSC-300 (30 amp) or PSC-550 (55 amp) or similar as specified by the vehicle manufacturer.**

FIGURE 1–17 The first step in the reprogramming procedure is to determine the current software installed using a scan tool. Not all scan tools can be used. In most cases using the factory scan tool is needed for reprogramming unless the scan tool is equipped to handle reprogramming.

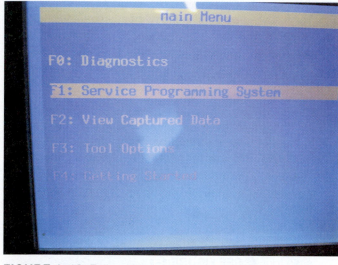

FIGURE 1–18 Follow the on-screen instructions.

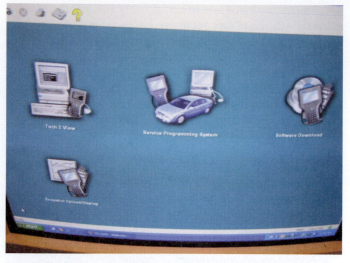

FIGURE 1–19 An Internet connection is usually needed to perform updates although some vehicle manufacturers use CDs which are updated regularly at a cost to the shop.

FIGURE 1–20 Connecting cables and a computer to perform off-board programming.

**DIRECT PROGRAMMING.** Direct programming does utilize a connection between the shop PC and the vehicle DLC.

**OFF-BOARD PROGRAMMING.** Off-board programming is used if the PCM must be programmed away from the vehicle. This is preformed using the off-board programming adapter. ● **SEE FIGURE 1–20.**

**J2534 REPROGRAMMING** Legislation has mandated that vehicle manufacturers meet the SAE J2534 standards for all emissions-related systems on all new vehicles starting with model year 2004. This standard enables independent service repair operators to program or reprogram emissions-related ECMs from a wide variety of vehicle manufacturers with a single tool. ● **SEE FIGURE 1–21.** A J2534 compliant

pass-through system is a standardized programming and diagnostic system. It uses a personal computer (PC) plus a standard interface to a software device driver, and a hardware vehicle communication interface. The interface connects to a PC, and to a programmable ECM on a vehicle through the J1962 data link connector (DLC). This system allows programming of all vehicle manufacturer ECMs using a single set of programming hardware. Programming software made available by the vehicle manufacturer must be functional with a J2534 compliant pass-through system.

The software for a typical pass-through application consists of two major components including:

■ The part delivered by the company that furnishes the hardware for J2534 enables the pass-through vehicle communication interface to communicate with the PC and provides

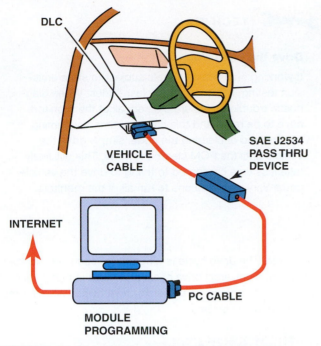

FIGURE 1–21 The J2534 pass-through reprogramming system does not need a scan tool to reflash the PCM on most 2004 and newer vehicles.

FIGURE 1–22 A typical J2534 universal reprogrammer that uses the J2534 standards.

for all Vehicle Communication Protocols as required by SAE J2534. It also provides for the software interface to work with the software applications as provided for by the vehicle manufacturers. ● SEE FIGURE 1–22.

■ The second part of the pass-through enabling software is provided for by the vehicle manufacturers. This is normally a subset of the software used with their original equipment manufacturer (OEM) tools and their website will indicate how to obtain this software and under what conditions it can be used. Refer to the National Automotive Service

Task Force (NASTF) website for the addresses for all vehicle manufacturers' service information and cost, *www.NASTF.org.*

Since the majority of vehicle manufacturers make this software available in downloadable form, having an Internet browser (Explorer/Netscape) and connection is a must.

## MANUFACTURER'S DIAGNOSTIC ROUTINES

Each vehicle manufacturer has established their own diagnostic routines and they should be followed. Most include the following steps:

**STEP 1** Retrieve diagnostic trouble codes.

**STEP 2** Check for all technical service bulletins that could be related to the stored DTC.

**STEP 3** If there are multiple DTCs, the diagnostic routine may include checking different components or systems instead of when only one DTC was stored.

**STEP 4** Perform system checks.

**STEP 5** Perform the necessary service or repair

**STEP 6** Perform a road test matching the parameters recorded in the freeze-frame to check that the repair has corrected the malfunction.

**STEP 7** Repeat the road test to cause the MIL to be extinguished.

**NOTE: Do not clear codes (DTCs) unless instructed by the service information.**

Following the vehicle manufacturer's specific diagnostic routines will ensure that the root cause is found and the repair verified. This is important for customer satisfaction.

## COMPLETING SYSTEM REPAIRS

After the repair has been successfully completed, the vehicle should be driven under similar conditions that caused the original concern. Verify that the problem has been corrected. To perform this test drive, it is helpful to have a copy of the freeze-frame parameters that were present when the DTC was set. By driving under similar conditions, the PCM may perform a test of the system and automatically extinguish the MIL. This is the method preferred by most vehicle manufacturers. The DTC can be cleared using a scan tool, but then that means that monitors will have to be run and the vehicle may fail an emission inspection if driven directly to the testing station.

# PROCEDURES FOR RESETTING THE PCM

The PCM can be reset or cleared of previously set DTCs and freeze-frame data in the following ways:

1. **Driving the Vehicle.** Drive the vehicle under similar conditions that were present when the fault occurred. If the conditions are similar and the PCM performed the noncontinuous monitor test and it passed three times, then the PCM will extinguish the MIL. This is the method preferred by most vehicle manufacturers, however, this method could be time consuming. If three passes cannot be achieved, the owner of the vehicle will have to be told that even though the check engine light (MIL) is on, the problem has been corrected and the MIL should go out in a few days of normal driving.

2. **Clear DTCs Using a Scan Tool.** A scan tool can be used to clear the diagnostic trouble code (DTC), which will also delete all of the freeze-frame data. The advantage of using a scan tool is that the check engine (MIL) will be out and the customer will be happy that the problem (MIL on) has been corrected. Do not use a scan tool to clear a DTC if the vehicle is going to be checked soon at a test station for state-mandated emission tests.

3. **Battery Disconnect.** Disconnecting the negative battery cable will clear the DTCs and freeze-frame on many vehicles but not all. Besides clearing the DTCs, disconnecting the battery for about 20 minutes will also erase radio station presets and other memory items in many cases. Most vehicle manufacturers do not recommend that the battery be disconnected to clear DTCs and it may not work on some vehicles.

# ROAD TEST (DRIVE CYCLE)

Use the freeze-frame data and test-drive the vehicle so that the vehicle is driven to match the conditions displayed on the freeze-frame. If the battery has been disconnected, then the vehicle may have to be driven under conditions that allow the PCM to conduct monitor tests. This drive pattern is called a **drive cycle.** The drive cycle is different for each vehicle manufacturer but a universal drive cycle may work in many cases. In many cases performing a universal drive cycle will reset most monitors in most vehicles.

## UNIVERSAL DRIVE CYCLE

**PRECONDITIONING: Phase 1.**

MIL must be off.

No DTCs present.

Fuel fill between 15% and 85%.

Cold start—Preferred = 8-hour soak at 68°F to 86°F.

Alternative = ECT below 86°F.

1. With the ignition off, connect scan tool.
2. Start engine and drive between 20 and 30 mph for 22 minutes, allowing speed to vary.
3. Stop and idle for 40 seconds, gradually accelerate to 55 mph.
4. Maintain 55 mph for 4 minutes using a steady throttle input.
5. Stop and idle for 30 seconds, then accelerate to 30 mph.
6. Maintain 30 mph for 12 minutes.
7. Repeat steps 4 and 5 four times.

Using scan tool, check readiness. If insufficient readiness set, continue to universal drive trace phase II.

**Important: (Do not shut off engine between phases).**
**Phase II:**

1. Vehicle at a stop and idle for 45 seconds, then accelerate to 30 mph.
2. Maintain 30 mph for 22 minutes.
3. Repeat steps 1 and 2 three times.
4. Bring vehicle to a stop and idle for 45 seconds, then accelerate to 35 mph.
5. Maintain speed between 30 and 35 mph for 4 minutes.
6. Bring vehicle to a stop and idle for 45 seconds, then accelerate to 30 mph.
7. Maintain 30 mph for 22 minutes.
8. Repeat steps 6 and 7 five times.
9. Using scan tool, check readiness.

## SUMMARY

1. Funnel diagnostics—Visual approach to a diagnostic procedure:
   **Step 1** Verify the problem (concern)
   **Step 2** Perform a thorough visual inspection and basic tests
   **Step 3** Retrieve the diagnostic trouble codes (DTCs)
   **Step 4** Check for technical service bulletins (TSBs)
   **Step 5** Look carefully at scan tool data
   **Step 6** Narrow the problem to a system or cylinder
   **Step 7** Repair the problem and determine the root cause
   **Step 8** Verify the repair and check for any stored DTCs

2. A thorough visual inspection is important during the diagnosis and troubleshooting of any engine performance problem or electrical malfunction.

3. If the MIL is on, retrieve the DTC and follow the manufacturer's recommended procedure to find the root cause of the problem.

4. OBD-II vehicles use a 16-pin DLC and common DTCs.

## REVIEW QUESTIONS

1. Explain the procedure to follow when diagnosing a vehicle with stored DTCs using a scan tool.

2. Discuss what the PCM does during a drive cycle to test emission-related components.

3. Explain the difference between a type A and type B OBD-II diagnostic trouble code.

4. List three things that should be checked as part of a thorough visual inspection.

5. List the eight-step funnel diagnostic procedure.

6. Explain why a bulletin search should be performed after stored DTCs are retrieved.

7. List the three methods that can be used to reprogram a PCM.

## CHAPTER QUIZ

1. Technician A says that the first step in the diagnostic process is to verify the problem (concern). Technician B says the second step is to perform a thorough visual inspection. Which technician is correct?
   a. Technician A only
   b. Technician B only
   c. Both Technicians A and B
   d. Neither Technician A nor B

2. Which item is *not* important to know before starting the diagnosis of an engine performance problem?
   a. List of previous repairs
   b. The brand of engine oil used
   c. The type of gasoline used
   d. The temperature of the engine when the problem occurs

3. A paper test can be used to check for a possible problem with _____.
   a. The ignition system (bad spark plug wire)
   b. A faulty injector on a multiport engine
   c. A burned valve
   d. All of the above

4. Which step should be performed *last* when diagnosing an engine performance problem?
   a. Checking for any stored diagnostic trouble codes
   b. Checking for any technical service bulletins (TSBs)
   c. Performing a thorough visual inspection
   d. Verify the repair

5. Technician A says that if the opposite DTC can be set, the problem is the component itself. Technician B says if the opposite DTC cannot be set, the problem is with the wiring or grounds. Which technician is correct?
   a. Technician A only
   b. Technician B only
   c. Both Technicians A and B
   d. Neither Technician A nor B

6. The preferred method to clear diagnostic trouble codes (DTCs) is to _____.
   a. Disconnect the negative battery cable for 10 seconds
   b. Use a scan tool
   c. Remove the computer (PCM) power feed fuse
   d. Cycle the ignition key on and off 40 times

7. Which is the factory scan tool for Chrysler brand vehicles equipped with CAN?
   a. Star Scan
   b. Tech 2
   c. NGS
   d. Master Tech

8. Technician A says that reprogramming a PCM using the J2534 system requires a factory scan tool. Technician B says that reprogramming a PCM using the J2534 system requires Internet access. Which technician is correct?
   a. Technician A only
   b. Technician B only
   c. Both Technicians A and B
   d. Neither Technician A nor B

9. Technician A says that knowing if there are any stored diagnostic trouble codes (DTCs) may be helpful when checking for related technical service bulletins (TSBs). Technician B says that only a factory scan tool should be used to retrieve DTCs. Which technician is correct?
   a. Technician A only
   b. Technician B only
   c. Both Technicians A and B
   d. Neither Technician A nor B

10. Which method can be used to reprogram a PCM?
    a. Remote
    b. Direct
    c. Off-board
    d. All of the above

# chapter 2

# CAN AND NETWORK COMMUNICATIONS

**OBJECTIVES:** **After studying Chapter 2, the reader will be able to:** • Prepare for ASE Electrical/Electronic Systems (A6) certification test content area "A" (General Electrical/Electronic Systems Diagnosis). • Describe the types of networks and serial communications used on vehicles. • Discuss how the networks connect to the data link connector and to other modules. • Explain how to diagnose module communication faults.

**KEY TERMS:** Breakout box (BOB) 31 • BUS 23 • CAN 23 • Chrysler Collision Detection (CCD) 27 • Class 2 23 • E & C 23 • GMLAN 23 • Keyword 23 • Multiplexing 20 • Network 20 • Node 20 • Plastic optical fiber (POF) 31 • Programmable controller interface (PCI) 28 • Protocol 23 • Serial communications interface (SCI) 28 • Serial data 20 • Splice pack 21 • Standard corporate protocol (SCP) 26 • State of health (SOH) 32 • SWCAN 24 • Terminating resistors 32 • Twisted pair 20 • UART 23 • UART-based protocol (UBP) 26

## MODULE COMMUNICATIONS AND NETWORKS

**NEED FOR NETWORK**   Since the 1990s, vehicles have used modules to control the operation of most electrical components. A typical vehicle will have 10 or more modules and they communicate with each other over data lines or hard wiring, depending on the application.

**ADVANTAGES**   Most modules are connected together in a network because of the following advantages.

- A decreased number of wires are needed, thereby saving weight and cost, as well as helping with installation at the factory and decreased complexity, making servicing easier.
- Common sensor data can be shared with those modules that may need the information, such as vehicle speed, outside air temperature, and engine coolant temperature.
  - ● SEE FIGURE 2–1.

## NETWORK FUNDAMENTALS

**MODULES AND NODES**   Each module, also called a **node,** must communicate to other modules. For example, if the driver depresses the window-down switch, the power window switch sends a window-down message to the body control module. The body control module then sends the request to the driver's side window

module. This module is responsible for actually performing the task by supplying power and ground to the window lift motor in the current polarity to cause the window to go down. The module also contains a circuit that monitors the current flow through the motor and will stop and/or reverse the window motor if an obstruction causes the window motor to draw more than the normal amount of current.

**TYPES OF COMMUNICATION**   The types of communications include the following:

- **Differential.** In the differential form of BUS communication, a difference in voltage is applied to two wires, which are twisted to help reduce electromagnetic interference (EMI). These transfer wires are called a **twisted pair.**
- **Parallel.** In the parallel type of BUS communication, the send and receive signals are on different wires.
- **Serial data.** The **serial data** is data transmitted by a series of rapidly changing voltage signals pulsed from low to high or from high to low.
- **Multiplexing.** The process of **multiplexing** involves the sending of multiple signals of information at the same time over a signal wire and then separating the signals at the receiving end.

  This system of intercommunication of computers or processors is referred to as a **network.** ● SEE FIGURE 2–2.

  By connecting the computers together on a communications network, they can easily share information back and forth. This multiplexing has the following advantages.

- Elimination of redundant sensors and dedicated wiring for these multiple sensors
- Reduction of the number of wires, connectors, and circuits

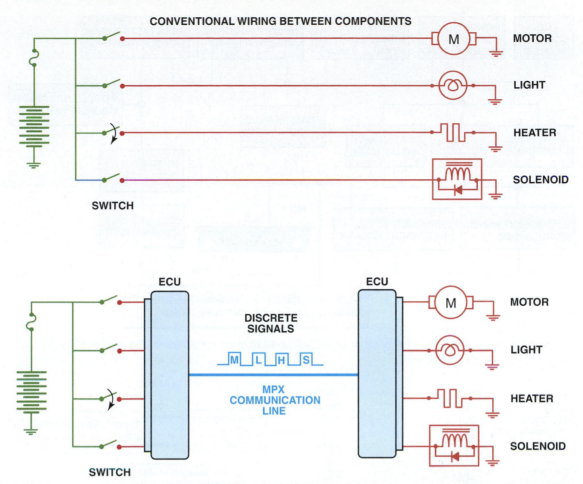

**CONVENTIONAL WIRING BETWEEN COMPONENTS**

MOTOR

LIGHT

HEATER

SOLENOID

SWITCH

ECU

ECU

MOTOR

DISCRETE
SIGNALS

LIGHT

MPX
COMMUNICATION
LINE

HEATER

SOLENOID

SWITCH

**FIGURE 2–1** Module communications makes controlling multiple electrical devices and accessories easier by utilizing simple low-current switches to signal another module, which does the actual switching of the current to the device.

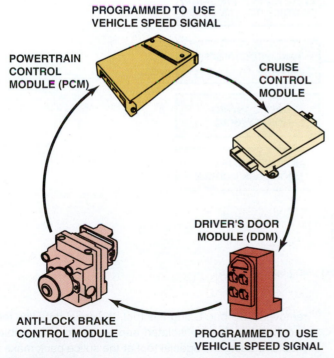

PROGRAMMED TO USE
VEHICLE SPEED SIGNAL

POWERTRAIN
CONTROL
MODULE (PCM)

CRUISE
CONTROL
MODULE

DRIVER'S DOOR
MODULE (DDM)

ANTI-LOCK BRAKE
CONTROL MODULE

PROGRAMMED TO USE
VEHICLE SPEED SIGNAL

**FIGURE 2–2** A network allows all modules to communicate with other modules.

- Addition of more features and option content to new vehicles
- Weight reduction due to fewer components, wires, and connectors, thereby increasing fuel economy
- Changeable features with software upgrades versus component replacement

# MODULE COMMUNICATIONS CONFIGURATION

The three most common types of networks used on vehicles include:

1. **Ring link networks.** In a ring-type network, all modules are connected to each other by a serial data line (in a line) until all are connected in a ring. ● **SEE FIGURE 2–3.**

2. **Star link networks.** In a star link network, a serial data line attaches to each module and then each is connected to a central point. This central point is called a **splice pack**, abbreviated SP such as in "SP 306." The splice pack uses a bar to splice all of the serial lines together. Some GM vehicles use two or more splice packs to tie the modules

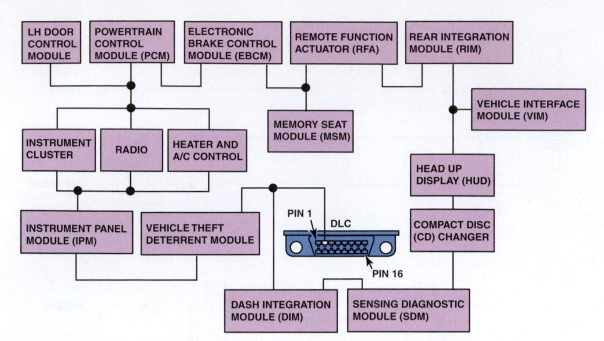

**FIGURE 2–3** A ring link network reduces the number of wires it takes to interconnect all of the modules.

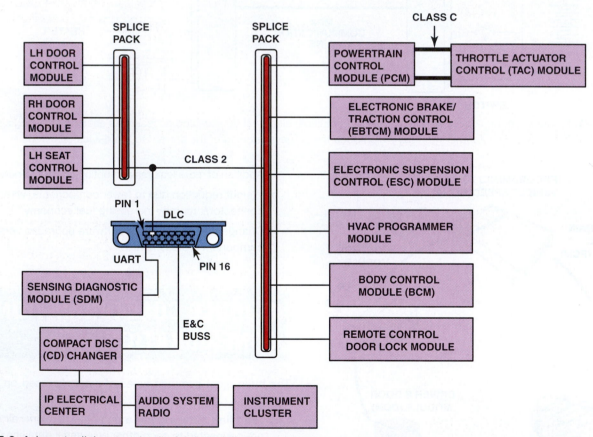

**FIGURE 2–4** In a star link network, all of the modules are connected using splice packs.

together. When more than one splice pack is used, a serial data line connects one splice pack to the others. In most applications, the BUS bar used in each splice pack can be removed. When the BUS bar is removed, a special tool (J 42236) can be installed in place of the removed BUS bar. Using this tool, the serial data line for each module can be isolated and tested for a possible problem. Using the special tool at the splice pack makes diagnosing this type of network easier than many others.
● **SEE FIGURE 2–4.**

3. **Ring/star hybrid.** In a ring/star network, the modules are connected using both types of network configurations. Check service information (SI) for details on how this network is connected on the vehicle being diagnosed and always follow the recommended diagnostic steps.

# NETWORK COMMUNICATIONS CLASSIFICATIONS

The Society of Automotive Engineers (SAE) standards include the following three categories of in-vehicle network communications.

**CLASS A** Low-speed networks, meaning less than 10,000 bits per second (bps, or 10 Kbs), are generally used for trip computers, entertainment, and other convenience features.

**CLASS B** Medium-speed networks, meaning 10,000 to 125,000 bps (10 to 125 Kbs), are generally used for information transfer among modules, such as instrument clusters, temperature sensor data, and other general uses.

**CLASS C** High-speed networks, meaning 125,000 to 1,000,000 bps, are generally used for real-time powertrain and vehicle dynamic control. High-speed BUS communication systems now use a **controller area network (CAN).** ● SEE FIGURE 2–5.

# GENERAL MOTORS COMMUNICATIONS PROTOCOLS

**UART** General Motors and others use UART communications for some electronic modules or systems. **UART** is a serial data communications protocol that stands for **universal asynchronous receive and transmit.** UART uses a master control module connected to one or more remote modules. The master

control module is used to control message traffic on the data line by poling all of the other UART modules. The remote modules send a response message back to the master module.

UART uses a fixed pulse-width switching between 0 and 5 V. The UART data BUS operates at a baud rate of 8,192 bps. ● SEE FIGURE 2–6.

### ENTERTAINMENT AND COMFORT COMMUNICATION

The GM **entertainment and comfort (E & C)** serial data is similar to UART, but uses a 0 to 12 V toggle. Like UART, the E & C serial data uses a master control module connected to other remote modules, which could include the following:

- Compact disc (CD) player
- Instrument panel (IP) electrical center
- Audio system (radio)
- Heating, ventilation, and air-conditioning (HVAC) programmer and control head
- Steering wheel controls
  ● SEE FIGURE 2–7.

### CLASS 2 COMMUNICATIONS
**Class 2** is a serial communications system that operates by toggling between 0 and 7 V at a transfer rate of 10.4 Kbs. Class 2 is used for most high-speed communications between the powertrain control module (PCM) and other control modules, plus to the scan tool. Class 2 is the primary high-speed serial communications system used by GMCAN (CAN). ● SEE FIGURE 2–8.

### KEYWORD COMMUNICATION
**Keyword** 81, 82, and 2000 serial data are also used for some module-to-module communication on GM vehicles. Keyword data BUS signals are toggled from 0 to 12 V when communicating. The voltage or the datastream is zero volt when not communicating. Keyword serial communication is used by the seat heater module and others, but is not connected to the data link connector (DLC). ● SEE FIGURE 2–9.

### GMLAN
General Motors, like all vehicle manufacturers, must use high-speed serial data to communicate with scan tools on all vehicles effective with the 2008 model year. As mentioned, the standard is called controller area network (CAN), which General Motors calls **GMLAN,** which stands for **GM local area network.**

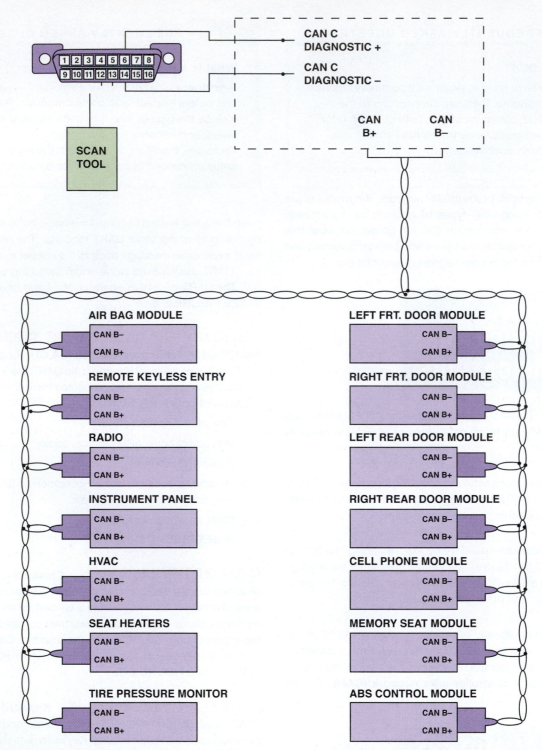

**FIGURE 2–5** A typical BUS system showing module CAN communications and twisted pairs of wire.

General Motors uses two versions of GMLAN.

- **Low-speed GMLAN.** The low-speed version is used for driver-controlled functions such as power windows and door locks. The baud rate for low-speed GMLAN is 33,300 bps. The GMLAN low-speed serial data is not connected directly to the data link connector and uses one wire. The voltage toggles between 0 and 5 V after an initial 12 V spike, which indicates to the modules to turn on or wake up and listen for data on the line. Low-speed GMLAN is also known as **single-wire CAN,** or **SWCAN.**

- **High-speed GMLAN.** The baud rate is almost real time at 500 Kbs. This serial data method uses a two-twisted-wire circuit which is connected to the data link connector on pins 6 and 14. ● **SEE FIGURE 2–10.**

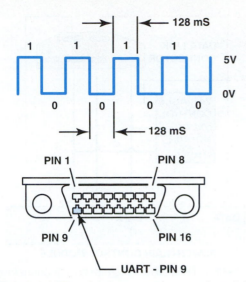

FIGURE 2–6 UART serial data master control module is connected to the data link connector at pin 9.

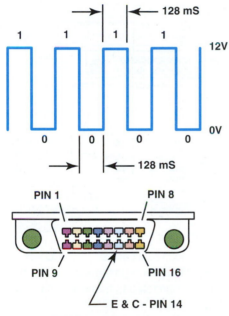

FIGURE 2–7 The E & C serial data is connected to the data link connector (DLC) at pin 14.

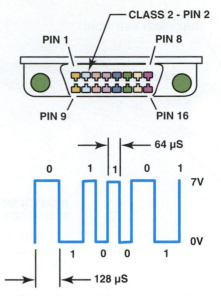

FIGURE 2–8 Class 2 serial data communication is accessible at the data link connector (DLC) at pin 2.

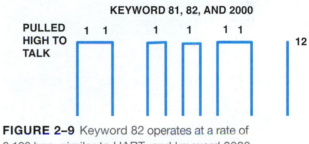

FIGURE 2–9 Keyword 82 operates at a rate of 8,192 bps, similar to UART, and keyword 2000 operates at a baud rate of 10,400 bps (the same as a Class 2 communicator).

? FREQUENTLY ASKED QUESTION

**Why Is a Twisted Pair Used?**

A twisted pair is where two wires are twisted to prevent electromagnetic radiation from affecting the signals passing through the wires. By twisting the two wires about once every inch (9 to 16 times per foot), the interference is canceled by the adjacent wire.
● **SEE FIGURE 2–11.**

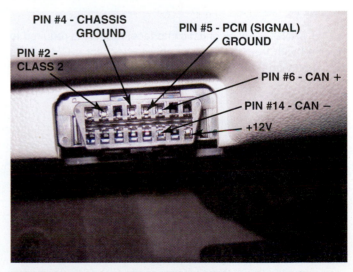

FIGURE 2–10 GMLAN uses pins at terminals 6 and 14.

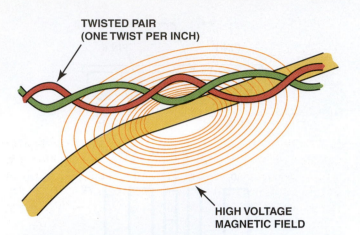

FIGURE 2–11 A twisted pair is used by several different network communications protocols to reduce interference that can be induced in the wiring from nearby electromagnetic sources.

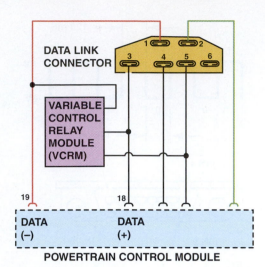

FIGURE 2–13 A Ford OBD-I diagnostic link connector showing that SCP communication uses terminals in cavities 1 (upper left) and 3 (lower left).

FIGURE 2–12 A CANDi module will flash the green LED rapidly if communication is detected.

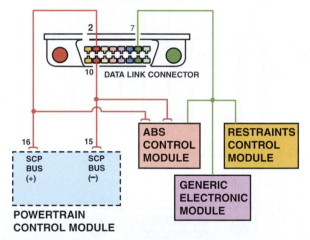

FIGURE 2–14 A scan tool can be used to check communications with the SCP BUS through terminals 2 and 10 and to the other modules connected to terminal 7 of the data link connector (DLC).

A CANDi (CAN diagnostic interface) module is required to be used with the Tech 2 to be able to connect a GM vehicle equipped with GMLAN. ● **SEE FIGURE 2–12.**

## FORD NETWORK COMMUNICATIONS PROTOCOLS

### STANDARD CORPORATE PROTOCOL
Only a few Fords had scan tool data accessible through the OBD-I data link connector. To identify an OBD-I (1988–1995) on a Ford vehicle that is equipped with **standard corporate protocol (SCP)** and be able to communicate through a scan tool, look for terminals in cavities 1 and 3 of the DLC. ● **SEE FIGURE 2–13.**

SCP uses the J-1850 protocol and is active with the key on. The SCP signal is from 4 V negative to 4.3 V positive, and a scan tool does not have to be connected for the signal to be detected on the terminals. OBD-II (EECV) Ford vehicles use terminals 2 (positive) and 10 (negative) of the 16 pin data link connector (DLC) for network communication, using the SCP module communications.

### UART-BASED PROTOCOL
Newer Fords use the CAN for scan tool diagnosis, but still retain SCP and **UART-based protocol (UBP)** for some modules. ● **SEE FIGURES 2–14 AND 2–15.**

# CHRYSLER COMMUNICATIONS PROTOCOLS

**CCD** Since the late 1980s, Chrysler has used **Chrysler Collision Detection (CCD)** multiplex network for scan tool and module communications. It is a differential-type communication and uses a twisted pair of wires. The modules connected to the network apply a bias voltage on each wire. CCD signals are divided into plus and minus (CCD+ and CCD−) and the voltage difference does not exceed 0.02 V. The baud rate is 7,812.5 bps.

**NOTE: The "collision" in CCD-type BUS communications refers to the program that avoids conflicts of information exchange within the BUS, and does not refer to airbags or other accident-related circuits of the vehicle.**

The circuit is active without a scan tool command. ● **SEE FIGURE 2–16.**

The modules on the CCD BUS apply a bias voltage on each wire by using termination resistors. ● **SEE FIGURE 2–17.**

The difference in voltage between CCD+ and CCD− is less than 20 mV. For example, using a digital meter with the black meter lead attached to ground and the red meter lead

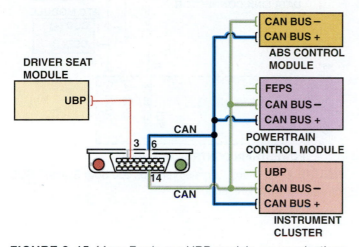

**FIGURE 2–15** Many Fords use UBP module communications along with CAN.

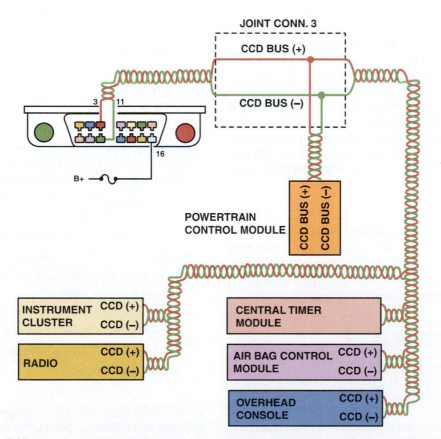

**FIGURE 2–16** Chrysler CCD signals are labeled plus and minus and use a twisted pair of wires. Notice that terminals 3 and 11 of the data link connector are used to access the CCD BUS from a scan tool. Pin 16 is used to supply 12 volts to the scan tool.

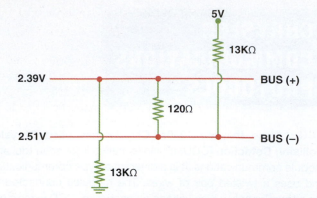

**FIGURE 2–17** The differential voltage for the CCD BUS is created by using resistors in a module.

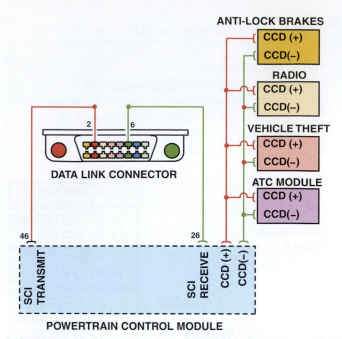

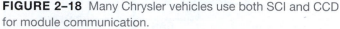

**FIGURE 2–18** Many Chrysler vehicles use both SCI and CCD for module communication.

attached at the data link connector (DLC), a normal reading could include:

- Terminal 3 = 2.45 volts
- Terminal 11 = 2.47 volts

This is an acceptable reading because the readings are 20 mV (0.020 volt) of each other. If both had been exactly 2.5 volts, then this could indicate that the two data lines are shorted together. The module providing the bias voltage is usually the body control module on passenger cars and the front control module on Jeeps and trucks.

## PROGRAMMABLE CONTROLLER INTERFACE

The Chrysler **programmable controller interface (PCI)** is a one-wire communication protocol that connects at the OBD-II DLC at terminal 2. The PCI BUS is connected to all modules on the BUS in a star configuration and operates at a baud rate of 10,200 bps. The voltage signal toggles between 7.5 and 0 V. If this voltage is checked at terminal 2 of the OBD-II DLC, a voltage of about 1 V indicates the average voltage and means that the BUS is functioning and is not shorted-to-ground. PCI and CCD are often used in the same vehicle. ● **SEE FIGURE 2–18.**

## SERIAL COMMUNICATIONS INTERFACE

Chrysler used **serial communications interface (SCI)** for most scan tool and flash reprogramming functions until it was replaced with CAN. SCI is connected at the OBD-II diagnostic link connector (DLC) at terminals 6 (SCI receive) and 7 (SCI transmit). A scan tool must be connected to test the circuit.

## CONTROLLER AREA NETWORK

**BACKGROUND** Robert Bosch Corporation developed the CAN protocol, which was called CAN 1.2, in 1993. The CAN protocol was approved by the Environmental Protection Agency (EPA)

for 2003 and newer vehicle diagnostics, and a legal requirement for all vehicles by 2008. The CAN diagnostic systems use pins 6 and 14 in the standard 16 pin OBD-II (J-1962) connector. Before CAN, the scan tool protocol had been manufacturer specific.

**CAN FEATURES** The CAN protocol offers the following features.

- Faster than other BUS communication protocols
- Cost effective because it is an easier system than others to use
- Less effected by electromagnetic interference (Data is transferred on two wires that are twisted together, called twisted pair, to help reduce EMI interference.)
- Message based rather than address based which makes it easier to expand
- No wakeup needed because it is a two-wire system
- Supports up to15 modules plus a scan tool
- Uses a 120 ohm resistor at the ends of each pair to reduce electrical noise
- Applies 2.5 volts on both wires:

  H (high) goes to 3.5 volts when active

  L (low) goes to 1.5 volts when active

  ● **SEE FIGURE 2–19.**

**CAN CLASS A, B, AND C** There are three classes of CAN and they operate at different speeds. The CAN A, B, and C networks can all be linked using a gateway within the same vehicle. The gateway is usually one of the many modules in the vehicle.

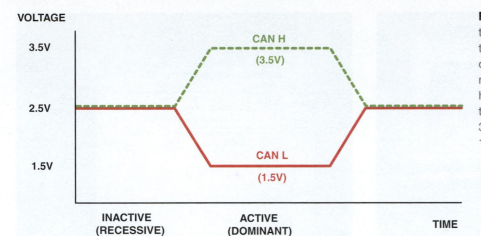

VOLTAGE

3.5V ··· CAN H
      (3.5V)

2.5V

1.5V ··· CAN L
      (1.5V)

INACTIVE
(RECESSIVE)

ACTIVE
(DOMINANT)

TIME

**FIGURE 2–19** CAN uses a differential type of module communication where the voltage on one wire is the equal but opposite voltage on the other wire. When no communication is occurring, both wires have 2.5 volts applied. When communication is occurring, CAN H goes up 1 volt to 3.5 volts and CAN L goes down 1 volt to 1.5 volts.

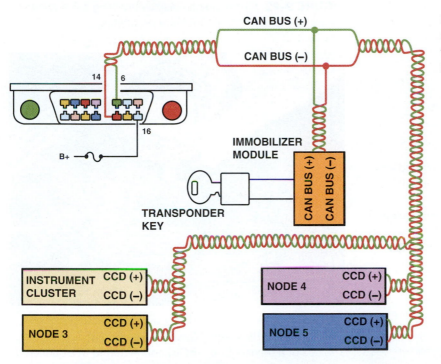

CAN BUS (+)

CAN BUS (−)

14  6

16

B+

IMMOBILIZER
MODULE

TRANSPONDER
KEY

CAN BUS (+)
CAN BUS (−)

INSTRUMENT
CLUSTER
CCD (+)
CCD (−)

NODE 3
CCD (+)
CCD (−)

NODE 4
CCD (+)
CCD (−)

NODE 5
CCD (+)
CCD (−)

**FIGURE 2–20** A typical (generic) system showing how the CAN BUS is connected to various electrical accessories and systems in the vehicle.

- **CAN A.** This class operates on only one wire at slow speeds and is therefore less expensive to build. CAN A operates a data transfer rate of 33.33 Kbs in normal mode and up to 83.33 Kbs during reprogramming mode. CAN A uses the vehicle ground as the signal return circuit.

- **CAN B.** This class operates on a two-wire network and does not use the vehicle ground as the signal return circuit. CAN B uses a data transfer rate of 95.2 Kbs. Instead, CAN B (and CAN C) uses two network wires for differential signaling. This means that the two data signal voltages are opposite to each other and used for error detection by constantly being compared. In this case, when the signal voltage at one of the CAN data wires goes high (CAN H), the other one goes low (CAN L), hence the name *differential signaling*. Differential signaling is also used for redundancy, in case one of the signal wires shorts out.

- **CAN C.** This class is the highest speed CAN protocol with speeds up to 500 Kbs. Beginning with 2008 models, all vehicles sold in the United States must use CAN BUS for scan tool communications. Most vehicle manufacturers started using CAN in older models; and it is easy to determine if a vehicle is equipped with CAN. The CAN BUS communicates to the scan tool through terminals 6 and 14 of the DLC indicating that the vehicle is equipped with CAN. ● **SEE FIGURE 2–20.**

The total voltage remains constant at all times and the electromagnetic field effects of the two data BUS lines cancel each other out. The data BUS line is protected against received radiation and is virtually neutral in sending radiation.

**FIGURE 2–21** A DLC from a pre-CAN Acura. It shows terminals in cavities 4, 5 (grounds), 7, 10, 14, and 16 (B+).

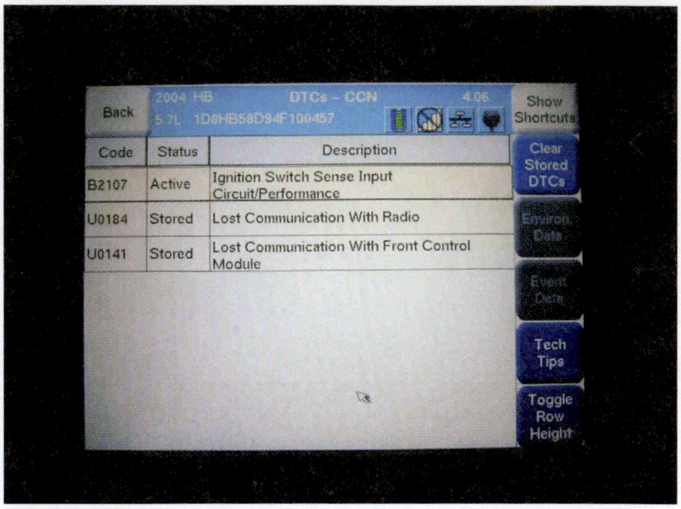

**FIGURE 2–22** A Honda scan display showing a B and two U codes, all indicating a BUS-related problem(s).

## HONDA/TOYOTA COMMUNICATIONS

The primary BUS communications on pre-CAN-equipped vehicles is ISO 9141-2 using terminals 7 and 15 at the OBD-II DLC. ● **SEE FIGURE 2–21.**

A factory scan tool or an aftermarket scan tool equipped with enhanced original equipment (OE) software is needed to access many of the BUS messages. ● **SEE FIGURE 2–22.**

## EUROPEAN BUS COMMUNICATIONS

### UNIQUE DIAGNOSTIC CONNECTOR
Many different types of module communications protocols are used on European vehicles such as Mercedes and BMW.

Most of these communication BUS messages cannot be accessed through the data link connector (DLC). To check the operation of the individual modules, a scan tool equipped with factory-type software will be needed to communicate with the module through the gateway module. ● **SEE FIGURE 2–23** for an alternative access method to the modules.

### MEDIA ORIENTED SYSTEM TRANSPORT BUS
The media oriented system transport (MOST) BUS uses fiber optics for module-to-module communications in a ring or star configuration. This BUS system is currently being used for entertainment equipment data communications for videos, CDs, and other media systems in the vehicle.

**FIGURE 2–23** A typical 38-cavity diagnostic connector as found on many BMW and Mercedes vehicles under the hood. The use of a breakout box (BOB) connected to this connector can often be used to gain access to module BUS information.

### MOTOROLA INTERCONNECT BUS
Motorola interconnect (MI) is a single-wire serial communications protocol, using one master control module and many slave modules. Typical application of the MI BUS protocol is with power and memory mirrors, seats, windows, and headlight levelers.

### DISTRIBUTED SYSTEM INTERFACE BUS
Distributed system interface (DSI) BUS protocol was developed by Motorola and uses a two-wire serial BUS. This BUS protocol is currently being used for safety-related sensors and components.

### BOSCH-SIEMANS-TEMIC BUS
The Bosch-Siemans-Temic (BST) BUS is another system that is used for safety-related components and sensors in a vehicle, such as airbags. The BST BUS is a two-wire system and operates up to 250,000 bps.

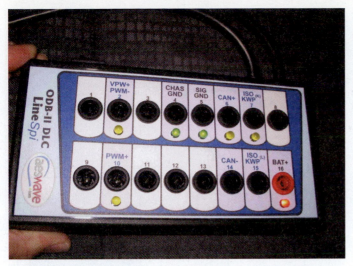

**FIGURE 2–24** A breakout box (BOB) used to access the BUS terminals while using a scan tool to activate the modules. This breakout box is equipped with LEDs that light when circuits are active.

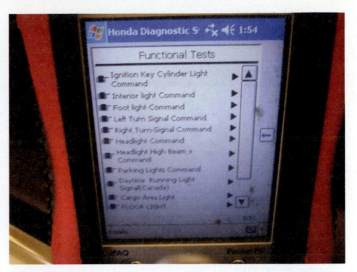

**FIGURE 2–25** This Honda scan tool allows the technician to turn on individual lights and operate individual power windows and other accessories that are connected to the BUS system.

 **FREQUENTLY ASKED QUESTION**

**How Do You Know What System Is Used?**

Use service information to determine which network communication protocol is used. However, due to the various systems on some vehicles, it may be easier to look at the data link connection to determine the system. All OBD-II vehicles have terminals in the following cavities.

Terminal 4: chassis ground

Terminal 5: computer (signal) ground

Terminal 16: 12 V positive

The terminals in cavities 6 and 14 mean that this vehicle is equipped with CAN as the only module communication protocol available at the DLC. To perform a test of the BUS, use a **breakout box (BOB)** to gain access to the terminals while connecting to the vehicle, using a scan tool. ● **SEE FIGURE 2–24** or a typical OBD-II connector breakout box.

**BYTEFLIGHT BUS** The byteflight BUS is used in safety critical systems, such as airbags, and uses the time division multiple access (TDMA) protocol, which operates at 10 million bps using a **plastic optical fiber (POF).**

**FLEXRAY BUS** FlexRay BUS is a version of byteflight, and is a high-speed serial communication system for in-vehicle networks. FlexRay is commonly used for steer-by-wire and brake-by-wire systems.

**DOMESTIC DIGITAL BUS** The domestic digital BUS, commonly designated D2B, is an optical BUS system connecting audio, video, computer, and telephone components in a single-ring structure with a speed of up to 5,600,000 bps.

**LOCAL INTERCONNECT NETWORK BUS** Local interconnect network (LIN) is a BUS protocol used between intelligent sensors and actuators, and has a BUS speed of 19,200 bps.

## NETWORK COMMUNICATIONS DIAGNOSIS

**STEPS TO FINDING A FAULT** When a network communications fault is suspected, perform the following steps.

STEP 1 **Check everything that does and does not work.** Often accessories that do not seem to be connected can help identify which module or BUS circuit is at fault.

STEP 2 **Perform module status test.** Use a factory level scan tool or an aftermarket scan tool equipped with enhanced software that allows OE-like functions. Check if the components or systems can be operated through the scan tool. ● **SEE FIGURE 2–25.**

- **Ping modules.** Start the Class 2 diagnosis by using a scan tool and select *diagnostic circuit check*. If no diagnostic trouble codes (DTCs) are shown, there could be a communication problem. Select

**Class 2 Message Monitor**

| Modules | Status | |
|---|---|---|
| BCM/BFC/DIM/SBM/TBC | Active | 1 |
| PCM/VCM | Active | 1 |
| ABS/TCS | Active | 1 |
| IPC | Active | 1 |
| SIR | Active | 1 |
| Radio | Active | 1 |
| ACM/HCM | Active | 1 |

00:00:03    1 / 9

BCM/BFC/DIM/SBM/TBC

| Sleep Mode | Ping Module | Ping All Modules |

**FIGURE 2–26** Modules used in a General Motors vehicle can be "pinged" using a Tech 2 scan tool.

**TECH TIP**

**No Communication? Try Bypass Mode.**

If a Tech 2 scan tool shows "no communication," try using the bypass mode to see what should be on the data display. To enter bypass mode, perform the following steps.

**STEP 1** Select tool option (F3).

**STEP 2** Set communications to bypass (F5).

**STEP 3** Select enable.

**STEP 4** Input make/model and year of vehicle.

**STEP 5** Note all parameters that should be included, as shown. The values will not be shown.

*message monitor,* which will display the status of all of the modules on the Class 2 BUS circuit. The modules that are awake will be shown as active and the scan tool can be used to ping individual modules or command all modules. The ping command should change the status from "active" to "inactive." ● **SEE FIGURE 2–26.**

**NOTE: If an excessive parasitic draw is being diagnosed, use a scan tool to ping the modules in one way to determine if one of the modules is not going to sleep and causing the excessive battery drain.**

● **Check state of health.** All modules on the Class 2 BUS circuit have at least one other module responsible for reporting **state of health (SOH).** If a module fails to send a state of health message within five seconds, the companion module will set a diagnostic trouble code for the module that did not respond. The defective module is not capable of sending this message.

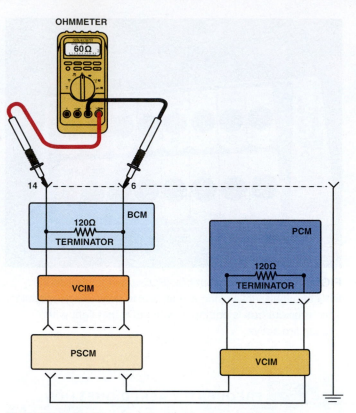

**FIGURE 2–27** Checking the terminating resistors using an ohmmeter at the DLC.

**STEP 3** **Check the resistance of the terminating resistors.** Most high-speed BUS systems use resistors at each end, called **terminating resistors.** These resistors are used to help reduce interference into other systems in the vehicle. Usually two 120 ohm resistors are installed at each end and are therefore connected electrically in parallel. Two 120 ohm resistors connected in parallel would measure 60 ohms if being tested using an ohmmeter. ● **SEE FIGURE 2–27.**

**STEP 4** **Check data BUS for voltages.** Use a digital multimeter set to DC volts, to monitor communications and check the BUS for proper operation. Some BUS conditions and possible causes include:

● **Signal is zero volt all of the time.** Check for short-to-ground by unplugging modules one at a time to check if one module is causing the problem.

● **Signal is high or 12 volts all of the time.** The BUS circuit could be shorted to 12 V. Check with the customer to see if any service or body repair work was done recently. Try unplugging each module one at a time to pin down which module is causing the communications problem.

● **A variable voltage usually indicates that messages are being sent and received.** CAN and Class 2 can be identified by looking at the data link connector (DLC) for a terminal in cavity number 2. Class 2 is active all of the time the ignition is on, and therefore voltage variation between 0 and 7 V can be measured using a DMM set to read DC volts. ● **SEE FIGURE 2–28.**

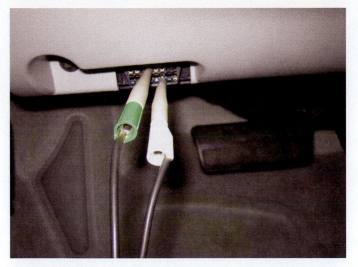

**FIGURE 2–28** Use front-probe terminals to access the data link connector. Always follow the specified back-probe and front-probe procedures as found in service information.

**STEP 5** **Use a digital storage oscilloscope to monitor the waveforms of the BUS circuit.** Using a scope on the data line terminals can show if communication is being transmitted. Typical faults and their causes include:

- **Normal operation.** Normal operation shows variable voltage signals on the data lines. It is impossible to know what information is being transmitted, but if there is activity with short sections of inactivity, this indicates normal data line transmission activity. ● **SEE FIGURE 2–29.**
- **High voltage.** If there is a constant high-voltage signal without any change, this indicates that the data line is shorted to voltage.
- **Zero or low voltage.** If the data line voltage is zero or almost zero and not showing any higher voltage signals, then the data line is short-to-ground.

**STEP 6** **Follow factory service information instructions to isolate the cause of the fault.** This step often involves disconnecting one module at a time to see if it is the cause of a short-to-ground or an open in the BUS circuit.

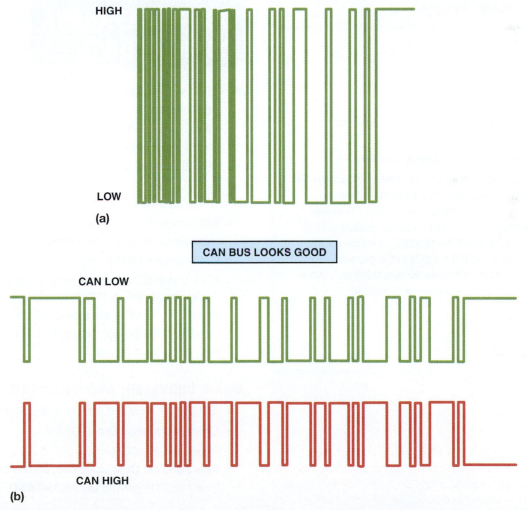

**FIGURE 2–29** (a) Data is sent in packets, so it is normal to see activity then a flat line between messages. (b) A CAN BUS should show voltages that are opposite when there is normal communications. CAN H (high) circuit should go from 2.5 volts at rest to 3.5 volts when active. The CAN L (low) circuit goes from 2.5 volts at rest to 1.5 volts when active.

### The Radio Caused No-Start Story

A 2005 Chevrolet Cobalt did not start. A technician checked with a subscription-based helpline service and discovered that a fault with the Class 2 data circuit could prevent the engine from starting. The advisor suggested that a module should be disconnected one at a time to see if one of them was taking the data line to ground. The two most common components on the Class 2 serial data line that have been known to cause a lack of communication and become shorted-to-ground are the radio and electronic brake control module (EBCM). The first one the technician disconnected was the radio. The engine started and ran. Apparently the Class 2 serial data line was shorted-to-ground inside the radio, which took the entire BUS down. When BUS communication is lost, the PCM is not able to energize the fuel pump, ignition, or fuel injectors so the engine would not start. The radio was replaced to solve the no-start condition.

**?** **FREQUENTLY ASKED QUESTION**

### Which Module Is the Gateway Module?

The gateway module is responsible for communicating with other modules and acts as the main communications module for scan tool data. Most General Motors vehicles use the body control module (BCM) or the instrument panel control (IPC) module as the gateway. To verify which module is the gateway, check the schematic and look for one that has voltage applied during all of the following conditions.

- Key on, engine off
- Engine cranking
- Engine running

| PIN NO. | ASSIGNMENTS |
|---|---|
| 1. | MANUFACTURER'S DISCRETION |
| 2. | BUS + LINE, SAE J1850 |
| 3. | MANUFACTURER'S DISCRETION |
| 4. | CHASSIS GROUND |
| 5. | SIGNAL GROUND |
| 6. | MANUFACTURER'S DISCRETION |
| 7. | K LINE, ISO 9141 |
| 8. | MANUFACTURER'S DISCRETION |
| 9. | MANUFACTURER'S DISCRETION |
| 10. | BUS – LINE, SAE J1850 |
| 11. | MANUFACTURER'S DISCRETION |
| 12. | MANUFACTURER'S DISCRETION |
| 13. | MANUFACTURER'S DISCRETION |
| 14. | MANUFACTURER'S DISCRETION |
| 15. | L LINE, ISO 9141 |
| 16. | VEHICLE BATTERY POSITIVE (4A MAX) |

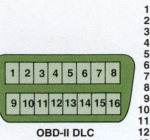

**OBD-II DLC**

**FIGURE 2–30** A 16 pin OBD-II DLC with terminals identified. Scan tools use the power pin (16) and ground pin (4) for power so that a separate cigarette lighter plug is not necessary on OBD-II vehicles.

## OBD-II DATA LINK CONNECTOR

All OBD-II vehicles use a 16 pin connector that includes:

Pin 4 = chassis ground

Pin 5 = signal ground

Pin 16 = battery power (4 A max)

● **SEE FIGURE 2–30.**

### GENERAL MOTORS VEHICLES

- SAE J-1850 (VPW, Class 2, 10.4 Kbs) standard, which uses pins 2, 4, 5, and 16, but not 10
- GM Domestic OBD-II

  Pin 1 and 9: CCM (comprehensive component monitor) slow baud rate, 8,192 UART

  Pins 2 and 10: OEM enhanced, fast rate, 40,500 baud rate

  Pins 7 and 15: generic OBD-II, ISO 9141, 10,400 baud rate

  Pins 6 and 14: GMLAN

### ASIAN, CHRYSLER, AND EUROPEAN VEHICLES

- ISO 9141-2 standard, which uses pins 4, 5, 7, 15, and 16
- Chrysler Domestic Group OBD-II

  Pins 2 and 10: CCM

  Pins 3 and 14: OEM enhanced, 60,500 baud rate

  Pins 7 and 15: generic OBD-II, ISO 9141, 10,400 baud rate

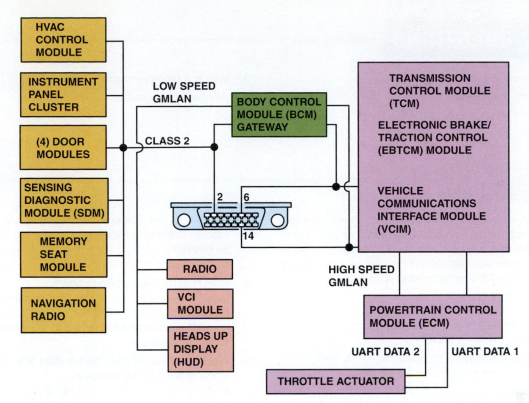

**FIGURE 2–31** This schematic of a Chevrolet Equinox shows that the vehicle uses a GMLAN BUS (DLC pins 6 and 14), plus a Class 2 (pin 2) and UART.

## FORD VEHICLES

- SAE J-1850 (PWM) (PWM, 41.6 Kbs) standard, which uses pins 2, 4, 5, 10, and 16
- Ford Domestic OBD-II

  Pins 2 and 10: CCM

  Pins 6 and 14: OEM enhanced, Class C, 40,500 baud rate

  Pins 7 and 15: generic OBD-II, ISO 9141, 10,400 baud rate

---

**TECH TIP**

**Check Computer Data Line Circuit Schematic**

Many General Motors vehicles use more than one type of BUS communications protocol. Check service information (SI) and look at the schematic for computer data line circuits which should show all of the data BUSes and their connectors to the diagnostic link connector (DLC). ● **SEE FIGURE 2–31.**

---

# SUMMARY

1. The use of a network for module communications reduces the number of wires and connections needed.

2. Module communication configurations include ring link, star link, and ring/star hybrid systems.

3. The SAE communication classifications for vehicle communications systems include Class A (low speed), Class B (medium speed), and Class C (high speed).

4. Various module communications used on General Motors vehicles include UART, E & C, Class 2, keyword communications, and GMLAN (CAN).

5. Types of module communications used on Ford vehicles include SCP, UBP, and CAN.

6. Chrysler brand vehicles use SCI, CCD, PCI, and CAN communications protocols.

7. Many European vehicles use an underhood electrical connector that can be used to access electrical components and modules using a breakout box (BOB) or special tester.

8. Diagnosis of network communications includes checking the terminating resistor value and checking for charging voltage signals at the DLC.

1. Why is a communication network used?

2. Why are the two wires twisted if used for network communications?

3. Why is a gateway module used?

4. What are U codes?

## CHAPTER QUIZ

1. Technician A says that module communications networks are used to reduce the number of wires in a vehicle. Technician B says that a communications network is used to share data from sensors, which can be used by many different modules. Which technician is correct?
   a. Technician A only
   b. Technician B only
   c. Both Technicians A and B
   d. Neither Technician A nor B

2. A module is also known as a _____.
   a. BUS
   b. Node
   c. Terminator
   d. Resistor pack

3. A high-speed CAN BUS communicates with a scan tool through which terminal(s)?
   a. 6 and 14
   b. 2
   c. 7 and 15
   d. 4 and 16

4. UART uses a _____ signal that toggles 0 V.
   a. 5 V
   b. 7 V
   c. 8 V
   d. 12 V

5. GM Class 2 communication toggles between _____.
   a. 5 and 7 V
   b. 0 and 12 V
   c. 7 and 12 V
   d. 0 and 7 V

6. Which terminal of the data link connector does General Motors use for Class 2 communication?
   a. 1
   b. 2
   c. 3
   d. 4

7. GMLAN is the General Motors term for which type of module communication?
   a. UART
   b. Class 2
   c. High-speed CAN
   d. Keyword 2000

8. CAN H and CAN L operate how?
   a. CAN H is at 2.5 volts when not transmitting.
   b. CAN L is at 2.5 volts when not transmitting.
   c. CAN H goes to 3.5 volts when transmitting.
   d. All of the above

9. Which terminal of the OBD-II data link connector is the signal ground for all vehicles?
   a. 1
   b. 3
   c. 4
   d. 5

10. Terminal 16 of the OBD-II data link connector is used for what?
    a. Chassis ground
    b. 12 V positive
    c. Module (signal ground)
    d. Manufacturer's discretion

# chapter 3

# ON-BOARD DIAGNOSIS

**OBJECTIVES:** **After studying Chapter 3, the reader will be able to:** • Prepare for ASE Engine Performance (A8) certification test content area "D" (Emission Control Systems Diagnosis and Repair including OBD II). • Explain the purpose and function of onboard diagnosis. • List the various duties of the diagnostic executive (task master). • List five continuous monitors. • List five noncontinuous monitors.

**KEY TERMS:** California Air Resources Board (CARB) 37 • Diagnostic Executive 38 • Enable Criteria 40 • Exponentially Weighted Moving Average (EWMA) Monitor 40 • Federal Test Procedure (FTP) 38 • Freeze-Frame 38 • Functionality 39 • Malfunction indicator lamp (MIL) 37 • Monitor identification (MID) 00 • On-Board Diagnosis (OBD) 37 • Rationality 39 • Society of Automotive Engineers (SAE) 41 • Task Manager 38

## ON-BOARD DIAGNOSTICS GENERATION-II (OBD-II) SYSTEMS

During the 1980s, most manufacturers began equipping their vehicles with full-function control systems capable of alerting the driver of a malfunction and of allowing the technician to retrieve codes that identify circuit faults. These early diagnostic systems were meant to reduce emissions and speed up vehicle repair.

The automotive industry calls these systems **On-Board Diagnostics (OBDs).** The **California Air Resources Board (CARB)** developed the first regulation requiring manufacturers selling vehicles in that state to install OBD. OBD Generation I (OBD I) applies to all vehicles sold in California beginning with the 1988 model year. It carries the following requirements:

1. An instrument panel warning lamp able to alert the driver of certain control system failures, now called a **malfunction indicator lamp (MIL).** ● **SEE FIGURE 3–1.**

2. The system's ability to record and transmit DTCs for emission-related failures.

3. Electronic system monitoring of the $HO_2S$, EGR valve, and evaporative purge solenoid. Although not U.S. EPA-required, during this time most manufacturers also equipped vehicles sold outside of California with OBD I.

By failing to monitor the catalytic converter, the evaporative system for leaks, and the presence of engine misfire, OBD I

**FIGURE 3–1** A typical malfunction indicator lamp (MIL) often labeled "check engine."

did not do enough to lower automotive emissions. This led the CARB and the EPA to develop OBD Generation II (OBD II).

**OBD-II OBJECTIVES** Generally, the CARB defines an OBD-II-equipped vehicle by its ability to do the following:

1. Detect component degradation or a faulty emission-related system that prevents compliance with federal emission standards.

2. Alert the driver of needed emission-related repair or maintenance.

3. Use standardized DTCs and accept a generic scan tool.

These requirements apply to all 1996 and later model light-duty vehicles. The Clean Air Act of 1990 directed the EPA to develop new regulations for OBD. The primary purpose of OBD II is emission-related, whereas the primary purpose of OBD I (1988) was to detect faults in sensors or sensor circuits. OBD-II regulations require that not only sensors be tested but also all exhaust emission control devices, and that they be verified for proper operation.

All new vehicles must pass the **Federal Test Procedure (FTP)** for exhaust emissions while being tested for 1874 seconds on dynamometer rollers that simulate the urban drive cycle around downtown Los Angeles.

**NOTE: IM 240 is simply a shorter 240-second version of the federal test procedure.**

The regulations for OBD-II vehicles state that the vehicle computer must be capable of testing for, and determining, if the exhaust emissions are within 1.5 times the FTP limits. To achieve this goal, the computer must do the following:

1. Test all exhaust emission system components for correct operation.

2. Actively operate the system and measure the results.

3. Continuously monitor all aspects of the engine operation to be certain that the exhaust emissions do not exceed 1.5 times the FTP.

4. Check engine operation for misfire.

5. Turn on the MIL (check engine) if the computer senses a fault in a circuit or system.

6. Record a **freeze-frame,** which is a snapshot of important engine data at the time the DTC was set.

7. Flash the MIL if an engine misfire occurs that could damage the catalytic converter.

## DIAGNOSTIC EXECUTIVE AND TASK MANAGER

On OBD-II Systems, the PCM incorporates a special segment of software. On Ford and GM systems, this software is called the **diagnostic executive.** On Chrysler systems, it is called the **task manager.** This software program is designed to manage the operation of all OBD-II monitors by controlling the sequence of steps necessary to execute the diagnostic tests and monitors.

## MONITORS

A monitor is an organized method of testing a specific part of the system. Monitors are simply tests that the computer performs to evaluate components and systems. If a component or system failure is detected while a monitor is running, a DTC will be stored and the MIL illuminated during the second trip. The two types of monitors are continuous and noncontinuous.

**CONTINUOUS MONITORS** As required conditions are met, continuous monitors begin to run. These continuous monitors will run for the remainder of the vehicle drive cycle. The three continuous monitors are as follows:

- **Comprehensive component monitor (CCM).** This monitor watches the sensors and actuators in the OBD-II system. Sensor values are constantly compared with known-good values stored in the PCM's memory.

  The CCM is an internal program in the PCM designed to monitor a failure in any electronic component or circuit (including emission-related and non-emission-related circuits) that provide input or output signals to the PCM. The PCM considers that an input or output signal is inoperative when a failure exists due to an open circuit, out-of-range value, or if an onboard rationality check fails. If an emission-related fault is detected, the PCM will set a code and activate the MIL (requires two consecutive trips).

  Many PCM sensors and output devices are tested at key-on or immediately after engine start-up. However, some devices, such as the IAC, are only tested by the CCM after the engine meets certain engine conditions. The number of times the CCM must detect a fault before it will activate the MIL depends upon the manufacturer, but most require two consecutive trips to activate the MIL. The components tested by the CCM include:

  Four-wheel-drive low switch

  Brake switch

  Camshaft (CMP) and crankshaft (CKP) sensors

  Clutch switch (manual transmissions/transaxles only)

  Cruise servo switch

  Engine coolant temperature (ECT) sensor

  EVAP purge sensor or switch

  Fuel composition sensor

  Intake air temperature (IAT) sensor

  Knock sensor (KS)

  Manifold absolute pressure (MAP) sensor

  Mass air-flow (MAF) sensor

  Throttle-position (TP) sensor

  Transmission temperature sensor

  Transmission turbine speed sensor

  Vacuum sensor

  Vehicle speed (VS) sensor

  EVAP canister purge and EVAP purge vent solenoid

  Idle air control (IAC) solenoid

  Ignition control system

  Transmission torque converter clutch solenoid

  Transmission shift solenoids

- **Misfire monitor.** This monitor watches for engine misfire. The PCM uses the information received from the crankshaft position sensor (CKP) to calculate the time between the edges of the reluctor, as well as the rotational speed and acceleration. By comparing the acceleration of each firing event, the PCM can determine if a cylinder is not firing correctly.

**Misfire type A.** Upon detection of a misfire type A (200 revolutions), which would cause catalyst damage, the MIL will blink once per second during the actual misfire, and a DTC will be stored.

**Misfire type B.** Upon detection of a misfire type B (1000 revolutions), which will exceed 1.5 times the EPA federal test procedure (FTP) standard or cause a vehicle to fail an inspection and maintenance tailpipe emissions test, the MIL will illuminate and a DTC will be stored.

The DTC associated with multiple cylinder misfire for a type A or type B misfire is DTC P0300. The DTCs associated with an individual cylinder misfire for a type A or type B misfire are DTCs P0301, P0302, P0303, P0304, P0305, P0306, P0307, P0308, P0309, and P0310.

- **Fuel trim monitor.** The PCM continuously monitors short- and long-term fuel trim. Constantly updated adaptive fuel tables are stored in long-term memory (KAM), and used by the PCM for compensation due to wear and aging of the fuel system components. The MIL will illuminate when the PCM determines the fuel trim values have reached and stayed at their limits.

### NONCONTINUOUS MONITORS

Noncontinuous monitors run (at most) once per vehicle drive cycle. The noncontinuous monitors are as follows:

O2S monitor

O2S heater monitor

Catalyst monitor

EGR monitor

EVAP monitor

Secondary AIR monitor

Transmission monitor

PCV system monitor

Thermostat monitor

Once a noncontinuous monitor has run to completion, it will not be run again until the conditions are met during the next vehicle drive cycle. Also after a noncontinuous monitor has run to completion, the readiness status on your scan tool will show "complete" or "done" for that monitor. Monitors that have not run to completion will show up on your scanner as "incomplete."

## OBD-II MONITOR INFORMATION

### COMPREHENSIVE COMPONENT MONITOR

The circuits and components covered by the comprehensive component monitor (CCM) do not include those directly monitored by another monitor.

However, OBD II also requires that inputs from powertrain components to the PCM be tested for **rationality,** and that outputs to powertrain components from the PCM be tested for **functionality.** Both inputs and outputs are to be checked *electrically.* Rationality checks refer to a PCM comparison of input value to values.

**Example**

| | |
|---|---|
| TPS | 3 V |
| MAP 18 | in./Hg |
| RPM 700 | RPM |
| PRNDL | Park |

**NOTE: Comprehensive component monitors are continuous. Therefore enabling conditions do not apply.**

- Monitor runs continuously
- Monitor includes sensors, switches, relays, solenoids, and PCM hardware
- All are checked for opens, shorts-to-ground, and shorts-to-voltage
- Inputs are checked for rationality
- Outputs are checked for functionality
- Most are one-trip DTCs
- Freeze-frame is priority 3
- Three consecutive good trips are used to extinguish the MIL
- Forty warm up cycles are necessary to self erase the DTC and freeze frame.
- Two minutes run time without reoccurrence of the fault constitutes a "good trip"

### CONTINUOUS RUNNING MONITORS

- Monitors run continuously, only stop if they fail
- Fuel system: rich/lean
- Misfire: catalyst damaging/FTP (emissions)
- Two-trip faults (except early generation catalyst damaging misfire)
- MIL, DTC, freeze-frame after two consecutive faults
- Freeze-frame is priority 2 on first trip
- Freeze-frame is priority 4 on maturing (second) trip
- Three consecutive good trips in a similar condition window are used to extinguish the MIL
- Forty warm-up cycles are used to erase DTC and freeze-frame (80 to erase one-trip failure if similar conditions cannot be met)

### ONCE PER TRIP MONITORS

- Monitor runs once per trip, pass or fail
- $O_2$ response, $O_2$ heaters, EGR, purge flow EVAP leak, secondary air, catalyst
- Two-trip DTCs
- MIL, DTC, freeze-frame after two consecutive faults

- Freeze-frame is priority 1 on first trip
- Freeze-frame is priority 3 on maturing trip
- Three consecutive good trips are used to extinguish the MIL
- Forty warm-up cycles are used to erase DTC and freeze-frame

## EXPONENTIALLY WEIGHTED MOVING AVERAGE (EWMA) MONITORS

The **exponentially weighted moving average (EWMA) monitor** is a mathematical method used to determine performance.

- Catalyst monitor
- EGR monitor
- PCM runs six consecutive failed tests; fails in one trip
- Three consecutive failed tests on next trip, then fails
- Freeze-frame is priority 3
- Three consecutive good trips are used to extinguish the MIL
- Forty warm-up cycles are used to erase DTC and freeze-frame

## ENABLING CRITERIA

With so many different tests (monitors) to run, the PCM needs an internal director to keep track of when each monitor should run. As mentioned, different manufacturers have different names for this director, such as the diagnostic executive or the task manager. Each monitor has enabling criteria. These criteria are a set of conditions that must be met before the task manager will give the go-ahead for each monitor to run. Most enabling criteria follow simple logic, for example:

- The task manager will not authorize the start of the O2S monitor until the engine has reached operating temperature and the system has entered closed loop.
- The task manager will not authorize the start of the EGR monitor when the engine is at idle, because the EGR is always closed at this time.

There may be a conflict if two monitors were to run at the same time. The results of one monitor might also be tainted if a second monitor were to run simultaneously. In such cases, the task manager decides which monitor has a higher priority. Some monitors also depend on the results of other monitors before they can run.

A monitor may be classified as pending if a failed sensor or other system fault is keeping it from running on schedule.

The task manager may suspend a monitor if the conditions are not correct to continue. For example, if the catalyst monitor is running during a road test and the PCM detects a misfire, the catalyst monitor will be suspended for the duration of the misfire.

**TRIP** A trip is defined as a key-on condition that contains the necessary conditions for a particular test to be performed followed by a key-off. These conditions are called the **enable**

criteria. For example, for the EGR test to be performed, the engine must be at normal operating temperature and decelerating for a minimum amount of time. Some tests are performed when the engine is cold, whereas others require that the vehicle be cruising at a steady highway speed.

**READINESS INDICATORS** Indicators of monitors running or not, are used by most states as an emission test along with a MIL check. Readiness indicators stay in PCM memory until power or ground is interrupted or until DTCs are cleared using a scan tool.

**WARM-UP CYCLE** Once a MIL is deactivated, the original code will remain in memory until 40 warm-up cycles are completed without the fault reappearing. A warm-up cycle is defined as a trip with an engine temperature increase of at least 40°F and where engine temperature reaches at least 160°F (71°C).

**MIL CONDITION: OFF** This condition indicates that the PCM has not detected any faults in an emissions-related component or system, or that the MIL circuit is not working.

**MIL CONDITION: ON STEADY** This condition indicates a fault in an emissions-related component or system that could affect the vehicle emission levels. The MIL is also turned on at key on, engine off (KOEO) for at least 20 seconds as a bulb check.

**MIL CONDITION: FLASHING** This condition indicates a misfire or fuel control system fault that could damage the catalytic converter.

**NOTE: In a misfire condition with the MIL on steady, if the driver reaches a vehicle speed and load condition with the engine misfiring at a level that could cause catalyst damage, the MIL would start flashing. It would continue to flash until engine speed and load conditions caused the level of misfire to subside. Then the MIL would go back to the on-steady condition. This situation might result in a customer complaint of a MIL with an intermittent flashing condition.**

**MIL: OFF** The PCM will turn off the MIL if any of the following actions or conditions occur:

- The codes are cleared with a scan tool.
- Power to the PCM is removed at the battery or with the PCM power fuse for an extended period of time (may be up to several hours or longer).
- A vehicle is driven on three consecutive trips with a warm-up cycle and meets all code set conditions without the PCM detecting any faults.

The PCM will record a failure if a fault is detected that could cause tailpipe emissions to exceed 1.5 times the FTP standard. For one trip failures the MIL is immediately illuminated and a DTC stored. For two trip faults, the MIL is not illuminated nor is the DTC matured until the component has been tested and failed on the next trip. Many failures require that the vehicle be driven under similar RPM, temperature, and load conditions to be given a good trip. Without entering a *similar conditions window (SCW)*, the MIL will remain illuminated.

## OBD-II DTC NUMBERING DESIGNATION

A scan tool is required to retrieve DTCs from an OBD-II vehicle. Every OBD-II scan tool will be able to read all generic **Society of Automotive Engineers (SAE)** DTCs from any vehicle. ● SEE **FIGURE 3–2** for definitions and explanations of OBD alphanumeric DTCs. The diagnostic trouble codes (DTCs) are grouped into major categories, depending on the location of the fault on the system involved.

- Pxxx codes—powertrain DTCs (engine, transmission-related faults)
- Bxxx codes—body DTCs (accessories, interior-related faults)
- Cxxx codes—chassis DTCs (suspension and steering-related faults)
- Uxxx codes—network DTCs (module communication-related faults)

**DTC NUMBERING EXPLANATION** The number in the hundredth position indicates the specific vehicle system or subgroup that failed. This position should be consistent for P0xxx and P1xxx type codes. The following numbers and systems were established by SAE:

- P0100—Air metering and fuel system fault
- P0200—Fuel system (fuel injector only) fault
- P0300—Ignition system or misfire fault
- P0400—Emission control system fault
- P0500—Idle speed control, vehicle speed (VS) sensor fault
- P0600—Computer output circuit (relay, solenoid, etc.) fault
- P0700—Transaxle, transmission faults

**NOTE: The number of the last two digits indicate the specific fault within the vehicle system.**

**TYPES OF DTCS** Not all OBD-II DTCs are of the same importance for exhaust emissions. Each type of DTC has different requirements for it to set, and the computer will only turn on the MIL for emissions-related DTCs.

**TYPE A CODES.** A type A DTC is emission-related and will cause the MIL to be turned on the *first trip* if the computer has detected a problem. Engine misfire or a very rich or lean air-fuel ratio, for example, would cause a type A DTC. These codes alert

the driver to an emission problem that may cause damage to the catalytic converter.

**TYPE B CODES.** A type B code will be stored and the MIL will be turned on during the *second consecutive trip,* alerting the driver to the fact that a diagnostic test was performed and failed.

**NOTE: Type A and B codes are emission-related codes that will cause the lighting of the malfunction indicator lamp (MIL), usually labeled "check engine" or "service engine soon."**

**TYPE C AND D CODES.** Type C and D codes are for use with non-emission-related diagnostic tests; they will cause the lighting of a "service" lamp (if the vehicle is so equipped). Type C codes are also called type C1 codes and D codes are also called type C0 codes.

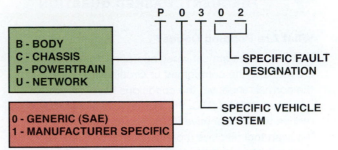

**EXAMPLE: P0302 = CYLINDER #2 MISFIRE DETECTED**

B - BODY
C - CHASSIS
P - POWERTRAIN
U - NETWORK

0 - GENERIC (SAE)
1 - MANUFACTURER SPECIFIC

SPECIFIC FAULT DESIGNATION

SPECIFIC VEHICLE SYSTEM

**FIGURE 3–2** OBD-II DTC identification format.

## DIAGNOSTIC TROUBLE CODE PRIORITY

CARB has also mandated that all diagnostic trouble codes (DTCs) be stored according to individual priority. DTCs with a higher priority overwrite those with a lower priority. The OBD-II System DTC Priority is listed below.

- Priority 0—Non-emission-related codes
- Priority 1—One-trip failure of two-trip fault for non-fuel, non-misfire codes
- Priority 2—One-trip failure of two-trip fault for fuel or misfire codes
- Priority 3—Two-trip failure or matured fault of non-fuel, non-misfire codes
- Priority 4—Two-trip failure or matured fault for fuel or misfire codes

**OBD-II FREEZE-FRAME** To assist the service technician, OBD II requires the computer to take a "snapshot" or freeze-frame of all data at the instant an emission-related DTC is set. A scan tool is required to retrieve this data.

**FREQUENTLY ASKED QUESTION**

### What Are Pending Codes?

Pending codes are set when operating conditions are met and the component or circuit is not within the normal range, yet the conditions have not yet been met to set a DTC. For example, a sensor may require two consecutive faults before a DTC is set. If a scan tool displays a pending code or a failure, a driveability concern could also be present. The pending code can help the technician to determine the root cause before the customer complains of a check engine light indication.

**NOTE: Although OBD II requires that just one freeze-frame of data be stored, the instant an emission-related DTC is set, vehicle manufacturers usually provide expanded data about the DTC beyond that required such as General Motor's *failure recorders*. However, retrieving this enhanced data usually requires the use of the vehicle-specific scan tool.**

Freeze-frame items include:

- Calculated load value
- Engine speed (RPM)
- Short-term and long-term fuel trim percent
- Fuel system pressure (on some vehicles)
- Vehicle speed (MPH)
- Engine coolant temperature
- Intake manifold pressure
- Closed/open-loop status
- Fault code that triggered the freeze-frame
- If a misfire code is set, identify which cylinder is misfiring

A DTC should not be cleared from the vehicle computer memory unless the fault has been corrected and the technician is so directed by the diagnostic procedure. If the problem that caused the DTC to be set has been corrected, the computer will automatically clear the DTC after 40 consecutive warm-up cycles with no further faults detected. It requires 80 warm-up cycles to erase the pending fault if similar conditions window cannot be met. The codes can also be erased by using a scan tool or by disconnecting the battery or PCM in most cases.

**NOTE: Disconnecting the battery may not erase OBD-II DTCs or freeze-frame data. Most vehicle manufacturers recommend using a scan tool to erase DTCs rather than disconnecting the battery, because the memory for the radio, seats, and learned engine operating parameters is lost if the battery is disconnected.**

# ENABLING CONDITIONS OR CRITERIA

These are the exact engine operating conditions required for a diagnostic monitor to run.

### Example

Specific RPM
Specific ECT, MAP, run time, VSS, etc.

**PENDING** Under some situations the PCM will not run a monitor if the MIL is illuminated and a fault is stored from another monitor. In these situations, the PCM postpones monitors pending a resolution of the original fault. The PCM does not run the test until the problem is remedied.

For example, when the MIL is illuminated for an oxygen sensor fault, the PCM does not run the catalyst monitor until the oxygen sensor fault is remedied. Since the catalyst monitor is based on signals from the oxygen sensor, running the test would produce inaccurate results.

**CONFLICT** There are also situations when the PCM does not run a monitor if another monitor is in progress. In these situations, the effects of another monitor running could result in an erroneous failure. If this conflict is present, the monitor is not run until the conflicting condition passes. Most likely, the monitor will run later after the conflicting monitor has passed.

For example, if the fuel system monitor is in progress, the PCM does not run the EGR monitor. Since both tests monitor changes in air-fuel ratio and adaptive fuel compensation, the monitors conflict with each other.

**SUSPEND** Occasionally, the PCM may not allow a two-trip fault to mature. The PCM will suspend the maturing fault if a condition exists that may induce erroneous failure. This prevents illuminating the MIL for the wrong fault and allows more precise diagnosis.

For example, if the PCM is storing a one-trip fault for the oxygen sensor and the EGR monitor, the PCM may still run the EGR monitor but will suspend the results until the oxygen sensor monitor either passes or fails. At that point, the PCM can determine if the EGR system is actually failing or if an oxygen sensor is failing.

**RATIONALITY TEST** While input signals to the PCM are constantly being monitored for electrical opens and shorts, they are also tested for rationality. This means that the input signal is compared against other inputs and information to see if it makes sense under the current conditions.

PCM sensor inputs that are checked for rationality include:

- MAP sensor
- $O_2$ sensor
- ECT

## PCM Determination of Faults Chart

| Monitor Name | Monitor Type (How Often It Completes) | Number of Faults on Separate Trips to Set a Pending DTC | Number of Separate Consecutive Trips to Light MIL, Store a DTC | Number of Trips with No Faults to Erase a pending DTC | Number of Trips with No Fault to Turn the MIL Off | Number of Warm-Up Cycles to Erase DTC after MIL Is Turned Off |
|---|---|---|---|---|---|---|
| CCM | Continuous (when trip conditions allow it) | 1 | 2 | 1 | 3–Trips | 40 |
| Catalyst | Once per drive cycle | 1 | 3 | 1 | 3–Trips | 40 |
| Misfire Type A | Continuous | | 1 | | 3–Similar conditions | 40 |
| Misfire Type B | Continuous | 1 | 2 | 1 | 3–Similar conditions | 40 |
| Fuel System | Continuous | 1 | 2 | 1 | 3–Similar conditions | 40 |
| Oxygen Sensor | Once per trip | 1 | 2 | 1 | 3–Trips | 40 |
| EGR | Once per trip | 1 | 2 | 1 | 3–Trips | 40 |
| EVAP | Once per trip | 1 | 1 | 1 | 3–Trips | 40 |
| AIR | Once per trip | 1 | 2 | 1 | 3–Trips | 40 |

- Camshaft position sensor (CMP)
- VS sensor
- Crankshaft position sensor (CKP)
- IAT sensor
- TP sensor
- Ambient air temperature sensor
- Power steering switch
- $O_2$ sensor heater
- Engine controller
- Brake switch
- P/N switch
- Transmission controls

## FUNCTIONALITY TEST
A functionality test refers to PCM inputs checking the operation of the outputs.

### Example

PCM commands the IAC open; expected change in engine RPM is not seen
IAC 60 counts (example of commanded position)
RPM 700 RPM (example of the desired engine speed)

PCM outputs that are checked for functionality include:

- EVAP canister purge solenoid
- EVAP purge vent solenoid
- Cooling fan

- Idle air control solenoid
- Ignition control system
- Transmission torque converter clutch solenoid
- Transmission shift solenoids (A, B, 1–2, etc.)

## ELECTRICAL TEST
Refers to the PCM check of both inputs and outputs for the following:

- Open
- Shorts
- Ground

### Example

ECT
Shorted high (input to PCM) above capable voltage, i.e., 5-volt sensor with 12-volt input to PCM would indicate a short to voltage or a short high.

| Monitor Type | Conditions to Set DTC and Illuminate MIL | Extinguish MIL | Clear DTC Criteria | Applicable DTC |
|---|---|---|---|---|
| Comprehensive Monitor | Continuous 1-trip monitor | Input and output failure—rationally, functionally, electrically | 3 consecutive pass trips | 40 warm-up cycles | P0123 |

**NOTE:** The number of times the comprehensive component monitor must detect a fault depends on the vehicle manufacturer. On some vehicles, the comprehensive component monitor will activate the MIL as soon as it detects a fault. On other vehicles, the comprehensive component monitor must fail two times in a row.

- Freeze-frame captured on first-trip failure.
- Enabling conditions: Many PCM sensors and output devices are tested at key-on or immediately after engine start-up. However, some devices (ECT, idle speed control) are only tested by the comprehensive component monitor after the engine meets particular engine conditions.
- Pending: No pending condition
- Conflict: No conflict conditions
- Suspend: No suspend conditions

## SUMMARY

1. If the MIL is on, retrieve the DTC and follow the manufacturer's recommended procedure to find the root cause of the problem.
2. All monitors must have the enable criteria achieved before a test is performed.
3. OBD-II vehicles use a 16-pin DLC and common DTCs.
4. OBD II includes generic (SAE), as well as vehicle manufacturer-specific DTCs, and data display.

## REVIEW QUESTIONS

1. What does the PCM do during a trip to test emission-related components?
2. What is the difference between a type A and type B OBD-II DTC?
3. What is the difference between a trip and a warm-up cycle?
4. What could cause the MIL to flash?

## CHAPTER QUIZ

1. A freeze-frame is generated on an OBD-II vehicle _____.
   a. When a type C or D diagnostic trouble code is set
   b. When a type A or B diagnostic trouble code is set
   c. Every other trip
   d. When the PCM detects a problem with the O2S

2. An ignition misfire or fuel mixture problem is an example of what type of DTC?
   a. Type A
   b. Type B
   c. Type C
   d. Type D

3. The comprehensive component monitor checks components for _____.
   a. opens
   b. rationality
   c. functionality
   d. All of the above

4. OBD II has been on all passenger vehicles in the United States since _____.
   a. 1986
   b. 1991
   c. 1996
   d. 2000

5. Fuel trim and misfires are continuously monitored.
   a. True
   b. False

6. DTC P0302 is a _____.
   a. Generic DTC
   b. Vehicle manufacturer-specific DTC
   c. Idle speed-related DTC
   d. Transmission/transaxle-related DTC

7. The MIL is turned off if _____.
   a. The codes are cleared with a scan tool
   b. Power to the PCM is disconnected
   c. The vehicle is driven on three consecutive trips with a warm-up cycle and meets all code set conditions without the PCM detecting any faults
   d. Any of the above occur

8. Which generic DTC could indicate that the gas cap is loose or a defective emission control system?
   a. P0221
   b. P1301
   c. P0442
   d. P1603

9. The computer will automatically clear a DTC if there are no additional detected faults after _____.
   a. Forty consecutive warm-up cycles
   b. Eighty warm-up cycles
   c. Two consecutive trips
   d. Four key-on/key-off cycles

10. A pending code is set when a fault is detected on _____.
    a. A one-trip fault item
    b. The first fault of a two-trip failure
    c. The catalytic converter efficiency
    d. Thermostat problem (too long to closed-loop status)

# GLOBAL OBD II AND MODE $06

**OBJECTIVES:** After studying Chapter 4, the reader will be able to: • Access global OBD II on a scan tool. • Identify mode $06 diagnostic steps. • Describe how mode $06 can be used to identify a problem. • Explain how to convert raw numbers to usable data.

**KEY TERMS:** CID 47 • Generic OBD II 46 • Global OBD II 46 • MID 47 • Mode $06 48 • PID 46 • TID 47

## WHAT IS GLOBAL OBD II?

**Global OBD II,** also called **generic OBD II,** is the standardized format of on-board diagnostics, following SAE standard J1962. Global OBD II was designed for engineers: when OBD II was first introduced, it was not intended to be used by service technicians.

**PURPOSES AND FUNCTIONS** The purposes and functions of Global OBD II include:

1. It can check the powertrain control module (PCM) to determine what it has detected about a failure.

2. It can be used by service technicians to verify a repair.

3. It can check the test results performed by the PCM to see if the results are close to a failure level. This information will show what is at fault even though no diagnostic trouble codes are set.

4. Since the data displayed is very technical, it often needs to be converted to give the service technician usable information.

5. An estimated 80% of the PCM DTCs can be diagnosed using the global OBD II function of the scan tool.

6. All global OBD-II functions are standardized, which is not the case when looking at original equipment manufacturer (OEM) data.

7. Some DTCs may be displayed using the global OBD-II function of the scan tool that is not displayed on an OEM, or by using the enhanced mode OBD-II function of the scan tool.

## GLOBAL OBD II MODES

All OBD-II vehicles must be able to display data on a global (generic) scan tool under nine different modes of operation. These modes include:

| | |
|---|---|
| **MODE ONE** | Current powertrain data (parameter identification display or **PID**) |
| **MODE TWO** | Freeze-frame data |
| **MODE THREE** | Diagnostic trouble codes |
| **MODE FOUR** | Clear and reset diagnostic trouble codes (DTCs), freeze-frame data, and readiness status monitors for noncontinuous monitors only |
| **MODE FIVE** | Oxygen sensor monitor test results |
| **MODE SIX** | Onboard monitoring of test results for non-continuous monitored systems |
| **MODE SEVEN** | Onboard monitoring of test results for continuously monitored systems |
| **MODE EIGHT** | Bidirectional control of onboard systems |
| **MODE NINE** | Module identification |

**HEXADECIMAL NUMBERS** Generic (global) data is used by most state emission programs. Generic OBD-II displays often use hexadecimal numbers, which use 16 numbers instead of 10. The numbers 0 to 9 (zero counts as a number) make up

### ? FREQUENTLY ASKED QUESTION

**How Can You Tell Global from Factory?**

When using a scan tool on an OBD-II equipped vehicle, if the display asks for make, model, and year, then the factory or enhanced part of the PCM is being accessed. This is true for most scan tools except the Chrysler DRB III and Star Scans being used on a Chrysler vehicle. These scan tools can determine vehicle information from the PCM and do not need to be entered by the service technician. If the global or generic part of the PCM is being scanned, then there is no need to know the vehicle details.

the first 10 and then capital letters A to F complete the 16 numbers. To help identify the number as being in a hexadecimal format, a dollar sign ($) is used in front of the number or letter. See the following conversion chart:

| Decimal Number | Hexadecimal Code |
|---|---|
| 0 | $0 |
| 1 | $1 |
| 2 | $2 |
| 3 | $3 |
| 4 | $4 |
| 5 | $5 |
| 6 | $6 |
| 7 | $7 |
| 8 | $8 |
| 9 | $9 |
| 10 | $A |
| 11 | $B |
| 12 | $C |
| 13 | $D |
| 14 | $E |
| 15 | $F |

Hexadecimal coding is also used to identify tests (**Test Identification [TID]** and **Component Identification [CID]**). CAN-equipped vehicles use **monitor identification (MID)** and TID.

## DIAGNOSING PROBLEMS USING MODE $06

Mode $06 information can be used to diagnose faults by following three steps:

**STEP 1** Check the monitor status before starting repairs. This step will show how the system failed.

**STEP 2** Look at the component or parameter that triggered the fault. This step will help pin down the root cause of the failure.

**STEP 3** Look to the monitor enable criteria, which will show what it takes to fail or pass the monitor.

## ACCESSING GLOBAL OBD II

Global (generic) OBD II is used by inspectors where emission testing is performed. Aftermarket scan tools are designed to retrieve global OBD II; however, some original equipment scan

**FIGURE 4–1** Global OBD II can be accessed from the main menu on all aftermarket and some original equipment scan tools.

**? FREQUENTLY ASKED QUESTION**

**What Is EOBD?**
EOBD stands for European on-board diagnostics. It is similar to the U.S. version and meets the standard specified for generic OBD data.

tools, such as the Tech 2 used on General Motors vehicles, are not able to retrieve the information without special software. Global OBD II is accessible using ISO-9141-2, KWP 2000, J1850 PWM, J1850 VPW, and CAN. ● **SEE FIGURE 4–1.**

**SNAP-ON 2500** An older Snap-on scan tool, often called "the brick" that was used in the aftermarket for many year.

**SNAP-ON SOLUS** From the main menu select "Generic OBD II/EOBD" and then follow the on-screen instructions to select the desired test.

**SNAP-ON MODIS** Select the scanner using the down arrow key and then select "Global OBD II." Follow on-screen instructions to get to "start communication" and then to the list of options to view.

**OTC GENISYS** From the main menu select "Global OBD II" and then follow the on-screen instructions. Select "special tests" to get access to mode $06 information and parameters.

**MASTER TECH** From the main menu, select "Global OBD II." At the next screen, select "OBD II functions," then "system tests," and then "other results" to obtain mode $06 data. ● **SEE FIGURE 4–2.**

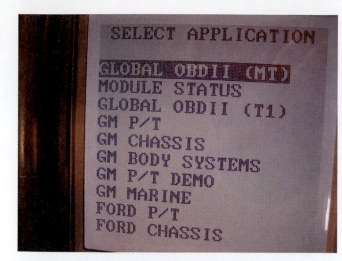

FIGURE 4–2 A photo of a Master Tech display, showing where to select global OBD II from the menu.

## MODE $06

Mode $06 is used by service technicians to monitor the PCM test results of various systems. While other modes are used for monitoring other functions, mode $06 is used to maintain all continuous and noncontinuous monitors and pending DTCs. The continuous monitors include fuel system monitors, misfire monitors, and comprehensive component monitors (CCM). The noncontinuous monitors include catalyst efficiency, EGR, EVAP, oxygen sensor monitors, oxygen sensor heater, secondary air injection (SAI), and thermostats.

**USING MODE $06** Mode $06 is used to monitor all of the tests of the system and components. Mode $06 allows the service technician to view what the computer is doing and see the results of all of the tests that are being performed. Mode $06 can be used for the following:

- **See test results that are close to failing.** This means that a diagnostic trouble code may be set in the future because results of the test are close to the set limit, which would cause a DTC to set. Therefore, by looking at mode $06 data, the technician can be forewarned of a problem; in that case the customer can be told that a "check engine" light may come on and why.
- **Verify a repair.** By looking at mode $06 test results, the service technician can determine whether or not the repair that caused the check engine light to come on was in fact repaired correctly. If the test results are close to the upper or lower limit allowed, the repair was not completed successfully. If, however, the test results are far from the upper or lower limit, the repair was successful

and the vehicle can be returned to the owner with the satisfaction of knowing that the check engine light will not come on again due to the same concern.

**READING MODE $06 DATA** Some scan tools translate the raw hexadecimal data into English, such as Auto Enginuity scan tool software, which is used with a PC. However, the data is difficult to read. In addition, data from Ford vehicles needs to be multiplied by a conversion factor to achieve a usable value.

**SELECT MONITOR** The first step is to select the monitor (fuel trim, misfire, catalyst, etc.). There could be three results:

- **Incomplete.** This means that the computer has not yet completed the test for the selected monitor.
- **Pass.** This means that the monitor was tested to completion and that the test passed. This pass could have been close to failing; looking at the test results will indicate how close it came to failing.
- **Fail.** The monitor test failed. Checking the test results will help the service technician determine why it failed and by how much, which will help in diagnosing the root cause.

**DATA DISPLAY** The test data displayed often includes upper limit and/or lower limit (often not both), test results, and units.

The "unit" may be just a number. However, by looking at the upper and lower limits, the technician can judge how close the test results were to failing the test. Many scan tools display component and test information in plain English while others just display the hexadecimal number. If just the hexadecimal number is shown, it has to be translated into English to show which component or test is being displayed. Check service information for the exact translation or refer to the following charts for a typical example.

### Chart 1

| | |
|---|---|
| $03 | Fuel System 1 |
| $03 | Fuel System 2 |
| $04 | Calculated Load Percentage |
| $05 | Engine Coolant Temp Sensor (Celsius) |
| $06 | Short-Term Fuel Trim Bank 1 (%) |
| $07 | Long-Term Fuel Trim Bank 1 (%) |
| $08 | Short-Term Fuel Trim Bank 2 (%) |
| $09 | Long-Term Fuel Trim Bank 2 (%) |
| $0A | Fuel Pressure Gauge (KPA) |
| $0B | Intake MAP (KPA) |
| $0C | Engine Speed (1/min) |
| $0D | Vehicle Speed (km/h) |
| $0E | Ignition Timing Advance (degrees) |
| $0F | Intake Air Temperature (Celsius) |
| $10 | Air Flow Rate (g/s) |
| $11 | Absolute Throttle Position (%) |

| | |
|---|---|
| $12 | Commanded Secondary AIR Status |
| $13 | O2S Bank 1-Sensor 1 |
| $13 | O2S Bank 1-Sensor 2 |
| $13 | O2S Bank 1-Sensor 3 |
| $13 | O2S Bank 1-Sensor 4 |
| $13 | O2S Bank 2-Sensor 1 |
| $13 | O2S Bank 2-Sensor 2 |
| $13 | O2S Bank 2-Sensor 3 |
| $13 | O2S Bank 2-Sensor 4 |
| $14 | O2S Voltage Bank 1-Sensor 1 (V) |
| $14 | Short-Term Fuel Trim Bank 1-Sensor 1 (%) |
| $15 | O2S Voltage Bank 1-Sensor 2 (V) |
| $15 | Short-Term Fuel Trim Bank 1-Sensor 2 (%) |
| $16 | O2S Voltage Bank 1-Sensor 3 (V) |
| $16 | Short-Term Fuel Trim Bank 1-Sensor 3 (%) |
| $17 | O2S Voltage Bank 1-Sensor 4 (V) |
| $17 | Short-Term Fuel Trim Bank 1-Sensor 4 (%) |
| $18 | O2S Voltage Bank 2-Sensor 1 (V) |
| $18 | O2S Voltage Bank 3-Sensor 1 (V) |
| $18 | Short-Term Fuel Trim Bank 2-Sensor 1 (%) |
| $18 | Short-Term Fuel Trim Bank 3-Sensor 1 (%) |
| $19 | O2S Voltage Bank 2-Sensor 2 (V) |
| $19 | O2S Voltage Bank 3-Sensor 2 (V) |
| $19 | Short-Term Fuel Trim Bank 2-Sensor 2 (%) |
| $19 | Short-Term Fuel Trim Bank 3-Sensor 2 (%) |
| $1A | O2S Voltage Bank 2-Sensor 3 (V) |
| $1A | O2S Voltage Bank 4-Sensor 1 (V) |
| $1A | Short-Term Fuel Trim Bank 2-Sensor 3 (%) |
| $1A | Short-Term Fuel Trim Bank 4-Sensor 1 (%) |
| $1B | O2S Voltage Bank 2-Sensor 4 (V) |
| $1B | O2S Voltage Bank 4-Sensor 2 (V) |
| $1B | Short-Term Fuel Trim Bank 2-Sensor 4 (%) |
| $1B | Short-Term Fuel Trim Bank 4-Sensor 2 (%) |
| $1C | OBD Requirements |
| $1D | O2S Bank 1-Sensor 1 |
| $1D | O2S Bank 1-Sensor 2 |
| $1D | O2S Bank 2-Sensor 1 |
| $1D | O2S Bank 2-Sensor 2 |
| $1D | O2S Bank 3-Sensor 1 |
| $1D | O2S Bank 3-Sensor 2 |
| $1D | O2S Bank 4-Sensor 1 |
| $1D | O2S Bank 4-Sensor 2 |
| $1E | Power Take Off Status |
| $1F | Time Since Engine Start(s) |
| $21 | Distance While MIL Active (km/miles) |
| $22 | Relative Fuel Pressure (kPa) |
| $23 | Fuel Pressure Gauge (kPa) |
| $24 | Equivalence Ratio Bank 1-Sensor 1 (:1) |
| $25 | Equivalence Ratio Bank 1-Sensor 2 (:1) |
| $26 | Equivalence Ratio Bank 1-Sensor 3 (:1) |
| $27 | Equivalence Ratio Bank 1-Sensor 4 (:1) |
| $28 | Equivalence Ratio Bank 2-Sensor 1 (:1) |
| $28 | Equivalence Ratio Bank 3-Sensor 1 (:1) |
| $29 | Equivalence Ratio Bank 2-Sensor 2 (:1) |
| $29 | Equivalence Ratio Bank 3-Sensor 2 (:1) |
| $2A | Equivalence Ratio Bank 2-Sensor 3 (:1) |
| $2A | Equivalence Ratio Bank 3-Sensor 3 (:1) |
| $2B | Equivalence Ratio Bank 2-Sensor 4 (:1) |
| $2B | Equivalence Ratio Bank 3-Sensor 4 (:1) |
| $2C | Commanded EGR (%) |
| $2D | EGR Error (%) |
| $2E | Commanded Evaporative Purge (%) |
| $2F | Fuel Level Input (%) |
| $30 | Number of Warm-Ups Since DTCs Cleared |
| $31 | Distance Since DTCs Cleared |
| $32 | EVAP System Vapor Pressure (Pa) |
| $33 | Barometric Pressure (kPa) |
| $34 | O2S Current Bank 1-Sensor 1 (ma) |
| $35 | O2S Current Bank 1-Sensor 2 (ma) |
| $36 | O2S Current Bank 1-Sensor 3 (ma) |
| $37 | O2S Current Bank 1-Sensor 4 (ma) |
| $38 | O2S Current Bank 2-Sensor 1 (ma) |
| $38 | O2S Current Bank 3-Sensor 1 (ma) |
| $39 | O2S Current Bank 2-Sensor 2 (ma) |
| $39 | O2S Current Bank 3-Sensor 2 (ma) |
| $3A | O2S Current Bank 2-Sensor 3 (ma) |
| $3A | O2S Current Bank 3-Sensor 3 (ma) |
| $3B | O2S Current Bank 2-Sensor 4 (ma) |
| $3B | O2S Current Bank 3-Sensor 4 (ma) |
| $3C | Catalyst Temperature Bank 1-Sensor 1°C |
| $3D | Catalyst Temperature Bank 2-Sensor 1°C |
| $3E | Catalyst Temperature Bank 1-Sensor 2°C |
| $3F | Catalyst Temperature Bank 2-Sensor 2°C |
| $42 | Control Module Voltage |
| $43 | Absolute Load Value (%) |
| $44 | Commanded Equivalence Ratio |
| $45 | Relative Throttle Position (%) |
| $46 | Ambient Air Temperature °C |
| $47 | Absolute Throttle Position B (%) |
| $48 | Absolute Throttle Position C (%) |
| $49 | Accelerator Pedal Position D (%) |
| $4A | Accelerator Pedal Position E (%) |
| $4B | Accelerator Pedal Position F (%) |
| $4C | Commanded Throttle ACT. Control (%) |
| $4D | Engine Run Time with MIL Active (min.) |
| $4E | Time Since DTCs Cleared (min.) |

## Chart 2

| Test ID | Numbers (oxygen sensor) |
|---|---|
| $01 | Rich to Lean Sensor Threshold |
| $02 | Lean to Rich Sensor Threshold |
| $03 | Low Sensor Voltage for Switch Time Calculation |
| $04 | High Sensor Voltage for Switch Time Calculation |
| $05 | Rich to Lean Sensor Switch Time |
| $06 | Lean to Rich Sensor Switch Time |
| $07 | Minimum Sensor Voltage for Test Cycle |
| $08 | Maximum Sensor Voltage for Test Cycle |
| $09 | Time Between Sensor Transitions |
| $0A | Sensor Period |

## OXYGEN SENSOR HEATER MODE $06 TEST (GENERAL MOTORS)

This fault can set a P0141 DTC for bank 1, sensor 1 (B1S1). Checking service information indicates the following enable criteria for the code to set:

1. Cold engine start
2. Engine at idle speed
3. Engine operating temperature below 150°F (66°C)

The following monitors are suspended:

1. EVAP
2. Oxygen sensor performance
3. Catalyst

Mode $06 data for B1S1 heater circuit in TID-06, CID-41:

1. The maximum limit—186
2. Measure value = 33
3. Minimum limit = -----
4. Result = passed

Note that the technician cannot determine what is being measured nor what the number 186 indicates. Also note that there is no minimum limit and the measured value of 33 is far below the maximum limit of 186. This means that the oxygen sensor heater test easily passed.

## ENGINE MISFIRE TESTS (FORD)

A misfire fault can set a random misfire DTC of P0300 or one or more individual misfire DTCs P0301 through P0310 for cylinders one through 10. The enable criteria for these codes to set include:

1. Time since engine start 5 seconds
2. Engine coolant temperature 20°F (−7°C) to 250°F (121°C)
3. RPM range from idle to redline or fuel cutoff
4. Fuel level 15% minimum

Test ID is used to identify several related tests including:

$50—Total engine misfire (updated every 1,000 revolutions)
$53—Cylinder specific misfire

For example, a Ford being checked using mode $06 for TID-50 had the following results:

Maximum limit = 1,180
Measured value = 0

Minimum value = -----
Result = passed

What is the percentage of misfire allowed? The value shown for maximum has to be converted to get the actual percentage.

According to service information, to get the actual percentage of misfire the value has to be multiplied by 0.000015. Therefore, the raw value for maximum misfire was 1,180 × 0.000015, which equals 1.7%. In other words, the maximum allowable misfire before a DTC is set is 1.7%. By looking at mode $06 data, the technician can determine how close the engine is to failing the misfire monitor.

For individual cylinder misfires, check test ID $53. For example, if a value of 17,482 is displayed, the test failed. Multiplying the test results (17,482) by the conversion factor (0.000015) shows a misfire of 26%.

Type A misfire codes are those that can cause damage to the catalytic converter. The misfire usually ranges from 40% at idle to about 4% at high engine speeds.

Type B misfire codes are set if the misfire exceeds 2% to 4%, depending on the engine, make, model, and year.

## FORD OXYGEN SENSOR MODE $06 TEST

Ford and other companies have many tests performed on the oxygen sensor, including voltage amplitude. For example, Ford TID $01, CID $21 for HO2S1 shows:

Minimum value = 512
Maximum value = N/A
Current value = 794

According to Ford service information, the numbers have to be converted into volts by multiplying the value by 0.00098. Therefore, the current value is 0.778 volts, which is above the minimum allowable voltage of 0.50 (512 × 0.0098 = 0.50).

## GENERAL MOTORS CAN OXYGEN SENSOR MODE $06 TEST

One of the oxygen sensor tests performed on a General Motors vehicle equipped with CAN (GMCAN) is the rich-to-lean sensor switch time. Typical test results show:

Monitor ID (MID) $01
Test ID $05

Maximum limit = 0.155 sec.

Measured value = 0.030 sec.

Minimum value = 0.000 sec.

Result = passed

This mode $06 test clearly shows that the oxygen sensor is able to reset very quickly to a change in air-fuel mixture from rich to lean by reacting in 30 ms (0.030 sec.). Normally this information can only be determined by a service technician using a scope of the waveform who forces the system lean and watches the reaction time on the scope display. Using mode $06 and a scan tool, especially on vehicles equipped with CAN, is a fast and easy way to determine oxygen sensor health without having to do time-consuming tests.

## FORD EGR TESTS

Ford checks many functions of the exhaust gas recirculation (EGR) system, including flow testing and tests of the sensor used to check the flow of exhaust gases. The duty cycle of the EGR solenoid can be checked using mode $06 by looking at the following:

TID $4B

CID $30

Maximum limit = 26,214

Measured value = 14,358

Minimum value = -----

Test results = passed

These results at the limits, like many other Ford mode $06 data, must be converted to give usable values. Multiply the measured set limit value by 0.0000305 to get the duty cycle as a percentage (%).

Maximum limit = 26,214 × 0.0000305 = 80%

Measured value = 14.358 × 0.0000305 = 43%

### FORD DELTA PRESSURE FOR EGR FLOW TEST In this test, the following occurred on a test vehicle:

TID 4A

CID 30

Maximum limit =

Measured value = 2,226

Minimum limit = 768

Result = passed

The values shown need to be compared and corrected as follows:

- If the value is greater than 32,767, the value is negative.

- If the value is less than 32,767, the value is positive.

- Multiply the value by 0.0078 to get inches of water.

The value was 2,226 × 0.0078 = 17.7 inches of water (in. $H_2O$) of vacuum (negative pressure).

## GENERAL MOTORS CATALYST EFFICIENCY TEST

The scan tool displays data that does not need to be converted, although the units are often unknown. The service technician can, however, see how close the test results come to either the maximum or the minimum limits. For example, a General Motors idle catalyst efficiency test could have the results following:

TID 0C

CID 60

Maximum limit = 33,234

Measured value = 17,708

Minimum limit = -----

Result = passed

What do the numbers represent? The numbers are created as a result of the test and cannot be determined by the technician. However, it is clear by the reading and the maximum limit that the catalyst efficiency test easily passed. This is an excellent test to check if the efficiency of the catalytic converter needs to be determined.

## GENERAL MOTORS EVAP TEST (CAN)

One of the evaporative (EVAP) system tests that can be monitored using a scan tool and mode $06 data is the engine off, natural vacuum test. An example of a typical result includes:

MID EVAP – 0.020

TID 201

Minimum value = 0.000

Maximum value = 0.601

Current value = 0.023

The values do not need to be converted, although the units are unknown. However, it is clear from the test results that the current value is not even close to the maximum limit, which means that the EVAP system being tested by the natural vacuum method is free from faults.

## WHERE TO GET MODE $06 INFORMATION

Many scan tools display all of the parameters and information needed so that additional mode $06 data is not needed. Many vehicle manufacturers post mode $06 information on the service information websites. This information is often free, unlike other service information. Refer to the National Automotive Service Task Force (NASTF) website for the website address of all vehicle manufacturers' service information sites (*www.NASTF.org*)

Two examples include:

*http://service.gm.com* (free access to mode $06 information)

*www.motorcraftservice.com* (search for mode $06 free access)

## SUMMARY

1. Global OBD II can be used by a service technician to do the following:
   a. Check the PCM regarding what it has detected as a fault
   b. Verify a repair
   c. Check if the test results are close to failure, which could trigger the MIL
2. Global OBD II has nine modes, each covering a certain aspect of the diagnostic system.
3. Mode $06 is the most commonly used mode of global OBD II because it includes data on the noncontinuous monitored system.
4. Most aftermarket scan tools and some original equipment scan tools can access global OBD II data.
5. Many Ford mode $06 data requires that the displayed number be converted to show usable values.

## REVIEW QUESTIONS

1. What are the nine modes of global (generic) OBD II?
2. How do hexadecimal numbers differ from base 10 numbers?
3. Why does some mode $06 data need to be translated into plain English?
4. Where can mode $06 data information be obtained?

## CHAPTER QUIZ

1. What is global (generic) OBD II?
   a. A standardized format that meets SAE standard J1962
   b. A format originally designed for engineers
   c. The same for all numbers and models of vehicles
   d. All of the above
2. Mode $06 can be used to verify a repair by checking _____.
   a. The component system test passed
   b. DTCs
   c. Sensor values
   d. A captured freeze-frame
3. Mode $06 is the mode that checks which systems?
   a. Oxygen sensors
   b. Continuously monitored systems
   c. Noncontinuously monitored systems
   d. Current powertrain data (PIDs)
4. The hexadecimal number for 12 is _____.
   a. 12
   b. $A
   c. $B
   d. $C

5. Technician A says that by looking at the mode $06 data, the technician can determine how close a component or system came to passing the onboard test. Technician B says that the data shown may have to be converted to obtain values that are meaningful to the technician. Which technician is correct?
   a. Technician A only
   b. Technician B only
   c. Both Technicians A and B
   d. Neither Technician A nor B

6. The data display usually shows what information?
   a. Upper limit and lower limit
   b. Upper limit or lower limit
   c. Test results
   d. Both b and c

7. An oxygen sensor switch time from rich to lean is identified as test identification (TID) _____.
   a. $05
   b. $0A
   c. $02
   d. $09

8. Type A misfire codes are those that can damage the catalytic converter and usually have misfires that range from _____ at idle to _____ at high engine speeds.
   a. 10%, 20%
   b. 40%, 4%
   c. 25%, 25%
   d. 2%, 4%

9. A General Motors vehicle is being checked using mode $06 for the proper operation of the oxygen sensor. The rich-to-lean sensor switch time is 0.030 seconds. Technician A says that this indicates a slow reacting oxygen sensor. Technician B says that the oxygen sensor is reacting correctly and is okay. Which technician is correct?
   a. Technician A only
   b. Technician B only
   c. Both Technicians A and B
   d. Neither Technician A nor B

10. Mode $06 information can be accessed at _____.
    a. http://service.gm.com
    b. www.motorcraftservice.com
    c. www.nastf.org
    d. All of the above

# chapter 5

# CIRCUIT TESTERS AND DIGITAL METERS

**OBJECTIVES:** **After studying Chapter 5, the reader will be able to:** • Prepare for ASE Electrical/Electronic Systems (A6) certification test content area "A" (General Electrical/Electronic System Diagnosis). • Discuss how to safely use a fused jumper wire, a test light, and a logic probe. • Explain how to set up and use a digital meter to read voltage, resistance, and current. • Explain meter terms and readings. • Interpret meter readings and compare to factory specifications. • Discuss how to properly and safely use meters.

**KEY TERMS:** AC/DC clamp-on DMM 61 • Continuity light 55 • DMM 56 • DVOM 56 • High-impedance test meter 56 • IEC 66 • Inductive ammeter 60 • Kilo (k) 62 • LED test light 55 • Logic probe 56 • Mega (M) 62 • Meter accuracy 65 • Meter resolution 64 • Milli (m) 62 • OL 58 • RMS 64 • Test light 55

## FUSED JUMPER WIRE

**DEFINITION** A fused jumper wire is used to check a circuit by bypassing the switch or to provide a power or ground to a component. A fused jumper wire, also called a lead, can be purchased or made by the service technician.
● **SEE FIGURE 5–1.**
　It should include the following features.

■ **Fused.** A typical fused jumper wire has a blade-type fuse that can be easily replaced. A 10 ampere fuse (red color) is often the value used.

■ **Alligator clip ends.** Alligator clips on the ends allow the fused jumper wire to be clipped to a ground or power source while the other end is attached to the power side or ground side of the unit being tested.

■ **Good-quality insulated wire.** Most purchased jumper wire is about 14 gauge stranded copper wire with a flexible rubberized insulation to allow it to move easily even in cold weather.

## USES OF A FUSED JUMPER WIRE
A fused jumper wire can be used to help diagnose a component or circuit by performing the following procedures.

■ **Supply power or ground.** If a component, such as a horn, does not work, a fused jumper wire can be used to supply a temporary power and/or ground. Start by unplugging the electrical connector from the device and

**FIGURE 5–1** A technician-made fused jumper lead, which is equipped with a red 10 ampere fuse. This fused jumper wire uses terminals for testing circuits at a connector instead of alligator clips.

connect a fused jumper lead to the power terminal. Another fused jumper wire may be needed to provide the ground. If the unit works, the problem is in the power side or ground side circuit.

**CAUTION: Never use a fused jumper wire to bypass any resistance or load in the circuit. The increased current flow could damage the wiring and could blow the fuse on the jumper lead.**

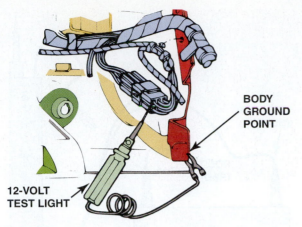

**FIGURE 5–2** A 12 volt test light is attached to a good ground while probing for power.

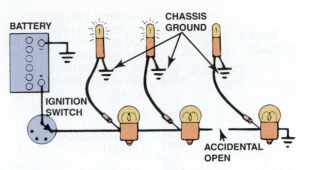

**FIGURE 5–3** A test light can be used to locate an open in a circuit. Note that the test light is grounded at a different location than the circuit itself.

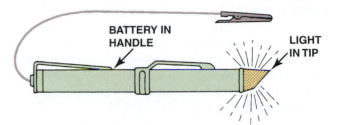

**FIGURE 5–4** A continuity light should not be used on computer circuits because the applied voltage can damage delicate electronic components or circuits.

## TEST LIGHTS

**NONPOWERED TEST LIGHT** A 12 volt test light is one of the simplest testers that can be used to detect electricity. A **test light** is simply a light bulb with a probe and a ground wire attached. ● **SEE FIGURE 5–2.**

It is used to detect battery voltage potential at various test points. Battery voltage cannot be seen or felt, and can be detected only with test equipment.

The ground clip is connected to a clean ground on either the negative terminal of the battery or a clean metal part of the body and the probe touched to terminals or components. If the test light comes on, this indicates that voltage is available. ● **SEE FIGURE 5–3.**

A purchased test light could be labeled a "12 volt test light." Do not purchase a test light designed for household current (110 or 220 volts), as it will not light with 12 to 14 volts.

**USES OF A 12 VOLT TEST LIGHT** A 12 volt test light can be used to check the following:

- **Electrical power.** If the test light lights, then there is power available. It will not, however, indicate the voltage level or if there is enough current available to operate an electrical load. This indicates only that there is enough voltage and current to light the test light (about 0.25 A).

- **Grounds.** A test light can be used to check for grounds by attaching the clip of the test light to the positive terminal of the battery or any 12 volt electrical terminal. The tip of the test light can then be used to touch the ground wire. If there is a ground connection, the test light will light.

**CONTINUITY TEST LIGHTS** A **continuity light** is similar to a test light but includes a battery for self-power. A continuity light illuminates whenever it is connected to both ends of a wire that has continuity or is not broken. ● **SEE FIGURE 5–4.**

**CAUTION: The use of a self-powered (continuity) test light is not recommended on any electronic circuit, because a continuity light contains a battery and applies voltage; therefore, it may harm delicate electronic components.**

**HIGH-IMPEDANCE TEST LIGHT** A high-impedance test light has a high internal resistance and therefore draws very low current in order to light. High-impedance test lights are safe to use on computer circuits because they will not affect the circuit current in the same way as conventional 12 volt test lights when connected to a circuit. There are two types of high-impedance test lights.

- Some test lights use an electronic circuit to limit the current flow, to avoid causing damage to electronic devices.

- An **LED test light** uses a light-emitting diode (LED) instead of a standard automotive bulb for a visual indication of voltage. An LED test light requires only about 25 milliamperes (0.025 ampere) to light; therefore, it can be used on electronic circuits as well as on standard circuits.

● **SEE FIGURE 5–5** for construction details for a homemade LED test light.

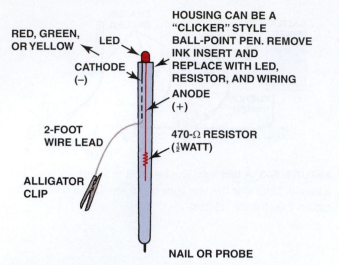

FIGURE 5–5 An LED test light can be easily made using low cost components and an old ink pen. With the 470 ohm resistor in series with the LED, this tester only draws 0.025 ampere (25 milliamperes) from the circuit being tested. This low current draw helps assure the technician that the circuit or component being tested will not be damaged by excessive current flow.

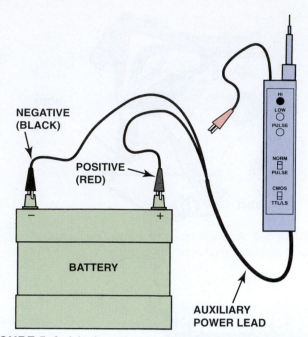

FIGURE 5–6 A logic probe connected to the vehicle battery. When the tip probe is connected to a circuit, it can check for power, ground, or a pulse.

## LOGIC PROBE

**PURPOSE AND FUNCTION** A **logic probe** is an electronic device that lights up a red (usually) LED if the probe is touched to battery voltage. If the probe is touched to ground, a green (usually) LED lights. ● **SEE FIGURE 5–6.**

A logic probe can "sense" the difference between high- and low-voltage levels, which explains the name *logic*.

- A typical logic probe can also light another light (often amber color) when a change in voltage levels occurs.
- Some logic probes will flash the red light when a pulsing voltage signal is detected.
- Some will flash the green light when a pulsing ground signal is detected.

This feature is helpful when checking for a variable voltage output from a computer or ignition sensor.

**USING A LOGIC PROBE** A logic probe must first be connected to a power and ground source such as the vehicle battery. This connection powers the probe and gives it a reference low (ground).

Most logic probes also make a distinctive sound for each high- and low-voltage level. This makes troubleshooting easier when probing connectors or component terminals. A sound (usually a beep) is heard when the probe tip is touched to a changing voltage source. The changing voltage also usually

lights the pulse light on the logic probe. Therefore, the probe can be used to check components such as:

- Pickup coils
- Hall-effect sensors
- Magnetic sensors

## DIGITAL MULTIMETERS

**TERMINOLOGY** Digital multimeter (DMM) and **digital volt-ohm-milliammeter (DVOM)** are terms commonly used for electronic **high-impedance test meters.** *High impedance* means that the electronic internal resistance of the meter is high enough to prevent excessive current draw from any circuit being tested. Most meters today have a minimum of 10 million ohms (10 megohms) of resistance. This high internal resistance between the meter leads is present only when measuring volts. The high resistance in the meter itself reduces the amount of current flowing through the meter when it is being used to measure voltage, leading to more accurate test results because the meter does not change the load on the circuit. High-impedance meters are required for measuring computer circuits.

**CAUTION: Analog (needle-type) meters are almost always lower than 10 megohms and should not be used to measure any computer or electronic circuit. Connecting an analog meter to a computer circuit could damage the computer or other electronic modules.**

A high-impedance meter can be used to measure any automotive circuit within the ranges of the meter. ● **SEE FIGURE 5–7.**

**FIGURE 5–7** Typical digital multimeter. The black meter lead always is placed in the COM terminal. The red meter test lead should be in the volt-ohm terminal except when measuring current in amperes.

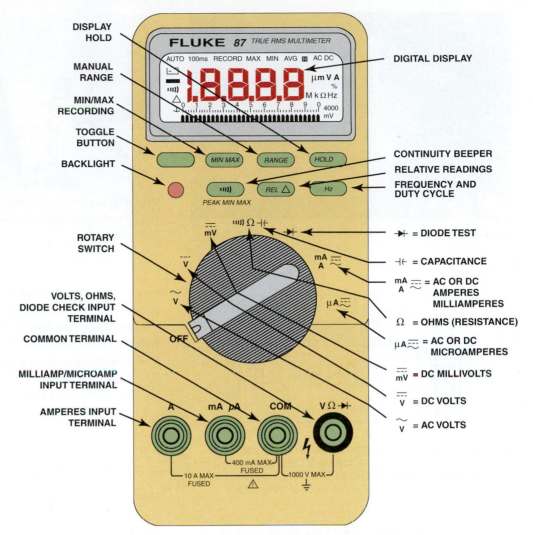

The common abbreviations for the units that many meters can measure are often confusing. ● **SEE CHART 5–1** for the most commonly used symbols and their meanings.

**MEASURING VOLTAGE**  A voltmeter measures the *pressure* or potential of electricity in units of volts. A voltmeter is connected to a circuit in parallel. Voltage can be measured by selecting either AC or DC volts.

- **DC volts (DCV).** This setting is the most common for automotive use. Use this setting to measure battery voltage and voltage to all lighting and accessory circuits.

- **AC volts (ACV).** This setting is used to check for unwanted AC voltage from alternators and some sensors.

- **Range.** The range is automatically set for most meters but can be manually ranged if needed.
  ● **SEE FIGURES 5–8 AND 5–9.**

**MEASURING RESISTANCE**  An ohmmeter measures the resistance in ohms of a component or circuit section when no current is flowing through the circuit. An ohmmeter contains a battery (or other power source) and is connected in series with the component

| SYMBOL | MEANING |
|--------|---------|
| AC | Alternating current or voltage |
| DC | Direct current or voltage |
| V | Volts |
| mV | Millivolts (1/1,000 volts) |
| A | Ampere (amps), current |
| mA | Milliampere (1/1,000 amps) |
| % | Percent (for duty cycle readings only) |
| Ω | Ohms, resistance |
| kΩ | Kilohm (1,000 ohms), resistance |
| MΩ | Megohm (1,000,000 ohms), resistance |
| Hz | Hertz (cycles per second), frequency |
| kHz | Kilohertz (1,000 cycles/sec.), frequency |
| Ms | Milliseconds (1/1,000 sec.) for pulse width measurements |

**CHART 5–1**

Common symbols and abbreviations used on digital meters.

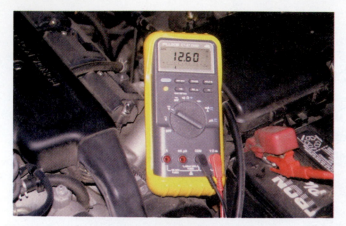

**FIGURE 5–8** Typical digital multimeter (DMM) set to read DC volts.

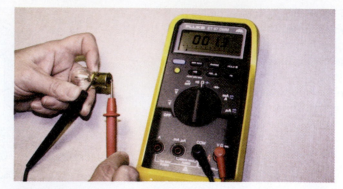

**FIGURE 5–10** Using a digital multimeter set to read ohms (Ω) to test this light bulb. The meter reads the resistance of the filament.

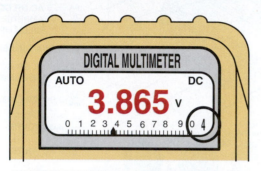

BECAUSE THE SIGNAL READING IS BELOW 4 VOLTS, THE METER AUTORANGES TO THE 4-VOLT SCALE. IN THE 4-VOLT SCALE, THIS METER PROVIDES THREE DECIMAL PLACES.

**(A)**

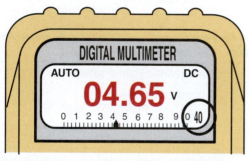

WHEN THE VOLTAGE EXCEEDED 4 VOLTS, THE METER AUTORANGES INTO THE 40-VOLT SCALE. THE DECIMAL POINT MOVES ONE PLACE TO THE RIGHT LEAVING ONLY TWO DECIMAL PLACES.

**(B)**

**FIGURE 5–9** A typical autoranging digital multimeter automatically selects the proper scale to read the voltage being tested. The scale selected is usually displayed on the meter face. (a) Note that the display indicates "4," meaning that this range can read up to 4 volts. (b) The range is now set to the 40 volt scale, meaning that the meter can read up to 40 volts on the scale. Any reading above this level will cause the meter to reset to a higher scale. If not set on autoranging, the meter display would indicate OL if a reading exceeds the limit of the scale selected.

or wire being measured. When the leads are connected to a component, current flows through the test leads and the difference in voltage (voltage drop) between the leads is measured as resistance. Note the following facts about using an ohmmeter.

- Zero ohms on the scale means that there is no resistance between the test leads, thus indicating continuity or a continuous path for the current to flow in a closed circuit.
- Infinity means no connection, as in an open circuit.
- Ohmmeters have no required polarity even though red and black test leads are used for resistance measurement.

**CAUTION: The circuit must be electrically open with no current flowing when using an ohmmeter. If current is flowing when an ohmmeter is connected, the reading will be incorrect and the meter can be destroyed.**

Different meters have different ways of indicating infinity resistance, or a reading higher than the scale allows. Examples of an over limit display include:

- **OL,** meaning **over limit** or overload
- Flashing or solid number 1
- Flashing or solid number 3 on the left side of the display

Check the meter instructions for the exact display used to indicate an open circuit or over range reading. ● **SEE FIGURES 5–10 AND 5–11.**

To summarize, open and zero readings are as follows:

0.00 Ω = Zero resistance (component or circuit has continuity)

OL = An open circuit or reading is higher than the scale selected (no current flows)

**MEASURING AMPERES** An ammeter measures the flow of *current* through a complete circuit in units of amperes. The ammeter has to be installed in the circuit (in series) so that it can measure all the current flow in that circuit, just as a water flow meter would measure the amount of water flow (cubic feet per minute, for example). ● **SEE FIGURE 5–12.**

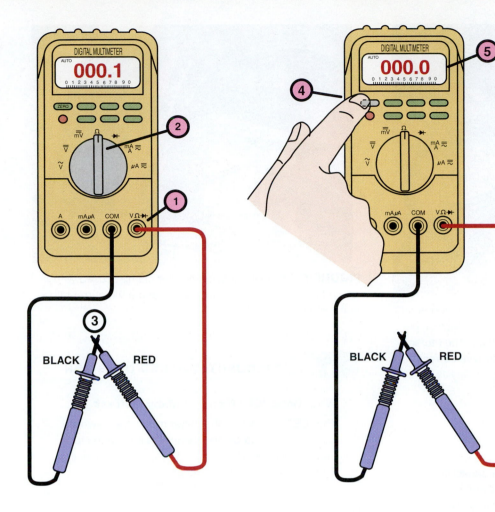

FIGURE 5-11 Many digital multimeters can have the display indicate zero to compensate for test lead resistance. (1) Connect leads in the V Ω and COM meter terminals. (2) Select the Ω scale. (3) Touch the two meter leads together. (4) Push the "zero" or "relative" button on the meter. (5) The meter display will now indicate zero ohms of resistance.

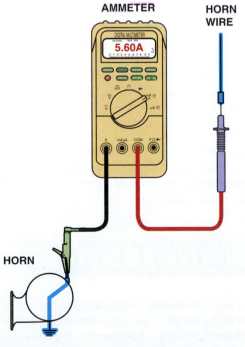

FIGURE 5-12 Measuring the current flow required by a horn requires that the ammeter be connected to the circuit in series and the horn button be depressed by an assistant.

## ? FREQUENTLY ASKED QUESTION

### How Much Voltage Does an Ohmmeter Apply?

Most digital meters that are set to measure ohms (resistance) apply 0.3 to 1 volt to the component being measured. The voltage comes from the meter itself to measure the resistance. Two things are important to remember about an ohmmeter.

1. The component or circuit must be disconnected from any electrical circuit while the resistance is being measured.

2. Because the meter itself applies a voltage (even though it is relatively low), a meter set to measure ohms can damage electronic circuits. Computer or electronic chips can be easily damaged if subjected to only a few milliamperes of current, similar to the amount an ohmmeter applies when a resistance measurement is being performed.

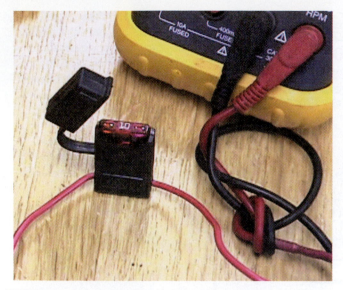

**FIGURE 5–13** Note the blade-type fuse holder soldered in series with one of the meter leads. A 10 ampere fuse helps protect the internal meter fuse (if equipped) and the meter itself from damage that may result from excessive current flow if accidentally used incorrectly.

**FIGURE 5–14** An inductive ammeter clamp is used with all starting and charging testers to measure the current flow through the battery cables.

**CAUTION: An ammeter must be installed in series with the circuit to measure the current flow in the circuit. If a meter set to read amperes is connected in parallel, such as across a battery, the meter or the leads may be destroyed, or the fuse will blow, by the current available across the battery. Some digital multimeters (DMMs) beep if the unit selection does not match the test lead connection on the meter. However, in a noisy shop, this beep sound may be inaudible.**

    Digital meters require that the meter leads be moved to the ammeter terminals. Most digital meters have an ampere scale that can accommodate a maximum of 10 amperes. See the Tech Tip, "Fuse Your Meter Leads!"

## INDUCTIVE AMMETERS

**OPERATION** **Inductive ammeters** do not make physical contact with the circuit. They measure the strength of the magnetic field surrounding the wire carrying the current, and use a Hall-effect sensor to measure current. The Hall-effect sensor detects the strength of the magnetic field that surrounds the wire carrying an electrical current. ● **SEE FIGURE 5–14.**

**FIGURE 5–15** A typical mini clamp-on-type digital multimeter. This meter is capable of measuring alternating current (AC) and direct current (DC) without requiring that the circuit be disconnected to install the meter in series. The jaws are simply placed over the wire and current flow through the circuit is displayed.

This means that the meter probe surrounds the wire(s) carrying the current and measures the strength of the magnetic field that surrounds any conductor carrying a current.

### AC/DC CLAMP-ON DIGITAL MULTIMETERS
An **AC/DC clamp-on digital multimeter (DMM)** is a useful meter for automotive diagnostic work. ● **SEE FIGURE 5–15.**

The major advantage of the clamp-on-type meter is that there is no need to break the circuit to measure current (amperes). Simply clamp the jaws of the meter around the power lead(s) or ground lead(s) of the component being measured and read the display. Most clamp-on meters can also measure alternating current, which is helpful in the diagnosis of an alternator problem. Volts, ohms, frequency, and temperature can also be measured with the typical clamp-on DMM, but use conventional meter leads. The inductive clamp is only used to measure amperes.

# DIODE CHECK, PULSE WIDTH, AND FREQUENCY

### DIODE CHECK
Diode check is a meter function that can be used to check diodes including light-emitting diodes (LEDs).

The meter is able to text diodes by way of the following:

- The meter applies roughly a 3 volt DC signal to the text leads.
- The voltage is high enough to cause a diode to work and the meter will display:
  1. 0.4 to 0.7 volt when testing silicon diodes such as found in alternators
  2. 1.5 to 2.3 volts when testing LEDs such as found in some lighting applications

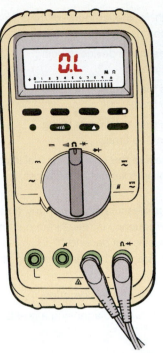

**FIGURE 5–16** Typical digital multimeter showing OL (over limit) on the readout with the ohms (Ω) unit selected. This usually means that the unit being measured is open (infinity resistance) and has no continuity.

🔧 **TECH TIP**

**Over Limit Display Does Not Mean the Meter Is Reading "Nothing"**

The meaning of the over limit display on a digital meter often confuses beginning technicians. When asked what the meter is reading when an over limit (OL) is displayed on the meter face, the response is often, "Nothing." Many meters indicate *over limit* or *over load,* which simply means that the reading is over the maximum that can be displayed for the selected range. For example, the meter will display OL if 12 volts are being measured but the meter has been set to read a maximum of 4 volts.

Autoranging meters adjust the range to match what is being measured. Here OL means a value higher than the meter can read (unlikely on the voltage scale for automobile usage), or infinity when measuring resistance (ohms). Therefore, OL means infinity when measuring resistance or an open circuit is being indicated. The meter will read 00.0 if the resistance is zero, so "nothing" in this case indicates continuity (zero resistance), whereas OL indicates infinity resistance. Therefore, when talking with another technician about a meter reading, make sure you know exactly what the reading on the face of the meter means. Also be sure that you are connecting the meter leads correctly. ● **SEE FIGURE 5–16.**

**PULSE WIDTH** Pulse width is the amount of time in a percentage that a signal is on compared to being off.

- 100% pulse width indicates that a device is being commanded on all of the time.
- 50% pulse width indicates that a device is being commanded on half of the time.
- 25% pulse width indicates that a device is being commanded on just 25% of the time.

Pulse width is used to measure the on time for fuel injectors and other computer-controlled solenoid and devices.

**FREQUENCY** Frequency is a measure of how many times per second a signal changes. Frequency is measured in a unit called hertz, formerly termed "cycles per second."

Frequency measurements are used when checking the following:

- Mass airflow (MAF) sensors for proper operation
- Ignition primary pulse signals when diagnosing a no-start condition
- Checking a wheel speed sensor

# ELECTRICAL UNIT PREFIXES

**DEFINITIONS** Electrical units are measured in numbers such as 12 volts, 150 amperes, and 470 ohms. Large units over 1,000 may be expressed in kilo units. **Kilo (k)** means 1,000.
● **SEE FIGURE 5–17.**

4,700 ohms = 4.7 kilohms (kΩ)

If the value is over 1 million (1,000,000), then the prefix **mega (M)** is often used. For example:

1,100,000 volts = 1.1 megavolts (MV)

4,700,000 ohms = 4.7 megohms (MΩ)

Sometimes a circuit conducts so little current that a smaller unit of measure is required. Small units of measure expressed in 1/1,000 are prefixed by **milli (m)**. To summarize:

mega (M) = 1,000,000 (decimal point six places to the right = 1,000,000)

kilo (k) = 1,000 (decimal point three places to the right = 1,000)

milli (m) = 1/1,000 (decimal point three places to the left = 0.001)

**HINT: Lowercase *m* equals a small unit (milli), whereas a capital *M* represents a large unit (mega).**

● **SEE CHART 5–2.**

**USE OF PREFIXES** The prefixes can be confusing because most digital meters can express values in more than one unit, especially if the meter is autoranging. For example, an ammeter reading may show 36.7 mA on autoranging. When the scale is changed to

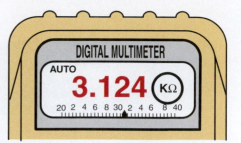

**THE SYMBOL ON THE RIGHT SIDE OF THE DISPLAY INDICATES WHAT RANGE THE METER HAS BEEN SET TO READ.**

Ω = **OHMS**
IF THE ONLY SYMBOL ON THE DISPLAY IS THE OHMS SYMBOL, THE READING ON THE DISPLAY IS EXACTLY THE RESISTANCE IN OHMS.

KΩ = **KILOHMS = OHMS TIMES 1000**
A "K" IN FRONT OF THE OHMS SYMBOL MEANS "KILOHMS"; THE READING ON THE DISPLAY IS IN KILOHMS. YOU HAVE TO MULTIPLY THE READING ON THE DISPLAY BY 1000 TO GET THE RESISTANCE IN OHMS.

MΩ = **MEGOHMS = OHMS TIMES 1,000,000**
A "M" IN FRONT OF THE OHMS SYMBOL MEANS "MEGOHMS"; THE READING ON THE DISPLAY IS IN MEGOHMS. YOU HAVE TO MULTIPLY THE READING ON THE DISPLAY BY 1,000,000 TO GET THE RESISTANCE IN OHMS.

**FIGURE 5–17** Always look at the meter display when a measurement is being made, especially if using an autoranging meter.

| TO/ FROM | MEGA | KILO | BASE | MILLI |
|---|---|---|---|---|
| Mega | 0 places | 3 places to the right | 6 places to the right | 9 places to the right |
| Kilo | 3 places to the left | 0 places | 3 places to the right | 6 places to the right |
| Base | 6 places to the left | 3 places to the left | 0 places | 3 places to the right |
| Milli | 9 places to the left | 6 places to the left | 3 places to the left | 0 places |

**CHART 5–2**

A conversion chart showing the decimal point location for the various prefixes.

amperes ("A" in the window of the display), the number displayed will be 0.037 A. Note that the resolution of the value is reduced.

**HINT: Always check the face of the meter display for the unit being measured. To best understand what is being displayed on the face of a digital meter, select a manual scale and move the selector until *whole units appear*, such as "A" for amperes instead of "mA" for milliamperes.**

**Think of Money**

Digital meter displays can often be confusing. The display for a battery measured as 12 1/2 volts would be 12.50 V, just as $12.50 is 12 dollars and 50 cents. A 1/2 volt reading on a digital meter will be displayed as 0.50 V, just as $0.50 is half of a dollar.

It is more confusing when low values are displayed. For example, if a voltage reading is 0.063 volt, an autoranging meter will display 63 millivolts (63 mV), or 63/1,000 of a volt, or $63 of $1,000. (It takes 1,000 mV to equal 1 volt.) Think of millivolts as one-tenth of a cent, with 1 volt being $1.00. Therefore, 630 millivolts are equal to $0.63 of $1.00 (630 tenths of a cent, or 63 cents).

To avoid confusion, try to manually range the meter to read base units (whole volts). If the meter is ranged to base unit volts, 63 millivolts would be displayed as 0.063 or maybe just 0.06, depending on the display capabilities of the meter.

# HOW TO READ DIGITAL METERS

**STEPS TO FOLLOW** Getting to know and use a digital meter takes time and practice. The first step is to read, understand, and follow all safety and operational instructions that come with the meter. Use of the meter usually involves the following steps.

**STEP 1** **Select the proper unit of electricity for what is being measured.** This unit could be volts, ohms (resistance), or amperes (amount of current flow). If the meter is not autoranging, select the proper scale for the anticipated reading. For example, if a 12 volt battery is being measured, select a meter reading range that is higher than the voltage but not too high. A 20 or 30 volt range will accurately show the voltage of a 12 volt battery. If a 1,000 volt scale is selected, a 12 volt reading may not be accurate.

**STEP 2** **Place the meter leads into the proper input terminals.**
- The black lead is inserted into the common (COM) terminal. This meter lead usually stays in this location for all meter functions.
- The red lead is inserted into the volt, ohm, or diode check terminal usually labeled "VΩ" when voltage, resistance, or diodes are being measured.
- When current flow in amperes is being measured, most digital meters require that the red test lead

be inserted in the ammeter terminal, usually labeled "A" or "mA."

**CAUTION: If the meter leads are inserted into ammeter terminals, even though the selector is set to volts, the meter may be damaged or an internal fuse may blow if the test leads touch both terminals of a battery.**

**STEP 3** **Measure the component being tested.** Carefully note the decimal point and the unit on the face of the meter.

- **Meter lead connections.** If the meter leads are connected to a battery backwards (red to the battery negative, for example), the display will still show the correct reading, but a negative sign (−) will be displayed in front of the number. The correct polarity is not important when measuring resistance (ohms) except where indicated, such as measuring a diode.
- **Autorange.** Many meters automatically default to the autorange position and the meter will display the value in the most readable scale. The meter can be manually ranged to select other levels or to lock in a scale for a value that is constantly changing.

  If a 12 volt battery is measured with an autoranging meter, the correct reading of 12.0 is given. "AUTO" and "V" should show on the face of the meter. For example, if a meter is manually set to the 2 kilohm scale, the highest that the meter will read is 2,000 ohms. If the reading is over 2,000 ohms, the meter will display OL. ● **SEE CHART 5–3.**

**STEP 4** **Interpret the reading.** This is especially difficult on autoranging meters, where the meter itself selects the proper scale. The following are two examples of different readings.

**Example 1:** A voltage drop is being measured. The specifications indicate a maximum voltage drop of 0.2 volt. The meter reads "AUTO" and "43.6 mV." This reading means that the voltage drop is 0.0436 volt, or 43.6 mV, which is far lower than the 0.2 volt (200 millivolts). Because the number showing on the meter face is much larger than the specifications, many beginner technicians are led to believe that the voltage drop is excessive.

**NOTE: Pay attention to the units displayed on the meter face and convert to whole units.**

**Example 2:** A spark plug wire is being measured. The reading should be less than 10,000 ohms for each foot in length if the wire is okay. The wire being tested is 3 ft long (maximum allowable resistance is 30,000 ohms). The meter reads "AUTO" and "14.85 kΩ." This reading is equivalent to 14,850 ohms.

**NOTE: When converting from kilohms to ohms, make the decimal point a comma.**

Because this reading is well below the specified maximum allowable, the spark plug wire is okay.

## VOLTAGE BEING MEASURED

| Scale Selected | 0.01 V (10 MV) | 0.150 V (150 MV) | 1.5 V | 10.0 V | 12.0 V | 120 V |
|---|---|---|---|---|---|---|
| | Voltmeter will display: | | | | | |
| 200 mV | 10.0 | 150.0 | OL | OL | OL | OL |
| 2 V | 0.100 | 0.150 | 1.500 | OL | OL | OL |
| 20 V | 0.1 | 1.50 | 1.50 | 10.00 | 12.00 | OL |
| 200 V | 00.0 | 01.5 | 01.5 | 10.0 | 12.0 | 120.0 |
| 2 kV | 00.00 | 00.00 | 000.1 | 00.10 | 00.12 | 0.120 |
| Autorange | 10.0 mV | 15.0 mV | 1.50 | 10.0 | 12.0 | 120.0 |

## RESISTANCE BEING MEASURED

| Scale Selected | 10 OHMS | 100 OHMS | 470 OHMS | 1 KILOHM | 220 KILOHMS | 1 MEGOHM |
|---|---|---|---|---|---|---|
| | Ohmmeter will display: | | | | | |
| 400 ohms | 10.0 | 100.0 | OL | OL | OL | OL |
| 4 kilohms | 010 | 100 | 0.470 k | 1000 | OL | OL |
| 40 kilohms | 00.0 | 0.10 k | 0.47 k | 1.00 k | OL | OL |
| 400 kilohms | 000.0 | 00.1 k | 00.5 k | 0.10 k | 220.0 k | OL |
| 4 megohms | 00.00 | 0.01 M | 0.05 M | 00.1 M | 0.22 M | 1.0 M |
| Autorange | 10.0 | 100.0 | 470.0 | 1.00 k | 220 k | 1.00 M |

## CURRENT BEING MEASURED

| Scale Selected | 50 MA | 150 MA | 1.0 A | 7.5 A | 15.0 A | 25.0 A |
|---|---|---|---|---|---|---|
| | Ammeter will display: | | | | | |
| 40 mA | OL | OL | OL | OL | OL | OL |
| 400 mA | 50.0 | 150 | OL | OL | OL | OL |
| 4 A | 0.05 | 0.00 | 1.00 | OL | OL | OL |
| 40 A | 0.00 | 0.000 | 01.0 | 7.5 | 15.0 | 25.0 |
| Autorange | 50.0 mA | 150.0 mA | 1.00 | 7.5 | 15.0 | 25.0 |

**CHART 5–3** Sample meter readings using manually set and autoranging selection on the digital meter control.

**RMS VERSUS AVERAGE** Alternating current voltage waveforms can be true sinusoidal or nonsinusoidal. A true sine wave pattern measurement will be the same for both **root-mean-square (RMS)** and average reading meters. RMS and averaging are two methods used to measure the true effective rating of a signal that is constantly changing. ● SEE FIGURE 5–18.

Only true RMS meters are accurate when measuring non-sinusoidal AC waveforms, which are seldom used in automotive applications.

**RESOLUTION, DIGITS, AND COUNTS** Meter resolution refers to how small or fine a measurement the meter can make. By knowing the resolution of a DMM you can determine whether the meter could measure down to only 1 volt or down to 1 millivolt (1/1,000 of a volt).

You would not buy a ruler marked in 1 in. segments (or centimeters) if you had to measure down to 1/4 in. (or 1 mm). A thermometer that only measured in whole degrees is not of

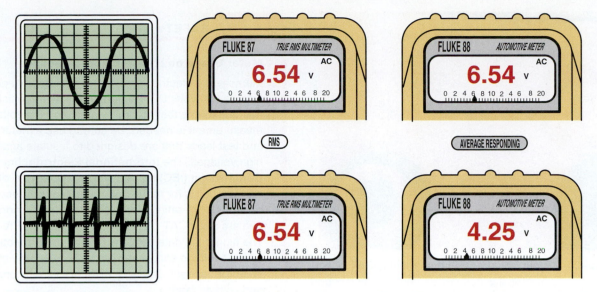

**FIGURE 5–18** When reading AC voltage signals, a true RMS meter (such as a Fluke 87) provides a different reading than an average responding meter (such as a Fluke 88). The only place this difference is important is when a reading is to be compared with a specification.

**FIGURE 5–19** This meter display shows 052.2 AC volts. Notice that the zero beside the 5 indicates that the meter can read over 100 volts AC with a resolution of 0.1 volt.

much use when your normal temperature is 98.6°F. You need a thermometer with 0.1° *resolution.*

The terms *digits* and *counts* are used to describe a meter's resolution. DMMs are grouped by the number of counts or digits they display.

- A 3 1/2-digit meter can display three full digits ranging from 0 to 9, and one "half" digit that displays only a 1 or is left blank. A 3 1/2-digit meter will display up to 1,999 counts of resolution.

- A 4 1/2-digit meter can display up to 19,000 counts of resolution. It is more precise to describe a meter by counts of resolution than by 3 1/2 or 4 1/2 digits. Some 3 1/2-digit meters have enhanced resolution of up to 3,200 or 4,000 counts.

Meters with more counts offer better resolution for certain measurements. For example, a 1,999 count meter will not be able to measure down to a tenth of a volt when measuring 200 volts or more. ● **SEE FIGURE 5–19.**

However, a 3,200 count meter will display a tenth of a volt up to 320 volts. Digits displayed to the far right of the display may at times flicker or constantly change. This is called *digit rattle* and represents a changing voltage being measured on the ground (COM terminal of the meter lead). High-quality meters are designed to reject this unwanted voltage.

**ACCURACY** Meter accuracy is the largest allowable error that will occur under specific operating conditions. In other words, it is an indication of how close the DMM's displayed measurement is to the actual value of the signal being measured.

Accuracy for a DMM is usually expressed as a percent of reading. An accuracy of ±1% of reading means that for a displayed reading of 100.0 V, the actual value of the voltage could be anywhere between 99.0 V and 101.0 V. Thus, the lower the percent of accuracy is, the better.

- Unacceptable = 1.00%
- Okay = 0.50% (1/2%)
- Good = 0.25% (1/4%)
- Excellent = 0.10% (1/10%)

**FIGURE 5–20** Be sure to only use a meter that is CAT III rated when taking electrical voltage measurements on a hybrid vehicle.

**FIGURE 5–21** Always use meter leads that are CAT III rated on a meter that is also CAT III rated, to maintain the protection needed when working on hybrid vehicles.

For example, if a battery had 12.6 volts, a meter could read between the following, based on its accuracy.

| | | |
|---|---|---|
| ±0.1% | high = | 12.61 |
| | low = | 12.59 |
| ±0.25% | high = | 12.63 |
| | low = | 12.57 |
| ±0.50% | high = | 12.66 |
| | low = | 12.54 |
| ±1.00% | high = | 12.73 |
| | low = | 12.47 |

Before you purchase a meter, check the accuracy. Accuracy is usually indicated on the specifications sheet for the meter.

**Meter Usage on Hybrid Electric Vehicles**

Many hybrid electric vehicles use system voltage as high as 650 volts DC. Be sure to follow all vehicle manufacturer's testing procedures; and if a voltage measurement is needed, be sure to use a meter and test leads that are designed to insulate against high voltages. The **International Electrotechnical Commission (IEC)** has several categories of voltage standards for meter and meter leads. These categories are ratings for overvoltage protection and are rated CAT I, CAT II, CAT III, and CAT IV. The higher the category, the greater the protection against voltage spikes caused by high-energy circuits. Under each category there are various energy and voltage ratings.

**CAT I**      Typically a CAT I meter is used for low-energy voltage measurements such as at wall outlets in the home. Meters with a CAT I rating are usually rated at 300 to 800 volts.

**CAT II**      This higher rated meter would be typically used for checking higher energy level voltages at the fuse panel in the home. Meters with a CAT II rating are usually rated at 300 to 600 volts.

**CAT III**      This minimum rated meter should be used for hybrid vehicles. The CAT III category is designed for high-energy levels and voltage measurements at the service pole at the transformer. Meters with this rating are usually rated at 600 to 1,000 volts.

**CAT IV**      CAT IV meters are for clamp-on meters only. If a clamp-on meter also has meter leads for voltage measurements, that part of the meter will be rated as CAT III.

**NOTE: Always use the highest CAT rating meter, especially when working with hybrid vehicles. A CAT III, 600 volt meter is safer than a CAT II, 1,000 volt meter because of the energy level of the CAT ratings.**

Therefore, for best personal protection, use only meters and meter leads that are CAT III or CAT IV rated when measuring voltage on a hybrid vehicle. ● **SEE FIGURES 5–20 AND 5–21.**

**1** For most electrical measurements, the black meter lead is inserted in the terminal labeled COM and the red meter lead is inserted into the terminal labeled V.

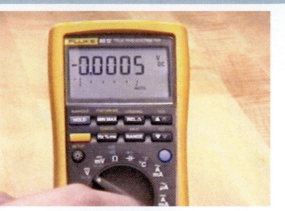

**2** To use a digital meter, turn the power switch and select the unit of electricity to be measured. In this case, the rotary switch is turned to select DC volts.

**3** For most automotive electrical use such as for measuring battery voltage, select DC volts.

**4** Connect the red meter lead to the positive (+) terminal of a battery and the black meter lead to the negative (−) terminal of a battery. The meter reads the voltage difference between the leads.

**5** This jump start battery unit measures 13.151 volts with the meter set on autoranging on the DC voltage scale.

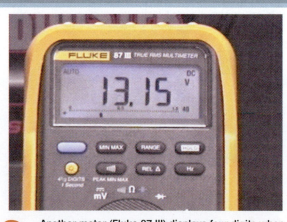

**6** Another meter (Fluke 87 III) displays four digits when measuring the voltage of the battery jump start unit.

CONTINUED ▶

**7** To measure resistance turn the rotary dial to the ohm (Ω) symbol. With the meter leads separated, the meter display reads OL (over limit).

**8** The meter can read your own body resistance if you grasp the meter lead terminals with your fingers. The reading on the display indicates 196.35 kΩ.

**9** When measuring anything; be sure to read the meter face. In this case, the meter is reading 291.10 kΩ.

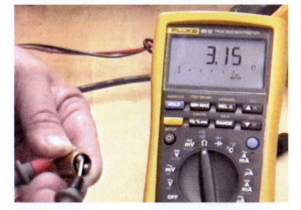

**10** A meter set on ohms can be used to check the resistance of a light bulb filament. In this case, the meter reads 3.15 ohms. If the bulb were bad (filament open), the meter would display OL.

**11** A digital meter set to read ohms should measure 0.00 as shown when the meter leads are touched together.

**12** The large letter V means volts and the wavy symbol over the V means that the meter measures alternating current (AC) voltage if this position is selected.

**13** The next symbol is a V with a dotted and a straight line overhead. This symbol stands for direct current (DC) volts. This position is most used for automotive service.

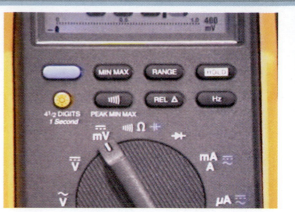

**14** The symbol mV indicates millivolts or 1/1000 of a volt (0.001). The solid and dashed line above the mV means DC mV.

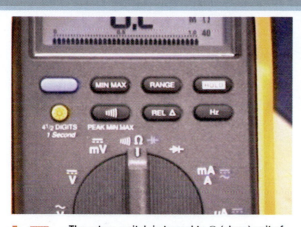

**15** The rotary switch is turned to Ω (ohms) unit of resistance measure. The symbol to the left of the Ω symbol is the beeper or continuity indicator.

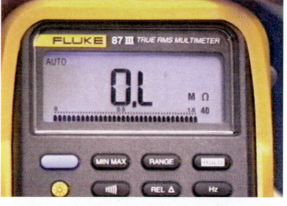

**16** Notice that auto is in the upper left and the MΩ is in the lower right. This MΩ means megaohms or that the meter is set to read in millions of ohms.

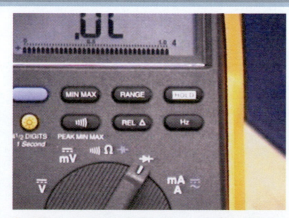

**17** The symbol shown is the symbol of a diode. In this position, the meter applies a voltage to a diode and the meter reads the voltage drop across the junction of a diode.

**18** One of the most useful features of this meter is the MIN/MAX feature. By pushing the MIN/MAX button, the meter will be able to display the highest (MAX) and the lowest (MIN) reading.

CONTINUED ▶

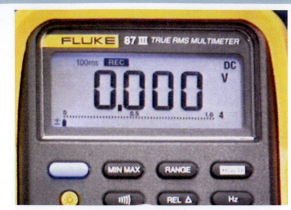

**19** Pushing the MIN/MAX button puts the meter into record mode. Note the 100 mS and "rec" on the display. In this position, the meter is capturing any voltage change that lasts 100 mS (0.1 sec) or longer.

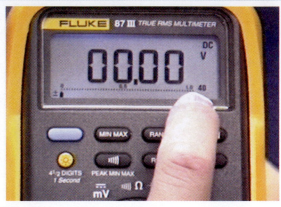

**20** To increase the range of the meter touch the range button. Now the meter is set to read voltage up to 40 volts DC.

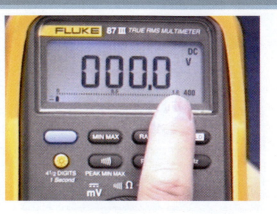

**21** Pushing the range button one more time changes the meter scale to the 400-voltage range. Notice that the decimal point has moved to the right.

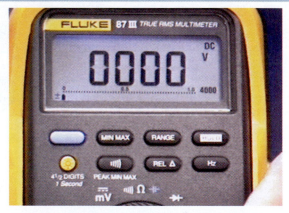

**22** Pushing the range button again changes the meter to the 4000-volt range. This range is not suitable to use in automotive applications.

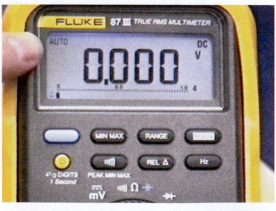

**23** By pushing and holding the range button, the meter will reset to autorange. Autorange is the preferred setting for most automotive measurements except when using MIN/MAX record mode.

## SUMMARY

1. Digital multimeter (DMM) and digital volt-ohm-milliammeter (DVOM) are terms commonly used for electronic high-impedance test meters.

2. Use of a high-impedance digital meter is required on any computer-related circuit or component.

3. Ammeters measure current and must be connected in series in the circuit.

4. Voltmeters measure voltage and are connected in parallel.

5. Ohmmeters measure resistance of a component and must be connected in parallel, with the circuit or component disconnected from power.

6. Logic probes can indicate the presence of power, ground, or pulsed signals.

## REVIEW QUESTIONS

1. Why should high-impedance meters be used when measuring voltage on computer-controlled circuits?

2. How is an ammeter connected to an electrical circuit?

3. Why must an ohmmeter be connected to a disconnected circuit or component?

## CHAPTER QUIZ

1. Inductive ammeters work because of what principle?
   a. Magic
   b. Electrostatic electricity
   c. A magnetic field surrounds any wire carrying a current
   d. Voltage drop as it flows through a conductor

2. A meter used to measure amperes is called a(n) _____.
   a. Amp meter
   b. Ampmeter
   c. Ammeter
   d. Coulomb meter

3. A voltmeter should be connected to the circuit being tested _____.
   a. In series
   b. In parallel
   c. Only when no power is flowing
   d. Both a and c

4. An ohmmeter should be connected to the circuit or component being tested _____.
   a. With current flowing in the circuit or through the component
   b. When connected to the battery of the vehicle to power the meter
   c. Only when no power is flowing (electrically open circuit)
   d. Both b and c

5. A high-impedance meter _____.
   a. Measures a high amount of current flow
   b. Measures a high amount of resistance
   c. Can measure a high voltage
   d. Has a high internal resistance

6. A meter is set to read DC volts on the 4 volt scale. The meter leads are connected at a 12 volt battery. The display will read _____.
   a. 0.00
   b. OL
   c. 12 V
   d. 0.012 V

7. What could happen if the meter leads were connected to the positive and negative terminals of the battery while the meter and leads were set to read amperes?
   a. Could blow an internal fuse or damage the meter
   b. Would read volts instead of amperes
   c. Would display OL
   d. Would display 0.00

8. The highest amount of resistance that can be read by the meter set to the 2 kΩ scale is _____.
   a. 2,000 ohms
   b. 200 ohms
   c. 200 kΩ (200,000 ohms)
   d. 20,000,000 ohms

9. If a digital meter face shows 0.93 when set to read kΩ, the reading means _____.
   a. 93 ohms
   b. 930 ohms
   c. 9,300 ohms
   d. 93,000 ohms

10. A reading of 432 shows on the face of the meter set to the millivolt scale. The reading means _____.
    a. 0.432 volt
    b. 4.32 volts
    c. 43.2 volts
    d. 4,320 volts

# OSCILLOSCOPES AND GRAPHING MULTIMETERS

**OBJECTIVES:** **After studying Chapter 6, the reader will be able to:** • Prepare for ASE Electrical/Electronic Systems (A6) certification test content area "A" (General Electrical/Electronic System Diagnosis). • Use a digital storage oscilloscope to measure voltage signals. • Interpret meter and scope readings and determine if the values are within factory specifications. • Explain time base and volts per division settings. • Explain how a graphing multimeter works.

**KEY TERMS:** AC coupling 74 • BNC connector 77 • Cathode ray tube (CRT) 72 • Channel 75 • DC coupling 74 • Digital storage oscilloscope (DSO) 72 • Division 73 • Duty cycle 75 • External trigger 76 • Frequency 75 • GMM 78 • Graticule 72 • Hertz 75 • Oscilloscope (scope) 72 • Pulse train 74 • Pulse width 75 • PWM 75 • Time base 73 • Trigger level 76 • Trigger slope 76

## TYPES OF OSCILLOSCOPES

**TERMINOLOGY** An **oscilloscope** (usually called a **scope**) is a visual voltmeter with a timer that shows when a voltage changes. Following are several types of oscilloscopes.

- An *analog scope* uses a **cathode ray tube (CRT)** similar to a television screen to display voltage patterns. The scope screen displays the electrical signal constantly.

- A *digital scope* commonly uses a liquid crystal display (LCD), but a CRT may also be used on some digital scopes. A digital scope takes samples of the signals that can be stopped or stored and is therefore called a **digital storage oscilloscope,** or **DSO.**

- A digital scope does not capture each change in voltage but instead captures voltage levels over time and stores them as dots. Each dot is a voltage level. Then the scope displays the waveforms using the thousands of dots (each representing a voltage level) and then electrically connects the dots to create a waveform.

- A DSO can be connected to a sensor output signal wire and can record over a long period of time the voltage signals. Then it can be replayed and a technician can see if any faults were detected. This feature makes a DSO the perfect tool to help diagnose intermittent problems.

- A digital storage scope, however, can sometimes miss faults called *glitches* that may occur between samples captured by the scope. This is why a DSO with a high "sampling rate" is preferred. Sampling rate means

that a scope is cable of capturing voltage changes that occur over a very short period of time. Some digital storage scopes have a capture rate of 25 million (25,000,000) samples per second. This means that the scope can capture a glitch (fault) that lasts just 40 nano (0.00000040) seconds long.

- A scope has been called "a voltmeter with a clock."

  - The voltmeter part means that a scope can capture and display changing voltage levels.

  - The clock part means that the scope can display these changes in voltage levels within a specific time period; and with a DSO it can be replayed so that any faults can be seen and studied.

**OSCILLOSCOPE DISPLAY GRID** A typical scope face usually has eight or ten grids vertically (up and down) and ten grids horizontally (left to right). The transparent scale (grid), used for reference measurements, is called a **graticule.** This arrangement is commonly 8 × 10 or 10 × 10 divisions. ● **SEE FIGURE 6–1.**

**NOTE: These numbers originally referred to the metric dimensions of the graticule in centimeters. Therefore, an 8 × 10 display would be 8 cm (80 mm or 3.14 in.) high and 10 cm (100 mm or 3.90 in.) wide.**

- Voltage is displayed on a scope starting with zero volts at the bottom and higher voltage being displayed vertically.

- The scope illustrates time left to right. The pattern starts on the left and sweeps across the screen from left to right.

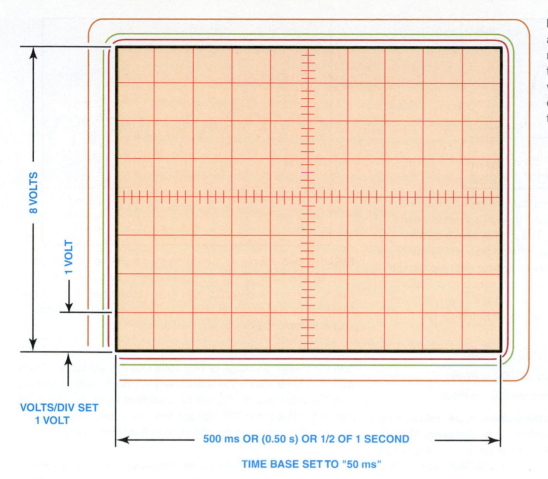

**FIGURE 6–1** A scope display allows technicians to take measurements of voltage patterns. In this example, each vertical division is 1 volt and each horizontal division is set to represent 50 milliseconds.

8 VOLTS

1 VOLT

VOLTS/DIV SET
1 VOLT

500 ms OR (0.50 s) OR 1/2 OF 1 SECOND

TIME BASE SET TO "50 ms"

## SCOPE SETUP AND ADJUSTMENTS

**SETTING THE TIME BASE** Most scopes use 10 graticules from left to right on the display. Setting the **time base** means setting how much time will be displayed in each block called a **division**. For example, if the scope is set to read 2 seconds per division (referred to as *s/div*), then the total displayed would be 20 seconds (2 × 10 divisions = 20 sec.). The time base should be set to an amount of time that allows two to four events to be displayed. Milliseconds (0.001 sec.) are commonly used in scopes when adjusting the time base. Sample time is milliseconds per division (indicated as *ms/div*) and total time. ● **SEE CHART 6–1.**

**NOTE: Increasing the time base reduces the number of samples per second.**

The horizontal scale is divided into 10 divisions (sometimes called *grats*). If each division represents 1 second of time, then the total time period displayed on the screen will be 10 seconds. The time per division is selected so that several

| MILLISECONDS PER DIVISION (MS/DIV) | TOTAL TIME DISPLAYED |
|---|---|
| 1 ms | 10 ms (0.010 sec.) |
| 10 ms | 100 ms (0.100 sec.) |
| 50 ms | 500 ms (0.500 sec.) |
| 100 ms | 1 sec. (1.000 sec.) |
| 500 ms | 5 sec. (5.0 sec.) |
| 1,000 ms | 10 sec. (10.0 sec.) |

**CHART 6–1**

The time base is milliseconds (ms) and total time of an event that can be displayed.

events of the waveform are displayed. Time per division settings can vary greatly in automotive use, including:

- MAP/MAF sensors: 2 ms/div (20 ms total)
- Network (CAN) communications network: 2 ms/div (20 ms total)
- Throttle position (TP) sensor: 100 ms per division (1 sec. total)
- Fuel injector: 2 ms/div (20 ms total)
- Oxygen sensor: 1 sec. per division (10 sec. total)

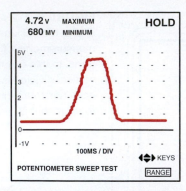

FIGURE 6–2 The display on a digital storage oscilloscope (DSO) displays the entire waveform from idle to wide-open throttle and then returns to idle. The display also indicates the maximum reading (4.72 V) and the minimum (680 mV or 0.68 V). The display does not show anything until the throttle is opened, because the scope has been set up to only start displaying a waveform after a certain voltage level has been reached. This voltage is called the trigger or trigger point.

- Primary ignition: 10 ms/div (100 ms total)
- Secondary ignition: 10 ms/div (100 ms total)
- Voltage measurements: 5 ms/div (50 ms total)

The total time displayed on the screen allows comparisons to see if the waveform is consistent or is changing. Multiple waveforms shown on the display at the same time also allow for measurements to be seen more easily. ● SEE FIGURE 6–2 for an example of a throttle position sensor waveform created by measuring the voltage output as the throttle was depressed and then released.

**VOLTS PER DIVISION** The volts per division, abbreviated *V/div*, should be set so that the entire anticipated waveform can be viewed. Examples include:

Throttle position (TP) sensor: 1 V/div (8 V total)

Battery, starting and charging: 2 V/div (16 V total)

Oxygen sensor: 200 mV/div (1.6 V total)

Notice from the examples that the total voltage to be displayed exceeds the voltage range of the component being tested. This ensures that all the waveform will be displayed. It also allows for some unexpected voltage readings. For example, an oxygen sensor should read between 0 V and 1 V (1,000 mV). By setting the V/div to 200 mV, up to 1.6 V (1,600 mV) will be displayed.

## DC AND AC COUPLING

**DC COUPLING** DC coupling is the most used position on a scope because it allows the scope to display both alternating current (AC) voltage signals and direct current (DC) voltage signals present in the circuit. The AC part of the signal will ride on top of the DC component. For example, if the engine is running

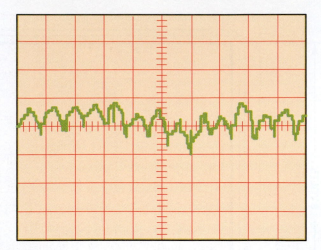

FIGURE 6–3 Ripple voltage is created from the AC voltage from an alternator. Some AC ripple voltage is normal but if the AC portion exceeds 0.5 volt, then a bad diode is the most likely cause. Excessive AC ripple can cause many electrical and electronic devices to work incorrectly.

and the charging voltage is 14.4 volts DC, this will be displayed as a horizontal line on the screen. Any AC ripple voltage leaking past the alternator diodes will be displayed as an AC signal on top of the horizontal DC voltage line. Therefore, both components of the signal can be observed at the same time.

**AC COUPLING** When the **AC coupling** position is selected, a capacitor is placed into the meter lead circuit, which effectively blocks all DC voltage signals but allows the AC portion of the signal to pass and be displayed. ● SEE FIGURE 6–3. AC coupling can be used to show output signal waveforms from sensors such as:

- Distributor pickup coils
- Magnetic wheel speed sensors
- Magnetic crankshaft position sensors
- Magnetic camshaft position sensors
- Magnetic vehicle speed sensors

**NOTE: Check the instructions from the scope manufacturer for the recommended settings to use. Sometimes it is necessary to switch from DC coupling to AC coupling or from AC coupling to DC coupling to properly see some waveforms.**

## PULSE TRAINS

**DEFINITION** Scopes can show all voltage signals. Among the most commonly found in automotive applications is a DC voltage that varies up and down and does not go below zero like an AC voltage. A DC voltage that turns on and off in a series of pulses is called a **pulse train**. Pulse trains differ from an AC

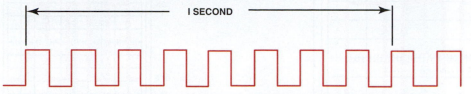

1. FREQUENCY - FREQUENCY IS THE NUMBER OF CYCLES THAT TAKE PLACE PER SECOND. THE MORE CYCLES THAT TAKE PLACE IN ONE SECOND, THE HIGHER THE FREQUENCY READING. FREQUENCIES ARE MEASURED IN HERTZ, WHICH IS THE NUMBER OF CYCLES PER SECOND. AN EIGHT HERTZ SIGNAL CYCLES EIGHT TIMES PER SECOND.

I SECOND

THIS IS WHAT AN 8 HERTZ WOULD LOOK LIKE - 8 HERTZ MEANS "8 CYCLES PER SECOND."

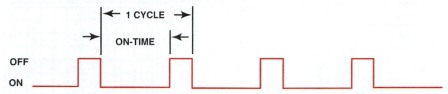

2. DUTY CYCLE - DUTY CYCLE IS A MEASUREMENT COMPARING THE SIGNAL ON-TIME TO THE LENGTH OF ONE COMPLETE CYCLE. AS ON-TIME INCREASES, OFF-TIME DECREASES. DUTY CYCLE IS MEASURED IN PERCENTAGE OF ON-TIME. A 60% DUTY CYCLE IS SIGNAL A THAT'S ON 60% OF THE TIME, AND OFF 40% OF THE TIME. ANOTHER WAY TO MEASURE DUTY CYCLE IS DWELL, WHICH IS MEASURED IN DEGREES INSTEAD OF PERCENT.

1 CYCLE
ON-TIME
OFF
ON

DUTY CYCLE IS THE RELATIONSHIP BETWEEN ONE COMPLETE CYCLE, AND THE SIGNAL'S ON-TIME. A SIGNAL CAN VARY IN DUTY CYCLE WITHOUT AFFECTING THE FREQUENCY.

3. PULSE WIDTH - PULSE WIDTH IS THE ACTUAL ON-TIME OF A SIGNAL, MEASURED IN MILLISECONDS. WITH PULSE WIDTH MEASUREMENTS, OFF-TIME DOESN'T REALLY MATTER - THE ONLY REAL CONCERN IS HOW LONG THE SIGNAL'S ON. THIS IS A USEFUL TEST FOR MEASURING CONVENTIONAL INJECTOR ON-TIME, TO SEE THAT THE SIGNAL VARIES WITH LOAD CHANGE.

PULSE WIDTH
OFF
ON

PULSE WIDTH IS THE ACTUAL TIME A SIGNAL'S ON, MEASURED IN MILLISECONDS. THE ONLY THING BEING MEASURED IS HOW LONG THE SIGNAL IS ON.

**FIGURE 6–4** A pulse train is any electrical signal that turns on and off, or goes high and low in a series of pulses. Ignition module and fuel-injector pulses are examples of a pulse train signal.

signal in that they do not go below zero. An alternating voltage goes above and below zero voltage. Pulse train signals can vary in several ways. ● SEE FIGURE 6–4.

**FREQUENCY** Frequency is the number of cycles per second measured in **hertz.** The engine revolutions per minute (RPM) signal is an example of a signal that can occur at various frequencies. At low engine speed, the ignition pulses occur fewer times per second (lower frequency) than when the engine is operated at higher engine speeds (RPM).

**DUTY CYCLE** Duty cycle refers to the percentage of on-time of the signal during one complete cycle. As on-time increases, the amount of time the signal is off decreases and is usually measured in percentage. Duty cycle is also called **pulse-width modulation (PWM)** and can be measured in degrees. ● SEE FIGURE 6–5.

**PULSE WIDTH** The **pulse width** is a measure of the actual on-time measured in milliseconds. Fuel injectors are usually controlled by varying the pulse width. ● SEE FIGURE 6–6.

## NUMBER OF CHANNELS

**DEFINITION** Scopes are available that allow the viewing of more than one sensor or event at the same time on the display. The number of events, which require leads for each, is called a **channel.** A channel is an input to a scope. Commonly available scopes include:

- **Single channel.** A single channel scope is capable of displaying only one sensor signal waveform at a time.
- **Two channel.** A two-channel scope can display the waveform from two separate sensors or components at the

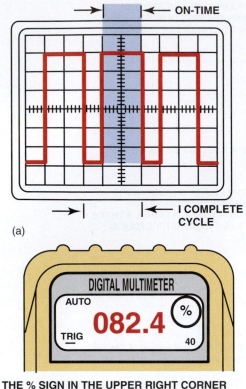

ON-TIME

I COMPLETE CYCLE

(a)

DIGITAL MULTIMETER

AUTO

082.4

%

TRIG

40

THE % SIGN IN THE UPPER RIGHT CORNER OF THE DISPLAY INDICATES THAT THE METER IS READING A DUTY CYCLE SIGNAL.

(b)

**FIGURE 6–5** (a) A scope representation of a complete cycle showing both on-time and off-time. (b) A meter display indicating the on-time duty cycle in a percentage (%). Note the trigger and negative (–) symbol. This indicates that the meter started to record the percentage of on-time when the voltage dropped (start of on-time).

same time. This feature is very helpful when testing the camshaft and crankshaft position sensors on an engine to see if they are properly timed. ● SEE FIGURE 6–7.

■ **Four channel.** A four-channel scope allows the technician to view up to four different sensors or actuators on one display.

**NOTE: Often the capture speed of the signals is slowed when using more than one channel.**

## TRIGGERS

**EXTERNAL TRIGGER**    An **external trigger** is when the waveform starts when a signal is received from another external source rather than from the signal pickup lead. A common example of an external trigger comes from the probe clamp around the cylinder #1 spark plug wire to trigger the start of an ignition pattern.

**TRIGGER LEVEL**    **Trigger level** is the voltage that must be detected by the scope before the pattern will be displayed. A scope will only start displaying a voltage signal when it is

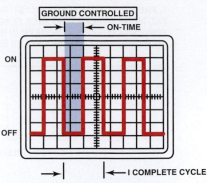

GROUND CONTROLLED

ON-TIME

ON

OFF

I COMPLETE CYCLE

ON A GROUND-CONTROLLED CIRCUIT, THE ON-TIME PULSE IS THE LOWER HORIZONTAL PULSE.

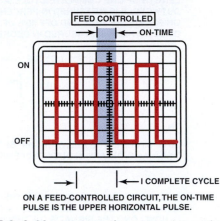

FEED CONTROLLED

ON-TIME

ON

OFF

I COMPLETE CYCLE

ON A FEED-CONTROLLED CIRCUIT, THE ON-TIME PULSE IS THE UPPER HORIZONTAL PULSE.

**FIGURE 6–6** Most automotive computer systems control the device by opening and closing the ground to the component.

triggered or is told to start. The trigger level must be set to start the display. If the pattern starts at 1 volt, then the trace will begin displaying on the left side of the screen *after* the trace has reached 1 volt.

**TRIGGER SLOPE**    The **trigger slope** is the voltage direction that a waveform must have in order to start the display. Most often, the trigger to start a waveform display is taken from the signal itself. Besides trigger voltage level, most scopes can be adjusted to trigger only when the voltage rises past the trigger-level voltage. This is called a *positive slope*. When the voltage falling past the higher level activates the trigger, this is called a *negative slope*.

The scope display indicates both a positive and a negative slope symbol. For example, if a waveform such as a magnetic sensor used for crankshaft position or wheel speed starts moving upward, a positive slope should be selected. If a negative slope is selected, the waveform will not start showing until the voltage reaches the trigger level in a downward direction. A negative slope should be used when a fuel-injector circuit is being analyzed. In this circuit, the computer provides the ground and the voltage level drops when the computer commands the injector on. Sometimes the technician needs to change from negative to positive or positive to negative trigger if a waveform is not being shown correctly. ● SEE FIGURE 6–8.

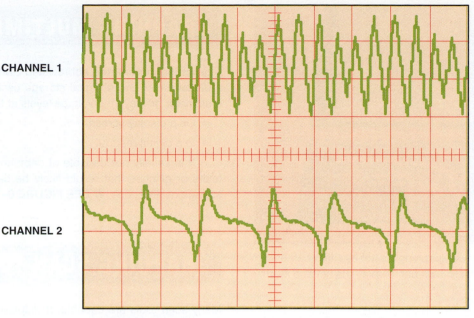

CHANNEL 1

CHANNEL 2

10mSec/Div 5Volts/Div

**FIGURE 6–7** A two-channel scope being used to compare two signals on the same vehicle.

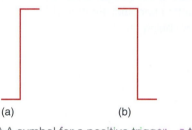

(a)          (b)

**FIGURE 6–8** (a) A symbol for a positive trigger—a trigger occurs at a rising (positive) edge of the signal (waveform). (b) A symbol for a negative trigger—a trigger occurs at a falling (negative) edge of the signal (waveform).

## USING A SCOPE

**USING SCOPE LEADS** Most scopes, both analog and digital, normally use the same test leads. These leads usually attach to the scope through a **BNC connector**, a miniature standard coaxial cable connector. BNC is an international standard that is used in the electronics industry. If using a BNC connector, be sure to connect one lead to a good clean, metal engine ground. The probe of the scope lead attaches to the circuit or component being tested. Many scopes use one ground lead and then each channel has it own signal pickup lead.

**MEASURING BATTERY VOLTAGE WITH A SCOPE** One of the easiest things to measure and observe on a scope is battery voltage. A lower voltage can be observed on the scope display as the engine is started and a higher voltage should be displayed after the engine starts. ● **SEE FIGURE 6–9.**

An analog scope displays rapidly and cannot be set to show or freeze a display. Therefore, even though an analog

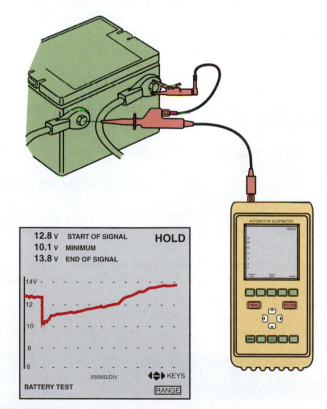

**FIGURE 6–9** Battery voltage is represented by a flat horizontal line. In this example, the engine was started and the battery voltage dropped to about 10 V as shown on the left side of the scope display. When the engine started, the alternator started to charge the battery and the voltage is shown as climbing.

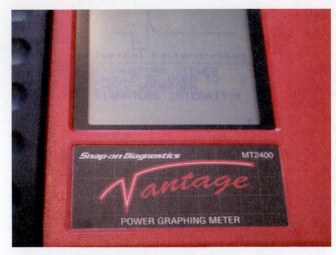

**FIGURE 6–10** A typical graphing multimeter that can be used as a digital meter, plus it can display the voltage levels on the display screen.

scope shows all voltage signals, it is easy to miss a momentary glitch on an analog scope.

**CAUTION: Check the instructions for the scope being used before attempting to scope household AC circuits. Some scopes, such as the Snap-On MODIS, are not designed to measure high-voltage AC circuits.**

## GRAPHING MULTIMETER

A **graphing multimeter**, abbreviated **GMM**, is a cross between a digital meter and a digital storage oscilloscope. A graphing multimeter displays the voltage levels at two places:

- On a display screen
- In a digital readout

It is usually not capable of capturing very short duration faults or glitches that would likely be captured with a digital storage oscilloscope. ● **SEE FIGURE 6–10.**

## GRAPHING SCAN TOOLS

Many scan tools are capable of displaying the voltage levels captured by the scan tool through the data link connector (DLC) on a screen. This feature is helpful where seeing changes in voltage levels is difficult to detect by looking at numbers that are constantly changing. Read and follow the instructions for the scan tool being used.

## SUMMARY

1. Analog oscilloscopes use a cathode ray tube to display voltage patterns.
2. The waveforms shown on an analog oscilloscope cannot be stored for later viewing.
3. A digital storage oscilloscope (DSO) creates an image or waveform on the display by connecting thousands of dots captured by the scope leads.
4. An oscilloscope display grid is called a graticule. Each of the 8 × 10 or 10 × 10 dividing boxes is called a division.
5. Setting the time base means establishing the amount of time each division represents.
6. Setting the volts per division allows the technician to view either the entire waveform or just part of it.
7. DC coupling and AC coupling are two selections that can be made to observe different types of waveforms.
8. A graphing multimeter is not capable of capturing short duration faults but can display usable waveforms.
9. Oscilloscopes display voltage over time. A DSO can capture and store a waveform for viewing later.

## REVIEW QUESTIONS

1. What are the differences between an analog and a digital oscilloscope?
2. What is the difference between DC coupling and AC coupling?
3. Why are DC signals that change called pulse trains?
4. What is the difference between an oscilloscope and a graphing multimeter?

1. Technician A says an analog scope can store the waveform for viewing later. Technician B says that the trigger level has to be set on most scopes to be able to view a changing waveform. Which technician is correct?
   a. Technician A only
   b. Technician B only
   c. Both Technicians A and B
   d. Neither Technician A nor B

2. An oscilloscope display is called a _____.
   a. Grid
   c. Division
   b. Graticule
   d. Box

3. A signal showing the voltage of a battery displayed on a digital storage oscilloscope (DSO) is being discussed. Technician A says that the display will show one horizontal line above the zero line. Technician B says that the display will show a line sloping upward from zero to the battery voltage level. Which technician is correct?
   a. Technician A only
   b. Technician B only
   c. Both Technicians A and B
   d. Neither Technician A nor B

4. Setting the time base to 50 ms per division will allow the technician to view a waveform how long in duration?
   a. 50 ms
   c. 400 ms
   b. 200 ms
   d. 500 ms

5. A throttle position sensor waveform is going to be observed. At what setting should the volts per division be set to see the entire waveform from 0 to 5 volts?
   a. 0.5 V/division
   c. 2.0 V/division
   b. 1.0 V/division
   d. 5.0 V/division

6. Two technicians are discussing the DC coupling setting on a DSO. Technician A says that the position allows both the DC and AC signals of the waveform to be displayed. Technician B says that this setting allows just the DC part of the waveform to be displayed. Which technician is correct?
   a. Technician A only
   b. Technician B only
   c. Both Technicians A and B
   d. Neither Technician A nor B

7. Voltage signals (waveforms) that do not go below zero are called _____.
   a. AC signals
   b. Pulse trains
   c. Pulse width
   d. DC coupled signals

8. Cycles per second are expressed in _____.
   a. Hertz
   c. Pulse width
   b. Duty cycle
   d. Slope

9. Oscilloscopes use what type of lead connector?
   a. Banana plugs
   b. Double banana plugs
   c. Single conductor plugs
   d. BNC

10. A digital meter that can show waveforms is called a _____.
    a. DVOM
    c. GMM
    b. DMM
    d. DSO

# STARTING AND CHARGING SYSTEM DIAGNOSIS

**OBJECTIVES:** **After studying Chapter 7, the reader will be able to:** • Prepare for ASE Engine Performance (A8) certification test content area "F" (Engine Electrical Systems Diagnosis and Repair). • Discuss methods that can be used to check the condition of a battery. • Describe how to perform a battery drain test and how to isolate the cause. • Explain how to test the condition of the starter. • List the steps necessary to perform a voltage-drop test. • Explain how to test the alternator.

**KEY TERMS:** AC ripple voltage 97 • Ampere-hour 81 • Battery 80 • Battery electrical drain test 86 • Battery voltage correction factor 81 • CA 81 • Capacity test 83 • CCA 80 • Charging circuit 80 • Conductance testing 84 • Cranking circuit 80 • DE 95 • ELD 100 • alternator 80 • IOD 87 • Load test 83 • LRC 100 • MCA 81 • Neutral safety switch 90 • Open-circuit battery voltage test 82 • Parasitic load 87 • Reserve capacity 81 • Ripple current 98 • SRE 95 • State of charge 85 • Surface charge 82 • Voltage-drop test 92

Just as in the old saying "If Mother isn't happy—no one is happy," the battery, the starter, and the charging system have to function correctly for the engine performance to be satisfactory.

## PURPOSE AND FUNCTION OF A BATTERY

The primary purpose of an automotive **battery** is to provide a source of electrical power for starting and for electrical demands that exceed alternator output. The battery also acts as a voltage stabilizer for the entire electrical system. The battery is a voltage stabilizer because it acts as a reservoir where large amounts of current (amperes) can be removed quickly during starting and replaced gradually by the **alternator** during charging. The battery *must* be in good (serviceable) condition before the charging system and the cranking system can be tested. For example, if a battery is discharged, the **cranking circuit** (starter motor) could test as being defective because the battery voltage might drop below specifications. The **charging circuit** could also test as being defective because of a weak or discharged battery. It is important to test the vehicle battery before further testing of the cranking or charging system.

## BATTERY RATINGS

Batteries are rated according to the amount of current they can produce under specific conditions.

**FIGURE 7–1** This battery shows a large "1000" on the front panel but this is the CA rating and not the more important CCA rating. Always compare batteries with the same rating.

**COLD-CRANKING AMPERES** Every automotive battery must be able to supply electrical power to crank the engine in cold weather and still provide voltage high enough to operate the ignition system for starting. The cold-cranking power of a battery is the number of amperes that can be supplied at 0°F (−18°C) for 30 seconds while the battery still maintains a voltage of 1.2 volts per cell or higher. This means that the battery voltage would be 7.2 volts for a 12-volt battery and 3.6 volts for a 6-volt battery. The cold-cranking performance rating is called **cold-cranking amperes (CCA).** Try to purchase a battery that offers the highest CCA for the money. ● **SEE FIGURE 7–1.**

**How Can a Defective Battery Affect Engine Performance?**

A weak or discharged battery should be replaced as soon as possible. A weak battery causes a constant load on the alternator that can cause the stator windings to overheat and fail. Low battery voltage also affects the electronic fuel-injection system. The computer senses low battery voltage and increases the fuel injector on-time to help compensate for the lower voltage to the fuel pump and fuel injectors. This increase in injector pulse time is added to the calculated pulse time and is sometimes called the **battery voltage correction factor.** Reduced fuel economy could therefore be the result of a weak or defective battery.

**Should Batteries Be Kept Off of Concrete Floors?**

All batteries should be stored in a cool, dry place when not in use. Many technicians have been warned not to store or place a battery on concrete. According to battery experts, it is the temperature difference between the top and the bottom of the battery that causes a difference in the voltage potential between the top (warmer section) and the bottom (colder section). It is this difference in temperature that causes self-discharge to occur.

In fact, submarines cycle seawater around their batteries to keep all sections of the battery at the same temperature to help prevent self-discharge.

Therefore, always store or place batteries up off the floor and in a location where the entire battery can be kept at the same temperature, avoiding extreme heat and freezing temperatures. Concrete cannot drain the battery directly, because the case of the battery is a very good electrical insulator.

**CRANKING AMPERES** **Cranking amperes (CA)** are not the same as CCA, but are often advertised and labeled on batteries. The designation CA refers to the number of amperes that can be supplied by the battery at 32°F (0°C). This rating results in a higher number than the more stringent rating of CCA.

**MARINE CRANKING AMPERES** **Marine cranking amperes (MCA)** rating is similar to the cranking amperes (CA) rating and is tested at 32°F (0°C).

**AMPERE-HOUR RATING** The **Ampere-Hour (Ah)** is how many amperes can be discharged from the battery before dropping to 10.5 volts over a 20-hour period. A battery that is able

**What Can Cause a Battery to Explode?**

Batteries discharge hydrogen gas and oxygen when being charged. If there happens to be a flame or spark, the hydrogen will burn. The oxygen can also help contribute to an explosion of a small pocket of hydrogen.

to supply 3.75 amperes for 20 hours has a rating of 75 ampere-hours ($3.75 \times 20 = 75$).

**RESERVE CAPACITY** The **reserve capacity** rating for batteries is *the number of minutes* for which the battery can produce 25 amperes and still have a battery voltage of 1.75 volts per cell (10.5 volts for a 12-volt battery). This rating is actually a measurement of the time for which a vehicle can be driven in the event of a charging system failure.

## BATTERY SERVICE SAFETY CONSIDERATIONS

Batteries contain acid and release explosive gases (hydrogen and oxygen) during normal charging and discharging cycles. To help prevent physical injury or damage to the vehicle, always adhere to the following safety procedures:

1. Whenever working on any electrical component on a vehicle, disconnect the negative battery cable from the battery. When the negative cable is disconnected, all electrical circuits in the vehicle will be open, which will prevent accidental electrical contact between an electrical component and ground. Any electrical spark has the potential to cause explosion and personal injury.

2. Wear eye protection whenever working around any battery.

3. Wear protective clothing to avoid skin contact with battery acid.

4. Always adhere to all safety precautions as stated in the service procedures for the equipment used for battery service and testing.

5. Never smoke or use an open flame around any battery.

## BATTERY VISUAL INSPECTION

The battery and battery cables should be included in the list of items checked during a thorough visual inspection. Check the battery cables for corrosion and tightness. ● **SEE FIGURE 7–2.**

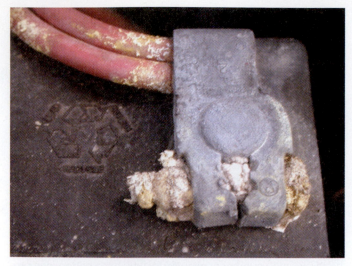

**FIGURE 7–2** Corrosion on a battery cable could be an indication that the battery is either being overcharged or is sulfated, creating a lot of gassing of the electrolyte.

**FIGURE 7–3** A visual inspection on this battery showed that the electrolyte level was below the plates in all cells.

**NOTE: On side-post batteries, grasp the battery cable near the battery and attempt to move the cable in a clockwise direction in an attempt to tighten the battery connection.**

If possible, remove the covers and observe the level of the electrolyte. ● **SEE FIGURE 7–3.**

## BATTERY VOLTAGE TEST

Testing the battery voltage with a voltmeter is a simple method for determining the state of charge of any battery. ● **SEE FIGURE 7–4.** The voltage of a battery does not necessarily indicate whether the battery can perform satisfactorily, but it does indicate to the technician more about the battery's condition than a simple visual inspection. A battery that *looks* good may

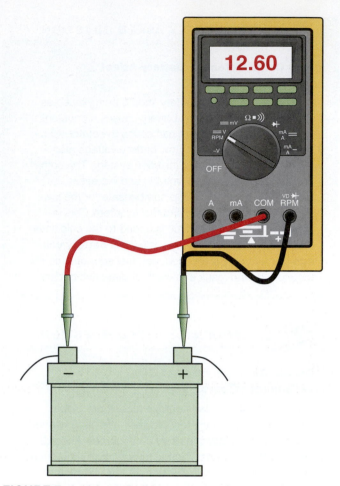

**FIGURE 7–4** Using a DMM to measure the open-circuit voltage of a battery.

not be good. This test is commonly called an **open-circuit battery voltage test** because it is conducted with an open circuit—with no current flowing and no load applied to the battery.

1. Connect a voltmeter to the positive (+) and negative (−) terminals of the battery. Set the voltmeter to read DC volts.

2. If the battery has just been charged or the vehicle has recently been driven, it is necessary to remove the surface charge from the battery before testing. A **surface charge** is a charge of higher-than-normal voltage that is only on the surface of the battery plates. The surface charge is quickly removed whenever the battery is loaded and therefore does not accurately represent the true state of charge of the battery.

3. To remove the surface charge, turn the headlights on high beam (brights) for 1 minute, then turn the headlights off and wait 2 minutes.

4. Read the voltmeter and compare the results with the following state-of-charge chart. The voltages shown are for a battery at or near room temperature (70° to 80°F or 21° to 27°C).

**NOTE: Watch the voltmeter when the headlights are turned on. A new good battery will indicate a gradual drop in voltage, whereas a weak battery will indicate a more rapid drop in voltage. Soon the voltage will stop dropping and will stabilize. A good**

(a)

(b)

**FIGURE 7–5** (a) Voltmeter showing the battery voltage after the headlights were on (engine off) for 1 minute. (b) Headlights were turned off and the battery voltage quickly recovered to indicate 12.6 volts.

new battery will likely stabilize above 12 volts. A weak older battery may drop below 11 volts. After turning off the headlights, the faster the recovery, generally, the better the battery. ● SEE FIGURE 7–5.

| Battery voltage (V) | State of charge |
|---|---|
| 12.6 or higher | 100% charged |
| 12.4 | 75% charged |
| 12.2 | 50% charged |
| 12.0 | 25% charged |
| 11.9 or lower | Discharged |

## BATTERY LOAD TESTING

One method to determine the condition of any battery is the **load test**, also known as a **capacity test.** Most automotive starting and charging testers use a carbon pile to create an electrical load on the battery. The amount of the load is determined by the original capacity of the battery being tested. The capacity is measured in cold-cranking amperes (CCA), which is the number of amperes that a battery can supply at

### TECH TIP

**Use a Scan Tool to Check the Battery, Starter, and Alternator!**

General Motors and Chrysler vehicles as well as selected others that can display data to a scan tool can be easily checked for proper operating voltage. Most scan tools can display battery or system voltage and engine speed in RPM (revolutions per minute). Connect a scan tool to the data link connector (DLC) and perform the following while watching the scan tool display. ● SEE FIGURE 7–6.

Many scan tools are also capable of recording or graphing engine data while cranking including:

- RPM during cranking should be 80 to 250 RPMs.
- Battery voltage during cranking should be above 9.6 volts.

**NOTE: Usually readings for a good battery and starter would be 10.5 to 11.5 volts.**

- Battery voltage after engine starts should be 13.5 to 15.0 volts.

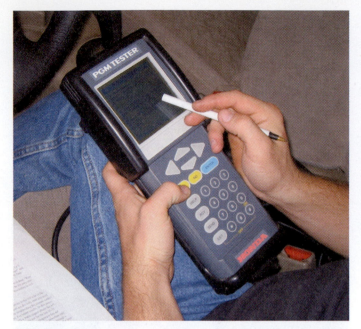

**FIGURE 7–6** Using a scan tool to check battery voltage.

**FIGURE 7–7** A Bear Automotive starting and charging tester. This tester automatically loads the battery for 15 seconds to remove the surface charge, waits 30 seconds to allow the battery to recover, and then loads the battery again. The LCD indicates the status of the battery.

0°F (−18°C) for 30 seconds. An older type of battery rating is called the ampere-hour rating. The proper electrical load to be used to test a battery is one-half of the CCA rating or three times the ampere-hour rating, with a minimum of a 150-ampere load. Apply the load for a full 15 seconds and observe the voltmeter at the end of the 15-second period while the battery is still under load. A good battery should indicate above 9.6 V.

**NOTE: This test is sometimes called the *1-minute test,* because many battery manufacturers recommend performing the load test twice, using the first load period (15 seconds) to remove the surface charge on the battery, then waiting for 30 seconds to allow time for the battery to recover, and then loading the battery again for 15 seconds. Total time required is 60 seconds (15 + 30 + 15 = 60 seconds or 1 minute). This method provides a true indication of the condition of the battery. ● SEE FIGURES 7–7 AND 7–8.**

If the battery fails the load test, recharge the battery and retest. If the battery fails the load test again, replace the battery.

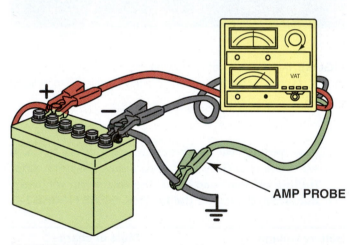

**FIGURE 7–8** This shows a typical battery load tester hookup.

## CONDUCTANCE TESTING

General Motors Corporation, Chrysler Corporation, Ford, and other vehicle manufacturers specify that a **conductance tester** be used to test batteries in vehicles still under factory warranty. The tester uses its internal electronic circuitry to determine the state of charge and capacity of the battery by measuring the voltage and conductance of the plates. ● SEE FIGURE 7–9.

**FIGURE 7–9** An electronic battery tester.

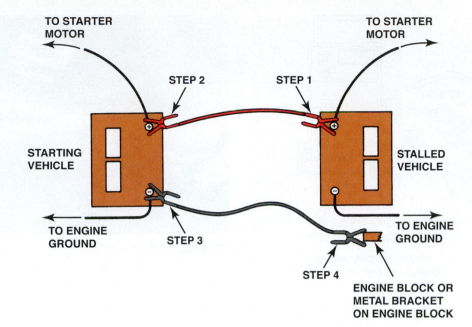

STEP 2

STEP 1

TO STARTER MOTOR

TO STARTER MOTOR

STARTING VEHICLE

STALLED VEHICLE

TO ENGINE GROUND

STEP 3

TO ENGINE GROUND

STEP 4

ENGINE BLOCK OR METAL BRACKET ON ENGINE BLOCK

**FIGURE 7–10** Jumper cable usage guide.

**?  FREQUENTLY ASKED QUESTION**

**What Are Some Symptoms of a Weak or Defective Battery?**

There are several warning signs that may indicate that a battery is near the end of its useful life, including:

- **Uses water in one or more cells.** This indicates that the plates are sulfated and that, during the charging process, the water in the electrolyte is being turned into separate hydrogen and oxygen gases.
- **Excessive corrosion on battery cables or connections.** Corrosion is more likely to occur if the battery is sulfated, creating hot spots on the plates. When the battery is being charged, the acid fumes are forced out of the vent holes and get onto the battery cables, connections, and even on the tray underneath the battery.
- **Slower-than-normal engine cranking.** When the capacity of the battery is reduced due to damage or age, it is less likely to supply the necessary current for starting the engine, especially during cold weather.

Connect the tester to the positive and negative terminals of the battery, and after entering the CCA rating (if known), push the arrow keys. The tester determines one of the following:

- **Good battery.** The battery can return to service.
- **Charge and retest.** Fully recharge the battery and return it to service.
- **Replace the battery.** The battery is not serviceable and should be replaced.
- **Bad cell—replace.** The battery is not serviceable and should be replaced.

**CAUTION: Test results can be incorrectly reported on the display if proper, clean connections to the battery are not made. Also be sure that all accessories and the ignition switch are in the off position.**

## JUMP STARTING

To safely jump start a vehicle without doing any harm, use the following procedure:

1. Be certain the ignition switch is off on both vehicles.
2. Connect good-quality copper jumper cables as indicated in the guide in ● **FIGURE 7–10.**
3. Start the vehicle with the good battery and allow it to run for 5 to 10 minutes. This allows the alternator of the good vehicle to charge the battery on the disabled vehicle.
4. Start the disabled vehicle and, after the engine is operating smoothly, disconnect the jumper cables in the reverse order of step 2.

**NOTE: To help prevent accidental touching of the jumper cables, simply separate them into two cables and attach using wire (cable) ties or tape so that the clamps are offset from each other, making it impossible for them to touch.**

## BATTERY CHARGING

If the **state of charge** of a battery is low, it must be recharged. It is best to slow-charge any battery to prevent possible overheating damage to the battery. Remember, it may take 8 hours or more to charge a fully discharged battery. The initial charge rate should be about 35 amperes for 30 minutes to help start the

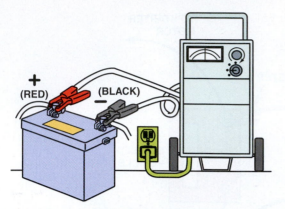

**FIGURE 7–11** To use a battery charger, make sure the charger is connected to the battery before plugging in the charger.

| OPEN CIRCUIT VOLTAGE, V | STATE OF CHARGE, % | CHARGING TIME (MIN) TO FULL CHARGE AT 80°F (27°C)* | | | | | |
|---|---|---|---|---|---|---|---|
| | | at 60 A | at 50 A | at 40 A | at 30 A | at 20 A | at 10 A |
| 12.6 | 100 | Full Charge | | | | | |
| 12.4 | 75 | 15 | 20 | 27 | 35 | 48 | 90 |
| 12.2 | 50 | 35 | 45 | 55 | 75 | 95 | 180 |
| 12.0 | 25 | 50 | 65 | 85 | 115 | 145 | 280 |
| 11.8 | 0 | 65 | 85 | 110 | 150 | 195 | 370 |

**CHART 7–1**

A chart that can be used to estimate the charging time based on battery voltage and charging rate.
* If colder, allow additional time.

charging process. Fast-charging a battery increases the temperature of the battery and can cause warping of the plates inside the battery. Fast-charging also increases the amount of gassing (release of hydrogen and oxygen), which can create a health and fire hazard. The battery temperature should not exceed 125°F (hot to the touch). Most batteries should be charged at a rate equal to 1% of the battery's CCA rating. ● **SEE FIGURE 7–11.**

Fast charge: 15 amperes maximum

Slow charge: 5 amperes maximum

● **SEE CHART 7–1** for battery charging times at various battery voltages and charging rates.

**CAUTION: Always use the "AGM" setting on the charger when charging absorbed glass mat batteries. AGM batteries should never be charged at a voltage higher than 15 volts.**

## BATTERY SERVICE

Before returning the vehicle to the customer, check and service the following items as necessary.

1. Neutralize and clean any corrosion from the battery terminals.
2. Carefully inspect the battery cables and hold-down brackets by visual inspection. ● **SEE FIGURE 7–12.**
3. Check the tightness and cleanliness of all battery connections.

**FIGURE 7–12** This battery cable was found corroded underneath. The corrosion had eaten through the insulation yet was not noticeable without careful inspection. This cable should be replaced.

**? FREQUENTLY ASKED QUESTION**

**How Should I Connect a Battery Charger So as Not to Do Harm to the Vehicle?**

Most vehicle manufacturers recommend disconnecting both battery cables from the battery before charging the battery. Side-post batteries require adapters or bolts with nuts attached to permit sufficient surface area around the battery terminal for proper current flow. The following steps will ensure a safe method of connecting a battery charger:

1. Make certain the battery charger is unplugged from the electrical outlet and the charger control is off.
2. Connect the leads of the charger to the battery—the red lead to the positive (+) terminal and the black lead to the negative (−) terminal.
3. Plug the charger into the electrical outlet.
4. Set the controls to the fast (high) rate for about 30 minutes or until the battery starts to take a charge. After 30 minutes, reduce the charge rate to about 1% of the CCA rating of the battery until the battery is charged.

## BATTERY ELECTRICAL DRAIN TEST

The **battery electrical drain test** determines if some component or circuit in a vehicle or truck is causing a drain on the battery when everything is off. This test is also called the **ignition**

## TECH TIP

### It Could Happen to You!

The owner of a Toyota replaced the battery. After replacing the battery, the owner noted that the "airbag" amber warning lamp was lit and the radio was locked out. The owner had purchased the vehicle used from a dealer and did not know the 4-digit security code needed to unlock the radio. Determined to fix it, the owner tried three 4-digit numbers, hoping that one of them would work. However, after three tries, the radio became permanently disabled.

Frustrated, the owner went to a dealer. It cost over $300 to fix the problem. A special tool was required to easily reset the airbag lamp. The radio had to be removed, sent to an out-of-state authorized radio service center, and then reinstalled into the vehicle.

Therefore, before disconnecting the battery, please be certain that the owner has the security code for a security-type radio. A "memory saver" may be needed to keep the radio powered when the battery is being disconnected. ● SEE FIGURE 7–13.

## TECH TIP

### Use a MIN/MAX Feature to Check for Battery Electrical Drain

Most digital multimeters that feature a "data hold," MIN/MAX, or recording feature can be used when the meter is set up to read DC amperes. This is especially helpful if the battery drain is not found during routine tests in the shop. The cause or source of this drain may only occur when the vehicle cools down at night or after it sits for several hours. Connect the ammeter in series with the disconnected negative battery cable and set the meter to record. Refer to the meter instruction booklet if necessary to be assured of a proper setup. The next morning, check the meter for the maximum, minimum, and average readings. For example,

MAX = 0.89 A (over specifications of 0.05 A)
MIN = 0.02 A (typical normal reading)
Average = 0.76 A

Because the average is close to the maximum, the battery electrical drain was taking place during most of the duration of the test.

off-draw (IOD) or parasitic load test. This test should be performed whenever one of the following conditions exists:

1. Whenever a battery is being charged or replaced (a battery drain could have been the cause for charging or replacing the battery)
2. Whenever the battery is suspected of being drained

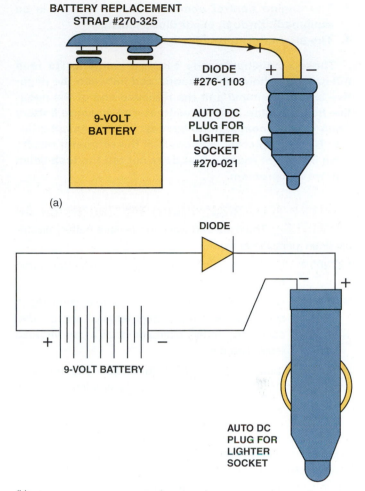

(a)

(b)

**FIGURE 7–13** (a) Memory saver. The part numbers represent components from Radio Shack®. (b) A schematic drawing of the same memory saver.

Normal battery drain on a vehicle equipped with electronic radio, climate control, computerized fuel injection, and so forth, is usually about 20 to 30 milliamperes (0.02 to 0.03 A). Most vehicle manufacturers recommend repairing the cause of any drain that exceeds 50 mA (0.05 A).

**NOTE: Some manufacturers relate maximum allowable parasitic load to the size of the battery. The higher the battery capacity, the greater the allowable load. The maximum allowable drain on a battery can be calculated by dividing the reserve capacity of the battery in minutes by 4 to get the maximum allowable drain in milliamps. For example, if a battery had a reserve capacity of 100 minutes, it would have a maximum allowable parasitic load of 25 mA (100 ÷ 4 = 25 mA).**

**NOTE: Many electronic components do draw a slight amount of current from the battery all the time with the ignition off. These components include:**

1. **Digital clocks**
2. **Electronically tuned radios for station memory and clock circuits (if the vehicle is so equipped)**

3. The engine control computer (if the vehicle is so equipped), through slight diode leakage

4. The alternator, through slight diode leakage

These components may cause a voltmeter to read full battery voltage if it is connected between the negative battery terminal and the removed end of the negative battery cable. Using a voltmeter to measure battery drain is *not* recommended by most vehicle manufacturers. The high internal resistance of the voltmeter results in an irrelevant reading that does not tell the technician if there is a problem.

## BATTERY ELECTRICAL DRAIN TESTING USING AN AMMETER
There are two ways to measure battery electrical drain (parasitic draw).

**METHOD 1** Use an inductive clamp-on ammeter (preferred method)

**METHOD 2** Connect a digital meter set to read amperes in series between the battery terminal and the disconnected battery clamp or install a parasitic load tester adapter.

Normal battery drain is 0.020 to 0.030 A and any drain greater than 0.050 A should be found and corrected.

## PROCEDURE FOR BATTERY ELECTRICAL DRAIN TEST
The fastest and easiest method to measure battery electrical drain is to connect an inductive DC ammeter that is capable of measuring low current (10 mA). ● SEE FIGURE 7–14 for an example of a clamp-on digital multimeter being used to measure battery drain.

Following is the procedure for performing the battery electrical drain test using a test light:

1. Make certain that all lights, accessories, and the ignition are off.

2. Check all vehicle doors to be certain that the interior courtesy (dome) lights are off.

3. Disconnect the *negative* (−) battery cable and install a parasitic load tool as shown in ● FIGURE 7–15.

4. Start the engine and drive the vehicle about 10 minutes, being sure to turn on all the lights and accessories, including the radio.

5. Turn the engine and all accessories off, including the underhood light.

6. Connect an ammeter across the parasitic load tool switch and wait 20 minutes or longer for all computers to go to sleep and circuits to shut down.

7. Open the switch on the load tool and read the battery electrical drain on the meter display.

Results: Normal = 10 to 30 mA (0.02 to 0.03 A)

Maximum allowable = 50 mA (0.05 A) (Industry standards—some vehicle manufacturers' specifications can vary)

Be sure to reset the clock and anti-theft radio, if equipped. ● SEE FIGURE 7–16.

**FIGURE 7–14** This mini clamp-on DMM is being used to measure the amount of battery electrical drain that is present. In this case, a reading of 20 mA (displayed on the meter as 00.02 A) is within the normal range of 20 to 30 mA. Be sure to clamp around all of the positive battery cables or all of the negative battery cables, whichever is easiest to clamp.

**FIGURE 7–15** After connecting the shutoff tool, start the engine and operate all accessories. Stop the engine and turn off everything. Connect the ammeter across the shutoff switch in parallel. Wait 20 minutes. This time allows all electronic circuits to "time out" or shut down. Open the switch—all current now will flow through the ammeter. A reading greater than specified, usually greater than 50 mA (0.05 A), indicates a problem that should be corrected.

## FINDING THE SOURCE OF THE DRAIN
If there is a drain, check and temporarily disconnect the following components:

1. Cell phone or MP3 player still connected to the vehicle

2. Glove compartment light

3. Trunk light

FIGURE 7–16 The battery was replaced in this Acura and the radio displayed "code" when the replacement battery was installed. Thankfully, the owner had the five-digit code required to unlock the radio.

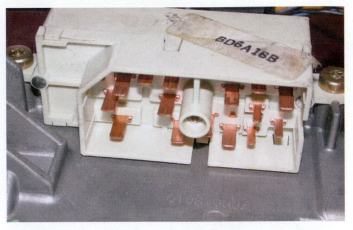

FIGURE 7–17 A typical ignition switch showing all of the electrical terminals after the connector has been removed.

If after disconnecting these components the battery drain can draw more than 50 mA (0.05 A), disconnect one fuse at a time from the fuse box until the ammeter reading drops. If the drain drops to normal after one fuse is disconnected, the source of the drain is located in that particular circuit, as labeled on the fuse box. As fuses are pulled, they should not be reinstalled until the end of the test. Reinstalling a fuse can reset a module and foul up the test. Start at the fuses farthest from the battery and work toward the battery until the faulty circuit is found. Note that many vehicles have multiple fuse boxes. Then disconnect the *power-side* wire connectors from each component included in that particular circuit until the ammeter reads a normal amount of draw. The source of the battery drain can then be traced to an individual component or part of one circuit. If none of the fuses causes the drain to stop, disconnect the alternator output lead. A shorted diode in the alternator could be the cause.

# CRANKING CIRCUIT

The cranking circuit includes those mechanical and electrical components required to crank the engine for starting. The cranking force in the early 1900s was the driver's arm. Modern cranking circuits include the following:

1. **Starter motor.** The starter is normally a 0.5 to 2.6 horsepower (0.4 to 2.0 kilowatts) electric motor that can develop nearly 8 horsepower (6 kilowatts) for a very short time when first cranking a cold engine.

2. **Battery.** The battery must be of the correct capacity and be at least 75% charged to provide the necessary current and voltage for correct operation of the starter.

3. **Starter solenoid or relay.** The high current required by the starter must be able to be turned on and off. A large switch would be required if the current were controlled by the driver directly. Instead, a small current switch (ignition switch) operates a solenoid or relay that controls the high starter current.

4. **Starter drive.** The starter drive uses a small gear that contacts the engine flywheel gear and transmits starter motor power to rotate the engine.

5. **Ignition switch.** The ignition switch and safety control switches control the starter motor operation. ● SEE FIGURES 7–17 AND 7–18.

The engine is cranked by an electric motor that is controlled by a key-operated ignition switch or the PCM on vehicles equipped with electronic starting. The ignition switch will not operate the starter unless the automatic transmission is in neutral or park. This is to prevent an accident that might result from the vehicle moving forward or backward when the engine is started. Many automobile manufacturers use a **neutral safety switch** that opens the circuit between the ignition switch and the starter to prevent starter motor operation unless the gear selector is in

FIGURE 7–18 Some column-mounted ignition switches act directly on the contact points, whereas others use a link from the lock cylinder to the ignition switch.

FIGURE 7–19 A typical solenoid-operated starter.

neutral or park. The safety switch can either be attached to the steering column inside the vehicle near the floor or on the side of the transmission/transaxle. According to vehicle manufacturing engineers, starters can be expected to start an engine 25,000 times during normal life of the vehicle. ● SEE FIGURE 7–19.

## DIAGNOSING STARTER PROBLEMS USING VISUAL INSPECTION

For proper operation, all starters require that the vehicle battery be at least 75% charged and that both power-side and ground-side battery cables be free from excessive voltage

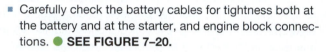

FIGURE 7–20 Carefully inspect all battery terminals for corrosion.

drops. The following should be carefully checked as part of a thorough visual inspection:

- Carefully check the battery cables for tightness both at the battery and at the starter, and engine block connections. ● SEE FIGURE 7–20.
- Check to see if the heat shield (if equipped) is in place.
- Check for any nonstock add-on accessories or equipment that may drain the battery such as a sound system, extra lighting, and so on.
- Crank the engine. Feel the battery cables and connections. If any cables or connections are hot to the touch, then an excessive voltage drop is present or the starter is drawing too much current. The engine itself could be binding. Repair or replace the components or connections as needed.

## STARTER TESTING ON THE VEHICLE

**CHECK BATTERY** Before performing a starter amperage test, be certain that the battery is sufficiently charged (75% or more) and capable of supplying adequate starting current.

**STARTER AMPERAGE TEST** A starter amperage test should be performed whenever the starter fails to operate normally (is slow in cranking) or as part of a routine electrical system inspection. Some service manuals specify normal starter amperage for starter motors being tested on the vehicle; however, most service manuals only give the specifications for bench-testing a starter without a load applied. These specifications are helpful in making certain that a repaired starter meets exact specifications, but they do not apply to starter testing on the vehicle. If exact

**FIGURE 7–21** When connecting a starter tester such as a Sun VAT 45 to the vehicle, make certain that the inductive probe is placed over all of the cables or wires from the battery.

**FIGURE 7–22** Always check the battery, using a conductance or load tester. A battery showing a green charge indicator does not mean that the battery is good.

specifications are not available, the following can be used as general maximum specifications for testing a starter on the vehicle. Any ampere reading lower than these are acceptable:

- 4-cylinder engines = 150 to 185 amperes (normally less than 100A)
- 6-cylinder engines = 160 to 200 amperes (normally less than 125A)
- 8-cylinder engines = 185 to 250 amperes (normally less than 150A)
  ● **SEE FIGURE 7-21.**

Excessive current draw may indicate one or more of the following:

1. Low battery voltage (discharged or defective battery).
   ● **SEE FIGURE 7–22.**
2. Binding of starter armature as a result of worn bushings
3. Oil too thick (viscosity too high) for weather conditions
4. Shorted or grounded starter windings or cables
5. Tight or seized engine

## TESTING A STARTER USING A SCAN TOOL

A scan tool can be used on most vehicles to check the cranking system. Follow these steps:

1. Connect the scan tool according to the manufacturer's instructions.
2. Select battery voltage and engine RPM on the scan tool.

**? REAL WORLD FIX**

**The Case of the No Crank**

A 4-cylinder engine would not crank. Previously the customer said that once in a while, the starter seemed to lock up when the vehicle sat overnight but would then finally crank. The problem only occurred in the morning and the engine would crank and start normally the rest of the day.

The vehicle finally would not start and was towed to the shop. The service technician checked the current draw of the starter and it read higher than the scale on the ammeter. The technician then attempted to rotate the engine by hand and found that the engine would not rotate. Based on this history of not cranking normally in the morning, the technician removed the spark plugs and attempted to crank the engine. This time the engine cranked and coolant was seen shooting from cylinders number two and three. Apparently coolant leaked into the cylinders, due to a fault with the head gasket, causing the engine to hydro-lock or not rotate due to liquid being trapped on top of the piston. Replacing the bad gasket solved the cranking problems in the morning.

3. Select "snapshot" and start recording or graphing if the scan tool is capable.
4. Crank the engine. Stop the scan tool recording.
5. Retrieve the scan data and record cranking RPM and battery voltage during cranking. Cranking RPM should be between 80 and 250 RPM. Battery voltage during cranking should be higher than 9.6 volts.

**Watch the Dome Light**

When diagnosing any starter-related problem, open the door of the vehicle and observe the brightness of the dome or interior light(s). The brightness of any electrical lamp is proportional to the voltage.

Normal operation of the starter results in a slight dimming of the dome light.

- *If the light remains bright,* the problem is usually an open circuit in the control circuit.
- *If the light goes out or almost goes out,* the problem is usually a shorted or grounded armature or field coils inside the starter.

A poor electrical connection that opens under load or a discharged battery could also be the cause.

🔧 TECH TIP

**Don't Hit That Starter!**

In the past, it was common to see service technicians hitting a starter in their effort to diagnose a no-crank condition. Often the shock of the blow to the starter aligned or moved the brushes, armature, and bushings. Many times, the starter functioned after being hit—even if only for a short time.

However, most of today's starters use permanent-magnet fields, and the magnets can be easily broken if hit. A magnet that is broken becomes two weaker magnets. Some early permanent-magnet (PM) starters used magnets that were glued or bonded to the field housing. If struck with a heavy tool, the magnets could be broken, with parts of the magnet falling onto the armature and into the bearing pockets, making the starter impossible to repair or rebuild.

# VOLTAGE-DROP TESTING

## PURPOSE OF VOLTAGE DROP TESTING
**Voltage drop** is the drop in voltage that occurs when current is flowing through a resistance. For example, a voltage drop is the difference between voltage at the source and voltage at the electrical device to which it is flowing. The higher the voltage drop, the greater the resistance in the circuit. Even though voltage-drop testing can be performed on any electrical circuit, the most common areas of testing include the cranking circuit and the charging circuit wiring and connections.

**Is Voltage Drop the Same as Resistance?**

Many technicians have asked the question: Why measure voltage drop when the resistance can be easily measured using an ohmmeter? Think of a battery cable with all the strands of the cable broken, except for one. If an ohmmeter is used to measure the resistance of the cable, the reading would be very low, probably less than 1 ohm. However, the cable is not capable of conducting the amount of current necessary to crank the engine. In less severe cases, several strands can be broken and affect the operation of the starter motor. Although the resistance of the battery cable will not indicate any increased resistance, the restriction to current flow will cause heat and a drop in the voltage available at the starter. Because resistance is not effective until current flows, measuring the voltage drop (differences in voltage between two points) is the most accurate method of determining the true resistance in a circuit.

How much is too much? According to Bosch Corporation, all electrical circuits should have a maximum of 3% loss of the voltage of the circuit to resistance. Therefore, in a 12-volt circuit, the maximum loss of voltage in cables and connections should be 0.36 volt (12 × 0.03 = 0.36 volt). The remaining 97% of the circuit voltage (11.64 volt) is available to operate the electrical device (load). Just remember:

- **Low voltage drop = low resistance**
- **High voltage drop = high resistance**

**RESULTS OF EXCESSIVE VOLTAGE DROP** A high voltage drop (high resistance) in the cranking circuit wiring can cause slow engine cranking with less-than-normal starter amperage drain as a result of the excessive circuit resistance. If the voltage drop is high enough, such as could be caused by dirty battery terminals, the starter may not operate. A typical symptom of low battery voltage or high resistance in the cranking circuit is a "clicking" of the starter solenoid.

**PERFORMING A VOLTAGE DROP TEST** Voltage-drop testing of the wire involves connecting any voltmeter (on the low scale) to the suspected high-resistance cable ends and cranking the engine. ● **SEE FIGURES 7–23, 7–24, AND 7–25.**

**NOTE: Before a difference in voltage (voltage drop) can be measured between the ends of a battery cable, current must be flowing through the cable. *Resistance is not effective unless current is flowing.* If the engine is not being cranked, current is not flowing through the battery cables and the voltage drop cannot be measured.**

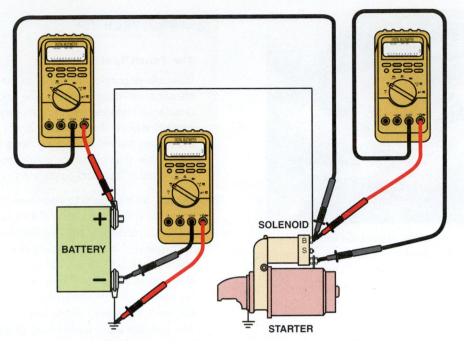

**FIGURE 7–23** Voltmeter hookups for voltage-drop testing of a GM-type cranking circuit.

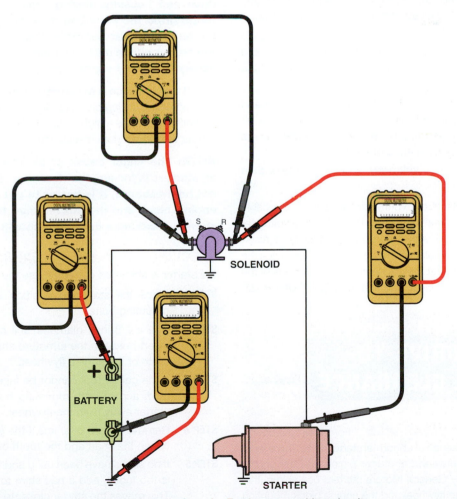

**FIGURE 7–24** Voltmeter hookups for voltage-drop testing of a Ford-type cranking circuit.

**FIGURE 7–25** To test the voltage drop of the battery cable connection, place one voltmeter lead on the battery terminal and the other voltmeter lead on the cable end and crank the engine. The voltmeter will read the difference in voltage between the two leads, which should not exceed 0.20 volt (200 mV).

Crank the engine with a voltmeter connected to the battery and record the reading. Crank the engine with the voltmeter connected across the starter and record the reading. If the difference in the two readings exceeds 0.5 volt, perform the following steps to determine the exact location of the voltage drop.

1. Connect the positive voltmeter test lead to the most positive end of the cable being tested. The most positive end of a cable is the end closest to the positive terminal of the battery.

2. Connect the negative voltmeter test lead to the other end of the cable being tested. With no current flowing through the cable, the voltmeter should read zero because there is the same voltage at both ends of the cable.

3. Crank the engine. The voltmeter should read less than 0.2 volt.

4. Evaluate the results. If the voltmeter reads zero, the cable being tested has no resistance and is good. If the voltmeter reads higher than 0.2 volt, the cable has excessive resistance and should be replaced. However, before replacing the cable, make certain that the connections at both ends of the cable being tested are clean and tight. ● SEE FIGURE 7–26.

# STARTER DRIVE-TO-FLYWHEEL CLEARANCE

**NEED FOR PROPER CLEARANCE** For the proper operation of the starter and absence of abnormal starter noise, there must be a slight clearance between the starter pinion and the engine flywheel ring gear. Many General Motors starters use shims (thin metal strips) between the flywheel and the engine block mounting pad to provide the proper clearance. ● SEE FIGURE 7–27.

**NOTE: Some manufacturers use shims under the starter drive end housings during production. Other manufacturers *grind* the mounting pads at the factory for proper starter pinion gear clearance. If *any* GM starter is replaced, the starter pinion *must* be checked and corrected as necessary to prevent starter damage and excessive noise.**

If the clearance is too great, the starter will produce a high-pitched whine *during* cranking. If the *clearance is too small,* the starter will produce a high-pitched whine *after* the engine starts, just as the ignition key is released.

**NOTE: The major cause of broken drive-end housings on starters is too small a clearance. If the clearance cannot be measured, it is better to put a shim between the engine block and the starter than to leave one out and chance breaking a drive-end housing.**

**CHECKING FOR PROPER CLEARANCE** To be sure that the starter is shimmed correctly, use the following procedure:

**STEP 1** Place the starter in position and finger-tighten the mounting bolts.

**STEP 2** Use a 1/8-inch-diameter drill bit (or gauge tool) and insert between the armature shaft of the starter and a tooth of the engine flywheel.

**STEP 3** If the gauge tool cannot be inserted, use a full-length shim across both mounting holes, which moves the starter away from the flywheel.

**STEP 4** Remove a shim or shims if the gauge tool is loose between the shaft and the tooth of the engine flywheel.

**STEP 5** If no shims have been used and the fit of the gauge tool is too loose, add a half shim to the outside pad only. This moves the starter closer to the teeth of the engine flywheel.

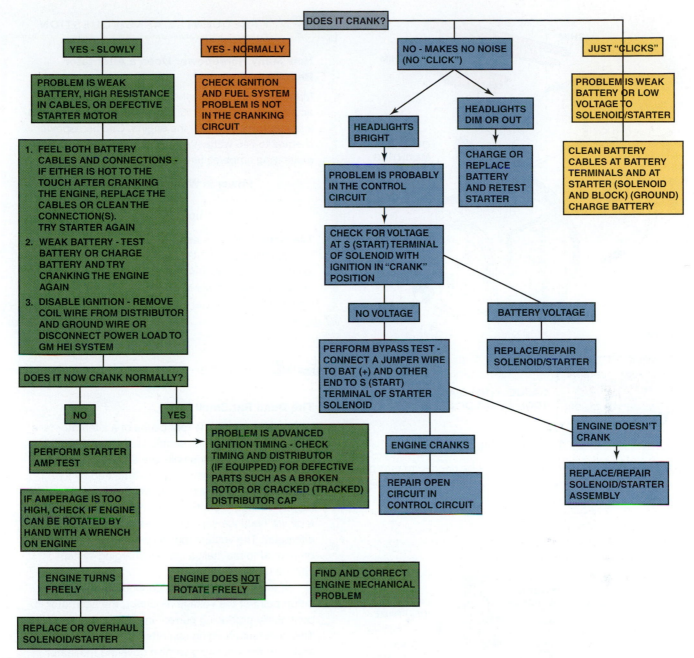

**FIGURE 7–26** Starter diagnosis chart.

The chart contains the following text:

DOES IT CRANK?

**YES - SLOWLY**

PROBLEM IS WEAK BATTERY, HIGH RESISTANCE IN CABLES, OR DEFECTIVE STARTER MOTOR

1. FEEL BOTH BATTERY CABLES AND CONNECTIONS - IF EITHER IS HOT TO THE TOUCH AFTER CRANKING THE ENGINE, REPLACE THE CABLES OR CLEAN THE CONNECTION(S). TRY STARTER AGAIN
2. WEAK BATTERY - TEST BATTERY OR CHARGE BATTERY AND TRY CRANKING THE ENGINE AGAIN
3. DISABLE IGNITION - REMOVE COIL WIRE FROM DISTRIBUTOR AND GROUND WIRE OR DISCONNECT POWER LOAD TO GM HEI SYSTEM

DOES IT NOW CRANK NORMALLY?

NO — PERFORM STARTER AMP TEST

IF AMPERAGE IS TOO HIGH, CHECK IF ENGINE CAN BE ROTATED BY HAND WITH A WRENCH ON ENGINE

ENGINE TURNS FREELY

ENGINE DOES NOT ROTATE FREELY

FIND AND CORRECT ENGINE MECHANICAL PROBLEM

REPLACE OR OVERHAUL SOLENOID/STARTER

YES — PROBLEM IS ADVANCED IGNITION TIMING - CHECK TIMING AND DISTRIBUTOR (IF EQUIPPED) FOR DEFECTIVE PARTS SUCH AS A BROKEN ROTOR OR CRACKED (TRACKED) DISTRIBUTOR CAP

**YES - NORMALLY**

CHECK IGNITION AND FUEL SYSTEM PROBLEM IS NOT IN THE CRANKING CIRCUIT

**NO - MAKES NO NOISE (NO "CLICK")**

HEADLIGHTS BRIGHT

PROBLEM IS PROBABLY IN THE CONTROL CIRCUIT

CHECK FOR VOLTAGE AT S (START) TERMINAL OF SOLENOID WITH IGNITION IN "CRANK" POSITION

NO VOLTAGE

PERFORM BYPASS TEST - CONNECT A JUMPER WIRE TO BAT (+) AND OTHER END TO S (START) TERMINAL OF STARTER SOLENOID

ENGINE CRANKS

REPAIR OPEN CIRCUIT IN CONTROL CIRCUIT

BATTERY VOLTAGE

REPLACE/REPAIR SOLENOID/STARTER

ENGINE DOESN'T CRANK

REPLACE/REPAIR SOLENOID/STARTER ASSEMBLY

HEADLIGHTS DIM OR OUT

CHARGE OR REPLACE BATTERY AND RETEST STARTER

**JUST "CLICKS"**

PROBLEM IS WEAK BATTERY OR LOW VOLTAGE TO SOLENOID/STARTER

CLEAN BATTERY CABLES AT BATTERY TERMINALS AND AT STARTER (SOLENOID AND BLOCK) (GROUND) CHARGE BATTERY

# ALTERNATORS

**CONSTRUCTION** A alternator is constructed of a two-piece cast-aluminum housing. Aluminum is used because of its lightweight, nonmagnetic properties and heat transfer properties which are needed to help keep the alternator cool. A front ball bearing is pressed into the front housing (called the **drive-end [DE] housing**) to provide the support and friction reduction necessary for the belt-driven rotor assembly. The rear housing (called the **slip ring end [SRE]**) usually contains a roller-bearing support for the rotor and mounting for the brushes, diodes, and internal voltage regulator (if the alternator is so equipped). ● **SEE FIGURE 7–28.**

**CHARGING SYSTEM VOLTAGE** The charge indicator light on the dash should be on with the ignition on, engine off (KOEO), but should be off when the engine is running (KOER). If the charge light remains on with the engine running, check the charging system voltage. To measure charging system voltage, connect the test leads of a digital multimeter to the positive (+) and negative (−) terminals of the battery. Set the multimeter to read DC volts.

**CHARGING SYSTEM VOLTAGE SPECIFICATIONS** Most alternators are designed to supply between 13.5 and 15.0 volts at 2,000 engine RPM. Be sure to check the vehicle manufacturer's specifications. For example, most General Motors Corporation vehicles specify a charging voltage of

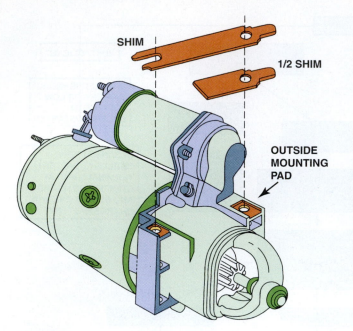

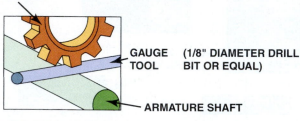

**FIGURE 7–27** A shim (or half shim) may be needed to provide the proper clearance between the flywheel teeth of the engine and the pinion teeth of the starter.

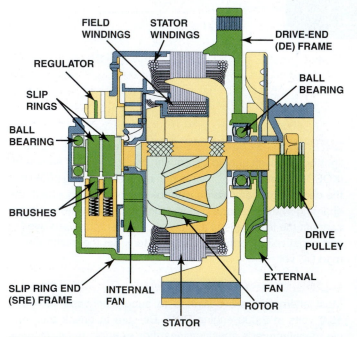

**FIGURE 7–28** Cutaway view of a typical AC alternator.

### How Many Horsepower Does a Alternator Require to Operate?

Many technicians are asked how much power certain accessories require. A 100 A alternator requires about 2 horsepower (hp) from the engine. One horsepower is equal to 746 watts (W). Watts are calculated by multiplying amperes times volts.

$$\text{Power in W} = 100\ A \times 14.5\ V$$
$$= 1450\ W$$
$$1\ hp = 746\ W$$

Therefore, 1450 W is about 2 hp.

Allowing about 20% for mechanical and electrical losses adds another 0.4 hp. Therefore, when anyone asks how much power it takes to produce 100 A from a alternator, the answer is about 2.4 hp.

**🔧** **TECH TIP**

### The Dead Rat Smell Test

When checking for the root cause of a alternator failure, the wise technician should sniff (smell) the alternator! If the alternator smells like a dead rat (rancid), the stator windings have been overheated by trying to charge a discharged or defective battery. If the battery voltage is continuously low, the voltage regulator will continue supplying full-field current to the alternator. The voltage regulator is designed to cycle on and off to maintain a narrow charging system voltage range.

If the battery voltage is continually below the cutoff point of the voltage regulator, the alternator is continually producing current in the stator windings. This constant charging can often overheat the stator and burn the insulating varnish covering the stator windings. If the alternator fails the sniff test, the technician should replace the alternator *and* replace or recharge and test the battery.

14.7 volts ± 0.5 (or between 14.2 and 15.2 volts) at 2000 RPM and no load.

### CHARGING SYSTEM VOLTAGE TEST PROCEDURE

Charging system voltage tests should be performed on a vehicle with a battery at least 75% charged. If the battery is discharged (or defective), the charging voltage may be below specifications. To measure charging system voltage, follow these steps:

1. Connect the voltmeter as shown in ● **FIGURE 7–29**.
2. Set the meter to read DC volts.

FIGURE 7–29 The digital multimeter should be set to read DC volts and the red lead connected to the battery positive (+) terminal and the black meter lead connected to the negative (−) battery terminal.

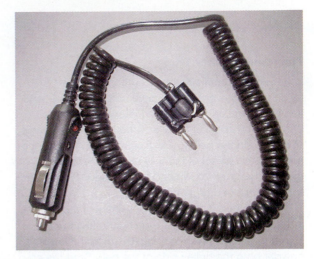

FIGURE 7–30 A simple and easy-to-use tester can be made from a lighter plug and double banana plug that fits the "COM" and "V" terminals of most digital meters. By plugging the lighter plug into the lighter, the charging circuit voltage can be easily measured.

**TECH TIP**

**The Lighter Plug Trick**

Battery voltage measurements can be read through the lighter socket. ● **SEE FIGURE 7–30.** Simply construct a test tool using a lighter plug at one end of a length of two-conductor wire and the other end connected to a double banana plug. The double banana plug will fit most meters in the common (COM) terminal and the volt terminal of the meter.

3. Start the engine and raise to a fast idle (about 2,000 RPM).
4. Read the voltmeter and compare with specifications. If lower than specifications, charge the battery and test for excessive charging circuit voltage drop and for a possible open in the sensing wire before replacing the alternator.

**NOTE: If the voltmeter reading rises, then becomes lower as the engine speed is increased, the alternator drive (accessory drive) belt is loose or slipping.**

**TESTING A ALTERNATOR USING A SCAN TOOL** A scan tool can be used on most vehicles that have datastream information on the battery and the charging system. Follow these steps:

1. Connect the scan tool according to the manufacturers' instructions.
2. Select battery voltage and engine RPM on the scan tool.
3. Start the engine and operate at 2,000 RPM.
4. Observe the battery voltage. This voltage should be between 13.5 and 15.0 volts (or within manufacturers' specifications).

**NOTE: The scan tool voltage should be within 0.5 volt of the charging voltage as tested at the battery. Some PCM controlled charging systems such as the General Motor's electrical power management (EPM) system, the charging voltage can vary from from 12 to 15 volts and be normal. Always check service information for the exact specification for the vehicle being tested to help avoid un-necessary repairs.**

## AC RIPPLE VOLTAGE CHECK

A good alternator should produce only a small amount of AC voltage. It is the purpose of the diodes in the alternator to rectify AC voltage into DC voltage. **AC ripple voltage** is the AC part of the DC charging voltage produced by the alternator. If the AC ripple voltage is higher than 0.5 volt this can cause engine performance problems because the AC voltage can interfere with sensor signals. The procedure to check for AC voltage includes the following steps:

1. Set the digital meter to read AC volts.
2. Start the engine and operate it at 2,000 RPM (fast idle).
3. Connect the voltmeter leads to the positive and negative battery terminals.
4. Turn on the headlights to provide an electrical load on the alternator.

**NOTE: A higher, more accurate reading can be obtained by touching the meter lead to the output terminal of the alternator as shown in ● FIGURE 7–31.**

### The Hand Cleaner Trick

Lower-than-normal alternator output could be the result of a loose or slipping drive belt. All belts (V and serpentine multigroove) use an interference angle between the angle of the V's of the belt and the angle of the V's on the pulley. A belt wears this interference angle off the edges of the V of the belt. As a result, the belt may start to slip and make a squealing sound even if tensioned properly.

A common trick used to determine if the noise is belt related is to use grit-type hand cleaner or scouring powder. With the engine off, sprinkle some powder onto the pulley side of the belt. Start the engine. The excess powder will fly into the air, so get away from under the hood when the engine starts. If the belts are now quieter, you know that it was the glazed belt that made the noise.

**NOTE: Often, the noise sounds exactly like a noisy bearing. Therefore, before you start removing and replacing parts, try the hand cleaner trick.**

The grit from the hand cleaner will often remove the glaze from the belt and the noise will not return. If the belt is worn or loose, however, the noise will return and the belt should be replaced. A fast, alternative method to check for belt noise is to spray water from a squirt bottle at the belt with the engine running. If the noise stops, the belt is the cause of the noise. The water quickly evaporates and therefore, unlike the gritty hand cleaner, water simply finds the problem—it does not provide a short-term fix.

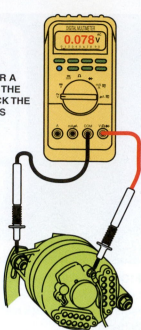

MEASURING THE AC RIPPLE FROM THE ALTERNATOR TELLS A LOT ABOUT ITS CONDITION. IF THE AC RIPPLE IS ABOVE 500 MILLIVOLTS, OR 0.5 VOLTS, LOOK FOR A PROBLEM IN THE DIODES OR STATOR. IF THE RIPPLE IS BELOW 500 MILLIVOLTS, CHECK THE ALTERNATOR OUTPUT TO DETERMINE ITS CONDITION.

**FIGURE 7–31** AC ripple at the output terminal of the alternator is more accurate than testing at the battery due to the resistance of the wiring between the alternator and the battery. The reading shown on the meter is only 78 mV (0.078 V), far below what the reading would be if a diode were defective.

**FIGURE 7–32** A mini clamp-on digital multimeter can be used to measure alternator output and unwanted AC current by switching the meter to read DC amperes.

The results should be interpreted as follows: If the diodes are good, the voltmeter should read *less* than 0.4 volt AC. If the reading is *over* 0.5 volt AC, the rectifier diodes or stator are defective indicating that the alternator should be replaced.

**NOTE: This test will *not* test for a defective diode trio, which is used in some alternators to power the field circuit internally and to turn off the dash charge light.**

## AC CURRENT CHECK

The amount of AC current (also called **ripple current**) in amperes flowing from the alternator to the battery can be measured using a clamp-on digital multimeter set to read AC amperes. Attach the clamp of the meter around the alternator output wire or all of the positive or negative battery cables if the output wire is not accessible. Start the engine and turn on all lights and accessories to load the alternator and read the meter display. The maximum allowable AC current (amperes) from the alternator is less than 10% of the rated output of the alternator. Because most newer alternators produce about 100 amperes DC, the maximum allowable AC amperes would be 10 amperes. If the reading is above 10 A (or 10%), this indicates that the rectifier diodes or a fault with the stator windings is present.
● SEE FIGURE 7–32.

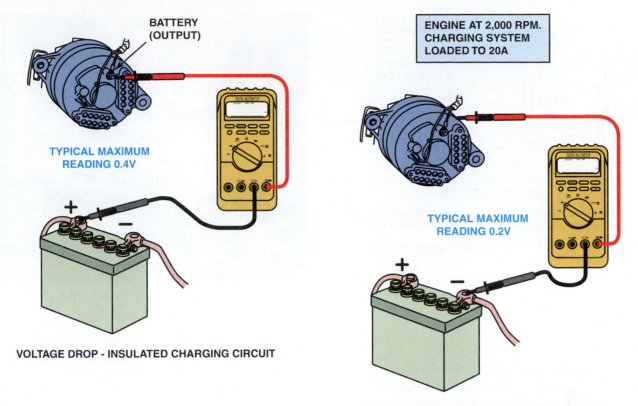

BATTERY
(OUTPUT)

TYPICAL MAXIMUM
READING 0.4V

VOLTAGE DROP - INSULATED CHARGING CIRCUIT

ENGINE AT 2,000 RPM.
CHARGING SYSTEM
LOADED TO 20A

TYPICAL MAXIMUM
READING 0.2V

VOLTAGE DROP - CHARGING GROUND CIRCUIT

**FIGURE 7-33** Voltmeter hookup to test the voltage drop of the charging circuit.

## CHARGING SYSTEM VOLTAGE-DROP TESTING

### PURPOSE OF CHARGING SYSTEM VOLTAGE DROP TESTING
For the proper operation of any charging system, there must be good electrical connections between the battery positive terminal and the alternator output terminal. The alternator must also be properly grounded to the engine block.

Many vehicle manufacturers run the lead from the output terminal of the alternator to other connectors or junction blocks that are electrically connected to the positive terminal of the battery. If there is high resistance (a high voltage drop) in these connections or in the wiring itself, the battery will not be properly charged.

### CHARGING SYSTEM VOLTAGE DROP TESTING PROCEDURE
When there is a suspected charging system problem (with or without a charge indicator light on), simply follow these steps to measure the voltage drop of the insulated (power-side) charging circuit:

1. Start the engine and run it at a fast idle (about 2000 engine RPM).

2. Turn on the headlights to ensure an electrical load on the charging system.

3. Using any voltmeter, connect the positive test lead (usually red) to the output terminal of the alternator. Attach the negative test lead (usually black) to the positive post of the battery.

The results should be interpreted as follows:

1. If there is less than a 0.4-volt reading, then all wiring and connections are satisfactory.

2. If the voltmeter reads higher than 0.4 volt, there is excessive resistance (voltage drop) between the alternator output terminal and the positive terminal of the battery.

3. If the voltmeter reads battery voltage (or close to battery voltage), there is an open circuit between the battery and the alternator output terminal (look for a positive open fusible link).

To determine whether the alternator is correctly grounded, maintain the engine speed at 2000 RPM with the headlights on. Connect the positive voltmeter lead to the case of the alternator and the negative voltmeter lead to the negative terminal of the battery. The voltmeter should read less than 0.2 volt if the alternator is properly grounded. If the reading is over 0.2 volt, connect one end of an auxiliary ground wire to the case of the alternator and the other end to a good engine ground. ● **SEE FIGURE 7-33.**

## ALTERNATOR OUTPUT TEST

A charging circuit may be able to produce correct charging circuit voltage, but not be able to produce adequate amperage output. If in doubt about charging system output, first check the condition of the alternator drive belt. With the engine off, attempt to rotate the fan of the alternator by hand. Replace tensioner or

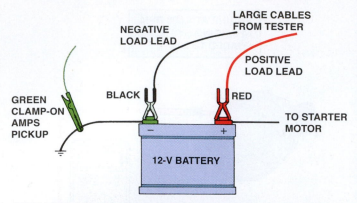

NEGATIVE LOAD LEAD

LARGE CABLES FROM TESTER

POSITIVE LOAD LEAD

GREEN CLAMP-ON AMPS PICKUP

BLACK

RED

TO STARTER MOTOR

12-V BATTERY

TEST LEAD CONNECTIONS FOR TESTING THE STARTING SYSTEM, CHARGING SYSTEM, VOLTAGE REGULATOR, AND DIODE STATOR.

**FIGURE 7–34** Typical hookup of a starting and charging tester.

OUTPUT RATING

**FIGURE 7–35** The output on this alternator is printed on a label.

## TECH TIP

### "2 to 4"

Most voltage-drop specifications range between 0.2 and 0.4 volt. Generally, if the voltage loss (voltage drop) in a circuit exceeds 0.5 volt (1/2 volt), the wiring in that circuit should be repaired or replaced. During automotive testing, it is sometimes difficult to remember the exact specification for each test; therefore, the technician can simply remember "2 to 4" and that any voltage drop over that may indicate a problem.

## ? REAL WORLD FIX

### The 2-Minute Alternator Repair

A Chevrolet pickup truck was brought to a dealer for routine service. The owner stated that the battery required a jump start after a weekend of sitting. The battery voltage was 12.4 volts (about 75% charged), but the charging voltage was also 12.4 volts at 2,000 RPM. Because normal charging voltage should be 13.5 to 15.0 volts, it was obvious that the charging system was not operating correctly.

The technician checked the dash and found that the "charge" light was not on. Before removing the alternator for service, the technician checked the wiring connection. When the connector was removed, it was discovered to be rusty. After the contacts were cleaned, the charging system was restored to normal operation. The technician had learned that the simple things should always be checked first before tearing into a big (or expensive) repair.

tighten drive belt if the alternator fan can be rotated by hand.

● **SEE FIGURE 7–34** for typical test equipment hookup.

The testing procedure for alternator output is as follows:

1. Connect the starting and charging test leads according to the manufacturers' instructions.

2. Turn the ignition switch on (engine off) and observe the ammeter. This is the ignition circuit current, and it should be about 2 to 8 amperes.

3. Start the engine and operate it at 2,000 RPM (fast idle). Turn the load increase control slowly to obtain the highest reading on the ammeter scale while maintaining a battery voltage of at least 13 volts. Note the ampere reading.

4. Total the amperes from steps 2 and 3. Results should be within 10% (or 15 amperes) of the rated output. Rated output may be stamped on the alternator as shown in ● **FIGURE 7–35.**

**NOTE: Almost all vehicle manufacturers are now using some load response control (LRC) also called electronic load detector (ELD), in the control of the voltage output (voltage regulators) of the alternator. This means that the regulator does not react immediately to a load change, but rather slowly increases the load on the alternator to avoid engine idle problems. This gradual increase of voltage may require as long as 15 seconds. This delay has convinced some technicians that a problem exists in the alternator/regulator or computer control of the alternator.**

**NOTE: When applying a load to the battery with a carbon pile tester during a alternator output test, do not permit the battery voltage to drop below 13 volts. Most alternators will produce their maximum output (in amperes) above 13 volts.**

**FIGURE 7–36** Normal alternator scope pattern. This AC ripple is on top of a DC voltage line. The ripple should be less than 0.50 V high.

**FIGURE 7–37** Alternator pattern indicating a shorted diode.

**FIGURE 7–38** Alternator pattern indicating an open diode.

## TESTING A ALTERNATOR USING A SCOPE

Defective diodes and open or shorted stators can be detected on an ignition scope. Connect the scope leads as usual, *except* for the coil negative connection, which attaches to the alternator output ("BAT") terminal. With the pattern selection set to "raster" (stacked), start the engine and run to approximately 1000 RPM (slightly higher-than-normal idle speed). The scope should show an even ripple pattern reflecting the slight alternating up-and-down level of the alternator output voltage.

If the alternator is controlled by an electronic voltage regulator, the rapid on-and-off cycling of the field current can create vertical spikes evenly throughout the pattern. These spikes are normal. If the ripple pattern is jagged or uneven, a defective diode (open or shorted) or a defective stator is indicated. ● **SEE FIGURES 7–36 THROUGH 7–38.** If the alternator scope pattern does not show even ripples, the alternator should be replaced.

### ? REAL WORLD FIX

**The Start/Stall/Start/Stall Problem**

A Chevrolet 4-cylinder engine would stall every time it was started. The engine cranked normally and the engine started quickly. It would just stall once it had run for about 1 second. After hours of troubleshooting, it was discovered that if the "gages" fuse was removed, the engine would start and run normally. Because the alternator was powered by the "gages" fuse, the charging voltage was checked and found to be over 16 volts just before the engine stalled. Replacing the alternator fixed the problem. The computer shut down to prevent damage when the voltage exceeded 16 volts.

**NOTE: A shorted throttle-body injector on a similar vehicle had the same characteristic problem. In this case, the lower resistance caused an increase in current flow (amperes) through the injector and through the computer switching transistor. To protect the transistor, the computer limited current to the injector after the engine started and the charging voltage increased to above 14 volts. As long as the alternator was disconnected, the current flow through the injector was okay and the engine ran when the alternator was disconnected.**

## SUMMARY

1. Batteries can be tested with a voltmeter to determine the state of charge. A battery load test loads the battery to one-half of its CCA rating. A good battery should be able to maintain above 9.6 volts for the entire 15-second test period.

2. A battery drain test should be performed if the battery runs down.

3. Proper operation of the starter motor depends on the battery being at least 75% charged and the battery cables being of the correct size (gauge) and having no more than a 0.2-volt drop.

4. Voltage-drop testing includes cranking the engine, measuring the drop in voltage from the battery to the starter, and measuring the drop in voltage from the negative terminal of the battery to the engine block.

5. The cranking circuit should be tested for proper amperage draw.

6. An open in the control circuit can prevent starter motor operation.

7. Charging system testing requires that the battery be at least 75% charged to be assured of accurate test results. The charge indicator light should be on with the ignition switch on, but should go out whenever the engine is running. Normal charging voltage (at 2000 engine RPM) is 13.5 to 15.0 volts.

8. To check for excessive resistance in the wiring between the alternator and the battery, perform a voltage-drop test.

1. Describe the results of a voltmeter battery state-of-charge test.
2. List the steps for performing a battery load test.
3. Explain how to perform a battery drain test.
4. Explain how to perform a voltage-drop test of the cranking circuit.
5. Describe how to test the voltage drop of the charging circuit.
6. Discuss how to measure the maximum amperage output of a alternator.

## CHAPTER QUIZ

1. A battery high-rate discharge (load capacity) test is being performed on a 12-volt battery. Technician A says that a good battery should have a voltage reading of higher than 9.6 volts while under load at the end of the 15-second test. Technician B says that the battery should be discharged (loaded to 2 times its CCA rating). Which technician is correct?
   a. Technician A only
   b. Technician B only
   c. Both Technicians A and B
   d. Neither Technician A nor B

2. Normal battery drain (parasitic drain) with a vehicle with many computer and electronic circuits is _____.
   a. 20 to 30 milliamperes
   b. 2 to 3 amperes
   c. 150 to 300 milliamperes
   d. None of the above

3. When jump starting, _____.
   a. The last connection should be the positive post of the dead battery
   b. The last connection should be the engine block of the dead vehicle
   c. The alternator must be disconnected on both vehicles
   d. Both a and c

4. Technician A says that a discharged battery (lower-than-normal battery voltage) can cause solenoid clicking. Technician B says that a discharged battery or dirty (corroded) battery cables can cause solenoid clicking. Which technician is correct?
   a. Technician A only
   b. Technician B only
   c. Both Technicians A and B
   d. Neither Technician A nor B

5. Slow cranking can be caused by all of the following *except* _____.
   a. A low or discharged battery
   b. Corroded or dirty battery cables
   c. Engine mechanical problems
   d. An open neutral safety switch

6. High resistance means _____.
   a. High voltage drop
   b. Low voltage drop
   c. Causes higher than normal current to flow
   d. Normally found in good battery cables

7. An acceptable charging circuit voltage on a 12-volt system is _____.
   a. 13.5 to 15.0 volts
   b. 12.6 to 15.6 volts
   c. 12.0 to 14.0 volts
   d. 14.9 to 16.1 volts

8. Technician A says that a voltage-drop test of the charging circuit should only be performed when current is flowing through the circuit. Technician B says to connect the leads of a voltmeter to the positive and negative terminals of the battery to measure the voltage drop of the charging system. Which technician is correct?
   a. Technician A only
   b. Technician B only
   c. Both Technicians A and B
   d. Neither Technician A nor B

9. Testing the electrical system through the lighter plug using a digital meter can test _____.
   a. Charging system current
   b. Charging system voltage
   c. Cranking system current
   d. All of the above

10. The maximum acceptable AC ripple voltage is _____.
    a. 0.010 V (10 mV)
    b. 0.050 V (50 mV)
    c. 0.100 V (100 mV)
    d. 0.400 V (400 mV)

# chapter 8

# IGNITION SYSTEM COMPONENTS AND OPERATION

**OBJECTIVES:** After studying Chapter 8, the reader will be able to: • Prepare for ASE Engine Performance (A8) certification test content area "B" (Ignition System Diagnosis and Repair). • Explain how ignition coils create 40,000 volts. • Discuss crankshaft position sensor and pickup coil operation. • Describe the operation of waste-spark and coil-on-plug ignition systems.

**KEY TERMS:** Bypass ignition 116 • Companion (paired) cylinder 110 • Compression-sensing ignition 111 • COP ignition 111 • Detonation 114 • DI 103 • DIS 110 • Dwell 115 • EI 104 • EMI 112 • EST 115 • Firing order 109 • Hall effect 106 • High voltage 107 • IC 115 • ICM 114 • Ion-sensing ignition 114 • Knock sensors 114 • Low voltage 107 • Magnetic sensor 106 • Optical sensors 107 • Paired cylinders 110 • Pickup coil 106 • Ping 114 • Primary winding 105 • Pulse generator 106 • Secondary winding 105 • Schmitt trigger 107 • Spark knock 114 • SPOUT 115 • Switching 105 • Transistor 106 • Trigger 106 • Turns ratio 105 • Up-integrated ignition 116

## IGNITION SYSTEM

**PURPOSE AND FUNCTION** The ignition system includes components and wiring necessary to create and distribute a high voltage (up to 40,000 volts or more) and send to the spark plug at the correct time. A high-voltage arc occurs across the gap of a spark plug inside the combustion chamber. The spark raises the temperature of the air-fuel mixture and starts the combustion process inside the cylinder.

**BACKGROUND** All ignition systems apply battery voltage (close to 12 volts) to the positive side of the ignition coil(s) and pulse the negative side to ground on and off.

- **Early ignition systems.** Before the mid-1970s, ignition systems used a mechanically opened set of contact points to make and break the electrical connection to ground. A cam lobe, located in and driven by the distributor, opened the points. There was one lobe for each cylinder. The points used a rubbing block that was lubricated by applying a thin layer of grease on the cam lobe at each service interval. Each time the points opened, a spark was created in the ignition coil. The high-voltage spark then traveled to each spark plug through the distributor cap and rotor and the spark plug wires. The distributor was used twice in the creation of the spark.
    - First, it connected to the camshaft that rotated the distributor cam causing the points to open and close.

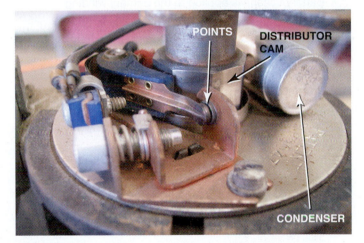

**FIGURE 8–1** A point-type distributor from a hot rod being tested on a distributor machine.

- Second, it used a rotor to direct the high-voltage spark from the coil entering the center of the distributor cap to inserts connected to spark plug wires to each cylinder.
- ● SEE FIGURE 8–1.
- **Electronic ignition.** Since the mid-1970s, ignition systems have used sensors, such as a pickup coil and reluctor (trigger wheel), to trigger or signal an electronic module that switches the primary ground circuit of the ignition coil. **Distributor ignition (DI)** is the term specified by the Society of Automotive Engineers (SAE) for an ignition system that uses a distributor. **Electronic**

ignition (EI) is the term specified by the SAE for an ignition system that does not use a distributor. Types of EI systems include:

1. **Waste-spark system.** This type of system uses one ignition coil to fire the spark plugs for two cylinders at the same time.

2. **Coil-on-plug system.** This type of system uses a single ignition coil for each cylinder with the coil placed above or near the spark plug.

## IGNITION COIL OPERATION

In an ignition coil there are two windings:

- Primary winding
- Secondary winding

All ignition systems use electromagnetic induction to produce a high-voltage spark from the ignition coil. Electromagnetic induction means that a current can be created in a conductor (coil winding) by a moving magnetic field. Current flowing through the primary winding of the coil produces the magnetic field in an ignition coil. An ignition coil is able to increase battery voltage to 40,000 volts or more in the following way.

- Battery voltage is applied to the primary winding.
- A ground is provided to the primary winding by the ignition control module (ICM), igniter, or powertrain control module (PCM).
- Current (approximately 2 to 6 amperes) flows in the primary coil creating a magnetic field.
- When the ground is opened by the ICM, the primary circuit is turned off and the built-up magnetic field in the secondary winding collapses.
- The movement of the collapsing magnetic field induces a voltage of 250 to 400 volts in the primary winding and 20,000 to 40,000 volts or more in the secondary winding with a current of 0.02 to 0.08 amperes (20 to 80 mA).
- The high voltage created in the secondary winding is high enough to jump the air gap at the spark plug.
- The electrical arc at the spark plug ignites the air-fuel mixture in the combustion chamber of the engine.
- For each spark that occurs, the coil must be charged with a magnetic field and then discharged.

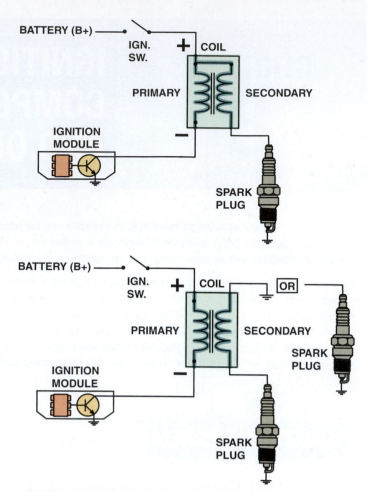

**FIGURE 8–2** The primary ignition system is used to trigger and therefore create the secondary (high-voltage) spark from the ignition coil. Some ignition coils are electrically connected, called married (top figure) whereas others use separated primary and secondary windings, called divorced (lower figure).

The ignition components in the coil primary winding are known collectively as the primary ignition circuit.

- When the primary circuit is carrying current, the secondary circuit is off.
- When the primary circuit is turned off, the secondary circuit has high voltage.
- The components necessary to create and distribute the high voltage produced in the secondary windings of the coil are called the secondary ignition circuit. ● **SEE FIGURE 8–2.**

These circuits include the following components.

- Primary ignition circuit

1. Battery
2. Ignition switch
3. Primary winding of coil
4. Pickup coil (if distributor ignition)
5. Crankshaft position sensor (CKP)
6. Ignition control module (ICM) or igniter

**FIGURE 8–3** The steel laminations used in an E coil increases the magnetic field strength, which helps the coil produce higher energy output for a more complete combustion in the cylinders.

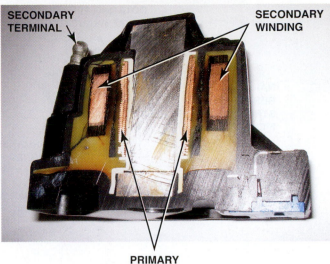

**FIGURE 8–4** The primary windings are inside the secondary windings on this General Motors coil.

- Secondary ignition circuit
  1. Secondary winding of coil
  2. Distributor cap and rotor (if the vehicle is so equipped)
  3. Spark plug wires
  4. Spark plugs

**IGNITION COIL CONSTRUCTION** Many ignition coils contain two separate but electrically connected windings of copper wire. Other coils are true transformers in which the primary and secondary windings are not electrically connected. ● **SEE FIGURE 8–3.**

The center of an ignition coil contains a core of laminated soft iron (thin strips of soft iron). This core increases the magnetic strength of the coil.

- **Secondary winding.** Surrounding the laminated core are approximately 20,000 turns of fine wire (approximately 42 gauge), which is smaller than a human hair. The winding is called the **secondary** coil winding.

- **Primary winding.** Surrounding the secondary windings are approximately 150 turns of heavy wire (approximately 21 gauge), which is about 0.028 inch in diameter. The winding is called the **primary** coil winding. The secondary winding has about 100 times the number of turns of the primary winding, referred to as the **turns ratio** (approximately 100:1).

In older coils, these windings are surrounded with a thin metal shield and insulating paper and placed into a metal container filled with transformer oil to help cool the coil windings. Other coil designs use an air-cooled, epoxy-sealed E coil. The *E coil* is so named because the laminated, soft iron core is E shaped, with the coil wire turns wrapped around the center "finger" of the E and the primary winding wrapped inside the secondary winding. ● **SEE FIGURES 8–4 AND 8–5.**

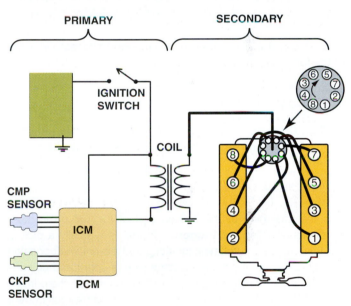

**FIGURE 8–5** The primary ignition system is used to trigger and therefore create the secondary (high-voltage) spark from the ignition coil.

## IGNITION SWITCHING AND TRIGGERING

**SWITCHING** For any ignition system to function, the primary current must be turned on to charge the coil and off to allow the coil to discharge, creating a high-voltage spark. This turning on and off of the primary circuit is called **switching**. The unit that does the switching is an electronic switch, such as a

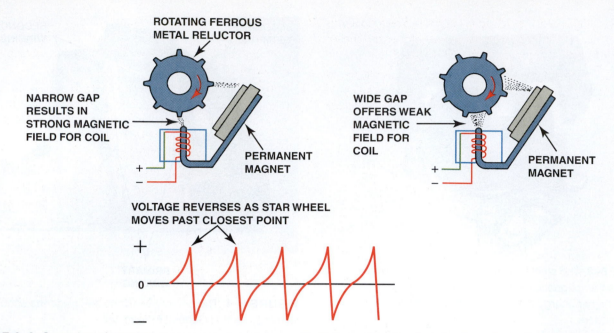

**FIGURE 8–6** Operation of a typical pulse generator (pickup coil). At the bottom is a line drawing of a typical scope pattern of the output voltage of a pickup coil. The ICM receives this voltage from the pickup coil and opens the ground circuit to the ignition coil when the voltage starts down from its peak (just as the reluctor teeth start moving away from the pickup coil).

power transistor. This power transistor can be located in either of the following locations.

- In the ICM or igniter
- In the PCM (computer)

**NOTE: On some coil-on-plug systems, the ICM is part of the ignition coil itself and is serviced as an assembly.**

## PRIMARY CIRCUIT OPERATION

The device that signals the switching of the coil on and off or just on in most instances is called the **trigger.** A trigger is typically a pickup coil in some distributor-type ignitions and a crankshaft position sensor (CKP) on electronic systems (waste-spark and coil-on-plug systems). To get a spark out of an ignition coil, the primary coil circuit must be turned on and off. The primary circuit current switching is controlled by a **transistor** (electronic switch) inside the ignition module or igniter, and is controlled by one of the following devices.

- **Magnetic sensor.** A simple and common ignition electronic switching device is the magnetic pulse generator system. This type of magnetic sensor is often called a magnetic **pulse generator** or **pickup coil,** and is installed in the distributor housing. The pulse generator consists of a trigger wheel (reluctor) and a pickup coil. The pickup coil consists of an iron core wrapped with fine wire, in a coil at one end and attached to a permanent magnet at the other end. The center of the coil is called the pole piece. The pickup coil signal triggers the transistor inside the module and is also used by the computer for piston position information and engine speed (RPM). The reluctor is shaped so that the

magnetic strength changes enough to create a usable varying signal for use by the module to trigger the coil. A magnetic pickup coil produces an analog AC signal.
● **SEE FIGURE 8–6.**

Magnetic crankshaft position sensors use the changing strength of the magnetic field surrounding a coil of wire to signal the ICM and PCM. This signal is used by the electronics in the ignition module and computer to determine piston position and engine speed (RPM). This sensor operates similarly to the distributor magnetic pickup coil. The crankshaft position sensor uses the strength of the magnetic field surrounding a coil of wire to signal the ICM. The rotating crankshaft has notches cut into it that trigger the magnetic position sensor, which change the strength of the magnetic field as the notches pass by the position sensor, creating an AC analog signal.
● **SEE FIGURE 8–7.**

- **Hall-effect switch.** This switch also uses a stationary sensor and rotating trigger wheel (shutter). Unlike the magnetic pulse generator, the Hall-effect switch requires a small input voltage to generate an output or signal voltage. **Hall effect** has the ability to generate a voltage signal in semiconductor material (gallium arsenate crystal) by passing current through it in one direction and applying a magnetic field to it at a right angle to its surface. If the input current is held steady and the magnetic field fluctuates, an output voltage is produced that changes in proportion to field strength. Most Hall-effect switches used in distributors have the following:

1. Hall element or device
2. Permanent magnet

3. Rotating ring of metal blades (shutters) similar to a trigger wheel (Another method uses a stationary sensor with a rotating magnet.) ● SEE FIGURE 8–8.

   Some blades are designed to hang down, typically found in Bosch and Chrysler systems; others may be on a separate ring on the distributor shaft, typically found in General Motors and Ford Hall-effect distributors.

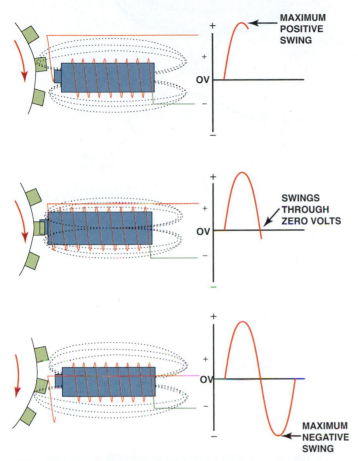

FIGURE 8–7 A magnetic sensor uses a permanent magnet surrounded by a coil of wire. The notches of the crankshaft (or camshaft) create a variable magnetic field strength around the coil. When a metallic section is close to the sensor, the magnetic field is stronger because metal is a better conductor of magnetic lines of force than air.

■ When the shutter blade enters the gap between the magnet and the Hall element, it creates a magnetic shunt that changes the field strength through the Hall element.

■ This analog signal is sent to a **Schmitt trigger** inside the sensor itself, which converts the analog signal into a digital signal. A digital (on or off) voltage signal is created at a varying frequency to the ignition module or onboard computer. ● SEE FIGURE 8–9.

■ **Optical sensors.** This type of sensor uses light from an LED and a phototransistor to signal the computer. An interrupter disc between the LED and the phototransistor has slits that allow the light from the LED to trigger the phototransistor on the other side of the disc. Most optical sensors (usually located inside the distributor) use two rows of slits to provide individual cylinder recognition (low-resolution) and precise distributor angle recognition (high-resolution) signals that are used for cylinder misfire detection. ● SEE FIGURE 8–10.

## DISTRIBUTOR IGNITION

**PURPOSE AND FUNCTION**   The purpose of a distributor is to distribute the high-voltage spark from the secondary terminal of the ignition coil to the spark plugs for each cylinder. A gear or shaft that is part of the distributor is meshed with a gear on the camshaft. The distributor is driven at camshaft speed (one-half of crankshaft speed). Most distributor ignition systems also use a sensor to trigger the ignition control module.

**OPERATION OF DISTRIBUTOR IGNITION**   The distributor is used twice in most ignition systems that use one.

■ The first time is when the **low voltage** triggers the ignition control module (ICM) by the use of the rotating distributor shaft.

■ The second time is when the **high voltage** is directed by rotating the rotor to distribute the high-voltage spark to the individual spark plugs.

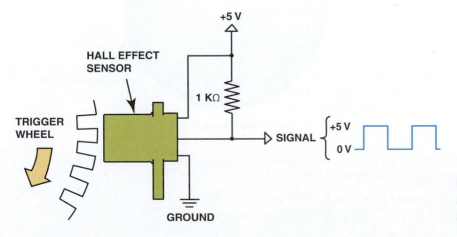

FIGURE 8–8 A Hall-effect sensor produces an on-off voltage signal whether it is used with a blade or a notched wheel.

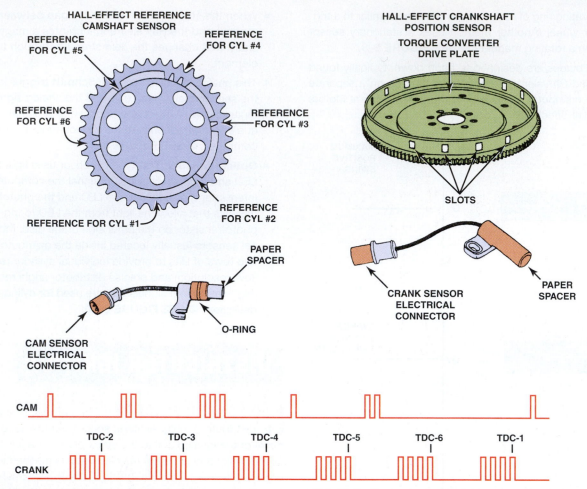

**FIGURE 8–9** Some Hall-effect sensors look like magnetic sensors. This Hall-effect camshaft reference sensor and crankshaft position sensor have an electronic circuit built in that creates a 0 to 5 volt signal as shown at the bottom. These Hall-effect sensors have three wires: a power supply (8 volts) from the computer (controller), a signal (0 to 5 volts), and a signal ground.

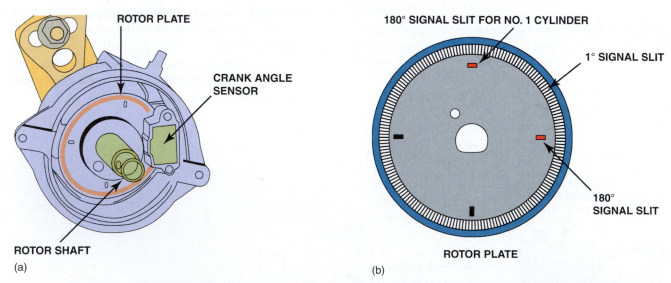

**FIGURE 8–10** (a) Typical optical distributor. (b) Cylinder I slit signals the computer the piston position for cylinder I. The 1-degree slits provide accurate engine speed information to the PCM.

### Optical Distributors Do Not Like Light

Optical distributors use the light emitted from LEDs to trigger phototransistors. Most optical distributors use a shield between the distributor rotor and the optical interrupter ring. Sparks jump the gap from the rotor tip to the distributor cap inserts. This shield blocks the light from the electrical arcs from interfering with the detection of the light from the LEDs. **SEE FIGURE 8–11.**

If this shield is not replaced during service, the light signals are reduced and the engine may not operate correctly. **SEE FIGURE 8–11.**

This can be difficult to detect because nothing looks wrong during a visual inspection. Remember that all optical distributors must be shielded between the rotor and the interrupter ring.

**FIGURE 8–11** A light shield being installed before the rotor is attached.

### The Tachometer Trick

When diagnosing a no-start or intermediate misfiring condition, check the operation of the tachometer. If the tachometer does not indicate engine speed (no-start condition) or drops toward zero (engine missing), then the problem is due to a defect in the *primary* ignition circuit. The tachometer gets its signal from the pulsing of the primary winding of the ignition coil. The following components in the primary circuit could cause the tachometer to not work when the engine is cranking.

- Pickup coil
- Crankshaft position (CKP) sensor
- Ignition control module (ICM) or igniter
- Coil primary wiring

If the vehicle is not equipped with a tachometer, use a scan tool to look at engine RPM. Results:

- No or an unstable engine RPM reading means the problem is in the primary ignition circuit.
- A steady engine RPM reading means the problem is in the secondary ignition circuit or is a fuel-related problem.

**FIGURE 8–12** The firing order is cast or stamped on the intake manifold on most engines that have a distributor ignition.

firing order is often cast into the intake manifold for easy reference. **SEE FIGURE 8–12.**

Service information also shows the firing order and the direction of the distributor rotor rotation, engine cylinder numbering, and the location of the spark plug wires on the distributor cap.

**Caution: Ford V-8s use two different firing orders depending on whether the engine is high output (HO) or standard. Using the incorrect firing order can cause the engine to backfire and could cause engine damage or personal injury. General Motors V-6 engines use different firing orders and different locations for cylinder 1 between the 60-degree V-6 and the 90-degree V-6. Using the incorrect firing order or cylinder number location chart could result in poor engine operation or a no-start condition. Firing order is also important for waste-spark-type ignition systems. The spark plug wire can often be installed on the wrong coil pack which can create a no-start condition or poor engine operation.**

**FIRING ORDER** **Firing order** means the order that the spark is distributed to the correct spark plug at the right time. The firing order of an engine is determined by crankshaft and camshaft design and the location of the spark plug wires in the distributor cap of an engine equipped with a distributor. The

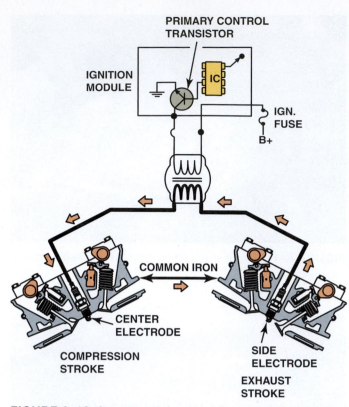

FIGURE 8–13 A waste-spark system fires one cylinder while its piston is on the compression stroke and into paired or companion cylinders while it is on the exhaust stroke. In a typical engine, it requires only about 2 to 3 kV to fire the cylinder on the exhaust stroke. The remaining coil energy is available to fire the spark plug under compression (typically about 8 to 12 kV).

# WASTE-SPARK IGNITION SYSTEMS

**PARTS INVOLVED** Waste-spark ignition is another name for the **distributorless ignition system (DIS)** or electronic ignition (EI). Waste-spark ignition was introduced in the mid-1980s and uses the ignition control module (ICM) and/or the powertrain control module (PCM) to fire the ignition coils. A 4-cylinder engine uses two ignition coils and a 6-cylinder engine uses three ignition coils. Each coil is a true transformer because the primary winding and secondary winding are not electrically connected. A waste-spark coil has four terminals:

- Two primary (Bat + and − to ICM)
- Two secondary (each connected to a spark plug)

Each end of the secondary winding is connected to the spark plug of the cylinder exactly opposite the other in the firing order, called a **companion (paired) cylinder**. ● SEE **FIGURE 8–13.**

**WASTE-SPARK SYSTEM OPERATION** *Both* spark plugs fire at the same time (within nanoseconds of each other).

- When one cylinder (for example, cylinder number 6) is on the compression stroke, the other cylinder (number 3) is on the exhaust stroke.
- The spark that occurs on the exhaust stroke is called the waste spark, because it does no useful work and is only used as a ground path for the secondary winding of the ignition coil. The voltage required to jump the spark plug gap on cylinder 3 (the exhaust stroke) is only 2 to 3 kV.
- The cylinder on the compression stroke uses the remaining coil energy.
- One spark plug of each pair always fires straight polarity (from the center electrode to the ground electrode of the spark plug) and the other cylinder always fires reverse polarity (from the ground electrode to the center electrode of the spark plug). Spark plug life is not greatly affected by the reverse polarity. If there is only one defective spark plug wire or spark plug, two cylinders may be affected.

The coil polarity is determined by the direction the coil is wound (left-hand rule for conventional current flow) and cannot be changed.

For example, if a V-6 engine has a firing order of 165432 when one cylinder is on compression, such as cylinder number 1, then the paired cylinder (number 4) is on the exhaust stroke. During the next rotation of the crankshaft, cylinder number 4 is on the compression stroke and cylinder number 1 is on the exhaust stroke.

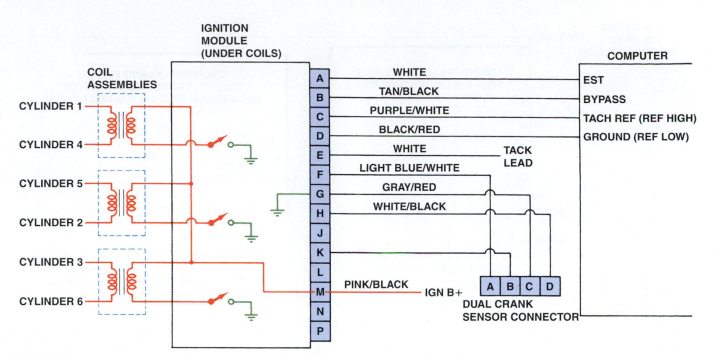

**FIGURE 8–14** Typical wiring diagram of a GM V-6 waste-spark ignition system.

**Odds Fire Straight**

Waste-spark ignition systems fire two spark plugs at the same time. Most vehicle manufacturers use a waste-spark system that fires the odd number cylinders (1, 3, and 5) by straight polarity (current flow from the top of the spark plug through the gap and to the ground electrode). The even number cylinders (2, 4, and 6) are fired reverse polarity, meaning that the spark jumps from the side electrode to the center electrode. Some vehicle manufacturers equip their vehicles with platinum plugs, with the expensive platinum alloy only on one electrode as follows:

- On odd number cylinders (1, 3, 5), the platinum is on the center electrode.
- On even number cylinders (2, 4, 6), the platinum is on the ground electrode.

Replacement spark plugs use platinum on both electrodes (double platinum) and, therefore, can be placed in any cylinder location.

**Cylinder 1.** Always fires straight polarity (from the center electrode to the ground electrode), one time requiring 10 to 12 kV, and one time requiring 3 to 4 kV.

**Cylinder 4.** Always fires reverse polarity (from the ground electrode to the center electrode), one time requiring 10 to 12 kV, and one time requiring 3 to 4 kV.

Waste-spark ignitions require a sensor (usually a crankshaft sensor) to trigger the coils at the correct time. ● **SEE FIGURE 8–14.**

The crankshaft sensor cannot be moved to adjust ignition timing, because ignition timing is not adjustable. The slight adjustment of the crankshaft sensor is designed to position the sensor exactly in the middle of the rotating metal disc for maximum clearance.

### COMPRESSION-SENSING WASTE-SPARK IGNITION

Some waste-spark ignition systems, such as on Saturns and others, use the voltage required to fire the cylinders to determine cylinder position. It requires a higher voltage to fire a spark plug under compression than it does when the spark plug is being fired on the exhaust stroke. The electronics in the coil and the PCM can detect which of the two companion (paired) cylinders that are fired at the same time requires the higher voltage, which indicates the cylinder that is on the compression stroke. For example, a typical 4-cylinder engine equipped with a waste-spark ignition system will fire both cylinders 1 and 4. If cylinder number 4 requires a higher voltage to fire, as determined by the electronics connected to the coil, then the PCM assumes that cylinder number 4 is on the compression stroke. Engines equipped with **compression-sensing ignition** systems do not require the use of a camshaft position sensor to determine specific cylinder numbers. ● **SEE FIGURE 8–15.**

## COIL-ON-PLUG IGNITION

**TERMINOLOGY** Coil-on-plug (COP) ignition uses one ignition coil for each spark plug. This system is also called *coil-by-plug, coil-near-plug,* or *coil-over-plug* ignition. ● **SEE FIGURES 8–16 AND 8–17.**

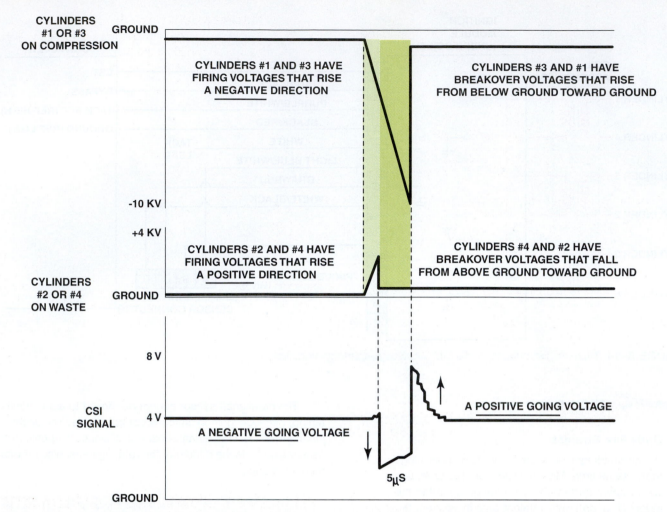

**FIGURE 8–15** The slight (5 microsecond) difference in the firing of the companion cylinders is enough time to allow the PCM to determine which cylinder is firing on the compression stroke. The compression sensing ignition (CSI) signal is then processed by the PCM which then determines which cylinder is on the compression stroke.

**ADVANTAGES** The coil-on-plug system eliminates the spark plug wires that are often the source of **electromagnetic interference (EMI)** that can cause problems to some computer signals. The vehicle computer controls the timing of the spark. Ignition timing also can be changed (retarded or advanced) on a cylinder-by-cylinder basis for maximum performance and to respond to knock sensor signals.

**TYPES OF COP SYSTEMS** There are two basic types of coil-on-plug ignition.

- **Two primary wires.** This design uses the vehicle computer to control the firing of the ignition coil. The two wires include ignition voltage feed and the pulse ground wire, which is controlled by the PCM. The ignition control module (ICM) is located in the PCM, which handles all ignition timing and coil on-time control.

- **Three primary wires.** This design includes an ignition module at each coil. The three wires include:
  - Ignition voltage
  - Ground
  - Pulse from the PCM to the built-in ignition module

Vehicles use a variety of coil-on-plug-type ignition systems, such as the following:

- Many General Motors V-8 engines use a coil-near-plug system with individual coils and modules for each individual cylinder placed on the valve covers. Short secondary ignition spark plug wires are used to connect the output terminal of the ignition coil to the spark plug, which explains why this system is called a *coil-near-plug* system.

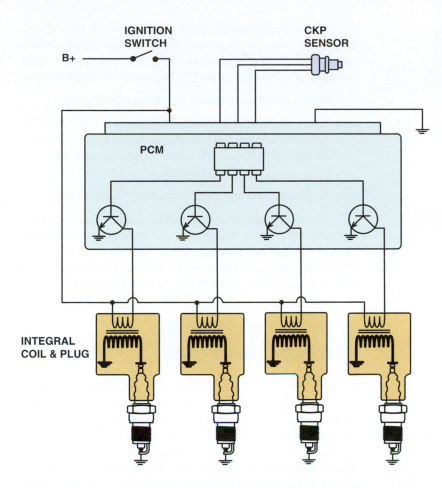

**FIGURE 8–16** A typical coil-on-plug ignition system showing the triggering and the switching being performed by the PCM via input from the crankshaft position sensor.

IGNITION SWITCH

CKP SENSOR

B+

PCM

INTEGRAL COIL & PLUG

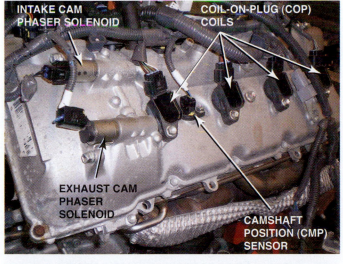

**FIGURE 8–17** An overhead camshaft engine equipped with variable valve timing on both the intake and exhaust camshafts and the coil-on-plug ignition.

INTAKE CAM PHASER SOLENOID

COIL-ON-PLUG (COP) COILS

EXHAUST CAM PHASER SOLENOID

CAMSHAFT POSITION (CMP) SENSOR

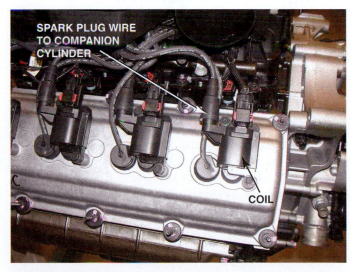

**FIGURE 8–18** A Chrysler Hemi V-8 that has two spark plugs per cylinder. The coil on top of one spark plug fires that plug and, through a spark plug wire, fires a plug in the companion cylinder.

SPARK PLUG WIRE TO COMPANION CYLINDER

COIL

■ A combination of coil-on-plug and waste-spark systems fires a spark plug attached to the coil and uses a spark plug wire attached to the other secondary terminal of the coil to fire another spark plug of the companion cylinder. This type of system is used in some Chrysler Hemi V-8 and Toyota V-6 engines. ● **SEE FIGURE 8–18.**

Most new engines use coil-over-plug-type ignition systems. Each coil is controlled by the PCM, which can vary the ignition timing separately for each cylinder based on signals the PCM receives from the knock sensor(s). For example, if the knock sensor detects that a spark knock has occurred after firing cylinder 3, then the PCM will continue to monitor cylinder 3

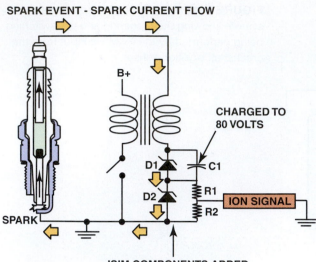

SPARK EVENT - SPARK CURRENT FLOW

B+

CHARGED TO
80 VOLTS

D1
D2
C1
R1
ION SIGNAL
R2

SPARK

ISIM COMPONENTS ADDED
TO SECONDARY CIRCUIT

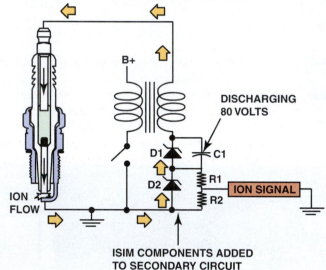

MEASUREMENT PERIOD - ION CURRENT FLOW

B+

DISCHARGING
80 VOLTS

D1
D2
C1
R1
ION SIGNAL
R2

ION
FLOW

ISIM COMPONENTS ADDED
TO SECONDARY CIRCUIT

**FIGURE 8–19** A DC voltage is applied across the spark plug gap after the plug fires and the circuit can determine if the correct air-fuel ratio was present in the cylinder and if knock occurred. The applied voltage for ion sensing does not jump the spark plug gap but rather determines the conductivity of the ionized gases left over from the combustion process.

and retard timing on just this one cylinder if necessary to prevent engine damaging detonation.

### ION-SENSING IGNITION
In an **ion-sensing ignition** system, the spark plug itself becomes a sensor. An ion-sensing ignition uses a coil-on-plug design where the **ignition control module (ICM)** applies a DC voltage across the spark plug gap *after* the ignition event to sense the ionized gases (called plasma) inside the cylinder. Ion-sensing ignition is used in the General Motors EcoTec 4-cylinder engines. ● **SEE FIGURE 8–19.**

The secondary coil discharge voltage (10 to 15 kV) is electrically isolated from the ion-sensing circuit. The combustion flame is ionized and will conduct some electricity, which can be accurately measured at the spark plug gap. The purpose of this circuit includes:

- Misfire detection (required by OBD-II regulations)
- Knock detection (eliminates the need for a knock sensor)
- Ignition timing control (to achieve the best spark timing for maximum power with lowest exhaust emissions)
- Exhaust gas recirculation (EGR) control
- Air-fuel ratio control on an individual cylinder basis

Ion-sensing ignition systems still function the same as conventional coil-on-plug designs, but the engine does not need to be equipped with a camshaft position sensor for misfire detection or a knock sensor, because both of these faults are achieved using the electronics inside the ignition control circuits.

## KNOCK SENSORS

**PURPOSE AND FUNCTION** **Knock sensors (KS)** are used to detect abnormal combustion, often called **ping, spark knock,** or **detonation.** Whenever abnormal combustion occurs, a rapid pressure increase occurs in the cylinder, creating a vibration in the engine block. It is this vibration that is detected by the knock sensor. The signal from the knock sensor is used by the PCM to retard the ignition timing until the knock is eliminated, thereby reducing the damaging effects of the abnormal combustion on pistons and other engine parts.

Inside the knock sensor is a piezoelectric element which is a type of crystal that produces a voltage when pressure or a vibration is applied to the unit. The knock sensor is tuned to the engine knock frequency, in a range from 5 to 10 kHz depending on the engine design. The voltage signal from the knock sensor is sent to the PCM, which then retards the ignition timing until the knocking stops. ● **SEE FIGURE 8–20.**

**DIAGNOSING THE KNOCK SENSOR** If a knock sensor diagnostic trouble code (DTC) is present, follow the specified testing procedure in the service information. A scan tool can be used to check the operation of the knock sensor, using the following procedure.

**STEP 1** Start the engine and connect a scan tool to monitor ignition timing and/or knock sensor activity.

**STEP 2** Create a simulated engine knocking sound by tapping on the engine block or cylinder head with a soft faced mallet or small ball peen hammer.

**STEP 3** Observe the scan tool display. The vibration from the tapping should have been interpreted by the knock sensor as a knock, resulting in a knock sensor signal and a reduction in the spark advance.

A knock sensor also can be tested using a digital storage oscilloscope. ● **SEE FIGURE 8–21.**

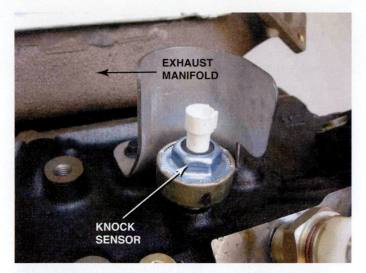

FIGURE 8–20 A typical knock sensor on the side of the block. Some are located in the "V" of a V-type engine and are not noticeable until the intake manifold has been removed.

 **REAL WORLD FIX**

**The Low Power Toyota**

A technician talked about the driver of a Toyota who complained about poor performance and low fuel economy. The technician checked everything, and even replaced all secondary ignition components. Then the technician connected a scan tool and noticed that the knock sensor was commanding the timing to be retarded. Careful visual inspection revealed a "chunk" missing from the serpentine belt, causing a "noise" similar to a spark knock. Apparently the knock sensor was "hearing" the accessory drive belt noise and kept retarding the ignition timing. After replacing the accessory drive belt, a test drive confirmed that normal engine power was restored.

Other items that can fool the knock sensor to retard the ignition timing include:

- Loose valve lifter adjustment
- Engine knocks
- Loose accessory brackets such as the air-conditioning compressor, power steering pumps, or alternator.

NOTE: **Some engine computers are programmed to ignore knock sensor signals when the engine is at idle speed, to avoid having the noise from a loose accessory drive belt or other accessory interpreted as engine knock. Always follow the vehicle manufacturer's recommended testing procedure.**

**REPLACING A KNOCK SENSOR** If replacing a knock sensor, be sure to purchase the exact replacement needed,

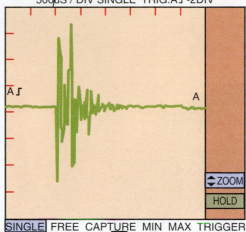

FIGURE 8–21 A typical waveform from a knock sensor during a spark knock event. This signal is sent to the computer which in turn retards the ignition timing. This timing retard is accomplished by an output command from the computer to either a spark advance control unit or directly to the ignition module.

because they often look the same, but the frequency range can vary according to engine design and location on the engine. Many engines also use two knock sensors, so check service information for exact details and locations of the sensors for the engine being serviced. Always tighten the knock sensor using a torque wrench and tighten to the specified torque to avoid causing damage to the piezoelectric element inside the sensor.

## IGNITION CONTROL CIRCUITS

**TERMINOLOGY** Ignition control (IC) is the OBD-II terminology for the output signal from the PCM to the ignition system that controls engine timing. Previously, each manufacturer used a different term to describe this signal. For instance, Ford referred to this signal as **spark output (SPOUT)** and General Motors referred to this signal as **electronic spark timing (EST)**. This signal is now referred to as the ignition control (IC) signal. The ignition control signal is usually a digital output that is sent to the ignition system as a timing signal. If the ignition system is equipped with an ignition module, then this signal is used by the ignition module to vary the timing as engine speed and load change. If the PCM directly controls the coils, such as most coil-on-plug ignition systems, then this IC signal directly controls the coil primary and there is a separate IC signal for each ignition coil. The IC signal controls the time that the coil fires and it can also either advance or retard the ignition timing. On many systems, this signal controls the duration of the primary current flow in the coil, referred to as the **dwell**. ● SEE **FIGURE 8–22.**

**FIGURE 8–22** A SPOUT connector on a Ford that is equipped with a distributor ignition. This connector has to be disconnected to separate the PCM in order to set base ignition timing.

### BYPASS IGNITION CONTROL SYSTEM

With **bypass ignition** control, the engine starts using the ignition module for timing control and then switches to the PCM for timing control after the engine starts. A bypass ignition is commonly used on General Motors engines equipped with distributor ignition (DI), as well as those equipped with waste-spark ignition.

The bypass circuit includes four wires.

- The *tach reference (purple/white)* wire comes from the ignition control (IC) module and is used by the PCM as engine speed information.
- The *ground (black/white)* wire is used to ensure that both the PCM and the ignition control module share the same ground.
- The *bypass (tan/black)* wire is used to conduct a 5 volt DC signal from the PCM to the ignition control module to switch the timing control from the module to the PCM.

**NOTE: It is this bypass wire that is disconnected before the ignition timing can be set on many General Motors engines equipped with a distributor ignition.**

- The *EST (ignition control) (white)* wire is the ignition timing control signal from the PCM to the ignition control module.

### UP-INTEGRATED IGNITION CONTROL

Most coil-on-plug and many waste-spark-type ignition systems use the PCM for ignition timing control. This type of ignition control is called **up-integrated ignition** because all timing functions are interpreted in the PCM, rather than being split between the ignition control module and the PCM. The ignition module, if even used, contains only the power transistor for coil switching. The signal as to when the coil fires is determined and controlled from the PCM.

Unlike a bypass ignition control circuit, it is not possible to separate the PCM from the ignition coil control to help isolate a fault.

## SUMMARY

1. All inductive ignition systems supply battery voltage to the positive side of the ignition coil and pulse the negative side of the coil on and off to ground to create a high-voltage spark.
2. If an ignition system uses a distributor, it is a distributor ignition (DI) system.
3. If an ignition system does not use a distributor, it is called an electronic ignition (EI) system.
4. A waste-spark ignition system fires two spark plugs at the same time.
5. A coil-on-plug ignition system uses an ignition coil for each spark plug.
6. Some waste-spark systems are capable of sensing which of the two spark plugs fires first; therefore, the engine can detect cylinder location.
7. Some COP ignition systems can be used to detect the plasma in the cylinder, which is used by the PCM to determine if the correct air-fuel mixture and ignition timing have been performed.

## REVIEW QUESTIONS

1. How can 12 volts from a battery be changed to 40,000 volts for ignition?
2. How does a magnetic sensor work?
3. How does a Hall-effect sensor work?
4. How does a waste-spark ignition system work?

1. The primary (low-voltage) ignition system must be working correctly before any spark occurs from a coil. Which component is not in the primary ignition circuit?
   a. Spark plug wiring
   b. Ignition module (igniter)
   c. Pickup coil (pulse generator)
   d. Ignition switch

2. The ignition module has direct control over the firing of the coil(s) of an EI system. Which component(s) triggers (controls) the module?
   a. Pickup coil
   b. Computer
   c. Crankshaft sensor
   d. All of the above

3. Distributor ignition systems can be triggered by a _____.
   a. Hall-effect sensor
   b. Magnetic sensor
   c. Spark sensor
   d. Either a or b

4. A compression-sensing ignition system uses a _____-type ignition.
   a. Distributor
   b. Coil-on-plug
   c. Waste-spark
   d. All of the above

5. Coil polarity is determined by the _____.
   a. Direction of rotation of the coil windings
   b. Turns ratio
   c. Direction of laminations
   d. Saturation direction

6. How does a waste-spark ignition system fire the spark plugs?
   a. The polarity reverses at each firing (flip flops).
   b. The same plug always is fired straight or reverse polarity
   c. The waste spark is sent to the cylinder next to the cylinder being fired.
   d. Both a and c

7. The pulse generator _____.
   a. Fires the spark plug directly
   b. Signals the electronic control unit (module)
   c. Signals the computer that fires the spark plug directly
   d. Is used as a tachometer reference signal by the computer and has no other function

8. Two technicians are discussing distributor ignition. Technician A says that the pickup coil or optical sensor in the distributor is used to pulse the ignition module (igniter). Technician B says that some distributor ignition systems use an optical sensor. Which technician is correct?
   a. Technician A only
   b. Technician B only
   c. Both Technicians A and B
   d. Neither Technician A nor B

9. A waste-spark-type ignition system fires _____.
   a. Two spark plugs at the same time
   b. One spark plug with reverse polarity
   c. One spark plug with straight polarity
   d. All of the above

10. Technician A says that a two-wire COP system uses the PCM to trigger the coil. Technician B says that a three-wire COP system has an ICM built into the coil assembly. Which technician is correct?
    a. Technician A only
    b. Technician B only
    c. Both Technicians A and B
    d. Neither Technician A nor B

# chapter 9

# IGNITION SYSTEM DIAGNOSIS AND SERVICE

**OBJECTIVES:** After studying Chapter 9, the reader will be able to: • Prepare for ASE Engine Performance (A8) certification test content area "B" (Ignition System Diagnosis and Repair). • Describe the procedure used to check for spark. • Discuss what to inspect and look for during a visual inspection of the ignition system. • Explain how to test pickup coils, ignition coils, and spark plug wires. • Discuss how to current ramp ignition coils using a low ampere current clamp and a scope. • Describe how to test the ignition system using an oscilloscope.

**KEY TERMS:** Burn kV 135 • Charging rise time 119 • Firing line 133 • Firing order 131 • Ignition timing 130 • Iridium spark plugs 127 • Millisecond (ms) sweep 136 • Module current limits 119 • Platinum spark plugs 127 • Spark line 133 • Spark tester 118

## CHECKING FOR SPARK

**SPARK TESTER** In the event of a no-start condition, the first step should be to check for secondary voltage out of the ignition coil or to the spark plugs. If the engine is equipped with a separate ignition coil, remove the coil wire from the center of the distributor cap, install a **spark tester,** and crank the engine. See the Tech Tip, "Always Use a Spark Tester." A good coil and ignition system should produce a blue spark at the spark tester.
● **SEE FIGURES 9–1 AND 9–2.**

If the ignition system being tested does not have a separate ignition coil, disconnect any spark plug wire from a spark plug and, while cranking the engine, test for spark available at the spark plug wire, again using a spark tester.

**NOTE: An intermittent spark should be considered a no-spark condition.**

Typical causes of a no-spark (intermittent spark) condition include the following:

1. Weak ignition coil
2. Low or no voltage to the primary (positive) side of the coil
3. High resistances or open coil wire, or spark plug wire
4. Negative side of the coil not being pulsed by the ignition module
5. Defective pickup coil or crankshaft position sensor
6. Defective ignition control module (ICM)
7. Defective main relay (can be labeled main, EFI, ASD [Chrysler products], or EEC [Ford vehicles] relay)

**FIGURE 9–1** A spark tester looks like a regular spark plug with an alligator clip attached to the shell. This tester has a specified gap that requires at least 25,000 volts (25 kV) to fire.

The triggering sensor has to work to create a spark from the ignition coil(s). If a no-spark condition occurs, then check for triggering by using a scan tool and check for engine RPM while cranking the engine.

- If the engine speed (RPM) shows zero or almost zero while cranking, the most likely cause is a defective triggering sensor or sensor circuit fault.
- If the engine speed (RPM) is shown on the scan tool while cranking the engine, then the triggering sensor is working (in most cases).

Check service information for the exact procedure to follow for testing triggering sensors.

**FIGURE 9–2** A close-up showing the recessed center electrode on a spark tester. It is recessed 3/8 in. into the shell and the spark must then jump another 3/8 in. to the shell for a total gap of 3/4 in.

# IGNITION COIL TESTING

**IGNITION COIL TESTING USING AN OHMMETER** If an ignition coil is suspected of being defective, a simple ohmmeter check can be performed to test the resistance of the primary and secondary winding inside the coil. For accurate resistance measurements, the wiring to the coil should be removed before testing. To test the primary coil winding resistance, take the following steps. ● **SEE FIGURE 9–3.**

**STEP 1** Set the meter to read low ohms.

**STEP 2** Measure the resistance between the positive terminal and the negative terminal of the ignition coil. Most coils will give a reading between 0.5 and 3 ohms. Check the manufacturer's specifications for the exact resistance values.

To test the secondary coil winding resistance, follow these steps.

**STEP 1** Set the meter to read kilohms (kΩ).

**STEP 2** Measure the resistance either between the primary terminal and the secondary coil tower or between the secondary towers. The normal resistance of most coils ranges between 6,000 and 30,000 ohms.

Check service information for the exact procedures and specifications.

**CURRENT RAMPING IGNITION COILS** Testing an ignition coil for resistance does not always find a coil problem that occurs under actual heat and loads. However, by using a digital storage oscilloscope and a low-current probe, the ignition system can be checked for module current limits and the charging rise time.

Ignition coil operation begins with the ignition control module (ICM) completing the primary circuit through the ignition coil winding. The module allows primary current to ramp upward (primary charging time) to a preset limit. Once ramped to the preset limit, the coil remains on for a set period of time (primary saturation), known as the *dwell period.* Coil current is then turned off (open circuit) allowing the magnetic field built up through the dwell cycle to collapse inward, cutting across many turns of secondary coil windings, inducing a higher output voltage to fire the coil. The ignition systems used today must provide voltages of at least 25,000 volts and maintain spark duration of over 2 ms to assure good ignition over extended service intervals.

Using the digital storage oscilloscope and a current probe, a quick check can be made of the overall primary condition of the two most important parameters of the ignition circuit, the **module current limits** and the **charging rise time** of the circuit. Actual circuit operation of the primary current control is a precise element in total ignition function and output. ● **SEE FIGURE 9–5.**

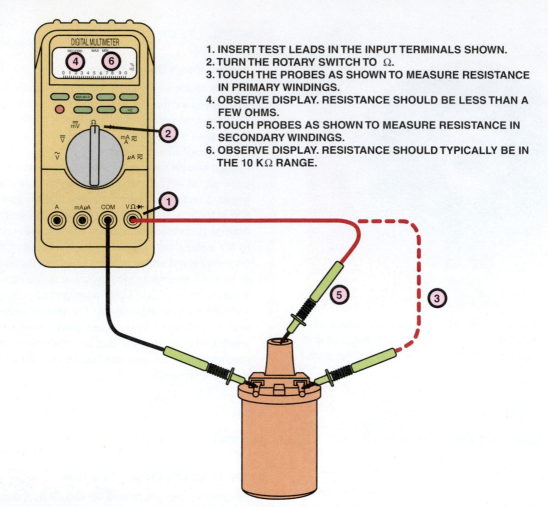

1. INSERT TEST LEADS IN THE INPUT TERMINALS SHOWN.
2. TURN THE ROTARY SWITCH TO Ω.
3. TOUCH THE PROBES AS SHOWN TO MEASURE RESISTANCE IN PRIMARY WINDINGS.
4. OBSERVE DISPLAY. RESISTANCE SHOULD BE LESS THAN A FEW OHMS.
5. TOUCH PROBES AS SHOWN TO MEASURE RESISTANCE IN SECONDARY WINDINGS.
6. OBSERVE DISPLAY. RESISTANCE SHOULD TYPICALLY BE IN THE 10 KΩ RANGE.

**FIGURE 9–3** Checking an ignition coil using a multimeter set to read ohms.

**FIGURE 9–4** If the coil is working, the end of the magnetic pickup tool will move with the changes in the magnetic field around the coil.

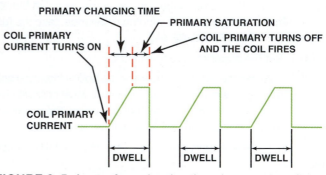

**FIGURE 9–5** A waveform showing the primary current flow through the primary windings of an ignition coil.

## CURRENT RAMP TEST PROCEDURE
To perform a current ramp test of the ignition coil(s), take the following steps.

**STEP 1** Every ignition system has a power feed circuit to the ignition coil(s). To perform current probe testing on the system, first locate the feed wire and make it current probe accessible. ● **SEE FIGURE 9–6**. This will serve as a common point on all ignition systems and include both the DI and EI units.

**STEP 2** Set up the scope to read approximately 100 mV per division and 2 ms per division. This may be adjusted to suit the waveform, but will give an initial reference point. ● **SEE CHART 9–1**.

A good current ramp waveform is shown in ● **FIGURE 9–7**. Examples of some faults that a current waveform can detect are shown in ● **FIGURE 9–8**.

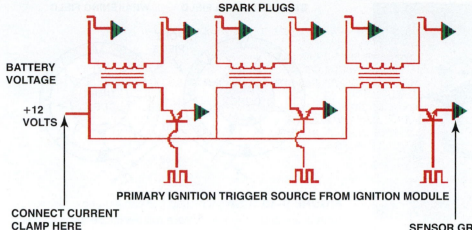

SPARK PLUGS

BATTERY VOLTAGE

+12 VOLTS

PRIMARY IGNITION TRIGGER SOURCE FROM IGNITION MODULE

CONNECT CURRENT CLAMP HERE

SENSOR GROUND

**FIGURE 9–6** Schematic of a typical waste-spark ignition system showing the location for the power feed and grounds. *(Courtesy of Fluke Corporation)*

| OBSERVED CURRENT RAMP TIMES | |
|---|---|
| GM electronic (DI) systems | 3.6 ms |
| GM late 1996 and up (DI) systems | 2.5 ms |
| GM electronic (EI) systems | 2.6 ms |
| Ford electronic (DI) systems | 3.6 ms |
| Ford electronic (EI) systems | 2.6 ms |
| Chrysler electronic (DI) systems | 3.8 ms |
| Chrysler electronic (EI) systems | 2.6 ms |

**CHART 9–1**

The ignition coil ramp times vary according to the type of ignition system.

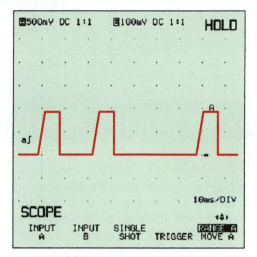

AN OPEN COIL PRIMARY WINDING WILL BE IDENTIFIED BY A MISSING PULSE IN THE CURRENT PATTERN.

(a)

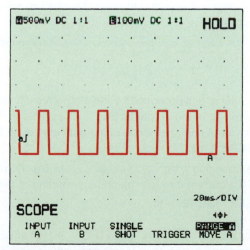

GOOD COIL PATTERN

**FIGURE 9–7** An example of a good coil current flow waveform pattern. Note the regular shape of the rise time and slope. Duration of the waveform may change as the module adjusts the dwell. The dwell is usually increased as the engine speed is increased. *(Courtesy of Fluke Corporation)*

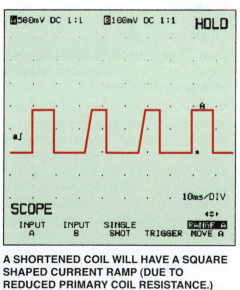

A SHORTENED COIL WILL HAVE A SQUARE SHAPED CURRENT RAMP (DUE TO REDUCED PRIMARY COIL RESISTANCE.)

(b)

**FIGURE 9–8** (a) A waveform pattern showing an open in the coil primary. (b) A shorted coil pattern waveform. *(Courtesy of Fluke Corporation)*

FIGURE 9–9 Measuring the resistance of an HEI pickup coil using a digital multimeter set to the ohms position. The reading on the face of the meter is 0.796 kΩ or 796 ohms in the middle of the 500 to 1,500 ohm specifications.

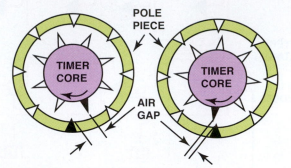

**STRENGTHENING FIELD**     **WEAKENING FIELD**

FIGURE 9–10 A typical pickup coil showing how the waveform is created as the timer core rotates inside the pole piece.

## IGNITION SENSOR TESTING

**MAGNETIC SENSOR TESTING** Magnetic sensors are found in pickup coils, located under the distributor cap on many distributor ignition (DI) equipped engines and in crankshaft position (CKP) sensors. If defective, they can cause a no-spark condition. Magnetic sensors must generate an AC voltage pulse to the ignition control module (ICM) so that the module can pulse the ignition coil.

A pickup coil or magnetic sensor contains a coil of wire, and the resistance of this coil should be within the range specified by the manufacturer.

Common tests for pickup coils and magnetic crankshaft position (CKP) sensors include:

- **Resistance.** The resistance is usually between 150 and 1,500 ohms (check service information for exact specifications). ● SEE FIGURE 9–9.

- **Short to ground.** Ensure that the coil windings are insulated from ground by checking for continuity using an ohmmeter. With one ohmmeter lead attached to ground, touch the other lead of the ohmmeter to either of the two pickup coil terminals. The ohmmeter should read OL (over limit or infinity) with the ohmmeter set on the highest ohms scale. If the ohmmeter shows a reading of any resistance or even zero, then the pickup coil is shorted to ground and should be replaced. If the pickup coil resistance is not within the specified range or if it has continuity to ground, then replace the pickup coil assembly.

- **AC voltage output.** The pickup coil also can be tested for proper voltage output. During cranking, most pickup coils should produce a minimum of 0.25 volt AC.

- **Scope testing.** A pickup coil can also be checked on a scope. The waveform created is an analog (continuously

variable) and is produced by the strengthening and weakening of the magnetic field as the points of the timer core rotate past the points of the pole pieces. ● SEE FIGURE 9–10.

The changing magnetic field is sent to the ICM where it turns off the current through the primary winding of the ignition coil. ● SEE FIGURE 9–11.

**HALL-EFFECT SENSOR TESTING** A Hall effect sensor uses a semiconductor chip to produce an on and off signal when exposed to a magnetic field. Using a digital voltmeter, check for the following:

- Power and ground to the sensor
- Changing voltage (pulsed on and off or digital DC voltage) when the engine is being cranked (The usual voltage

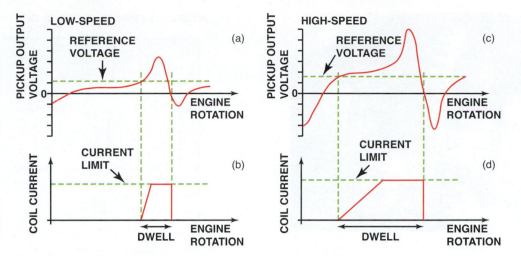

**FIGURE 9–11** (a) A voltage waveform of a pickup coil at low engine speed. (b) A current waveform of the current through the primary windings of the ignition coil at low engine speed. (c) A voltage waveform of a pickup coil at high speed. (d) A current waveform through the primary winding of the ignition coil at high engine speed.

 **REAL WORLD FIX**

**The Hard-to-Start Chevrolet HHR**

The owner of a 2008 Chevrolet HHR complained that the engine was hard to start and required a long period of cranking. Once the engine started, it ran great all day. A P0336 crankshaft position (CKP) sensor fault code was stored. ● **SEE FIGURE 9–12.**

The CKP sensor had been replaced several times before and the sensor output was scope tested yet everything appeared to be normal. Then one time when the engine started, the technician noticed that while it was running the engine speed (RPM) displayed on the Tech 2 scan tool was zero. ● **SEE FIGURE 9–13.**

After replacing the crankshaft position sensor again and checking the wiring, the technician looked at the reluctor wheel using a boroscope. Some blades of the reluctor wheel were bent. The cause was likely when the first sensor failed and possibly damaged the reluctor. As a result of the testing, the local Chevrolet dealer replaced the crankshaft under warranty. ● **SEE FIGURE 9–14.**

range is 0 to 5 volts, or 0 to 8 volts depending on the sensors and the application.)

Another test is to use an oscilloscope and observe the waveform. ● **SEE FIGURE 9–15.**

**OPTICAL SENSOR TESTING** Optical sensors will not operate if dirty or covered in oil. Perform a thorough visual inspection and look for an oil leak that could cause dirty oil to

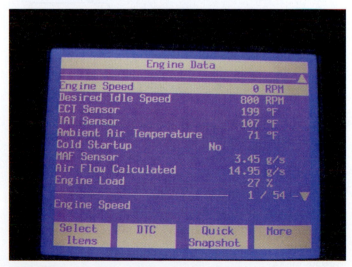

**FIGURE 9–12** A diagnostic trouble code P0336 was displayed on a Tech 2 scan tool as the only code.

**FIGURE 9–13** The engine started and was running, but the Tech 2 displayed zero RPM.

**FIGURE 9–14** The old crankshaft showing the reluctor notches. The damage was not visible, but the engine started each time after the crankshaft was replaced.

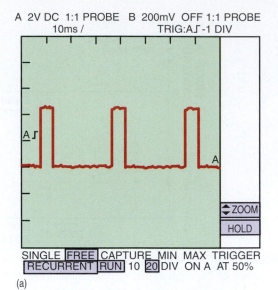

(a)

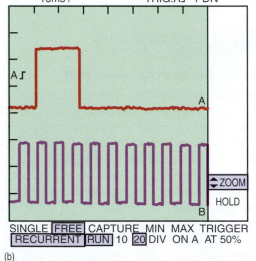

(b)

**FIGURE 9–16** (a) The low-resolution signal has the same number of pulses as the engine has cylinders. (b) A dual trace pattern showing both the low-resolution and the high-resolution signals that usually represent 1 degree of rotation.

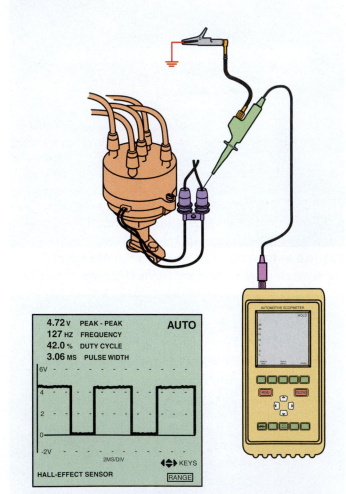

**FIGURE 9–15** The connection required to test a Hall-effect sensor. A typical waveform from a Hall-effect sensor is a digital square wave. Check service information for the signal wire location.

get on the LED or phototransistor. Also be sure that the light shield is securely fastened and that the seal is lightproof. An optical sensor also can be checked using an oscilloscope.
● **SEE FIGURE 9–16.**

Because of the speed of the engine and the number of slits in the optical sensor disk, a scope is one of the only tools that can capture useful information. For example, a Nissan has 360 slits and if it is running at 2,000 RPM, a signal is generated 720,000 times per minute or 12,000 times per second.

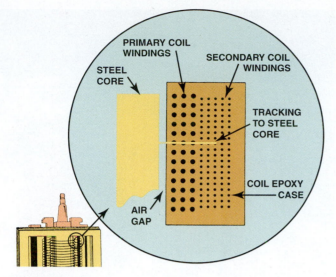

FIGURE 9–17 A track inside an ignition coil is not a short, but a low-resistance path or hole that has been burned through from the secondary wiring to the steel core.

FIGURE 9–18 Corroded terminals on a waste-spark coil can cause misfire diagnostic trouble codes to be set.

## TECH TIP

### Bad Wire? Replace the Coil!

When performing engine testing (such as a compression test), always ground the coil wire or disable the primary ignition circuit by removing the ignition fuse. If the spark cannot spark to ground, the coil energy can (and usually does) arc inside the coil itself, creating a low-resistance path to the primary windings or the steel laminations of the coil. ● SEE FIGURE 9–17.

    This low-resistance path is called a *track* and could cause an engine miss under load even though all of the remaining component parts of the ignition system are functioning correctly. Often these tracks do not show up on any coil test, including most scopes. Because the track is a lower resistance path to ground than normal, it requires that the ignition system be put under a load for it to be detected; and even then, the problem such as an engine misfire may be intermittent.

## TECH TIP

### Spark Plug Wire Pliers Are a Good Investment

Spark plug wires are often difficult to remove. Using good-quality spark plug wire pliers, as shown in ● FIGURE 9–18, saves time and reduces the chance of harming the wire during removal.

## SPARK PLUG WIRE INSPECTION

**VISUAL INSPECTION** Spark plug wires should be visually inspected for cuts or defective insulation. Faulty spark plug wire insulation can cause hard starting or no starting in rainy or damp weather conditions. When removing a spark plug wire, be sure to rotate the boot of the wire at the plug before pulling it off the spark plug. This will help prevent damaging the wire as many wires are stuck to the spark plug and are often difficult to remove.

    Make a thorough visual inspection of the following items.

- Check all spark plug wires for proper routing. All plug wires should be in the factory wiring separators and be clear of any metallic object that could damage the insulation and cause a short-to-ground fault.
- Check that all spark plug wires are securely attached to the spark plugs and to the distributor cap or ignition coil(s).
- Check that all spark plug wires are clean and free from excessive dirt or oil. Check that all protective covers normally covering the coil and/or distributor cap are in place and not damaged.
- Carefully check the cap and distributor rotor for faults or coil secondary terminal on waste spark coils. ● SEE FIGURE 9–19.

    Visually check the wires and boots for damage. ● SEE FIGURE 9–20.

FIGURE 9–19 This spark plug boot on an overhead camshaft engine has been arcing to the valve cover causing a misfire to occur.

FIGURE 9–20 Measuring the resistance of a spark plug wire with a multimeter set to the ohms position. The reading of 16.03 kΩ (16,030 ohms) is okay because the wire is about 2 ft long. Maximum allowable resistance for a spark plug wire this long would be 20 kΩ (20,000 ohms).

FIGURE 9–21 Spark plug wire boot pliers are a handy addition to any tool box.

**OHMMETER TESTING**    Check all spark plug wires with an ohmmeter for proper resistance. Good spark plug wires should measure less than 10,000 ohms per foot of length. ● SEE FIGURE 9–21.

FIGURE 9–22 A water spray bottle is an excellent diagnostic tool to help find an intermittent engine misfire caused by a break in a secondary ignition circuit component.

## SPARK PLUGS

**SPARK PLUG CONSTRUCTION**    Spark plugs are manufactured from ceramic insulators inside a steel shell. The threads of the shell are rolled and a seat is formed to create a gas-tight seal with the cylinder head. ● SEE FIGURE 9–23.

Physical differences in spark plugs include the following:

- **Reach.** The reach is the length of the threaded part of the plug.
- **Heat range.** The heat range of the spark plug refers to how rapidly the heat created at the tip is transferred to

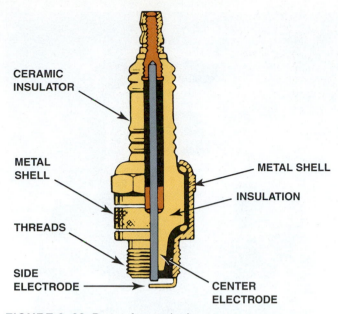

FIGURE 9–23 Parts of a spark plug.

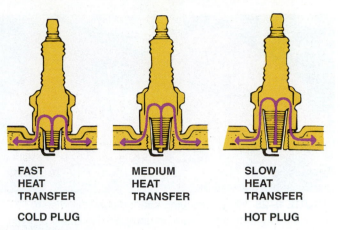

FAST HEAT TRANSFER — COLD PLUG

MEDIUM HEAT TRANSFER

SLOW HEAT TRANSFER — HOT PLUG

FIGURE 9–24 The heat range of a spark plug is determined by the distance the heat flows from the tip to the cylinder head.

the cylinder head. A plug with a long ceramic insulator path will run hotter at the tip than a spark plug that has a shorter path because the heat must travel farther. ● SEE FIGURE 9–24.

- **Type of seat.** Some spark plugs use a gasket and others rely on a tapered seat to seal.

## RESISTOR SPARK PLUGS
Most spark plugs include a resistor in the center electrode, to reduce electromagnetic noise or radiation from the ignition system. The closer the resistor is to the actual spark or arc, the more effective it becomes. The value of the resistor is usually between 2,500 and 7,500 ohms.

## PLATINUM SPARK PLUGS
**Platinum spark plugs** have a small amount of the precious metal platinum included onto the end of the center electrode, as well as on the ground or side electrode. Platinum is a gray-white metal that does not react with oxygen and, therefore, will not erode away as can occur with conventional nickel alloy spark plug electrodes. Platinum is also used as a catalyst in catalytic converters where it is able to start a chemical reaction without itself being consumed.

## IRIDIUM SPARK PLUGS
Iridium is a white precious metal and is the most corrosion-resistant metal known. Most **iridium spark plugs** use a small amount of iridium welded onto the tip of a small center electrode 0.0015 to 0.002 in. (0.4 to 0.6 mm) in diameter. The small diameter reduces the voltage required to jump the gap between the center and the side electrode, thereby reducing possible misfires. The ground or side electrode is usually tipped with platinum to help reduce electrode gap wear.

Spark plugs should be inspected when an engine performance problem occurs and should be replaced at specified intervals to ensure proper ignition system performance.

- Nonplatinum spark plugs have a service life of over 20,000 miles (32,000 km).
- Platinum-tipped original equipment spark plugs have a typical service life of 60,000 to 100,000 miles (100,000 to 160,000 km) or longer.

Used *Platinum-tipped spark plugs should not be regapped!* Using a gapping tool can break the platinum after it has been used in an engine. Check service information regarding the recommended type of spark plugs and the specified service procedures.

## SPARK PLUG SERVICE
When replacing spark plugs, perform the following steps.

STEP 1 **Check service information.** Check for the exact spark plug to use and the specified instructions and/or technical service bulletins that affect the part number of plug to be used or a revised replacement procedure.

STEP 2 **Allow the engine to cool before removing spark plugs.** This step is especially critical on engines with aluminum cylinder heads.

STEP 3 **Use compressed air or a brush to remove dirt from around the spark plug before removal.** This step helps prevent dirt from getting into the cylinder of an engine while removing a spark plug.

STEP 4 **Check the spark plug gap and correct as needed.** Be careful not to damage the tip on the center electrode if adjusting a platinum or iridium type of spark plug.

STEP 5 **Install the spark plugs.** Be sure the threads are clean by using a thread chaser. Then install the spark plug by hand, then using the proper spark plug socket and a torque wrench, tighten the plugs to factory specifications.
● SEE FIGURES 9–25 AND 9–26.

FIGURE 9–25 When removing spark plugs, it is wise to arrange them so that they can be compared and any problem can be identified with a particular cylinder.

FIGURE 9–26 A spark plug thread chaser is a low-cost tool that hopefully will not be used often, but is necessary in order to clean the threads before installing new spark plugs.

Spark plugs are the windows to the inside of the combustion chamber. A thorough visual inspection of the spark plugs often can lead to the root cause of an engine performance problem. Two indications on spark plugs and their possible root causes in engine performance include the following:

1.  **Carbon fouling.** If the spark plug(s) has *dry black carbon* (soot), the usual causes include:
    - Excessive idling
    - Defective thermostat
    - Overly rich air-fuel mixture due to a fuel system fault
    - Weak ignition system output
2.  **Oil fouling.** If the spark plug has *wet, oily* deposits with little electrode wear, oil may be getting into the combustion chamber from the following:
    - Worn or broken piston rings
    - Worn valve guides
    - Defective or missing valve stem seals

When removing spark plugs, place them in order so that they can be inspected to check for engine problems that might affect one or more cylinders. All spark plugs should be in the same condition, and the color of the center insulator should be light tan or gray. If all the spark plugs are black or dark, the engine should be checked for conditions that could cause an

FIGURE 9–27 A normally worn spark plug that uses a tapered platinum-tipped center electrode.

FIGURE 9–28 A worn spark plug showing fuel and/or oil deposits.

overly rich air-fuel mixture or possible oil burning. If only one or a few spark plugs are black, check those cylinders for proper firing (possible defective spark plug wire) or an engine condition affecting only those particular cylinders. ● **SEE FIGURES 9–27 THROUGH 9–30**.

If all spark plugs are white, check for possible overadvanced ignition timing or a vacuum leak causing a lean air-fuel mixture. If only one or a few spark plugs are white, check for a

**FIGURE 9–29** A spark plug from an engine that had a blown head gasket. The white deposits could be from the aluminum of the position or from the additives in the coolant.

**FIGURE 9–30** A platinum tipped spark plug that is fuel soaked indicating a fault with the fuel system or the ignition system causing the spark plug to not fire.

| SPARK PLUG TYPE | TORQUE WITH TORQUE WRENCH (LB-FT) | | TORQUE WITHOUT TORQUE WRENCH (TURNS AFTER SEATED) | |
|---|---|---|---|---|
| | CAST-IRON HEAD | ALUMINUM HEAD | CAST-IRON HEAD | ALUMINUM HEAD |
| Gasket | | | | |
| 14 mm | 26–30 | 18–22 | 1/4 | 1/4 |
| 18 mm | 32–38 | 28–34 | 1/4 | 1/4 |
| Tapered seat | | | | |
| 14 mm | 7–15 | 7–15 | 1/16 (snug) | 1/16 (snug) |
| 18 mm | 15–20 | 15–20 | 1/16 (snug) | 1/16 (snug) |

**CHART 9–2**

Typical spark plug installation torque.

vacuum leak or injector fault affecting the air-fuel mixture only to those particular cylinders.

**NOTE: The PCM "senses" rich or lean air-fuel ratios by means of input from the oxygen sensor(s). If one cylinder is lean, the PCM may make all other cylinders richer to compensate.**

Inspect all spark plugs for wear by first checking the condition of the center electrode. As a spark plug wears, the center electrode becomes rounded. If the center electrode is rounded, higher ignition system voltage is required to fire the spark plug. When installing spark plugs, always use the correct tightening torque to ensure proper heat transfer from the spark plug shell to the cylinder head. ● **SEE CHART 9–2.**

**NOTE: General Motors does not recommend the use of antiseize compound on the threads of spark plugs being installed in an aluminum cylinder head, because the**

 **TECH TIP**

**Two-Finger Trick**

To help prevent overtightening a spark plug when a torque wrench is not available, simply use two fingers on the ratchet handle. Even the strongest service technician cannot overtighten a spark plug by using two fingers.

**spark plug will be overtightened. This excessive tightening torque places the threaded portion of the spark plug too far into the combustion chamber where carbon can accumulate and result in the spark plugs being difficult to remove. If antiseize compound is used on spark plug threads, reduce the tightening torque by 40%. Always follow the vehicle manufacturer's recommendations.**

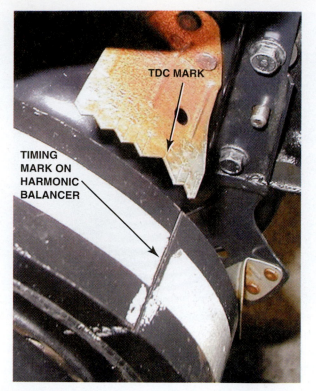

**FIGURE 9–31** Ignition timing marks are found on the harmonic balancers on engines equipped with distributors that can be adjusted for timing.

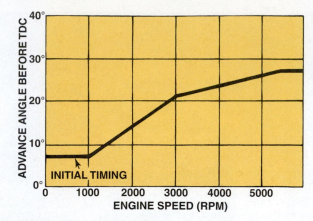

**FIGURE 9–32** The initial (base) timing is where the spark plug fires at idle speed. The PCM then advances the timing based primarily on engine speed.

## IGNITION TIMING

**PURPOSE** **Ignition timing** refers to when the spark plug fires in relation to piston position. The time when the spark occurs depends on engine speed, and therefore, it must be advanced (spark plugs fire sooner) as the engine rotates faster. The ignition process in the cylinder takes a certain amount of time, usually 30 ms (30/1,000 of a second) and remains constant regardless of engine speed. Therefore, to maintain the most efficient combustion, the ignition sequence has to occur sooner as the engine speed increases. For maximum efficiency from the expanding gases inside the combustion chamber, the burning of the air-fuel mixture should end by about 10 degrees after top dead center (ATDC). If the burning of the mixture is still occurring after that point, the expanding gases do not exert much force on the piston because the gases are "chasing" the piston as it moves downward.

Therefore, to achieve the goal of having the air-fuel mixture be completely burned by the time the piston reaches 10° after top dead center (ATDC), the spark must be advanced (occur sooner) as the engine speed increases. This timing advance is determined and controlled by the PCM on most vehicles. ● **SEE FIGURE 9–31.**

If the engine is equipped with a distributor, it *may* or *may not* be possible to adjust the base or the initial timing. Check service information for details regarding the vehicle being serviced.

The initial timing is usually set to fire the spark plug between zero degrees (top dead center, or TDC) or slightly before TDC (BTDC). Initial (base) ignition timing changes as mechanical wear occurs on the following:

- Timing chain
- Distributor gear
- Camshaft drive gear
  ● **SEE FIGURE 9–32.**

**CHECKING IGNITION TIMING** To be assured of the proper ignition timing, follow the exact timing procedure indicated on the underhood vehicle emission control information (VECI) decal. If the decal is missing, check with service information for the timing procedure.

**NOTE: The ignition timing for waste-spark and coil-on-plug ignition systems cannot be adjusted.**

FIGURE 9–33 The firing order is cast or stamped on the intake manifold of most engines that have a distributor ignition.

FIGURE 9–34 Always take the time to install spark plug wires back into the original holding brackets (wiring combs).

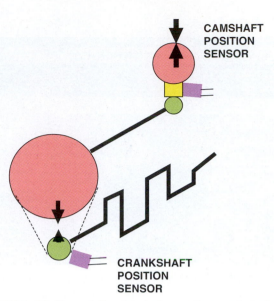

FIGURE 9–35 The relationship between the crankshaft position (CKP) sensor and the camshaft position (CMP) sensor is affected by wear in the timing gear and/or chain.

## FIRING ORDER

**Firing order** is the order that the spark is distributed to the correct spark plug at the right time. The firing order of an engine is determined by crankshaft and camshaft design. The ignition firing order is determined by the location of the spark plug wires in the distributor cap of an engine equipped with a distributor and how the spark plug wires are installed on the waste-spark coils. The firing order is often cast into the intake manifold for easy reference. ● SEE FIGURE 9–33.

NOTE: **Most service manuals also show the firing order and the direction of the distributor rotor rotation, how the cylinders are numbered, and the location of the spark plug wires on the distributor cap.**

Firing order is also important for waste-spark-type ignition systems. The spark plug wire can often be installed on the wrong coil pack, creating a no-start condition or poor engine operation.

## DISTRIBUTOR INDEXING

A few engines using a distributor also use it to house a camshaft position (CMP) sensor. One purpose of this sensor is to properly initiate the fuel-injection sequence. Some of these engines use a positive distributor position notch or clamp that allows the distributor to be placed in only one position, while others use a method of indexing to verify the distributor position. ● SEE FIGURE 9–35.

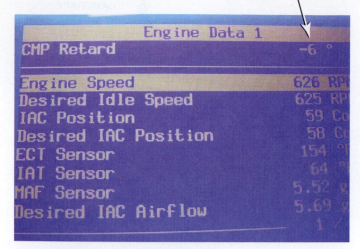

**FIGURE 9–36** A scan tool displays excessive cam retard on a Chevrolet pickup truck V-6. The cam retard value should be ± 2 degrees.

**FIGURE 9–37** A worn distributor drive gear can be the cause of an out-of-specification camshaft position (CMP) signal.

If a distributor is not indexed correctly, the following symptoms may occur.

- Surging (especially at idle speed)
- Light bucking
- Intermittent engine misfiring

This will most likely occur when the vehicle is at operating temperature, and under a light load at approximately 2,000 RPM. A misindexed distributor may cause these conditions.

**NOTE: This is *not* the same as setting the ignition timing. Indexing the distributor does not affect the ignition timing.**

Always use the factory procedure as stated in service information. Some of the methods may require a scan tool, while others require the use of a voltmeter to verify position. Jeep, late model Chrysler V-6 and V-8 engines, and some GM trucks require indexing. ● **SEE FIGURES 9–36 AND 9–37.**

## NO-START DIAGNOSIS

A no-start condition (with normal engine cranking speed) can be the result of either no spark or no fuel delivery.

The PCM uses the ignition primary pulses as a signal to inject fuel in a fuel-injection system. If there is no pulse, then there is no squirt of fuel. To determine exactly what is wrong, follow these steps.

**STEP 1** Test the output signal from the crankshaft sensor. Most engines with waste-spark or COP ignitions use a crankshaft position (CKP) sensor. These sensors are either the Hall-effect or the magnetic type. The sensors must be able to produce a variable (either analog or digital) signal. A voltmeter set to read DC volts for a Hall-effect sensor or set to read AC volts for a magnetic sensor should read a voltage across the sensor leads when the engine is being cranked. If there is no changing voltage output, replace the sensor.

**STEP 2** If the sensor tests okay in step 1, check for a changing voltage signal at the ignition module.

**NOTE: Step 2 checks the wiring between the crankshaft position (CKP) sensor and the ignition control module.**

**STEP 3** If the ignition control module is receiving a changing signal from the crankshaft position sensor, it must be capable of switching the power to the ignition coils on and off. Remove a coil or coil package, and with the ignition switched to on (run), check for voltage at the positive terminal of the coil(s).

**NOTE: Several manufacturers program the current to the coils to be turned off within several seconds of the ignition being switched to on if no pulse is received by the PCM. This circuit design helps prevent ignition coil damage in the event of a failure in the control circuit or driver error, by keeping the ignition switch on (run) without operating the starter (start position). Some Chrysler brand engines do not supply power to the positive (+) side of the coil through the automatic shutdown (ASD) relay until a crank pulse is received by the PCM.**

**CAUTION: Most ignition systems can produce 40,000 volts or more, with energy levels high enough to cause personal injury. Do not disconnect a spark plug wire while the engine is running, because it may damage the ignition system or create a shock hazard.**

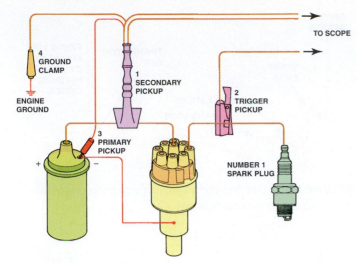

FIGURE 9–38 Typical engine analyzer hookup that includes a scope display. (1) Coil wire on top of the distributor cap if integral type of coil; (2) number 1 spark plug connection; (3) negative side of the ignition coil; (4) ground (negative) connection of the battery.

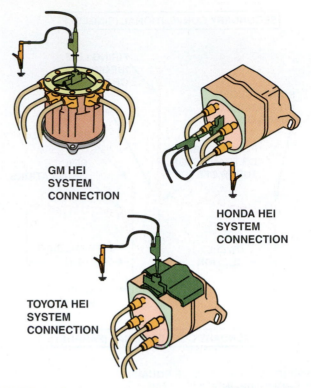

GM HEI SYSTEM CONNECTION

HONDA HEI SYSTEM CONNECTION

TOYOTA HEI SYSTEM CONNECTION

FIGURE 9–39 Clip-on adapters are used with an ignition system that uses an integral ignition coil.

## IGNITION SCOPE TESTING

**TERMINOLOGY** All ignition systems must charge and discharge an ignition coil. With the engine off, ignition scopes will display a horizontal line. With the engine running, this horizontal (zero) line is changed to a pattern that will have sections both above and below the zero line. Sections of this pattern that are above the zero line indicate that the ignition coil is discharging. Sections of the scope pattern below the zero line indicate charging of the ignition coil. The height of the scope pattern indicates voltage. The length (from left to right) of the scope pattern indicates time. ● SEE FIGURES 9–38 AND 9–39 for typical scope hookups.

**FIRING LINE** The leftmost vertical (upward) line is called the **firing line**. The height of the firing line should be between 5,000 and 15,000 volts (5 and 15 kV) with not more than a 3 kV difference between the highest and the lowest cylinder's firing line. ● SEE FIGURES 9–40 AND 9–41.

The height of the firing line indicates the *voltage* required to fire the spark plug. It requires a high voltage to make the air inside the cylinder electrically conductive (to ionize the air). One or more of the following conditions may cause higher-than-normal height firing lines.

1. Spark plug gapped too wide
2. Lean fuel mixture
3. Defective spark plug wire (excessive resistance or electrically open)

If the firing lines are higher than normal for *all* cylinders, then possible causes include one or more of the following:

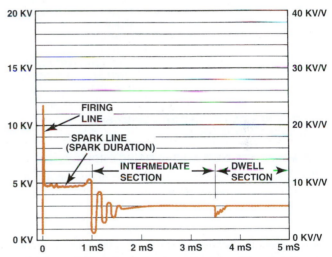

FIGURE 9–40 Typical secondary ignition oscilloscope pattern.

1. Worn distributor cap and/or rotor (if the vehicle is so equipped)
2. Excessive wearing of all spark plugs
3. Defective coil wire (the high voltage could still jump across the open section of the wire to fire the spark plugs)

**SPARK LINE** The **spark line** is a short horizontal line connected to the firing line. The height of the spark line represents the voltage required to maintain the spark across the spark plug

## SECONDARY CONVENTIONAL (SINGLE)

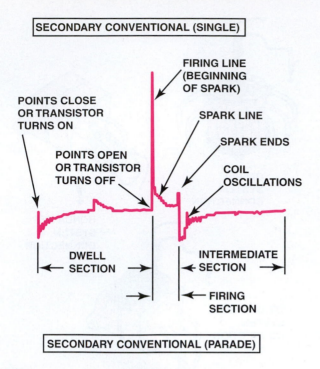

POINTS CLOSE
OR TRANSISTOR
TURNS ON

POINTS OPEN
OR TRANSISTOR
TURNS OFF

FIRING LINE
(BEGINNING
OF SPARK)

SPARK LINE

SPARK ENDS

COIL
OSCILLATIONS

DWELL
SECTION

INTERMEDIATE
SECTION

FIRING
SECTION

## SECONDARY CONVENTIONAL (PARADE)

FIRING LINES SHOULD BE EQUAL.
A SHORT LINE INDICATES LOW
RESISTANCE IN THE WIRE. A HIGH
LINE INDICATES HIGH RESISTANCE
IN THE WIRE.

AVAILABLE VOLTAGE
SHOULD BE ABOUT
10 KV ON A
CONVENTIONAL
IGNITION SYSTEM
AND EVEN GREATER
WITH AN ELECTRONIC
SYSTEM

SPARK LINES CAN BE VIEWED SIDE-BY-SIDE
FOR EASE OF COMPARISON

CYLINDERS ARE DISPLAYED IN FIRING ORDER

**FIGURE 9–41** A single cylinder is shown at the top and a 4-cylinder engine at the bottom.

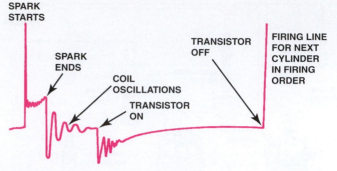

SPARK
STARTS

SPARK
ENDS

COIL
OSCILLATIONS

TRANSISTOR
ON

TRANSISTOR
OFF

FIRING LINE
FOR NEXT
CYLINDER
IN FIRING
ORDER

**FIGURE 9–42** Drawing shows what is occurring electrically at each part of the scope pattern.

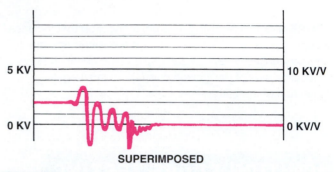

5 KV

0 KV

10 KV/V

0 KV/V

SUPERIMPOSED

**FIGURE 9–43** Typical secondary ignition pattern. Note the lack of firing lines on the superimposed pattern.

after the spark has started. The height of the spark line should be one-fourth of the height of the firing line (between 1.5 and 2.5 kV). The length (from left to right) of the line represents the length of time for which the spark lasts (duration). The spark duration should be between 0.8 and 2.2 milliseconds (usually between 1.0 and 2.0 ms). The spark stops at the end (right side) of the spark line, as shown in ● **FIGURE 9–42.**

### INTERMEDIATE OSCILLATIONS
After the spark has stopped, some energy remains in the coil. This remaining energy dissipates in the coil windings and the entire secondary circuit. The oscillations are also called the "ringing" of the coil as it is pulsed.

The secondary pattern amplifies any voltage variation occurring in the primary circuit because of the turns ratio between

the primary and secondary windings of the ignition coil. A correctly operating ignition system should display five or more "bumps" (oscillations) (three or more for a GM HEI system).

### TRANSISTOR-ON POINT
After the intermediate oscillations, the coil is empty (not charged), as indicated by the scope pattern being on the zero line for a short period. When the transistor turns on in an electronic ignition system, the coil is being charged. Note that the charging of the coil occurs slowly (coil-charging oscillations) because of the inductive reactance of the coil.

### DWELL SECTION
Dwell is the amount of time that the current is charging the coil from the transistor-on point to the transistor-off point. The end of the dwell section marks the beginning of the next firing line. This point is called "transistor off," and indicates that the primary current of the coil is stopped, resulting in a high-voltage spark out of the coil.

### PATTERN SELECTION
The entire pattern is not seen on a scope. Ignition oscilloscopes use three positions to view certain sections of the basic pattern more closely. These three positions are as follows:

1. **Superimposed.** This superimposed position is used to look at differences in patterns between cylinders in all areas except the firing line. There are no firing lines illustrated in superimposed positions. ● **SEE FIGURE 9–43.**

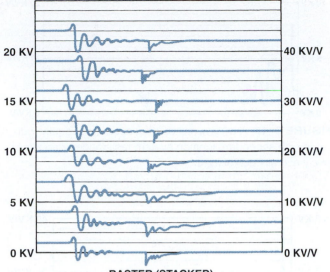

RASTER (STACKED)

**FIGURE 9–44** Raster is the best scope position to view the spark lines of all the cylinders to check for differences. Most scopes display cylinder 1 at the bottom. The other cylinders are positioned by firing order above cylinder 1.

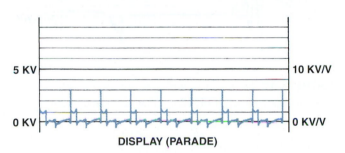

DISPLAY (PARADE)

**FIGURE 9–45** Display is the only position to view the firing lines of all cylinders. Cylinder 1 is displayed on the left (except for its firing line, which is shown on the right). The cylinders are displayed from left to right by firing order.

2. **Raster (stacked).** Cylinder 1 appears at the bottom of the screen and all other cylinder patterns are displayed upward in the engine's firing order. Use the raster (stacked) position to look at the spark line length and transistor-on point. The raster pattern shows all areas of the scope pattern except the firing lines. ● **SEE FIGURE 9–44**.

3. **Display (parade).** Display (parade) is the only position in which firing lines are visible and the cylinders are displayed on the screen from left to right in the engine's firing order. This selection is used to compare the height of firing lines among all cylinders. ● **SEE FIGURE 9–45**.

**READING THE SCOPE ON DISPLAY (PARADE)**   Start the engine and operate at approximately 1,000 RPM to ensure a smooth and accurate scope pattern. Firing lines are visible only on the display (parade) position. The firing lines should all be 5 to 15 kV in height and be within 3 kV of each other. If one or more cylinders have high firing lines, this could indicate a

 **REAL WORLD FIX**

**A Technician's Toughie**

A vehicle ran poorly, yet its scope patterns were "perfect." Remembering that the scope indicates only that a spark has occurred (not necessarily inside the engine), the technician grounded one spark plug wire at a time using a vacuum hose and a test light. Every time a plug wire was grounded, the engine ran worse, until the last cylinder was checked. When the last spark plug wire was grounded, the engine ran the same. The technician checked the spark plug wire with an ohmmeter; it tested within specifications (less than 10,000 ohms per foot of length). The technician also removed and inspected the spark plug. The spark plug looked normal. The spark plug was reinstalled and the engine tested again. The test had the same results as before—the engine seemed to be running on seven cylinders, yet the scope pattern was perfect.

The technician then replaced the spark plug for the affected cylinder. The engine ran correctly. Very close examination of the spark plug showed a thin crack between the wire terminal and the shell of the plug. Why didn't the cracked plug show on the scope? The scope simply indicated that a spark had occurred. The scope cannot distinguish between a spark inside and outside the engine. In this case, the voltage required to travel through the spark plug crack to ground was about the same voltage required to jump the spark plug electrodes inside the engine. The spark that occurred across the cracked spark plug, however, may have been visible at night with the engine running.

defective (open) spark plug wire, a spark plug gapped too far, or a lean fuel mixture affecting only those cylinders.

A lean mixture (not enough fuel) requires a higher voltage to ignite because there are fewer droplets of fuel in the cylinder for the spark to use as "stepping stones" for the voltage to jump across. Therefore, a lean mixture is less conductive than a rich mixture.

**READING THE SPARK LINES**   Spark lines can easily be seen on either superimposed or raster (stacked) position. On the raster position, each individual spark line can be viewed.

The spark lines should be level and one-fourth as high as the firing lines (1.5 to 2.5 kV, but usually less than 2 kV). The spark line voltage is called the **burn kV**. The *length* of the spark line is the critical factor for determining proper operation of the engine because it represents the spark duration time. There is only a limited amount of energy in an ignition coil. If most of the energy is used to ionize the air gaps of the rotor

| NORMAL SPARK LINE LENGTH (AT 700 TO 1200 RPM) | | | |
|---|---|---|---|
| Number of Cylinders | Milliseconds | Percentage (%) of Dwell Scale | Degrees |
| 4 | 1–2 | 3–6 | 3–5 |
| 6 | 1–2 | 4–9 | 2–5 |
| 8 | 1–2 | 6–13 | 3–6 |

**CHART 9–3**

Converting between units is sometimes needed depending on the type of scope used.

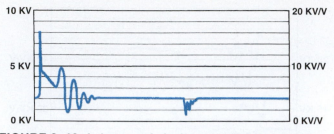

**FIGURE 9–46** A downward-sloping spark line usually indicates high secondary ignition system resistance or an excessively rich air-fuel mixture.

and the spark plug, there may not be enough energy remaining to create a spark duration long enough to completely burn the air-fuel mixture. Many scopes are equipped with a **millisecond (ms) sweep.** This means that the scope will sweep only that portion of the pattern that can be shown during a 5 ms or 25 ms setting.

Following are guidelines for spark line length.

- 0.8 ms: too short
- 1.5 ms: average
- 2.2 ms: too long

If the spark line is too short, possible causes include the following:

1. Spark plug(s) gapped too widely
2. Rotor tip to distributor cap insert distance gapped too widely (worn cap or rotor)
3. High-resistance spark plug wire
4. Air-fuel mixture too lean (vacuum leak, broken valve spring, etc.)

If the spark line is too long, possible causes include the following:

1. Fouled spark plug(s)
2. Spark plug(s) gapped too closely
3. Shorted spark plug or spark plug wire

Many scopes do not have a millisecond scale. Some scopes are labeled in degrees and/or percentage (%) of dwell. ● **CHART 9–3** can be used to determine acceptable spark line length.

### SPARK LINE SLOPE
Downward-sloping spark lines indicate that the voltage required to maintain the spark duration is decreasing during the firing of the spark plug. Although it is normal for the spark line to angle downward slightly, a steep slope indicates that the spark energy is finding ground through spark plug deposits (the plug is fouled) or other ignition problems. ● **SEE FIGURE 9–46.**

An upward-sloping spark line usually indicates a mechanical engine problem. A defective piston ring or valve would tend to seal better in the increasing pressures of combustion. As the spark plug fires, the effective increase in pressures increases

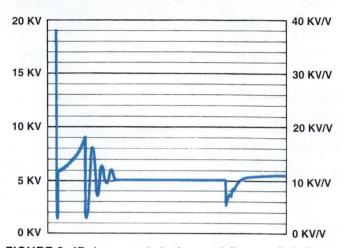

**FIGURE 9–47** An upward-sloping spark line usually indicates a mechanical engine problem or a lean air-fuel mixture.

the voltage required to maintain the spark, and the height of the spark line rises during the duration of the spark. ● **SEE FIGURE 9–47.**

An upward-sloping spark line can also indicate a lean air-fuel mixture. Typical causes include:

1. Clogged injector(s)
2. Vacuum leak
3. Sticking intake valve

● **SEE FIGURE 9–48** for an example showing the relationship between the firing line and the spark line.

### READING THE INTERMEDIATE SECTION
The intermediate section should have three or more oscillations (bumps) for a correctly operating ignition system. Because approximately 250 volts are in the primary ignition circuit when the spark stops flowing across the spark plugs, this voltage is reduced by about 75 volts per oscillation. Additional resistances in the primary circuit would decrease the number of oscillations. If there are fewer than three oscillations, possible problems include the following:

1. Shorted ignition coil
2. Loose or high-resistance primary connections on the ignition coil or primary ignition wiring

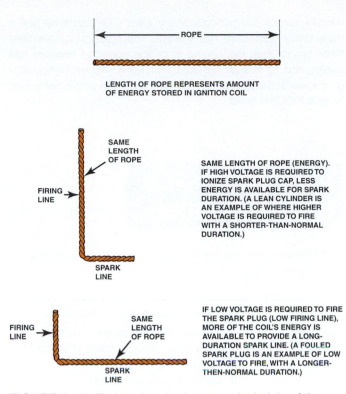

LENGTH OF ROPE REPRESENTS AMOUNT OF ENERGY STORED IN IGNITION COIL

SAME LENGTH OF ROPE (ENERGY). IF HIGH VOLTAGE IS REQUIRED TO IONIZE SPARK PLUG CAP, LESS ENERGY IS AVAILABLE FOR SPARK DURATION. (A LEAN CYLINDER IS AN EXAMPLE OF WHERE HIGHER VOLTAGE IS REQUIRED TO FIRE WITH A SHORTER-THAN-NORMAL DURATION.)

IF LOW VOLTAGE IS REQUIRED TO FIRE THE SPARK PLUG (LOW FIRING LINE), MORE OF THE COIL'S ENERGY IS AVAILABLE TO PROVIDE A LONG-DURATION SPARK LINE. (A FOULED SPARK PLUG IS AN EXAMPLE OF LOW VOLTAGE TO FIRE, WITH A LONGER-THEN-NORMAL DURATION.)

**FIGURE 9–48** The relationship between the height of the firing line and length of the spark line can be illustrated using a rope. Because energy cannot be destroyed, the stored energy in an ignition coil must dissipate totally, regardless of engine operating conditions.

### DWELL AND CURRENT-LIMITING HUMP

Ignition systems use a dwell period to charge the coil. Dwell is the time that current is charging the coil, and changes with increasing RPM in many electronic ignition systems. This change in dwell with RPM should be considered normal.

Many EI systems also produce a "hump" in the dwell section, which reflects a current-limiting circuit in the control module. These current-limiting humps may have slightly different shapes depending on the exact module used. For example, the humps produced by various GM HEI modules differ slightly.

### DWELL VARIATION (DISTRIBUTOR IGNITION)

A worn distributor gear, worn camshaft gear, or other distributor problem may cause engine performance problems, because the signal created in the distributor will be affected by the inaccurate distributor operation. However, many electronic ignitions vary the length of the dwell period electronically in the module to maintain acceptable current flow levels through the ignition coil and ignition control module (ICM).

Different EI systems use one of three different designs. The dwell length characteristic and the types of EI systems that use each design are as follows:

1. Dwell time remains *constant* as the engine speed is increased.
2. Dwell time *decreases* as the engine speed is increased.
3. Dwell time *increases* as the engine speed is increased.

**NOTE: Waste-spark and coil-on-plug ignition systems also vary dwell time electronically within the PCM or ignition module.**

### ACCELERATION CHECK

With the scope selector set on the display (parade) position, rapidly accelerate the engine (gear selector in park or neutral with the parking brake on). The results should be interpreted as follows:

1. All firing lines should rise evenly (not to exceed 75% of maximum coil output) for properly operating spark plugs.
2. If the firing lines on one or more cylinders fail to rise, this indicates fouled spark plugs.

### ROTOR GAP VOLTAGE (DI SYSTEMS)

The rotor gap voltage test measures the voltage required to jump the gap (0.03 to 0.05 in., or 0.8 to 1.3 mm) between the rotor and the inserts (segments) of the distributor cap. Select the display (parade) scope pattern and remove a spark plug wire (at the spark plug end), then using a jumper connected to a good ground, insert the jumper into the spark plug boot making sure it contacts the plug wire terminal. Start the engine and observe the height of the firing line for the cylinder being tested. Because the spark plug wire is connected directly to ground, the firing line height on the scope will indicate the voltage required to jump the air gap between the rotor and the distributor cap insert. The normal rotor gap voltage is 3 to 7 kV, and the voltage should not exceed 8 kV. If the rotor gap voltage indicated is near or above 8 kV, inspect and replace the distributor cap and/or rotor as required.

## SCOPE-TESTING A WASTE-SPARK SYSTEM

A handheld digital storage oscilloscope can be used to check the pattern of individual cylinders. Some larger scopes can be connected to all spark plug wires and therefore are able to display both power and waste-spark waveforms. ● **SEE FIGURE 9–49.**

Because the waste spark does not require as high a voltage level as the cylinder on the power stroke, the waste-spark firing line will be normally lower. The high and low firing lines will alternately change from high to low as the "paired" cylinders change from the compression to the exhaust strokes.

## SCOPE-TESTING A COP SYSTEM

On a coil-on-plug (COP) type of ignition system, the individual coils can be shown on a scope and using the proper cables and adapters, the waveform for all of the cylinders can be viewed at the same time. Always follow the scope equipment

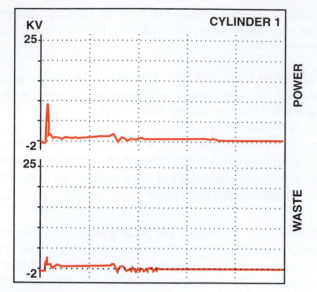

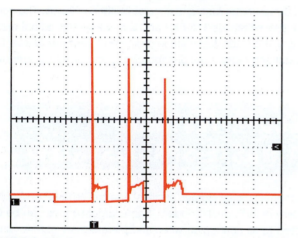

FIGURE 9–49 A dual trace scope pattern showing both the power and the waste spark from the same coil (cylinders 1 and 6). Note that the firing line is higher on the cylinder that is under compression (power); otherwise, both patterns are almost identical.

FIGURE 9–50 A secondary waveform of a Ford 4.6 liter V-8, showing three sparks occurring at idle speed.

manufacturer's instructions. Many Ford COP systems use a triple-strike secondary spark event. The spark plugs are fired three times when the engine is at idle speed to improve idle quality and to reduce exhaust emissions. Above certain engine speeds, the ignition system switches to a single-fire event.
● SEE FIGURE 9–50.

## IGNITION SYSTEM SYMPTOM GUIDE

The following list will assist technicians in troubleshooting ignition system problems.

| Problem | Possible Causes and/or Solutions |
|---|---|
| No spark out of the coil | 1. Open in the ignition switch circuit<br>2. Defective ignition module (if electronic ignition coil)<br>3. Defective trigger sensor<br>4. Open ignition fuse or power feed circuit |
| Weak spark out of the coil | 1. High-resistance coil wire or spark plug wire<br>2. Poor ground between the distributor or module and the engine block |
| Engine misfiring | 1. Defective (open) spark plug wire<br>2. Worn, cracked, or fouled spark plugs<br>3. Defective pickup coil<br>4. Defective module<br>5. Poor electrical connections at the pickup coil and/or module |

## SUMMARY

1. A thorough visual inspection should be performed on all ignition components when diagnosing an engine performance problem.

2. Platinum spark plugs should not be regapped after use in an engine.

3. Magnetic, Hall-effect, and optical sensors can be tested using a scope.

4. A secondary ignition scope pattern includes a firing line, spark line, intermediate oscillations, and transistor-on and transistor-off points.

5. The slope of the spark line can indicate incorrect air-fuel ratio or other engine problems.

1. Why should a spark tester be used to check for spark rather than a standard spark plug?

2. How do you test a pickup coil for resistance and AC voltage output?

3. What harm can occur if the engine is cranked or run with an open (defective) spark plug wire?

4. What are the sections of a secondary ignition scope pattern?

5. What can the slope of the spark line indicate about the engine?

## CHAPTER QUIZ

1. Technician A says that a pickup coil (pulse generator) can be tested with an ohmmeter. Technician B says that ignition coils can be tested with an ohmmeter. Which technician is correct?
   a. Technician A only
   b. Technician B only
   c. Both Technicians A and B
   d. Neither Technician A nor B

2. Technician A says that a defective spark plug wire can cause an engine misfire. Technician B says that a defective spark plug can cause an engine misfire. Which technician is correct?
   a. Technician A only
   b. Technician B only
   c. Both Technicians A and B
   d. Neither Technician A nor B

3. A spark tester should be used to check for spark because _____.
   a. A spark tester requires at least 25,000 volts to fire
   b. It is connected to the CKP sensor to check its output
   c. It can detect a cracked spark plug
   d. It can detect the gap of the spark plugs

4. Typical primary coil resistance specifications usually range from _____ ohms.
   a. 100 to 450
   b. 500 to 1,500
   c. 0.5 to 3
   d. 6,000 to 30,000

5. Typical secondary coil resistance specifications usually range from _____ ohms.
   a. 100 to 450
   b. 500 to 1,500
   c. 1 to 3
   d. 6,000 to 30,000

6. A coil is being tested using current ramping. The waveform should _____.
   a. Slope downward
   b. Slope upward
   c. Remain flat
   d. Start off flat then slope upward

7. Camshaft variation as displayed on a scan tool on an engine with a distributor-mounted CMP sensor should be ± _____ degrees.
   a. 10
   b. 5
   c. 2
   d. None of the above

8. The spark plug threads in the cylinder head should be cleaned using a(n) _____ before installing new plugs.
   a. Wire brush
   b. Tap
   c. Old toothbrush
   d. Thread chaser

9. Two technicians are discussing a no-start condition. During cranking, a magnet held over the coil moves and the engine backfires at times. Technician A says that a bad pickup coil or CKP sensor is the most likely cause. Technician B says that an open coil primary is the most likely cause. Which technician is correct?
   a. Technician A only
   b. Technician B only
   c. Both Technicians A and B
   d. Neither Technician A nor B

10. Which sensor produces a digital signal?
    a. Magnetic sensor
    b. Hall-effect sensor
    c. Pickup coil
    d. Both b and c

# chapter 10

# GASOLINE, ALTERNATIVE FUELS, AND DIESEL FUELS

**OBJECTIVES:** After studying Chapter 10, the reader will be able to: • Describe how the proper grade of gasoline affects engine performance. • List gasoline purchasing considerations. • Discuss how volatility affects driveability. • Explain how oxygenated fuels can reduce CO exhaust emissions. • Discuss safety precautions when working with gasoline.

**KEY TERMS:** AFV 150 • Air-fuel ratio 142 • Antiknock index (AKI) 144 • API gravity 159 • ASTM 142 • B5 159 • B20 159 • Biodiesel 159 • Biomass 152 • Catalytic cracking 140 • Cetane number 158 • Cloud point 158 • Coal to liquid (CTL) 157 • Compressed natural gas (CNG) 153 • Cracking 140 • Detonation 143 • Diesohol 161 • Distillation 140 • E10 146 • E85 150 • E-diesel 161 • Ethanol 146 • Ethyl alcohol 150 • FFV 150 • Fischer-Tropsch 156 • Flex fuel 150 • FTD 156 • Fuel compensation sensor 151 • Fungible 141 • Gasoline 140 • Grain alcohol 150 • GTL 156 • Hydrocracking 141 • Liquified petroleum gas (LPG) 153 • LP gas 153 • M85 153 • Methanol 152 • Methanol to gasoline (MTG) 157 • NGV 153 • Octane rating 143 • Oxygenated fuels 145 • Petrodiesel 160 • Ping 143 • PPO 160 • Propane 153 • RVP 142 • Spark knock 143 • Stoichiometric 143 • SVO 160 • Syncrude 157 • Syn-gas 152 • UCO 160 • ULSD 159 • Underground coal gasification (UCG) 157 • Variable fuel sensor 151 • V-FFV 152 • Volatility 141 • WVO 160 • WWFC 148

## INTRODUCTION

Using the proper fuel is important for the proper operation of any engine. Although gasoline is the most commonly used fuel today, there are several alternative fuels that can be used in some vehicles. Diesel fuel contains much lower amounts of sulfur than before 2007 and this allows the introduction of many new clean burning diesel engines.

## GASOLINE

**Gasoline** is a term used to describe a complex mixture of various hydrocarbons refined from crude petroleum oil for use as a fuel in engines. Gasoline and air burns in the cylinder of the engine and produces heat and pressure which is transferred to rotary motion inside the engine and eventually powers the drive wheels of a vehicle. When the combustion process in the engine is perfect, all of the fuel and air are consumed and only carbon dioxide and water are produced.

## REFINING

**DISTILLATION** In the late 1800s, crude was separated into different products by boiling in a process called **distillation.** Distillation works because crude oil is composed of hydrocarbons with a broad range of boiling points.

In a distillation column, the vapor of the lowest boiling hydrocarbons, propane and butane, rises to the top. The straight-run gasoline (also called naphtha), kerosene, and diesel fuel cuts are drawn off at successively lower positions in the column.

**CRACKING** **Cracking** is the process during which hydrocarbons with higher boiling points can be broken down (cracked) into lower boiling hydrocarbons by treating them to very high temperatures. This process, called thermal cracking, was used to increase gasoline production starting in 1913.

Today, instead of high heat, cracking is performed using a catalyst and is called **catalytic cracking.** A catalyst is a material that speeds up or otherwise facilitates a chemical reaction without undergoing a permanent chemical change itself. Catalytic cracking produces gasoline of higher quality than thermal cracking.

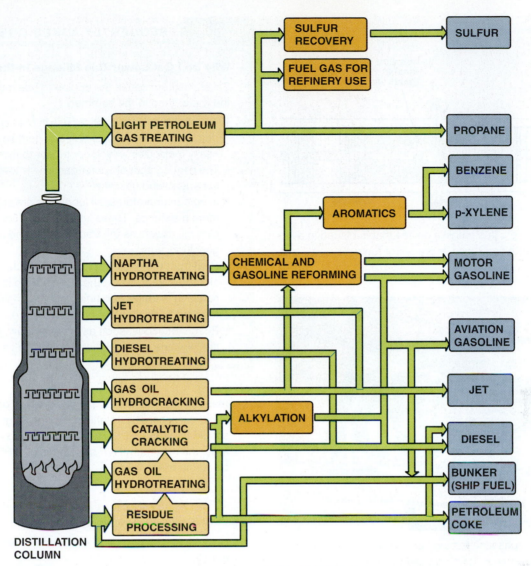

FIGURE 10–1 The crude oil refining process showing most of the major steps and processes.

**Hydrocracking** is similar to catalytic cracking in that it uses a catalyst, but the catalyst is in a hydrogen atmosphere. Hydrocracking can break down hydrocarbons that are resistant to catalytic cracking alone and it is used to produce diesel fuel rather than gasoline.

Other types of refining processes include:

- Reforming
- Alkylation
- Isomerization
- Hydrotreating
- Desulfurization
  - ● SEE FIGURE 10–1.

**SHIPPING** The gasoline is transported to regional storage facilities by tank railway car or by pipeline. In the pipeline method, all gasoline from many refiners is often sent through the same pipeline and can become mixed. All gasoline is said to be **fungible,** meaning that it is capable of being interchanged because each grade is created to specification so there is no reason to keep the different gasoline brands separated except for grade. Regular grade, midgrade, and premium grades are separated by using a device, called a pig, in the pipeline and sent to regional storage facilities. ● SEE FIGURE 10–2.

It is at these regional or local storage facilities where the additives and dye (if any) are added and then shipped by truck to individual gas stations.

## VOLATILITY

**DEFINITION** **Volatility** describes how easily the gasoline evaporates (forms a vapor). The definition of volatility assumes that the vapors will remain in the fuel tank or fuel line and will cause a certain pressure based on the temperature of the fuel.

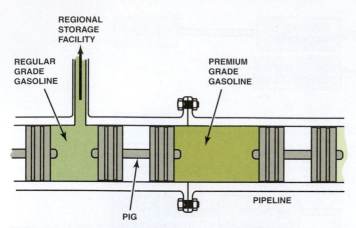

FIGURE 10–2 A pig is a pluglike device that is placed in a pipeline to separate two types or grades of fuel.

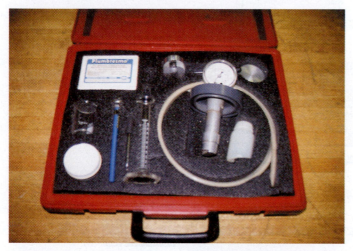

FIGURE 10–3 A gasoline testing kit, including an insulated container where water at 100°F is used to heat a container holding a small sample of gasoline. The reading on the pressure gauge is the Reid vapor pressure (RVP).

**REID VAPOR PRESSURE** Reid vapor pressure (RVP) is the pressure of the vapor above the fuel when the fuel is at 100°F (38°C). Increased vapor pressure permits the engine to start in cold weather. Gasoline without air will not burn. Gasoline must be vaporized (mixed with air) to burn in an engine. ● SEE FIGURE 10–3.

**SEASONAL BLENDING** Cold temperatures reduce the normal vaporization of gasoline; therefore, winter-blended gasoline is specially formulated to vaporize at lower temperatures for proper starting and driveability at low ambient temperatures.

- **Winter blend.** The **American Society for Testing and Materials (ASTM)** standards for winter-blend gasoline allow volatility of up to 15 pounds per square inch (PSI) RVP.

- **Summer blend.** At warm ambient temperatures, gasoline vaporizes easily. However, the fuel system (fuel pump,

**Why Do I Get Lower Gas Mileage in the Winter?**
Several factors cause the engine to use more fuel in the winter than in the summer.

- Gasoline that is blended for use in cold climates is designed for ease of starting and contains fewer heavy molecules, which contribute to fuel economy. The heat content of winter gasoline is lower than summer-blend gasoline.
- In cold temperatures, all lubricants are stiff, causing more resistance. These lubricants include the engine oil, as well as the transmission and differential gear lubricants.
- Heat from the engine is radiated into the outside air more rapidly when the temperature is cold, resulting in longer run time until the engine has reached normal operating temperature.
- Road conditions, such as ice and snow, can cause tire slippage or additional drag on the vehicle.

fuel-injector nozzles, etc.) is designed to operate with liquid gasoline. The volatility of summer-grade gasoline should be about 7 PSI RVP. According to ASTM standards, the maximum RVP should be 10.5 PSI for summer-blend gasoline.

**VOLATILITY-RELATED PROBLEMS** If using winter-grade fuel during warm weather, the following may occur.

- Heat causes some fuel to evaporate, thereby causing bubbles.
- When the fuel is full of bubbles (sometimes called vapor lock), the engine is not being supplied with enough fuel and the engine runs lean. A lean engine will lead to the following:

1. Rough idle
2. Stalling
3. Hesitation on acceleration
4. Surging

If using summer-grade fuel in cold temperatures, then the engine will be hard to start (long cranking before starting) due to the lack of volatility to allow the engine to start easily.

## AIR-FUEL RATIOS

**DEFINITION** The **air-fuel ratio** is the proportion by weight of air and gasoline that the injection system mixes as needed for engine combustion. Air-fuel ratios in which a gasoline engine can operate without stalling range from 8:1 to 18.5:1. ● SEE FIGURE 10–4.

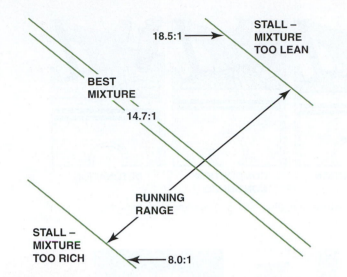

FIGURE 10–4 An engine will not run if the air-fuel mixture is either too rich or too lean.

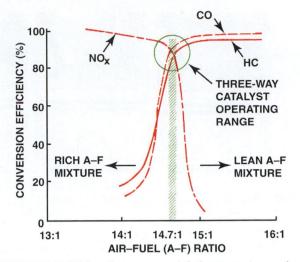

FIGURE 10–5 With a three-way catalytic converter, emission control is most efficient with an air-fuel ratio between 14.65:1 and 14.75:1.

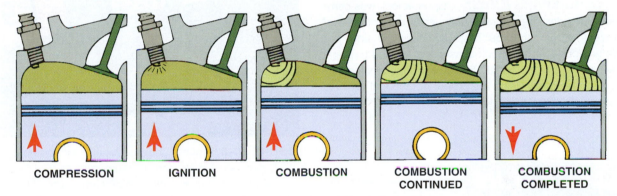

FIGURE 10–6 Normal combustion is a smooth, controlled burning of the air-fuel mixture.

These ratios are usually stated by weight, as follows:

- 8 parts of air by weight combined with 1 part of gasoline by weight (8:1), which is the richest mixture that an engine can tolerate and still fire reliably

- 18.5 parts of air mixed with 1 part of gasoline (18.5:1), which is the leanest practical ratio

Richer or leaner air-fuel ratios cause the engine to misfire badly or not run at all.

### STOICHIOMETRIC AIR-FUEL RATIO   The ideal mixture
or ratio at which all of the fuel combines with all of the oxygen in the air and burns completely is called the **stoichiometric** ratio, a chemically perfect combination. In theory, this ratio for gasoline is an air-fuel mixture of 14.7:1. The stoichiometric ratio is a compromise between maximum power and maximum economy. ● SEE FIGURE 10–5.

## NORMAL AND ABNORMAL COMBUSTION

### TERMINOLOGY   The **octane rating** of gasoline is the mea-
sure of its antiknock properties. **Spark knock** (also called **detonation** or **ping**) is a metallic noise an engine makes, usually during acceleration, resulting from abnormal or uncontrolled combustion inside the cylinder. Normal combustion occurs smoothly and progresses across the combustion chamber from the point of ignition.
● SEE FIGURE 10–6.

Normal flame-front combustion travels between 45 and 90 mph (72 and 145 km/h). The speed of the flame front depends on air-fuel ratio, combustion chamber design (determining amount of turbulence), and temperature.

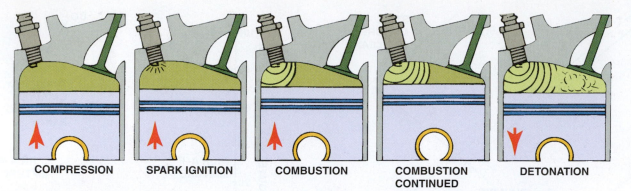

| COMPRESSION | SPARK IGNITION | COMBUSTION | COMBUSTION CONTINUED | DETONATION |

**FIGURE 10–7** Detonation is a secondary ignition of the air-fuel mixture. It is also called spark knock or pinging.

**ABNORMAL COMBUSTION** During periods of abnormal combustion, called spark knock or detonation, the combustion speed increases by up to 10 times to near the speed of sound. The increased combustion speed also causes increased temperatures and pressures, which can damage pistons, gaskets, and cylinder heads. ● SEE FIGURE 10–7.

**CONTROLLING SPARK KNOCK** Spark knock was commonly heard in older engines especially when under load and in warm weather temperatures. Most engines built since the 1990s are equipped with a knock sensor that is used to signal the powertrain control module (PCM) to retard the ignition timing if knock is detected. Using the proper octane fuel helps to ensure that spark knock does not occur.

## OCTANE RATING

**RATING METHODS** The two basic methods used to rate gasoline for antiknock properties (octane rating) include the Research method and the Motor method.

Each uses a model of the special cooperative fuel research (CFR) single-cylinder engine to test the octane of a fuel sample, and the two methods use different engine settings. The research method typically results in readings that are 6 to 10 points higher than those of the motor method. For example, a fuel with a research octane number (RON) of 93 might have a motor octane number (MON) of 85.

**GASOLINE GRADES** The octane rating posted on pumps in the United States is the average of the two methods and is referred to as (R + M) ÷ 2, meaning that, for the fuel used in the previous example, the rating posted on the pumps would be:

$$\frac{RON + MON}{2} = \frac{93 + 85}{2} = 89$$

This pump octane rating is often called the **antiknock index (AKI)**.
● SEE FIGURE 10–8.

**FIGURE 10–8** A pump showing regular with a pump octane of 87, plus rated at 89, and premium rated at 93. These ratings can vary with brand as well as in different parts of the country.

| Grades | Octane Rating |
|--------|---------------|
| Regular | 87 |
| Midgrade (also called Plus) | 89 |
| Premium | 91 or higher |

**CHART 10–1**

The octane rating displayed on the fuel pumps can vary depending on climate.

Except in high-altitude areas, the grades and octane ratings are shown in ● CHART 10–1.

**OCTANE EFFECTS OF ALTITUDE** As the altitude increases, atmospheric pressure drops. The air is less dense because a pound of air takes more volume. The octane rating of fuel does not need to be as high because the engine cannot take in as much air. This process will reduce the combustion (compression) pressures inside the engine. In mountainous areas, gasoline (R + M) ÷ 2 octane ratings are two or more

**What Grade of Gasoline Does the EPA Use When Testing Engines?**

Due to the various grades and additives used in commercial fuel, the government (EPA) uses a liquid called indolene, which has a research method octane number of 96.5 and a motor method octane rating of 88, resulting in a $(R + M) \div 2$ rating of 92.25.

 TECH TIP

**Horsepower and Fuel Flow**

To produce 1 hp, the engine must be supplied with 0.50 lb of fuel per hour (lb/hr). Fuel injectors are rated in pounds per hour. For example, a V-8 engine equipped with 25 lb/hr fuel injectors could produce 50 hp per cylinder (per injector) or 400 hp. Even if the cylinder head or block is modified to produce more horsepower, the limiting factor may be the injector flow rate.

The following are flow rates and resulting horsepower for a V-8 engine.

- 30 lb/hr: 60 hp per cylinder, or 480 hp
- 35 lb/hr: 70 hp per cylinder, or 560 hp
- 40 lb/hr: 80 hp per cylinder, or 640 hp

Of course, injector flow rate is only one of many variables that affect power output. Installing larger injectors without other major engine modifications could decrease engine output and drastically increase exhaust emissions.

**FIGURE 10–9** The posted octane rating in most high-altitude areas shows regular at 85 instead of the usual 87.

numbers lower than normal (according to the SAE, about one octane number lower per 1,000 ft or 300 m in altitude). ● **SEE FIGURE 10–9.**

A second reason for the lowered octane requirement of engines running at higher altitudes is the normal enrichment of the air-fuel ratio and lower engine vacuum with the decreased air density. Some problems, therefore, may occur when driving out of high-altitude areas into lower areas where the octane rating must be higher. Most electronic fuel injection systems can compensate for changes in altitude and modify air-fuel ratio and ignition timing for best operation.

Because the combustion burn rate slows at high altitude, the ignition (spark) timing can be advanced to improve power. The amount of timing advance can be about 1 degree per 1,000 ft over 5,000 ft. Therefore, if driving at 8,000 ft of altitude, the ignition timing can be advanced 3 degrees.

**VOLATILITY EFFECTS OF ALTITUDE** High altitude also allows fuel to evaporate more easily. The volatility of fuel should be reduced at higher altitudes to prevent vapor from forming

in sections of the fuel system, which can cause driveability and stalling problems. The extra heat generated in climbing to higher altitudes plus the lower atmospheric pressure at higher altitudes combine to cause possible driveability problems as the vehicle goes to higher altitudes.

# GASOLINE ADDITIVES

**DYE** Dye is usually added to gasoline at the distributor to help identify the grade and/or brand of fuel. Fuels are required to be colored using a fuel soluble dye in many countries. In the United States and Canada, diesel fuel used for off-road use and not taxed is required to be dyed red for identification. Gasoline sold for off-road use in Canada is dyed purple.

**OXYGENATED FUEL ADDITIVES** Oxygenated fuels contain oxygen in the molecule of the fuel itself. Examples of oxygenated fuels include:

- **Methyl tertiary butyl ether (MTBE).** This fuel is manufactured by means of the chemical reaction of methanol and isobutylene. Unlike methanol, MTBE does not increase the volatility of the fuel, and is not as sensitive to water as are other alcohols. The maximum allowable volume level, according to the EPA, is 15% but is currently being phased out due to health concerns, as well as MTBE contamination of drinking water if spilled from storage tanks.

- **Tertiary-amyl methyl ether (TAME).** This fuel contains an oxygen atom bonded to two carbon atoms, and is added to gasoline to provide oxygen to the fuel. It is slightly soluble in water, very soluble in ethers and alcohol, and soluble in most organic solvents including hydrocarbons.

- **Ethyl tertiary butyl ether (ETBE).** This fuel is derived from ethanol. The maximum allowable volume level is

FIGURE 10–10 This fuel tank indicates that the gasoline is blended with 10% ethanol (ethyl alcohol) and can be used in any gasoline vehicle. E85 contains 85% ethanol and can only be used in vehicles specifically designed to use it.

FIGURE 10–11 A container with gasoline containing water and alcohol. Notice the separation line where the alcohol-water mixture separated from the gasoline and sank to the bottom.

17.2%. The use of ETBE is the cause of much of the odor from the exhaust of vehicles if using reformulated gasoline, as mandated for use in some parts of the country.

■ **Ethanol.** Also called ethyl alcohol, **ethanol** is drinkable alcohol and is usually made from grain. Adding 10% ethanol (ethyl alcohol or grain alcohol) increases the $(R + M) \div 2$ octane rating by three points.

The alcohol added to the base gasoline, however, also raises the volatility of the fuel about 0.5 PSI. Most automobile manufacturers permit up to 10% ethanol if driveability problems are not experienced.

The oxygen content of a 10% blend of ethanol in gasoline, called **E10,** is 3.5% oxygen by weight. ● SEE FIGURE 10–10.

## GASOLINE BLENDING

Gasoline additives, such as ethanol and dyes, are usually added to the fuel at the distributor. Adding ethanol to gasoline is a way to add oxygen to the fuel itself. There are three basic methods

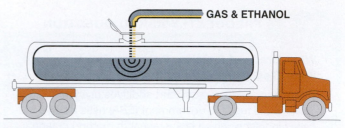

FIGURE 10–12 In-line blending is the most accurate method for blending ethanol with gasoline because computers are used to calculate the correct ratio.

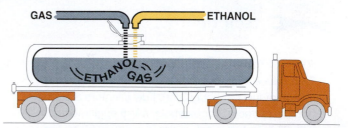

FIGURE 10–13 Sequential blending uses a computer to calculate the correct ratio as well as the prescribed order that the products are loaded.

used to blend ethanol with gasoline to create E10 (10% ethanol, 90% gasoline).

1. **In-line blending.** Gasoline and ethanol are mixed in a storage tank or in the tank of a transport truck while it is being filled. Because the quantities of each can be accurately measured, this method is most likely to produce a well-mixed blend of ethanol and gasoline. ● SEE FIGURE 10–12.

2. **Sequential blending.** This method is usually performed at the wholesale terminal and involves adding a measured amount of ethanol to a tank truck followed by a measured amount of gasoline. ● SEE FIGURE 10–13.

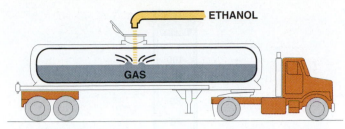

**FIGURE 10–14** Splash blending occurs when the ethanol is added to a tanker with gasoline and is mixed as the truck travels to the retail outlet.

**?** **FREQUENTLY ASKED QUESTION**

**Is Water Heavier than Gasoline?**

Yes. Water weighs about 8 lb per gallon, whereas gasoline weighs about 6 lb per gallon. The density as measured by specific gravity includes:

Water = 1.000 (the baseline for specific gravity)

Gasoline = 0.730 to 0.760

This means that any water that gets into the fuel tank will sink to the bottom.

3. **Splash blending.** This method can be done at the retail outlet or distributor and involves separate purchases of ethanol and gasoline. In a typical case, a distributor can purchase gasoline, and then drive to another supplier and purchase ethanol. The ethanol is then added (splashed) into the tank of gasoline. This method is the least accurate method of blending and can result in ethanol concentration for E10 that should be 10% to range from 5% to over 20% in some cases. ● **SEE FIGURE 10–14.**

# TESTING GASOLINE FOR ALCOHOL CONTENT

Take the following steps when testing gasoline for alcohol content.

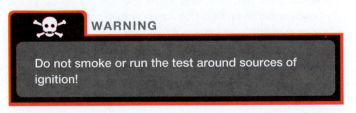

**WARNING**

Do not smoke or run the test around sources of ignition!

1. Pour suspect gasoline into a graduated cylinder.
2. Carefully fill the graduated cylinder to the 90 mL mark.
3. Add 10 mL of water to the graduated cylinder by counting the number of drops from an eyedropper.

4. Put the stopper in the cylinder and shake vigorously for one minute. Relieve built-up pressure by occasionally removing the stopper. Alcohol dissolves in water and will drop to the bottom of the cylinder.
5. Place the cylinder on a flat surface and let it stand for two minutes.
6. Take a reading near the bottom of the cylinder at the boundary between the two liquids.
7. For percent of alcohol in gasoline, subtract 10 to get the percentage.

    For example,
    The reading is 20 mL: 20 − 10 = 10% alcohol

If the increase in volume is 0.2% or less, it may be assumed that the test gasoline contains no alcohol. ● **SEE FIGURE 10–15.**

Alcohol content can also be checked using an electronic tester. See the photo sequence at the end of the chapter.

# GENERAL GASOLINE RECOMMENDATIONS

The fuel used by an engine is a major expense in the operation cost of the vehicle. The proper operation of the engine depends on clean fuel of the proper octane rating and vapor pressure for the atmospheric conditions.

To help ensure proper engine operation and keep fuel costs to a minimum, follow these guidelines.

1. Purchase fuel from a busy station to help ensure that it is fresh and less likely to be contaminated with water or moisture.
2. Keep the fuel tank above one-quarter full, especially during seasons in which the temperature rises and falls by more than 20°F between daytime highs and nighttime lows. This helps to reduce condensed moisture in the fuel tank and could prevent gas line freeze-up in cold weather.

    **NOTE: Gas line freeze-up occurs when the water in the gasoline freezes and forms an ice blockage in the fuel line.**

3. Do not purchase fuel with a higher octane rating than is necessary. Try using premium high-octane fuel to check for operating differences. Most newer engines are equipped with a detonation (knock) sensor that signals the vehicle computer to retard the ignition timing when spark knock occurs. Therefore, an operating difference may not be noticeable to the driver when using a low-octane fuel, except for a decrease in power and fuel economy. In other words, the engine with a knock sensor will tend to operate knock free on regular fuel, even if premium, higher octane fuel is specified. Using premium fuel may result in more power

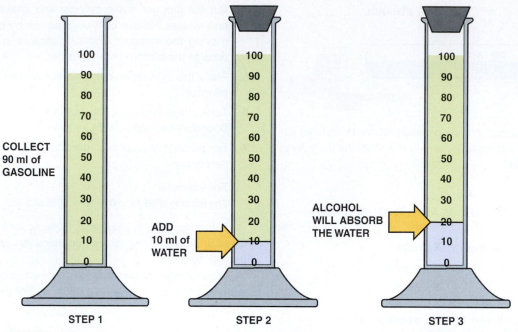

FIGURE 10–15 Checking gasoline for alcohol involves using a graduated cylinder and adding water to check if the alcohol absorbs the water.

? **FREQUENTLY ASKED QUESTION**

**What Is "Top-Tier" Gasoline?**

Top-tier gasoline has specific standards for quality, including enough detergent to keep all intake valves clean. Four automobile manufacturers (BMW, General Motors, Honda, and Toyota) developed the standards. Top-tier gasoline exceeds the quality standards developed by the **World Wide Fuel Charter (WWFC)** in 2002 by vehicle and engine manufacturers. The gasoline companies that agreed to make fuel that matches or exceeds the standards as a top-tier fuel include ChevronTexaco, Shell, and ConocoPhillips. Ford has specified that BP fuel, sold in many parts of the country, is the recommended fuel to use in Ford vehicles.

● **SEE FIGURE 10–16.**

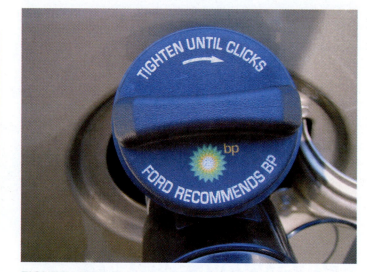

FIGURE 10–16 The gas cap on a Ford vehicle notes that BP fuel is recommended.

and greater fuel economy. The increase in fuel economy, however, would have to be substantial to justify the increased cost of high-octane premium fuel. Some drivers find a good compromise by using midgrade (plus) fuel to benefit from the engine power and fuel economy gains without the cost of using premium fuel all the time.

4. Try to avoid using gasoline with alcohol in warm weather, even though many alcohol blends do not affect engine driveability. If warm-engine stumble, stalling, or rough idle occurs, change brands of gasoline.

5. Do not purchase fuel from a retail outlet when a tanker truck is filling the underground tanks. During the refilling procedure, dirt, rust, and water may be stirred up in the underground tanks. This undesirable material may be pumped into your vehicle's fuel tank.

6. Do not overfill the gas tank. After the nozzle clicks off, add just enough fuel to round up to the next dime. Adding additional gasoline will cause the excess to be drawn into the charcoal canister. This can lead to engine flooding and excessive exhaust emissions.

7. Be careful when filling gasoline containers. Always fill a gas can on the ground to help prevent the possibility of static electricity buildup during the refueling process. ● **SEE FIGURE 10–17.**

FIGURE 10–17 Many service stations have signs posted warning customers to place plastic fuel containers on the ground while filling. If placed in a trunk or pickup truck bed equipped with a plastic liner, static electricity could build up during fueling and discharge from the container to the metal nozzle, creating a spark and possible explosion. Some service stations have warning signs not to use cell phones while fueling to help avoid the possibility of an accidental spark creating a fire hazard.

? FREQUENTLY ASKED QUESTION

### Why Should I Keep the Fuel Gauge Above One-Quarter Tank?

The fuel pickup inside the fuel tank can help keep water from being drawn into the fuel system unless water is all that is left at the bottom of the tank. Over time, moisture in the air inside the fuel tank can condense, causing liquid water to drop to the bottom of the fuel tank. (Recall that water is heavier than gasoline—about 8 lb per gallon for water and about 6 lb per gallon for gasoline.) If alcohol-blended gasoline is used, the alcohol can absorb the water and the alcohol-water combination can be burned inside the engine. However, when water combines with alcohol, a separation layer occurs between the gasoline at the top of the tank and the alcohol-water combination at the bottom. When the fuel level is low, the fuel pump will draw from this concentrated level of alcohol and water. Because alcohol and water do not burn as well as pure gasoline, severe driveability problems can occur such as stalling, rough idle, hard starting, and missing.

 TECH TIP

### Do Not Overfill the Fuel Tank

Gasoline fuel tanks have an expansion volume area at the top. The volume of this expansion area is equal to 10% to 15% of the volume of the tank. This area is normally not filled with gasoline, but rather is designed to provide a place for the gasoline to expand into, if the vehicle is parked in the hot sun and the gasoline expands. This prevents raw gasoline from escaping from the fuel system. A small restriction is usually present to control the amount of air and vapors that can escape the tank and flow to the charcoal canister.

This volume area could be filled with gasoline if the fuel is slowly pumped into the tank. Since it can hold an extra 10% (2 gallons in a 20 gallon tank), some people deliberately try to fill the tank completely. When this expansion volume is filled, liquid fuel (rather than vapors) can be drawn into the charcoal canister. When the purge valve opens, liquid fuel can be drawn into the engine, causing an excessively rich air-fuel mixture. Not only can this liquid fuel harm vapor recovery parts, but overfilling the gas tank could also cause the vehicle to fail an exhaust emission test, particularly during an enhanced test when the tank could be purged while on the rollers.

TECH TIP

### The Sniff Test

Problems can occur with stale gasoline from which the lighter parts of the gasoline have evaporated. Stale gasoline usually results in a no-start situation. If stale gasoline is suspected, sniff it. If it smells rancid, replace it with fresh gasoline.

**NOTE: If storing a vehicle, boat, or lawnmower over the winter, put some gasoline stabilizer into the gasoline to reduce the evaporation and separation that can occur during storage. Gasoline stabilizer is frequently available at lawnmower repair shops or marinas.**

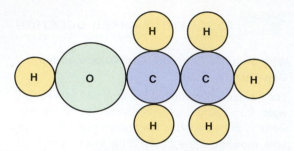

**FIGURE 10–18** The ethanol molecule showing two carbon atoms, six hydrogen atoms, and one oxygen atom.

**FIGURE 10–19** Some retail stations offer a variety of fuel choices, such as this station in Ohio where E10 and E85 are available.

## E85

**WHAT IS E85?** Vehicle manufacturers have available vehicles that are capable of operating on gasoline plus ethanol or a combination of gasoline and ethanol called **E85,** composed of 85% ethanol and 15% gasoline. Ethanol is also called **ethyl alcohol** or **grain alcohol,** because it is usually made from grain and is the type of alcohol found in alcoholic drinks such as beer, wine, and distilled spirits like whiskey. Ethanol is composed of two carbon atoms and six hydrogen atoms with one added oxygen atom. ● **SEE FIGURE 10–18.**

Pure ethanol has an octane rating of about 113. E85, which contains 35% oxygen by weight, has an octane rating of 100 to 105. This compares to a regular unleaded gasoline which has a rating of 87. ● **SEE FIGURE 10–19.**

**NOTE: The octane rating of E85 depends on the exact percent of ethanol used, which can vary from 81% to 85%. It also depends on the octane rating of the gasoline used to make E85.**

**HEAT ENERGY OF E85** E85 has less heat energy than gasoline.

Gasoline: 114,000 BTUs per gallon

E85: 87,000 BTUs per gallon

This means that the fuel economy is reduced by 20% to 30% if E85 is used instead of gasoline.

**Example:** A Chevrolet Tahoe 5.3 liter V-8 with an automatic transmission has an EPA rating using gasoline of 15 mpg in the city and 20 mpg on the highway. If this same vehicle is fueled with E85, the EPA fuel economy rating drops to 11 mpg in the city and 15 mpg on the highway.

## ALTERNATIVE FUEL VEHICLES

The 15% gasoline in the E85 blend helps the engine start, especially in cold weather. Vehicles equipped with this capability are commonly referred to as:

- **Alternative fuel vehicles (AFVs)**
- **Flex fuels**
- **Flexible fuel vehicles (FFVs)**

Using E85 in a flex fuel vehicle can result in a power increase of about 5%. For example, an engine rated at 200 hp using gasoline or E10 could produce 210 hp if using E85.

**NOTE: E85 may test as containing less than 85% ethanol if tested because it is often blended according to outside temperature. A lower percentage of ethanol with a slightly higher percentage of gasoline helps engines start in cold climates.**

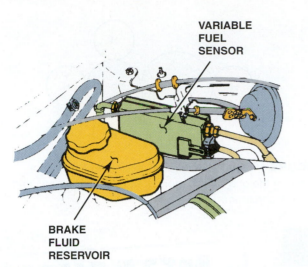

**FIGURE 10–20** The location of the variable fuel sensor can vary, depending on the make and model of vehicle, but it is always in the fuel line between the fuel tank and the fuel injectors.

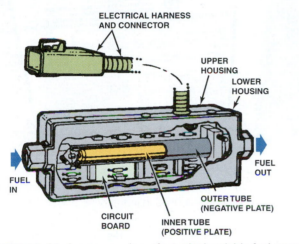

**FIGURE 10–21** A cutaway view of a typical variable fuel sensor.

These vehicles are equipped with an electronic sensor in the fuel supply line that detects the presence and percentage of ethanol. The PCM then adjusts the fuel injector on-time and ignition timing to match the needs of the fuel being used.

E85 contains less heat energy, and therefore will use more fuel, but the benefits include a lower cost of the fuel and less environmental impact associated with using an oxygenated fuel.

General Motors, Ford, Chrysler, and Mazda are a few of the manufacturers offering E85 compatible vehicles. E85 vehicles use fuel system parts designed to withstand the additional alcohol content, modified driveability programs that adjust fuel delivery and timing to compensate for the various percentages of ethanol fuel, and a **fuel compensation sensor** that measures both the percentage of ethanol blend and the temperature of the fuel. This sensor is also called a **variable fuel sensor.** ● SEE FIGURES 10–20 AND 10–21.

**E85 FUEL SYSTEM REQUIREMENTS** Most E85 vehicles are very similar to non-E85 vehicles. Fuel system components may be redesigned to withstand the effects of higher

**FIGURE 10–22** A flex fuel vehicle often has a yellow gas cap, which is labeled E85/gasoline.

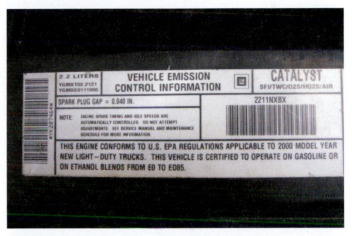

**FIGURE 10–23** A vehicle emission control information (VECI) sticker on a flexible fuel vehicle indicating that it can use ethanol from 0% to 85%.

concentrations of ethanol. In addition, since the stoichiometric point for ethanol is 9:1 instead of 14.7:1 as for gasoline, the air-fuel mixture has to be adjusted for the percentage of ethanol present in the fuel tank.

The benefits of E85 vehicles include:

- Reduced pollution
- Less $CO_2$ production
- Less dependence on imported oil

**FLEX FUEL VEHICLE IDENTIFICATION** Flexible fuel vehicles (FFVs) can be identified by:

- Emblems on the side, front, and/or rear of the vehicle
- Yellow fuel cap showing E85/gasoline (● SEE FIGURE 10–22.)
- Vehicle emission control information (VECI) label under the hood (● SEE FIGURE 10–23.)
- Vehicle identification number (VIN)

### How Does a Sensorless Flex Fuel System Work?

Many General Motors flex fuel vehicles do not use a fuel compensation sensor and instead use the oxygen sensor to detect the presence of the lean mixture and the extra oxygen in the fuel.

The powertrain control module (PCM) then adjusts the injector pulse width and the ignition timing to optimize engine operation to the use of E85. This type of vehicle is called a **virtual flexible fuel vehicle (V-FFV)**. It can operate on pure gasoline or blends up to 85% ethanol.

### How Long Can Oxygenated Fuel Be Stored Before All of the Oxygen Escapes?

The oxygen in oxygenated fuels, such as E10 and E85, is not in a gaseous state like the $CO_2$ in soft drinks. The oxygen is part of the molecule of ethanol or other oxygenates and does not bubble out of the fuel. Oxygenated fuels, like any fuel, have a shelf life of about 90 days.

NOTE: For additional information on E85 and for the location of E85 stations in your area, go to www.e85fuel.com.

## METHANOL

**METHANOL TERMINOLOGY**    **Methanol,** also known as methyl alcohol, wood alcohol, or methyl hydrate, is a chemical compound formula that includes one carbon atom, four hydrogen atoms, and one oxygen atom. ● **SEE FIGURE 10–24.**

Methanol is a light, volatile, colorless, tasteless, flammable, poisonous liquid with a very faint odor. Methanol can be used in the following ways.

- As an antifreeze, a solvent, or a fuel
- To denature ethanol (to make undrinkable)

Methanol burns in air, forming $CO_2$ (carbon dioxide) and $H_2O$ (water). A methanol flame is almost colorless. Methanol is often called wood alcohol because it was once produced chiefly

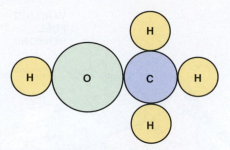

**FIGURE 10–24** The molecular structure of methanol showing the one carbon atom, four hydrogen atoms, and one oxygen atom.

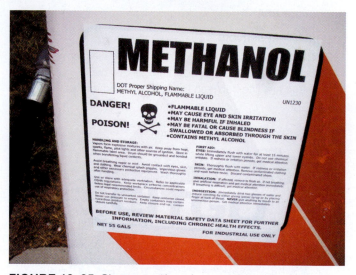

**FIGURE 10–25** Sign on methanol pump shows that methyl alcohol is a poison and can cause skin irritation and other personal injury. Methanol is used in industry as well as being a fuel.

as a by-product of the destructive distillation of wood. ● **SEE FIGURE 12–25.**

**PRODUCTION OF METHANOL**    The biggest source of methanol in the United States is coal. Using a simple reaction between coal and steam, a gas mixture called **syn-gas** (synthesis gas) is formed. The components of this mixture are carbon monoxide and hydrogen, which, through an additional chemical reaction, are converted to methanol.

Natural gas can also be used to create methanol and is reformed or converted to synthesis gas, which is later made into methanol.

**Biomass** can be converted to synthesis gas by a process called partial oxidation, and later converted to methanol. Biomass is organic material, and includes:

- Urban wood wastes
- Primary mill residues
- Forest residues
- Agricultural residues
- Dedicated energy crops (e.g., sugarcane and sugar beets) that can be made into fuel

**FIGURE 10–26** Propane fuel storage tank in the trunk of a Ford taxi.

**FIGURE 10–27** The blue sticker on the rear of this vehicle indicates that it is designed to use compressed natural gas. This Ford truck also has a sticker that allows it to be driven in the high occupancy vehicle (HOV) lane, even if there is just the driver, because it is a CNG vehicle.

Electricity can be used to convert water into hydrogen, which is then reacted with carbon dioxide to produce methanol.

Methanol is toxic and can cause blindness and death. It can enter the body by ingestion, inhalation, or absorption through the skin. Dangerous doses will build up if a person is regularly exposed to fumes or handles liquid without skin protection. If methanol has been ingested, a doctor should be contacted immediately. The usual fatal dose is 4 fl oz (100 to 125 mL).

**M85** Some flexible fuel vehicles are designed to operate on 85% methanol and 15% gasoline, called **M85**. Methanol is very corrosive and requires that the fuel system components be constructed of stainless steel and other alcohol-resistant rubber and plastic components. The heat content of M85 is about 60% of that of gasoline.

## PROPANE

**Propane** is the most widely used of all the alternative fuels mainly because of its use in fleets, which utilize a central refueling station. Propane is normally a gas but is easily compressed into a liquid and stored in inexpensive containers. When sold as a fuel, it is also known as **liquefied petroleum gas (LPG)** or **LP gas,** because the propane is often mixed with about 10% of other gases, including:

- Butane
- Propylene
- Butylenes
- Mercaptan, to give the colorless and odorless propane a smell

Propane is nontoxic, but if inhaled can cause asphyxiation through lack of oxygen. Propane is heavier than air and lays near the floor if released into the atmosphere. Propane is

commonly used in forklifts and other equipment located inside warehouses and factories, because the exhaust from the engine using propane is not harmful. Propane is a by-product of petroleum refining of natural gas. In order to liquefy the fuel, it is stored in strong tanks at about 300 PSI (2,000 kPa). The heating value of propane is less than that of gasoline; therefore, more is required, which reduces the fuel economy. ● **SEE FIGURE 10–26.**

## COMPRESSED NATURAL GAS

**CNG VEHICLE DESIGN** Another alternative fuel that is often used in fleet vehicles is **compressed natural gas (CNG)**. Vehicles using this fuel are often referred to as **natural gas vehicles (NGVs)**. Look for the blue CNG label on vehicles designed to operate on compressed natural gas. ● **SEE FIGURE 10–27.**

Because natural gas must be compressed to 3,000 PSI (20,000 kPa) or more, the weight and cost of the storage container are major factors when it comes to preparing a vehicle to run on CNG. The tanks needed for CNG are typically constructed of 0.5 in. (3 mm) thick aluminum reinforced with fiberglass. ● **SEE FIGURE 10–28.**

The octane rating of CNG is about 130 and the cost per gallon is roughly half of the cost of gasoline. However, the heat value of CNG is also less, and therefore more is required to produce the same power; and the miles per gallon is less.

**FIGURE 10–28** A CNG storage tank from a Honda Civic GX shown with the fixture used to support it while it is being removed or installed in the vehicle. Honda specifies that three technicians be used to remove or install the tank through the rear door of the vehicle due to the size and weight of the tank.

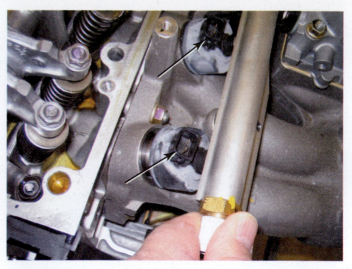

**FIGURE 10–29** The fuel injectors used on this Honda Civic GX CNG engine are designed to flow gaseous fuel instead of liquid fuel and cannot be interchanged with any other type of injector.

 **FREQUENTLY ASKED QUESTION**

**What Is the Amount of CNG Equal to in Gasoline?**

To achieve the amount of energy of 1 gallon of gasoline, 122 ft$^3$ of compressed natural gas (CNG) is needed. While the octane rating of CNG is much higher than gasoline (130 octane), using CNG instead of gasoline in the same engine would result in a 10% to 20% reduction of power due to the lower heat energy that is released when CNG is burned in the engine.

**CNG COMPOSITION** Compressed natural gas is a blend of the following:

- Methane
- Propane
- Ethane
- N-butane
- Carbon dioxide
- Nitrogen

Once it is processed, compressed natural gas is at least 93% methane. Natural gas is nontoxic, odorless, and colorless in its natural state. It is odorized during processing, using ethyl mercaptan ("skunk"), to allow for easy leak detection. Natural gas is lighter than air and will rise when released into the air. Since CNG is already a vapor, it does not need heat to vaporize before it will burn, which improves cold start-up and results in lower emissions during cold operation. However, because

it is already in a gaseous state, it displaces some of the air charge in the intake manifold, leading to a 10% reduction in engine power as compared to an engine operating on gasoline. Natural gas also burns slower than gasoline; therefore, the ignition timing must be advanced more when the vehicle operates on natural gas. The stoichiometric ratio, the point at which all the air and fuel is used or burned, is 16.5:1 compared to 14.7:1 for gasoline. This means that more air is required to burn 1 lb of natural gas than is required to burn 1 lb of gasoline. ● **SEE FIGURE 10–29.**

The CNG engine is designed to include:

- Increased compression ratio
- Strong pistons and connecting rods
- Heat-resistant valves
- Fuel injectors designed for gaseous fuel instead of liquid fuel

**CNG FUEL SYSTEMS** When completely filled, the CNG tank has 3,600 PSI of pressure in the tank. When the ignition is turned on, the alternate fuel electronic control unit activates the high-pressure lock-off, which allows high-pressure gas to pass to the high-pressure regulator.

- The high-pressure regulator reduces the high-pressure CNG to approximately 150 to 170 PSI and sends it to the low-pressure lock-off. The low-pressure lock-off is also controlled by the alternate fuel electronic control unit and is activated at the same time as the high-pressure lock-off.

- From the low-pressure lock-off, the CNG is directed to the low-pressure regulator. This is a two-stage regulator that first reduces the pressure to approximately 4 to 6 PSI in the first stage and then to about 0.5 PSI in the second stage.

From here, the low-pressure gas is delivered to the gas mass sensor/mixture control valve. This valve controls the air-fuel mixture. The CNG gas distributor adapter then delivers the gas to the intake stream.

CNG vehicles are designed for fleet use that usually have their own refueling capabilities. One of the drawbacks to using CNG is the time that it takes to refuel a vehicle. The ideal method of refueling is the slow-fill method. The slow filling method compresses the natural gas as the tank is being fueled. This method ensures that the tank will receive a full charge of CNG; however, this method can take three to five hours to accomplish. If more than one vehicle needs filling, the facility will need multiple CNG compressors to refuel the vehicles.

There are three commonly used CNG refilling station pressures.

P24: 2,400 PSI

P30: 3,000 PSI

P36: 3,600 PSI

Try to find and use a station with the highest refilling pressure. Filling at lower pressures will result in less compressed natural gas being installed in the storage tank, thereby reducing the driving range. ● **SEE FIGURE 10–30.**

The fast-fill method uses CNG that is already compressed. However, as the CNG tank is filled rapidly, the internal temperature of the tank will rise, which causes a rise in tank pressure.

**FIGURE 10–30** This CNG pump is capable of supplying compressed natural gas at either 3,000 PSI or 3,600 PSI. The price per gallon is higher for the higher pressure.

Once the temperature drops in the CNG tank, the pressure in the tank also drops, resulting in an incomplete charge in the CNG tank. This refueling method may take only about five minutes, but it will result in an incomplete charge to the CNG tank, reducing the driving range. ● **SEE CHART 10–2** for a comparison of the most frequently used alternative fuels.

| ALTERNATE FUEL COMPARISON CHART | | | | | |
|---|---|---|---|---|---|
| Characteristic | Propane | CNG | Methanol | Ethanol | Regular Unleaded Gas |
| Octane | 104 | 130 | 100 | 100 | 87–93 |
| BTU per gallon | 91,000 | NA | 70,000 | 83,000 | 114,000–125,000 |
| Gallon equivalent | 1.15 | 122 ft³ to 1 gallon of gasoline | 1.8 | 1.5 | 1 |
| Onboard fuel storage | Liquid | Gas | Liquid | Liquid | Liquid |
| Miles/gallon as compared to gas | 85% | Varies with pressure | 55% | 70% | 100% |
| Relative tank size required to yield driving range equivalent to gas | Tank is 1.25 times larger | Tank is 3.5 times larger | Tank is 1.8 times larger | Tank is 1.5 times larger | |
| Pressure | 200 PSI | 3,000–3,600 PSI | NA | NA | NA |
| Cold weather capability | Good | Good | Poor | Poor | Good |
| Vehicle power | 5%–10% power loss | 10%–20% power loss | 4% power increase | 5% power increase | Standard |
| Toxicity | Nontoxic | Nontoxic | Highly toxic | Toxic | Toxic |
| Corrosiveness | Noncorrosive | Noncorrosive | Corrosive | Corrosive | Minimally corrosive |
| Source | Natural gas/ petroleum refining | Natural gas/ crude oil | Natural gas/coal | Sugar and starch crops/biomass | Crude oil |

**CHART 10–2**

The characteristics of alternative fuels compared to regular unleaded gasoline show that all have advantages and disadvantages.

# LIQUIFIED NATURAL GAS

Natural gas can be turned into a liquid if cooled to below −260°F (−127°C). The natural gas condenses into a liquid at normal atmospheric pressure and the volume is reduced by about 600 times. This means that the natural gas can be more efficiently transported over long distances where no pipelines are present when liquefied.

Because the temperature of liquefied natural gas (LNG) must be kept low, it is best used for fleets where a central LPG station can be used to refuel the vehicles.

# P-SERIES FUELS

P-series alternative fuel is patented by Princeton University and is a nonpetroleum or natural gas based fuel suitable for use in flexible fuel vehicles or any vehicle designed to operate on E85 (85% ethanol, 15% gasoline). P-series fuel is recognized by the U.S. Department of Energy as being an alternative fuel, but is not yet available to the public. P-series fuels are blends of the following:

- Ethanol (ethyl alcohol)
- Methyltetrahydrofuron (MTHF)
- Natural gas liquids, such as pentanes
- Butane

The ethanol and MTHF are produced from renewable feedstocks, such as corn, waste paper, biomass, agricultural waste, and wood waste (scraps and sawdust). The components used in P-series fuel can be varied to produce regular grade, premium grade, or fuel suitable for cold climates. ● SEE CHART 10–3 for the percentages of the ingredients based on fuel grade.

# SYNTHETIC FUELS

**INTRODUCTION**   Synthetic fuels can be made from a variety of products, using several different processes. Synthetic fuel must, however, make these alternatives practical only when conventional petroleum products are either very expensive or not available.

**FISCHER-TROPSCH**   Synthetic fuels were first developed using the **Fischer-Tropsch** method, and have been in use since the 1920s to convert coal, natural gas, and other fossil fuel products into a fuel that is high in quality and clean burning. The process for producing Fischer-Tropsch fuels was patented by two German scientists, Franz Fischer and Hans Tropsch, during World War I. The Fischer-Tropsch method uses carbon monoxide and hydrogen (the same synthesis gas used to produce

| COMPOSITION OF P-SERIES FUELS (BY VOLUME) | | | |
|---|---|---|---|
| Component | Regular Grade | Premium Grade | Cold Weather |
| Pentanes plus | 32.5% | 27.5% | 16% |
| MTHF | 32.5% | 17.5% | 26% |
| Ethanol | 35% | 55% | 47% |
| Butane | 0% | 0% | 11% |

**CHART 10–3**

P-series fuel varies in composition, depending on the octane rating and temperature.

hydrogen fuel) to convert coal and other hydrocarbons to liquid fuels in a process similar to hydrogenation, another method for hydrocarbon conversion. The process using natural gas, also called **gas-to-liquid (GTL)** technology, uses a catalyst, usually iron or cobalt, and incorporates steam reforming to give off the by-products of carbon dioxide, hydrogen, and carbon monoxide. ● SEE FIGURE 10–31.

Whereas traditional fuels emit environmentally harmful particulates and chemicals, namely sulfur compounds, Fischer-Tropsch fuels combust with no soot or odors and emit only low levels of toxins. Fischer-Tropsch fuels can also be blended with traditional transportation fuels with little equipment modification, as they use the same engine and equipment technology as traditional fuels.

The fuels contain a very low sulfur and aromatic content and they produce virtually no particulate emissions. Researchers also expect reductions in hydrocarbon and carbon monoxide emissions. Fischer-Tropsch fuels do not differ in fuel performance from gasoline and diesel. At present, Fischer-Tropsch fuels are very expensive to produce on a large scale, although research is under way to lower processing costs. Diesel fuel created using the **Fischer-Tropsch diesel (FTD)** process is often called GTL diesel. GTL diesel can also be combined with petroleum diesel to produce a GTL blend. This fuel product is currently being sold in Europe and plans are in place to introduce it in North America.

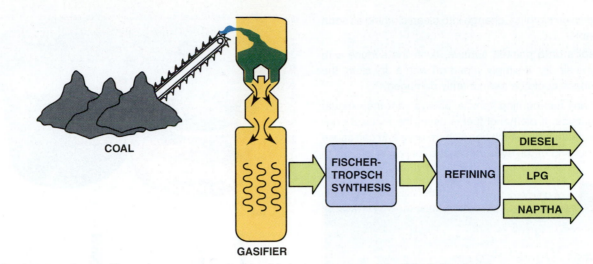

**FIGURE 10–31** A Fischer-Tropsch processing plant is able to produce a variety of fuels from coal.

**COAL TO LIQUID** Coal is very abundant in the United States and can be converted to a liquid fuel through a process called **coal to liquid (CTL).** The huge cost of processing is the main obstacle to this type of fuel. The need to invest $1.4 billion per plant before it can make product is the reason no one has built a CTL plant yet in the United States. Investors need to be convinced that the cost of oil is going to remain high in order to get them to commit this kind of money.

A large plant might be able to produce 120,000 barrels of liquid fuel a day and would consume about 50,000 tons of coal per day. However, such a plant would create about 6,000 tons of $CO_2$ per day, which could contribute to global warming. With this factor and with the costs involved, CTL technology is not likely to expand.

Despite the limitations, two procedures can be used to convert CTL fuel.

1. **Direct method.** In the direct method, coal is broken down to create liquid products. First the coal is reacted with hydrogen ($H_2$) at high temperatures and pressure with a catalyst. This process creates a synthetic crude, called **syncrude,** which is then refined to produce gasoline or diesel fuel.

2. **Indirect method.** In the indirect method, coal is first turned into a gas and the molecules are reassembled to create the desired product. This process involves turning coal into syngas, which is then converted into liquid, using the Fischer-Tropsch (FTD) process.

Russia has been using CTL by injecting air into the underground coal seams. Ignition is provided and the resulting gases are trapped and converted to liquid gasoline and diesel fuel through the Fischer-Tropsch process. This underground method is called **underground coal gasification (UCG).**

**METHANOL TO GASOLINE** Exxon Mobil has developed a process for converting methanol (methyl alcohol) into gasoline in a process called **methanol to gasoline (MTG).** The MTG process was discovered by accident when a gasoline additive

made from methanol was being created. The process instead created olefins (alkenes), paraffins (alkenes), and aromatic compounds, which in combination are known as gasoline. The process uses a catalyst and is currently being produced in New Zealand.

**FUTURE OF SYNTHETIC FUELS** Producing gasoline and diesel fuels by other methods besides refining from crude oil has usually been more expensive. With the increasing cost of crude oil, alternative methods are now becoming economically feasible. Whether the diesel fuel or gasoline is created from coal, natural gas, or methanol, or created by refining crude oil, the transportation and service pumps are already in place. Compared to using compressed natural gas or other similar alternative fuels, synthetic fuels represent the lowest cost.

## SAFETY PROCEDURES WHEN WORKING WITH ALTERNATIVE FUELS

All fuels are flammable and many are explosive under certain conditions. Whenever working around compressed gases of any kind (CNG, LNG, propane, or LPG), always wear personal protective equipment (PPE), including at least the following items.

1. Safety glasses and/or face shield

2. Protective gloves

3. Long-sleeve shirt and pants, to help protect bare skin from the freezing effects of gases under pressure in the event that the pressure is lost

If a spill should occur, take the following actions.

4. If any fuel gets on the skin, the area should be washed immediately.

5. If fuel spills on clothing, change into clean clothing as soon as possible.

6. If fuel spills on a painted surface, flush the surface with water and air dry. If simply wiped off with a dry cloth, the paint surface could be permanently damaged.

7. As with any fuel-burning vehicle, always vent the exhaust to the outside. If methanol fuel is used, the exhaust contains formaldehyde, which has a sharp odor and can cause severe burning of the eyes, nose, and throat.

 **WARNING**

Do not smoke or have an open flame in the area when working around or refueling any vehicle.

(a)

# DIESEL FUEL

**FEATURES OF DIESEL FUEL** Diesel fuel must meet an entirely different set of standards than gasoline. Diesel fuel contains 12% more heat energy than the same amount of gasoline. The fuel in a diesel engine is not ignited with a spark, but is ignited by the heat generated b y high compression. The pressure of compression (400 to 700 PSI, or 2,800 to 4,800 kPa) generates temperatures of 1,200°F to 1,600°F (700°C to 900°C), which speeds the preflame reaction to start the ignition of fuel injected into the cylinder.

**DIESEL FUEL REQUIREMENTS** All diesel fuel must have the following characteristics.

- **Cleanliness.** It is imperative that the fuel used in a diesel engine be clean and free from water. Unlike the case with gasoline engines, the fuel is the lubricant and coolant for the diesel injector pump and injectors. Good-quality diesel fuel contains additives such as oxidation inhibitors, detergents, dispersants, rust preventatives, and metal deactivators.

- **Low-temperature fluidity.** Diesel fuel must be able to flow freely at all expected ambient temperatures. One specification for diesel fuel is its "pour point," which is the temperature below which the fuel would stop flowing.

- **Cloud point.** Another concern with diesel fuel at lower temperatures concerns **cloud point,** the low-temperature point when the waxes present in most diesel fuels tend to form crystals that can clog the fuel filter. Most diesel fuel suppliers distribute fuel with the proper pour point and cloud point for the climate conditions of the area.

**CETANE NUMBER** The cetane number for diesel fuel is the opposite of the octane number for gasoline. The **cetane number** is a measure of the ease with which the fuel can be ignited. The cetane rating of the fuel determines, to a great extent, its

(b)

**FIGURE 10–32** (a) Regular diesel fuel on the left has a clear or greenish tint, whereas fuel for off-road use is tinted red for identification. (b) This fuel pump in a farming area clearly states the red diesel fuel is for off-road use only.

ability to start the engine at low temperatures and to provide smooth warmup and even combustion. The cetane rating of diesel fuel should be between 45 and 50. The higher the cetane rating, the more easily the fuel is ignited.

**SULFUR CONTENT** The sulfur content of diesel fuel is very important to the life of the engine. Sulfur in the fuel creates sulfuric acid during the combustion process, which can damage engine components and cause piston ring wear. Federal regulations are getting extremely tight on sulfur content to less than 15 parts per million (PPM). High-sulfur fuel contributes to acid rain.

**DIESEL FUEL COLOR** Diesel fuel intended for use on the streets and highways is either clear or green. Diesel fuel to be used on farms and off-road use is dyed red. ● **SEE FIGURE 10–32.**

## GRADES OF DIESEL FUEL
ASTM also classifies diesel fuel by volatility (boiling range) into the following grades.

| | |
|---|---|
| Grade 1 | This grade of diesel fuel has the lowest boiling point and the lowest cloud and pour points, as well as a lower BTU content (less heat per pound of fuel). As a result, grade 1 is suitable for use during low-temperature (winter) operation. Grade 1 produces less heat per pound of fuel compared to grade 2, and may be specified for use in diesel engines involved in frequent changes in load and speed, such as those found in city buses and delivery trucks. |
| Grade 2 | This grade has a higher boiling point, cloud point, and pour point as compared with grade 1. It is usually specified where constant speed and high loads are encountered, such as in long-haul trucking and automotive diesel applications. |

**FIGURE 10–33** Testing the API viscosity of a diesel fuel sample using a hydrometer.

## DIESEL FUEL SPECIFIC GRAVITY TESTING
The density of diesel fuel should be tested whenever there is a driveability concern. The density or specific gravity of diesel fuel is measured in units of **API gravity,** which is an arbitrary scale expressing the gravity or density of liquid petroleum products devised jointly by the American Petroleum Institute and the National Bureau of Standards. The measuring scale is calibrated in terms of degrees API. Oil with the least specific gravity has the highest API gravity. The formula for determining API gravity is as follows:

$$\text{Degrees API gravity} = (141.5 \div \text{Specific gravity at } 60°F) - 131.5$$

The normal API gravity for grade 1 diesel fuel is 39 to 44 (typically 40). The normal API gravity for grade 2 diesel fuel is 30 to 39 (typically 35). A hydrometer calibrated in API gravity units should be used to test diesel fuel. ● **SEE FIGURE 10–33.**

## ULTRA-LOW-SULFUR DIESEL FUEL
Diesel fuel is used in diesel engines and is usually readily available throughout the United States, Canada, and Europe, where many more cars are equipped with diesel engines. Diesel engines manufactured to 2007 or newer standards must use **ultra-low-sulfur diesel (ULSD)** fuel containing less than 15 PPM of sulfur compared to the older, low-sulfur specification of 500 PPM. The purpose of the lower sulfur amount in diesel fuel is to reduce emissions of sulfur oxides (SOx) and particulate matter (PM) from heavy-duty highway engines and vehicles that use diesel fuel. The emission controls used on 2007 and newer diesel engines require the use of ULSD for reliable operation.

ULSD will eventually replace the current highway diesel fuel, low-sulfur diesel, which can have as much as 500 PPM of sulfur. ULSD is required for use in all model year 2007 and newer vehicles equipped with advanced emission control systems. ULSD looks lighter in color and has less smell than other diesel fuels.

## BIODIESEL

### DEFINITION OF BIODIESEL
**Biodiesel** is a domestically produced, renewable fuel that can be manufactured from vegetable oils, animal fats, or recycled restaurant greases. Biodiesel is safe, biodegradable, and reduces serious air pollutants such as particulate matter (PM), carbon monoxide, and hydrocarbons. Biodiesel is defined as mono-alkyl esters of long-chain fatty acids derived from vegetable oils or animal fats which conform to ASTM D6751 specifications for use in diesel engines. Biodiesel refers to the pure fuel before blending with diesel fuel. ● **SEE FIGURE 10–34.**

Biodiesel blends are denoted as BXX, with the "XX" representing the percentage of biodiesel contained in the blend (i.e., **B20** is 20% biodiesel, 80% petroleum diesel). Blends of 5% biodiesel with 95% petroleum diesel, called **B5,** can generally be used in unmodified diesel engines. Some diesel-powered

**FIGURE 10–34** A biodiesel pump decal indicating that the diesel fuel is ultra-low-sulfur diesel (ULSD) and must be used in 2007 and newer diesel vehicles.

vehicles can use B20 (20% biodiesel). Dodge, for example, allows the use of B5 in all diesel vehicles and B20 only if the optional additional fuel filter is installed. Biodiesel can also be used in its pure form (B100), but it may require certain engine modifications to avoid maintenance and performance problems and may not be suitable for wintertime use. Users should consult their engine warranty statement for more information on fuel blends of greater than 20% biodiesel.

In general, B20 costs 30 to 40 cents more per gallon than conventional diesel. Although biodiesel costs more than regular diesel fuel, often called **petrodiesel,** fleet managers can make the switch to alternative fuels without purchasing new vehicles, acquiring new spare parts inventories, rebuilding refueling stations, or hiring new service technicians.

### FEATURES OF BIODIESEL   Biodiesel has the following characteristics.

1. Purchasing biodiesel in bulk quantities decreases the cost of fuel.
2. Biodiesel maintains similar horsepower, torque, and fuel economy.
3. Biodiesel has a higher cetane number than conventional diesel, which increases the engine's performance.
4. Biodiesel has a high flash point and low volatility so it does not ignite as easily as petrodiesel, which increases the margin of safety in fuel handling. In fact, it degrades four times faster than petrodiesel and is not particularly soluble in water.

**? FREQUENTLY ASKED QUESTION**

**I Thought Biodiesel Was Vegetable Oil?**

Biodiesel is vegetable oil with the glycerin component removed by means of reacting the vegetable oil with a catalyst. The resulting hydrocarbon esters are 16 to 18 carbon atoms in length, almost identical to the petroleum diesel fuel atoms. This allows the use of biodiesel fuel in a diesel engine with no modifications needed. Biodiesel-powered vehicles do not need a second fuel tank, whereas vehicles powered with vegetable oil do.

There are three main types of fuel used in diesel engines.

- Petroleum diesel, a fossil hydrocarbon with a carbon chain length of about 16 carbon atoms
- Biodiesel, a hydrocarbon with a carbon chain length of 16 to 18 carbon atoms
- Vegetable oil, a triglyceride with a glycerin component joining three hydrocarbon chains of 16 to 18 carbon atoms each, called **straight vegetable oil (SVO)**

Other terms used when describing vegetable oil include:

- **Pure plant oil (PPO)**, a term most often used in Europe to describe SVO
- **Waste vegetable oil (WVO)**, which could include animal or fish oils from cooking
- **Used cooking oil (UCO)**, a term used when the oil may or may not be pure vegetable oil

Vegetable oil is not liquid enough at common ambient temperatures for use in a diesel engine fuel delivery system designed for the lower viscosity petroleum diesel fuel. Vegetable oil needs to be heated to obtain a similar viscosity to biodiesel and petroleum diesel. This means that a heat source needs to be provided before the fuel can be used in a diesel engine. This is achieved by starting on petroleum diesel or biodiesel fuel until the engine heat can be used to sufficiently warm a tank containing the vegetable oil. It also requires purging the fuel system of vegetable oil with petroleum diesel or biodiesel fuel prior to stopping the engine to avoid the vegetable oil thickening and solidifying in the fuel system away from the heated tank. The use of vegetable oil in its natural state does, however, eliminate the need to remove the glycerin component.

Many vehicle and diesel engine fuel system suppliers permit the use of biodiesel fuel that is certified as meeting testing standards. None permit the use of vegetable oil in its natural state.

5. It is nontoxic, which makes it safe to handle, transport, and store. Maintenance requirements for B20 vehicles and petrodiesel vehicles are the same.

6. Biodiesel acts as a lubricant, which can add to the life of the fuel system components.

**NOTE: For additional information on biodiesel and the locations where it can be purchased, visit www .biodiesel.org.**

## E-DIESEL FUEL

**DEFINITION**    E-diesel, also called **diesohol** outside of the United States, is standard No. 2 diesel fuel that contains up to 15% ethanol. While E-diesel can have up to 15% ethanol by volume, typical blend levels are from 8% to 10%.

**CETANE RATING OF E-DIESEL**    The higher the cetane number, the shorter the delay between injection and ignition. Normal diesel fuel has a cetane number of about 50. Adding 15% ethanol lowers the cetane number. To increase the cetane number back to that of conventional diesel fuel, a cetane-enhancing additive is added to E-diesel. The additive used to increase the cetane rating of E-diesel is ethylhexylnitrate or ditertbutyl peroxide.

E-diesel has better cold-flow properties than conventional diesel. The heat content of E-diesel is about 6% less than conventional diesel, but the particulate matter (PM) emissions are reduced by as much as 40%, carbon monoxide by 20%, and oxides of nitrogen (NOx) by 5%.

Currently, E-diesel is considered to be experimental and can be used legally in off-road applications or in mass-transit buses with EPA approval. For additional information, visit www.e-diesel.org.

**? FREQUENTLY ASKED QUESTION**

**What Are the Pump Nozzle Sizes?**
Unleaded gasoline nozzles are smaller than those used for diesel fuel to help prevent fueling errors. However, it is still possible to fuel a diesel vehicle with gasoline.
● **SEE CHART 10–4** for the sizes and colors used for fuel pump nozzles.

| Fuel | Nozzle Diameter | Pump Handle Color (Varies—no established standard) |
|------|-----------------|----------------------------------------------------|
| Gasoline | 13/16 in. (21 mm) | Black, red, white, green, or blue |
| E10 | 13/16 in. (21 mm) | Black, red, white, green, or blue |
| E85 | 13/16 in. (21 mm) | Yellow or black |
| Diesel fuel | 15/16 in. (24 mm) | Yellow, green, or black |
| Biodiesel | 15/16 in. (24 mm) | Green |
| Truckstop diesel | 1 1/14 or 1 1/2 in. (32 or 38 mm) | Varies |

**CHART 10–4**

Fuel pump nozzle size is standardized except for use by over-the-road truckstops where high fuel volumes and speedy refills require larger nozzle sizes compared to passenger vehicle filling station nozzles.

# TESTING FOR ALCOHOL CONTENT IN GASOLINE

**1** A fuel composition tester (SPX Kent-Moore J-44175) is the recommended tool to use to test the alcohol content of gasoline.

**2** This battery-powered tester uses light-emitting diodes (LEDs), meter lead terminals, and two small openings for the fuel sample.

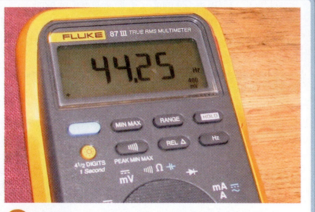

**3** The first step is to verify the proper operation of the tester by measuring the air frequency by selecting AC hertz on the meter. The air frequency should be between 35 Hz and 48 Hz.

**4** After verifying that the tester is capable of correctly reading the air frequency, gasoline is poured into the testing cell of the tool.

**5** Record the AC frequency as shown on the meter and subtract 50 from the reading (e.g., 60.50 − 50.00 = 10.5). This number (10.5) is the percentage of alcohol in the gasoline sample.

**6** Adding additional amounts of ethyl alcohol (ethanol) increases the frequency reading.

## SUMMARY

1. Gasoline is a complex blend of hydrocarbons. Gasoline is blended for seasonal usage to achieve the correct volatility for easy starting and maximum fuel economy under all driving conditions.

2. Winter-blend fuel used in a vehicle during warm weather can cause a rough idle and stalling because of its higher Reid vapor pressure (RVP).

3. Abnormal combustion (also called detonation or spark knock) increases both the temperature and the pressure inside the combustion chamber.

4. Most regular grade gasoline today, using the $(R + M) \div 2$ rating method, is 87 octane; midgrade (plus) is 89 and premium grade is 91 or higher.

5. Oxygenated fuels contain oxygen to lower CO exhaust emissions.

6. Flexible fuel vehicles (FFVs) are designed to operate on gasoline or gasoline-ethanol blends up to 85% ethanol (E85).

7. E85 has fewer BTUs of energy per gallon compared with gasoline and will therefore provide lower fuel economy.

8. Methanol is also called methyl alcohol or wood alcohol and, while it can be made from wood, it is mostly made from natural gas.

9. Propane is the most widely used alternative fuel. Propane is also called liquefied petroleum gas (LPG).

10. Compressed natural gas (CNG) is available for refilling in several pressures, including 2,400 PSI, 3,000 PSI, and 3,600 PSI.

11. Safety procedures when working around alternative fuel include wearing the necessary personal protective equipment (PPE), including safety glasses and protective gloves.

12. Diesel fuel requirements include cleanliness, low-temperature fluidity, and proper cetane rating.

13. Emission control devices used on 2007 and newer engines require the use of ultra-low-sulfur diesel (ULSD) that has less than 15 parts per million (PPM) of sulfur.

14. Biodiesel is the blend of vegetable-based liquid with regular diesel fuel. Most diesel engine manufacturers allow the use of a 5% blend, called B5, without any changes to the fuel system or engine.

## REVIEW QUESTIONS

1. What is the difference between summer-blend and winter-blend gasoline?

2. What is Reid vapor pressure?

3. What does the $(R + M) \div 2$ gasoline pump octane rating indicate?

4. What is stoichiometric?

5. How is a flexible fuel vehicle identified?

6. What other gases are often mixed with propane?

7. Why is it desirable to fill a compressed natural gas (CNG) vehicle with the highest pressure available?

8. P-series fuel is made of what products?

9. The Fischer-Tropsch method can be used to change what into gasoline?

10. Biodiesel blends are identified by what designation?

## CHAPTER QUIZ

1. Winter-blend gasoline _____.
   a. Vaporizes more easily than summer-blend gasoline
   b. Has a higher RVP
   c. Can cause engine driveability problems if used during warm weather
   d. All of the above

2. Technician A says that spark knock, ping, and detonation are different names for abnormal combustion. Technician B says that any abnormal combustion raises the temperature and pressure inside the combustion chamber and can cause severe engine damage. Which technician is correct?
   a. Technician A only
   b. Technician B only
   c. Both Technicians A and B
   d. Neither Technician A nor B

3. Technician A says that the research octane number is higher than the motor octane number. Technician B says that the octane rating posted on fuel pumps is an average of the two ratings. Which technician is correct?
   a. Technician A only
   b. Technician B only
   c. Both Technicians A and B
   d. Neither Technician A nor B

4. Technician A says that in going to high altitudes, engines produce lower power. Technician B says that most engine control systems can compensate the air-fuel mixture for changes in altitude. Which technician is correct?
   a. Technician A only
   b. Technician B only
   c. Both Technicians A and B
   d. Neither Technician A nor B

5. Which method of blending ethanol with gasoline is the most accurate?
   a. In-line
   b. Sequential
   c. Splash
   d. All of the above

6. What can be used to measure the alcohol content in gasoline?
   a. Graduated cylinder
   b. Electronic tester
   c. Scan tool
   d. Both a and b

7. E85 means that the fuel is made from _____.
   a. 85% gasoline and 15% ethanol
   b. 85% ethanol and 15% gasoline
   c. Ethanol that has 15% water
   d. Pure ethyl alcohol

8. A flex fuel vehicle can be identified by _____.
   a. Emblems on the side, front, and/or rear of the vehicle
   b. VECI
   c. VIN
   d. All of the above

9. When refueling a CNG vehicle, why is it recommended that the tank be filled to a high pressure?
   a. The range of the vehicle is increased.
   b. The cost of the fuel is lower.
   c. Less of the fuel is lost to evaporation.
   d. Both a and c

10. What color is diesel fuel dyed if it is for off-road use only?
    a. Red
    b. Green
    c. Blue
    d. Yellow

# chapter 11

# TEMPERATURE SENSORS

**OBJECTIVES:** After studying Chapter 11, the reader will be able to: • Prepare for ASE Engine Performance (A8) certification test content area "E" (Computerized Engine Controls Diagnosis and Repair). • Explain the purpose and function of the ECT and IAT temperature sensors. • Describe how to test temperature sensors. • Discuss how automatic transmission fluid temperature sensor values can affect transmission operation.

**KEY TERMS:** Cylinder head temperature (CHT) 173 • Engine coolant temperature (ECT) 165 • Engine fuel temperature (EFT) 173 • Negative temperature coefficient (NTC) 165 • Throttle-body temperature (TBT) 171 • Transmission fluid temperature (TFT) 172

## ENGINE COOLANT TEMPERATURE SENSORS

**PURPOSE AND FUNCTION** Computer-equipped vehicles use an **engine coolant temperature (ECT)** sensor. When the engine is cold, the fuel mixture must be richer to prevent stalling and engine stumble. When the engine is warm, the fuel mixture can be leaner to provide maximum fuel economy with the lowest possible exhaust emissions. Because the computer controls spark timing and fuel mixture, it will need to know the engine temperature. An engine coolant temperature sensor (ECT) screwed into the engine coolant passage will provide the computer with this information. ● SEE FIGURE 11–1. This will be the most important (high-authority) sensor while the engine is cold. The ignition timing can also be tailored to engine (coolant) temperature. A hot engine cannot have the spark timing as far advanced as can a cold engine. The ECT sensor is also used as an important input for the following:

- Idle air control (IAC) position
- Oxygen sensor closed-loop status
- Canister purge on/off times
- Idle speed

**ECT SENSOR CONSTRUCTION** Engine coolant temperature sensors are constructed of a semiconductor material that decreases in resistance as the temperature of the sensor increases. Coolant sensors have very high resistance when the coolant is cold and low resistance when the coolant is hot. This is referred to as having a **negative temperature coefficient (NTC),** which is opposite to the situation with most other electrical components. ● SEE FIGURE 11–2. Therefore, if the coolant sensor has a poor connection (high resistance) at the wiring connector, the

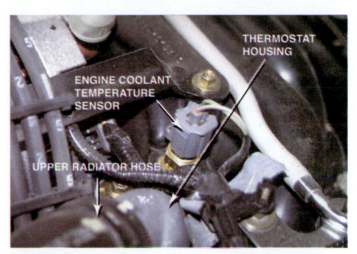

**FIGURE 11–1** A typical engine coolant temperature (ECT) sensor. ECT sensors are located near the thermostat housing on most engines.

computer will supply a richer-than-normal fuel mixture based on the resistance of the coolant sensor. Poor fuel economy and a possible-rich code can be caused by a defective sensor or high resistance in the sensor wiring. If the sensor was shorted or defective and had too low a resistance, a leaner-than-normal fuel mixture would be supplied to the engine. A too-lean fuel mixture can cause driveability problems and a possible-lean computer code.

**STEPPED ECT CIRCUITS** Some vehicle manufacturers use a step-up resistor to effectively broaden the range of the ECT sensor. Chrysler and General Motors vehicles use the same sensor as a non-stepped ECT circuit, but instead apply the sensor voltage through two different resistors.

- When the temperature is cold, usually below 120°F (50°C), the ECT sensor voltage is applied through a high-value resistor inside the PCM.

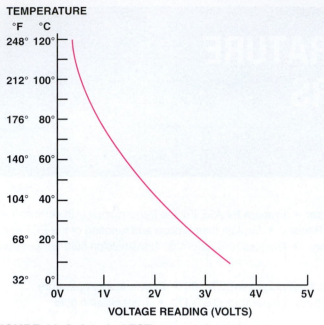

TEMPERATURE

VOLTAGE READING (VOLTS)

**FIGURE 11–2** A typical ECT sensor temperature versus voltage curve.

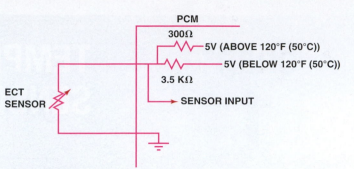

**FIGURE 11–3** A typical two-step ECT circuit showing that when the coolant temperature is low, the PCM applies a 5-volt reference voltage to the ECT sensor through a higher resistance compared to when the temperature is higher.

■ When the temperature is warm, usually above 120°F (50°C), the ECT sensor voltage is applied through a much lower resistance value inside the PCM. ● **SEE FIGURE 11–3.**

The purpose of this extra circuit is to give the PCM a more accurate reading of the engine coolant temperature compared to the same sensor with only one circuit. ● **SEE FIGURE 11–4.**

## TESTING THE ENGINE COOLANT TEMPERATURE SENSOR

**TESTING THE ENGINE COOLANT TEMPERATURE BY VISUAL INSPECTION** The correct functioning of the engine coolant temperature (ECT) sensor depends on the following items that should be checked or inspected:

■ **Properly filled cooling system.** Check that the radiator reservoir bottle is full and that the radiator itself is filled to the top.

**CAUTION: Be sure that the radiator is cool before removing the radiator cap to avoid being scalded by hot coolant.**

The ECT sensor must be submerged in coolant to be able to indicate the proper coolant temperature.

■ **Proper pressure maintained by the radiator cap.** If the radiator cap is defective and cannot allow the cooling system to become pressurized, air pockets could develop. These air pockets could cause the engine to operate at a hotter-than-normal temperature and prevent proper temperature measurement, especially if the air pockets occur around the sensor.

■ **Proper antifreeze–water mixture.** Most vehicle manufacturers recommend a 50/50 mixture of antifreeze and water as the best compromise between freezing protection and heat transfer ability.

■ **Proper operation of the cooling fan.** If the cooling fan does not operate correctly, the engine may overheat.

**TESTING THE ECT USING A MULTIMETER** Both the resistance (in ohms) and the voltage drop across the sensor can be measured and compared with specifications. ● **SEE FIGURE 11–5.** See the following charts showing examples of typical engine coolant temperature sensor specifications. Some vehicles use the PCM to attach another resistor in the ECT circuit to provide a more accurate measure of the engine temperature. ● **SEE FIGURE 11–6.**

If resistance values match the approximate coolant temperature and there is still a coolant sensor trouble code, the problem is generally in the wiring between the sensor and the computer. Always consult the manufacturers' recommended procedures for checking this wiring. If the resistance values do not match, the sensor may need to be replaced.

**General Motors ECT Sensor with Pull-up Resistor**

| °F | °C | Ohms | Voltage Drop Across Sensor |
|---|---|---|---|
| −40 | −40 | 100,000 + | 4.95 |
| 18 | −8 | 14,628 | 4.68 |
| 32 | 0 | 9,420 | 4.52 |
| 50 | 10 | 5,670 | 4.25 |
| 68 | 20 | 3,520 | 3.89 |
| 86 | 30 | 2,238 | 3.46 |
| 104 | 40 | 1,459 | 2.97 |
| 122 | 50 | 973 | 2.47 |
| 140 | 60 | 667 | 2.00 |
| 158 | 70 | 467 | 1.59 |
| 176 | 80 | 332 | 1.25 |
| 194 | 90 | 241 | 0.97 |
| 212 | 100 | 177 | 0.75 |

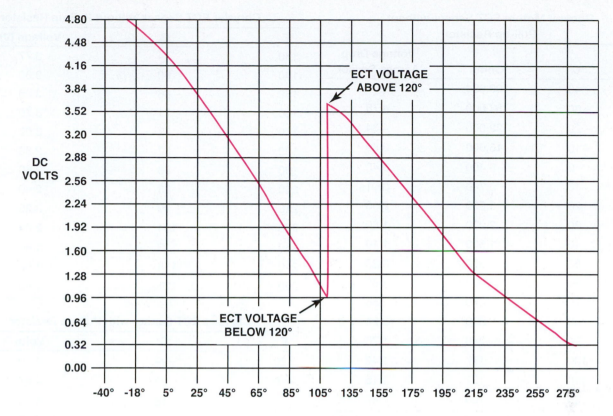

**FIGURE 11–4** The transition between steps usually occurs at a temperature that would not interfere with cold engine starts or the cooling fan operation. In this example, the transition occurs when the sensor voltage is about 1 volt and rises to about 3.6 volts.

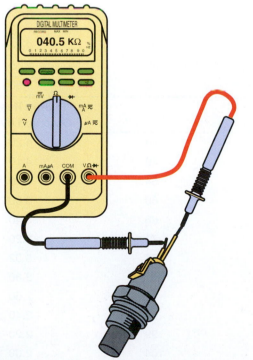

**FIGURE 11–5** Measuring the resistance of the ECT sensor. The resistance measurement can then be compared with specifications. *(Courtesy of Fluke Corporation)*

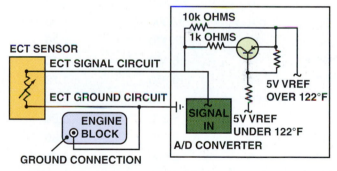

**FIGURE 11–6** When the voltage drop reaches approximately 1.20 volts, the PCM turns on a transistor. The transistor connects a 1-kΩ resistor in parallel with the 10-kΩ resistor. Total circuit resistance now drops to around 909 ohms. This function allows the PCM to have full binary control at cold temperatures up to approximately 122°F, and a second full binary control at temperatures greater than 122°F.

## General Motors ECT Sensor without Pull-up Resistor

| °F | °C | Ohms | Voltage Drop Across Sensor |
|---|---|---|---|
| −40 | −40 | 100,000 | 5 |
| −22 | −30 | 53,000 | 4.78 |
| −4 | −20 | 29,000 | 4.34 |
| 14 | −10 | 16,000 | 3.89 |
| 32 | 0 | 9,400 | 3.45 |
| 50 | 10 | 5,700 | 3.01 |
| 68 | 20 | 3,500 | 2.56 |
| 86 | 30 | 2,200 | 1.80 |
| 104 | 40 | 1,500 | 1.10 |
| 122 | 50 | 970 | 3.25 |
| 140 | 60 | 670 | 2.88 |
| 158 | 70 | 470 | 2.56 |
| 176 | 80 | 330 | 2.24 |
| 194 | 90 | 240 | 1.70 |
| 212 | 100 | 177 | 1.42 |
| 230 | 110 | 132 | 1.15 |
| 248 | 120 | 100 | .87 |

## Ford ECT Sensor

| °F | °C | Resistance (Ω) | Voltage (V) |
|---|---|---|---|
| 50 | 10 | 58,750 | 3.52 |
| 68 | 20 | 37,300 | 3.06 |
| 86 | 30 | 24,270 | 2.26 |
| 104 | 40 | 16,150 | 2.16 |
| 122 | 50 | 10,970 | 1.72 |
| 140 | 60 | 7,600 | 1.35 |
| 158 | 70 | 5,370 | 1.04 |
| 176 | 80 | 3,840 | 0.80 |
| 194 | 90 | 2,800 | 0.61 |
| 212 | 100 | 2,070 | 0.47 |
| 230 | 110 | 1,550 | 0.36 |
| 248 | 120 | 1,180 | 0.28 |

## Chrysler ECT Sensor without Pull-up Resistor

| °F | °C | Voltage (V) |
|---|---|---|
| 130 | 54 | 3.77 |
| 140 | 60 | 3.60 |
| 150 | 66 | 3.40 |
| 160 | 71 | 3.20 |
| 170 | 77 | 3.02 |
| 180 | 82 | 2.80 |
| 190 | 88 | 2.60 |
| 200 | 93 | 2.40 |
| 210 | 99 | 2.20 |
| 220 | 104 | 2.00 |
| 230 | 110 | 1.80 |
| 240 | 116 | 1.62 |
| 250 | 121 | 1.45 |

## Chrysler ECT Sensor with Pull-up Resistor

| °F | °C | Volts |
|---|---|---|
| −20 | −29 | 4.70 |
| −10 | −23 | 4.57 |
| 0 | −18 | 4.45 |
| 10 | −12 | 4.30 |
| 20 | −7 | 4.10 |
| 30 | −1 | 3.90 |
| 40 | 4 | 3.60 |
| 50 | 10 | 3.30 |
| 60 | 16 | 3.00 |
| 70 | 21 | 2.75 |
| 80 | 27 | 2.44 |
| 90 | 32 | 2.15 |
| 100 | 38 | 1.83 |

|  |  | Pull-up Resistor Switched by PCM |
|---|---|---|
| 110 | 43 | 4.20 |
| 120 | 49 | 4.10 |
| 130 | 54 | 4.00 |
| 140 | 60 | 3.60 |
| 150 | 66 | 3.40 |
| 160 | 71 | 3.20 |
| 170 | 77 | 3.02 |
| 180 | 82 | 2.80 |
| 190 | 88 | 2.60 |
| 200 | 93 | 2.40 |
| 210 | 99 | 2.20 |
| 220 | 104 | 2.00 |
| 230 | 110 | 1.80 |
| 240 | 116 | 1.62 |
| 250 | 121 | 1.45 |

## Nissan ECT Sensor

| °F | °C | Resistance (Ω) |
|---|---|---|
| 14 | −10 | 7,000–11,400 |
| 68 | 20 | 2,100–2,900 |
| 122 | 50 | 680–1,000 |
| 176 | 80 | 260–390 |
| 212 | 100 | 180–200 |

## Mercedes ECT

| °F | °C | Voltage (DCV) |
|---|---|---|
| 60 | 20 | 3.5 |
| 86 | 30 | 3.1 |
| 104 | 40 | 2.7 |
| 122 | 50 | 2.3 |
| 140 | 60 | 1.9 |
| 158 | 70 | 1.5 |
| 176 | 80 | 1.2 |
| 194 | 90 | 1.0 |
| 212 | 100 | 0.8 |

## European Bosch ECT Sensor

| °F | °C | Resistance (Ω) |
|---|---|---|
| 32 | 0 | 6,500 |
| 50 | 10 | 4,000 |
| 68 | 20 | 3,000 |
| 86 | 30 | 2,000 |
| 104 | 40 | 1,500 |
| 122 | 50 | 900 |
| 140 | 60 | 650 |
| 158 | 70 | 500 |
| 176 | 80 | 375 |
| 194 | 90 | 295 |
| 212 | 100 | 230 |

## Honda ECT Sensor (Resistance Chart)

| °F | °C | Resistance (Ω) |
|---|---|---|
| 0 | −18 | 15,000 |
| 32 | 0 | 5,000 |
| 68 | 20 | 3,000 |
| 104 | 40 | 1,000 |
| 140 | 60 | 500 |
| 176 | 80 | 400 |
| 212 | 100 | 250 |

## Honda ECT Sensor (Voltage Chart)

| °F | °C | Voltage (V) |
|---|---|---|
| 0 | −18 | 4.70 |
| 10 | −12 | 4.50 |
| 20 | −7 | 4.29 |
| 30 | −1 | 4.10 |
| 40 | 4 | 3.86 |
| 50 | 10 | 3.61 |
| 60 | 16 | 3.35 |
| 70 | 21 | 3.08 |
| 80 | 27 | 2.81 |
| 90 | 32 | 2.50 |
| 100 | 38 | 2.26 |
| 110 | 43 | 2.00 |
| 120 | 49 | 1.74 |
| 130 | 54 | 1.52 |
| 140 | 60 | 1.33 |
| 150 | 66 | 1.15 |
| 160 | 71 | 1.00 |
| 170 | 77 | 0.88 |
| 180 | 82 | 0.74 |
| 190 | 88 | 0.64 |
| 200 | 93 | 0.55 |
| 210 | 99 | 0.47 |

Normal operating temperature varies with vehicle make and model. Some vehicles are equipped with a thermostat with an opening temperature of 180°F (82°C), whereas other vehicles use a thermostat that is 195°F (90°C) or higher. Before replacing the ECT sensor, be sure that the engine is operating at the temperature specified by the manufacturer. Most manufacturers recommend checking the ECT sensor after the cooling fan has cycled twice, indicating a fully warmed engine. To test for voltage at the ECT sensor, select DC volts on a digital meter and carefully back probe the sensor wire and read the voltage. ● SEE FIGURE 11–7.

## TESTING THE ECT SENSOR USING A SCAN TOOL

Follow the scan tool manufacturer's instructions and connect a scan tool to the data link connector (DLC) of the vehicle. Comparing the temperature of the engine coolant as displayed on a scan tool with the actual temperature of the engine is an excellent method to test an engine coolant temperature sensor.

REMARKS:
ECT Voltage
2001 Jeep Wrangler Warm-up Cycle
AUTO 202 - Fuel and Emissions Systems

SHOW DATA: ALL GRAPH VIEW: ALL

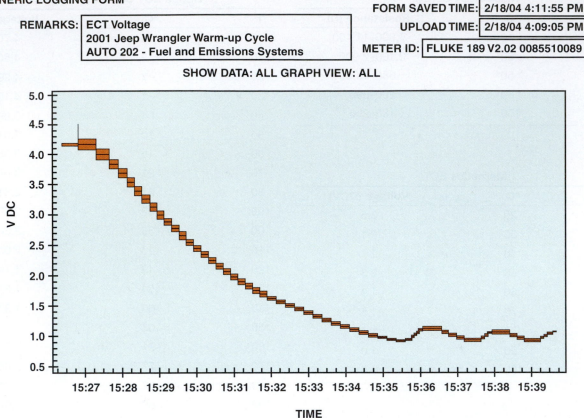

**FIGURE 11–7** An ECT sensor being tested using a digital meter set to DC volts. A chart showing the voltage decrease of the ECT sensor as the temperature increases from a cold start. The bumps at the bottom of the waveform represent temperature decreases when the thermostat opens and is controlling coolant temperature.

1. Record the scan tool temperature of the coolant (ECT).
2. Measure the actual temperature of the coolant using an infrared pyrometer or contact-type temperature probe.

**NOTE: Often the coolant temperature gauge in the dash of the vehicle can be used to compare with the scan tool temperature. Although not necessarily accurate, it may help to diagnose a faulty sensor, especially if the temperature shown on the scan tool varies greatly from the temperature indicated on the dash gauge.**

The maximum difference between the two readings should be 10°F (5°C). If the actual temperature varies by more than 10°F from the temperature indicated on the scan tool, check the ECT sensor wiring and connector for damage or corrosion. If the connector and wiring are okay, check the sensor with a DVOM for resistance and compare to the actual engine temperature chart. If that checks out okay, check the computer.

**NOTE: Some manufacturers use two coolant sensors, one for the dash gauge and another one for the computer.**

## INTAKE AIR TEMPERATURE SENSOR

**PURPOSE AND FUNCTION** The intake air temperature (IAT) sensor is a negative temperature coefficient (NTC) thermistor that decreases in resistance as the temperature of the sensor increases. The IAT sensor can be located in one of the following locations:

- In the air cleaner housing
- In the air duct between the air filter and the throttle body, as shown in ● **FIGURE 11–8**
- Built into the mass air flow (MAF) or airflow sensor
- Screwed into the intake manifold where it senses the temperature of the air entering the cylinders

**NOTE: An IAT installed in the intake manifold is the most likely to suffer damage due to an engine backfire, which can often destroy the sensor.**

The purpose and function of the intake air temperature sensor is to provide the engine computer (PCM) the temperature

**FIGURE 11–8** The IAT sensor on this General Motors 3800 V-6 engine is in the air passage duct between the air cleaner housing and the throttle body.

of the air entering the engine. The IAT sensor information is used for fuel control (adding or subtracting fuel) and spark timing, depending on the temperature of incoming air.

- If the air temperature is cold, the PCM will modify the amount of fuel delivery and add fuel.
- If the air temperature is hot, the PCM will subtract the calculated amount of fuel.
- Spark timing is also changed, depending on the temperature of the air entering the engine. The timing is advanced if the temperature is cold and retarded from the base-programmed timing if the temperature is hot.
- Cold air is more dense, contains more oxygen, and therefore requires a richer mixture to achieve the proper air–fuel mixture. Air at 32°F (0°C) is 14% denser than air at 100°F (38°C).
- Hot air is less dense, contains less oxygen, and therefore requires less fuel to achieve the proper air–fuel mixture.

The IAT sensor is a low-authority sensor and is used by the computer to modify the amount of fuel and ignition timing as determined by the engine coolant temperature sensor.

The IAT sensor is used by the PCM as a backup in the event that the ECT sensor is determined to be inoperative.

**NOTE: Some engines use a throttle-body temperature (TBT) sensor to sense the temperature of the air entering the engine, instead of an intake air temperature sensor.**

Engine temperature is most accurately determined by looking at the engine coolant temperature (ECT) sensor. In certain conditions, the IAT has an effect on performance

---

## TECH TIP

### Quick and Easy ECT Test

To check that the wiring and the computer are functioning, regarding the ECT sensor, connect a scan tool and look at the ECT temperature display.

**STEP 1** Unplug the connector from the ECT sensor. The temperature displayed on the scan tool should read about −40.

> **NOTE: −40° Celsius is also −40° Fahrenheit. This is the point where both temperature scales meet.**

**STEP 2** With the connector still removed from the ECT sensor, use a fused jumper lead and connect the two terminals of the connector together. The scan tool should display about 285°F (140°C).

This same test procedure will work for the IAT and most other temperature sensors.

---

## TECH TIP

### Poor Fuel Economy? Black Exhaust Smoke? Look at the IAT

If the intake air temperature sensor is defective, it may be signaling the computer that the intake air temperature is extremely cold when in fact it is warm. In such a case the computer will supply a mixture that is much richer than normal.

If a sensor is physically damaged or electrically open, the computer will often set a diagnostic trouble code (DTC). This DTC is based on the fact that the sensor temperature did not change for a certain amount of time, usually about 8 minutes. If, however, the wiring or the sensor itself has excessive resistance, a DTC will not be set and the result will be lower-than-normal fuel economy, and in serious cases, black exhaust smoke from the tailpipe during acceleration.

---

and driveability. One such condition is a warm engine being stopped in very cold weather. In this case, when the engine is restarted, the ECT may be near normal operating temperature such as 200°F (93°C) yet the air temperature could be −20°F (−30°C). In this case, the engine requires a richer mixture due to the cold air than the ECT would seem to indicate.

# TESTING THE INTAKE AIR TEMPERATURE SENSOR

If the intake air temperature sensor circuit is damaged or faulty, a diagnostic trouble code (DTC) is set and the malfunction indicator lamp (MIL) may or may not turn on depending on the condition and the type and model of the vehicle. To diagnose the IAT sensor follow these steps:

**STEP 1** After the vehicle has been allowed to cool for several hours, use a scan tool, observe the IAT temperature on a scan tool and compare it to the engine coolant temperature (ECT). The two temperatures should be within 5°F of each other.

**STEP 2** Perform a thorough visual inspection of the sensor and the wiring. If the IAT is screwed into the intake manifold, remove the sensor and check for damage.

**STEP 3** Check the voltage and compare to the following chart.

### Intake Air Temperature Sensor Temperature vs. Resistance and Voltage Drop (Approximate)

| °F | °C | Ohms | Voltage Drop Across the Sensor |
|---|---|---|---|
| −40 | −40 | 100,000 | 4.95 |
| +18 | −8 | 15,000 | 4.68 |
| 32 | 0 | 9,400 | 4.52 |
| 50 | 10 | 5,700 | 4.25 |
| 68 | 20 | 3,500 | 3.89 |
| 86 | 30 | 2,200 | 3.46 |
| 104 | 40 | 1,500 | 2.97 |
| 122 | 50 | 1,000 | 2.47 |
| 140 | 60 | 700 | 2.00 |
| 158 | 70 | 500 | 1.59 |
| 176 | 80 | 300 | 1.25 |
| 194 | 90 | 250 | 0.97 |
| 212 | 100 | 200 | 0.75 |

# TRANSMISSION FLUID TEMPERATURE SENSOR

The **transmission fluid temperature (TFT),** also called *transmission oil temperature (TOT),* sensor is an important sensor for the proper operation of the automatic transmission. A TFT sensor is a negative temperature coefficient (NTC) thermistor that decreases in resistance as the temperature of the sensor increases.

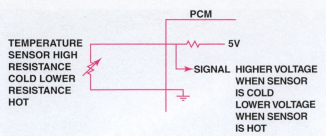

**FIGURE 11–9** A typical temperature sensor circuit.

**What Exactly Is an NTC Sensor?**

A negative temperature coefficient (NTC) thermistor is a semiconductor whose resistance decreases as the temperature increases. In other words, the sensor becomes more electrically conductive as the temperature increases. Therefore, when a voltage is applied, typically 5 volts, the signal voltage is high when the sensor is cold because the sensor has a high resistance and little current flows through to ground. ● SEE FIGURE 11–9.

However, when the temperature increases, the sensor becomes more electrically conductive and takes more of the 5 volts to ground, resulting in a lower signal voltage as the sensor warms.

### General Motors
*Transaxle Sensor—Temperature to Resistance (approximate)*

| °F | °C | Resistance Ohms |
|---|---|---|
| 32 | 0 | 7,987–10,859 |
| 50 | 10 | 4,934–6,407 |
| 68 | 20 | 3,106–3,923 |
| 86 | 30 | 1,991–2,483 |
| 104 | 40 | 1,307–1,611 |
| 122 | 50 | 878–1,067 |
| 140 | 60 | 605–728 |
| 158 | 70 | 425–507 |
| 176 | 80 | 304–359 |
| 194 | 90 | 221–259 |
| 212 | 100 | 163–190 |

## Chrysler
### Sensor Resistance (Ohms)—Transmission Temperature Sensor

| °F | °C | Resistance Ohms |
|---|---|---|
| −40 | −40 | 291,490–381,710 |
| −4 | −20 | 85,850–108,390 |
| 14 | −10 | 49,250–61,430 |
| 32 | 0 | 29,330–35,990 |
| 50 | 10 | 17,990–21,810 |
| 68 | 20 | 11,370–13,610 |
| 77 | 25 | 9,120–10,880 |
| 86 | 30 | 7,370–8,750 |
| 104 | 40 | 4,900–5,750 |
| 122 | 50 | 3,330–3,880 |
| 140 | 60 | 2,310–2,670 |
| 158 | 70 | 1,630–1,870 |
| 176 | 80 | 1,170–1,340 |
| 194 | 90 | 860–970 |
| 212 | 100 | 640–720 |
| 230 | 110 | 480–540 |
| 248 | 120 | 370–410 |

## Ford
### Transmission Fluid Temperature

| °F | °C | Resistance Ohms |
|---|---|---|
| −40 to −4 | −40 to −20 | 967K–284K |
| −3 to 31 | −19 to −1 | 284K–100K |
| 32 to 68 | 0 to 20 | 100K–37K |
| 69 to 104 | 21 to 40 | 37K–16K |
| 105 to 158 | 41 to 70 | 16K–5K |
| 159 to 194 | 71 to 90 | 5K–2.7K |
| 195 to 230 | 91 to 110 | 2.7K–1.5K |
| 231 to 266 | 111 to 130 | 1.5K–0.8K |
| 267 to 302 | 131 to 150 | 0.8K–0.54K |

The transmission fluid temperature signal is used by the Powertrain Control Module (PCM) to perform certain strategies based on the temperature of the automatic transmission fluid. For example:

- If the temperature of the automatic transmission fluid is low (typically below 32°F [0°C]), the shift points may be delayed and overdrive disabled. The torque converter clutch also may not be applied to assist in the heating of the fluid.

- If the temperature of the automatic transmission fluid is high (typically above 260°F [130°C]), the overdrive is disabled and the torque converter clutch is applied to help reduce the temperature of the fluid.

**NOTE: Check service information for the exact shift strategy based on high and low transmission fluid temperatures for the vehicle being serviced.**

## CYLINDER HEAD TEMPERATURE SENSOR

Some vehicles are equipped with **cylinder head temperature (CHT)** sensors.

**VW Golf**

$$14°F\ (−10°C) = 11{,}600\ \Omega$$
$$68°F\ (20°C) = 2{,}900\ \Omega$$
$$176°F\ (80°C) = 390\ \Omega$$

## ENGINE FUEL TEMPERATURE (EFT) SENSOR

Some vehicles, such as many Ford vehicles that are equipped with an electronic returnless type of fuel injection, use an **engine fuel temperature (EFT)** sensor to give the PCM information regarding the temperature and, therefore, the density of the fuel.

## EXHAUST GAS RECIRCULATION (EGR) TEMPERATURE SENSOR

Some engines, such as Toyota, are equipped with exhaust gas recirculation (EGR) temperature sensors. EGR is a well-established method for reduction of $NO_x$ emissions in internal combustion engines. The exhaust gas contains unburned hydrocarbons, which are recirculated in the combustion process. Recirculation is controlled by valves, which operate as a function of exhaust gas speed, load, and temperature. The gas reaches a temperature of about 850°F (450°C) for which a special heavy-duty glass-encapsulated NTC sensor is available.

The PCM monitors the temperature in the exhaust passage between the EGR valve and the intake manifold. If the temperature increases when the EGR is commanded on, the PCM can determine that the valve or related components are functioning.

# ENGINE OIL TEMPERATURE SENSOR

Engine oil temperature sensors are used on many General Motors vehicles and are used as an input to the oil life monitoring system. The computer program inside the PCM calculates engine oil life based on run time, engine RPM, and oil temperature.

# TEMPERATURE SENSOR DIAGNOSTIC TROUBLE CODES

The OBD-II diagnostic trouble codes that relate to temperature sensors include both high- and low-voltage codes, as well as intermittent codes.

| Diagnostic Trouble Code | Description | Possible Causes |
|---|---|---|
| P0112 | IAT sensor low voltage | • IAT sensor internally shorted-to-ground<br>• IAT sensor wiring shorted-to-ground<br>• IAT sensor damaged by backfire (usually associated with IAT sensors that are mounted in the intake manifold)<br>• Possible defective PCM |
| P0113 | IAT sensor high voltage | • IAT sensor internally (electrically) open<br>• IAT sensor signal, circuit, or ground circuit open<br>• Possible defective PCM |
| P0117 | ECT sensor low voltage | • ECT sensor internally shorted-to-ground<br>• The ECT sensor circuit wiring shorted-to-ground<br>• Possible defective PCM |
| P0118 | ECT sensor high voltage | • ECT sensor internally (electrically) open<br>• ECT sensor signal, circuit, or ground circuit open<br>• Engine operating in an overheated condition<br>• Possible defective PCM |

# SUMMARY

1. The ECT sensor is a high-authority sensor at engine start-up and is used for closed-loop control, as well as idle speed.

2. All temperature sensors decrease in resistance as the temperature increases. This is called negative temperature coefficient (NTC).

3. The ECT and IAT sensors can be tested visually, as well as by using a digital multimeter or a scan tool.

4. Some vehicle manufacturers use a stepped ECT circuit inside the PCM to broaden the accuracy of the sensor.

5. Other temperature sensors include transmission fluid temperature (TFT), engine fuel temperature (EFT), exhaust gas recirculation (EGR) temperature, and engine oil temperature.

# REVIEW QUESTIONS

1. How does a typical NTC temperature sensor work?

2. What is the difference between a stepped and a non-stepped ECT circuit?

3. What temperature should be displayed on a scan tool if the ECT sensor is unplugged with the key on, engine off?

4. What are the three ways that temperature sensors can be tested?

5. If the transmission fluid temperature (TFT) sensor were to fail open (as if it were unplugged), what would the PCM do to the transmission shifting points?

1. The sensor that most determines fuel delivery when a fuel-injected engine is first started is the _____.
   a. O2S
   b. ECT sensor
   c. Engine MAP sensor
   d. IAT sensor

2. What happens to the voltage measured at the ECT sensor when the thermostat opens?
   a. Increases slightly
   b. Increases about 1 volt
   c. Decreases slightly
   d. Decreases about 1 volt

3. Two technicians are discussing a stepped ECT circuit. Technician A says that the sensor used for a stepped circuit is different than one used in a non-stepped circuit. Technician B says that a stepped ECT circuit uses different internal resistance inside the PCM. Which technician is correct?
   a. Technician A only
   b. Technician B only
   c. Both Technicians A and B
   d. Neither Technician A nor B

4. When testing an ECT sensor on a vehicle, a digital multimeter can be used and the signal wires back probed. What setting should the technician use to test the sensor?
   a. AC volts
   b. DC volts
   c. Ohms
   d. Hz (hertz)

5. When testing the ECT sensor with the connector disconnected, the technician should select what position on the DMM?
   a. AC volts
   b. DC volts
   c. Ohms
   d. Hz (hertz)

6. When checking the ECT sensor with a scan tool, about what temperature should be displayed if the connector is removed from the sensor with the key on, engine off?
   a. 284°F (140°C)
   b. 230°F (110°C)
   c. 120°F (50°C)
   d. −40°F (−40°C)

7. Two technicians are discussing the IAT sensor. Technician A says that the IAT sensor is more important to the operation of the engine (higher authority) than the ECT sensor. Technician B says that the PCM will add fuel if the IAT indicates that the incoming air temperature is cold. Which technician is correct?
   a. Technician A only
   b. Technician B only
   c. Both Technicians A and B
   d. Neither Technician A nor B

8. A typical IAT or ECT sensor reads about 3,000 ohms when tested using a DMM. This resistance represents a temperature of about _____.
   a. −40°F (−40°C)
   b. 70°F (20°C)
   c. 120°F (50°C)
   d. 284°F (140°C)

9. If the transmission fluid temperature (TFT) sensor indicates cold automatic transmission fluid temperature, what would the PCM do to the shifts?
   a. Normal shifts and normal operation of the torque converter clutch
   b. Disable torque converter clutch; normal shift points
   c. Delayed shift points and torque converter clutch disabled
   d. Normal shifts but overdrive will be disabled

10. A P0118 DTC is being discussed. Technician A says that the ECT sensor could be shorted internally. Technician B says that the signal wire could be open. Which technician is correct?
    a. Technician A only
    b. Technician B only
    c. Both Technicians A and B
    d. Neither Technician A nor B

# chapter 12

# THROTTLE POSITION (TP) SENSORS

**OBJECTIVES:** **After studying Chapter 12, the reader will be able to:** • Prepare for ASE Engine Performance (A8) certification test content area "E" (Computerized Engine Controls Diagnosis and Repair). • Discuss how throttle position sensors work. • List the methods that can be used to test TP sensors. • Describe the symptoms of a failed TP sensor. • List how the operation of the TP sensor affects vehicle operation. • Discuss TP sensor rationality tests.

**KEY TERMS:** Potentiometer 176 • Skewed 179 • Throttle position (TP) sensor 176

## THROTTLE POSITION SENSOR CONSTRUCTION

Most computer-equipped engines use a **throttle position (TP) sensor** to signal to the computer the position of the throttle.
● **SEE FIGURE 12–1**. The TP sensor consists of a **potentiometer,** a type of variable resistor.

**POTENTIOMETERS** A potentiometer is a variable-resistance sensor with three terminals. One end of the resistor receives reference voltage, while the other end is grounded. The third terminal is attached to a movable contact that slides across the resistor to vary its resistance. Depending on whether the contact is near the supply end or the ground end of the resistor, return voltage is high or low. ● **SEE FIGURE 12–2**.

Throttle position (TP) sensors are among the most common potentiometer-type sensors. The computer uses their input to determine the amount of throttle opening and the rate of change.

A typical sensor has three wires:

■ A 5-volt reference feed wire from the computer

■ Signal return (A ground wire back to the computer)

■ A voltage signal wire back to the computer; as the throttle is opened, the voltage to the computer changes

Normal throttle position voltage on most vehicles is about 0.5 volt at idle (closed throttle) and 4.5 volts at wide-open throttle (WOT).

**NOTE: The TP sensor voltage at idle is usually about 10% of the TP sensor voltage when the throttle is wide open, but can vary from as low as 0.3 volt to 1.2 volts, depending on the make and model of vehicle.**

**FIGURE 12–1** A typical TP sensor mounted on the throttle plate of this port-injected engine.

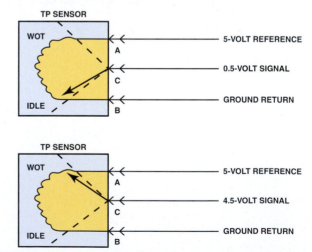

**FIGURE 12–2** The signal voltage from a throttle position increases as the throttle is opened because the wiper arm is closer to the 5-volt reference. At idle, the resistance of the sensor winding effectively reduces the signal voltage output to the computer.

# TP SENSOR COMPUTER INPUT FUNCTIONS

- The computer senses any change in throttle position and changes the fuel mixture and ignition timing. The actual change in fuel mixture and ignition timing is also partly determined by the other sensors, such as the manifold pressure (engine vacuum), engine RPM, the coolant temperature, and oxygen sensor(s). Some throttle position sensors are adjustable and should be set according to the exact engine manufacturer's specifications.

- The throttle position (TP) sensor used on fuel-injected vehicles acts as an "electronic accelerator pump." This means that the computer will pulse additional fuel from the injectors when the throttle is depressed. Because the air can quickly flow into the engine when the throttle is opened, additional fuel must be supplied to prevent the air–fuel mixture from going lean, causing the engine to hesitate when the throttle is depressed. If the TP sensor is unplugged or defective, the engine may still operate satisfactorily, but hesitate upon acceleration.

- The PCM supplies the TP sensor with a regulated voltage that ranges from 4.8 to 5.1 volts. This reference voltage is usually referred to as a 5-volt reference or "Vref." The TP output signal is an input to the PCM, and the TP sensor ground also flows through the PCM.

See the Ford throttle position (TP) sensor chart for an example of how sensor voltage changes with throttle angle.

### Ford Throttle Position (TP) Sensor Chart

| Throttle Angle (Degrees) | Voltage (V) |
| --- | --- |
| 0 | 0.50 |
| 10 | 0.97 |
| 20 | 1.44 |
| 30 | 1.90 |
| 40 | 2.37 |
| 50 | 2.84 |
| 60 | 3.31 |
| 70 | 3.78 |
| 80 | 4.24 |

**NOTE: Generally, any reading higher than 80% represents wide-open throttle to the computer.**

# PCM USES FOR THE TP SENSOR

The TP sensor is used by the Powertrain Control Module (PCM) for the following reasons.

**CLEAR FLOOD MODE** If the throttle is depressed to the floor during engine cranking, the PCM will either greatly reduce or entirely eliminate any fuel-injector pulses to aid in cleaning a flooded engine. If the throttle is depressed to the floor and the engine is not flooded with excessive fuel, the engine may not start.

**TORQUE CONVERTER CLUTCH ENGAGEMENT AND RELEASE** The torque converter clutch will be released if the PCM detects rapid acceleration to help the transmission deliver maximum torque to the drive wheels. The torque converter clutch is applied when the vehicle is lightly accelerating and during cruise conditions to help improve fuel economy.

**RATIONALITY TESTING FOR MAP AND MAF SENSORS** As part of the rationality tests for the MAP and/or MAF sensor, the TP sensor signal is compared to the reading from other sensors to determine if they match. For example, if the throttle position sensor is showing wide-open throttle (WOT), the MAP and/or MAF reading should also indicate that this engine is under a heavy load. If not, a diagnostic trouble code could be set for the TP, as well as the MAP and/or MAF sensors.

**AUTOMATIC TRANSMISSION SHIFT POINTS** The shift points are delayed if the throttle is opened wide to allow the engine speed to increase, thereby producing more power and aiding in the acceleration of the vehicle. If the throttle is barely open, the shift point occurs at the minimum speed designed for the vehicle.

**TARGET IDLE SPEED (IDLE CONTROL STRATEGY)** When the TP sensor voltage is at idle, the PCM then controls idle speed using the idle air control (IAC) and/or spark timing variation to maintain the commanded idle speed. If the TP sensor indicates that the throttle has moved off idle, fuel delivery and spark timing are programmed for acceleration. Therefore, if the throttle linkage is stuck or binding, the idle speed may not be correct.

**AIR-CONDITIONING COMPRESSOR OPERATION** The TP sensor is also used as an input sensor for air-conditioning compressor operation. If the PCM detects that the throttle is at or close to wide open, the air-conditioning compressor is disengaged.

**BACKS UP OTHER SENSORS** The TP sensor is used as a backup to the MAP sensor and/or MAF in the event the PCM detects that one or both are not functioning correctly. The PCM then calculates fuel needs and spark timing based on the engine speed (RPM) and throttle position.

FIGURE 12–3 A meter lead connected to a T-pin that was gently pushed along the signal wire of the TP sensor until the point of the pin touched the metal terminal inside the plastic connector.

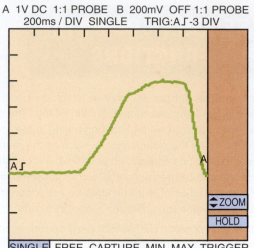

A 1V DC 1:1 PROBE   B 200mV OFF 1:1 PROBE
200ms / DIV SINGLE     TRIG:A⌐-3 DIV

SINGLE FREE CAPTURE MIN MAX TRIGGER
RECURRENT RUN 10 20 DIV ON A AT 50%

FIGURE 12–4 A typical waveform of a TP sensor signal as recorded on a DSO when the accelerator pedal was depressed with the ignition switch on (engine off). Clean transitions and the lack of any glitches in this waveform indicate a good sensor. *(Courtesy of Fluke Corporation)*

# TESTING THE THROTTLE POSITION SENSOR

A TP sensor can be tested using one or more of the following tools:

- A digital voltmeter with three test leads connected in series between the sensor and the wiring harness connector or back probing using T-pins or other recommended tool that will not cause harm to the connector or wiring.
- A scan tool or a specific tool recommended by the vehicle manufacturer.
- A breakout box that is connected in series between the computer and the wiring harness connector(s). A typical breakout box includes test points at which TP voltages can be measured with a digital voltmeter.
- An oscilloscope.

Use jumper wires, T-pins to back-probe the wires, or a breakout box to gain electrical access to the wiring to the TP sensor. ● SEE FIGURE 12–3.

NOTE: The procedure that follows is the usual method used by many manufacturers. Always refer to service information for the exact recommended procedure and specifications for the vehicle being tested.

The procedure for testing the sensor using a digital multimeter is as follows:

1. Turn the ignition switch on (engine off).
2. Set the digital meter to read to DC volts and measure the voltage between the signal wire and ground (reference low) wire. The voltage should be about 0.5 volt.

NOTE: Consult the service information for exact wire colors or locations.

3. With the engine still not running (but with the ignition still on), slowly increase the throttle opening. The voltage signal from the TP sensor should also increase. Look for any "dead spots" or open circuit readings as the throttle is increased to the wide-open position. ● SEE FIGURE 12–4 for an example of how a good TP sensor would look when tested with a digital storage oscilloscope (DSO).

NOTE: Use the accelerator pedal to depress the throttle because this applies the same forces on the TP sensor as the driver does during normal driving. Moving the throttle by hand under the hood may not accurately test the TP sensor.

4. With the voltmeter still connected, slowly return the throttle down to the idle position. The voltage from the TP sensor should also decrease evenly on the return to idle.

The TP sensor voltage at idle should be within the acceptable range as specified by the manufacturer. Some TP sensors can be adjusted by loosening their retaining screws and moving the sensor in relation to the throttle opening. This movement changes the output voltage of the sensor.

All TP sensors should also provide a smooth transition voltage reading from idle to WOT and back to idle. Replace the TP sensor if erratic voltage readings are obtained or if the correct setting at idle cannot be obtained.

**FIGURE 12-5** Checking the 5-volt reference from the computer being applied to the TP sensor with the ignition switch on (engine off). The reading for this vehicle (5.02 volts DC) is within the normal range for the five voltage reference voltage of 4.9 to 5.1 volts.

---

⚒ **TECH TIP**

### Check Power and Ground Before Condemning a Bad Sensor

Most engine sensors use a 5-volt reference and a ground. If the 5 volts to the sensor is too high (shorted to voltage) or too low (high resistance), then the sensor output will be **skewed** or out of range. Before replacing the sensor that did not read correctly, measure both the 5-volt reference and ground. To measure the ground, simply turn the ignition on (engine off) and touch one test lead of a DMM set to read DC volts to the sensor ground and the other to the negative terminal of the battery. Any reading higher than 0.2 volt (200 mV) represents a poor ground. ● **SEE FIGURES 12-5 AND 12-6.**

---

# TESTING A TP SENSOR USING THE MIN/MAX FUNCTION

Many digital multimeters are capable of recording voltage readings over time and then displaying the minimum, maximum, and average readings. To perform a MIN/MAX test of the TP sensor, manually set the meter to read higher than 4 volts.

**FIGURE 12-6** Checking the voltage drop between the TP sensor ground and a good engine ground with the ignition on (engine off). A reading of greater than 0.2 volt (200 mV) represents a bad computer ground.

**STEP 1** Connect the red meter lead to the signal wire and the black meter lead to a good ground or the ground return wire at the TP sensor.

**STEP 2** With the ignition on, engine off, slowly depress and release the accelerator pedal from inside the vehicle.

**STEP 3** Check the minimum and maximum voltage reading on the meter display. Any 0- or 5-volt reading would indicate a fault or short in the TP sensor.

---

# TESTING THE TP SENSOR USING A SCAN TOOL

A scan tool can be used to check for proper operation of the throttle position sensor using the following steps.

**STEP 1** With the key on, engine off, the TP sensor voltage display should be about 0.5 volt, but can vary from as low as 0.3 volt to as high as 1.2 volts.

**STEP 2** Check the scan tool display for the percentage of throttle opening. The reading should be zero and gradually increase in percentage as the throttle is depressed.

**STEP 3** The idle air control (IAC) counts should increase as the throttle is opened and decrease as the throttle is closed. Start the engine and observe the IAC counts as the throttle is depressed.

**STEP 4** Start the engine and observe the TP sensor reading. Use a wedge at the throttle stop to increase the throttle opening slightly. The throttle percentage reading should increase. Shut off and restart the engine. If the percentage of throttle opening returns to 0%, the PCM determines that the increased throttle opening is now the new minimum and resets the idle position of the TP sensor. Remove the wedge and cycle the ignition key. The throttle position sensor should again read zero percentage.

**NOTE:** Some engine computers are not capable of resetting the throttle position sensor.

# TP SENSOR DIAGNOSTIC TROUBLE CODES

The diagnostic trouble codes (DTCs) associated with the throttle position sensor include the following.

| Diagnostic Trouble Code | Description | Possible Causes |
|---|---|---|
| P0122 | TP sensor low voltage | • TP sensor internally shorted-to-ground<br>• TP sensor wiring shorted-to-ground<br>• TP sensor or wiring open |
| P0123 | TP sensor high voltage | • TP sensor internally shorted to 5-volt reference<br>• TP sensor ground open<br>• TP sensor wiring shorted-to-voltage |
| P0121 | TP sensor signal does not agree with MAP | • Defective TP sensor<br>• Incorrect vehicle-speed (VS) sensor signal<br>• MAP sensor out-of-calibration or defective |

## SUMMARY

1. A throttle position (TP) sensor is a three-wire variable resistor called a potentiometer.

2. The three wires on the TP sensor include a 5-volt reference voltage from the PCM, plus the signal wire to the PCM, and a ground, which also goes to the PCM.

3. The TP sensor is used by the PCM for clear flood mode, torque converter engagement and release, and automotive transmission shift points, as well as for rationality testing for the MAP and MAF sensors.

4. The TP sensor signal voltage should be about 0.5 volt at idle and increase to about 4.5 volts at wide-open throttle (WOT).

5. A TP sensor can be tested using a digital multimeter, a digital storage oscilloscope (DSO), or a scan tool.

## REVIEW QUESTIONS

1. What is the purpose of each of the three wires on a typical TP sensor?

2. What all does the PCM do with the TP sensor signal voltage?

3. What is the procedure to follow when checking the 5-volt reference and TP sensor ground?

4. How can a TP sensor be diagnosed using a scan tool?

## CHAPTER QUIZ

1. Which sensor is generally considered to be the electronic accelerator pump of a fuel-injected engine?
   a. O2S
   b. ECT sensor
   c. Engine MAP sensor
   d. TP sensor

2. Typical TP sensor voltage at idle is about _____.
   a. 2.50 to 2.80 volts
   b. 0.5 volt or 10% of WOT TP sensor voltage
   c. 1.5 to 2.8 volts
   d. 13.5 to 15.0 volts

3. A TP sensor is what type of sensor?
   a. Rheostat
   b. Voltage generating
   c. Potentiometer
   d. Piezoelectric

4. Most TP sensors have how many wires?
   a. 1
   b. 2
   c. 3
   d. 4

5. Which sensor does the TP sensor back up if the PCM determines that a failure has occurred?
   a. Oxygen sensor
   b. MAF sensor
   c. MAP sensor
   d. Either b or c

6. Which wire on a TP sensor should be back-probed to check the voltage signal to the PCM?
   a. 5-volt reference (Vref)
   b. Signal
   c. Ground
   d. Meter should be connected between the 5-volt reference and the ground

7. After a TP sensor has been tested using the MIN/MAX function on a DMM, a reading of zero volts is displayed. What does this reading indicate?
   a. The TP sensor is open at one point during the test.
   b. The TP sensor is shorted.
   c. The TP sensor signal is shorted to 5-volt reference.
   d. Both b and c are possible.

8. After a TP sensor has been tested using the MIN/MAX function on a DMM, a reading of 5 volts is displayed. What does this reading indicate?
   a. The TP sensor is open at one point during the test.
   b. The TP sensor is shorted.
   c. The TP sensor signal is shorted to 5-volt reference.
   d. Both b and c are possible.

9. A technician attaches one lead of a digital voltmeter to the ground terminal of the TP sensor and the other meter lead to the negative terminal of the battery. The ignition is switched to on, engine off and the meter displays 37.3 mV. Technician A says that this is the signal voltage and is a little low. Technician B says that the TP sensor ground circuit has excessive resistance. Which technician is correct?
   a. Technician A only
   b. Technician B only
   c. Both Technicians A and B
   d. Neither Technician A nor B

10. A P0122 DTC is retrieved using a scan tool. This DTC means _____.
    a. The TP sensor voltage is low
    b. The TP sensor could be shorted-to-ground
    c. The TP sensor signal circuit could be shorted-to-ground
    d. All of the above are correct.

# chapter 13

# MAP/BARO SENSORS

**OBJECTIVES:** **After studying Chapter 13, the reader will be able to:** • Prepare for ASE Engine Performance (A8) certification test content area "E" (Computerized Engine Controls Diagnosis and Repair). • Discuss how MAP sensors work. • List the methods that can be used to test MAP sensors. • Describe the symptoms of a failed MAP sensor. • List how the operation of the MAP sensor affects vehicle operation. • Discuss MAP sensor rationality tests. • Describe how the BARO sensor is used to determine altitude.

**KEY TERMS:** Barometric manifold absolute pressure (BMAP) sensor 187 • Barometric pressure (BARO) sensor 187 • Manifold absolute pressure (MAP) sensor 182 • Piezoresistivity 184 • Pressure differential 182 • Speed density 185 • Vacuum 182

## AIR PRESSURE—HIGH AND LOW

Think of an internal combustion engine as a big air pump. As the pistons move up and down in the cylinders, they pump in air and fuel for combustion and pump out exhaust gases. They do this by creating a difference in air pressure. The air outside an engine has weight and exerts pressure, as does the air inside an engine.

As a piston moves down on an intake stroke with the intake valve open, it creates a larger area inside the cylinder for the air to fill. This lowers the air pressure within the engine. Because the pressure inside the engine is lower than the pressure outside, air flows into the engine to fill the low-pressure area and equalize the pressure.

The low pressure within the engine is called **vacuum.** Vacuum causes the higher-pressure air on the outside to flow into the low-pressure area inside the cylinder. The difference in pressure between the two areas is called a **pressure differential.** ● SEE FIGURE 13–1.

## PRINCIPLES OF PRESSURE SENSORS

Intake manifold pressure changes with changing throttle positions. At wide-open throttle, manifold pressure is almost the same as atmospheric pressure. On deceleration or at idle, manifold pressure is below atmospheric pressure, thus creating a vacuum. In cases where turbo- or supercharging is used, under part- or full-load condition, intake manifold pressure rises above

atmospheric pressure. Also, oxygen content and barometric pressure change with differences in altitude, and the computer must be able to compensate by making changes in the flow of fuel entering the engine. To provide the computer with changing airflow information, a fuel-injection system may use the following:

- Manifold absolute pressure (MAP) sensor
- Manifold absolute pressure (MAP) sensor plus barometric absolute pressure (BARO) sensor
- Barometric and manifold absolute pressure sensors combined (BMAP)

The **manifold absolute pressure (MAP) sensor** may be a ceramic capacitor diaphragm, an aneroid bellows, or a piezoresistive crystal. It has a sealed vacuum reference input on one side; the other side is connected (vented) to the intake manifold. This sensor housing also contains signal conditioning circuitry. ● SEE FIGURE 13–2. Pressure changes in the manifold cause the sensor to deflect, varying its analog or digital return signal to the computer. As the air pressure increases, the MAP sensor generates a higher voltage or frequency return signal to the computer.

## CONSTRUCTION OF MANIFOLD ABSOLUTE PRESSURE (MAP) SENSORS

The manifold absolute pressure (MAP) sensor is used by the engine computer to sense engine load. The typical MAP sensor consists of a ceramic or silicon wafer sealed on one side with a perfect vacuum and exposed to intake manifold vacuum on the other side.

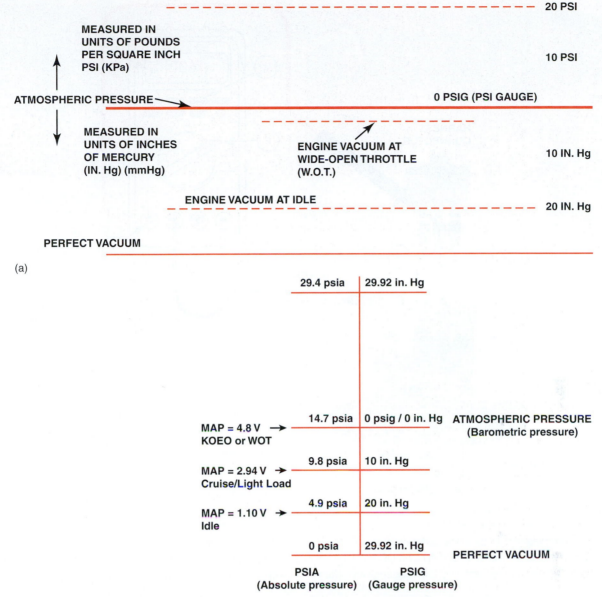

**FIGURE 13–1** (a) As an engine is accelerated under a load, the engine vacuum drops. This drop in vacuum is actually an increase in absolute pressure in the intake manifold. A MAP sensor senses all pressures greater than that of a perfect vacuum. (b) The relationship between absolute pressure, vacuum and gauge pressure.

**FIGURE 13–2** A clear plastic MAP sensor used for training purposes showing the electronic circuit board and electrical connections.

As the engine vacuum changes, the pressure difference on the wafer changes the output voltage or frequency of the MAP sensor.

A manifold absolute pressure (MAP) sensor is used on many engines for the PCM to determine the load on the engine.

The relationship among barometer pressure, engine vacuum, and MAP sensor voltage includes:

- Absolute pressure is equal to barometric pressure minus intake manifold vacuum.

- A decrease in manifold vacuum means an increase in manifold pressure.

- The MAP sensor compares manifold vacuum to a perfect vacuum.

- Barometric pressure minus MAP sensor reading equals intake manifold vacuum. Normal engine vacuum is 17–21 in. Hg.

- Supercharged and turbocharged engines require a MAP sensor that is calibrated for pressures above atmospheric, as well as for vacuum.

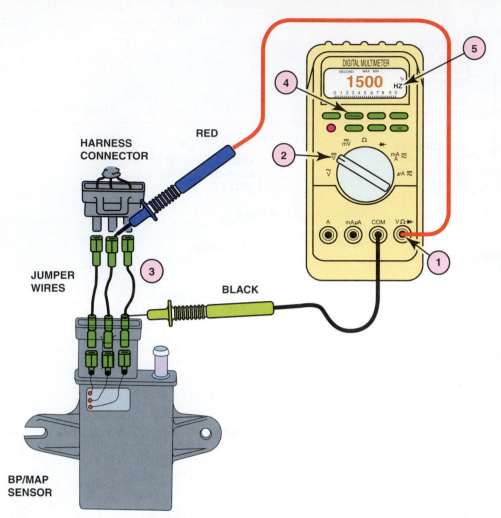

**FIGURE 13–3** MAP sensors use three wires: 1. 5-volt reference from the PCM 2. Sensor signal (output signal) 3. Ground. A DMM set to test a MAP sensor. (1) Connect the red meter lead to the V meter terminal and the black meter lead to the COM meter terminal. (2) Select DC volts. (3) Connect the test leads to the sensor signal wire and the ground wire. (4) Select hertz (Hz) if testing a MAP sensor whose output is a varying frequency; otherwise keep it on DC volts. (5) Read the change of voltage (frequency) as the vacuum is applied to the sensor. Compare the vacuum reading and the frequency (or voltage) reading to the specifications. *(Courtesy of Fluke Corporation)*

## SILICON-DIAPHRAGM STRAIN GAUGE MAP SENSOR

This is the most commonly used design for a MAP sensor and the output is a DC analog (variable) voltage. One side of a silicon wafer is exposed to engine vacuum and the other side is exposed to a perfect vacuum.

There are four resistors attached to the silicon wafer, which changes in resistance when strain is applied to the wafer. This change in resistance due to strain is called **piezoresistivity.** The resistors are electrically connected to a Wheatstone bridge circuit and then to a differential amplifier, which creates a voltage in proportion to the vacuum applied.

A typical General Motors MAP sensor voltage varies from 0.88 to 1.62 at engine idle.

- 17 in. Hg is equal to about 1.62 volts
- 21 in. Hg is equal to about 0.88 volts

Therefore, a good reading should be about 1.0 volt from the MAP sensor on a sound engine at idle speed. See the following chart that shows engine load, engine vacuum, and MAP.

| Engine Load | Manifold Vacuum | Manifold Absolute Pressure | MAP Sensor Volt Signal |
|---|---|---|---|
| Heavy (WOT) | Low (almost 0 in. Hg) | High (almost atmospheric) | High (4.6–4.8 V) |
| Light (idle) | High (17–21 in. Hg) | Low (lower than atmospheric) | Low (0.8–1.6 V) |

## CAPACITOR-CAPSULE MAP SENSOR
A capacitor-capsule is a type of MAP sensor used by Ford which uses two ceramic (alumina) plates with an insulating washer spacer in the center to create a capacitor. Changes in engine vacuum cause the plates to deflect, which changes the capacitance. The electronics in the sensor then generate a varying digital frequency output signal, which is proportional to the engine vacuum. ● SEE FIGURE 13–3. ● SEE FIGURE 13–4 for a scope waveform of a digital MAP sensor. Also see the Ford MAP sensor chart.

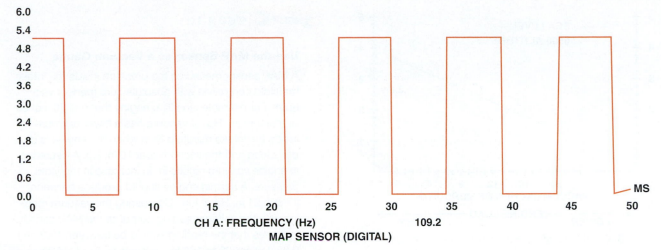

CH A: FREQUENCY (Hz)      109.2

MAP SENSOR (DIGITAL)

**FIGURE 13–4** A waveform of a typical digital MAP sensor.

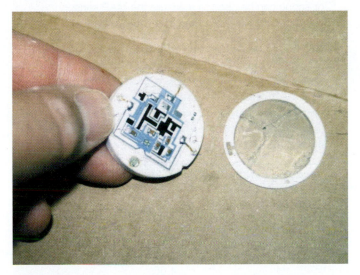

**FIGURE 13–5** Shown is the electronic circuit inside a ceramic disc MAP sensor used on many Chrysler engines. The black areas are carbon resistors that are applied to the ceramic, and lasers are used to cut lines into these resistors during testing to achieve the proper operating calibration.

### Ford MAP Sensor Chart

| MAP Sensor Output (Hz) | Engine Operating Conditions | Intake Manifold Vacuum (in. Hg) |
|---|---|---|
| 156–159 Hz | Key on, engine off | 0 in. Hg |
| 102–109 Hz | Engine at idle (sea level) | 17–21 in. Hg |
| 156–159 Hz | Engine at wide-open throttle (WOT) | About 0 in. Hg |

**CERAMIC DISC MAP SENSOR** The ceramic disc MAP sensor is used by Chrysler and it converts manifold pressure into a capacitance discharge. The discharge controls the amount of voltage delivered by the sensor to the PCM. The output is the same as the previously used strain gauge/Wheatstone bridge design and is interchangeable. ● **SEE FIGURE 13–5.** See the Chrysler MAP sensor chart.

### Chrysler MAP Sensor Chart

| Vacuum (in. Hg) | MAP Sensor Signal Voltage (V) |
|---|---|
| 0.5 | 4.8 |
| 1.0 | 4.6 |
| 3.0 | 4.1 |
| 5.0 | 3.8 |
| 7.0 | 3.5 |
| 10.0 | 2.9 |
| 15.0 | 2.1 |
| 20.0 | 1.2 |
| 25.0 | 0.5 |

## PCM USES OF THE MAP SENSOR

Engines that rely on calculating the amount of air entering the engine by using the MAP sensor to determine the amount of fuel required is called a **speed density** system. The PCM uses the MAP sensor to determine the following:

- **The load on the engine.** The MAP sensor is used on a speed density-type fuel-injection system to determine the load on the engine, and therefore the amount of fuel

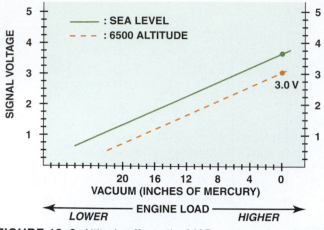

**FIGURE 13–6** Altitude affects the MAP sensor voltage.

needed. On engines equipped with a mass air flow (MAF) sensor, the MAP is used as a backup to the MAF, for diagnosis of other sensors, and systems such as the EGR system.

- **Altitude, fuel, and spark control calculations.** At key on, the MAP sensor determines the altitude (acts as a BARO sensor) and adjusts the fuel delivery and spark timing accordingly.

  - If the altitude is high, generally over 5,000 feet (1,500 meters), the PCM will reduce fuel delivery and advance the ignition timing.

  - The altitude is also reset when the engine is accelerated to wide-open throttle and the MAP sensor is used to reset the altitude reading. ● **SEE FIGURE 13–6.**

- **EGR system operation.** As part of the OBD-II standards, the exhaust gas recirculation (EGR) system must be checked for proper operation. One method used by many vehicle manufacturers is to command the EGR valve on and then watch the MAP sensor signal. The opening of the EGR pintle should decrease engine vacuum. If the MAP sensor does not react with the specified drop in manifold vacuum (increase in manifold pressure), an EGR flow rate problem diagnostic trouble code is set.

- **Detect deceleration (vacuum increases).** The engine vacuum rises when the accelerator is released, which changes the MAP sensor voltage. When deceleration is detected by the PCM, fuel is either stopped or greatly reduced to improve exhaust emissions.

- **Monitor engine condition.** As an engine wears, the intake manifold vacuum usually decreases. The PCM is programmed to detect the gradual change in vacuum and is able to keep the air–fuel mixture in the correct range. If the PCM were not capable of making adjustments for engine wear, the lower vacuum could be interpreted as increased load on the engine, resulting in too much fuel being injected, thereby reducing fuel economy and increasing exhaust emissions.

- **Load detection for returnless-type fuel injection.** On fuel delivery systems that do not use a return line back to the fuel tank, the engine load calculation for the fuel needed is determined by the signals from the MAP sensor.

- **Altitude and MAP sensor values.** On an engine equipped with a speed-density-type fuel injection, the MAP sensor is the most important sensor needed to determine injection pulse width. Variations in altitude and changes in the weather will cause the air density to change. Barometric pressure and altitude are inversely related:

  - As altitude increases—barometric pressure decreases
  - As altitude decreases—barometric pressure increases

As the ignition switch is turned from off to the start position, the PCM reads the MAP sensor value to determine atmospheric and air pressure conditions. This barometric pressure reading is updated every time the engine is started and whenever wide-open throttle is detected. The barometric pressure reading at that time is updated. See the chart that compares altitude to MAP sensor voltage.

### Altitude and MAP Sensor Voltage

| Altitude | MAP Sensor Voltage (key on, engine off) |
|---|---|
| Sea level | 4.6 to 4.8 volts |
| 2,500 (760 m) | 4.0 volts |
| 5,000 (1,520 m) | 3.7 volts |
| 7,500 (2,300 m) | 3.35 volts |
| 10,000 (3,050 m) | 3.05 volts |
| 12,500 (3,800 m) | 2.80 volts |
| 15,000 (4,600 m) | 2.45 volts |

# BAROMETRIC PRESSURE SENSOR

A **barometric pressure (BARO) sensor** is similar in design, but senses more subtle changes in barometric absolute pressure (atmospheric air pressure). It is vented directly to the atmosphere. The **barometric manifold absolute pressure (BMAP) sensor** is actually a combination of a BARO and MAP sensor in the same housing. The BMAP sensor has individual circuits to measure barometric and manifold pressure. This input not

REAL WORLD FIX

**The Cavalier Convertible Story**

The owner of a Cavalier convertible stated to a service technician that the "check engine" (MIL) was on. The technician found a diagnostic trouble code (DTC) for a MAP sensor. The technician removed the hose at the MAP sensor and discovered that gasoline had accumulated in the sensor and dripped out of the hose as it was being removed. The technician replaced the MAP sensor and test drove the vehicle to confirm the repair. Almost at once the check engine light came on with the same MAP sensor code. After several hours of troubleshooting without success in determining the cause, the technician decided to start over again. Almost at once, the technician discovered that no vacuum was getting to the MAP sensor where a vacuum gauge was connected with a T-fitting in the vacuum line to the MAP sensor. The vacuum port in the base of the throttle body was clogged with carbon. After a thorough cleaning, and clearing the DTC, the Cavalier again performed properly and the check engine light did not come on again. The technician had assumed that if gasoline was able to reach the sensor through the vacuum hose, surely vacuum could reach the sensor. The technician learned to stop assuming when diagnosing a vehicle and concentrate more on testing the simple things first.

only allows the computer to adjust for changes in atmospheric pressure due to weather, but also is the primary sensor used to determine altitude.

**NOTE: A MAP sensor and a BARO sensor are usually the same sensor, but the MAP sensor is connected to the manifold and a BARO sensor is open to the atmosphere. The MAP sensor is capable of reading barometric pressure just as the ignition switch is turned to the on position before the engine starts. Therefore, altitude and weather changes are available to the computer. During mountainous driving, it may be an advantage to stop and then restart the engine so that the engine computer can take another barometric pressure reading and recalibrate fuel delivery based on the new altitude. See the Ford/BARO altitude chart for an example of how altitude affects intake manifold pressure. The computer on some vehicles will monitor the throttle position sensor and use the MAP sensor reading at wide-open throttle (WOT) to update the BARO sensor if it has changed during driving.**

## Ford MAP/BARO Altitude Chart

| Altitude (feet) | Volts (V) |
|---|---|
| 0 | 1.59 |
| 1,000 | 1.56 |
| 2,000 | 1.53 |
| 3,000 | 1.50 |
| 4,000 | 1.47 |
| 5,000 | 1.44 |
| 6,000 | 1.41 |
| 7,000 | 1.39 |

**NOTE: Some older Chrysler brand vehicles were equipped with a combination BARO and IAT sensor. The sensor was mounted on the bulkhead (firewall) and sensed the underhood air temperature.**

# TESTING THE MAP SENSOR

Most pressure sensors operate on 5 volts from the computer and return a signal (voltage or frequency) based on the pressure (vacuum) applied to the sensor. If a MAP sensor is being tested, make certain that the vacuum hose and hose fittings are sound and making a good, tight connection to a manifold vacuum source on the engine.

Four different types of test instruments can be used to test a pressure sensor:

1. A digital voltmeter with three test leads connected in series between the sensor and the wiring harness connector or back-probe the terminals.

2. A scope connected to the sensor output, power, and ground.

3. A scan tool or a specific tool recommended by the vehicle manufacturer.

4. A breakout box connected in series between the computer and the wiring harness connection(s). A typical breakout box includes test points at which pressure sensor values can be measured with a digital voltmeter set on DC volts (or frequency counter, if a frequency-type MAP sensor is being tested).

**NOTE: Always check service information for the exact testing procedures and specifications for the vehicle being tested.**

## TESTING THE MAP SENSOR USING A DMM OR SCOPE

Use jumper wires, T-pins to back-probe the connector, or a breakout box to gain electrical access to the wiring to the pressure sensor. Most pressure sensors use three wires:

1. A 5-volt wire from the computer

2. A variable-signal wire back to the computer

3. A ground or reference low wire

The procedure for testing the sensor is as follows:

1. Turn the ignition on (engine off)

2. Measure the voltage (or frequency) of the sensor output

3. Using a hand-operated vacuum pump (or other variable vacuum source), apply vacuum to the sensor

A good pressure sensor should change voltage (or frequency) in relation to the applied vacuum. If the signal does not change or the values are out of range according to the manufacturers' specifications, the sensor must be replaced.

**TESTING THE MAP SENSOR USING A SCAN TOOL**   A scan tool can be used to test a MAP sensor by monitoring the injector pulse width (in milliseconds) when vacuum is being applied to the MAP sensor using a hand-operated vacuum pump. ● **SEE FIGURE 13–7.**

**STEP 1**   Apply about 20 in. Hg of vacuum to the MAP sensor and start the engine.

**STEP 2**   Observe the injector pulse width. On a warm engine, the injector pulse width will normally be 1.5 to 3.5 ms.

**STEP 3**   Slowly reduce the vacuum to the MAP sensor and observe the pulse width. A lower vacuum to the MAP sensor indicates a heavier load on the engine and the injector pulse width should increase.

**NOTE: If 23 in. Hg or more vacuum is applied to the MAP sensor with the engine running, this high vacuum will often stall the engine. The engine stalls because the high vacuum is interpreted by the PCM to indicate that the engine is being decelerated, which shuts off the fuel. During engine deceleration, the PCM shuts off the fuel injectors to reduce exhaust emissions and increase fuel economy.**

**FIGURE 13–7** A typical hand-operated vacuum pump.

## MAP/BARO DIAGNOSTIC TROUBLE CODES

The diagnostic trouble codes (DTCs) associated with the MAP and BARO sensors include:

| Diagnostic Trouble Code | Description | Possible Causes |
|---|---|---|
| P0106 | BARO sensor out-of-range at key on | • MAP sensor fault<br>• MAP sensor O-ring damaged or missing |
| P0107 | MAP sensor low voltage | • MAP sensor fault<br>• MAP sensor signal circuit shorted-to-ground<br>• MAP sensor 5-volt supply circuit open |
| P0108 | Map sensor high voltage | • MAP sensor fault<br>• MAP sensor O-ring damaged or missing<br>• MAP sensor signal circuit shorted-to-voltage |

## FUEL-RAIL PRESSURE SENSOR

A fuel-rail pressure (FRP) sensor is used on some vehicles such as Fords that are equipped with electronic returnless fuel injection. This sensor provides fuel pressure information to the PCM for fuel injection pulse width calculations.

## SUMMARY

1. Pressure below atmospheric pressure is called vacuum and is measured in inches of mercury.
2. A manifold absolute pressure sensor uses a perfect vacuum (zero absolute pressure) in the sensor to determine the pressure.
3. Three types of MAP sensors include:
   • Silicon-diaphragm strain gauge
   • Capacitor-capsule design
   • Ceramic disc design
4. A heavy engine load results in low intake manifold vacuum and a high MAP sensor signal voltage.
5. A light engine load results in high intake manifold vacuum and a low MAP sensor signal voltage.
6. A MAP sensor is used to detect changes in altitude, as well as check other sensors and engine systems.
7. A MAP sensor can be tested by visual inspection, testing the output using a digital meter or scan tool.

## REVIEW QUESTIONS

1. What is the relationship among atmospheric pressure, vacuum, and boost pressure in PSI?
2. What are two types (construction) of MAP sensors?
3. What is the MAP sensor signal voltage or frequency at idle on a typical General Motors, Chrysler, and Ford engine?
4. What are three uses of a MAP sensor by the PCM?

1. As the load on an engine increases, the manifold vacuum decreases and the manifold absolute pressure _____.
   a. Increases
   b. Decreases
   c. Changes with barometric pressure only (altitude or weather)
   d. Remains constant (absolute)

2. A typical MAP sensor compares the vacuum in the intake manifold to _____.
   a. Atmospheric pressure
   b. A perfect vacuum
   c. Barometric pressure
   d. The value of the IAT sensor

3. Which statement is *false*?
   a. Absolute pressure is equal to barometric pressure plus intake manifold vacuum.
   b. A decrease in manifold vacuum means an increase in manifold pressure.
   c. The MAP sensor compares manifold vacuum to a perfect vacuum.
   d. Barometric pressure minus the MAP sensor reading equals intake manifold vacuum.

4. Which design of MAP sensor produces a frequency (digital) output signal?
   a. Silicon-diaphragm strain gauge
   b. Piezoresistivity design
   c. Capacitor-capsule
   d. Ceramic disc

5. The frequency output of a digital MAP sensor is reading 114 Hz. What is the approximate engine vacuum?
   a. Zero
   b. 5 in. Hg
   c. 10 in. Hg
   d. 15 in. Hg

6. Which is *not* a purpose or function of the MAP sensor?
   a. Measures the load on the engine
   b. Measures engine speed
   c. Calculates fuel delivery based on altitude
   d. Helps diagnose the EGR system

7. When measuring the output signal of a MAP sensor on a General Motors vehicle, the digital multimeter should be set to read _____.
   a. DC V
   b. AC V
   c. Hz
   d. DC A

8. Two technicians are discussing testing MAP sensors. Technician A says that the MAP sensor voltage on a General Motors vehicle at idle should be about 1.0 volt. Technician B says that the MAP sensor frequency on a Ford vehicle at idle should be about 105–108 Hz. Which technician is correct?
   a. Technician A only
   b. Technician B only
   c. Both Technicians A and B
   d. Neither Technician A nor B

9. Technician A says that MAP sensors use a 5-volt reference voltage from the PCM. Technician B says that the MAP sensor voltage will be higher at idle at high altitudes compared to when the engine is operating at near sea level. Which technician is correct?
   a. Technician A only
   b. Technician B only
   c. Both Technicians A and B
   d. Neither Technician A nor B

10. A P0107 DTC is being discussed. Technician A says that a defective MAP sensor could be the cause. Technician B says that a MAP sensor signal wire shorted-to-ground could be the cause. Which technician is correct?
    a. Technician A only
    b. Technician B only
    c. Both Technicians A and B
    d. Neither Technician A nor B

# Chapter 14

# MASS AIR FLOW SENSORS

**OBJECTIVES:** After studying Chapter 14, the reader will be able to: • Prepare for ASE Engine Performance (A8) certification test content area "E" (Computerized Engine Controls Diagnosis and Repair). • Discuss how MAF sensors work. • List the methods that can be used to test MAF sensors. • Describe the symptoms of a failed MAF sensor. • List how the operation of the MAF sensor affects vehicle operation. • Discuss MAF sensor rationality tests.

**KEY TERMS:** False air 195 • Mass airflow (MAF) sensor 192 • Speed density 191 • Tap test 194 • Vane airflow (VAF) sensor 191

## AIRFLOW SENSORS

Electronic fuel injection systems that do not use the "speed density" system for fuel calculation measure the airflow volume delivered to the engine. Older systems use a movable vane in the intake stream called a **vane airflow (VAF)** sensor. The vane is deflected by intake airflow. ● **SEE FIGURE 14–1.**

The vane airflow sensor used in Bosch L-Jetronic, Ford, and most Japanese electronic port fuel-injection systems is a movable vane connected to a laser-calibrated potentiometer. The vane is mounted on a pivot pin and is deflected by intake airflow proportionate to air velocity. As the vane moves, it also moves the potentiometer. This causes a change in the signal voltage supplied to the computer. ● **SEE FIGURE 14–2.** For example, if the reference voltage is 5 volts, the potentiometer's signal to the computer will vary from a 0 voltage signal (no

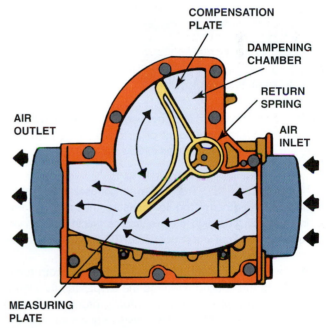

**FIGURE 14–1** A vane air flow (VAF) sensor. An air vane sensor measures the volume of the air, and the intake air temperature sensor is used by the PCM to calculate the mass of the air entering the engine.

COMPENSATION PLATE

DAMPENING CHAMBER

RETURN SPRING

AIR OUTLET

AIR INLET

MEASURING PLATE

---

**? FREQUENTLY ASKED QUESTION**

**What Is the Difference Between an Analog and a Digital MAF Sensor?**

Some MAF sensors produce a digital DC voltage signal whose frequency changes with the amount of airflow through the sensor. The frequency range also varies with the make of sensor and can range from 0- to 300-Hz for older General Motors MAF sensors to 1,000- to 9,000-Hz for most newer designs.

Some MAF sensors, such as those used by Ford and others, produce a changing DC voltage, rather than frequency, and range from 0- to 5-volts DC.

---

airflow) to almost a 5-volt signal (maximum airflow). In this way, the potentiometer provides the information the computer needs to vary the injector pulse width proportionate to airflow. There is a special "dampening chamber" built into the VAF to smooth out vane pulsations which would be created by intake manifold air-pressure fluctuations caused by the valve opening and closing. Many vane airflow sensors include a switch to energize the electric fuel pump. This is a safety feature that prevents the operation of the fuel pump if the engine stalls.

**FIGURE 14–2** A typical air vane sensor with the cover removed. The movable arm contacts a carbon resistance path as the vane opens. Many air vane sensors also have contacts that close to supply voltage to the electric fuel pump as the air vane starts to open when the engine is being cranked and air is being drawn into the engine.

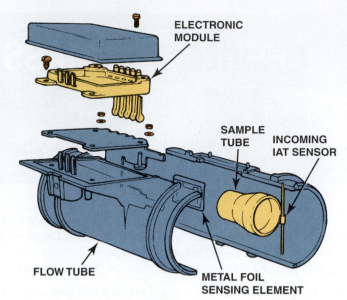

**FIGURE 14–3** This five-wire mass air flow sensor consists of a metal foil sensing unit, an intake air temperature (IAT) sensor, and the electronic module.

## MASS AIRFLOW SENSOR TYPES

Most newer fuel injection systems use a **Mass Air Flow (MAF)** sensor to measure the amount of air delivered to the engine. There are several types of mass airflow sensors.

**HOT FILM SENSOR** The hot film sensor uses a temperature-sensing resistor (thermistor) to measure the temperature of the incoming air. Through the electronics within the sensor, a conductive film is kept at a temperature 70°C above the temperature of the incoming air. ● SEE FIGURE 14–3.

Because the amount and density of the air both tend to contribute to the cooling effect as the air passes through the sensor, this type of sensor can actually produce an output based on the mass of the airflow. Mass equals volume times density. For example, cold air is denser than warm air so a small amount of cold air may have the same mass as a larger amount of warm air. Therefore, a mass airflow sensor is designed to measure the mass, not the volume, of the air entering the engine.

The output of this type of sensor is usually a frequency based on the amount of air entering the sensor. The more air that enters the sensor, the more the hot film is cooled. The electronics inside the sensor, therefore, increase the current flow through the hot film to maintain the 70°C temperature differential between the air temperature and the temperature of the hot film. This change in current flow is converted to a frequency output that the computer can use as a measurement of airflow. Most of these types of sensors are referred to as **mass airflow (MAF) sensors** because, unlike the air vane sensor, the MAF

**FIGURE 14–4** The sensing wire in a typical hot wire mass air flow sensor.

sensor takes into account relative humidity, altitude, and temperature of the air. The denser the air, the greater the cooling effect on the hot film sensor and the greater the amount of fuel required for proper combustion.

**HOT WIRE SENSOR** The hot wire sensor is similar to the hot film type, but uses a hot wire to sense the mass airflow instead of the hot film. Like the hot film sensor, the hot wire sensor uses a temperature-sensing resistor (thermistor) to measure the temperature of the air entering the sensor. ● SEE FIGURE 14–4. The electronic circuitry within the sensor keeps the temperature of the wire at 70°C above the temperature of the incoming air.

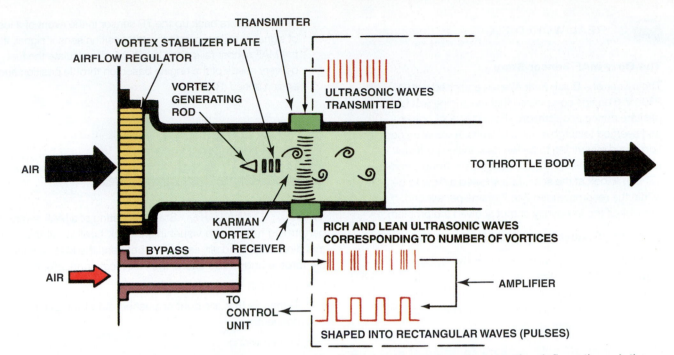

**FIGURE 14–5** A Karman Vortex air flow sensor uses a triangle-shaped rod to create vortexes as the air flows through the sensor. The electronics in the sensor itself converts these vortexes to a digital square wave signal.

Both designs operate in essentially the same way. A resistor wire or screen installed in the path of intake airflow is heated to a constant temperature by electric current provided by the computer. Air flowing past the screen or wire cools it. The degree of cooling varies with air velocity, temperature, density, and humidity. These factors combine to indicate the mass of air entering the engine. As the screen or wire cools, more current is required to maintain the specified temperature. As the screen or wire heats up, less current is required. The operating principle can be summarized as follows:

- More intake air volume = cooler sensor, more current.
- Less intake air volume = warmer sensor, less current.

The computer constantly monitors the change in current and translates it into a voltage signal that is used to determine injector pulse width.

**BURN-OFF CIRCUIT.** Some hot wire-type MAF sensors use a burn-off circuit to keep the sensing wire clean of dust and dirt. A high current is passed through the sensing wire for a short time, but long enough to cause the wire to glow due to the heat. The burn-off circuit is turned on when the ignition switch is switched off after the engine has been operating long enough to achieve normal operating temperature.

## KARMAN VORTEX SENSORS

In 1912, a Hungarian scientist named Theodore Van Karman observed that vortexes were created when air passed over a pointed surface. This type of sensor sends a sound wave

through the turbulence created by incoming air passing through the sensor. Air mass is calculated based on the time required for the sound waves to cross the turbulent air passage.

There are two basic designs of Karman Vortex air flow sensors. The two types include:

- **Ultrasonic.** This type of sensor uses ultrasonic waves to detect the vortexes that are produced, and produce a digital (on-and-off) signal where frequency is proportional to the amount of air passing through the sensor. ● **SEE FIGURE 14–5.**

- **Pressure-type.** Chrysler uses a pressure-type Karman Vortex sensor that uses a pressure sensor to detect the vortexes. As the airflow through the sensor increases, so do the number of pressure variations. The electronics in the sensor convert these pressure variations to a square wave (digital DC voltage) signal, whose frequency is in proportion to the airflow through the sensor.

## PCM USES FOR AIRFLOW SENSORS

The PCM uses the information from the airflow sensor for the following purposes:

- Airflow sensors are used mostly to determine the amount of fuel needed and base pulse-width numbers. The greater the mass of the incoming air, the longer the injectors are pulsed on.

### The Dirty MAF Sensor Story

The owner of a Buick Park Avenue equipped with a 3800 V-6 engine complained that the engine would hesitate during acceleration, showed lack of power, and seemed to surge or miss at times. A visual inspection found everything to be like new, including a new air filter. There were no stored diagnostic trouble codes (DTCs). A look at the scan data showed airflow to be within the recommended 3 to 7 grams per second. A check of the frequency output showed the problem.

**Idle frequency = 2.177 kHz (2,177 Hz)**

Normal frequency at idle speed should be 2.37 to 2.52 kHz. Cleaning the hot wire of the MAF sensor restored proper operation. The sensor wire was covered with what looked like fine fibers, possibly from the replacement air filter.

**NOTE: Older GM MAF sensors operated at a lower frequency of 32 to 150 Hz, with 32 Hz being the average reading at idle and 150 Hz for wide-open throttle.**

### What Is Meant By a "High-Authority Sensor"?

A high-authority sensor is a sensor that has a major influence over the amount of fuel being delivered to the engine. For example, at engine start-up, the engine coolant temperature (ECT) sensor is a high-authority sensor and the oxygen sensor (O2S) is a low-authority sensor. However, as the engine reaches operating temperature, the oxygen sensor becomes a high-authority sensor and can greatly affect the amount of fuel being supplied to the engine. See the chart.

| High-Authority Sensors | Low-Authority Sensors |
|---|---|
| ECT (especially when the engine starts and is warming up) | IAT (intake air temperature) sensors modify and back up the ECT |
| O2S (after the engine reaches closed-loop operation) | TFT (transmission fluid temperature) |
| MAP | PRNDL (shift position sensor) |
| MAF | KS (knock sensor) |
| TP (high authority during acceleration and deceleration) | EFT (engine fuel temperature) |

- Airflow sensors back up the TP sensor in the event of a loss of signal or an inaccurate throttle position sensor signal. If the MAF sensor fails, then the PCM will calculate the fuel delivery needs of the engine based on throttle position and engine speed (RPM).

## TESTING MASS AIRFLOW SENSORS

**VISUAL INSPECTION** Start the testing of a MAF sensor by performing a thorough visual inspection. Look at all the hoses that direct and send air, especially between the MAF sensor and the throttle body. Also check the electrical connector for:

- Corrosion
- Terminals that are bent or pushed out of the plastic connector
- Frayed wiring

**MAF SENSOR OUTPUT TEST** MAF sensors calculate air mass by weight in a given amount of time usually in grams per second (gm/sec.) A digital multimeter, set to read DC volts and connected to the signal wire circuit, can be used to check the MAF sensor. See the chart that shows the voltage output compared with the grams per second of airflow through the sensor. Normal airflow is 3 to 7 grams per second.

**Analog MAF Sensor Grams per Second/Voltage Chart**

| Grams per Second | Sensor Voltage |
|---|---|
| 0 | 0.2 |
| 2 | 0.7 |
| 4 | 1.0 (typical idle value) |
| 8 | 1.5 |
| 15 | 2.0 |
| 30 | 2.5 |
| 50 | 3.0 |
| 80 | 3.5 |
| 110 | 4.0 |
| 150 | 4.5 |
| 175 | 4.8 |

**TAP TEST** With the engine running at idle speed, gently tap the MAF sensor with the fingers of an open hand. If the engine stumbles or stalls, the MAF sensor is defective. This test is commonly called the **tap test.**

**DIGITAL METER TEST OF A MAF SENSOR** A digital multimeter can be used to measure the frequency (Hz) output of the sensor and compare the reading with specifications.

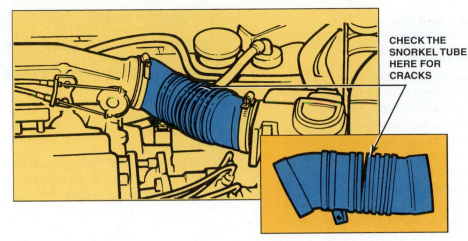

CHECK THE
SNORKEL TUBE
HERE FOR
CRACKS

**FIGURE 14–6** Carefully check the hose between the MAF sensor and the throttle body assembly for cracks or splits that could create extra (false) air into the engine that is not measured by the MAF sensor.

### What Is False Air?

Airflow sensors and mass airflow (MAF) sensors are designed to measure *all* the air entering the engine. If an air hose between the MAF sensor and throttle body was loose or had a hole, extra air could enter the engine without being measured. This extra air is often called **false air**.
● **SEE FIGURE 14–6.** Because this extra air is unmeasured, the computer does not provide enough fuel delivery and the engine operates too lean, especially at idle. A small hole in the air inlet hose would represent a fairly large percentage of false air at idle, but would represent a very small percentage of extra air at highway speeds.

To diagnose for false air, look at long-term fuel trim numbers at idle and at 3000 RPM.

**NOTE: If the engine runs well in reverse, yet runs terrible in any forward gear, carefully look at the inlet hose for air leaks that would open when the engine torque moves the engine slightly on its mounts.**

### The Unplug It Test

If a sensor is defective yet still produces a signal to the computer, the computer will often accept the reading and make the required changes in fuel delivery and spark advance. If, however, the sensor is not reading correctly, the computer will process this wrong information and perform an action assuming that information being supplied is accurate. For example, if a mass airflow (MAF) sensor is telling the computer that 12 grams of air per second is going into the engine, the computer will then pulse the injector for 6.4 ms or whatever figure it is programmed to provide. However, if the air going into the engine is actually 14 grams per second, the amount of fuel supplied by the injectors will not be enough to provide proper engine operation. If the MAF sensor is unplugged, the computer knows that the sensor is not capable of supplying airflow information, so it defaults to a fixed amount of fuel based on the values of other sensors such as the TP and MAP sensors. "If in doubt, take it out."

If the engine operates better with a sensor unplugged, then suspect that the sensor is defective. A sensor that is not supplying the correct information is said to be skewed. The computer will not set a diagnostic trouble code for this condition because the computer can often not detect that the sensor is supplying wrong information.

The frequency output and engine speed in RPM can also be plotted on a graph to check to see if the frequency and RPM are proportional, resulting in a straight line on the graph.

## MAF SENSOR CONTAMINATION

Dirt, oil, silicon, or even spiderwebs can coat the sensing wire. Because it tends to insulate the sensing wire at low airflow rates, a contaminated sensor often overestimates the amount of air entering the engine at idle, and therefore causes the fuel system to go rich. At higher engine speeds near wide-open throttle (WOT), the contamination can cause the sensor to underestimate the amount of air entering the engine. As a result, the fuel system will go lean, causing spark knock and lack of power concerns. To check for contamination, check the fuel trim numbers.

**The Rich Running Toyota**

A Toyota failed an enhanced emission test for excessive carbon monoxide, which is caused by a rich (too much fuel) air–fuel ratio problem. After checking all of the basics and not finding any fault in the fuel system, the technician checked the archives of the International Automotive Technicians Network *(www.iatn.net)* and discovered that a broken spring inside the air flow sensor was a possible cause. The sensor was checked and a broken vane return spring was discovered. Replacing the air flow sensor restored the engine to proper operating conditions and it passed the emission test.

If the fuel trim is negative (removing fuel) at idle, yet is positive (adding fuel) at higher engine speeds, a contaminated MAF sensor is a likely cause. Other tests for a contaminated MAF sensor include:

- At WOT, the grams per second, as read on a scan tool, should exceed 100.
- At WOT, the voltage, as read on a digital voltmeter, should exceed 4 volts for an analog sensor.
- At WOT, the frequency, as read on a meter or scan tool, should exceed 7 kHz for a digital sensor.

If the readings do not exceed these values, then the MAF sensor is contaminated.

# MAF-RELATED DIAGNOSTIC TROUBLE CODES

The diagnostic trouble codes (DTCs) associated with the mass airflow and air vane sensors include:

| Diagnostic Trouble Code | Description | Possible Causes |
|---|---|---|
| P0100 | Mass or volume airflow circuit problems | • Open or short in mass airflow circuit<br>• Defective MAF sensor |
| P0101 | Mass airflow circuit range problems | • Defective MAF sensor (check for false air) |
| P0102 | Mass airflow circuit low output | • Defective MAF sensor<br>• MAF sensor circuit open or shorted-to-ground<br>• Open 12-volt supply voltage circuit |
| P0103 | Mass airflow circuit high output | • Defective MAF sensor<br>• MAF sensor circuit shorted-to-voltage |

## SUMMARY

1. A mass airflow sensor actually measures the density and amount of air flowing into the engine, which results in accurate engine control.

2. An air vane sensor measures the volume of the air, and the intake air temperature sensor is used by the PCM to calculate the mass of the air entering the engine.

3. A hot wire MAF sensor uses the electronics in the sensor itself to heat a wire 70°C above the temperature of the air entering the engine.

## REVIEW QUESTIONS

1. How does a hot film MAF sensor work?

2. What type of voltage signal is produced by a MAF?

3. What change in the signal will occur if engine speed is increased?

4. How is a MAF sensor tested?

5. What is the purpose of a MAF sensor?

6. What are the types of airflow sensors?

1. A fuel-injection system that does not use a sensor to measure the amount (or mass) of air entering the engine is usually called a(n) _____ type of system.
   a. Air vane-controlled
   b. Speed density
   c. Mass airflow
   d. Hot wire

2. Which type of sensor uses a burn-off circuit?
   a. Hot wire MAF sensor
   b. Hot film MAF sensor
   c. Vane-type airflow sensor
   d. Both a and b

3. Which sensor has a switch that controls the electric fuel pump?
   a. VAF
   b. Hot wire MAF
   c. Hot filter MAF
   d. Karman Vortex sensor

4. Two technicians are discussing Karman Vortex sensors. Technician A says that they contain a burn-off circuit to keep them clean. Technician B says that they contain a movable vane. Which technician is correct?
   a. Technician A only
   b. Technicians B only
   c. Both Technicians A and B
   d. Neither Technician A nor B

5. The typical MAF reading on a scan tool with the engine at idle speed and normal operating temperature is _____.
   a. 1 to 3 grams per second
   b. 3 to 7 grams per second
   c. 8 to 12 grams per second
   d. 14 to 24 grams per second

6. Two technicians are diagnosing a poorly running engine. There are no diagnostic trouble codes. When the MAF sensor is unplugged, the engine runs better. Technician A says that this means that the MAF is supplying incorrect airflow information to the PCM. Technician B says that this indicates that the PCM is defective. Which technician is correct?
   a. Technician A only
   b. Technician B only
   c. Both Technicians A and B
   d. Neither Technician A nor B

7. A MAF sensor on a General Motors 3800 V-6 is being tested for contamination. Technician A says that the sensor should show over 100 grams per second on a scan tool display when the accelerator is depressed to WOT on a running engine. Technician B says that the output frequency should exceed 7,000 Hz when the accelerator pedal is depressed to WOT on a running engine. Which technician is correct?
   a. Technician A only
   b. Technician B only
   c. Both Technicians A and B
   d. Neither Technician A nor B

8. Which airflow sensor has a dampening chamber?
   a. A vane airflow
   b. A hot film MAF
   c. A hot wire MAF
   d. A Karman Vortex

9. Air that enters the engine without passing through the airflow sensor is called _____.
   a. Bypass air
   b. Dirty air
   c. False air
   d. Measured air

10. A P0102 DTC is being discussed. Technician A says that a sensor circuit shorted-to-ground can be the cause. Technician B says that an open sensor voltage supply circuit could be the cause. Which technician is correct?
    a. Technician A only
    b. Technician B only
    c. Both Technicians A and B
    d. Neither Technician A nor B

**OBJECTIVES:** After studying Chapter 15, the reader will be able to: • Prepare for ASE Engine Performance (A8) certification test content area "E" (Computerized Engine Controls Diagnosis and Repair). • Discuss how O2S sensors work. • List the methods that can be used to test O2S sensors. • Describe the symptoms of a failed O2S sensor. • List how the operation of the O2S sensor affects vehicle operation.

**KEY TERMS:** Bias voltage 202 • Closed-loop operation 200 • Cross counts 203 • False lean indication 211 • False rich indication 211 • Open-loop operation 200 • Oxygen sensor (O2S) 198

## OXYGEN SENSORS

### PURPOSE AND FUNCTION
Automotive computer systems use a sensor in the exhaust system to measure the oxygen content of the exhaust. These sensors are called **oxygen sensors (O2S).** The oxygen sensor is installed in the exhaust manifold or located downstream from the manifold in the exhaust pipe. ● SEE FIGURE 15–1. The oxygen sensor is directly in the path of the exhaust gas stream where it monitors oxygen level in both the exhaust stream and the ambient air. In a zirconia oxygen sensor, the tip contains a thimble made of zirconium dioxide ($ZrO_2$), an electrically conductive material capable of generating a small voltage in the presence of oxygen. The oxygen sensor is used by the PCM to control fuel delivery.

### CONSTRUCTION AND OPERATION
Exhaust from the engine passes through the end of the sensor where the gases contact the outer side of the thimble. Atmospheric air enters through the other end of the sensor or through the wire of the sensor and contacts the inner side of the thimble. The inner and outer surfaces of the thimble are plated with platinum. The inner surface becomes a negative electrode; the outer surface is a positive electrode. The atmosphere contains a relatively constant 21% of oxygen. Rich exhaust gases contain little oxygen. Exhaust from a lean mixture contains more oxygen.

Negatively charged oxygen ions are drawn to the thimble where they collect on both the inner and outer surfaces. ● SEE FIGURE 15–2. Because the percentage of oxygen present in the atmosphere exceeds that in the exhaust gases, the atmosphere side of the thimble draws more negative oxygen ions than the exhaust side. The difference between the two sides creates an electrical potential, or voltage. When the concentration of oxygen

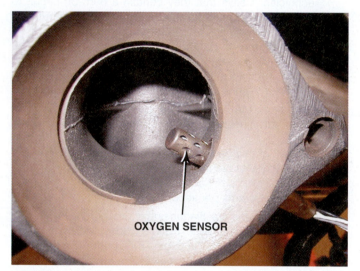

**FIGURE 15–1** Many fuel-control oxygen sensors are located in the exhaust manifold near its outlet so that the sensor can detect the presence or absence of oxygen in the exhaust stream for all cylinders that feed into the manifold.

on the exhaust side of the thimble is low (rich exhaust), a high voltage (0.60 to 1.0 volts) is generated between the electrodes. As the oxygen concentration on the exhaust side increases (lean exhaust), the voltage generated drops low (0.00 to 0.3 volts). ● SEE FIGURE 15–3.

This voltage signal is sent to the computer where it passes through the input conditioner for amplification. The computer interprets a high-voltage signal (low-oxygen content) as a rich air–fuel ratio, and a low-voltage signal (high-oxygen content) as a lean air–fuel ratio. Based on the O2S signal (above or below 0.45 volts), the computer compensates by making the mixture either leaner or richer as required to continually vary close to a 14.7:1 air–fuel ratio to satisfy the needs of the three-way catalytic

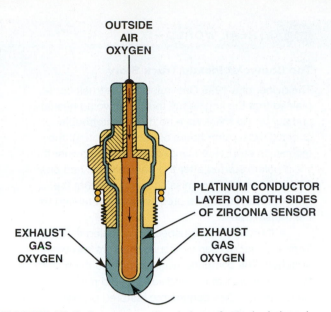

**FIGURE 15–2** A cross-sectional view of a typical zirconia oxygen sensor.

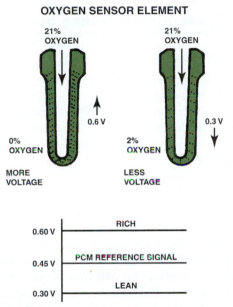

**FIGURE 15–3** A difference in oxygen content between the atmosphere and the exhaust gases enables an O2S sensor to generate voltage.

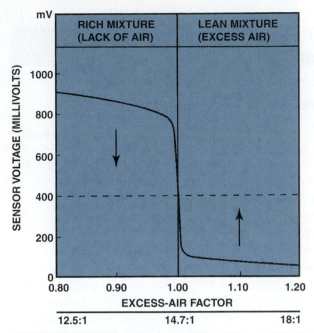

**FIGURE 15–4** The oxygen sensor provides a quick response at the stoichiometric air–fuel ratio of 14.7:1.

converter. The O2S is a high-authority sensor of an electronically controlled fuel metering system for emission control.

An O2S does not send a voltage signal until its tip reaches a temperature of about 572°F (300°C). Also, O2 sensors provide their fastest response to mixture changes at about 1472°F (800°C). When the engine starts and the O2S is cold, the computer runs the engine in the open-loop mode, drawing on prerecorded data in the PROM for fuel control on a cold engine, or when O2S output is not within certain limits.

If the exhaust contains very little oxygen (O2S), the computer assumes that the intake charge is rich (too much fuel) and reduces fuel delivery. ● **SEE FIGURE 15–4.** However, when the oxygen level is high, the computer assumes that the intake charge is lean (not enough fuel) and increases fuel delivery. There are several different designs of oxygen sensors, including:

- **One-wire oxygen sensor.** In the one-wire oxygen sensor, the single wire is used for the O2S signal wire and the ground circuit is provided through the shell and threads of the sensor and through the exhaust manifold.

- **Two-wire oxygen sensor.** The two-wire sensor has a signal wire and a ground wire for the O2S.

- **Three-wire oxygen sensor.** The three-wire sensor design uses an electric resistance heater to help get the O2S up to temperature more quickly and to help keep the sensor at operating temperature even at idle speeds. The three wires include the O2S signal, the power, and ground for the heater.

- **Four-wire oxygen sensor.** The four-wire sensor is a heated O2S (HO2S) that uses an O2S signal wire and signal ground. The other two wires are the power and ground for the heater.

## ZIRCONIA OXYGEN SENSORS

The most common type of oxygen sensor is made from zirconia (zirconium dioxide). It is usually constructed using powder that is pressed into a thimble shape and coated with porous platinum material that acts as electrodes. All zirconia sensors use 18-mm-diameter threads with a washer. ● **SEE FIGURE 15–5.**

Zirconia oxygen sensors (O2S) are constructed so that oxygen ions flow through the sensor when there is a difference

**FIGURE 15–5** A typical zirconia oxygen sensor.

between the oxygen content inside and outside of the sensor. An ion is an electrically charged particle. The greater the differences between the oxygen content between the inside and outside of the sensor the higher the voltage created.

- **Rich mixture.** A rich mixture results in little oxygen in the exhaust stream. Compared to the outside air, this represents a large difference and the sensor creates a relatively high voltage of about 1.0 volt (1,000 mV).

- **Lean mixture.** A lean mixture leaves some oxygen in the exhaust stream that did not combine with the fuel. This leftover oxygen reduces the difference between the oxygen content of the exhaust compared to the oxygen content of the outside air. As a result, the sensor voltage is low or almost 0 volts.

- **O2S voltage above 450 mV.** This is produced by the sensor when the oxygen content in the exhaust is low. This is interpreted by the engine computer (PCM) as being a rich exhaust.

- **O2S voltage below 450 mV.** This is produced by the sensor when the oxygen content is high. This is interpreted by the engine computer (PCM) as being a lean exhaust.

## TITANIA OXYGEN SENSOR

The titania (titanium dioxide) oxygen sensor does not produce a voltage but rather changes in resistance with the presence of oxygen in the exhaust. All titania oxygen sensors use a four-terminal variable resistance unit with a heating element. A titania sensor samples exhaust air only and uses a reference voltage from the PCM. Titania oxide oxygen sensors use a 14-mm thread and are not interchangeable with zirconia oxygen sensors. One volt is applied to the sensor and the changing resistance of the titania oxygen sensor changes the voltage of the sensor circuit. As with a zirconia oxygen sensor, the voltage signal is above 450 mV when the exhaust is rich, and low (below 450 mV) when the exhaust is lean.

## CLOSED LOOP AND OPEN LOOP

The amount of fuel delivered to an engine is determined by the Powertrain Control Module (PCM) based on inputs from the engine coolant temperature (ECT), throttle position (TP)

**REAL WORLD FIX**

**The Chevrolet Pickup Truck Story**

The owner of a 1996 Chevrolet pickup truck complained that the engine ran terribly. It would hesitate and surge, yet there were no diagnostic trouble codes (DTCs). After hours of troubleshooting, the technician discovered while talking to the owner that the problem started after the transmission had been repaired, yet the transmission shop said that the problem was an engine problem and not related to the transmission.

A thorough visual inspection revealed that the front and rear oxygen sensor connectors had been switched. The computer was trying to compensate for an air–fuel mixture condition that did not exist. Reversing the O2S connectors restored proper operation of the truck.

**?** **FREQUENTLY ASKED QUESTION**

**Where is HO2S1?**

Oxygen sensors are numbered according to their location in the engine. On a V-type engine, heated oxygen sensor number 1 (HO2S1) is located in the exhaust manifold on the side of the engine where the number one cylinder is located. ● **SEE FIGURE 15–6.**

sensor, and others until the oxygen sensor is capable of supplying a usable signal. When the PCM alone (without feedback) is determining the amount of fuel needed, it is called **open-loop operation.** As soon as the oxygen sensor (O2S) is capable of supplying rich and lean signals, adjustments by the computer can be made to fine-tune the correct air–fuel mixture. This checking and adjusting by the computer is called **closed-loop operation.**

## PCM USES OF THE OXYGEN SENSOR

**FUEL CONTROL**    The upstream oxygen sensors are among the main sensor(s) used for fuel control while operating in closed loop. Before the oxygen sensors are hot enough to give accurate exhaust oxygen information to the computer, fuel control is determined by other sensors and the anticipated injector pulse width determined by those sensors. After the control system achieves closed-loop status, the oxygen sensor provides feedback with actual exhaust gas oxygen content.

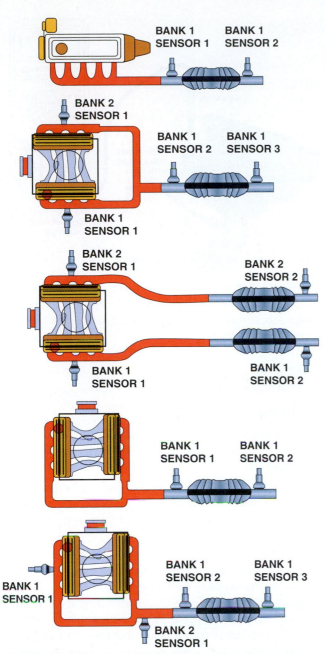

BANK 1 SENSOR 1   BANK 1 SENSOR 2

BANK 2 SENSOR 1

BANK 1 SENSOR 2   BANK 1 SENSOR 3

BANK 1 SENSOR 1

BANK 2 SENSOR 1

BANK 2 SENSOR 2

BANK 1 SENSOR 1   BANK 1 SENSOR 2

BANK 1 SENSOR 1   BANK 1 SENSOR 2

BANK 1 SENSOR 1   BANK 1 SENSOR 2

BANK 1 SENSOR 1   BANK 1 SENSOR 2   BANK 1 SENSOR 3

BANK 2 SENSOR 1

**FIGURE 15–6** Number and label designations for oxygen sensors. Bank 1 is the bank where cylinder number 1 is located.

**FUEL TRIM** Fuel trim is a computer program that is used to compensate for a too rich or a too lean air–fuel exhaust as detected by the oxygen sensor(s). Fuel trim is necessary to keep the air–fuel mixture within limits to allow the catalytic converter to operate efficiently. If the exhaust is too lean or too rich for a long time, the catalytic converter can be damaged. The fuel trim numbers are determined from the signals from the oxygen sensor(s). If the engine has been operating too lean, short-term and long-term fuel time programming inside the PCM can cause an increase in the commanded injector pulse width to bring the air–fuel mixture back into the proper range. Fuel trim can be negative (subtracting fuel) or positive (adding fuel).

**What Happens to the Bias Voltage?**

Some vehicle manufacturers such as General Motors Corporation have the computer apply 450 mV (0.450 V) to the O2S signal wire. This voltage is called the bias voltage and represents the threshold voltage for the transition from rich to lean.

This **bias voltage** is displayed on a scan tool when the ignition switch is turned on with the engine off. When the engine is started, the O2S becomes warm enough to produce a usable voltage and bias voltage "disappears" as the O2S responds to a rich and lean mixture. What happened to the bias voltage that the computer applied to the O2S? The voltage from the O2S simply overcame the very weak voltage signal from the computer. This bias voltage is so weak that even a 20-megohm impedance DMM will affect the strength enough to cause the voltage to drop to 426 mV. Other meters with only 10 megohms of impedance will cause the bias voltage to read less than 400 mV.

Therefore, even though the O2S voltage is relatively low powered, it is more than strong enough to override the very weak bias voltage the computer sends to the O2S.

## OXYGEN SENSOR DIAGNOSIS

The oxygen sensors are used for diagnosis of other systems and components. For example, the exhaust gas recirculation (EGR) system is tested by the PCM by commanding the valve to open during the test. Some PCMs determine whether enough exhaust gas flows into the engine by looking at the oxygen sensor response (fuel trim numbers). The upstream and downstream oxygen sensors are also used to determine the efficiency of the catalytic converter. ● **SEE FIGURE 15–7.**

**TESTING AN OXYGEN SENSOR USING A DIGITAL VOLTMETER** The oxygen sensor can be checked for proper operation using a digital high-impedance voltmeter.

1. With the engine off, connect the red lead of the meter to the oxygen sensor signal wire. ● **SEE FIGURE 15–8.**

2. Start the engine and allow it to reach closed-loop operation.

3. In closed-loop operation, the oxygen sensor voltage should be constantly changing as the fuel mixture is being controlled.

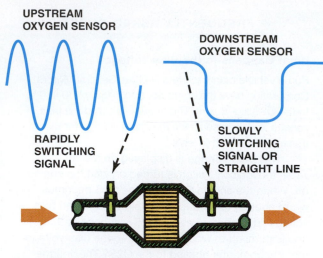

UPSTREAM OXYGEN SENSOR

DOWNSTREAM OXYGEN SENSOR

RAPIDLY SWITCHING SIGNAL

SLOWLY SWITCHING SIGNAL OR STRAIGHT LINE

CATALYTIC CONVERTER

**FIGURE 15–7** The OBD-II catalytic converter monitor compares the signals of the upstream and downstream oxygen sensor to determine converter efficiency.

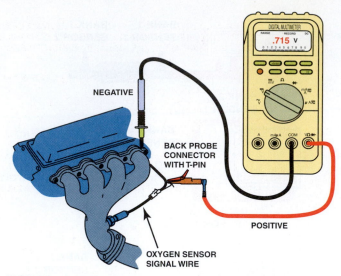

NEGATIVE

BACK PROBE CONNECTOR WITH T-PIN

OXYGEN SENSOR SIGNAL WIRE

POSITIVE

**FIGURE 15–8** Testing an oxygen sensor using a DMM set on DC volts. With the engine operating in closed loop, the oxygen voltage should read over 800 mV and lower than 200 mV and be constantly fluctuating.

 **REAL WORLD FIX**

### The Oxygen Sensor Is Lying to You

A technician was trying to solve a driveability problem with an older V-6 passenger car. The car idled roughly, hesitated, and accelerated poorly. A thorough visual inspection did not indicate any possible problems and there were no diagnostic trouble codes stored.

A check was made on the oxygen sensor activity using a DMM. The voltage stayed above 600 mV most of the time. If a large vacuum hose was removed, the oxygen sensor voltage would temporarily drop to below 450 mV and then return to a reading of over 600 mV. Remember:

- High O2S readings = rich exhaust (low $O_2$ content in the exhaust)
- Low O2S readings = lean exhaust (high $O_2$ content in the exhaust)

As part of a thorough visual inspection, the technician removed and inspected the spark plugs. All the spark plugs were white, indicating a lean mixture, not the rich mixture that the oxygen sensor was indicating. The high O2S reading signaled the computer to reduce the amount of fuel, resulting in an excessively lean operation.

After replacing the oxygen sensor, the engine ran great. But what killed the oxygen sensor? The technician finally learned from the owner that the head gasket had been replaced over a year ago. The phosphate and silicate additives in the antifreeze coolant had coated the oxygen sensor. Because the oxygen sensor was coated, the oxygen content of the exhaust could not be detected—the result: a false rich signal from the oxygen sensor.

 **REAL WORLD FIX**

### The Missing Ford Escort

A Ford Escort was being analyzed for poor engine operation. The engine ran perfectly during the following conditions:

1. With the engine cold or operating in open loop
2. With the engine at idle
3. With the engine operating at or near wide-open throttle

After hours of troubleshooting, the cause was found to be a poor ground connection for the oxygen sensor. The engine ran okay during times when the computer ignored the oxygen sensor. Unfortunately, the service technician did not have a definite plan during the diagnostic process and as a result checked and replaced many unnecessary parts. An oxygen sensor test early in the diagnostic procedure would have indicated that the oxygen (O2S) signal was not correct. The poor ground caused the oxygen sensor voltage level to be too high, indicating to the computer that the mixture was too rich. The computer then subtracted fuel, which caused the engine to miss and run rough as the result of the now too lean air–fuel mixture.

The results should be interpreted as follows:

- If the oxygen sensor fails to respond, and its voltage remains at about 450 millivolts, the sensor may be defective and require replacement. Before replacing the oxygen sensor, check the manufacturer's recommended procedures.
- If the oxygen sensor reads high all the time (above 550 millivolts), the fuel system could be supplying too

WATCH ANALOG POINTER SWEEP AS O2 VOLTAGE CHANGES.
DEPENDING ON THE DRIVING CONDITIONS, THE O2 VOLTAGE
WILL RISE AND FALL, BUT IT USUALLY AVERAGES AROUND 0.45V

1. SHUT THE ENGINE OFF AND INSERT TEST LEAD IN THE INPUT
   TERMINALS SHOWN.
2. SET THE ROTARY SWITCH TO VOLTS DC.
3. MANUALLY SELECT THE 4V.
4. CONNECT THE TEST LEADS AS SHOWN.
5. START THE ENGINE. IF THE O2 SENSOR IS UNHEATED, FAST IDLE
   THE CAR FOR A FEW MINUTES.
6. PRESS MIN / MAX BUTTON TO DISPLAY MAXIMUM (MAX)
   O2 VOLTAGE; PRESS AGAIN TO DISPLAY MINIMUM (MIN)
   VOLTAGE; PRESS AGAIN TO DISPLAY AVERAGE (AVG) VOLTAGE;
   PRESS AND HOLD DOWN MIN / MAX FOR 2 SECONDS TO EXIT.

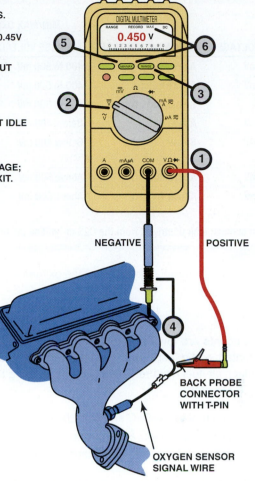

NEGATIVE        POSITIVE

BACK PROBE
CONNECTOR
WITH T-PIN

OXYGEN SENSOR
SIGNAL WIRE

**FIGURE 15–9** Using a digital multimeter to test an oxygen sensor using the MIN/MAX record function of the meter.

---

rich a fuel mixture or the oxygen sensor may be contaminated.

■ If the oxygen sensor voltage remains low (below 350 millivolts), the fuel system could be supplying too lean a fuel mixture. Check for a vacuum leak or partially clogged fuel injector(s). Before replacing the oxygen sensor, check the manufacturer's recommended procedures.

## TESTING THE OXYGEN SENSOR USING THE MIN/MAX METHOD

A digital meter set on DC volts can be used to record the minimum and maximum voltage with the engine running. A good oxygen sensor should be able to produce a value of less than 300 millivolts and a maximum voltage above 800 millivolts. Replace any oxygen sensor that fails to go above 700 millivolts or lower than 300 millivolts. ● **SEE FIGURE 15–9 AND CHART 15–1.**

## TESTING AN OXYGEN SENSOR USING A SCAN TOOL

A good oxygen sensor should be able to sense the oxygen content and change voltage outputs rapidly. How fast an oxygen sensor switches from high (above 450 millivolts) to low (below 350 millivolts) is measured in oxygen sensor **cross counts**. Cross counts are the number of times an oxygen sensor changes voltage from high to low (from low to high voltage is not counted) in 1 second (or 1.25 second, depending on scan tool and computer speed).

**NOTE: On a fuel-injected engine at 2,000 engine RPM, 8 to 10 cross counts is normal.**

Oxygen sensor cross counts can only be determined using a scan tool or other suitable tester that reads computer data.

| MIN/MAX Oxygen Sensor Test Chart | | | |
|---|---|---|---|
| **MINIMUM VOLTAGE** | **MAXIMUM VOLTAGE** | **AVERAGE VOLTAGE** | **TEST RESULTS** |
| Below 200 mV | Above 800 mV | 400 to 500 mV | Oxygen sensor is okay. |
| Above 200 mV | Any reading | 400 to 500 mV | Oxygen sensor is defective. |
| Any reading | Below 800 mV | 400 to 500 mV | Oxygen sensor is defective. |
| Below 200 mV | Above 800 mV | Below 400 mV | System is operating lean.* |
| Below 200 mV | Below 800 mV | Below 400 mV | System is operating lean. (Add propane to the intake air to see if the oxygen sensor reacts. If not, the sensor is defective.) |
| Below 200 mV | Above 800 mV | Above 500 mV | System is operating rich. |
| Above 200 mV | Above 800 mV | Above 500 mV | System is operating rich. (Remove a vacuum hose to see if the oxygen sensor reacts. If not, the sensor is defective.) |

*Check for an exhaust leak upstream from the O2S or ignition misfire that can cause a false lean indication before further diagnosis.

**CHART 15–1**

Use this chart to check for proper operation of the oxygen sensors and fuel system after checking them using a multimeter set to read Min/Max.

If the cross counts are low (or zero), the oxygen sensor may be contaminated, or the fuel delivery system is delivering a constant rich or lean air–fuel mixture. To test an engine using a scan tool, follow these steps:

1. Connect the scan tool to the DLC and start the engine.

2. Operate the engine at a fast idle (2,500 RPM) for 2 minutes to allow time for the oxygen sensor to warm to operating temperature.

3. Observe the oxygen sensor activity on the scan tool to verify closed-loop operation. Select "snapshot" mode and hold the engine speed steady and start recording.

4. Play back snapshot and place a mark beside each range of oxygen sensor voltage for each frame of the snapshot.

A good oxygen sensor and computer system should result in most snapshot values at both extremes of the sensor readings (0 to 300 and 600 to 1,000 mV). If most of the readings are in the middle, the oxygen sensor is not working correctly.

## TESTING AN OXYGEN SENSOR USING A SCOPE
An oscilloscope (scope) can also be used to test an oxygen sensor. Connect the scope to the signal wire and ground for the sensor (if it is so equipped). ● **SEE FIGURE 15–10.** With the engine operating in closed loop, the voltage signal of the sensor should be constantly changing. ● **SEE FIGURE 15–11.** Check for rapid switching from rich to lean and lean to rich and change between once every 2 seconds and five times per second (0.5 to 5.0 Hz). ● **SEE FIGURES 15–12, 15–13, AND 15–14.**

**NOTE: General Motors warns not to base the diagnosis of an oxygen sensor problem solely on its scope pattern. The varying voltage output of an oxygen sensor can easily be mistaken for a fault in the sensor itself, rather than a fault in the fuel delivery system.**

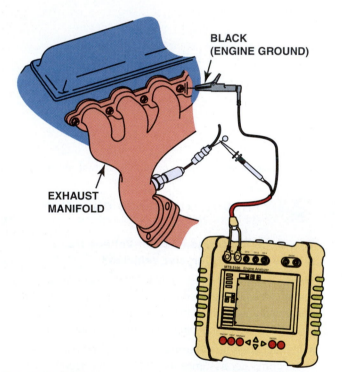

**BLACK (ENGINE GROUND)**

**EXHAUST MANIFOLD**

**FIGURE 15–10** Connecting a handheld digital storage oscilloscope to an oxygen sensor signal wire. The use of the low-pass filter helps eliminate any low-frequency interference from affecting the scope display.

## OXYGEN SENSOR WAVEFORM ANALYSIS

As the $O_2$ sensor warms up, the sensor voltage begins to rise. When the sensor voltage rises above 450 mV, the PCM determines that the sensor is up to operating temperature, takes

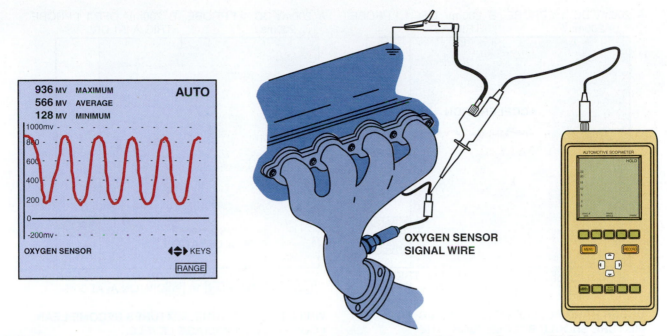

**FIGURE 15–11** The waveform of a good oxygen sensor as displayed on a digital storage oscilloscope (DSO). Note that the maximum reading is above 800 mV and the minimum reading is less than 200 mV.

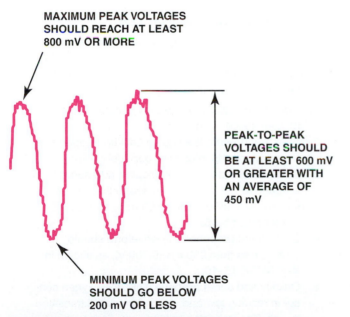

MAXIMUM PEAK VOLTAGES
SHOULD REACH AT LEAST
800 mV OR MORE

PEAK-TO-PEAK
VOLTAGES SHOULD
BE AT LEAST 600 mV
OR GREATER WITH
AN AVERAGE OF
450 mV

MINIMUM PEAK VOLTAGES
SHOULD GO BELOW
200 mV OR LESS

**FIGURE 15–12** A typical good oxygen sensor waveform as displayed on a digital storage oscilloscope. Look for transitions that occur between once every two seconds at idle and five times per second at higher engine speeds (0.5 and 5 Hz). *(Courtesy of Fluke Corporation)*

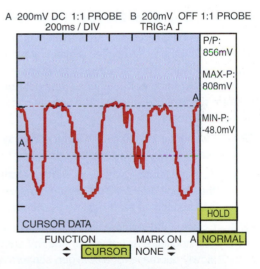

ONCE YOU'VE ACTIVATED "PEAK-TO-PEAK,"
"MAX-PEAK," AND "MIN-PEAK," FRAME THE
WAVEFORM WITH CURSORS - LOOK FOR
THE MINIMUM AND MAXIMUM VOLTAGES
AND THE DIFFERENCE BETWEEN THEM IN
THE RIGHT DISPLAY.

**FIGURE 15–13** Using the cursors on the oscilloscope, the high- and low-oxygen sensor values can be displayed on the screen. *(Courtesy of Fluke Corporation)*

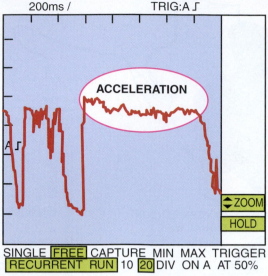

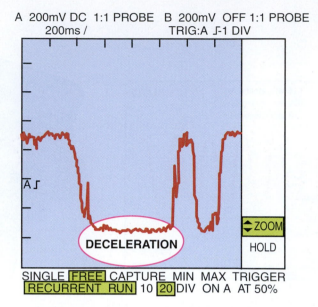

UNDER HARD ACCELERATION, THE AIR–FUEL MIXTURE SHOULD BECOME RICH - THE VOLTAGE SHOULD STAY FAIRLY HIGH

WHILE DECELERATING, MIXTURES BECOME LEAN. LOOK FOR LOW VOLTAGE LEVELS.

**FIGURE 15–14** When the air–fuel mixture rapidly changes such as during a rapid acceleration, look for a rapid response. The transition from low to high should be less than 100 ms. (*Courtesy of Fluke Corporation*)

---

🔧 **TECH TIP**

**The Key On, Engine Off Oxygen Sensor Test**

This test works on General Motors vehicles and may work on others if the PCM applies a bias voltage to the oxygen sensors. Zirconia oxygen sensors become more electrically conductive as they get hot. To perform this test, be sure that the vehicle has not run for several hours.

**STEP 1** Connect a scan tool and get the display ready to show oxygen sensor data.

**STEP 2** Turn the ignition switch on without starting the engine (KOEO). The heater in the oxygen sensor will start heating the sensor.

**STEP 3** Observe the voltage of the oxygen sensor. The applied bias voltage of 450 mV should slowly decrease for all oxygen sensors as they become more electrically conductive and other bias voltage is flowing to ground.

**STEP 4** A good oxygen sensor should indicate a voltage of less than 100 mV after 3 minutes. Any sensor that displays a higher-than-usual voltage or seems to stay higher longer than the others could be defective or skewed high.

🔧 **TECH TIP**

**The Propane Oxygen Sensor Test**

Adding propane to the air inlet of a running engine is an excellent way to check if the oxygen sensor is able to react to changes in air–fuel mixture. Follow these steps in performing the propane trick:

1. Connect a digital storage oscilloscope to the oxygen sensor signal wire.
2. Start and operate the engine until up to operating temperature and in closed-loop fuel control.
3. While watching the scope display, add some propane to the air inlet. The scope display should read full rich (over 800 mV), as shown in ● **FIGURE 15–15**.
4. Shut off the propane. The waveform should drop to less than 200 mV (0.200 V), as shown in ● **FIGURE 15–16**.
5. Quickly add some propane while the oxygen sensor is reading low and watch for a rapid transition to rich. The transition should occur in less than 100 milliseconds (ms).

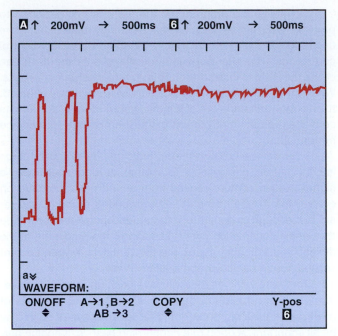

**FIGURE 15–15** Adding propane to the air inlet of an engine operating in closed loop with a working oxygen sensor causes the oxygen sensor voltage to read high.

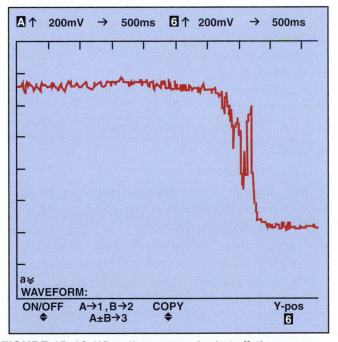

**FIGURE 15–16** When the propane is shut off, the oxygen sensor should read below 200 mV.

control of the fuel mixture, and begins to cycle rich and lean. At this point, the system is considered to be in closed loop. ● **SEE FIGURE 15–17.**

**FREQUENCY**   The frequency of the $O_2$ sensor is important in determining the condition of the fuel control system. The higher the frequency the better, but the frequency must not exceed

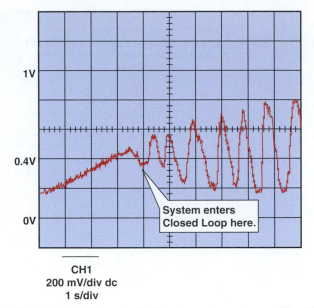

**FIGURE 15–17** When the O2S voltage rises above 450 mV, the PCM starts to control the fuel mixture based on oxygen sensor activity.

6 Hz. For its OBD-II standards, the government has stated that a frequency greater than 6 Hz represents a misfire.

**THROTTLE-BODY FUEL-INJECTION SYSTEMS.**   Normal TBI system rich/lean switching frequencies are from about 0.5 Hz at idle to about 3 Hz at 2500 RPM. Additionally, due to the TBI design limitations, fuel distribution to individual cylinders may not always be equal (due to unequal intake runner length, etc.). This may be normal unless certain other conditions are present at the same time.

**PORT FUEL-INJECTION SYSTEMS.**   Specification for port fuel-injection systems is 0.5 Hz at idle to 5 Hz at 2500 RPM. ● **SEE FIGURE 15–18.** Port fuel-injection systems have more rich/lean O2S voltage transitions (cross counts) for a given amount of time than any other type of system, due to the greatly improved system design compared to TBI units.

Port fuel-injection systems take the least amount of time to react to the fuel adaptive command (for example, changing injector pulse width).

## HASH

**BACKGROUND INFORMATION**   Hash on the O2S waveform is defined as a series of high-frequency spikes, or the fuzz (or noise) viewed on some O2S waveforms, or more specifically, oscillation frequencies higher than those created by the PCM normal feedback operation (normal rich/lean oscillations).

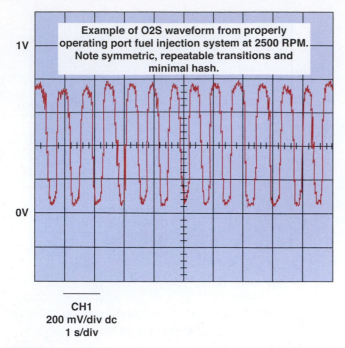

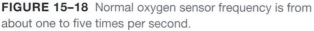

**CH1**
**200 mV/div dc**
**1 s/div**

**FIGURE 15–18** Normal oxygen sensor frequency is from about one to five times per second.

Hash is the critical indicator of reduced combustion efficiency. Hash on the O2S waveform can warn of reduced performance in individual engine cylinders. Hash also impedes proper operation of the PCM feedback fuel control program. The feedback program is the active software program that interprets the $O_2$ sensor voltage and calculates a corrective mixture control command.

Generally, the program for the PCM is not designed to process O2S signal frequencies efficiently that result from events other than normal system operation and fuel control commands. The high-frequency oscillations of the hash can cause the PCM to lose control. This, in turn, has several effects. When the operating strategy of the PCM is adversely affected, the air–fuel ratio drifts out of the catalyst window, which affects converter operating efficiency, exhaust emissions, and engine performance.

Hash on the O2S waveform indicates an exhaust charge imbalance from one cylinder to another, or more specifically, a higher oxygen content sensed from an individual combustion event. Most oxygen sensors, when working properly, can react fast enough to generate voltage deflections corresponding to a single combustion event. The bigger the amplitude of the deflection (hash), the greater the differential in oxygen content sensed from a particular combustion event.

There are vehicles that will have hash on their O2S waveforms and are operating perfectly normal. Small amounts of hash may not be of concern and larger amounts of hash may be all important. A good rule concerning hash is, if engine performance is good, there are no vacuum leaks, and if exhaust HC (hydrocarbon) and oxygen levels are okay while hash is present on the O2S waveform, then the hash is nothing to worry about.

**CAUSES OF HASH** Hash on the O2S signal can be caused by the following:

1. Misfiring cylinders
   - Ignition misfire
   - Lean misfire
   - Rich misfire
   - Compression-related misfire
   - Vacuum leaks
   - Injector imbalance
2. System design, such as different intake runner length
3. System design amplified by engine and component degradation caused by aging and wear
4. System manufacturing variances, such as intake runner blockage and valve stem mismachining

The spikes and hash on the waveform during a misfire event are created by incomplete combustion, which results in only partial use of the available oxygen in the cylinder. The leftover oxygen goes out the exhaust port and travels past the oxygen sensor. When the oxygen sensor "sees" the oxygen-filled exhaust charge, it quickly generates a low voltage, or spike. A series of these high-frequency spikes make up what we are calling "hash."

**CLASSIFICATIONS OF HASH**

**CLASS 1: AMPLIFIED AND SIGNIFICANT HASH.** Amplified hash is the somewhat unimportant hash that is often present between 300 and 600 millivolts on the O2S waveform. This type of hash is usually not important for diagnosis. That is because amplified hash is created largely as a result of the electrochemical

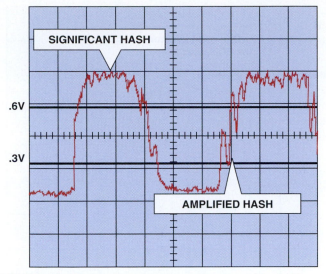

FIGURE 15–19 Significant hash can be caused by faults in one or more cylinders, whereas amplified hash is not as important for diagnosis.

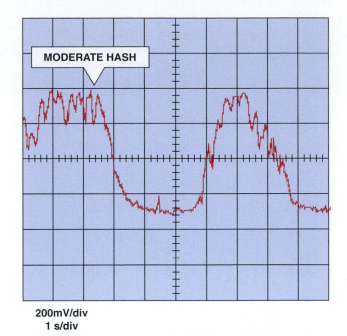

200mV/div
1 s/div

FIGURE 15–20 Moderate hash may or may not be significant for diagnosis.

properties of the O2S itself and many times not an engine or other unrelated problem. Hash between 300 and 600 mV is not particularly conclusive, so for all practical purposes it is insignificant. ● SEE FIGURE 15–19.

Significant hash is defined as the hash that occurs above 600 mV and below 300 mV on the O2S waveform. This is the area of the waveform that the PCM is watching to determine the fuel mixture. Significant hash is important for diagnosis because it is caused by a combustion event. If the waveform exhibits class 1 hash, the combustion event problem is probably occurring in only one of the cylinders. If the event happens in a greater number of the cylinders the waveform will become class 3 or be fixed lean or rich the majority of the time.

**CLASS 2: MODERATE HASH.** Moderate hash is defined as spikes shooting downward from the top arc of the waveform as the waveform carves its arc through the rich phase. Moderate hash spikes are not greater than 150 mV in amplitude. They may get as large as 200 mV in amplitude as the O2S waveform goes through 450 mV. Moderate hash may or may not be significant to a particular diagnosis. ● SEE FIGURE 15–20. For instance, most vehicles will exhibit more hash on the O2S waveform at idle. Additionally, the engine family or type of O2S could be important factors when considering the significance of moderate hash on the O2S waveform.

**CLASS 3: SEVERE HASH.** Severe hash is defined as hash whose amplitude is greater than 200 mV. Severe hash may even cover the entire voltage range of the sensor for an extended period of operation. Severe hash on the DSO display appears as spikes that shoot downward, over 200 mV from the top of the operating range of the sensor, or as far as to the bottom of the sensor's operating range. ● SEE FIGURE 15–21. If severe hash is present for several seconds during a steady state engine operating mode, say 2500 RPM, it is almost always significant to the diagnosis of any vehicle. Severe hash of this nature is almost never caused by a normal system design. It is caused by cylinder misfire or mixture imbalance.

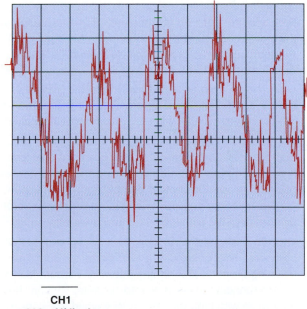

CH1
200 mV/div dc
500 ms/div

FIGURE 15–21 Severe hash is almost always caused by cylinder misfire conditions.

## HASH INTERPRETATION
### TYPES OF MISFIRES THAT CAN CAUSE HASH.

1. Ignition misfire caused by a bad spark plug, spark plug wire, distributor cap, rotor, ignition coil, or ignition primary problem. Usually an engine analyzer is used to eliminate these possibilities or confirm these problems. ● SEE FIGURE 15–22.

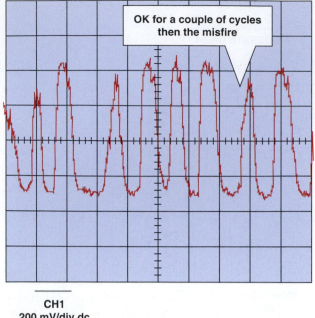

CH1
200 mV/div dc
500 ms/div

**FIGURE 15–22** An ignition- or mixture-related misfire can cause hash on the oxygen sensor waveform.

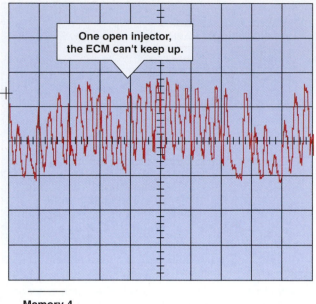

Memory 4
200 mV/div
200 ms/div

**FIGURE 15–23** An injector imbalance can cause a lean or a rich misfire.

2. Rich misfire from an excessively rich fuel delivery to an individual cylinder (various potential root causes). Air–fuel ratio in a given cylinder ventured below approximately 13:1.

3. Lean misfire from an excessively lean fuel delivery to an individual cylinder (various potential root causes). Air–fuel ratio in a given cylinder ventured above approximately 17:1.

4. Compression-related misfire from a mechanical problem that reduces compression to the point that not enough heat is generated from compressing the air–fuel mixture prior to ignition, preventing combustion. This raises O2S content in the exhaust (for example, a burned valve, broken or worn ring, flat cam lobe, or sticking valve).

5. Vacuum leak misfire unique to one or two individual cylinders. This possibility is eliminated or confirmed by inducing propane around any potential vacuum leak area (intake runners, intake manifold gaskets, vacuum hoses, etc.) while watching the DSO to see when the signal goes rich and the hash changes from ingesting the propane. Vacuum leak misfires are caused when a vacuum leak unique to one cylinder or a few individual cylinders causes the air–fuel ratio in the affected cylinder(s) to venture above approximately 17:1, causing a lean misfire.

6. Injector imbalance misfire (on port fuel-injected engines only); one cylinder has a rich or lean misfire due to an individual injector(s) delivering the wrong quantity of fuel. Injector imbalance misfires are caused when an injector on one cylinder or a few individual cylinders causes the air–fuel ratio in its cylinder(s) to venture above approximately

17:1, causing a lean misfire, or below approximately 13.7:1, causing a rich misfire. ● **SEE FIGURE 15–23.**

### OTHER RULES CONCERNING HASH ON THE O2S WAVEFORM

If there is significant hash on the O2S signal that is not normal for that type of system, it will usually be accompanied by a repeatable and generally detectable engine miss at idle (for example, a thump, thump, thump every time the cylinder fires). Generally, if the hash is significant, the engine miss will correlate in time with individual spikes seen on the waveform.

Hash that may be difficult to get rid of (and is normal in some cases) will not be accompanied by a significant engine miss that corresponds with the hash. When the individual spikes that make up the hash on the waveform do not correlate in time with an engine miss, less success can usually be found in getting rid of them by performing repairs.

A fair rule of thumb is if you are sure there are no intake vacuum leaks, and the exhaust gas HC (hydrocarbon) and oxygen levels are normal, and the engine does not run or idle rough, the hash is probably acceptable or normal.

## NEGATIVE O2S VOLTAGE

When testing O2S waveforms, some $O_2$ sensors will exhibit some negative voltage. The acceptable amount of negative O2S voltage is −0.75 mV, providing that the maximum voltage

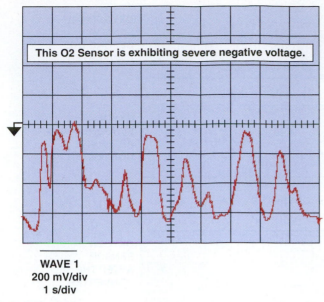

This O2 Sensor is exhibiting severe negative voltage.

WAVE 1
200 mV/div
1 s/div

**FIGURE 15–24** Negative reading oxygen sensor voltage can be caused by several problems.

peak exceeds 850 mV. ● **SEE FIGURE 15–24.** Testing has shown that negative voltage signals from an $O_2$ sensor have usually been caused by the following:

1. Chemical poisoning of sensing element (silicon, oil, etc.).
2. Overheated engines.
3. Mishandling of new $O_2$ sensors (dropped and banged around, resulting in a cracked insulator).
4. Poor $O_2$ sensor ground.

## LOW O2S READINGS

An oxygen sensor reading that is low could be due to other things besides a lean air–fuel mixture. Remember, an oxygen sensor senses oxygen, not unburned gas, even though a high reading generally indicates a rich exhaust (lack of oxygen) and a low reading indicates a lean mixture (excess oxygen).

**FALSE LEAN** If an oxygen sensor reads low as a result of a factor besides a lean mixture, it is often called a **false lean indication.**

False lean indications (low O2S readings) can be attributed to the following:

1. **Ignition misfire.** An ignition misfire due to a defective spark plug wire, fouled spark plug, and so forth, causes no burned air and fuel to be exhausted past the O2S. The O2S "sees" the oxygen (not the unburned gasoline) and the O2S voltage is low.
2. **Exhaust leak in front of the O2S.** An exhaust leak between the engine and the oxygen sensor causes outside oxygen to be drawn into the exhaust and past the O2S. This oxygen is "read" by the O2S and produces a lower-than-normal voltage. The computer interrupts the lower-than-normal voltage signal from the O2S as meaning that the air–fuel mixture is lean. The computer will cause the fuel system to deliver a richer air–fuel mixture.
3. **A spark plug misfire represents a false lean signal to the oxygen sensor.** The computer does not know that the extra oxygen going past the oxygen sensor is not due to a lean air–fuel mixture. The computer commands a richer mixture, which could cause the spark plugs to foul, increasing the rate of misfirings.

## HIGH O2S READINGS

An oxygen sensor reading that is high could be due to other things beside a rich air–fuel mixture. When the O2S reads high as a result of other factors besides a rich mixture, it is often called a **false rich indication.**

False rich indication (high O2S readings) can be attributed to the following:

1. Contaminated O2S due to additives in the engine coolant or due to silicon poisoning
2. A stuck-open EGR valve (especially at idle)
3. A spark plug wire too close to the oxygen sensor signal wire, which can induce a higher-than-normal voltage in the signal wire, thereby indicating to the computer a false rich condition
4. A loose oxygen sensor ground connection, which can cause a higher-than-normal voltage and a false rich signal
5. A break or contamination of the wiring and its connectors, which could prevent reference oxygen from reaching the oxygen sensor, resulting in a false rich indication. (All oxygen sensors require an oxygen supply inside the sensor itself for reference to be able to sense exhaust gas oxygen.)

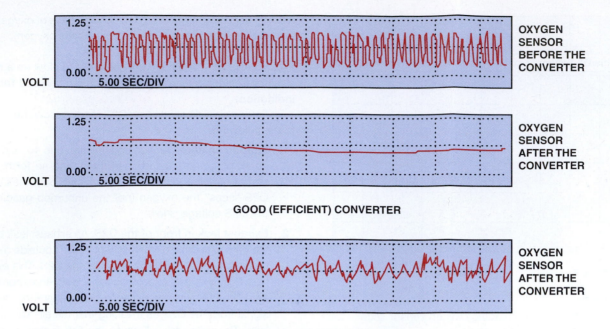

1.25

0.00

VOLT    5.00 SEC/DIV

OXYGEN SENSOR BEFORE THE CONVERTER

1.25

0.00

VOLT    5.00 SEC/DIV

OXYGEN SENSOR AFTER THE CONVERTER

**GOOD (EFFICIENT) CONVERTER**

1.25

0.00

VOLT    5.00 SEC/DIV

OXYGEN SENSOR AFTER THE CONVERTER

**BAD (INEFFICIENT) CONVERTER**

**FIGURE 15–25** The post-catalytic converter oxygen sensor should display very little activity if the catalytic converter is efficient.

## POST-CATALYTIC CONVERTER OXYGEN SENSOR TESTING

The oxygen sensor located behind the catalytic converter is used on OBD-II vehicles to monitor converter efficiency. A changing air–fuel mixture is required for the most efficient operation of the converter. If the converter is working correctly, the oxygen content after the converter should be fairly constant. ● **SEE FIGURE 15–25.**

## OXYGEN SENSOR VISUAL INSPECTION

Whenever an oxygen sensor is replaced, the old sensor should be carefully inspected to help determine the cause of the failure. This is an important step because if the cause of the failure is not discovered, it could lead to another sensor failure.

Inspection may reveal the following:

1. **Black sooty deposits** usually indicate a rich air–fuel mixture.

**? FREQUENTLY ASKED QUESTION**

**What Is Lambda?**

An oxygen sensor is also called a lambda sensor because the voltage changes at the air–fuel ratio of 14.7:1, which is the stoichiometric rate for gasoline. If this mixture of gasoline and air is burned, all of the gasoline is burned and uses all of the oxygen in the mixture. This exact ratio represents a lambda of 1.0. If the mixture is richer (more fuel or less air), the number is less than 1.0, such as 0.850. If the mixture is leaner than 14.7:1 (less fuel or more air), the lambda number is higher than 1.0, such as 1.130. Often, the target lambda is displayed on a scan tool. ● **SEE FIGURE 15–26.**

2. **White chalky deposits** are characteristic of silica contamination. Usual causes for this type of sensor failure include silica deposits in the fuel or a technician having used the wrong type of silicone sealant during the servicing of the engine.

3. **White sandy or gritty deposits** are characteristic of antifreeze (ethylene glycol) contamination. A defective cylinder head or intake manifold gasket could be the cause, or a cracked cylinder head or engine block. Antifreeze may also

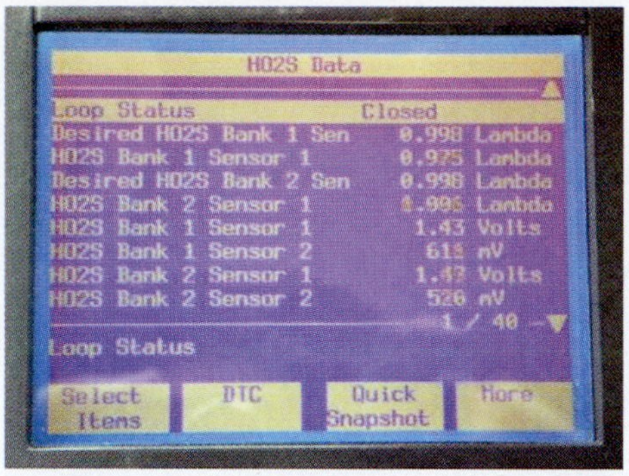

**FIGURE 15–26** The target lambda on this vehicle is slightly lower than 1.0 indicating that the PCM is attempting to supply the engine with an air–fuel mixture that is slightly richer than stoichiometric. Multiply the lambda number by 14.7 to find the actual air–fuel ratio.

cause the oxygen sensor to become green as a result of the dye used in antifreeze.

4. **Dark brown deposits** are an indication of excessive oil consumption. Possible causes include a defective positive crankcase ventilation (PCV) system or a mechanical engine problem such as defective valve stem seals or piston rings.

**CAUTION: Do not spray any silicone spray near the engine where the engine vacuum could draw the fumes into the engine. This can also cause silica damage to the oxygen sensor. Also be sure that the silicone sealer used for gaskets is rated oxygen-sensor safe.**

# OXYGEN SENSOR-RELATED DIAGNOSTIC TROUBLE CODES

Diagnostic trouble codes (DTCs) associated with the oxygen sensor include:

| Diagnostic Trouble Code | Description | Possible Causes |
|---|---|---|
| P0131 | Upstream HO2S grounded | • Exhaust leak upstream of HO2S (bank 1)<br>• Extremely lean air–fuel mixture<br>• HO2S defective or contaminated<br>• HO2S signal wire shorted-to-ground |
| P0132 | Upstream HO2S shorted | • Upstream HO2S (bank 1) shorted<br>• Defective HO2S<br>• Fuel-contaminated HO2S |
| P0133 | Upstream HO2S slow response | • Open or short in heater circuit<br>• Defective or fuel-contaminated HO2S<br>• EGR or fuel-system fault |

# SUMMARY

1. An oxygen sensor produces a voltage output signal based on the oxygen content of the exhaust stream.

2. If the exhaust has little oxygen, the voltage of the oxygen sensor will be close to 1 volt (1,000 mV) and close to zero if there is high oxygen content in the exhaust.

3. Oxygen sensors can have one, two, three, four, or more wires, depending on the style and design.

4. The oxygen sensor signal determines fuel trim, which is used to tailor the air–fuel mixture for the catalytic converter.

5. Conditions can occur that cause the oxygen sensor to be fooled and give a false lean or false rich signals to the PCM.

6. Oxygen sensors can be tested using a digital meter, a scope, or a scan tool.

1. How does an oxygen sensor detect oxygen levels in the exhaust?

2. What are four basic designs of oxygen sensors and how many wires may be used for each?

3. What is the difference between open-loop and closed-loop engine operation?

4. What are three ways oxygen sensors can be tested?

5. How can the oxygen sensor be fooled and provide the wrong information to the PCM?

## CHAPTER QUIZ

1. The sensor that must be warmed and functioning before the engine management computer will go to closed loop is the _____.
   a. O2S
   b. ECT sensor
   c. Engine MAP sensor
   d. BARO sensor

2. The voltage output of a zirconia oxygen sensor when the exhaust stream is lean (excess oxygen) is _____.
   a. Relatively high (close to 1 volt)
   b. About in the middle of the voltage range
   c. Relatively low (close to 0 volt)
   d. Either a or b, depending on atmospheric pressure

3. Where is sensor 1, bank 1 located on a V-type engine?
   a. On the same bank where number 1 cylinder is located
   b. In the exhaust manifold
   c. On the bank opposite cylinder number 1
   d. Both a and b

4. A heated zirconia oxygen sensor will have how many wires?
   a. 2
   b. 3
   c. 4
   d. Either b or c

5. A high O2S voltage could be due to _____.
   a. A rich exhaust
   b. A lean exhaust
   c. A defective spark plug wire
   d. Both a and c

6. A low O2S voltage could be due to _____.
   a. A rich exhaust
   b. A lean exhaust
   c. A defective spark plug wire
   d. Both b and c

7. An oxygen sensor is being tested with digital multimeter (DMM), using the MIN/MAX function. The readings are: minimum = 78 mV; maximum = 932 mV; average = 442 mV. Technician A says that the engine is operating correctly. Technician B says that the oxygen sensor is skewed too rich. Which technician is correct?
   a. Technician A only
   b. Technician B only
   c. Both Technicians A and B
   d. Neither Technician A nor B

8. An oxygen sensor is being tested using a digital storage oscilloscope (DSO). A good oxygen sensor should display how many switches per second?
   a. 1 to 5
   b. 5 to 10
   c. 10 to 15
   d. 15 to 20

9. When testing an oxygen sensor using a digital storage oscilloscope (DSO), how quickly should the voltage change when either propane is added to the intake stream or when a vacuum leak is created?
   a. Less than 100 ms
   b. 1 to 3 seconds
   c. 100 to 200 ms
   d. 450 to 550 ms

10. A P0133 DTC is being discussed. Technician A says that a defective heater circuit could be the cause. Technician B says that a contaminated sensor could be the cause. Which technician is correct?
    a. Technician A only
    b. Technician B only
    c. Both Technicians A and B
    d. Neither Technician A nor B

# chapter 16

# WIDE-BAND OXYGEN SENSORS

**OBJECTIVES:** After studying Chapter 16, the reader will be able to: • Prepare for the ASE certification test content Engine Performance (A8) content area "E" (Computerized Engine Controls Diagnosis and Repair) • Describe the difference between a two-band and a wide-band oxygen sensor. • Explain the difference between a thimble design and a planar design. • Discuss the operation of a wide-band oxygen sensor. • List the test procedure for testing a dual cell and a single cell wide-band oxygen sensor.

**KEY TERMS:** Air–fuel ratio sensor 220 • Air reference chamber 218 • Ambient air electrode 217 • Ambient side electrode 217 • Cup design 217 • Diffusion chamber 218 • Dual cell 218 • Exhaust side electrode 217 • Finger design 217 • Lean air–fuel (LAF) sensor 215 • Light-off time (LOT) 217 • Nernst cell 218 • Planar design 217 • Pump cell 218 • Reference electrode 217 • Reference voltage 218 • Signal electrode 217 • Single cell 220 • Thimble design 217

## TERMINOLOGY

Honda was the first manufacturer to use wide band oxygen sensors beginning in 1992. Wide-band oxygen sensors are used by most vehicle manufacturers to ensure that the exhaust emissions can meet the current standard. Wide-band oxygen sensors are also called by various names, depending on the vehicle and/or oxygen sensor manufacturer. The terms used include:

- **Wide-band oxygen sensor**
- **Broadband oxygen sensor**
- **Wide-range oxygen sensor**
- **Air–fuel ratio (AFR) sensor**
- **Wide-range air–fuel (WRAF) sensor**
- **Lean air–fuel (LAF) sensor**
- **Air–fuel (AF) sensor**

Wide-band oxygen sensors are also manufactured in dual cell and single cell designs.

## NEED FOR WIDE-BAND SENSORS

**INTRODUCTION** A conventional zirconia oxygen sensor reacts to an air–fuel mixture of either richer or leaner than 14.7:1. This means that the sensor cannot be used to detect the exact air–fuel mixture. ● **SEE FIGURE 16–1**.

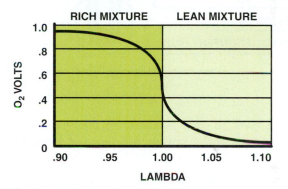

**FIGURE 16–1** A conventional zirconia oxygen sensor can only reset to exhaust mixtures that are richer or leaner than 14.7:1 (lambda 1.00).

The need for more stringent exhaust emission standards such as the natural low-emission vehicle (NLEV), plus the ultra low-emission vehicle (ULEV), and the super ultra low-emission vehicle (SULEV) require more accurate fuel control than can be provided by a traditional oxygen sensor.

**PURPOSE AND FUNCTION** A wide-band oxygen sensor is capable of supplying air–fuel ratio information to the PCM over a much broader range. The use of a wide-band oxygen sensor compared with a conventional zirconia oxygen sensor differs as follows:

1. Able to detect exhaust air–fuel ratios from as rich as 10:1 and as lean as 23:1 in some cases.

2. Cold-start activity within as little as 10 seconds.

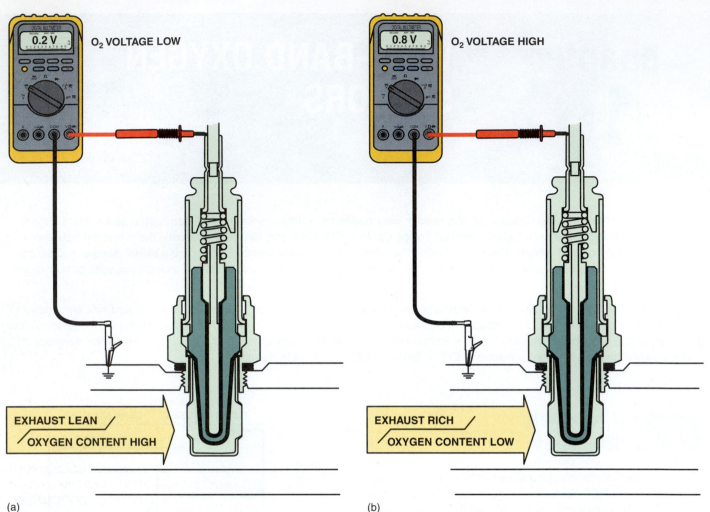

O₂ VOLTAGE LOW

O₂ VOLTAGE HIGH

**EXHAUST LEAN**
**OXYGEN CONTENT HIGH**

**EXHAUST RICH**
**OXYGEN CONTENT LOW**

(a)

(b)

**FIGURE 16–2** (a) When the exhaust is lean, the output of a zirconia oxygen sensor is below 450 mV. (b) When the exhaust is rich, the output of a zirconia oxygen sensor is above 450 mV.

**? FREQUENTLY ASKED QUESTION**

**How Quickly Can a Wide-Band Oxygen Sensor Achieve Closed Loop?**

In a Toyota Highlander hybrid electric vehicle, the operation of the gasoline engine is delayed for a short time when the vehicle is first driven. During this time of electric operation, the ICE oxygen sensor heaters are turned on in readiness for the gasoline engine starting. The gasoline engine often achieves closed loop operation during *cranking* because the oxygen sensors are fully warm and ready to go at the same time the engine is started. Having the gasoline engine achieve closed loop quickly, allows it to meet the stringent SULEV standards.

# CONVENTIONAL O2S REVIEW

**NARROW BAND**  A conventional zirconia oxygen sensor (O2S) is only able to detect if the exhaust is richer or leaner than 14.7:1. A conventional oxygen sensor is therefore referred to as:

- **2-step sensor**—either rich or lean
- **Narrow band sensor**—informs the PCM whether the exhaust is rich or lean only

The voltage value where a zirconia oxygen sensor switches from rich to lean or from lean to rich is 0.450 V (450 mV).

- Above 0.450 V = rich
- Below 0.450 V = lean
  - **SEE FIGURE 16–2.**

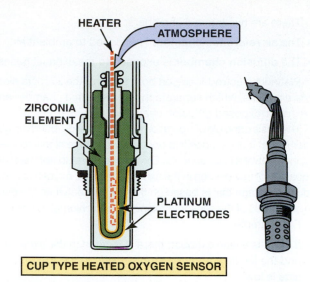

FIGURE 16–3 Most conventional zirconia oxygen sensors and some wide-band oxygen sensors use the cup-type design.

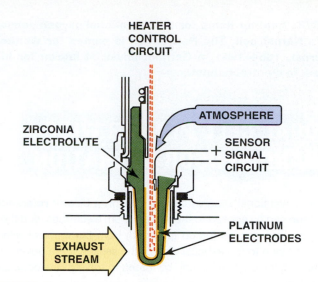

FIGURE 16–4 A typical heated zirconia oxygen sensor, showing the sensor signal circuit that uses the outer (exhaust) electrode as negative and the ambient air side electrode as the positive.

## CONSTRUCTION
A typical zirconia oxygen sensor has the sensing element in the shape of a thimble and is often referred to as:

- **Thimble design**
- **Cup design**
- **Finger design**
  - ● SEE FIGURE 16–3.

A typical zirconia oxygen sensor has a heater inside the thimble and does not touch the inside of the sensor. The sensor is similar to a battery that has two electrodes and an electrolyte. The electrolyte is solid and is the zirconia (zirconium dioxide). There are also two porous platinum electrodes, which have the following functions:

- **Exhaust side electrode**—This electrode is exposed to the exhaust stream.
- **Ambient side electrode**—This electrode is exposed to outside (ambient) air and is the **signal electrode,** also called the **reference electrode** or **ambient air electrode.**
  - ● SEE FIGURE 16–4.

The electrolyte (zirconia) is able to conduct electrons as follows:

- If the exhaust is rich, $O_2$ from the reference (inner) electrode wants to flow to the exhaust side electrode, which results in the generation of a voltage.
- If the exhaust is lean, $O_2$ flow is not needed and as a result, there is little if any electron movement and, therefore, no voltage is being produced.

## HEATER CIRCUITS
The heater circuit on conventional oxygen sensors requires 0.8 to 2.0 amperes and it keeps the sensor at about 600°F (315°C).

A wide-band oxygen sensor operates at a higher temperature than a conventional HO2S from 1,200°F to 1,400°F (650°C to 760°C). The amount of electrical current needed for a wide-band oxygen sensor is about 8 to 10 amperes.

## PLANAR DESIGN
In 1998, Bosch introduced a wide-band oxygen sensor that is flat and thin (1.5 mm or 0.006 inch) and not in the shape of a thimble, as previously constructed. Now several manufacturers produce a similar planar design wide-band oxygen sensor. Because it is thin, it is easier to heat than older styles of oxygen sensors and as a result can achieve closed loop in less than 10 seconds. This fast heating, called **light-off time (LOT),** helps improve fuel economy and reduces cold-start exhaust emissions. The type of construction is not noticed by the technician, nor does it affect the testing procedures.

A conventional oxygen sensor can be constructed using a **planar design** instead of the thimble-type design. A planar design has the following features:

- The elements including the zirconia electrolyte and the two electrodes and heater are stacked together in a flat-type design.
- The planar design allows faster warm-up because the heater is in direct contact with the other elements.
- Planar oxygen sensors are the most commonly used. Some planar designs are used as a conventional narrow-band oxygen sensor.

The sandwich-type design of the planar style of oxygen sensor has the same elements and operates the same, but is stacked in the following way from the exhaust side to the ambient air side:

Exhaust stream

Outer electrode

Zirconia ($ZiO_2$) (electrolyte)

Inner electrode (reference or signal)

Outside (ambient) air

Heater

● SEE FIGURE 16–5.

**NOTE: Another name for a conventional oxygen sensor is a Nernst cell. The Nernst cell is named for Walther Nernst, 1864–1941, a German physicist known for his work in electrochemistry.**

# DUAL CELL PLANAR WIDE-BAND SENSOR OPERATION

In a conventional zirconia oxygen sensor, a bias or **reference voltage** can be applied to the two platinum electrodes, and then oxygen ions can be forced (pumped) from the ambient reference air side to the exhaust side of the sensor. If the polarity is reversed, the oxygen ion can be forced to travel in the opposite direction.

A **dual cell** planar-type wide-band oxygen sensor is made like a conventional planar O2S and is labeled Nernst cell. Above the Nernst cell is another zirconia layer with two electrodes, which is called the **pump cell.** The two cells share a common ground, which is called the reference.

There are two internal chambers:

- The **air reference chamber** is exposed to ambient air.
- The **diffusion chamber** is exposed to the exhaust gases.

Platinum electrodes are on both sides of the zirconia electrolyte elements, which separate the air reference chamber and the exhaust-exposed diffusion chamber.

The basic principle of operation of a typical wide-band oxygen sensor is that it uses a positive or negative voltage signal to keep a balance between two sensors. Oxygen sensors do not measure the quantity of free oxygen in the exhaust. Instead, oxygen sensors produce a voltage that is based on the ion flow between the platinum electrodes of the sensor to maintain a stoichiometric balance.

For example:

- If there is a lean exhaust, there is oxygen in the exhaust and the ion flow from the ambient side to the exhaust side is low.
- If there were rich exhaust, the ion flow is increased to help maintain balance between the ambient air side and the exhaust side of the sensor.

The PCM can apply a small current to the pump cell electrodes, which causes oxygen ions through the zirconia into or out of the diffusion chamber. The PCM pumps $O_2$ ions in and out of the diffusion chamber to bring the voltage back to 0.450, using the pump cell.

The operation of a wide-band oxygen sensor is best described by looking at what occurs when the exhaust is stoichiometric, rich, and lean. ● SEE FIGURE 16–6.

## STOICHIOMETRIC

- When the exhaust is at stoichiometric (14.7:1 air–fuel ratio), the voltage of the Nernst cell is 450 mV (0.450 V).
- The voltage between the diffusion chamber and the air reference chamber changes from 0.450 V. This voltage will be:

  - Higher if the exhaust is rich
  - Lower if the exhaust is lean

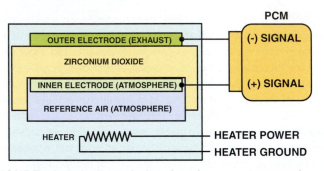

**FIGURE 16–5** A planar design zirconia oxygen sensor places all of the elements together, which allows the sensor to reach operating temperature quickly.

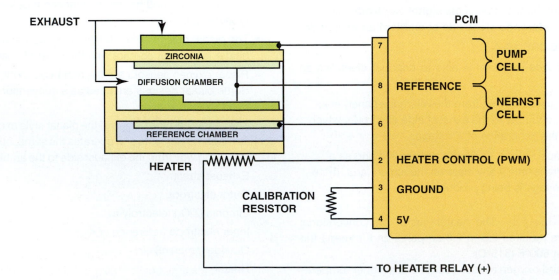

**FIGURE 16–6** The reference electrodes are shared by the Nernst cell and the pump cell.

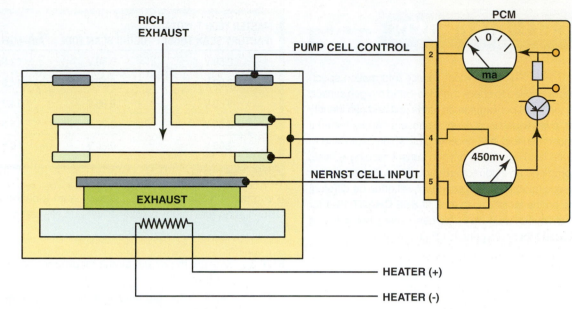

**FIGURE 16–7** When the exhaust is rich, the PCM applies a negative current into the pump cell.

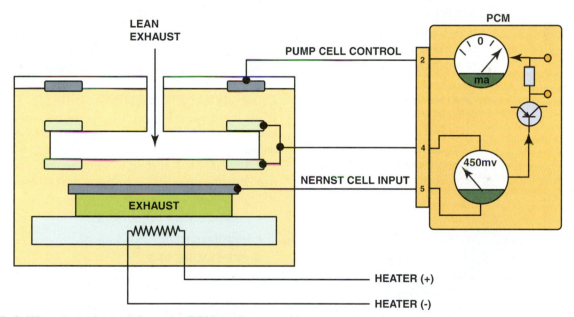

**FIGURE 16–8** When the exhaust is lean, the PCM applies a positive current into the pump cell.

The reference voltage remains constant, usually at 2.5 volts, but can vary depending on the year, make, and model of vehicle and the type of sensor. Typical reference voltages include:

- 2.2
- 2.5
- 2.7
- 3.3
- 3.6

**RICH EXHAUST.** When the exhaust is rich, the voltage between the common (reference) electrode and the Nernst cell electrode that is exposed to ambient air is higher than 0.450 V. The PCM applies a negative current in milliamperes to the pump cell electrode to bring the circuit back into balance. ● **SEE FIGURE 16–7.**

**LEAN EXHAUST.** When the exhaust is lean, the voltage between the common (reference) electrode and the Nernst cell electrode is lower than 0.450 V. The PCM applies a positive current in milliamperes to the pump cell to bring the circuit back into balance. ● **SEE FIGURE 16–8.**

# DUAL CELL DIAGNOSIS

**SCAN TOOL DIAGNOSIS** Most service information specifies that a scan tool be used to check the wide-band oxygen sensor. This is because the PCM performs tests of the unit and can identify faults. However, even wide-band oxygen sensors can be fooled if there is an exhaust manifold leak or other fault which could lead to false or inaccurate readings. If the oxygen sensor reading is false, the PCM will command an incorrect amount of fuel. The scan data shown on a generic (global) OBD-II scan tool will often be different than the reading on the factory scan tool. ● **SEE CHART 16–1** for an example of a Toyota wide-band oxygen sensor being tested using a factory scan tool and a generic OBD-II scan tool.

**SCAN TOOL DATA (PID)** The following information will be displayed on a scan tool when looking at data for a wide-band oxygen sensor:

| HO2S1 = _____ mA | If the current is positive, this means that the PCM is pumping current in the diffusion gap due to a rich exhaust. |
| --- | --- |
| | If the current is negative, the PCM is pumping current out of the diffusion gap due to a lean exhaust. |
| Air–fuel ratio = _____ | Usually expressed in lambda. One means that the exhaust is at stoichiometric (14.7:1 air–fuel ratio) and numbers higher than 1 indicate a lean exhaust and numbers lower than 1 indicate a rich exhaust. |

# DIGITAL MULTIMETER TESTING

When testing a wide-band oxygen sensor for proper operation, perform the following steps:

**STEP 1** Check service information and determine the circuit and connector terminal identification.

**STEP 2** Measure the calibration resistor. While the value of this resistor can vary widely, depending on the type of sensor, the calibrating resistor should still be checked for opens and shorts.

> **NOTE: The calibration resistor is usually located within the connector itself.**

- If open, the ohmmeter will read OL (infinity ohms).
- If shorted, the ohmmeter will read zero or close to zero.

| MASTER TECH TOYOTA (FACTORY SCAN TOOL) | OBD-II SCAN TOOL | AIR–FUEL RATIO |
| --- | --- | --- |
| 2.50 V | 0.50 V | 12.5:1 |
| 3.00 V | 0.60 V | 14.0:1 |
| 3.30 V | 0.66 V | 14.7:1 |
| 3.50 V | 0.70 V | 15.5:1 |
| 4.00 V | 0.80 V | 18.5:1 |

**CHART 16–1**

A comparison showing what a factory scan tool and a generic OBD-II scan tool might display at various air–fuel ratios.

**STEP 3** Measure the heater circuit for proper resistance or current flow.

**STEP 4** Measure the reference voltage relative to ground. This can vary but is generally 2.4 to 2.6 volts.

**STEP 5** Using jumper wires, connect an ammeter and measure the current in the pump cell control wire.

**RICH EXHAUST (LAMBDA LESS THAN 1.00)** When the exhaust is rich, the Nernst cell voltage will move higher than 0.45 volts. The PCM will pump oxygen from the exhaust into the diffusion gap by applying a negative voltage to the pump cell.

**LEAN EXHAUST (LAMBDA HIGHER THAN 1.00)** When the exhaust is lean, the Nernst cell voltage will move lower than 0.45 volts. The PCM will pump oxygen out of the diffusion gap by applying a positive voltage to the pump cell.

The pump cell is used to pump oxygen into the diffusion gap when the exhaust is rich. The pump cell applies a negative voltage to do this.

- Positive current = lean exhaust
- Negative current = rich exhaust
- ● **SEE FIGURE 16–9.**

# SINGLE CELL WIDE-BAND OXYGEN SENSORS

**CONSTRUCTION** A typical **single cell** wide-band oxygen sensor looks similar to a conventional four-wire zirconia oxygen sensor. The typical single cell wide-band oxygen sensor, usually called an **air–fuel ratio sensor,** has the following construction features:

- Can be made using the cup or planar design
- Oxygen ($O_2$) is pumped into the diffusion layer similar to the operation of a dual cell wide-band oxygen sensor.
- ● **SEE FIGURE 16–10.**

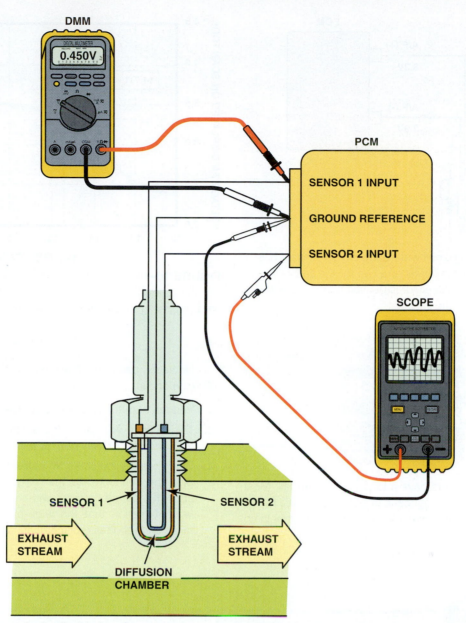

**FIGURE 16–9** Testing a dual cell wide-band oxygen sensor can be done using a voltmeter or a scope. The meter reading is attached to the Nernst cell and should read stoichiometric (450 mV) at all times. The scope is showing activity to the pump cell with commands from the PCM to keep the Nernst cell at 14.7:1 air–fuel ratio.

- Current flow reverses positive and negative
- Consists of two cell wires and two heater wires (power and ground)
- The heater usually requires 6 amperes and the ground side is pulse-width modulated.

### TESTING WITH A MILLIAMMETER
The PCM controls the single cell wide-band oxygen sensor by maintaining a voltage difference of 300 mV (0.3 V) between the two sensor leads. The PCM keeps the voltage difference constant under all operating conditions by increasing or decreasing current between the element of the cell.

- Zero (0 mA) represents lambda or stoichiometric air–fuel ratio of 14.7:1
- +10 mA indicates a lean condition
- −10 mA indicates a rich condition

### TESTING USING A SCAN TOOL
A scan tool will display a voltage reading but can vary depending on the type and maker of scan tool. ● **SEE FIGURE 16–11.**

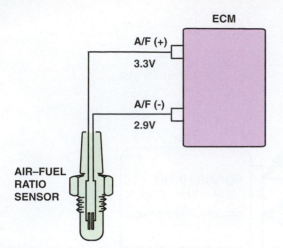

FIGURE 16–10 A single cell wide-band oxygen sensor has four wires with two for the heater and two for the sensor itself. The voltage applied to the sensor is 0.4 volt (3.3 − 2.9 = 0.4) across the two leads of the sensor.

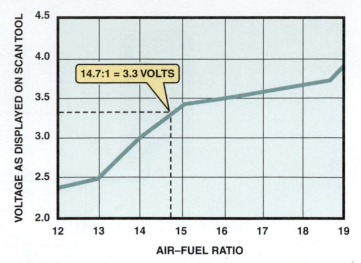

FIGURE 16–11 The scan tool can display various voltages but will often show 3.3 volts because the PCM is controlling the sensor by applying a low current to the sensor to achieve balance.

# WIDE-BAND OXYGEN SENSOR PATTERN FAILURES

Wide-band oxygen sensors have a long life but can fail. Most of the failures will cause a diagnostic trouble code (DTC) to set, usually causing the malfunction indicator (check engine) lamp to light.

However, one type of failure may not set a DTC when the following occurs:

1. Voltage from the heater circuit bleeds into the Nernst cell.

2. This voltage will cause the engine to operate extremely lean and may or may not set a diagnostic trouble code.

3. When testing indicates an extremely lean condition, unplug the connector to the oxygen sensor. If the engine starts to operate correctly with the sensor unplugged, this is confirmation that the wide-band oxygen sensor has failed and requires replacement.

## SUMMARY

1. Wide-band oxygen sensors are known by many different terms, including:
   - Broadband oxygen sensor
   - Wide-range oxygen sensor
   - Air–fuel ratio (AFR) sensor
   - Wide-range air–fuel (WRAF) sensor
   - Lean air–fuel (LAF) sensor
   - Air–fuel (AF) sensor

2. Wide-band oxygen sensors are manufactured using a cup or planar design and are dual cell or single cell design.

3. A wide-band oxygen sensor is capable of furnishing the PCM with exhaust air–fuel ratios as rich as 10:1 and as lean as 23:1.

4. The use of a wide-band oxygen sensor allows the engine to achieve more stringent exhaust emission standards.

5. A conventional zirconia oxygen sensor can be made in a cup shape or planar design and is sometimes called a narrow band or 2-step sensor.

6. The heater used on a conventional zirconia oxygen sensor uses up to 2 amperes and heats the sensor to about 600°F (315°C). A broadband sensor heater has to heat the sensor to 1,200°F to 1,400°F (650°C to 760°C) and requires up to 8 to 10 amperes.

7. A typical dual cell wide-band oxygen sensor uses the PCM to apply a current to the pump cell to keep the Nernst cell at 14.7:1.
   - When the exhaust is rich, the PCM applies a negative current to the pump cell.
   - When the exhaust is lean, the PCM applies a positive current to the pump cell.

8. Wide-band oxygen sensors can also be made using a single cell design.

9. Wide-band oxygen sensors can be best tested using a scan tool, but dual cell sensors can be checked with a voltmeter or scope. Single cell sensors can be checked using a milliammeter.

1. What type of construction is used to make wide-band oxygen sensors?

2. Why are wide-band oxygen sensors used instead of conventional zirconia sensors?

3. How is the heater different for a wide-band oxygen sensor compared with a conventional zirconia oxygen sensor?

4. How does a wide-range oxygen sensor work?

5. How can a wide-band oxygen sensor be tested?

## CHAPTER QUIZ

1. A wide-band oxygen sensor was first used on a Honda in what model year?
   a. 1992
   b. 1996
   c. 2000
   d. 2006

2. A wide-band oxygen sensor is capable of detecting the air–fuel mixture in the exhaust from _____ (rich) to _____ (lean).
   a. 12:1 to 15:1
   b. 13:1 to 16.7:1
   c. 10:1 to 23:1
   d. 8:1 to 18:1

3. A wide-band oxygen sensor and a conventional zirconia oxygen sensor can be made with what designs?
   a. Cup and thimble
   b. Cup and planar
   c. Finger and thimble
   d. Dual cell and single cell

4. A wide-band oxygen sensor can be made using what design?
   a. Cup and thimble
   b. Cup and planar
   c. Finger and thimble
   d. Dual cell and single cell

5. A wide-band oxygen sensor heater could draw how much current (amperes)?
   a. 0.8 to 2.0 A
   b. 2 to 4 A
   c. 6 to 8 A
   d. 8 to 10 A

6. A wide-band oxygen sensor needs to be heated to what operating temperature?
   a. 600°F (315°C)
   b. 800°F (427°C)
   c. 1,400°F (760°C)
   d. 2,000°F (1,093°C)

7. The two internal chambers of a dual cell wide-band oxygen sensor include _____.
   a. Single and dual
   b. Nernst and pump
   c. Air reference and diffusion
   d. Inside and outside

8. When the exhaust is rich, the PCM applies a _____ current into the pump cell.
   a. Positive
   b. Negative

9. When the exhaust is lean, the PCM applies a _____ current into the pump cell.
   a. Positive
   b. Negative

10. A dual cell wide-band oxygen sensor can be tested using a _____.
    a. Scan tool
    b. Voltmeter
    c. Scope
    d. All of the above

# chapter 17
# FUEL TRIM DIAGNOSIS

**OBJECTIVES:** **After studying Chapter 17, the reader will be able to:** • Explain the purpose and function of fuel trim. • Discuss the difference between speed density and mass air flow fuel control. • Describe how knowing the volumetric efficiency of the engine can help diagnose engine performance concerns. • Explain how to tell if a volumetric efficiency concern in an engine is due to a mechanical or an airflow measurement problem.

**KEY TERMS:** Alpha 230 • Base Pulse Width 225 • Equivalence Ratio (ER) 224 • Fuel Trim 225 • Fuel Trim Cells 228 • Lambda 224 • Long-Term Fuel Trim (LTFT) 228 • Short-Term Fuel Trim (STFT) 227 • Stoichiometric 224 • Volumetric Efficiency (VE) 230

## FUEL TRIM

**PURPOSE AND FUNCTION** The powertrain control module (PCM) does not measure or check the air-fuel mixture entering the cylinders. Instead, the PCM measures the air mass, and then calculates the amount of fuel needed. Fuel trim provides a method that is capable of changing the amount of fuel delivered to the engine based on feedback from the oxygen sensors. The primary purpose of the fuel trim is to keep the air-fuel mixture as close to 14.7:1 as possible. When the air-fuel ratio is kept at 14.7:1, the efficiency of the catalytic converter is the highest, which results in the lowest possible exhaust emissions. ● **SEE FIGURE 17–1.**

**LAMBDA** Lambda is a Greek letter used to represent ratio, as in air-fuel ratio. If an engine is operating at exactly 14.7:1, the air-fuel ratio on gasoline, the ratio is called **stoichiometric** and is assigned a lambda of 1.0.

- Air-fuel ratios lower than 1.0 indicate a rich mixture.
- Air-fuel ratios higher than 1.0 indicate a lean mixture.

To determine the air-fuel ratio if lambda is given, multiply lambda times 14.7.

### Example 1:
A lambda of 1.05 means that the engine is operating 5% lean and has an air-fuel mixture of 15.4:1 (14.7 × 1.05 = 15.4).

### Example 2:
A lambda of 0.97 means that the engine is operating 3% rich and has an air-fuel mixture of 14.3:1 (0.97 × 1.47 = 14.28).

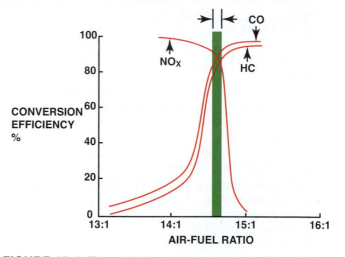

**FIGURE 17–1** The catalytic converter is most efficient when the exhaust ratio is closest to 14.7:1.

The usual lambda limits include:

- 0.9 lambda (13.2:1) is 10% rich and results in maximum power.
- 1.15 lambda (16.9:1) is 15% lean; in this case, a lean misfire is likely to occur.

Most newer vehicles are designed to operate between 0.98 and 1.02 lambda or, stated another way, within 2% of stoichiometric.

**EQUIVALENCE RATIO** The **equivalence ratio (ER)** is the inverse of lambda, with 1.0 equal to 1.0 lambda; however, 0.9 ER is equal to 1.1 lambda. Equivalence ratio (ER) = $1/\lambda$ (lambda), which is the inverse of lambda.

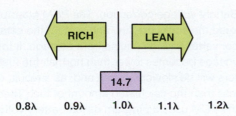

**FIGURE 17–2** Shown is lambda. The equivalence ratio is opposite lambda.

Therefore, a rich air-fuel mixture has an equivalence ratio of greater than 1 and a lean mixture less than 1. ● **SEE FIGURE 17–2.**

**NOTE: Engineers and many technical articles of fuel trim use equivalence ratios instead of lambda.**

## BASE PULSE WIDTH

**PURPOSE AND FUNCTION** The **base pulse width** is the injector pulse width that is calculated by the PCM using information from sensors before the oxygen senor(s) is operating and supplying air-fuel ratio information. The PCM uses information from the following sensors to determine the base pulse width for the fuel injectors.

- RPM (engine speed)
- Load
- Intake air temperature (IAT)
- Engine coolant temperature (ECT) (used mostly when the engine is cold)
- Amount of exhaust gas recirculation
- Canister purge flow amount
- Manifold absolute pressure
- BARO (altitude)
- Volumetric efficiency calculation

**MASS AIR FLOW VERSUS SPEED DENSITY** All throttle-body injected engines and some port fuel-injected engines use the speed density method for fuel control. The speed density uses the MAP sensor as the high authority sensor to determine the amount of fuel that will be needed. Although a speed density system can compensate for altitude, it is not as accurate as an engine equipped with a Mass Air Flow sensor that measures the actual amount of air entering the engine.

**SPEED DENSITY MODIFIER** Besides the MAP sensor, other sensors are used to fine tune or modify the mathematical calculations needed to determine the injector pulse width. The

input sensors that affect fuel trim in a speed density system include:

**BARO.** The BARO sensor or MAP sensor reading at key on determines the atmospheric pressure.

**IAT.** The intake air temperature (IAT) sensor measures the temperature of the air entering the engine. The PCM uses this information to calculate the density of the air.

**RPM.** All speed density calculations need the speed of the engine to calculate injector pulse width.

**EGR.** The PCM needs to determine the amount of exhaust gases being recirculated into the intake manifold to make an accurate measurement of air mass entering the cylinders. Various vehicle designs are used for this calculation and include one or more of the following:

- EGR valve pintle position
- EGR passage temperature sensor
- Pressure differential in the EGR passage
- ECT. The engine coolant temperature is used to add fuel when the engine is cold but has little effect on

### Is There less Oxygen in the Air at High Altitude?

No. At altitudes above sea level, the atmospheric pressure and air density are lower but the amount of oxygen (21%) remains the same at all altitudes. Three basic altitude-related factors are:

- **Physical altitude.** This is the altitude measured above sea level.
- **Pressure altitude.** This is the atmospheric pressure corrected to sea level according to the International Standard Atmosphere (ISA). Pressure altitude is primarily used for airplane performance calculations using 101 kPa as the standard for atmospheric pressure at sea level. See the following chart.

| Pressure Altitude (ft) | Static Pressure (kPa) | In. Hg | PSI |
|---|---|---|---|
| 0 | 101.325 | 29.92 | 14.7 |
| 1,000 | 97.715 | 28.86 | 14.2 |
| 2,500 | 92.500 | 27.32 | 13.4 |
| 5,000 | 84.306 | 24.90 | 12.2 |
| 10,000 | 69.681 | 20.58 | 10.1 |
| 20,000 | 46.563 | 13.75 | 6.8 |
| 30,000 | 30.089 | 8.89 | 4.4 |
| 36,090 | 22.631 | | |

- **Density altitude.** This altitude factor is important for engine operation. Density altitude is the number of oxygen molecules that are entering the engine. The density is affected by temperature; therefore, the use of the intake air temperature sensor data is important in determining air density.

fuel trim after the engine has been run for a while on newer vehicles.

- TP sensor. The PCM uses the position of the throttle in three places to determine basic calculations. These three positions are:
  - Idle
  - Cruise
  - Wide-open throttle (WOT)
- The TP sensor is also monitored for rate of change. If the throttle is rapidly depressed, this indicates that a large gulp of air is going to be entering the engine and additional fuel will need to be provided up to about five times (500%) more than normal. If the throttle is rapidly released, the fuel needs to be removed (fuel cut off) from the cylinders to keep the engine from stalling.

- Battery voltage correction. The PCM attempts to keep the emissions low and protect the catalytic converter and the engine from damage. If the battery voltage becomes lower than normal, the fuel injectors will be slower to open and, as a result, deliver less than the calculated amount of fuel. Therefore, the PCM uses a program called battery voltage correction that adds time to the injector pulse width if battery voltage is low. This correction will prevent a possible lean air-fuel condition, which could cause damage to the catalytic converter and/or the engine itself.

**MAF SYSTEM MODIFIERS** Using a mass air flow (MAF) sensor provides the PCM with a direct reading of the volume of air entering the engine. As a result, a MAF-equipped engine is able to provide a more accurate air-fuel ratio under all conditions. A MAF system has the following advantages compared with a speed density system:

- The system measures the actual mass of the air entering the engine.
- Altitude and temperature correction are not needed.
- The amount of exhaust gas recirculation does not need to be calculated.

However, some calculations need to be made to the air-fuel ratios if the throttle is rapidly depressed. Many General Motors systems use both a MAP sensor and a MAF sensor. One of the purposes of the MAP sensor, besides helping to diagnose the proper operation of the EGR system, is to provide the PCM with intake manifold pressure changes that occur when the throttle is rapidly closed or opened.

Electronic throttle control (ETC) systems help the PCM maintain proper air-fuel mixtures because the computer can control the rate of change of throttle opening. Therefore, it can determine what is happening directly rather than indicating it through information provided by the MAP sensor.

## MEASURING PULSE WIDTH

The PCM determines the base injector pulse width based on the reading from the sensors and the calculations from look-up tables stored in read-only memory. This base pulse width is the best guess as to the correct amount of fuel that the engine needs. Pulse width is measured in milliseconds (ms) and represents the amount of time the fuel injectors are commanded on. A typical engine at idle speed will have a pulse width of about 2 to 5 milliseconds, depending on the size of the engine. If there is a fault in one of the sensors, the calculated base pulse width may be incorrect. Because the air-fuel ratio is very important for the proper operation of the catalytic converter, the PCM uses data from the oxygen sensor to modify,

**One Millisecond per Liter**

A rule-of-thumb that usually works to determine if the pulse width is within reason is to remember that the size of the engine does affect the amount of fuel needed. While injector flow rates are higher for larger engines, it is generally true that, at idle on a warm engine, the injector pulse width will be about 1 millisecond per liter of displacement.

2 liters = 2 milliseconds
3 liters = 3 milliseconds
4 liters = 4 milliseconds
5 liters = 5 milliseconds
6 liters = 6 milliseconds

Therefore, if the injector pulse width is far from being normal, determine if the engine has a vacuum leak (if numbers are too high) or if the purge valve is stuck open (if the numbers are too low).

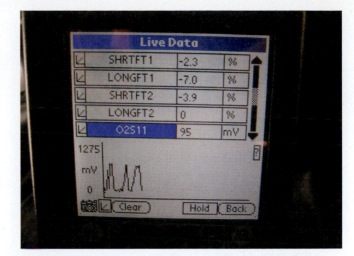

**FIGURE 17–3** Scan tool display, showing both long-term and short-term fuel trim. Both LTFT and STFT should be less than 10%.

if needed, the commanded pulse width. This correction from the base pulse width using data from the oxygen sensor is called fuel trim.

## FUEL TRIM

Based on the oxygen sensor activity, the PCM tries to keep the air-fuel mixture at 14.7:1 under most conditions.

**NOTE: If the vehicle is operating under full load, the oxygen sensor data is ignored and the PCM commands the richer-than-normal air-fuel mixture needed for maximum power based on inputs from the other sensors.**

## THE NEED FOR FUEL TRIM

The purpose of fuel trim is to provide the catalytic converter with a stoichiometric air-fuel mixture, which it needs to reduce $NO_x$ exhaust emissions and to help oxidize HC and CO into harmless carbon dioxide ($CO_2$) and water ($H_2O$) vapor.

If the exhaust is always rich, the catalytic converter cannot reduce CO and HC emissions. If the exhaust is always lean, the catalytic converter cannot reduce $NO_x$ emissions; therefore, the air-fuel mixture must alternate between rich and lean. The computer is therefore designed to provide as close to a 14.7:1 mixture as possible by using the oxygen sensor, as well as the short-term and long-term fuel trim program, to accomplish this feat. ● **SEE FIGURE 17–3.**

## SHORT-TERM FUEL TRIM

**Short-term fuel trim (STFT)** is a percentage measurement of the amount the computer is adding or subtracting from a calculated value. Electronic fuel-injector systems use the oxygen sensor (O2S) to determine whether the exhaust is rich or lean. Without the O2S, fuel delivery is controlled by the computer alone using the programmed pulse width commands based on other sensor inputs such as engine coolant temperature (ECT), throttle position (TP), and engine load (MAP). When the engine is operating in closed loop, the O2S signal can modify or change the preprogrammed fuel delivery. Fuel trim is expressed as a percentage (%), either positive (+) or negative (−), and represents the amount of fuel different from the anticipated amount. For example, if a small vacuum leak occurs, the O2S produces a lower voltage signal which is interpreted by the computer as meaning the air-fuel mixture is too lean. As a result, the pulse width is increased slightly to compensate for this slight vacuum leak. The amount of this additional fuel is seen on a scan tool as a positive short-term fuel trim.

**NOTE: Before 1993, General Motors referred to short-term fuel trim as the *integrator* and expressed it in binary numbers. A reading of 128 was the midpoint and a reading of + or − 10 from 128 (118–138) was usually considered to be a normal reading.**

A short-term fuel trim of +20% indicates that 20% additional fuel had to be added to achieve the proper air-fuel mixture. A −20% short-term fuel trim indicates that fuel had to be removed by shortening the injector pulse width to achieve the proper air-fuel mixture.

Short-term fuel trim represents actions by the computer over a relatively short time. The purpose of the STFT is to provide a varying air-fuel mixture so that the catalytic converter can efficiently reduce HC, CO, and $NO_x$ exhaust emissions. If, for example, a large vacuum leak were to occur, then the fuel delivery would have to be increased even more and for a longer

## REAL WORLD FIX

### The Red S-10 Pickup Truck Story

A 4-cylinder 2.2-liter engine was replaced under the new vehicle warranty due to excessive oil consumption. The replacement engine never did run correctly, especially at idle and low speeds. The scan tool data showed a −25% long-term fuel trim, indicating that the oxygen sensor was measuring a very rich (low oxygen content) exhaust stream. Because the engine was operating so badly, the service technician believed the oxygen sensor was indicating a false rich condition. The service technician then checked the following:

- Poor $O_2$ sensor ground (this can cause a higher-than-normal $O_2$ sensor voltage)
- $O_2$ sensor wiring shorted to voltage or near a spark plug wire
- A contaminated (coated) $O_2$ sensor that will read higher than normal

None of the false rich conditions was found. Remembering that the engine ran terribly even when cold and the problem started after the engine was replaced, the technician started to look for faults that could have occurred when parts were switched from the original engine to the replacement engine. The technician found an incorrect EGR gasket. This caused exhaust gases to flow into the cylinders all the time. The exhaust gases also displaced the oxygen that normally would be in the cylinder, thereby reducing the amount of oxygen measured by the $O_2$ sensor. Replacing the EGR gasket restored proper engine operation.

time. Therefore, electronic fuel-injection system computers also incorporate a long-term fuel trim program.

## LONG-TERM FUEL TRIM

**Long-term fuel trim (LTFT)** is designed to add or subtract fuel for a longer amount of time than short-term fuel trim. For this reason, LTFT should be looked at by the service technician as a guide to whether the computer has been adding or subtracting fuel in order to achieve the proper air-fuel mixture. For example, if a vacuum hose splits open, the engine will be leaner than normal. Short-term fuel trim will attempt to add fuel right away to adjust. If the resulting air (vacuum) leak remains for longer than a few seconds to a minute, the computer will revise the long-term fuel trim to compensate for the leak over a larger period of time.

When the LTFT makes an adjustment, the STFT can still make short and quick changes in the air-fuel mixture needed to provide the catalytic converter with an alternating rich, then lean, then rich exhaust. *The purpose of long-term fuel trim is to keep short-term fuel trim as close to zero as possible.*

## USING FUEL TRIM AS A DIAGNOSTIC AID

Fuel trim values can only be observed with a scan tool. A scan tool will display both short-term and long-term fuel trim. For system diagnosis, refer to the long-term fuel trim because it represents a longer amount of time (history) and a greater amount of mixture correction.

**NOTE: The object of STFT and LTFT is to be able to make corrections to the amount of fuel delivered to the engine to achieve the proper air-fuel mixture. For example, a reading of +30% LTFT will indicate the computer must deliver 30% more than the calibrated amount of fuel to achieve the proper air-fuel mixture. This also means that the engine is now operating with the correct air-fuel mixture. The LTFT number simply tells the technician what the computer had to do to achieve the proper mixture.**

The following are three examples of readings and possible explanations:

### Example

**Vehicle 1.**   STFT = +5%, LTFT = 20%
Explanation: The computer is responding to a lean condition. The LTFT indicates that the programmed amount of fuel had to be increased by 20% to achieve the proper air-fuel mixture to the level where the STFT could "toggle" the mixture rich and lean for the most catalytic converter efficiency. Look for a vacuum leak or low fuel pressure.

### Example

**Vehicle 2.**   STFT = +10%, LTFT = 0%
Explanation: These readings are perfect. It is normal for the STFT to add or subtract up to 20% to achieve the proper air-fuel mixture.

### Example

**Vehicle 3.**   STFT = −10%, LTFT = −30%
Explanation: The engine was rich because the LTFT had to remove 30% of the anticipated amount of fuel to achieve the proper air-fuel mixture. Look for a defective (stuck-open) injector, defective fuel pressure regulator, or a restriction in the intake air passage.

## FUEL TRIM CELLS

Both STFTs and LTFTs react to oxygen sensor voltage to modify fuel delivery. Most vehicles set aside different **fuel trim cells** for each combination of engine speed (RPM) and load. The computer can then correct for slight differences in fuel mixture separately for each cell. For example, General Motors uses 16 cells plus 2 for deceleration and 2 for idle only.

**Think of a Small Faucet and a Large Faucet**

The purpose of fuel trim is to add or subtract fuel as needed to maintain the proper air-fuel mixture so the catalytic converter can operate properly. STFT is fast but can add or subtract only a small amount of fuel. This can be visualized as being similar to a small water faucet adding water to a sink. For example, if a small vacuum hose becomes disconnected, the STFT will add a little extra fuel to compensate for the added amount of air being drawn into the engine. If a large hose becomes disconnected, the STFT cannot supply the needed fuel required; therefore, the LTFT is needed to supply additional fuel to overcome the large air leak. This can be visualized as being similar to a large water faucet adding a greater amount of water to a sink. Because the LTFT indicates a larger amount of fuel being added or subtracted than STFT, many service technicians simply ignore the STFT readings and use the LTFT numbers to see if they are within 10%. If LTFT is greater than 10%, either positive (+) or negative (−), then a fault should be corrected. The maximum value for STFT and LTFT depends on the exact make, model, and year of vehicle but is usually limited to 25% to 30% for either.

| Load | | | |
|---|---|---|---|
| 12 | 13 | 14 | 15 |
| 8 | 9 | 10 | 11 |
| 4 | 5 | 6 | 7 |
| 0 | 1 | 2 | 3 |

RPM ⟶

| Deceleration Cells | Idle Cells |
|---|---|
| Greater than 1225 RPM = 17 | A/C on = 18 |
| Less than 1225 RPM = 16 | A/C off = 19 |

# FUEL TRIM CELL DIAGNOSIS

To use fuel trim as a diagnostic aid, the data should be observed during the same condition as the problem. For example, notice that there are two cells for idle—one with the air conditioning (A/C) on and one for the A/C off. If the problem or customer's concern only occurs when the A/C is on, then observe the fuel trim numbers on the scan tool with the engine operating at idle and with the A/C on.

The same thing is true of a problem that may be occurring at 55 MPH (90 km/h). Looking at fuel trim in the service bay (stall) with the engine at idle will not help the technician at all. The vehicle must be driven under similar conditions to best duplicate

**Movie Mode Diagnosis**

A scan tool will display fuel trim values but only those in the cell where the engine is operating. For example, if an engine lacks power while towing a trailer up a hill, looking at the fuel trim values at idle in the shop will show the values in the cell or cells that the engine is operating. To observe the true fuel trim values, the vehicle will have to be operated under similar conditions and the data recorded on the scan tool. Use snap-shot or movie mode during the test drive, scroll through the recorded values, and look for the fuel trim cell and the LTFT and STFT values to help determine if there is a fuel delivery or other fuel trim-related problem.

the condition when the problem occurs. Only then will the correct fuel cell be displayed. Then the long-term fuel trim information should be valid. See the following fuel trim diagnostic chart.

**Fuel Trim Diagnostic Chart**

| Fuel Trim @ Idle | Fuel Trim @ 3000 RPM | Possible Cause(s) |
|---|---|---|
| Adding fuel | No correction | Vacuum leak |
| No correction | Adding fuel | Low fuel volume, weak fuel pump, or restricted fuel filter |
| Adding fuel | Adding fuel | Dirty (clogged) fuel injectors, low fuel pump pressure |
| Subtracting fuel | No correction | Gasoline in the engine oil (drawn into the engine through the PCV valve) |
| Subtracting fuel | Subtracting fuel | High fuel pressure, defective fuel pressure regulator, leaking or stuck-open injector(s) |

# MAF SENSOR ACCURACY

In an engine equipped with a MAF sensor, the accuracy of the sensor is critical for the PCM to provide the current pulse-width command to the fuel injectors. Factors that can affect the accuracy of the MAF sensor readings include:

1. **Vacuum leaks.** A vacuum leak represents air entering the combustion chambers that was not measured by the MAF sensor, and affects the air-fuel mixture mostly at idle. Above idle, the effects of a vacuum leak are reduced.

2. **False air.** False or unmeasured air is air that is entering the intake system after the MAF sensor. This false air can have a

**FIGURE 17–4** Any fault in the air cleaner assembly can disrupt the airflow through the MAF sensor.

**? FREQUENTLY ASKED QUESTION**

**What Is the Alpha PID?**

**Alpha** is the air-fuel ratio parameter displayed on Nissan/Infinity vehicles.

100 = 14.7:1

Higher than 100 = PCM is adding fuel

Lower than 100 = PCM is subtracting fuel

Alpha is used as a single parameter that replaces both long-term fuel trim and short-term fuel trim.

great effect on the air-fuel mixture at idle and, like a vacuum leak, tends to have less of an effect at higher engine speeds.

3. **PCV airflow.** The airflow through the PCV system is not measured by the MAF sensor. Therefore, all openings to the crankcase must be sealed to prevent unmeasured air from entering.

4. **Airflow disturbance (disruption).** If the incorrect air filter is installed or the air inlet system is modified, airflow through the MAF sensor may not be straight. If air turbulence passes through the MAF sensor, the accuracy of the amount of airflow will not be correct. ● **SEE FIGURE 17–4.**

# VOLUMETRIC EFFICIENCY

**DEFINITION OF VOLUMETRIC EFFICIENCY** Volumetric efficiency (VE) is the percentage of air entering the engine compared to the theoretical airflow. Typical normally aspirated engines will test having a VE of 75% to 90%. Older two-valve cylinder head engines will test lower than newer engines equipped with four valves per cylinder. Percentages above 100% are possible on supercharged or turbocharged engines. A VE calculator can be downloaded here (free):

*www.lindertech.com/guru3*

User name: GURU3

Password: LTS2004

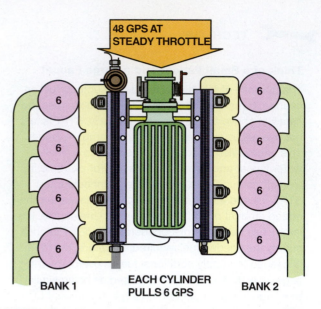

**FIGURE 17–5** This properly operating engine is drawing in 48 grams per second of air for all eight cylinders. This indicates that each cylinder will be receiving 6 grams per second (GPS).

**🚗 REAL WORLD FIX**

**Negative Fuel Trim Bank #1; Positive Fuel Trim Bank #2**

If one bank of a V-6 or V-8 engine has a restricted exhaust on one bank, the fuel trim numbers will be negative on the bank that is restricted and positive on the bank that is not restricted. ● **SEE FIGURES 17–5 THROUGH 17–8.**

The calculation requires data to be captured using a scan tool while the vehicle is being driven at wide-open throttle. This test should be conducted in a safe location away from traffic and does not need to be performed at high vehicle speeds. The data needed includes:

- Engine size in cubic inches
- Engine speed (RPM)
- MAF (grams per second)
- Intake air temperature (IAT)

### Example 1

A Chevrolet Trailblazer equipped with a 4.2-liter 6-cylinder engine is tested using the following information and results:

Engine size = 256 cu. in. (4.2 liters)

Engine RPM = 6097

MAF (gm/s) = 225.4

IAT (°F) = 66

The calculated airflow through the engine is 395 cu. ft per sec. The theoretical airflow through the engine is 451 cu. ft per second. The VE is 87%.

This result indicates that the MAF sensor is accurately measuring the airflow and the engine is in good mechanical condition.

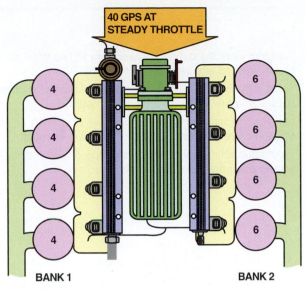

**LEFT EXHAUST IS PARTIALLY RESTRICTED**

40 GPS AT STEADY THROTTLE

BANK 1          BANK 2

**FIGURE 17–6** If the exhaust system on the left bank (bank #1) were to become restricted, the total airflow through the MAF sensor would also decrease. The cylinders on the right bank (bank #2) would draw the same 6 GPS as before and the cylinders on bank #1, which have a restricted exhaust, would draw just 4 GPS.

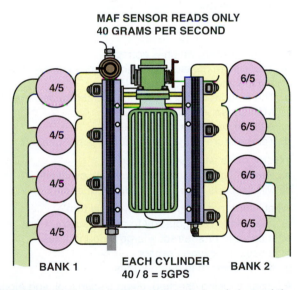

MAF SENSOR READS ONLY 40 GRAMS PER SECOND

BANK 1     EACH CYLINDER     BANK 2
           40 / 8 = 5GPS

**FIGURE 17–7** If all cylinders were equal and showed the 40 grams per second, then each cylinder will be drawing 5 grams per second (5 × 8 cylinders = 40 GPS). Bank 1 is being supplied 4/5ths of the air needed whereas bank 2 is being supplied 6/5ths of the air needed causing bank 1 to operate too rich and bank 2 to operate too lean.

### Example 2

A Cadillac Deville is equipped with a 4.6-liter V-8. The customer's concern is poor performance. Fuel trim numbers are within ± 2% from idle to cruise. A check of the VE indicates the following:
Engine size = 281 cu. in. (4.6 liters)
Engine RPM = 3400

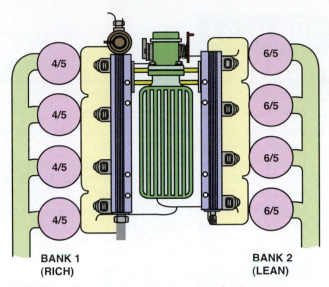

BANK 1              BANK 2
(RICH)              (LEAN)

**FIGURE 17–8** As a result of the restricted exhaust on bank #1, the restricted bank will operate too rich and bank #2 will operate too lean. The long-term fuel trim will be negative for bank #1 and positive for bank #2.

🔧 **TECH TIP**

### MAF Sensor or Airflow Problem?

If a MAF sensor reading is lower than normal, such as at wide-open throttle, it could be an engine breathing problem or a defective/contaminated MAF sensor. To determine which is the case, check the following:

- If the fuel trim numbers follow the airflow, then there is an airflow measurement error (MAF sensor-related problem).
- If the fuel trim numbers are okay, the MAF is okay.
- If the BARO reading is lower than normal, then there is an engine breathing issue, such as a restricted intake or exhaust.

🔧 **TECH TIP**

### Possible Restricted Exhaust? Check the IAT.

If the exhaust system is restricted, all of the exhaust will be unable to exit the engine, especially at wide-open throttle. Using a scan tool, look at the values displayed for the intake air temperature (IAT) sensor. The IAT temperature should decrease slightly at WOT normally due to the increased airflow. If the IAT temperature reading increases, this is an indication of a restricted exhaust.

MAF (gm/s) = 80
IAT (°F) = 95
The calculated volumetric efficiency is 53%. A clogged catalytic converter is discovered to be the cause.

## SUMMARY

1. Lambda is a Greek letter used to represent air-fuel ratio. Lambda of 1.0 is equal to an air-fuel rate of 14.7:1.

2. Equivalence ratio is the inverse of lambda.

3. Base pulse width is determined by the PCM based on input from many sensors.

4. Speed density fuel control uses calculations based on the input from various sensors such as the TP and MAP sensor to determine the amount of fuel needed.

5. Mass air flow systems use a mass air flow sensor to measure the mass of the air entering the engine directly.

6. Fuel trim uses the oxygen sensor data to fine tune the air-fuel mixture to ensure lowest emissions.

7. Short-term fuel trim (STFT) is capable of quickly adding or subtracting fuel, but only a limited amount.

8. Long-term fuel trim (LTFT) is capable of adding or subtracting more fuel than STFT, but is slower to react.

9. Volumetric efficiency is the percentage of air entering the engine compared to the theoretical airflow.

## REVIEW QUESTIONS

1. What is the difference between lambda and equivalence ratio?

2. How is base pulse width determined?

3. Why is fuel trim needed?

4. What is the difference between short-term and long-term fuel trim?

## CHAPTER QUIZ

1. If the air-fuel ratio is 14.7:1, what is lambda?
   a. 1.0
   b. 0.9
   c. 1.1
   d. 14.7

2. If lambda is 0.98, this means the _____.
   a. Mixture is lean
   b. Air-fuel mixture is within 2% of stoichiometric
   c. Air-fuel mixture is slightly rich
   d. Both b and c

3. Base pulse width is determined by _____.
   a. Oxygen sensor data
   b. Computer calculations
   c. Input from many sensors, except the oxygen sensor
   d. Both b and c

4. The air at high altitude has _____.
   a. 21% oxygen
   b. Less than 21% oxygen
   c. A higher pressure
   d. A higher density

5. In a speed density system, what does not need to be corrected for?
   a. Air temperature
   b. Oxygen in the exhaust from the oxygen sensor
   c. Amount of EGR
   d. BARO sensor data

6. In a MAF system, which is correct?
   a. The system measures the actual mass of the air entering the engine.
   b. The amount of EGR flow must be subtracted from the MAF sensor reading.
   c. Altitude correction is not needed.
   d. Temperature of the air correction is not needed.

7. Injector pulse width is measured in _____.
   a. Percentage (%)          c. Duty cycle (%)
   b. Milliseconds (ms)       d. Frequency (Hz)

8. What is not true about short-term fuel trim?
   a. It is able to react quickly to add or subtract fuel.
   b. It can add or subtract a large amount of fuel.
   c. It uses the oxygen sensor.
   d. It is expressed in percentages.

9. A Nissan is being checked, using a scan tool, and Alpha is 107. This means _____.
   a. The PCM is adding fuel
   b. The PCM is subtracting fuel
   c. The PCM represents STFT only
   d. The PCM represents LTFT only

10. A contaminated or defective MAF sensor is indicated if _____.
   a. The fuel trim number follows the airflow
   b. The VE is bad
   c. The fuel trim numbers are within ±2%
   d. The BARO reading is lower than normal

# chapter 18

# FUEL PUMPS, LINES, AND FILTERS

**OBJECTIVES:** After studying Chapter 18, the reader will be able to: • Prepare for ASE Engine Performance (A8) certification test content area "C" (Fuel, Air Induction, and Exhaust Systems Diagnosis and Repair). • Describe the construction and operation of fuel tanks, lines and filters. • Describe how to check an electric fuel pump for proper pressure and volume delivery. • Explain how to check a fuel-pressure regulator. • Describe how to test fuel injectors. • Explain how to diagnose electronic fuel-injection problems.

**KEY TERMS:** Accumulator 241 • Baffle 233 • Check valve 235 • Delivery system 233 • Filter basket 243 • Gerotor 239 • Hydrokinetic pump 239 • Inertia switch 235 • Onboard refueling vapor recovery (ORVR) 234 • Residual (rest) pressure 239 • Roller cell 238 • Rotary vane pump 239 • Turbine pump 239 • Vacuum lock 235 • Vapor lock 235 • Volatile organic compound (VOC) 238

## FUEL DELIVERY SYSTEM

Creating and maintaining a correct air-fuel mixture requires a properly functioning fuel and air **delivery system.** Fuel delivery (and return) systems use many if not all of the following components to make certain that fuel is available under the right conditions to the fuel-injection system.

- Fuel storage tank, filler neck, and gas cap
- Fuel tank pressure sensor
- Fuel pump
- Fuel filter(s)
- Fuel delivery lines and fuel rail
- Fuel pressure regulator
- Evaporative emission controls (discussed in Chapter 19)
- Fuel return line

## FUEL TANKS

A vehicle fuel tank is made of corrosion-resistant steel usually, or polyethylene plastic. Some models, such as sport utility vehicles (SUVs) and light trucks, may have an auxiliary fuel tank in addition to the main tank.

Tank design and capacity are a compromise between available space, filler location, fuel expansion room, and fuel

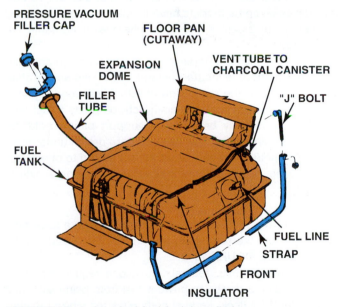

**FIGURE 18–1** A typical fuel tank installation.

movement. Newer tanks deliberately limit tank capacity by extending the filler tube neck into the tank low enough to prevent complete filling, or by providing for expansion room. ● **SEE FIGURE 18–1.**

A vertical **baffle** in fuel tanks limits fuel sloshing as the vehicle moves.

Regardless of size and shape, all fuel tanks incorporate most if not all of the following features.

- Inlet or filler tube through which fuel enters the tank
- Filler cap with pressure holding and relief features

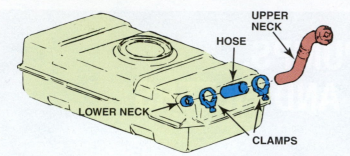

FIGURE 18–2 A three-piece filler tube assembly.

- Outlet to the fuel line leading to the fuel pump or fuel injector
- Fuel pump mounted within the tank
- Tank vent system
- Fuel pickup tube and fuel level sending unit

**TANK LOCATION AND MOUNTING** Most vehicles use a horizontally suspended fuel tank, usually mounted below the rear of the floor pan, just ahead of or behind the rear axle. Fuel tanks are located there so that frame rails and body components protect the tank in the event of a crash. To prevent squeaks, some models have insulated strips cemented on the top or sides of the tank wherever it contacts the underbody.

Fuel inlet location depends on the tank design and filler tube placement. It is located behind a filler cap and is often a hinged door in the outer side of either rear fender panel. Generally, a pair of metal retaining straps holds a fuel tank in place. Underbody brackets or support panels hold the strap ends using bolts. The free ends are drawn underneath the tank to hold it in place, and then are bolted to other support brackets or to a frame member on the opposite side of the tank.

**FILLER TUBES** Fuel enters the tank through a large tube extending from the tank to an opening on the outside of the vehicle. ● SEE FIGURE 18–2.

Effective in 1993, federal regulations require manufacturers to install a device to prevent fuel from being siphoned through the filler neck. Federal authorities recognized methanol as a poison, and methanol used in gasoline is a definite health hazard. Additionally, gasoline is a suspected carcinogen (cancer-causing agent). To prevent siphoning, manufacturers welded a filler-neck check-ball tube in fuel tanks. To drain check-ball-equipped fuel tanks, a technician must disconnect the check-ball tube at the tank and attach a siphon directly to the tank. ● SEE FIGURE 18–3.

**Onboard refueling vapor recovery (ORVR)** systems have been developed to reduce evaporative emissions during refueling. ● SEE FIGURE 18–4.

These systems add components to the filler neck and the tank. One ORVR system utilizes a tapered filler neck with

FIGURE 18–3 A view of a typical filler tube with the fuel tank removed. Notice the ground strap used to help prevent the buildup of static electricity as the fuel flows into the plastic tank. The check ball looks exactly like a ping-pong ball.

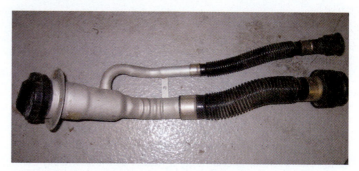

FIGURE 18–4 Vehicles equipped with onboard refueling vapor recovery usually have a reduced-size fill tube.

a smaller diameter tube and a check valve. When fuel flows down the neck, it opens the normally closed check valve. The vapor passage to the charcoal canister is opened. The decreased-size neck and the opened air passage allow fuel and vapor to flow rapidly into the tank and the canister respectively. When the fuel reaches a predetermined level, the check valve closes, and the fuel tank pressure increases. This forces the nozzle to shut off, thereby preventing the tank from being overfilled.

**PRESSURE VACUUM FILLER CAP** Fuel and vapors are sealed in the tank by the safety filler cap. The safety cap must release excess pressure or excess vacuum. Either condition could cause fuel tank damage, fuel spills, and vapor escape. Typically, the cap will release if the pressure is over 1.5 to 2 psi (10 to 14 kPa) or if the vacuum is 0.15 to 0.3 psi (1 to 2 kPa).

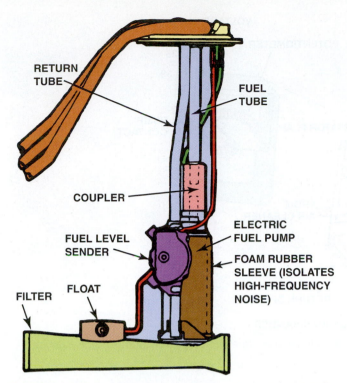

**FIGURE 18–5** The fuel pickup tube is part of the fuel sender and pump assembly.

**FUEL PICKUP TUBE** The fuel pickup tube is usually a part of the fuel sender assembly or the electric fuel pump assembly. Since dirt and sediment eventually gather on the bottom of a fuel tank, the fuel pickup tube is fitted with a filter sock or strainer to prevent contamination from entering the fuel lines. The filter sock usually is designed to filter out particles that are larger than 70 to 100 microns, or 30 microns if a gerotor-type fuel pump is used. One micron is 0.000039 in. ● **SEE FIGURE 18–5.**

**NOTE: The human eye cannot see anything smaller than about 40 microns.**

The filter is made from woven Saran resin (a copolymer of vinylidene chloride and vinyl chloride). The filter blocks any water that may be in the fuel tank, unless the filter is completely submerged in water. In that case, it will allow water through the filter. This filter should be replaced whenever the fuel pump is replaced.

**TANK VENTING REQUIREMENTS** Fuel tanks must be vented to prevent a **vacuum lock** as fuel is drawn from the tank. As fuel is used and its level drops in the tank, the space above the fuel increases. As the air in the tank expands to fill this greater space, its pressure drops. Without a vent, the air pressure inside the tank would drop below atmospheric pressure, developing a vacuum that prevents the flow of fuel. Under extreme pressure variance, the tank could collapse. Venting allows outside air to

enter the tank as the fuel level drops, preventing a vacuum from developing.

An EVAP system vents gasoline vapors from the fuel tank directly to a charcoal-filled vapor storage canister, and uses an unvented filler cap. Many filler caps contain valves that open to relieve pressure or vacuum above specified safety levels. Because fuel tanks are not vented directly to the atmosphere, the tank must allow for fuel expansion, contraction, and overflow that can result from changes in temperature or overfilling. One way is to use a dome in the top of the tank. Many General Motors vehicles use a design that includes a vertical slosh baffle which reserves up to 12% of the total tank capacity for fuel expansion.

**ROLLOVER LEAKAGE PROTECTION** All vehicles have one or more devices to prevent fuel leaks in case of vehicle rollover or a collision in which fuel may spill.

Variations of the basic one-way **check valve** may be installed in any number of places between the fuel tank and the engine. The valve may be installed in the fuel return line, vapor vent line, or fuel tank filler cap.

In addition to the rollover protection devices, some vehicles use devices to ensure that the fuel pump shuts off when an accident occurs. On some air vane sensors, a microswitch is built into the sensor to switch on the fuel pump as soon as intake airflow causes the vane to lift from its rest position. ● **SEE FIGURE 18–6.**

Ford vehicles use an **inertia switch.** ● **SEE FIGURE 18–7.** The inertia switch is installed in the rear of most passenger cars and behind the kick panel inside the passenger compartment in most pickup trucks. The switch is electrically connected between the electric fuel pump and its power supply. With any sudden impact, such as a jolt from another vehicle in a parking lot, the inertia switch opens and shuts off power to the fuel pump. The switch must be reset manually by pushing a button to restore current to the pump. Check with service information for the exact location of the inertia switch.

## FUEL LINES

**PURPOSE AND FUNCTION** Fuel and vapor lines made of steel, nylon tubing, or fuel-resistant rubber hoses connect the parts of the fuel system. Fuel lines supply fuel to the throttle body or fuel rail. They also return excess fuel and vapors to the tank. Depending on their function, fuel and vapor lines may be either rigid or flexible.

Fuel lines must remain as cool as possible. If any part of the line is located near too much heat, the gasoline passing through it vaporizes and **vapor lock** occurs. When this happens, the fuel pump supplies only vapor that passes into the injectors. Without liquid gasoline, the engine stalls and a hot restart problem develops.

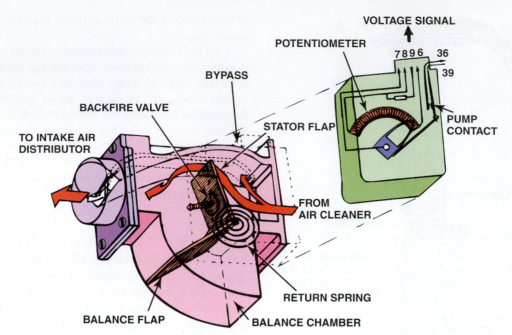

FIGURE 18–6 On some vehicles equipped with an airflow sensor, a switch is used to energize the fuel pump. In the event of a collision, the switch opens and the fuel flow stops.

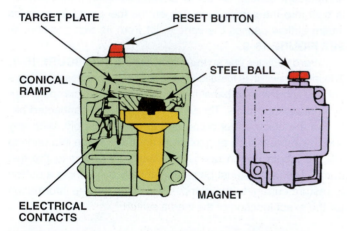

FIGURE 18–7 Ford uses an inertia switch to turn off the electric fuel pump in an accident.

The fuel delivery system supplies the following fuel system pressure depending on the type of fuel-injection system.

- Up to 35 psi (241 kPa) to many throttle-body injection units
- Up to 70 to 90 PSI (345 kPa) for port fuel-injection systems
- Up to 60 PSI (345 kPa) for gasoline direct-injection (GDI) systems (GDI system pressure is increased by a high-pressure engine-mounted fuel pump to 500 to 2,900 PSI [3,450 to 20,000 kPa].)

### RIGID LINES
All fuel lines fastened to the body, frame, or engine are made of seamless steel tubing or nylon reinforced plastic. Steel springs may be wound around the tubing at certain points to protect against impact damage.

Only steel tubing, or that recommended by the manufacturer, should be used when replacing rigid fuel lines. *Never substitute copper or aluminum tubing for steel tubing.* These materials do not withstand normal vehicle vibration and could combine with the fuel to cause a chemical reaction.

### FLEXIBLE LINES
Most fuel systems use synthetic rubber or nylon hose sections where flexibility is needed. Short hose sections often connect steel fuel lines to other system components. The fuel delivery hose inside diameter (ID) is generally larger (3/16 to 3/8 in., or 8 to 10 mm) than the fuel return hose ID (1/4 in., or 6 mm).

Fuel-injection systems require special composition–reinforced hoses specifically made for these higher pressure systems. Similarly, vapor vent lines must be made of materials that resist fuel vapors. Replacement vent hoses are usually marked with the designation "EVAP" to indicate their intended use.

### FUEL LINE MOUNTING
Fuel supply lines from the tank to a throttle body or fuel rail are routed to follow the frame along the underbody of the vehicle. Vapor and return lines may be routed with the fuel supply line. All rigid lines are fastened to the frame rail or underbody with screws and clamps, or clips.
● SEE FIGURE 18–8.

### FUEL-INJECTION LINES AND CLAMPS
Hoses used for fuel-injection systems are made of materials with high resistance to oxidation and deterioration. Replacement hoses for injection systems should always be equivalent to original equipment manufacturer (OEM) hoses.

Screw-type clamps are essential on injected engines and should have rolled edges to prevent hose damage.

**CAUTION:** *Do not use spring-type clamps on fuel-injected engines—they cannot withstand the fuel pressures involved.*

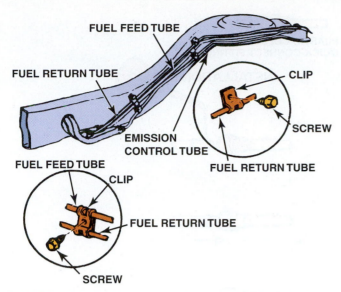

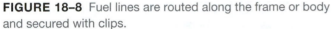

FIGURE 18–8 Fuel lines are routed along the frame or body and secured with clips.

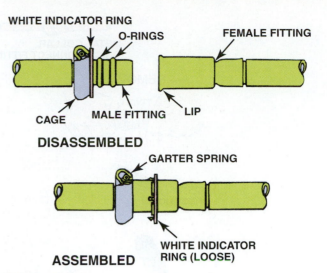

FIGURE 18–9 Some metal line connections use spring locks and O-rings. The purpose of the indicator ring is to keep the garter spring from falling out when the fitting is disconnected.

**FUEL-INJECTION FITTINGS AND NYLON LINES** Because of their operating pressures, fuel-injection systems often use special kinds of fittings to ensure leakproof connections. Some high-pressure fittings with port fuel-injection systems use O-ring seals instead of the traditional flare connections. When disconnecting such a fitting, inspect the O-ring for damage and replace it if necessary. *Always* tighten O-ring fittings to the specified torque value to prevent damage.

Other manufacturers also use O-ring seals on fuel line connections. In all cases, the O-rings are made of special materials that withstand contact with gasoline and oxygenated fuel blends. Some manufacturers specify that the O-rings be replaced every time the fuel system connection is opened. When replacing one of these O-rings, a new part specifically designed for fuel system service must be used.

Some vehicle manufacturers use spring-lock connectors to join male and female ends of steel tubing. ● SEE FIGURE 18–9.

The coupling is held together by a garter spring inside a circular cage. The flared end of the female fitting slips behind the spring to lock the coupling together.

General Motors has used nylon fuel lines with quick-connect fittings at the fuel tank and fuel filter since the early 1990s. Like the GM threaded couplings used with steel lines, nylon line couplings use internal O-ring seals. Unlocking the metal connectors requires a special quick-connector separator tool; plastic connectors can be released without the tool. ● SEE FIGURES 18–10 AND 18–11.

**FUEL LINE LAYOUT** Fuel pressures have tended to become higher to prevent vapor lock, and a major portion of the fuel routed to the fuel-injection system returns to the tank by way of a fuel return line or return-type systems. This allows better control, within limits, of heat absorbed by the gasoline as it is routed through the engine compartment. Throttle-body and multiport injection systems have typically used a pressure regulator to control fuel pressure in the throttle body or fuel rail,

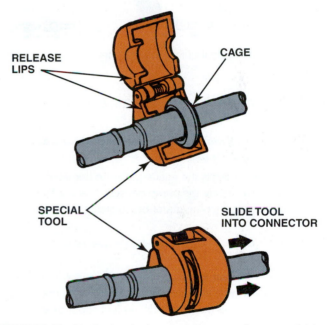

FIGURE 18–10 Spring-lock connectors require a special tool for disassembly.

**?** **FREQUENTLY ASKED QUESTION**

**Just How Much Fuel Is Recirculated?**

Approximately 80% of the available fuel pump volume is released to the fuel tank by the fuel-pressure regulator at idle speed. As an example, a passenger vehicle cruising down the road at 60 mph gets 30 mpg. With a typical return-style fuel system pumping about 30 gallons per hour from the tank, it would therefore burn 2 gallons per hour, and return about 28 gallons per hour to the tank.

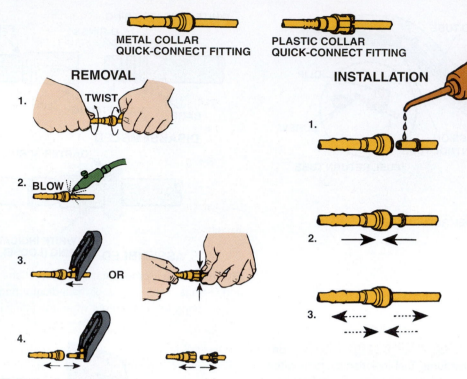

METAL COLLAR
QUICK-CONNECT FITTING

PLASTIC COLLAR
QUICK-CONNECT FITTING

REMOVAL

INSTALLATION

OIL

1. TWIST

2. BLOW

3. OR

4.

1.

2.

3.

**FIGURE 18–11** Typical quick-connect steps.

**? FREQUENTLY ASKED QUESTION**

**How Can an Electric Pump Work Inside a Gas Tank and Not Cause a Fire?**

Even though fuel fills the entire pump, no burnable mixture exists inside the pump because there is no air and no danger of commutator brush arcing, igniting the fuel.

and also allow excess fuel not used by the injectors to return to the tank. However, the warmer fuel in the tank may create problems, such as an excessive rise in fuel vapor pressures in the tank.

With late-model vehicles, there has been some concern about too much heat being sent back to the fuel tank, which causes rising in-tank temperatures and increasing fuel vaporization and **volatile organic compound (VOC)** (hydrocarbon) emissions. To reduce this problem, manufacturers have placed the pressure regulator back by the tank instead of under the hood on mechanical returnless systems. As a result the returned fuel is not subjected to the heat generated by the engine and the underhood environment. To prevent vapor lock in these systems, pressures have been raised in the fuel rail, and injectors tend to have smaller openings to maintain control of the fuel spray under pressure.

Not only must the fuel be filtered and supplied under adequate pressure, but also there must be a consistent *volume* of fuel to ensure smooth engine performance even under the heaviest of loads.

# ELECTRIC FUEL PUMPS

**LOCATION** The electric fuel pump is a pusher unit. When the pump is mounted in the tank, the entire fuel supply line to the engine can be pressurized. Because the fuel, when pressurized, has a higher boiling point, it is unlikely that vapor will form to interfere with fuel flow.

**POSITIVE DISPLACEMENT PUMP** A positive displacement pump is a design that forces everything that enters the pump to leave the pump. Most vehicles use the impeller or turbine pumps.

All electrical pumps are driven by a small electric motor, but the turbine pump turns at higher speeds and is quieter than the others.

In the **roller cell** or *vane pump,* the impeller draws fuel into the pump and then pushes it out through the fuel line to the injection system. All designs of pumps use a variable-sized chamber to draw in fuel. When the maximum volume has been reached, the supply port closes and the discharge opens. Fuel is then forced out the discharge as this volume decreases. Rollers or gears in a rotor plate form the chambers. Because this type of pump uses no valves to move the fuel, the fuel flows steadily through the pump housing. Fuel flows steadily through the entire pump, including the electrical portion, so the pump stays cool. Usually, only when a vehicle runs out of fuel is there a risk of pump damage. ● **SEE FIGURE 18–12.**

Most electric fuel pumps are equipped with a fuel outlet check valve that closes to maintain fuel pressure when the

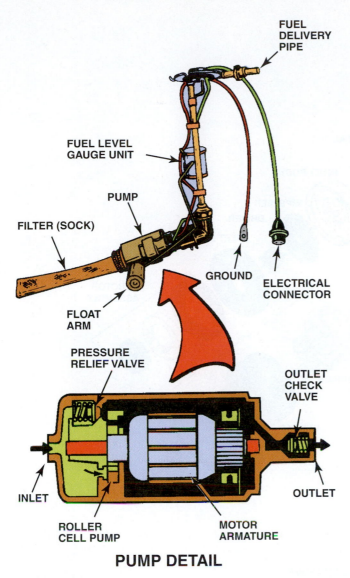

FIGURE 18–12 A roller cell-type electric fuel pump.

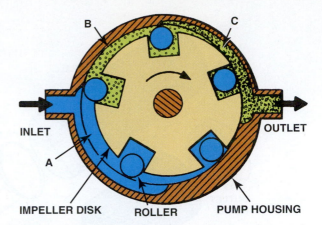

FIGURE 18–13 The pumping action of an impeller or rotary vane pump.

pump shuts off. **Residual** or **rest pressure** prevents vapor lock and hot-start problems on these systems.

● **FIGURE 18–13** shows the pumping action of a **rotary vane pump.**

The rotary vane pump consists of a central impeller disk, several rollers or vanes that ride in notches in the impeller, and a pump housing that is offset from the impeller centerline. The impeller is mounted on the end of the motor armature and spins whenever the motor is running. The rollers are free to slide in and out within the notches in the impeller to maintain sealing contact. Unpressurized fuel enters the pump, fills the spaces between the rollers, and is trapped between the impeller, the housing, and two rollers. An internal gear pump, called a **gerotor,** is another type of positive displacement pump that is often used in engine oil pumps. It uses the meshing of internal and external gear teeth to pressurize the fuel. A gerotor-type fuel pump uses an impeller as the first stage and is used to move the fuel to the gerotor section where it is pressurized. ● **SEE FIGURE 18–14.**

**HYDROKINETIC FLOW PUMP DESIGN** The word *hydro* means "liquid," and the term *kinetic* refers to motion, so the term **hydrokinetic pump** means that this design of pump rapidly moves the fuel to create pressure. This type of pump follows a nonpositive displacement pump design.

A **turbine pump** is the most common because it tends to be less noisy. Using a different number of impeller blades, and in some cases a higher number of impellers, or different shapes along the side discharge channels, controls actual pump volume. These units are fitted more toward lower operating pressures of less than 60 psi. Some are two-stage turbine pumps. ● **SEE FIGURE 18–15.**

The turbine impeller has a staggered blade design to minimize pump harmonic noise and to separate vapor from the liquid fuel. The end cap assembly contains a pressure relief valve and a radio frequency interference (RFI) suppression module. The check valve is usually located in the upper fuel pipe connector assembly.

After fuel passes through the strainer, it is drawn into the lower housing inlet port by the impellers. It is pressurized and delivered to the convoluted fuel tube for transfer through a check valve into the fuel feed pipe. A typical electric fuel pump used on a fuel-injection system delivers about 40 to 50 gallons per hour or 0.6 to 0.8 gallon per minute at a pressure of 70 to 90 psi.

**MODULAR FUEL SENDER ASSEMBLY** The modular fuel sender consists of a fuel level sensor, a turbine pump, and a jet pump. The reservoir housing is attached to the cover containing fuel pipes and the electrical connector. Fuel is transferred from the pump to the fuel pipe through a convoluted (flexible) fuel pipe. The convoluted fuel pipe eliminates the need for rubber hoses, nylon pipes, and clamps. The reservoir dampens fuel slosh to maintain a constant fuel level available to the roller vane pump; it also reduces noise.

Some of the flow, however, is returned to the jet pump for recirculation. Excess fuel is returned to the reservoir through one of the three hollow support pipes. The hot fuel quickly mixes with the cooler fuel in the reservoir; this minimizes the possibility of vapor lock. In these modules, the jet pump fills the

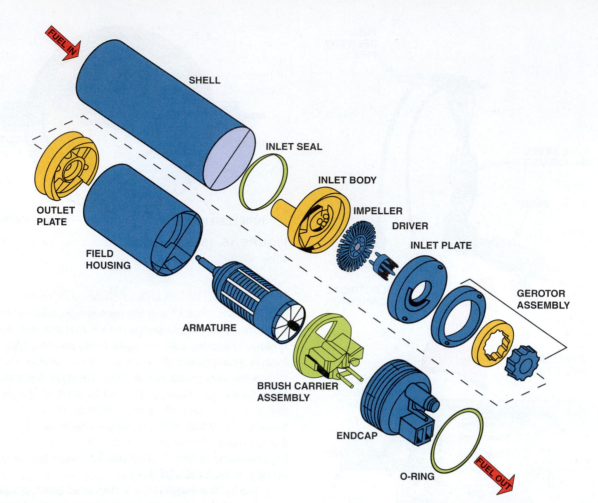

**FIGURE 18–14** An exploded view of a gerotor electric fuel pump.

FUEL IN

SHELL

INLET SEAL

INLET BODY

IMPELLER

OUTLET
PLATE

DRIVER

INLET PLATE

FIELD
HOUSING

GEROTOR
ASSEMBLY

ARMATURE

BRUSH CARRIER
ASSEMBLY

ENDCAP

O-RING

FUEL OUT

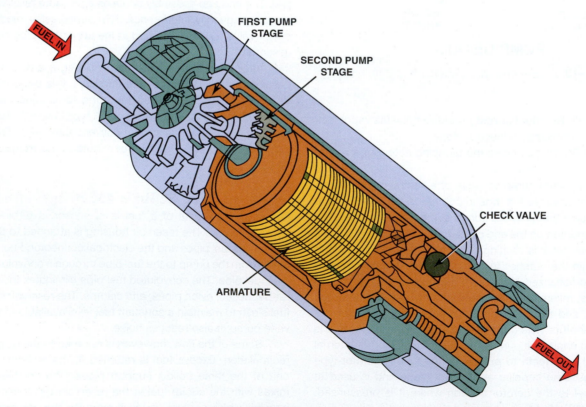

FIRST PUMP
STAGE

FUEL IN

SECOND PUMP
STAGE

CHECK VALVE

ARMATURE

FUEL OUT

**FIGURE 18–15** A cutaway view of a typical two-stage turbine electric fuel pump. A turbine type pump is the most commonly used type.

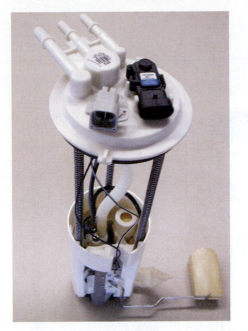

**FIGURE 18–16** A typical fuel pump module assembly, which includes the pickup strainer and fuel pump, as well as the fuel-pressure sensor and fuel level sensing unit.

**? FREQUENTLY ASKED QUESTION**

**Why Are Many Fuel Pump Modules Spring Loaded?**

Fuel modules that contain the fuel pickup sock, fuel pump, and fuel level sensor are often spring loaded when fitted to a plastic fuel tank. The plastic material shrinks when cold and expands when hot, so having the fuel module spring loaded ensures that the fuel pickup sock will always be the same distance from the bottom of the tank. ● SEE FIGURE 18–16.

reservoir. Some of the fuel from the pump is sent through the jet pump to lift fuel from the tank into the reservoir.

### ELECTRIC PUMP CONTROL CIRCUITS

Fuel pump circuits are controlled by the fuel pump relay. Fuel pump relays are activated initially by turning the ignition key to on, which allows the pump to pressurize the fuel system. As a safety precaution, the relay de-energizes after a few seconds until the key is moved to the crank position. Once an ignition coil signal, or "tach" signal, is received by the PCM, indicating the engine is rotating, the relay remains energized even with the key released to the run position.

### CHRYSLER

On Chrysler vehicles, the PCM must receive an engine speed (RPM) signal during cranking before it can energize a circuit driver inside the power module to activate an automatic shutdown (ASD) relay to power the fuel pump, ignition coil, and injectors. As a safety precaution, if the RPM signal to the PCM is interrupted, the PCM deactivates the ASD, turning off the pump, coil, and injectors. In some vehicles, the oil pressure switch circuit may be used as a safety circuit to activate the pump in the ignition switch run position.

### GENERAL MOTORS

General Motors systems energize the pump with the ignition switch to initially pressurize the fuel lines, but then deactivates the pump if an RPM signal is not received within one or two seconds. The pump is reactivated as soon as engine cranking is detected. The oil pressure sending unit serves as a backup to the fuel pump relay on some vehicles. In case of pump relay failure, the oil pressure switch will operate the fuel pump once oil pressure reaches about 4 psi (28 kPa).

### FORD

Most Fords with fuel injection have an inertia switch in the trunk between the fuel pump relay and fuel pump. When the ignition switch is turned to the on position, the electronic engine control (EEC) power relay energizes, providing current to the fuel pump relay and a timing circuit in the EEC module. If the ignition key is not turned to the start position within about one second, the timing circuit opens the ground circuit to de-energize the fuel pump relay and shut down the pump. This circuit is designed to pre-pressurize the system. Once the key is turned to the start position, power to the pump is sent through the relay and inertia switch.

The inertia switch opens under a specified impact, such as a collision. When the switch opens, current to the pump shuts off because the fuel pump relay will not energize. The switch must be reset manually by depressing the reset button before current flow to the pump can be restored. ● SEE FIGURE 18–17 for a schematic of a typical fuel system that uses an inertia switch in the power feed circuit to the electric fuel pump.

### PUMP PULSATION DAMPENING

Some manufacturers use an **accumulator** in the system to reduce pressure pulses and noise. Others use a pulsator located at the outlet of the fuel pump to absorb pressure pulsations that are created by the pump. These pulsators are often used on roller vane pumps and are a source of many internal fuel leaks. ● SEE FIGURE 18–18.

**NOTE: Some experts suggest that the pulsator be removed and replaced with a standard section of fuel line to prevent the loss of fuel pressure that results when the connections on the pulsator loosen and leak fuel back into the tank.**

### VARIABLE SPEED PUMPS

Another way to help reduce noise, current draw, and pump wear is to reduce the speed of the pump when less than maximum output is required. Pump speed and pressure can be regulated by controlling the voltage supplied to the pump with a resistor switched into the circuit, or by letting the engine-control computer pulse-width modulate (PWM) the voltage supply to the pump, through a separate fuel pump driver electronic module. With slower pump speed and pressure, less noise is produced.

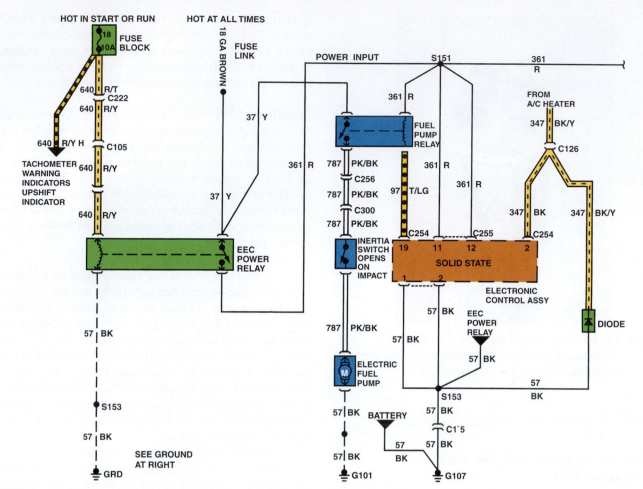

**FIGURE 18–17** A schematic showing that an inertia switch is connected in series between the fuel pump relay and the fuel pump.

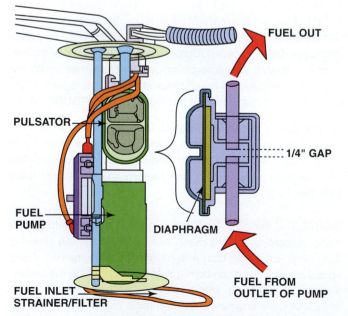

**FIGURE 18–18** A typical fuel pulsator used mostly with roller vane-type pumps to help even out the pulsation in pressure that can cause noise.

# FUEL FILTERS

**PURPOSE AND FUNCTION**   Despite the care generally taken in refining, storing, and delivering gasoline, some impurities get into the automotive fuel system. Fuel filters remove dirt, rust, water, and other contamination from the gasoline before it can reach the fuel injectors. Most fuel filters are designed to filter particles that are 10 to 20 microns or larger in size.

The useful life of many filters is limited, but vehicles that use a returnless-type fuel-injection system often use filters that are part of the fuel pump assembly and do not have any specified replacement interval. If fuel filters are not replaced according to the manufacturer's recommendations, they can become clogged and restrict fuel flow.

The filter is located in the line between the fuel pump and the throttle body or fuel rail. ● **SEE FIGURE 18–19.**

This filter protects the system from contamination, but does not protect the fuel pump. The inline filter usually is a metal or plastic container with a pleated paper element sealed inside.

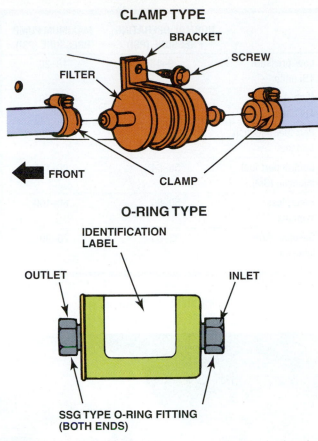

**CLAMP TYPE**

BRACKET

SCREW

FILTER

FRONT

CLAMP

**O-RING TYPE**

IDENTIFICATION
LABEL

OUTLET

INLET

SSG TYPE O-RING FITTING
(BOTH ENDS)

**FIGURE 18–19** Inline fuel filters are usually attached to the fuel line with screw clamps, quick disconnects or threaded connections. The fuel filter must be installed in the proper direction or a restricted fuel flow can result.

 **TECH TIP**

**Be Sure the Fuel Filter Is Installed Correctly**

The fuel filter has flow direction, so if it is installed backwards, the vehicle may act like a restricted exhaust (low power at higher engine speeds and loads).

**LOCATIONS**  Filters may be mounted on a bracket on the fender panel, a shock tower, or another convenient place in the engine compartment. They may also be installed under the vehicle near the fuel tank. Fuel filters should be replaced according to the vehicle manufacturer's recommendations, which range from every 30,000 miles (48,000 km) to 100,000 miles (160,000 km) or larger. Fuel filters that are part of the fuel pump module assemblies usually have no specified service interval.

All injectors, throttle body or port type, are fitted with one or more filter screens or strainers to remove any particles (generally 10 microns, or 0.00039 in.) that might have passed through the other filters. These screens, which surround the fuel inlet, are on the side of throttle-body injectors and are inserted in the top of port injectors. ● **SEE FIGURE 18–20.**

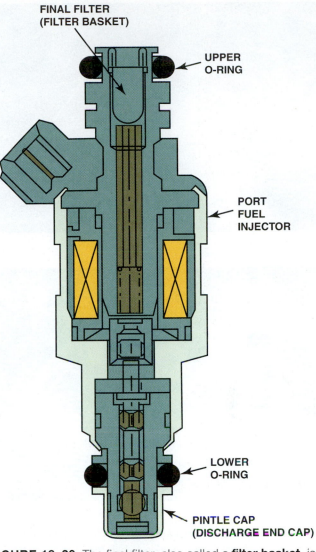

FINAL FILTER
(FILTER BASKET)

UPPER
O-RING

PORT
FUEL
INJECTOR

LOWER
O-RING

PINTLE CAP
(DISCHARGE END CAP)

**FIGURE 18–20** The final filter, also called a **filter basket,** is the last filter in the fuel system.

**TECH TIP**

**The Ear Test**

No, this is not a test of your hearing, but rather using your ear to check that the electric fuel pump is operating. The electric fuel pump inside the fuel tank is often difficult to hear running, especially in a noisy shop environment. A common trick to better hear the pump is to use a funnel in the fuel filter neck. ● **SEE FIGURE 18–21.**

## FUEL PUMP TESTING

Fuel pump testing includes varied tests and procedures. Even though a fuel pump can pass one test, this does not indicate that there is no fuel pump problem. For example, if the pump

(a)

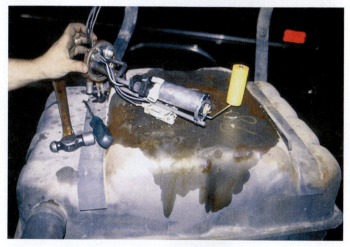

(b)

**FIGURE 18–21** (a) A funnel helps in hearing if the electric fuel pump inside the gas tank is working. (b) If the pump is not running, check the wiring and current flow before going through the process of dropping the fuel tank to remove the pump.

| | NORMAL OPERATING PRESSURE (PSI) | MAXIMUM PUMP PRESSURE (PSI) |
|---|---|---|
| Low-pressure TBI units | 9–13 | 18–20 |
| High-pressure TBI units | 25–35 | 50–70 |
| Port fuel-injection systems | 35–65 | 70–90 |
| Central port fuel injection (GM) | 55–64 | 90–110 |
| Returnless systems | 50–65 | 80–100 |
| Gasoline direct injection | 35–65 | 70–90 |

**CHART 18–1**

Typical fuel pressures for selected systems.

**FIGURE 18–22** The Schrader valve on this General Motors 3800 V-6 is located next to the fuel-pressure regulator.

motor is rotating slower than normal, it may be able to produce the specified pressure, but not enough volume to meet the needs of the engine while operating under a heavy load.

**FUEL PUMP PRESSURE TESTING** Fuel-pump-regulated pressure has become more important than ever with a more exact fuel control. Some engines will not start when fuel pressure is just a few PSI lower than specifications. Correct fuel pressure is very important for proper engine operation. Most fuel-injection systems operate at either a low pressure of about 10 psi or a high pressure of between 35 and 45 psi. ● SEE CHART 18–1.

In both types of systems, maximum fuel pump pressure is about double the normal operating pressure to ensure that a continuous flow of cool fuel is being supplied to the injector(s) to help prevent vapor from forming in the fuel system. Although vapor or foaming in a fuel system can greatly affect engine operation, the cooling and lubricating flow of

**TECH TIP**

**The Rubber Mallet Trick**

Often a no-start condition is due to an inoperative electric fuel pump. A common trick is to tap on the bottom of the fuel tank with a rubber mallet in an attempt to jar the pump motor enough to work. Instead of pushing a vehicle into the shop, simply tap on the fuel tank and attempt to start the engine. This is not a repair, but a confirmation that the fuel pump indeed requires replacement.

the fuel must be maintained to ensure the durability of injector nozzles.

To measure fuel pump pressure, locate the Schrader valve and attach a fuel-pressure gauge. ● SEE FIGURE 18–22.

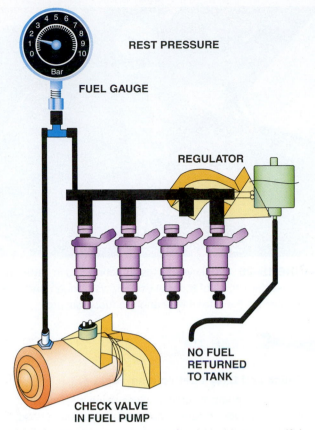

**FIGURE 18–23** The fuel system should hold pressure if the system is leak free.

**NOTE: Some vehicles, such as those with General Motors TBI fuel-injection systems, require a specific fuel-pressure gauge that connects to the fuel system. Always follow the manufacturer's recommendations and procedures.**

**REST PRESSURE TEST**    If the fuel pressure is acceptable, then check the system for leakdown. Observe the pressure gauge after five minutes. ● **SEE FIGURE 18–23.**

The pressure should be the same as the initial reading. If not, then the pressure regulator, fuel pump check valve, or the injectors are leaking down. To determine the reason for the drop in pressure, proceed as follows:

**STEP 1**    Energize the fuel pump to pressurize the system. To energize the pump, remove the fuel pump relay and, using a fused jumper lead, jumper the power to load terminals of the fuel pump relay (usually terminals 30 and 87). Check service information for the exact procedure to follow.

**STEP 2**    Connect fuel test hoses with shutoff valves and close the return line. If the leakdown stops, then the regulator is defective.

**STEP 3**    If leakdown continues, then pressurize the system again and close the supply and return lines.

**STEP 4**    If the leakdown stops now, then the fuel pump check valve is defective.

**FIGURE 18–24** If the vacuum hose is removed from the fuel-pressure regulator when the engine is running, the fuel pressure should increase. If it does not increase, then the fuel pump is not capable of supplying adequate pressure or the fuel-pressure regulator is defective. If gasoline is visible in the vacuum hose, the regulator is leaking and should be replaced.

**STEP 5**    If leakdown continues, then the injectors are leaking. (Some pumps have an internal bleed orifice to prevent vapor lock and will not hold rest pressure. It is more important that the pump be able to supply instant pressure when the key is turned on. If the pump is capable of supplying the specified pressure immediately at start-up, the bleeddown is not important.)

**DYNAMIC PRESSURE TEST**    To test the pressure dynamically, start the engine. If the pressure is vacuum referenced, then the pressure should change when the throttle is cycled. If it does not, then check the vacuum supply circuit. Remove the vacuum line from the regulator and inspect for any presence of fuel. ● **SEE FIGURE 18–24.**

There should never be any fuel present on the vacuum side of the regulator diaphragm. When the engine speed is increased, the pressure reading should remain within the specifications.

FIGURE 18–25 Fuel should be heard returning to the fuel tank at the fuel return line if the fuel pump and fuel-pressure regulator are functioning correctly.

FIGURE 18–26 A fuel system tester connected in series in the fuel system so all of the fuel used flows through the meter which displays the rate of flow and the fuel pressure.

Some engines do not use a vacuum-referenced regulator. The running pressure remains constant, which is typical for a mechanical returnless-type fuel system. On these systems, the pressure is higher than on return-type systems to help reduce the formation of fuel vapors in the system.

**FUEL PUMP VOLUME TESTING**   Fuel pressure alone is not enough for proper engine operation. Fuel flow specifications are usually expressed in gallons per minute. A typical specification would be 0.5 gallon per minute or more. Check service information for the exact fuel volume and pressure specifications. For example, specifications shown for one year of trucks is 0.85 to 1 U.S. gallon per hour (GPH) while another year of the same truck has a specification 0.92 to 1.08 GPH. This difference (however so slight) could cause a borderline problem with the vehicle if in fact the wrong pump has been installed.

   A fuel system tester is needed to test the fuel volume and must be connected into the fuel system in series. ● **SEE FIGURE 18–26.**

FUEL PUMP

**FIGURE 18–27** Removing the bed from a pickup truck makes gaining access to the fuel pump much easier.

**SYMPTOMS OF LOW FUEL VOLUME** If the fuel filter becomes partially clogged, the following symptoms are likely to occur.

1. There will be low power at higher engine speeds. The vehicle usually will not go faster than a certain speed (engine acts as if it has a built-in speed governor).
2. The engine will cut out or miss on acceleration, especially when climbing hills or during heavy load acceleration.

A weak or defective fuel pump can also be the cause of the symptoms just listed. If an electric fuel pump for a fuel-injected engine becomes weak, additional problems include the following:

1. The engine may be hard to start.
2. There may be a rough idle and stalling.

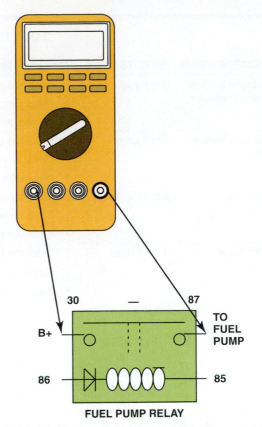

```
        30        —        87
  B+  ○                    ○   TO
                              FUEL
                              PUMP
  86  ─▷|──◉◉◉◉◉──          85
```
**FUEL PUMP RELAY**

**FIGURE 18–28** Hookup for testing fuel pump current draw on any vehicle equipped with a fuel pump relay.

3. There may be erratic shifting of the automatic transmission as a result of engine missing due to lack of fuel pump pressure and/or volume.

**CAUTION: Be certain to consult the vehicle manufacturer's recommended service and testing procedures before attempting to test or replace any component of a high-pressure electronic fuel-injection system.**

## FUEL PUMP CURRENT DRAW TEST

**PURPOSE** Another test that can and should be performed on a fuel pump is to measure the current draw in amperes. A fuel pump current draw test is performed by connecting a digital multimeter set to read DC amperes in series in the fuel pump circuit. Most vehicle fuel pumps are tested by connecting an ammeter into the fuel pump circuit at the fuel pump relay or by using a clamp-type inductive ammeter. ● **SEE FIGURE 18–28.**

Compare the reading to factory specifications. ● **SEE CHART 18–2.**

**NOTE: Testing the current draw of an electric fuel pump may not indicate whether the pump is good. A pump that is not rotating may draw normal current.**

## FUEL PUMP CURRENT DRAW

| AMPERAGE READING | EXPECTED VALUE | AMPERAGE TOO HIGH | AMPERAGE TOO LOW |
|---|---|---|---|
| Throttle-Body Fuel-Injection Engines | 2 to 5 amps | • Check the fuel filter. <br> • Check for restrictions in other fuel line areas. <br> • Replace the fuel pump. | • Check for a high-resistance connection. <br> • Check for a high-resistance ground fault. <br> • Replace the fuel pump. |
| Port Fuel-Injection Engines | 4 to 8 amps | • Check the fuel filter. <br> • Check for restrictions in other fuel line areas. <br> • Replace the fuel pump. | • Check for a high-resistance connection. <br> • Check for a high-resistance ground fault. <br> • Replace the fuel pump. |
| Turbocharged Engines | 6 to 10 amps | • Check the fuel filter. <br> • Check for restrictions in other fuel line areas. <br> • Replace the fuel pump. | • Check for a high-resistance connection. <br> • Check for a high-resistance ground fault. <br> • Replace the fuel pump. |
| GM CPI Truck Engines | 8 to 12 amps | • Check the fuel filter. <br> • Check for restrictions in other fuel line areas. <br> • Replace the fuel pump. | • Check for a high-resistance connection. <br> • Check for a high-resistance ground fault. <br> • Replace the fuel pump. |

**CHART 18–2**

Typical fuel pump current draw based on the type of fuel injection used.

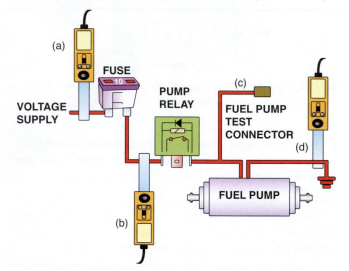

**FIGURE 18–29** A low-amp current probe can be connected anywhere in the fuel pump circuit that is the most convenient, including (a) at the fuse, (b) at the relay, and (c) at the test connector or even the ground wire for the pump. To test at the fuel pump test lead, apply 12 volts to the test lead using a fused jumper wire.

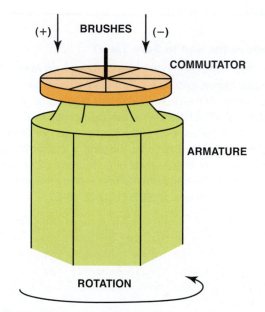

**FIGURE 18–30** A typical electric fuel pump motor that uses triangular commutator segments and horizontal brushes.

# FUEL PUMP CURRENT RAMPING

**PURPOSE** Current ramping means to observe the current (amperes) waveform. By checking the current waveform of the fuel pump, possible problems can be detected. To perform a current ramping test, the following test equipment is required.

- Digital storage oscilloscope
- Current probe

Current ramping is considered to be "nonintrusive," meaning that nothing has to be disconnected or disassembled in order to perform the test procedure. Most electric fuel pumps can be tested at one of three locations.

1. Fuel pump test lead (most 1981–1995 General Motors fuel-injected vehicles)
2. Fuel pump relay (use a fused jumper wire for the probe)
3. Fuel pump fuse (use a fused jumper wire for the probe)

A current probe detects the current flow to the motor of the electric fuel pump. ● **SEE FIGURE 18–29.**

The typical electric fuel pump motor has commutator segments and two brushes—a positive brush and a negative brush. ● **SEE FIGURE 18–30.**

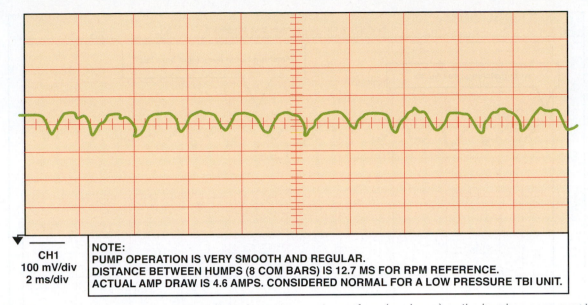

CH1
100 mV/div
2 ms/div

NOTE:
PUMP OPERATION IS VERY SMOOTH AND REGULAR.
DISTANCE BETWEEN HUMPS (8 COM BARS) IS 12.7 MS FOR RPM REFERENCE.
ACTUAL AMP DRAW IS 4.6 AMPS. CONSIDERED NORMAL FOR A LOW PRESSURE TBI UNIT.

**FIGURE 18–31** As the fuel pump motor rotates, it produces a current waveform (as shown) as the brushes pass over the commutator segments. Each horizontal line represents 1 ampere therefore the waveform shows that the pump is requiring a little over 4.5 amperes.

As the motor rotates, the current through the brushes changes as the commutator segments rotate past the brushes. ● **SEE FIGURE 18–31.**

### SCOPE SETUP
The majority of scopes used for fuel pump testing use a voltage setting of 100 mV per division and a time setting of 2 ms. In some cases, the time base can be expanded to 5 ms for a better look at the waveform produced by the pump.

### CURRENT DRAW
Current draw will increase with load and decrease with lack of load. Poor brush contact also will lower current draw; and brush spring tension is critical to the motor operation. The negative (ground) brush always seems to be the first to fail, and the spring behind the brushes will be the one to show heat and loss of spring tension.

### MOTOR COMMUTATOR BARS AND MOTOR SPEED
Most electric fuel pumps use a motor that has 8, 10, or 12 commutator segments. As the brushes pass over each commutator segment, a unique pattern is often visible. Counting the number of segments (usually eight) indicates one revolution of the pump motor. Using that number and the time base of the scope, the actual operational RPM of the pump motor can be determined. ● **SEE FIGURE 18–32.**

### PUMP MOTOR SPEED
The speed of a good pump motor should be greater than 3,000 RPM. Most pumps will operate from 3,000 to 6,000 RPM. A pump motor that is not rotating fast enough will not be able to supply the correct volume of fuel necessary for proper engine operation. To determine the speed of the pump motor, use the curves on the scope display and determine the time interval between the unique

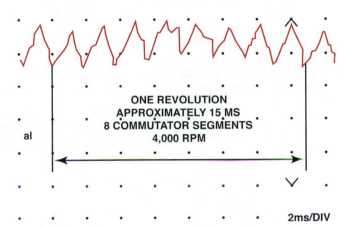

ONE REVOLUTION
APPROXIMATELY 15 MS
8 COMMUTATOR SEGMENTS
4,000 RPM

al

2ms/DIV

**FIGURE 18–32** The speed of the fuel pump motor can be determined by the time it takes the motor to make one revolution, as determined by looking for unique commutator segment patterns.

commutators and divide that number into 60,000 to determine the RPM.

$$\text{Pump RPM} = \frac{\text{time (ms)}}{60,000}$$

For example, if the pump motor rotates one revolution every 10 ms, then the motor is operating at 6,000 RPM. ● **SEE FIGURE 18–33.**

A pump that is operating at less than 3,000 RPM will likely be unable to supply enough fuel, resulting in a lack of power concern.

### CASE STUDY 1: GOOD FUEL PUMP WAVEFORM
A known good pump will produce the proper waveform. ● **SEE FIGURE 18–34.**

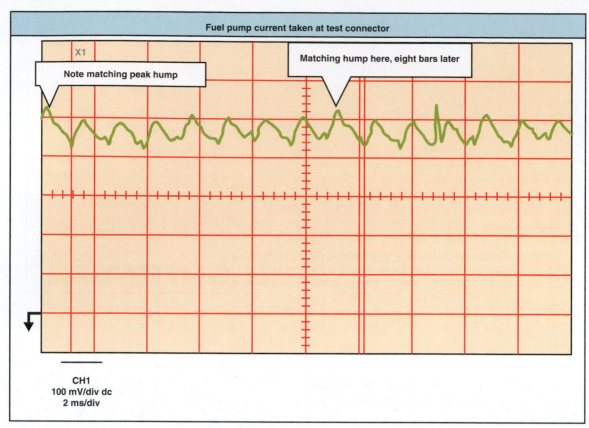

**FIGURE 18–33** The RPM of a pump is determined by first locating unique humps in the voltage waveform. Counting the number of divisions between unique humps and then multiplying it by the time per division determines the time for one revolution.

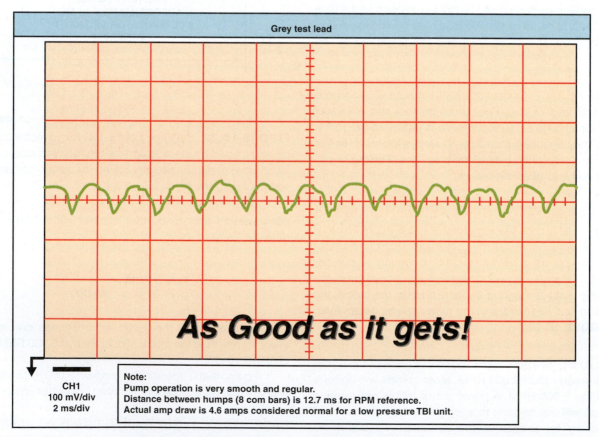

**FIGURE 18–34** This fuel pump voltage waveform shows good pump speed (4,724 RPM) and current draw. Each horizontal line represents 1 ampere therefore the waveform shows that the pump is requiring a little over 4.5 amperes.

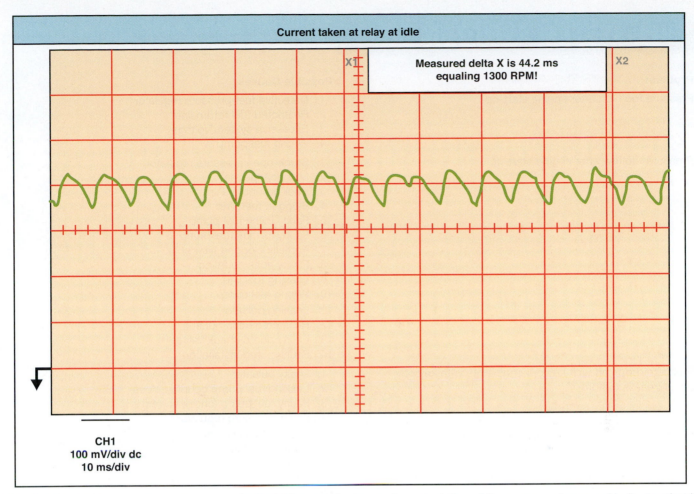

Current taken at relay at idle

Measured delta X is 44.2 ms
equaling 1300 RPM!

X1          X2

CH1
100 mV/div dc
10 ms/div

**FIGURE 18–35** Although the voltage waveform of this pump looks good, a calculation of the pump motor speed indicates that it is rotating far below the 3,000 RPM minimum acceptable speed.

The waveform indicated that the amp draw is correct and within specifications for the vehicle being tested. Higher fuel pressure equals higher current draw or motor load. Also, the brush contact is regular and consistent.

### CASH STUDY 2: GOOD PRESSURE, LOW VOLUME
This pump motor is rotating at only 1,300 RPM, indicating a very slow rotating pump. ● **SEE FIGURE 18–35.**

## FUEL PUMP REPLACEMENT

The following recommendations should be followed whenever replacing an electric fuel pump.

- The fuel pump strainer (sock) should be replaced with the new pump.
- If the original pump had a defector shield, it should always be used to prevent fuel return bubbles from blocking the inlet to the pump.
- Always check the interior of the fuel tank for evidence of contamination or dirt.
- Double-check that the replacement pump is correct for the application.

# FUEL SYSTEM SYMPTOM GUIDE

| Problem | Possible Causes |
|---|---|
| Pressure too high after engine start-up | 1. Defective fuel-pressure regulator<br>2. Restricted fuel return line<br>3. Excessive system voltage<br>4. Wrong fuel pump |
| Pressure too low after engine start-up | 1. Stuck-open pressure regulator<br>2. Low voltage<br>3. Poor ground<br>4. Plugged fuel filter<br>5. Faulty inline fuel pump<br>6. Faulty in-tank fuel pump<br>7. Partially clogged filter sock<br>8. Faulty hose coupling<br>9. Leaking fuel line<br>10. Wrong fuel pump<br>11. Leaking pulsator<br>12. Restricted accumulator<br>13. Faulty pump check valves<br>14. Faulty pump installation |
| Pressure drops off with key on, engine off; with key off, pressure fails to hold | 1. Leaky pulsator<br>2. Leaking fuel pump coupling hose<br>3. Faulty fuel pump (check valves)<br>4. Faulty pressure regulator<br>5. Leaking fuel injector<br>6. Faulty installation<br>7. Lines leaking |

# SUMMARY

1. The fuel delivery system includes the following items.
   - Fuel tank
   - Fuel pump
   - Fuel filter(s)
   - Fuel lines
2. A fuel tank is either constructed of corrosion-resistant steel or polyethylene plastic.
3. Fuel tank filler tubes contain an antisiphoning device.
4. Accident and rollover protection devices include check valves and inertia switches.
5. Fuel lines are made of steel, nylon tubing or fuel-resistant rubber hose.
6. Electric fuel pump types include roller cell, gerotor, and turbine.
7. Fuel filters remove particles that are 10 to 20 microns or larger in size.
8. Fuel pumps can be tested by checking:
   - Pressure
   - Volume
   - Pump motor speed (RPM) as determined by current ramping
   - Specified current draw

# REVIEW QUESTIONS

1. What are the two materials used to construct fuel tanks?
2. What are the most common pump designs?
3. What is the proper way to disconnect and connect plastic fuel line connections?
4. Where are the fuel filters located in the fuel system?
5. What accident and rollover devices are installed in a fuel delivery system?
6. What four methods can be used to test a fuel pump?

1. The first fuel filter in the sock inside the fuel tank normally filters particles larger than _____.
   a. 0.001 to 0.003 in.
   b. 0.01 to 0.03 in.
   c. 10 to 20 microns
   d. 70 to 100 microns

2. Which type of safety device will keep the electric fuel pump from operating if it is tripped?
   a. Rollover valve
   b. Inertia switch
   c. Antisiphoning valve
   d. Check valve

3. Fuel lines are constructed from _____.
   a. Seamless steel tubing
   b. Nylon plastic
   c. Copper and/or aluminum tubing
   d. Both a and b

4. Which is the most common type of fuel pump design?
   a. Gerotor
   c. Rotor cell
   b. Impeller
   d. Turbine

5. A good fuel pump should supply how much fuel per minute?
   a. 0.25 pint
   c. 1 pint
   b. 0.5 pint
   d. 0.5 to 1 gallon

6. Technician A says that fuel pump modules are spring loaded so that they can be compressed to fit into the opening. Technician B says that they are spring loaded to allow for expansion and contraction of plastic fuel tanks. Which technician is correct?
   a. Technician A only
   b. Technician B only
   c. Both Technicians A and B
   d. Neither Technician A nor B

7. Most fuel filters are designed to remove particles larger than _____.
   a. 1 micron
   b. 10 to 20 microns
   c. 70 microns
   d. 100 microns

8. The amperage draw of an electric fuel pump is *higher* than specified. All of the following are possible causes *except:*
   a. Corroded electrical connections at the pump motor
   b. Clogged fuel filter
   c. Restriction in the fuel line
   d. Defective fuel pump

9. A fuel pump is being tested with an amp probe and a digital storage oscilloscope. Technician A says that most fuel pumps have four commutator segments. Technician B says that the speed of the pump motor should be higher than 3,000 RPM. Which technician is correct?
   a. Technician A only
   b. Technician B only
   c. Both Technicians A and B
   d. Neither Technician A nor B

10. A fuel filter has been accidentally installed backwards. What is the most likely result?
    a. Nothing will be noticed
    b. Reduced fuel economy
    c. Lower power at higher engine speeds and loads
    d. Fuel system pulsation noises may be heard

# chapter 19

# FUEL-INJECTION COMPONENTS AND OPERATION

**OBJECTIVES:** After studying Chapter 19, the reader will be able to: • Prepare for ASE Engine Performance (A8) certification test content area "C" (Fuel, Air Induction, and Exhaust Systems Diagnosis and Repair). • Describe how a port fuel-injection system works. • Describe the fuel injection modes of operation. • Discuss central port injection (CPI) systems. • Explain how a stepper motor works. • Discuss the purpose and function of the fuel-pressure regulator. • List the types of fuel-injection systems.

**KEY TERMS:** Demand delivery system (DDS) 261 • Electronic air control (EAC) 265 • Electronic returnless fuel system (ERFS) 260 • Flare 265 • Fuel rail 262 • Gang fired 257 • Idle speed control (ISC) motor 266 • Mechanical returnless fuel system (MRFS) 261 • Nonchecking 260 • Port fuel-injection 254 • Pressure control valve (PCV) 261 • Pressure vent valve (PVV) 261 • Sequential fuel injection (SFI) 257 • Throttle-body injection (TBI) 254

## ELECTRONIC FUEL-INJECTION OPERATION

Electronic fuel-injection systems use the powertrain control module (PCM) to control the operation of fuel injectors and other functions based on information sent to the PCM from the various sensors. Most electronic fuel-injection systems share the following:

1. Electric fuel pump (usually located inside the fuel tank)
2. Fuel-pump relay (usually controlled by the computer)
3. Fuel-pressure regulator (mechanically operated spring-loaded rubber diaphragm maintains proper fuel pressure)
4. Fuel-injector nozzle or nozzles

● **SEE FIGURE 19–1.** Most electronic fuel-injection systems use the computer to control these aspects of their operation:

1. **Pulsing the fuel injectors on and off.** The longer the injectors are held open, the greater the amount of fuel injected into the cylinder.
2. **Operating the fuel pump relay circuit.** The computer usually controls the operation of the electric fuel pump located inside (or near) the fuel tank. The computer uses signals from the ignition switch and RPM signals from the ignition module or system to energize the fuel-pump relay circuit.

**NOTE: This is a safety feature, because if the engine stalls and the tachometer (engine speed) signal is lost, the computer will shut off (de-energize) the fuel-pump relay and stop the fuel pump.**

Computer-controlled fuel-injection systems are normally reliable systems if the proper service procedures are followed.

Fuel-injection systems use the gasoline flowing through the injectors to lubricate and cool the injector electrical windings and pintle valves.

**NOTE: The fuel does not actually make contact with the electrical windings because the injectors have O-rings at the top and bottom of the winding spool to keep fuel out.**

There are two types of electronic fuel-injection systems:

- **Throttle-body-injection (TBI)** type. A TBI system delivers fuel from a nozzle(s) into the air above the throttle plate. ● **SEE FIGURE 19–2.**
- **Port fuel-injection**-type. A port fuel-injection design uses a nozzle for each cylinder and the fuel is squirted into the intake manifold about 2 to 3 inches (70 to 100 mm) from the intake valve. ● **SEE FIGURE 19–3.**

## SPEED-DENSITY FUEL-INJECTION SYSTEMS

Fuel-injection computer systems require a method for measuring the amount of air the engine is breathing in, in order to match the correct fuel delivery. There are two basic methods used:

1. Speed density
2. Mass airflow

The speed-density method does not require an air quantity sensor, but rather calculates the amount of fuel required by the

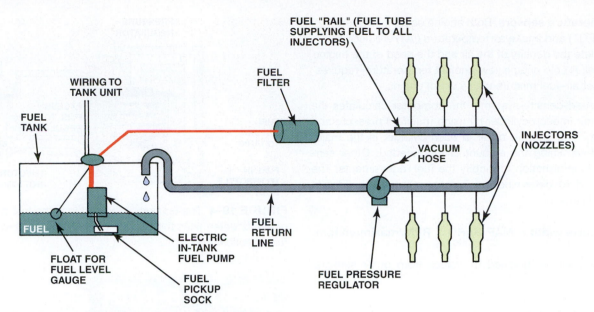

**FIGURE 19–1** Typical port fuel-injection system, indicating the location of various components. Notice that the fuel-pressure regulator is located on the fuel return side of the system. The computer does not control fuel pressure. But does control the operation of the electric fuel pump (on most systems) and the pulsing on and off of the injectors.

**FIGURE 19–2** A dual-nozzle TBI unit on a Chevrolet 4.3-L V-6 engine. The fuel is squirted above the throttle plate where the fuel mixes with air before entering the intake manifold.

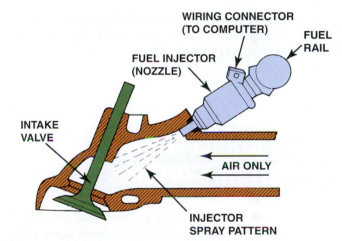

**FIGURE 19–3** A typical port fuel-injection system squirts fuel into the low pressure (vacuum) of the intake manifold, about 2 to 3 in. (70 to 100 mm) from the intake valve.

engine. The computer uses information from sensors such as the MAP and TP to calculate the needed amount of fuel.

- **MAP sensor.** The value of the intake (inlet) manifold pressure (vacuum) is a direct indication of engine load.
- **TP sensor.** The position of the throttle plate and its rate of change are used as part of the equation to calculate the proper amount of fuel to inject.

---

🔧 **TECH TIP**

**"Two Must-Do's"**

For long service life of the fuel system always do the following:

1. Avoid operating the vehicle on a near-empty tank of fuel. The water or alcohol that may be in the tank becomes more concentrated when the fuel level is low. Dirt that settles near the bottom of the fuel tank can be drawn through the fuel system and cause damage to the pump and injector nozzles.
2. Replace the fuel filter at regular service intervals.

---

- **Temperature sensors.** Both engine coolant temperature (ECT) and intake air temperature (IAT) are used to calculate the density of the air and the need of the engine for fuel. A cold engine (low-coolant temperature) requires a richer air–fuel mixture than a warm engine.

On speed-density systems, the computer calculates the amount of air in each cylinder by using manifold pressure and engine rpm. The amount of air in each cylinder is the major factor in determining the amount of fuel needed. Other sensors provide information to modify the fuel requirements. The formula used to determine the injector pulse width (PW) in milliseconds (ms) is:

$$\text{Injector pulse width} = \text{MAP/BARO} \times \text{RPM/maximum rpm}$$

The formula is modified by values from other sensors, including:

- Throttle position (TP)
- Engine coolant temperature (ECT)
- Intake air temperature (IAT)
- Oxygen sensor voltage (O2S)
- Adaptive memory

A fuel injector delivers atomized fuel into the airstream where it is instantly vaporized. All throttle-body (TB) fuel-injection systems and many multipoint (port) injection systems use the speed-density method of fuel calculation.

## MASS AIRFLOW FUEL-INJECTION SYSTEMS

The formula used by fuel-injection systems that use a mass airflow (MAF) sensor to calculate the injection base pulse width is:

$$\text{Injector pulse width} = \text{airflow/rpm}$$

The formula is modified by other sensor values such as:

- Throttle position
- Engine coolant temperature
- Barometric pressure
- Adaptive memory

**NOTE: Many four-cylinder engines do not use a MAF sensor because, due to the time interval between intake events, some reverse airflow can occur in the intake manifold. The MAF sensor would "read" this flow of air as being additional air entering the engine, giving the PCM incorrect airflow information. Therefore, most four-cylinder engines use the speed-density method of fuel control.**

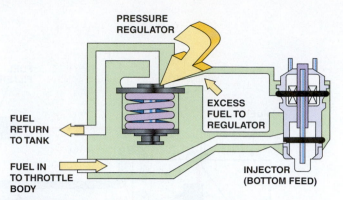

**FIGURE 19–4** The tension of the spring in the fuel-pressure regulator determines the operating pressure on a throttle-body fuel-injection unit.

## THROTTLE-BODY INJECTION

The computer controls injector pulses in one of two ways:

- Synchronized
- Nonsynchronized

If the system uses a synchronized mode, the injector pulses once for each distributor reference pulse. In some vehicles, when dual injectors are used in a synchronized system, the injectors pulse alternately. In a nonsynchronized system, the injectors are pulsed once during a given period (which varies according to calibration) completely independent of distributor reference pulses.

The injector always opens the same distance, and the fuel pressure is maintained at a controlled value by the pressure regulator. The regulators used on throttle-body injection systems are not connected to a vacuum like many port fuel-injection systems. The strength of the spring inside the regulator determines at what pressure the valve is unseated, sending the fuel back to the tank and lowering the pressure. ● **SEE FIGURE 19–4.** The amount of fuel delivered by the injector depends on the amount of time (on-time) that the nozzle is open. This is the injector pulse width—the on-time in milliseconds that the nozzle is open.

The PCM commands a variety of pulse widths to supply the amount of fuel that an engine needs at any specific moment.

- A long pulse width delivers more fuel.
- A short pulse width delivers less fuel.

## PORT-FUEL INJECTION

The advantages of port fuel-injection design also are related to characteristics of intake manifolds:

- Fuel distribution is equal to all cylinders because each cylinder has its own injector. ● **SEE FIGURE 19–5.**

### How Do the Sensors Affect the Pulse Width?

The base pulse width of a fuel-injection system is primarily determined by the value of the MAF or MAP sensor and engine speed (RPM). However, the PCM relies on the input from many other sensors to modify the base pulse width as needed. For example,

- **TP Sensor.** This sensor causes the PCM to command up to 500% (5 times) the base pulse width if the accelerator pedal is depressed rapidly to the floor. It can also reduce the pulse width by about 70% if the throttle is rapidly closed.
- **ECT.** The value of this sensor determines the temperature of the engine coolant, helps determine the base pulse width, and can account for up to 60% of the determining factors.
- **BARO.** The BARO sensor compensates for altitude and adds up to about 10% under high-pressure conditions and subtracts as much as 50% from the base pulse width at high altitudes.
- **IAT.** The intake air temperature is used to modify the base pulse width based on the temperature of the air entering the engine. It is usually capable of adding as much as 20% if very cold air is entering the engine or reduce the pulse width by up to 20% if very hot air is entering the engine.
- **O2S.** This is one of the main modifiers to the base pulse width and can add or subtract up to about 20% to 25% or more, depending on the oxygen sensor activity.

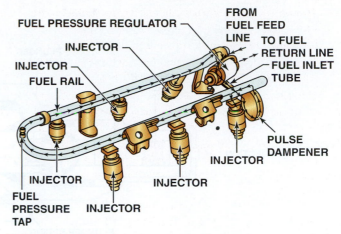

**FIGURE 19–5** The injectors receive fuel and are supported by the fuel rail.

- The fuel is injected almost directly into the combustion chamber, so there is no chance for it to condense on the walls of a cold intake manifold.
- Because the manifold does not have to carry fuel to properly position a TBI unit, it can be shaped and sized to tune the intake airflow to achieve specific engine performance characteristics.

An EFI injector is simply a specialized solenoid. ● **SEE FIGURE 19–6.** It has an armature winding to create a magnetic field, and a needle (pintle), a disc, or a ball valve. A spring holds the needle, disc, or ball closed against the valve seat, and when energized, the armature winding pulls open the valve when it receives a current pulse from the Powertrain Control Module (PCM). When the solenoid is energized, it unseats the valve to inject fuel.

Electronic fuel-injection systems use a solenoid-operated injector to spray atomized fuel in timed pulses into the manifold or near the intake valve. ● **SEE FIGURE 19–7.** Injectors may be sequenced and fired in one of several ways, but their pulse width is determined and controlled by the engine computer.

Port systems have an injector for each cylinder, but they do not all fire the injectors in the same way. Domestic systems use one of three ways to trigger the injectors:

- Grouped double-fire
- Simultaneous double-fire
- Sequential

**GROUPED DOUBLE-FIRE** This system divides the injectors into two equalized groups. The groups fire alternately; each group fires once each crankshaft revolution, or twice per four-stroke cycle. The fuel injected remains near the intake valve and enters the engine when the valve opens. This method of pulsing injectors in groups is sometimes called **gang fired**.

**SIMULTANEOUS DOUBLE-FIRE** This design fires all of the injectors at the same time once every engine revolution: two pulses per four-stroke cycle. Many port fuel-injection systems on four-cylinder engines use this pattern of injector firing. It is easier for engineers to program this system and it can make relatively quick adjustments in the air–fuel ratio, but it still requires the intake charge to wait in the manifold for varying lengths of time.

**SEQUENTIAL** Sequential firing of the injectors according to engine firing order is the most accurate and desirable method of regulating port fuel injection. However, it is also the most complex and expensive to design and manufacture. In this system, the injectors are timed and pulsed individually, much like the spark plugs are sequentially operated in firing order of the engine. This system is often called **sequential fuel injection** or **SFI.** Each cylinder receives one charge every two crankshaft revolutions, just before the intake valve opens. This means that the mixture is never static in the intake manifold and mixture adjustments can be made almost instantaneously between the firing of one injector and the next. A camshaft position sensor (CMP) signal or a special distributor reference pulse informs the PCM when the No. 1 cylinder is on its compression stroke. If the sensor fails or the reference pulse is interrupted, some injection systems shut down, while others revert to pulsing the injectors simultaneously.

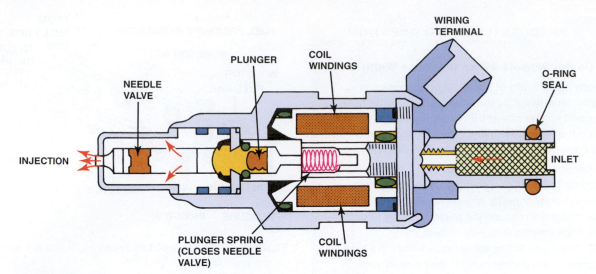

FIGURE 19–6 Cross-section of a typical port fuel-injection nozzle assembly. These injectors are serviced as an assembly only; no part replacement or service is possible except for replacement of external O-ring seals.

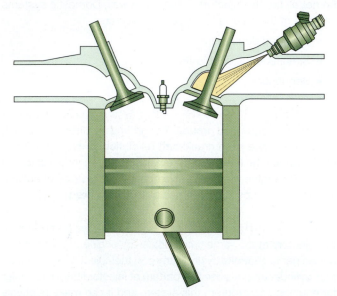

FIGURE 19–7 Port fuel injectors spray atomized fuel into the intake manifold about 3 inches (75 mm) from the intake valve.

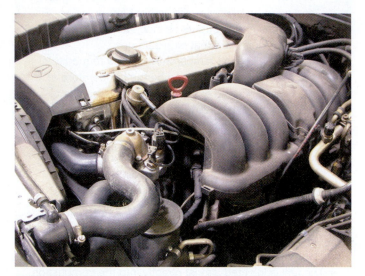

FIGURE 19–8 A port fuel-injected engine that is equipped with long, tuned intake manifold runners.

The major advantage of using port injection instead of the simpler throttle-body injection is that the intake manifolds on port fuel-injected engines only contain air, not a mixture of air and fuel. This allows the engine design engineer the opportunity to design long, "tuned" intake-manifold runners that help the engine produce increased torque at low engine speeds. ● SEE FIGURE 19–8.

NOTE: Some port fuel-injection systems used on engines with four or more valves per cylinder may use two injectors per cylinder. One injector is used all the time, and the second injector is operated by the computer when high engine speed and high-load conditions are detected by the computer. Typically, the second injector injects fuel into the high-speed intake ports of the manifold. This system permits good low-speed power and throttle responses as well as superior high-speed power.

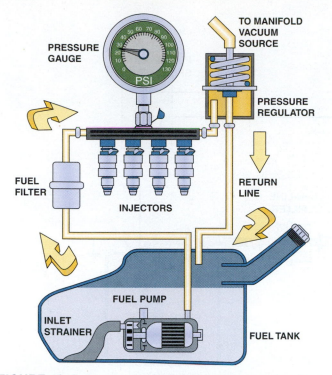

FIGURE 19-9 A typical port fuel-injected system showing a vacuum-controlled fuel-pressure regulator.

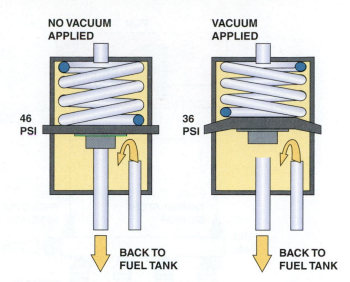

FIGURE 19-10 A typical fuel-pressure regulator that has a spring that exerts 46 pounds of force against the fuel. If 20 inches of vacuum are applied above the spring, the vacuum reduces the force exerted by the spring on the fuel, allowing the fuel to return to the tank at a lower pressure.

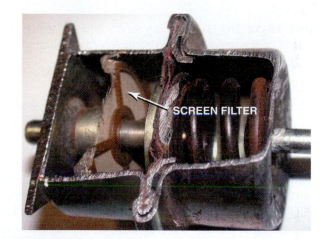

FIGURE 19-11 A lack of fuel flow could be due to a restricted fuel-pressure regulator. Notice the fine screen filter. If this filter were to become clogged, higher than normal fuel pressure would occur.

# FUEL-PRESSURE REGULATOR

The pressure regulator and fuel pump work together to maintain the required pressure drop at the injector tips. The fuel-pressure regulator typically consists of a spring-loaded, diaphragm-operated valve in a metal housing.

Fuel-pressure regulators on fuel-return-type fuel-injection systems are installed on the return (downstream) side of the injectors at the end of the fuel rail, or are built into or mounted upon the throttle-body housing. Downstream regulation minimizes fuel-pressure pulsations caused by pressure drop across the injectors as the nozzles open. It also ensures positive fuel pressure at the injectors at all times and holds residual pressure in the lines when the engine is off. On mechanical returnless systems, the regulator is located back at the tank with the fuel filter.

In order for excess fuel (about 80% to 90% of the fuel delivered) to return to the tank, fuel pressure must overcome spring pressure on the spring-loaded diaphragm to uncover the return line to the tank. This happens when system pressure exceeds operating requirements. With TBI, the regulator is close to the injector tip, so the regulator senses essentially the same air pressure as the injector.

The pressure regulator used in a port fuel-injection system has an intake manifold vacuum line connection on the regulator vacuum chamber. This allows fuel pressure to be modulated by a combination of spring pressure and manifold vacuum acting on the diaphragm. ● SEE FIGURES 19-9 AND 19-10.

TECH TIP

**Don't Forget the Regulator**

Some fuel-pressure regulators contain a 10-micron filter. If this filter becomes clogged, a lack of fuel flow would result. ● SEE FIGURE 19-11.

In both TBI and port fuel-injection systems, the regulator shuts off the return line when the fuel pump is not running. This maintains pressure at the injectors for easy restarting after hot soak as well as reducing vapor lock.

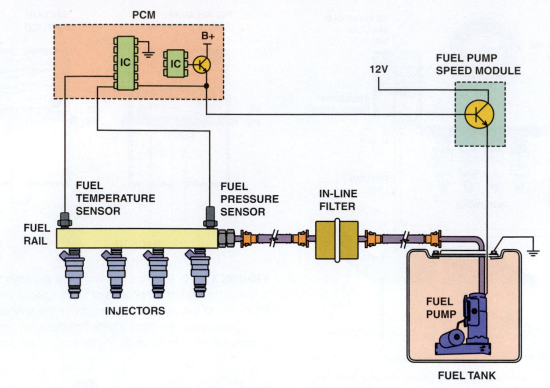

**FIGURE 19–12** The fuel-pressure sensor and fuel-temperature sensor are often constructed together in one assembly to help give the PCM the needed data to control the fuel-pump speed.

NOTE: **Some General Motors throttle-body units do not hold pressure and are called nonchecking.**

Port fuel-injection systems generally operate with pressures at the injector of about 30 to 55 PSI (207 to 379 kPa), while TBI systems work with injector pressures of about 10 to 20 PSI (69 to 138 kPa). The difference in system pressures results from the difference in how the systems operate. Since injectors in a TBI system inject the fuel into the airflow at the manifold inlet (above the throttle), there is more time for atomization in the manifold before the air–fuel charge reaches the intake valve. This allows TBI injectors to work at lower pressures than injectors used in a port system.

| Engine Operating Condition | Intake Manifold Vacuum | Fuel Pressure |
|---|---|---|
| Idle or cruise | High | Lower |
| Heavy load | Low | Higher |

The computer can best calculate injector pulse width based on all sensors if the pressure drop across the injector is the same under all operating conditions. A vacuum-controlled fuel-pressure regulator allows the equal pressure drop by reducing the force exerted by the regulator spring at high vacuum (low-load condition), yet allowing the full force of the regulator spring to be exerted when the vacuum is low (high-engine-load condition).

## VACUUM-BIASED FUEL-PRESSURE REGULATOR

The primary reason why many port fuel-injected systems use a vacuum-controlled fuel-pressure regulator is to ensure that there is a constant pressure drop across the injectors. In a throttle-body fuel-injection system, the injector squirts into the atmospheric pressure regardless of the load on the engine. In a port fuel-injected engine, however, the pressure inside the intake manifold changes as the load on the engine increases.

## ELECTRONIC RETURNLESS FUEL SYSTEM

This system is unique because it does not use a mechanical valve to regulate rail pressure. Fuel pressure at the rail is sensed by a pressure transducer, which sends a low-level signal to a controller. The controller contains logic to calculate a signal to the pump power driver. The power driver contains a high-current transistor that controls the pump speed using pulse width modulation (PWM). This system is called the **electronic returnless fuel system (ERFS)**. ● **SEE FIGURE 19–12.** This

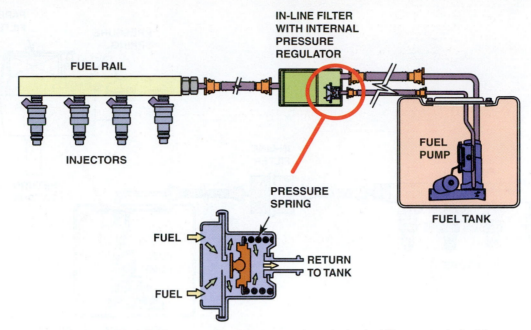

**FIGURE 19-13** A mechanical returnless fuel system. The bypass regulator in the fuel filter controls fuel line pressure.

transducer can be differentially referenced to manifold pressure for closed-loop feedback, correcting and maintaining the output of the pump to a desired rail setting. This system is capable of continuously varying rail pressure as a result of engine vacuum, engine fuel demand, and fuel temperature (as sensed by an external temperature transducer, if necessary). A **pressure vent valve (PVV)** is employed at the tank to relieve overpressure due to thermal expansion of fuel. In addition, a supply-side bleed, by means of an in-tank reservoir using a supply-side jet pump, is necessary for proper pump operation.

## MECHANICAL RETURNLESS FUEL SYSTEM

The first production returnless systems employed the **mechanical returnless fuel system (MRFS)** approach. This system has a bypass regulator to control rail pressure that is located in close proximity to the fuel tank. Fuel is sent by the in-tank pump to a chassis-mounted inline filter with excess fuel returning to the tank through a short return line. ● **SEE FIGURE 19-13.** The inline filter may be mounted directly to the tank, thereby eliminating the shortened return line. Supply pressure is regulated on the downstream side of the inline filter to accommodate changing restrictions throughout the filter's service life. This system is limited to constant rail pressure (*CRP) system calibrations, whereas with ERFS, the pressure transducer can be referenced to atmospheric pressure for CRP systems or differentially referenced to intake manifold pressure for constant differential injector pressure (**CIP) systems.

**NOTE: *CRP is referenced to atmospheric pressure, has lower operating pressure, and is desirable for calibrations using speed/air density sensing. **CIP is referenced to manifold pressure, varies rail pressure, and is desirable in engines that use mass airflow sensing.**

## DEMAND DELIVERY SYSTEM (DDS)

Given the experience with both ERFS and MRFS, a need was recognized to develop new returnless technologies that could combine the speed control and constant injector pressure attributes of ERFS together with the cost savings, simplicity, and reliability of MRFS. This new technology also needed to address pulsation dampening/hammering and fuel transient response. Therefore, the **demand delivery system (DDS)** technology was developed.

A different form of demand pressure regulator has been applied to the fuel rail. It mounts at the head or port entry and regulates the pressure downstream at the injectors by admitting the precise quantity of fuel into the rail as consumed by the engine. Having demand regulation at the rail improves pressure response to flow transients and provides rail pulsation dampening. A fuel pump and a low-cost, high-performance bypass regulator are used within the appropriate fuel sender. ● **SEE FIGURE 19-14.** They supply a pressure somewhat higher than the required rail set pressure to accommodate dynamic line and filter pressure losses. Electronic pump speed control is accomplished using a smart regulator as an integral flow sensor. A **pressure control valve (PCV)** may also be used and can readily reconfigure an existing design fuel sender into a returnless sender.

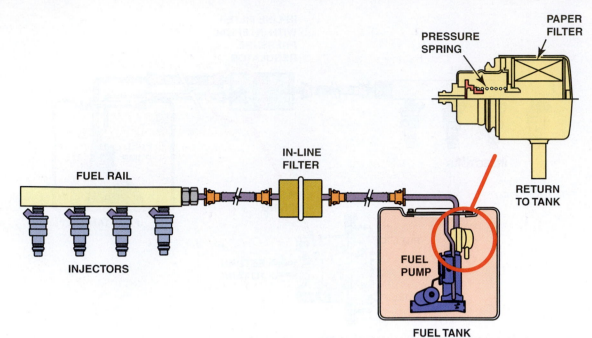

**FIGURE 19–14** A demand delivery system uses a fuel pressure regulator attached to the fuel pump assembly.

**?** **FREQUENTLY ASKED QUESTION**

**Why Are Some Fuel Rails Rectangular Shaped?**

A port fuel-injection system uses a pipe or tubes to deliver fuel from the fuel line to the intended fuel injectors. This pipe or tube is called the **fuel rail**. Some vehicle manufacturers construct the fuel rail in a rectangular cross-section. ● **SEE FIGURE 19–15.** The sides of the fuel rail are able to move in and out slightly, thereby acting as a fuel pulsator evening out the pressure pulses created by the opening and closing of the injectors to reduce underhood noise. A round cross-section fuel rail is not able to deform and, as a result, some manufacturers have had to use a separate dampener.

**FIGURE 19–15** A rectangular-shaped fuel rail is used to help dampen fuel system pulsations and noise caused by the injectors opening and closing.

# FUEL INJECTORS

EFI systems use a 12 volt solenoid-operated injectors. ● **SEE FIGURE 19–16.** This electromagnetic device contains an armature and a spring-loaded needle valve or ball valve assembly. When the computer energizes the solenoid, voltage is applied to the solenoid coil until the current reaches a specified level. This permits a quick pull-in of the armature during turn-on. The armature is pulled off of its seat against spring force, allowing fuel to flow through the inlet filter screen to the spray nozzle, where it is sprayed in a pattern that varies with application. ● **SEE FIGURE 19–17.** The injector opens the same amount each time it is energized, so the amount of fuel injected depends on the length of time the injector remains open. By angling the director

hole plates, the injector sprays fuel more directly at the intake valves, which further atomizes and vaporizes the fuel before it enters the combustion chamber. PFI injectors typically are a top-feed design in which fuel enters the top of the injector and passes through its entire length to keep it cool before being injected.

Ford introduced two basic designs of deposit-resistant injectors on some engines. The design, manufactured by Bosch, uses a four-hole director/metering plate similar to that used by the Rochester Multec injectors. The design manufactured by Nippondenso uses an internal upstream orifice in the adjusting tube. It also has a redesigned pintle/seat containing a wider tip opening that tolerates deposit buildup without affecting injector performance.

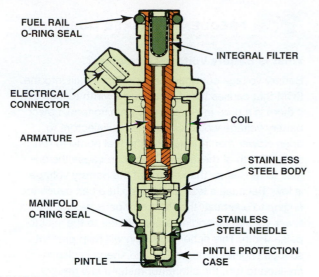

FIGURE 19–16 A multiport fuel injector. Notice that the fuel flows straight through and does not come in contact with the coil windings.

FIGURE 19–17 Each of the eight injectors shown are producing a correct spray pattern for the applications. While all throttle-body injectors spray a conical pattern, most port fuel injections do not.

## CENTRAL PORT INJECTION

A cross between port fuel injection and throttle-body injection, CPI was introduced in the early 1990s by General Motors. The CPI assembly consists of a single fuel injector, a pressure regulator, and six poppet nozzle assemblies with nozzle tubes. ● SEE FIGURE 19–18. The central sequential fuel injection (CSFI) system has six injectors in place of just one used on the CPI unit.

When the injector is energized, its armature lifts off of the six fuel tube seats and pressurized fuel flows through the nozzle tubes to each poppet nozzle. The increased pressure causes each poppet nozzle ball to also lift from its seat, allowing fuel to flow from the nozzle. This hybrid injection system combines the single injector of a TBI system with the equalized fuel

**How Can the Proper Injector Size Be Determined?**

Most people want to increase the output of fuel to increase engine performance. Injector sizing can sometimes be a challenge, especially if the size of injector is not known. In most cases, manufacturers publish the rating of injectors, in pounds of fuel per hour (lb/hr). The rate is figured with the injector held open at 3 bars (43.5 PSI). An important consideration is that larger flow injectors have a higher minimum flow rating. Here is a formula to calculate injector sizing when changing the mechanical characteristics of an engine.

**Flow rate = hp × BSFC/# of cylinders × maximum duty cycle (% of on-time of the injectors)**

- **hp** is the projected horsepower. Be realistic!
- **BSFC** is brake-specific fuel consumption in pounds per horsepower-hour. Calculated values are used for this, 0.4 to 0.8 lb. In most cases, start on the low side for naturally aspirated engines and the high side for engines with forced induction.
- **# of cylinders** is actually the number of injectors being used.
- **Maximum duty cycle** is considered at 0.8 (80%). Above this, the injector may overheat, lose consistency, or not work at all.

For example:

**5.7 liter V-8 = 240 hp × 0.65/8 cylinders × 8**
**= 24.37 lb/hr injectors required**

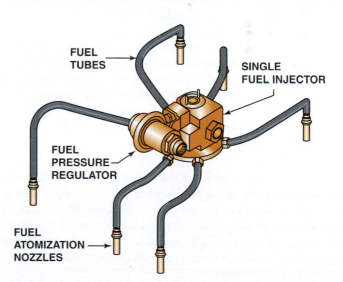

FIGURE 19–18 A central port fuel-injection system.

distribution of a PFI system. It eliminates the individual fuel rail while allowing more efficient manifold tuning than is otherwise possible with a TBI system. Newer versions use six individual solenoids to fire one for each cylinder. ● SEE FIGURE 19–19.

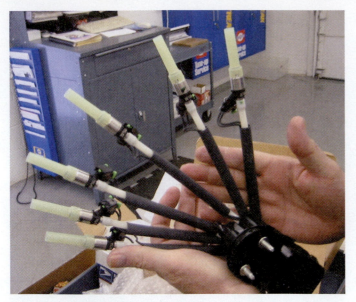

**FIGURE 19–19** A factory replacement unit for a CSFI unit that has individual injectors at the ends that go into the intake manifold instead of poppet valves.

**?  FREQUENTLY ASKED QUESTION**

**What Is Battery Voltage Correction?**

Battery voltage correction is a program built into the PCM that causes the injector pulse width to increase if there is a drop in electrical system voltage. Lower battery voltage would cause the fuel injectors to open slower than normal and the fuel pump to run slower. Both of these conditions can cause the engine to run leaner than normal if the battery voltage is low. Because a lean air–fuel mixture can cause the engine to overheat, the PCM compensates for the lower voltage by adding a percentage to the injector pulse width. This richer condition will help prevent serious engine damage. The idle speed is also increased to turn the alternator faster if low battery voltage is detect.

# FUEL-INJECTION MODES OF OPERATION

All fuel-injection systems are designed to supply the correct amount of fuel under a wide range of engine operating conditions. These modes of operation include:

| | |
|---|---|
| Starting (cranking) | Acceleration enrichment |
| Clear flood | Deceleration enleanment |
| Idle (run) | Fuel shutoff |

**STARTING MODE**   When the ignition is turned to the start position, the engine cranks and the PCM energizes the fuel pump relay. The PCM also pulses the injectors on, basing the pulse width on engine speed and engine coolant temperature. The colder the engine is, the greater the pulse width. Cranking mode air–fuel ratio varies from about 1.5:1 at −40°F (−40°C) to 14.7:1 at 200°F (93°C).

**CLEAR FLOOD MODE**   If the engine becomes flooded with too much fuel, the driver can depress the accelerator pedal to greater than 80% to enter the clear flood mode. When the PCM detects that the engine speed is low (usually below 600 RPM) and the throttle-position (TP) sensor voltage is high (WOT), the injector pulse width is greatly reduced or even shut off entirely, depending on the vehicle.

**OPEN-LOOP MODE**   Open-loop operation occurs during warm-up before the oxygen sensor can supply accurate information to the PCM. The PCM determines injector pulse width based on values from the MAF, MAP, TP, ECT, and IAT sensors.

**CLOSED-LOOP MODE**   Closed-loop operation is used to modify the base injector pulse width as determined by feedback from the oxygen sensor to achieve proper fuel control.

**ACCELERATION ENRICHMENT MODE**   During acceleration, the throttle-position (TP) voltage increases, indicating that a richer air–fuel mixture is required. The PCM then supplies a longer injector pulse width and may even supply extra pulses to supply the needed fuel for acceleration.

**DECELERATION ENLEANMENT MODE**   When the engine decelerates, a leaner air–fuel mixture is required to help reduce emissions and to prevent deceleration backfire. If the deceleration is rapid, the injector may be shut off entirely for a short time and then pulsed on enough to keep the engine running.

**FUEL SHUTOFF MODE**   Besides shutting off fuel entirely during periods of rapid deceleration, PCM also shuts off the injector when the ignition is turned off to prevent the engine from continuing to run.

# IDLE CONTROL

Port fuel-injection systems generally use an auxiliary air bypass to control idle speed. ● **SEE FIGURE 19–20.** This air bypass or regulator provides needed additional airflow, and thus more fuel. The engine needs more power when cold to maintain its normal idle speed to overcome the increased friction from cold lubricating oil. It does this by opening an intake air passage to let more air into the engine just as depressing the accelerator pedal would open the throttle valve, allowing more air into the engine. The system is calibrated to maintain engine idle speed at a specified value regardless of engine temperature.

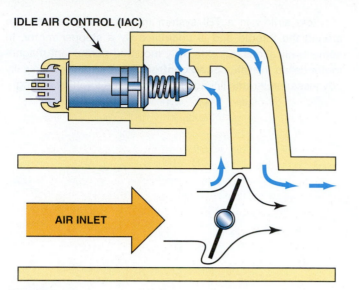

**FIGURE 19–20** The small arrows indicate the air bypassing the throttle plate in the closed throttle position. This air is called minimum air. The air flowing through the IAC (blue arrows) is the airflow that determines the idle speed.

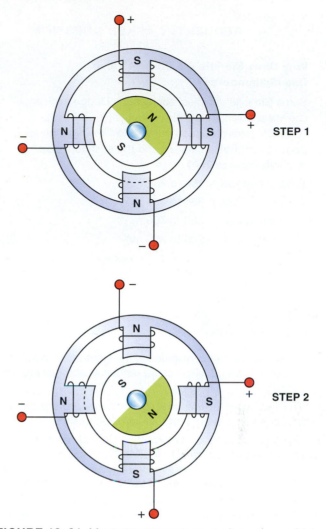

**FIGURE 19–21** Most stepper motors use four wires, which are pulsed by the computer to rotate the armature in steps.

Most PFI systems use an idle air control (IAC) motor to regulate idle bypass air. The IAC is computer-controlled, and is either a solenoid-operated valve or a stepper motor that regulates the airflow around the throttle. The idle air control valve is also called an **electronic air control (EAC)** valve.

When the engine stops, most IAC units will retract outward to get ready for the next engine start. When the engine starts, the engine speed is high to provide for proper operation when the engine is cold. Then, as the engine gets warmer, the computer reduces engine idle speed gradually by reducing the number of counts or steps commanded by the IAC.

When the engine is warm and restarted, the idle speed should momentarily increase, then decrease to normal idle speed. This increase and then decrease in engine speed is often called an engine **flare**. If the engine speed does not flare, then the IAC may not be working (it may be stuck in one position).

## STEPPER MOTOR OPERATION

A digital output is used to control stepper motors. Stepper motors are direct-current motors that move in fixed steps or increments from de-energized (no voltage) to fully energized (full voltage). A stepper motor often has as many as 120 steps of motion.

A common use for stepper motors is as an idle air control (IAC) valve, which controls engine idle speeds and prevents stalls due to changes in engine load. When used as an IAC, the stepper motor is usually a reversible DC motor that moves in increments, or steps. The motor moves a shaft back and forth to operate a conical valve. When the conical valve is moved back,

more air bypasses the throttle plates and enters the engine, increasing idle speed. As the conical valve moves inward, the idle speed decreases.

When using a stepper motor that is controlled by the PCM, it is very easy for the PCM to keep track of the position of the stepper motor. By counting the number of steps that have been sent to the stepper motor, the PCM can determine the relative position of the stepper motor. While the PCM does not actually receive a feedback signal from the stepper motor, it does know how many steps forward or backward the motor should have moved.

A typical stepper motor uses a permanent magnet and two electromagnets. Each of the two electromagnetic windings is controlled by the computer. The computer pulses the windings and changes the polarity of the windings to cause the armature of the stepper motor to rotate 90 degrees at a time. Each 90-degree pulse is recorded by the computer as a "count" or "step"; therefore, the name given to this type of motor. ● **SEE FIGURE 19–21.**

**Why Does the Idle Air Control Valve Use Milliamperes?**

Some Chrysler vehicles, such as the Dodge minivan, use linear solenoid idle air control valves (LSIAC). The PCM uses regulated current flow through the solenoid to control idle speed and the scan tool display is in milliamperes (mA).

Closed position = 180 to 200 mA

Idle = 300 to 450 mA

Light cruise = 500 to 700 mA

Fully open = 900 to 950 mA

Idle airflow in a TBI system travels through a passage around the throttle and is controlled by a stepper motor. In some applications, an externally mounted permanent magnet motor called the **idle speed control (ISC) motor** mechanically advances the throttle linkage to advance the throttle opening.

## SUMMARY

1. A fuel-injection system includes the electric fuel pump and fuel pump relay, fuel-pressure regulator, and fuel injectors (nozzles).

2. The two types of fuel-injection systems are the throttle-body design and the port fuel-injection design.

3. The two methods of fuel-injection control are the speed-density system, which uses the MAP to measure the load on the engine, and the mass airflow, which uses the MAF sensor to directly measure the amount of air entering the engine.

4. The amount of fuel supplied by fuel injectors is determined by how long they are kept open. This opening time is called the pulse width and is measured in milliseconds.

5. The fuel-pressure regulator is usually located on the fuel return on return-type fuel-injection systems.

6. TBI-type fuel-injection systems do not use a vacuum-controlled fuel-pressure regulator, whereas many port fuel-injection systems use a vacuum-controlled regulator to monitor equal pressure drop across the injectors.

7. Other fuel designs include the electronic returnless, the mechanical returnless, and the demand delivery systems.

## REVIEW QUESTIONS

1. What are the two basic types of fuel-injection systems?

2. What is the purpose of the vacuum-controlled (biased) fuel-pressure regulator?

3. How many sensors are used to determine the base pulse width on a speed-density system?

4. How many sensors are used to determine the base pulse width on a mass airflow system?

5. What are the three types of returnless fuel injection systems?

## CHAPTER QUIZ

1. Technician A says that the fuel pump relay is usually controlled by the PCM. Technician B says that a TBI injector squirts fuel above the throttle plate. Which technician is correct?
   a. Technician A only
   b. Technician B only
   c. Both Technicians A and B
   d. Neither Technician A nor B

2. Why are some fuel rails rectangular in shape?
   a. Increases fuel pressure
   b. Helps keep air out of the injectors
   c. Reduces noise
   d. Increases the speed of the fuel through the fuel rail

3. Which fuel-injection system uses the MAP sensor as the primary sensor to determine the base pulse width?
   a. Speed density
   b. Mass airflow
   c. Demand delivery
   d. Mechanical returnless

4. Why is a vacuum line attached to a fuel-pressure regulator on many port-fuel-injected engines?
   a. To draw fuel back into the intake manifold through the vacuum hose
   b. To create an equal pressure drop across the injectors
   c. To raise the fuel pressure at idle
   d. To lower the fuel pressure under heavy engine load conditions to help improve fuel economy

5. Which sensor has the greatest influence on injector pulse width besides the MAF sensor?
   a. IAT                    c. ECT
   b. BARO                   d. TP

6. Technician A says that the port fuel-injection injectors operate using 5 volts from the computer. Technician B says that sequential fuel injectors all use a different wire color on the injectors. Which technician is correct?
   a. Technician A only
   b. Technician B only
   c. Both Technicians A and B
   d. Neither Technician A nor B

7. Which type of port fuel-injection system uses a fuel temperature and/or fuel-pressure sensor?
   a. All port-fuel-injected engines
   b. TBI units only
   c. Electronic returnless systems
   d. Demand delivery systems

8. Dampeners are used on some fuel rails to _____.
   a. Increase the fuel pressure in the rail
   b. Reduce (decrease) the fuel pressure in the rail
   c. Reduce noise
   d. Trap dirt and keep it away from the injectors

9. Where is the fuel-pressure regulator located on a vacuum-biased port fuel-injection system?
   a. In the tank
   b. At the inlet of the fuel rail
   c. At the outlet of the fuel rail
   d. Near or on the fuel filter

10. What type of device is used in a typical idle air control?
    a. DC motor
    b. Stepper motor
    c. Pulsator-type actuator
    d. Solenoid

# GASOLINE DIRECT-INJECTION SYSTEMS

**OBJECTIVES:** **After studying Chapter 20, the reader will be able to:** • Prepare for the ASE certification test content area "C" (Fuel, Air Induction, and Exhaust Systems Diagnosis). • Describe the differences between port fuel-injection and gasoline direct-injection systems. • List the various modes of operation of a gasoline direct-injection system. • Explain how a gasoline direct-injection system works. • Perform a visual inspection of the gasoline direct-injection system and identify the parts.

**KEY TERMS:** Gasoline direct injection (GDI) 268 • Homogeneous mode 270 • Spark ignition direct injection (SIDI) 268 • Stratified mode 270

## DIRECT FUEL INJECTION

Several vehicle manufacturers such as Audi, Mitsubishi, Mercedes, BMW, Toyota/Lexus, Mazda, Ford, and General Motors are using **gasoline direct injection (GDI)** systems, which General Motors refers to as a **Spark Ignition Direct Injection (SIDI)** system. A direct-injection system sprays high-pressure fuel, up to 2,900 PSI, into the combustion chamber as the piston approaches the top of the compression stroke. With the combination of high-pressure swirl injectors and modified combustion chamber, almost instantaneous vaporization of the fuel occurs. This combined with a higher compression ratio allows a direct-injected engine to operate using a leaner-than-normal air–fuel ratio, which results in improved fuel economy with higher power output and reduced exhaust emissions. ●
**SEE FIGURE 20–1.**

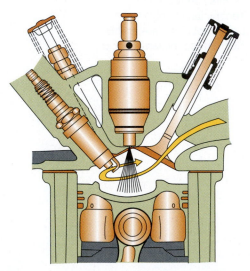

**FIGURE 20–1** A gasoline direct-injection system injects fuel under high pressure directly into the combustion chamber.

### ADVANTAGES OF GASOLINE DIRECT INJECTION

The use of direct injection compared with port fuel-injection has many advantages including:

- Improved fuel economy due to reduced pumping losses and heat loss
- Allows a higher compression ratio for higher engine efficiency
- Allows the use of lower-octane gasoline
- The volumetric efficiency is higher
- Less need for extra fuel for acceleration
- Improved cold starting and throttle response
- Allows the use of higher percentage of EGR to reduce exhaust emissions

- Up to 25% improvement in fuel economy
- 12% to 15% reduction in exhaust emissions

### DISADVANTAGES OF GASOLINE DIRECT INJECTION

- Higher cost due to high-pressure pump and injectors
- More components compared with port fuel-injection
- Due to the high compression, a $NO_x$ storage catalyst is sometimes required to meet emission standards, especially in Europe (● **SEE FIGURE 20–2).**
- Uses up to six operating modes depending on engine load and speed, which requires more calculations to be performed by the Powertrain Control Module (PCM).

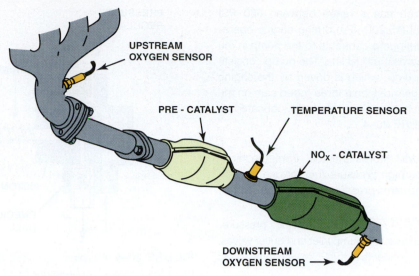

**FIGURE 20–2** An engine equipped with a gasoline direct injection (GDI) sometimes requires a $NO_x$ catalyst to meet exhaust emission standards.

UPSTREAM OXYGEN SENSOR

PRE - CATALYST

TEMPERATURE SENSOR

$NO_x$ - CATALYST

DOWNSTREAM OXYGEN SENSOR

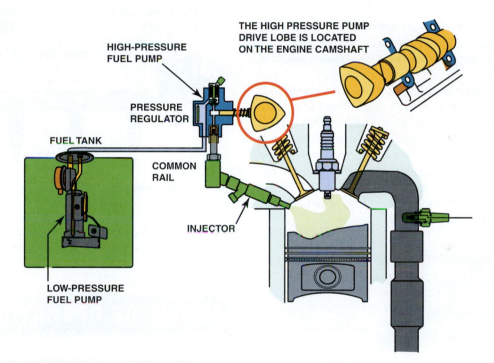

THE HIGH PRESSURE PUMP DRIVE LOBE IS LOCATED ON THE ENGINE CAMSHAFT

HIGH-PRESSURE FUEL PUMP

PRESSURE REGULATOR

FUEL TANK

COMMON RAIL

INJECTOR

LOW-PRESSURE FUEL PUMP

**FIGURE 20–3** A typical direct-injection system uses two pumps—one low-pressure electric pump in the fuel tank and the other a high-pressure pump driven by the camshaft. The high pressure fuel system operates at a pressure as low as 500 PSI during light load conditions and as high as 2,900 PSI under heavy loads.

## DIRECT-INJECTION FUEL DELIVERY SYSTEM

**LOW-PRESSURE SUPPLY PUMP** The fuel pump in the fuel tank supplies fuel to the high-pressure fuel pump at a pressure of approximately 60 PSI. The fuel filter is located in the fuel tank and is part of the fuel pump assembly. It is not usually serviceable as a separate component. The engine control module (ECM) controls the output of the high-pressure pump, which has a range between 500 PSI (3,440 kPa) and 2,900 PSI (15,200 kPa) during engine operation. ● **SEE FIGURE 20–3.**

**HIGH-PRESSURE PUMP** In a General Motors system, the engine control module (ECM) controls the output of the high-pressure pump, which has a range between 500 PSI (3,440 kPa) and 2,900 PSI (15,200 kPa) during engine operation. The high-pressure fuel pump connects to the pump in the fuel tank through the low-pressure fuel line. The pump consists of a single-barrel piston pump, which is driven by the engine camshaft. The pump plunger rides on a three-lobed cam on the camshaft. The high-pressure pump is cooled and lubricated by the fuel itself. ● SEE FIGURE 20–4.

**FUEL RAIL** The fuel rail stores the fuel from the high-pressure pump and stores high pressure fuel for use to each injector. All injectors get the same pressure fuel from the fuel rail.

**FUEL PRESSURE REGULATOR** An electric pressure-control valve is installed between the pump inlet and outlet valves. The fuel rail pressure sensor connects to the PCM with three wires:

- 5-volt reference
- ground
- signal

The sensor signal provides an analog signal to the PCM that varies in voltage as fuel rail pressure changes. Low pressure results in a low-voltage signal and high pressure results in a high-voltage signal.

The PCM uses internal drivers to control the power feed and ground for the pressure control valve. When both PCM drivers are deactivated, the inlet valve is held open by spring pressure. This causes the high pressure fuel pump to default to low-pressure mode. The fuel from the high-pressure fuel pump flows through a line to the fuel rail and injectors. The actual operating pressure can vary from as low as 900 PSI (6,200 kPa) at idle to over 2,000 PSI (13,800 kPa) during high speed or heavy load conditions. ● SEE FIGURE 20–5.

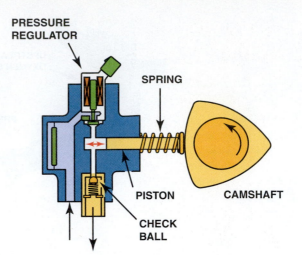

**FIGURE 20–4** A typical camshaft-driven high-pressure pump used to increase fuel pressure to 2,000 PSI or higher.

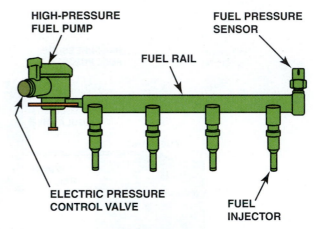

**FIGURE 20–5** A gasoline direct-injection (GDI) fuel rail and pump assembly with the electric pressure control valve.

## GASOLINE DIRECT-INJECTION FUEL INJECTORS

Each high-pressure fuel injector assembly is an electrically magnetic injector mounted in the cylinder head. In the GDI system, the PCM controls each fuel injector with 50 to 90 volts (usually 60–70 volts), depending on the system, which is created by a boost capacitor in the PCM. During the high-voltage boost phase, the capacitor is discharged through an injector, allowing for initial injector opening. The injector is then held open with 12 volts. The high-pressure fuel injector has a small slit or six precision-machined holes that generate the desired spray pattern. The injector also has an extended tip to allow for cooling from a water jacket in the cylinder head.

● **SEE CHART 20–1** for an overview of the differences between a port fuel-injection system and a gasoline direct-injection system.

## MODES OF OPERATION

The two basic modes of operation include:

1. **Stratified mode.** In this mode of operation, the air–fuel mixture is richer around the spark plug than it is in the rest of the cylinder.

2. **Homogeneous mode.** In this mode of operation, the air–fuel mixture is the same throughout the cylinder.

There are variations of these modes that can be used to fine-tune the air–fuel mixture inside the cylinder. For example, Bosch, a supplier to many vehicle manufacturers, uses six modes of operation including:

- **Homogeneous mode.** In this mode, the injector is pulsed one time to create an even air–fuel mixture in the cylinder. The injection occurs during the intake stroke. This mode is used during high-speed and/or high-torque conditions.

## PORT FUEL-INJECTION SYSTEM COMPARED WITH GDI SYSTEM

|  | PORT FUEL-INJECTION | GASOLINE DIRECT INJECTION |
|---|---|---|
| Fuel pressure | 35 to 60 PSI | Lift pump—50 to 60 PSI High-pressure pump—500 to 2,900 PSI |
| Injection pulse width at idle | 1.5 to 3.5 ms | About 0.4 ms (400 μs) |
| Injector resistance | 12 to 16 ohms | 1 to 3 ohms |
| Injector voltage | 6 V for low-resistance injectors, 12 V for most injectors | 50 to 90 V |
| Number of injections per event | One | 1 to 3 |
| Engine compression ratio | 8:1 to 11:1 | 11:1 to 13:1 |

**CHART 20–1**

A comparison chart showing the major differences between a port fuel-injection system and a gasoline direct-injection system.

- **Homogeneous lean mode.** Similar to the homogeneous mode except that the overall air–fuel mixture is slightly lean for better fuel economy. The injection occurs during the intake stroke. This mode is used under steady, light-load conditions.

- **Stratified mode.** In this mode of operation, the injection occurs just before the spark occurs resulting in lean combustion, reducing fuel consumption.

- **Homogeneous stratified mode.** In this mode, there are two injections of fuel:
  - The first injection is during the intake stroke.
  - The second injection is during the compression stroke. As a result of these double injections, the rich air–fuel mixture around the spark plug is ignited first. Then, the rich mixture ignites the leaner mixture. The advantages of this mode include lower exhaust emissions than the stratified mode and less fuel consumption than the homogeneous lean mode.

- **Homogeneous knock protection mode.** The purpose of this mode is to reduce the possibility of spark knock from occurring under heavy loads at low engine speeds. There are two injections of fuel:
  - The first injection occurs on the intake stroke.
  - The second injection occurs during the compression stroke with the overall mixture being stoichiometric.

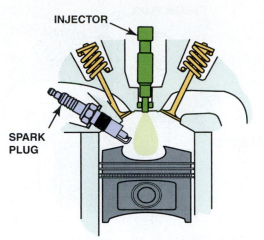

**FIGURE 20–6** In this design, the fuel injector is at the top of the cylinder and sprays fuel into the cavity of the piston.

As a result of this mode, the PCM does not need to retard ignition timing as much to operate knock-free.

- **Stratified catalyst heating mode.** In this mode, there are two injections:
  - The first injection is on the compression stroke just before combustion.
  - The second injection occurs after combustion occurs to heat the exhaust. This mode is used to quickly warm the catalytic converter and to burn the sulfur from the $NO_x$ catalyst.

## PISTON TOP DESIGNS

Gasoline direct injection (GDI) systems use a variety of shapes of piston and injector locations depending on make and model of engine. Three of the most commonly used designs include:

- **Spray-guided combustion.** In this design, the injector is placed in the center of the combustion chamber and injects fuel into the dished out portion of the piston. The shape of the piston helps guide and direct the mist of fuel in the combustion chamber. ● SEE FIGURE 20–6.

- **Swirl combustion.** This design uses the shape of the piston and the position of the injector at the side of the combustion chamber to create turbulence and swirl of the air–fuel mixture. ● SEE FIGURE 20–7.

- **Tumble combustion.** Depending on when the fuel is injected into the combustion chamber, helps determine how the air–fuel is moved or tumbled. ● SEE FIGURE 20–8.

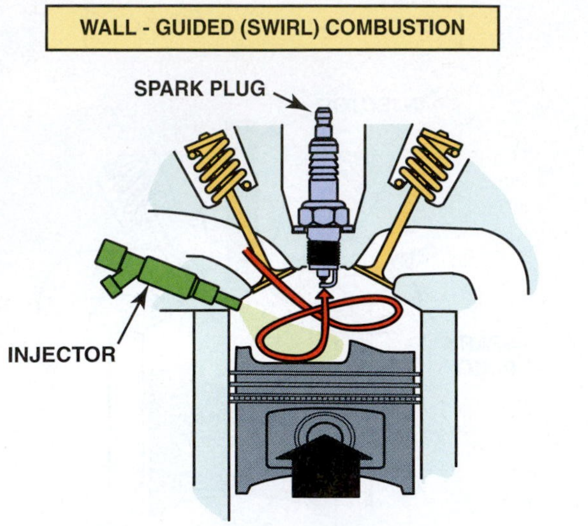

## WALL - GUIDED (SWIRL) COMBUSTION

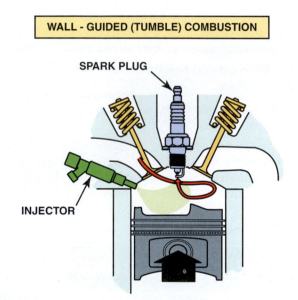

**FIGURE 20–7** The side injector combines with the shape of the piston to create a swirl as the piston moves up on the compression stroke.

## WALL - GUIDED (TUMBLE) COMBUSTION

**FIGURE 20–8** The piston creates a tumbling force as the piston moves upward.

## LEXUS PORT- AND DIRECT-INJECTION SYSTEMS

**OVERVIEW** Many Lexus vehicles use gasoline direct injection (GDI) and in some engines, they also use a conventional port fuel-injection system. The Lexus D-4S system combines direct-injection injectors located in the combustion chamber with port fuel-injectors in the intake manifold near the intake valve. The two injection systems work together to supply the fuel needed by the engine. ● **SEE FIGURE 20–9**

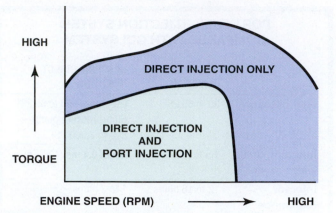

**FIGURE 20–9** Notice that there are conditions when the port fuel-injector located in the intake manifold, and the gasoline direct injector, located in the cylinder both operate to provide the proper air–fuel mixture.

for how the two systems are used throughout the various stages of engine operation.

**COLD-START WARM-UP** To help reduce exhaust emissions after a cold start, the fuel system uses a stratified change mode. This results in a richer air–fuel mixture near the spark plug and allows for the spark to be retarded to increase the temperature of the exhaust. As a result of the increased exhaust temperature, the catalytic converter rapidly reaches operating temperature, which reduces exhaust emissions.

## ENGINE START SYSTEM

An engine equipped with gasoline direct injection could use the system to start the engine. This is most useful during idle stop mode when the engine is stopped while the vehicle is at a traffic light to save fuel. The steps used in the Mitsubishi start-stop system, called the *smart idle stop system (SISS)*, allow the engine to be started without a starter motor and include the following steps:

**STEP 1** The engine is stopped. The normal stopping position of an engine when it stops is 70 degrees before top dead center, plus or minus 20 degrees. This is because the engine stops with one cylinder on the compression stroke and the PCM can determine the cylinder position, using the crankshaft and camshaft position sensors.

**STEP 2** When a command is made to start the engine by the PCM, fuel is injected into the cylinder that is on the compression stroke and ignited by the spark plug.

**STEP 3** The piston on the compression stroke is forced downward forcing the crankshaft to rotate counterclockwise or in the opposite direction to normal operation.

**STEP 4** The rotation of the crankshaft then forces the companion cylinder toward the top of the cylinder.

**STEP 5** Fuel is injected and the spark plug is fired, forcing the piston down, causing the crankshaft to rotate in the normal (clockwise) direction. Normal combustion events continue allowing the engine to keep running.

## GASOLINE DIRECT-INJECTION SERVICE

**NOISE ISSUES** Gasoline direct injection (GDI) systems operate at high pressure and the injectors can often be heard with the engine running and the hood open. This noise can be a customer concern because the clicking sound is similar to noisy valves. If a noise issue is the customer concern, check the following:

- Check a similar vehicle to determine if the sound is louder or more noticeable than normal.
- Check that nothing under the hood is touching the fuel rail. If another line or hose is in contact with the fuel rail, the sound of the injectors clicking can be transmitted throughout the engine, making the sound more noticeable.
- Check for any technical service bulletins (TSBs) that may include new clips or sound insulators to help reduce the noise.

**CARBON ISSUES** Carbon is often an issue in engines equipped with gasoline direct-injection systems. Carbon can affect engine operation by accumulating in two places:

- **On the injector itself.** Because the injector tip is in the combustion chamber, fuel residue can accumulate on the injector, reducing its ability to provide the proper spray pattern and amount of fuel. Some injector designs are more likely to be affected by carbon than others. For example, if the injector uses small holes, these tend to become clogged more often than an injector that uses a single slit opening where the fuel being sprayed out tends to blast away any carbon. ● **SEE FIGURE 20–10.**

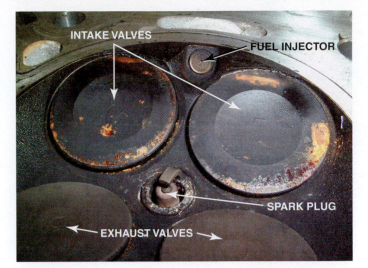

**FIGURE 20–10** There may become a driveability issue because the gasoline direct-injection injector is exposed to combustion carbon and fuel residue.

- **The backside of the intake valve.** This is a common place for fuel residue and carbon to accumulate on engines equipped with gasoline direct injection. The accumulation of carbon on the intake valve can become so severe that the engine will start and idle, but lack power to accelerate the vehicle. The carbon deposits restrict the airflow into the cylinder enough to decrease engine power.

**NOTE: Lexus engines that use both port and gasoline direct-injection injectors do not show intake valve deposits. It is thought that the fuel being sprayed onto the intake valve from the port injector helps keep the intake valve clean.**

**CARBON CLEANING.** Most experts recommend the use of Techron®, a fuel system dispersant, to help keep carbon from accumulating. The use of a dispersant every six months or every 6,000 miles has proven to help prevent injector and intake valve deposits.

If the lack of power is discovered and there are no stored diagnostic trouble codes, a conventional carbon cleaning procedure will likely restore power if the intake valves are coated.

## SUMMARY

1. A gasoline direct-injection system uses a fuel injector that delivers a short squirt of fuel directly into the combustion chamber rather than in the intake manifold, near the intake valve on a port fuel-injection system.

2. The advantages of using gasoline direct injection instead of port fuel-injection include:
   - Improved fuel economy
   - Reduced exhaust emissions
   - Greater engine power

3. Some of the disadvantages of gasoline direct-injection systems compared with a port fuel-injection system include:
   - Higher cost
   - The need for $NO_x$ storage catalyst in some applications
   - More components

4. The operating pressure can vary from as low as 500 PSI during some low-demand conditions to as high as 2,900 PSI.

5. The fuel injectors are open for a very short period of time and are pulsed using a 50 to 90 V pulse from a capacitor circuit.

6. GDI systems can operate in many modes, which are separated into the two basic modes:
   - Stratified mode
   - Homogeneous mode
7. GDI can be used to start an engine without the use of a starter motor for idle-stop functions.

8. GDI does create a louder clicking noise from the fuel injectors than port fuel-injection injectors.
9. Carbon deposits on the injector and the backside of the intake valve are a common problem with engines equipped with gasoline direct-injection systems.

## REVIEW QUESTIONS

1. What are two advantages of gasoline direct injection compared with port fuel-injection?
2. What are two disadvantages of gasoline direct injection compared with port fuel-injection?
3. How is the fuel delivery system different from a port fuel-injection system?
4. What are the basic modes of operation of a GDI system?

## CHAPTER QUIZ

1. Where is the fuel injected in an engine equipped with gasoline direct injection?
   a. Into the intake manifold near the intake valve
   b. Directly into the combustion chamber
   c. Above the intake port
   d. In the exhaust port
2. The fuel pump inside the fuel tank on a vehicle equipped with gasoline direct injection produces about what fuel pressure?
   a. 5 to 10 PSI
   b. 10 to 20 PSI
   c. 20 to 40 PSI
   d. 50 to 60 PSI
3. The high-pressure fuel pumps used in gasoline direct injection (GDI) systems are powered by _____.
   a. Electricity (DC motor)
   b. Electricity (AC motor)
   c. The camshaft
   d. The crankshaft
4. The high-pressure fuel pressure is regulated by using _____.
   a. An electric pressure-control valve
   b. A vacuum-biased regulator
   c. A mechanical regulator at the inlet to the fuel rail
   d. A non-vacuum biased regulator
5. The fuel injectors operate under a fuel pressure of about _____.
   a. 35 to 45 PSI
   b. 90 to 150 PSI
   c. 500 to 2,900 PSI
   d. 2,000 to 5,000 PSI

6. The fuel injectors used on a gasoline direct-injection system are pulsed on using what voltage?
   a. 12 to 14 V
   b. 50 to 90 V
   c. 100 to 110 V
   d. 200 to 220 V
7. Which mode of operation results in a richer air–fuel mixture near the spark plug?
   a. Stoichiometric
   b. Homogeneous
   c. Stratified
   d. Knock protection
8. Some engines that use a gasoline direct-injection system also have port injection.
   a. True
   b. False
9. A gasoline direct-injection system can be used to start an engine without the need for a starter.
   a. True
   b. False
10. A lack of power from an engine equipped with gasoline direct injection could be due to _____.
    a. Noisy injectors
    b. Carbon on the injectors
    c. Carbon on the intake valves
    d. Both b and c

# ELECTRONIC THROTTLE CONTROL SYSTEM

**OBJECTIVES:** After studying Chapter 21, the reader will be able to: • Prepare for ASE test content area "E" (Computerized Engine Controls Diagnosis and Repair). • Describe the purpose and function of an electronic throttle control (ETC) system. • Explain how an electronic throttle control system works. • List the parts of a typical electronic throttle control system. • Describe how to diagnose faults in an electronic throttle control system.

**KEY TERMS:** Accelerator pedal position (APP) sensor 275 • Coast-down stall 281 • Default position 277 • Drive-by-wire 275 • Electronic throttle control (ETC) 275 • Fail safe position 277 • Neutral position 277 • Servomotor 277 • Throttle position (TP) sensor 275

## ELECTRONIC THROTTLE CONTROL (ETC) SYSTEM

**ADVANTAGES OF ETC** The absence of any mechanical linkage between the throttle pedal and the throttle body requires the use of an electric actuator motor. The electronic throttle system has the following advantages over the conventional cable:

- Eliminates the mechanical throttle cable, thereby reducing the number of moving parts.

- Eliminates the need for cruise control actuators and controllers.

- Helps reduce engine power for traction control (TC) and electronic stability control (ESC) systems.

- Used to delay rapid applications of torque to the transmission/transaxle to help improve driveability and to smooth shifts.

- Helps reduce pumping losses by using the electronic throttle to open at highway speeds with greater fuel economy. The electronic throttle control (ETC) opens the throttle to maintain engine and vehicle speed as the Powertrain Control Module (PCM) leans the air–fuel ratio, retards ignition timing, and introduces additional exhaust gas recirculation (EGR) to reducing pumping losses.

- Used to provide smooth engine operation, especially during rapid acceleration.

- Eliminates the need for an idle air control valve.

The electronic throttle can be called **drive-by-wire,** but most vehicle manufacturers use the term **electronic throttle control (ETC)** to describe the system that opens the throttle valve electrically.

**PARTS INVOLVED** The typical ETC system includes the following components:

1. **Accelerator pedal position (APP)** sensor, also called accelerator pedal sensor (APS)

2. The electronic throttle actuator (servomotor), which is part of the electronic throttle body

3. A **throttle position (TP) sensor**

4. An electronic control unit, which is usually the Powertrain Control Module (PCM)
   ● SEE FIGURE 21–1.

## NORMAL OPERATION OF THE ETC SYSTEM

Driving a vehicle equipped with an electronic throttle control (ETC) system is about the same as driving a vehicle with a conventional mechanical throttle cable and throttle valve. However, the driver may notice some differences, which are to be considered normal. These normal conditions include:

- The engine may not increase above idle speed when depressing the accelerator pedal when the gear selector is in PARK.

- If the engine speed does increase when the accelerator is depressed with the transmission in PARK or NEUTRAL, the engine speed will likely be limited to less than 2000 RPM.

- While accelerating rapidly, there is often a slight delay before the engine responds. ● SEE FIGURE 21–2.

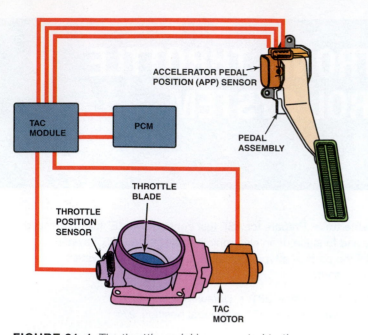

**FIGURE 21–1** The throttle pedal is connected to the accelerator pedal position (APP) sensor. The electronic throttle body includes a throttle position sensor to provide throttle angle feedback to the vehicle computer. Some systems use a Throttle Actuator Control (TAC) module to operate the throttle blade (plate).

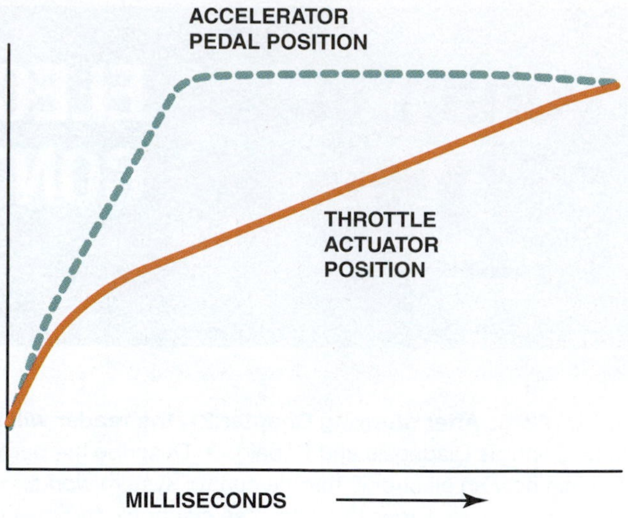

- While at cruise speed, the accelerator pedal may or may not cause the engine speed to increase if the accelerator pedal is moved slightly.

## ACCELERATOR PEDAL POSITION SENSOR

**CABLE-OPERATED SYSTEM** Honda Accords until 2008 model year used a cable attached to the accelerator pedal to operate the APP sensor located under the hood. A similar arrangement was used in Dodge RAM trucks in 2003. In both of these applications, the throttle cable was simply moving the APP sensor and not moving the throttle plate. The throttle plate is controlled by the PCM and moved by the electronic throttle control motor.

**TWO SENSORS** The accelerator pedal position sensor uses two and sometimes three separate sensors, which act together to give accurate accelerator pedal position information to the controller, but also are used to check that the sensor is working properly. They function just like a throttle position sensor, and two are needed for proper system function. One APP sensor output signal increases as the pedal is depressed and the other signal decreases. The controller compares the signals with a look-up table to determine the pedal position. Using two or three signals improves redundancy should one sensor fail, and allows the PCM to quickly detect a malfunction. When

**FIGURE 21–2** The opening of the throttle plate can be delayed as long as 30 milliseconds (0.030 sec.) to allow time for the amount of fuel needed to catch up to the opening of the throttle plate.

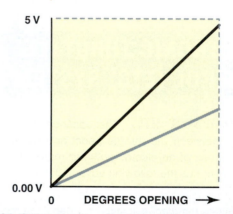

**FIGURE 21–3** A typical accelerator pedal position (APP) sensor, showing two different output voltage signals that are used by the PCM to determine accelerator pedal position. Two (or three in some applications) are used as a double check because this is a safety-related sensor.

three sensors are used, the third signal can either decrease or increase with pedal position, but its voltage range will still be different from the other two. ● **SEE FIGURE 21–3.**

## THROTTLE BODY ASSEMBLY

The throttle body assembly contains the following components:

- Throttle plate
- Electric actuator DC motor
- Dual throttle position (TP) sensors
- Gears used to multiply the torque of the DC motor
- Springs used to hold the throttle plate in the default location

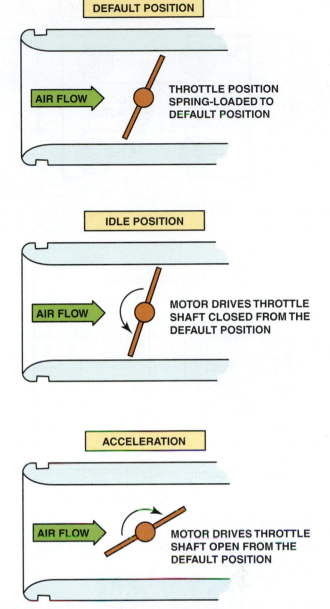

### What Is the "Spring Test"?

The spring test is a self-test performed by the PCM whenever the engine is started. The PCM operates the throttle to check if it can react to the command and return to the default (home) position. This self-test is used by the PCM to determine that the spring and motor are working correctly and may be noticed by some vehicle owners by the following factors:

• A slight delay in the operation of the starter motor. The PCM performs this test when the ignition switch is turned to the "on" position. While it takes just a short time to perform the test, it can be sensed by the driver that there could be a fault in the ignition switch or starter motor circuits.
• A slight "clicking" sound may also be heard coming from under the hood when the ignition is turned on. This is normal and is related to the self-test on the throttle as it opens and closes.

**THROTTLE PLATE AND SPRING** The throttle plate is held slightly open by a concentric clock spring. The spring applies a force that will close the throttle plate if power is lost to the actuator motor. The spring is also used to open the throttle plate slightly from the fully closed position.

**ELECTRONIC THROTTLE BODY MOTOR** The actuator is a DC electric motor and is often called a **servomotor.** The throttle plate is held in a **default position** by a spring inside the throttle body assembly. This partially open position, also called the **neutral position** or the **fail safe position,** is about 16% to 20% open. This default position varies depending on the vehicle and usually results in an engine speed of 1200 to 1500 RPM.

■ The throttle plate is driven closed to achieve speeds lower than the default position, such as idle speed.
■ The throttle plate is driven open to achieve speeds higher than the default position, such as during acceleration.
● **SEE FIGURE 21–4.**

The throttle plate motor is driven by a bidirectional pulse-width modulated (PWM) signal from the PCM or electronic throttle control module using an H-bridge circuit. ● **SEE FIGURE 21–5a, b.**

The H-bridge circuit is controlled by the Powertrain Control Module (PCM) by:

■ Reversing the polarity of power and ground brushes to the DC motor
■ Pulse-width modulating (PWM) the current through the motor

The PCM monitors the position of the throttle from the two throttle position (TP) sensors. The PCM then commands the throttle plate to the desired position. ● **SEE FIGURE 21–6.**

**FIGURE 21–4** The default position for the throttle plate is in slightly open position. The servomotor then is used to close it for idle and open it during acceleration.

### Why Not Use a Stepper Motor for ETC?

A stepper motor is a type of motor that has multiple windings and is pulsed by a computer to rotate a certain number of degrees when pulsed. The disadvantage is that a stepper motor is too slow to react compared with a conventional DC electric motor and is the reason a stepper motor is not used in electronic throttle control systems.

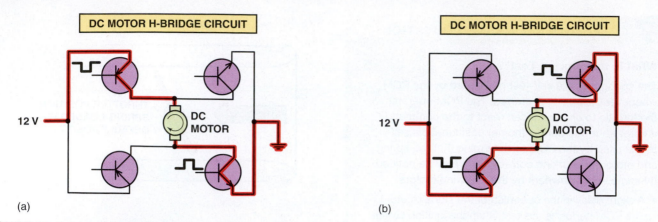

DC MOTOR H-BRIDGE CIRCUIT          DC MOTOR H-BRIDGE CIRCUIT

12 V    DC MOTOR                    12 V    DC MOTOR

(a)                                 (b)

**FIGURE 21–5** (a) An H-bridge circuit is used to control the direction of the DC electric motor of the electronic throttle control unit. (b) To reverse the direction of operation, the polarity of the current through the motor is reversed.

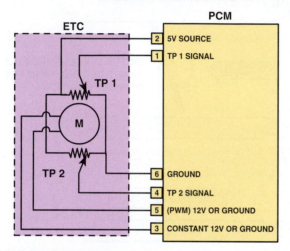

**FIGURE 21–6** Schematic of a typical electronic throttle control (ETC) system. Note that terminal #5 is always pulse-width modulated and that terminal #3 is always constant, but both power and ground are switched to change the direction of the motor.

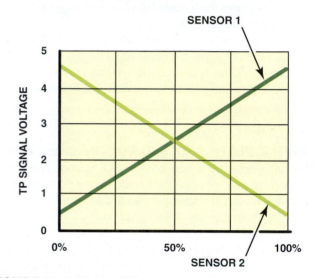

**FIGURE 21–7** The two TP sensors used on the throttle body of an electronic throttle body assembly produce opposite voltage signals as the throttle is opened. The total voltage of both combined at any throttle plate position is 5 volts.

# THROTTLE POSITION (TP) SENSOR

Two throttle position (TP) sensors are used in the throttle body assembly to provide throttle position signals to the PCM. Two sensors are used as a fail-safe measure and for diagnosis. There are two types of TP sensors used in electronic throttle control (ETC) systems: potentiometers and Hall-effect.

**THREE-WIRE POTENTIOMETER SENSORS** These sensors use a 5-volt reference from the PCM and produce an analog (variable) voltage signal that is proportional to the throttle plate position. The two sensors produce opposite signals as the throttle plate opens:

- One sensor starts at low voltage (about 0.5 V) and increases as the throttle plate is opened.
- The second sensor starts at a higher voltage (about 4.5 V) and produces a lower voltage as the throttle plate is opened. ● **SEE FIGURE 21–7.**

(a)

(b)

**FIGURE 21–8** (a) A "reduced power" warning light indicates a fault with the electronic throttle control system on some General Motors vehicles. (b) A symbol showing an engine with an arrow pointing down is used on some General Motors vehicles to indicate a fault with the electronic throttle control system.

**HALL-EFFECT TP SENSORS**  Some vehicle manufacturers, Honda for example, use a non-contact Hall-effect throttle position sensor. Because there is not physical contact, this type of sensor is less likely to fail due to wear.

## DIAGNOSIS OF ELECTRONIC THROTTLE CONTROL SYSTEMS

**FAULT MODE**  Electronic throttle control (ETC) systems can have faults like any other automatic system. Due to the redundant sensors in accelerator pedal position (APP) sensors and throttle position (TP) sensor, many faults result in a "*limp home*" situation instead of a total failure. The limp home mode is also called the "*fail-safe mode*" and indicates the following actions performed by the Powertrain Control Module (PCM).

- Engine speed is limited to the default speed (about 1200 to 1600 RPM).
- There is slow or no response when the accelerator pedal is depressed.
- The cruise control system is disabled.
- A diagnostic trouble code (DTC) is set.
- An ETC warning lamp on the dash will light. The warning lamp may be labeled differently, depending on the vehicle manufacturer. For example:
  - General Motors vehicle—Reduced power lamp (● **SEE FIGURE 21–8**)
  - Ford—Wrench symbol (amber or green) (● **SEE FIGURE 21–9**)

**FIGURE 21–9** A wrench symbol warning lamp on a Ford vehicle. The symbol can also be green.

- Chrysler—Red lightning bolt symbol (● **SEE FIGURE 21–10**)
- The engine will run and can be driven slowly. This limp-in mode operation allows the vehicle to be driven off of the road and to a safe location.

The ETC may enter the limp-in mode if any of the following has occurred:

- Low battery voltage has been detected
- PCM failure
- One TP and the MAP sensor have failed
- Both TP sensors have failed
- The ETC actuator motor has failed
- The ETC throttle spring has failed

**FIGURE 21-10** A symbol used on a Chrysler vehicle indicating a fault with the electronic throttle control.

**FIGURE 21-11** The throttle plate stayed where it was moved, which indicates that there is a problem with the electronic throttle body control assembly.

**REAL WORLD FIX**

**The High Idle Toyota**

The owner of a Toyota Camry complained that the engine would idle at over 1200 RPM compared with a normal 600 to 700 RPM. The vehicle would also not accelerate. Using a scan tool, a check for diagnostic trouble codes showed one code: P2101—"TAC motor circuit low."

Checking service information led to the inspection of the electronic throttle control throttle body assembly. With the ignition key out of the ignition and the inlet air duct off the throttle body, the technician used a screwdriver to push gently to see if the throttle plate worked.

**Normal operation**—The throttle plate should move and then spring back quickly to the default position.

**Abnormal operation**—If the throttle plate stays where it is moved or does not return to the default position, there is a fault with the throttle body assembly. ● SEE FIGURE 21-11.

**Solution:** The technician replaced the throttle body assembly with an updated version and proper engine operation was restored. The technician disassembled the old throttle body and found it was corroded inside due to moisture entering the unit through the vent hose. ● SEE FIGURE 21-12.

**VACUUM LEAKS** The electronic throttle control (ETC) system is able to compensate for many vacuum leaks. A vacuum leak at the intake manifold for example will allow air into the engine that is not measured by the mass airflow sensor. The ETC system will simply move the throttle as needed to achieve the proper idle speed to compensate for the leak.

**DIAGNOSTIC PROCEDURE** If a fault occurs in the ETC system, check service information for the specified procedure to follow for the vehicle being checked. Most vehicle service information includes the following steps:

**STEP 1** Verify the customer concern.

**STEP 2** Use a factory scan tool or an aftermarket scan tool with original equipment capability and check for diagnostic trouble codes (DTCs).

**STEP 3** If there are stored diagnostic trouble codes, follow service information instructions for diagnosing the system.

**STEP 4** If there are no stored diagnostic trouble codes, check scan tool data for possible fault areas in the system.

**SCAN TOOL DATA** Scan data related to the electronic throttle control system can be confusing. Typical data and the meaning include:

- **APP indicated angle.** The scan tool will display a percentage ranging from 0% to 100%. When the throttle is released, the indicated angle should be 0%. When the throttle is depressed to wide open, the reading should indicate 100%.

- **TP desired angle.** The scan tool will display a percentage ranging from 0% to 100%. This represents the desired throttle angle as commanded by the driver of the vehicle.

- **TP indicated angle.** The TP indicated angle is the angle of the measured throttle opening and it should agree with the TP desired angle.

- **TP sensors 1 and 2.** The scan tool will display "agree" or "disagree." If the PCM or throttle actuator control (TAC) module receives a voltage signal from one of the TP sensors that is not in the proper relationship to the other TP sensor, the scan tool will display disagree.

**FIGURE 21-12** A corroded electronic throttle control assembly shown with the cover removed.

**FIGURE 21-13** Notice the small motor gear on the left drives a larger plastic gear (black), which then drives the small gear in mesh with the section of a gear attached to the throttle plate. This results in a huge torque increase from the small motor and helps explain why it could be dangerous to insert a finger into the throttle body assembly.

## ETC THROTTLE FOLLOWER TEST

On some vehicles, such as many Chrysler vehicles, the operation of the electronic throttle control can be tested using a factory or factory-level scan tool. To perform this test, use the "throttle follower test" procedure as shown on the scan tool. An assistant is needed to check that the throttle plate is moving as the accelerator pedal is depressed. This test cannot be done normally because the PCM does not normally allow the throttle plate to be moved unless the engine is running.

## SERVICING ELECTRONIC THROTTLE SYSTEMS

**ETC-RELATED PERFORMANCE ISSUES** The only service that an electronic throttle control system may require is a cleaning of the throttle body. Throttle body cleaning is a routine service procedure on port fuel-injected engines and is still needed when the throttle is being opened by an electric motor rather than a throttle cable tied to a mechanical accelerator pedal. The throttle body may need cleaning if one or more of the following symptoms are present:

- Lower than normal idle speed
- Rough idle
- Engine stalls when coming to a stop (called a **coast-down stall**)

If any of the above conditions exists, a throttle body cleaning will often correct these faults.

**CAUTION: Some vehicle manufacturers add a nonstick coating to the throttle assembly and warn that cleaning could remove this protective coating. Always follow the vehicle manufacturer's recommended procedures.**

**THROTTLE BODY CLEANING PROCEDURE** Before attempting to clean a throttle body on an engine equipped with an electronic throttle control system, be sure that the ignition key is out of the vehicle and the ready light is off if working on a Toyota/Lexus hybrid electric vehicle to avoid the possibility of personal injury.

> ☠ **WARNING**
>
> The electric motor that operates the throttle plate is strong enough to cut off a finger. ● SEE FIGURE 21-13.

To clean the throttle, perform the following steps:

**STEP 1** With the ignition off and the key removed from the ignition, remove the air inlet hose from the throttle body.

**STEP 2** Spray throttle body cleaner onto a shop cloth.

**STEP 3** Open the throttle body and use the shop cloth to remove the varnish and carbon deposits from the throttle body housing and throttle plate.

**CAUTION: Do not spray cleaner into the throttle body assembly. The liquid cleaner could flow into and damage the throttle position (TP) sensors.**

**STEP 4** Reinstall the inlet hose being sure that there are no air leaks between the hose and the throttle body assembly.

**STEP 5** Start the engine and allow the PCM to learn the correct idle. If the idle is not correct, check service information for the specified procedures to follow to perform a throttle relearn.

**THROTTLE BODY RELEARN PROCEDURE** When installing a new throttle body or Powertrain Control Module (PCM) or sometimes after cleaning the throttle body, the throttle position has to be learned by the PCM. After the following conditions have been met, a typical throttle body relearn procedure for a General Motors vehicle includes:

- Accelerator pedal released
- Battery voltage higher than 8 volts
- Vehicle speed must be zero
- Engine coolant temperature (ECT) higher than 40°F (5°C) and lower than 212°F (100°C)
- Intake air temperature (IAT) higher than 40°F (5°C)
- No throttle diagnostic trouble codes set

If all of the above conditions are met, perform the following steps:

**STEP 1** Turn the ignition on (engine off) for 30 seconds.

**STEP 2** Turn the ignition off and wait 30 seconds.

Start the engine and the idle learn procedure should cause the engine to idle at the correct speed.

## SUMMARY

1. Using an electronic throttle control (ETC) system on an engine has many advantages over a conventional method that uses a mechanical cable between the accelerator pedal and the throttle valve.

2. The major components of an electronic throttle control system include:
   - Accelerator pedal position (APP) sensor
   - Electronic throttle control actuator motor and spring
   - Throttle position (TP) sensor
   - Electronic control unit

3. The throttle position (TP) sensor is actually two sensors that share the 5-volt reference from the PCM and produce opposite signals as a redundant check.

4. Limp-in mode is commanded if there is a major fault in the system, which can allow the vehicle to be driven enough to be pulled off the road to safety.

5. The diagnostic procedure for the ETC system includes verifying the customer concern, using a scan tool to check for diagnostic trouble codes, and checking the value of the TP and APP sensors.

6. Servicing the ETC system includes cleaning the throttle body and throttle plate.

## REVIEW QUESTIONS

1. What parts can be deleted if an engine uses an electronic throttle control (ETC) system instead of a conventional accelerator pedal and cable to operate the throttle valve?

2. How can the use of an electronic throttle control (ETC) system improve fuel economy?

3. How is the operation of the throttle different on a system that uses an electronic throttle control system compared with a conventional mechanical system?

4. What component parts are included in an electronic throttle control system?

5. What is the default or limp-in position of the throttle plate?

6. What dash warning light indicates a fault with the ETC system?

## CHAPTER QUIZ

1. The use of an electronic throttle control (ETC) system allows the elimination of all except _____.
   a. Accelerator pedal
   b. Mechanical throttle cable (most systems)
   c. Cruise control actuator
   d. Idle air control

2. The throttle plate is spring loaded to hold the throttle slightly open how far?
   a. 3% to 5%
   b. 8% to 10%
   c. 16% to 20%
   d. 22% to 28%

3. The throttle plate actuator motor is what type of electric motor?
   a. Stepper motor
   b. DC motor
   c. AC motor
   d. Brushless motor

4. The actuator motor is controlled by the PCM through what type of circuit?
   a. Series
   b. Parallel
   c. H-bridge
   d. Series-parallel

5. When does the PCM perform a self-test of the ETC system?
   a. During cruise speed when the throttle is steady
   b. During deceleration
   c. During acceleration
   d. When the ignition switch is first rotated to the on position before the engine starts

6. The throttle position sensor used in the throttle body assembly of an electronic throttle control (ETC) system is what type?
   a. A single potentiometer
   b. Two potentiometers that read in the opposite direction
   c. A Hall-effect sensor
   d. Either b or c

7. A green wrench symbol is displayed on the dash. What does this mean?
   a. A fault in the ETC in a Ford has been detected
   b. A fault in the ETC in a Honda has been detected
   c. A fault in the ETC in a Chrysler has been detected
   d. A fault in the ETC in a General Motors vehicle has been detected

8. A technician is checking the operation of the electronic throttle control system by depressing the accelerator pedal with the ignition in the on (run) position (engine off). What is the most likely result if the system is functioning correctly?
   a. The throttle goes to wide open when the accelerator pedal is depressed all the way
   b. No throttle movement
   c. The throttle will open partially but not all of the way
   d. The throttle will perform a self-test by closing and then opening to the default position

9. With the ignition off and the key out of the ignition, what should happen if a technician uses a screwdriver and pushes gently on the throttle plate in an attempt to open the valve?
   a. Nothing. The throttle should be kept from moving by the motor, which is not energized with the key off.
   b. The throttle should move and stay where it is moved and not go back unless moved back.
   c. The throttle should move, and then spring back to the home position when released.
   d. The throttle should move closed, but not open further than the default position.

10. The throttle body may be cleaned (if recommended by the vehicle manufacturer) if what conditions are occurring?
    a. Coast-down stall
    b. Rough idle
    c. Lower-than-normal idle speed
    d. Any of the above

# FUEL-INJECTION SYSTEM DIAGNOSIS AND SERVICE

**OBJECTIVES:** **After studying Chapter 22, the reader will be able to:** • Prepare for ASE Engine Performance (A8) certification test content area "C" (Fuel, Air Induction, and Exhaust Systems Diagnosis and Repair). • Explain how to test the fuel injection system using a scan tool. • Explain how to check a fuel-pressure regulator. • Describe how to test fuel injectors. • Explain how to diagnose electronic fuel-injection problems. • Describe how to service the fuel-injection system.

**KEY TERMS:** Graphing multimeter (GMM) 285 • IAC counts 286 • Idle air control (IAC) 293 • Noid light 287 • Peak-and-hold injector 292 • Pressure transducer 285 • Saturation 292

## PORT FUEL-INJECTION PRESSURE REGULATOR DIAGNOSIS

Most port-fuel-injected engines use a vacuum hose connected to the fuel-pressure regulator. At idle, the pressure inside the intake manifold is low (high vacuum). Manifold vacuum is applied above the diaphragm inside the fuel-pressure regulator. This reduces the pressure exerted on the diaphragm and results in a lower, about 10 PSI (69 kPa), fuel pressure applied to the injectors. To test a vacuum-controlled fuel-pressure regulator, follow these steps:

1. Connect a fuel-pressure gauge to monitor the fuel pressure.

2. Locate the fuel-pressure regulator and disconnect the vacuum hose from the regulator.

   **NOTE: If gasoline drips out of the vacuum hose when removed from the fuel-pressure regulator, the regulator is defective and will require replacement.**

3. With the engine running at idle speed, reconnect the vacuum hose to the fuel-pressure regulator while watching the fuel-pressure gauge. The fuel pressure should drop (about 10 PSI or 69 kPa) when the hose is reattached to the regulator.

4. Using a hand-operated vacuum pump, apply vacuum (20 in. Hg) to the regulator. The regulator should hold

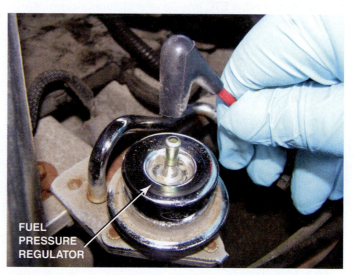

FUEL PRESSURE REGULATOR

**FIGURE 22–1** If the vacuum hose is removed from the fuel-pressure regulator when the engine is running, the fuel pressure should increase. If it does not increase, then the fuel pump is not capable of supplying adequate pressure or the fuel-pressure regulator is defective. If gasoline is visible in the vacuum hose, the regulator is leaking and should be replaced.

vacuum. If the vacuum drops, replace the fuel-pressure regulator. ● **SEE FIGURE 22–1.**

**NOTE: Some vehicles do not use a vacuum-regulated fuel-pressure regulator. Many of these vehicles use a regulator located inside the fuel tank that supplies a constant fuel pressure to the fuel injectors.**

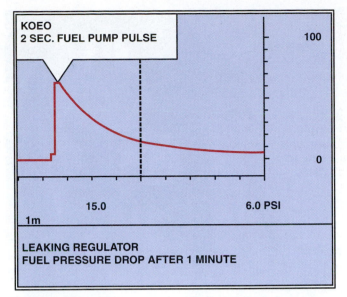

KOEO
2 SEC. FUEL PUMP PULSE

100

0

15.0                          6.0 PSI

1m

LEAKING REGULATOR
FUEL PRESSURE DROP AFTER 1 MINUTE

(a)

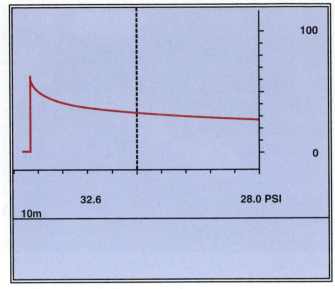

100

0

32.6                          28.0 PSI

10m

(b)

**FIGURE 22–2** (a) A fuel-pressure graph after key on, engine off (KOEO) on a TBI system. (b) Pressure drop after 10 minutes on a normal port fuel-injection system.

---

🔧 **TECH TIP**

**Pressure Transducer Fuel Pressure Test**

Using a **pressure transducer** and a **graphing multimeter (GMM)** or digital storage oscilloscope (DSO) allows the service technician to view the fuel pressure over time. ● **SEE FIGURE 22–2(a).** Note that the fuel pressure dropped from 15 PSI down to 6 PSI on a TBI-equipped vehicle after just one minute. A normal pressure holding capability is shown in ● **FIGURE 22–2(b)** when the pressure dropped only about 10% after 10 minutes on a port-fuel injection system.

**FIGURE 22–3** A clogged PCV system caused the engine oil fumes to be drawn into the air cleaner assembly. This is what the technician discovered during a visual inspection on this TBI system.

# DIAGNOSING ELECTRONIC FUEL-INJECTION PROBLEMS USING VISUAL INSPECTION

All fuel-injection systems require the proper amount of clean fuel delivered to the system at the proper pressure and the correct amount of filtered air. The following items should be carefully inspected before proceeding to more detailed tests.

- Check the air filter and replace as needed.
- Check the air induction system for obstructions.
- Check the conditions of all vacuum hoses. Replace any hose that is split, soft (mushy), or brittle.

- Check the positive crankcase ventilation (PCV) valve for proper operation or replacement as needed. ● **SEE FIGURE 22–3.**

  **NOTE: The use of an incorrect PCV valve can cause a rough idle or stalling.**

- Check all fuel-injection electrical connections for corrosion or damage.
- Check for gasoline at the vacuum port of the fuel-pressure regulator if the vehicle is so equipped. Gasoline in the vacuum hose at the fuel-pressure regulator indicates that the regulator is defective and requires replacement.

FIGURE 22–4 All fuel injectors should make the same sound with the engine running at idle speed. A lack of sound indicates a possible electrically open injector or a break in the wiring. A defective computer could also be the cause of a lack of clicking (pulsing) of the injectors.

FUEL PRESSURE REGULATOR

FUEL RETURN LINE TO TANK

FIGURE 22–5 Fuel should be heard returning to the fuel tank at the fuel return line if the fuel-pump and fuel-pressure regulator are functioning correctly.

**TECH TIP**

**Stethoscope Fuel-Injection Test**

A commonly used test for injector operation is to listen to the injector using a stethoscope with the engine operating at idle speed. ● SEE FIGURE 22–4. All injectors should produce the same clicking sound. If any injector makes a clunking or rattling sound, it should be tested further or replaced. With the engine still running, place the end of the stethoscope probe to the return line from the fuel-pressure regulator. ● SEE FIGURE 22–5. Fuel should be heard flowing back to the fuel tank if the fuel-pump pressure is higher than the fuel-regulator pressure. If no sound of fuel is heard, then either the fuel pump or the fuel-pressure regulator is at fault.

**TECH TIP**

**Quick and Easy Leaking Injector Test**

Leaking injectors may be found by disabling the ignition, unhooking all injectors, and checking exhaust for hydrocarbons (HC) using a gas analyzer while cranking the engine (maximum HC = 300 PPM). This test does not identify which injector is leaking, but it does confirm that one or more injector is leaking.

- The computer increases the injector pulse width slightly longer due to the signal from the MAP sensor.
- The air–fuel mixture remains unchanged.
- The idle air control (IAC) counts will decrease, thereby attempting to reduce the engine speed to the target idle speed stored in the computer memory. ● SEE FIGURE 22–6.

Therefore, one of the best indicators of a vacuum leak on a speed-density fuel-injection system is to look at the IAC counts or percentage. Normal **IAC counts** or percentage is usually 15 to 25. A reading of less than 5 indicates a vacuum leak.

If a vacuum leak occurs on an engine equipped with a mass airflow-type fuel-injection system, the extra air causes the following to occur:

- The engine will operate leaner-than-normal because the extra air has not been measured by the MAF sensor.
- The idle speed will likely be lower due to the leaner-than-normal air–fuel mixture.
- The idle air control (IAC) counts or percentage will often increase in an attempt to return the engine speed to the target speed stored in the computer.

# SCAN TOOL VACUUM LEAK DIAGNOSIS

If a vacuum (air) leak occurs on an engine equipped with a speed-density-type of fuel injection, the extra air would cause the following to occur:

- The idle speed increases due to the extra air just as if the throttle pedal was depressed.
- The MAP sensor reacts to the increased air from the vacuum leak as an additional load on the engine.

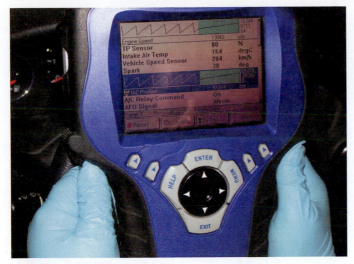

**FIGURE 22–6** Using a scan tool to check for IAC counts or percentage as part of a diagnostic routine.

**FIGURE 22–7** Checking the fuel pressure using a fuel-pressure gauge connected to the Schrader valve.

## TECH TIP

**No Spark, No Squirt**

Most electronic fuel-injection computer systems use the ignition primary (pickup coil or crank sensor) pulse as the trigger for when to inject (squirt) fuel from the injectors (nozzles). If this signal were not present, no fuel would be injected. Because this pulse is also necessary to trigger the module to create a spark from the coil, it can be said that "no spark" could also mean "no squirt." Therefore, if the cause of a no-start condition is observed to be a lack of fuel injection, do not start testing or replacing fuel-system components until the ignition system is checked for proper operation.

## PORT FUEL-INJECTION SYSTEM DIAGNOSIS

To determine if a port fuel-injection system—including the fuel pump, injectors, and fuel-pressure regulator—is operating correctly, take the following steps.

1. Attach a fuel-pressure gauge to the Schrader valve on the fuel rail. ● **SEE FIGURE 22–7.**

2. Turn the ignition key on or start the engine to build up the fuel-pump pressure (often about 35 to 45 PSI. Always check service information for the specified fuel pressure).

3. Wait 20 minutes and observe the fuel pressure retained in the fuel rail and note the PSI reading. The fuel pressure should not drop more than 20 PSI (140 kPa) in 20 minutes. If the drop is less than 20 PSI in 20 minutes, everything is

okay; if the drop is *greater,* then there is a possible problem with:

- The check valve in the fuel pump
- Leaking injectors, lines, or fittings
- A defective (leaking) fuel-pressure regulator

To determine which unit is defective, perform the following:

- Reenergize the electric fuel pump.
- Clamp the fuel *supply* line, and wait 10 minutes (see Caution box). If the pressure drop does not occur, replace the fuel pump. If the pressure drop still occurs, continue with the next step.
- Repeat the pressure buildup of the electric pump and clamp the fuel return line. If the pressure drop time is now okay, replace the fuel-pressure regulator.
- If the pressure drop still occurs, one or more of the injectors is leaking. Remove the injectors with the fuel rail and hold over paper. Replace those injectors that drip one or more drops after 10 minutes with pressurized fuel.

**CAUTION: Do not clamp plastic fuel lines. Connect shut-off valves to the fuel system to shut off supply and return lines.** ● **SEE FIGURE 22–8.**

## TESTING FOR AN INJECTOR PULSE

One of the first checks that should be performed when diagnosing a no-start condition is whether the fuel injectors are being pulsed by the computer. Checking for proper pulsing of the injector is also important in diagnosing a weak or dead cylinder.

A **noid light** is designed to electrically replace the injector in the circuit and to flash if the injector circuit is working correctly. ● **SEE FIGURE 22–9.** To use a noid light, disconnect the

**FIGURE 22–8** Shutoff valves must be used on vehicles equipped with plastic fuel lines to isolate the cause of a pressure drop in the fuel system.

(a)

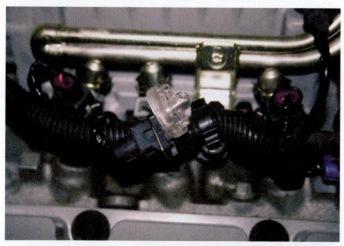

(b)

**FIGURE 22–9** (a) Noid lights are usually purchased as an assortment so that one is available for any type or size of injector wiring connector. (b) The connector is unplugged from the injector and a noid light is plugged into the harness side of the connector. The noid light should flash when the engine is being cranked if the power circuit and the pulsing to ground by the computer are functioning normally.

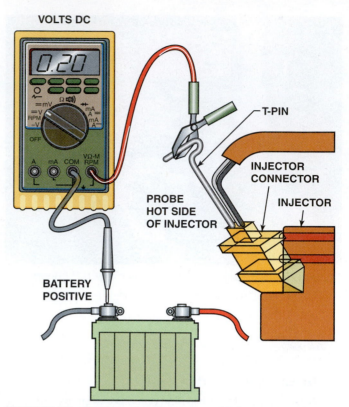

**FIGURE 22–10** Use a DMM set to read DC volts to check the voltage drop of the positive circuit to the fuel injector. A reading of 0.5 volt or less is generally considered to be acceptable.

electrical connector at the fuel injector and plug the noid light into the injector harness connections. Crank or start the engine. The noid light should flash regularly.

**NOTE: The term *noid* is simply an abbreviation of the word *solenoid*. Injectors use a movable iron core and are therefore solenoids. Therefore, a noid light is a replacement for the solenoid (injector).**

Possible noid light problems and causes include the following:

1. **The light is off and does not flash.** The problem is an open in either the power side or ground side (or both) of the injector circuit.

2. **The noid light flashes dimly.** A dim noid light indicates excessive resistance or low voltage available to the injector. Both the power and ground side must be checked.

3. **The noid light is on and does not flash.** If the noid light is on, then both a power and a ground are present. Because the light does not flash (blink) when the engine is being cranked or started, then a short-to-ground fault exists either in the computer itself or in the wiring between the injector and the computer.

**CAUTION: A noid lamp must be used with caution. The computer may show a good noid light operation and have low supply voltage. ● SEE FIGURE 22–10.**

# CHECKING FUEL-INJECTOR RESISTANCE

Each port fuel injector must deliver an equal amount of fuel or the engine will idle roughly or perform poorly.

The electrical balance test involves measuring the injector coil-winding resistance. For best engine operation, all injectors should have the same electrical resistance. To measure the resistance, carefully release the locking feature of the connector and remove the connector from the injector.

### Injector Resistance Table

| Manufacturer | Injector Application | Resistance Values |
|---|---|---|
| General Motors | | |
| | Quad 4 | 1.95–2.15 Ω |
| | CPI Vortec 4.3L | 1.48–1.52 Ω |
| | MFI Bosch Style Injector (1985–1989) 2.8L | 15.95–16.35 Ω |
| | MFI Black Multec Injector 2.8L, 3.1L, 3.3L, 3.4L | 11.8–12.6 Ω |
| | MFI 3800 | 14.3–14.7 Ω |
| | MFI 3.8L, 5.0L, 5.7L | 15.8–16.6 Ω |
| | MFI 5.7 LT5-ZR1 | 11.8–12.6 Ω |
| | TBI 220 Series 2.8L, 3.1L, 4.3L, 5.0L, 5.7L, 7.4L | 1.16–1.36 Ω |
| | TBI 295 Series 4.3L, 6.0L, 7.0L | 1.42–1.62 Ω |
| | TBI 700 Series 2.0L, 2.2L, 2.5L | 1.42–1.62 Ω |
| Chrysler Brand | | |
| | MFI Early Years through 1992 (majority of) | 2.4 Ω |
| | MFI Later Years after 1992 (majority of) | 14.5 Ω |
| | TBI Low-Pressure Systems (majority of) | 1.3 Ω |
| | TBI High-Pressure Systems (majority of) | 0.7 Ω |
| Ford | | |
| | MFI (majority of) | 15.0–18.0 Ω |
| | TBI Low-Pressure 1.9L (1987–1990) | 1.0–2.0 Ω |
| | TBI Low-Pressure 2.3L (1985–1987) | 1.0–2.0 Ω |
| | TBI Low-Pressure 2.5L (1986–1990) | 1.0–2.0 Ω |
| | TBI High-Pressure 3.8L (1984–1987) | 1.5–2.5 Ω |
| | TBI High-Pressure 5.0L (1981–1985) | 1.5–3.5 Ω |

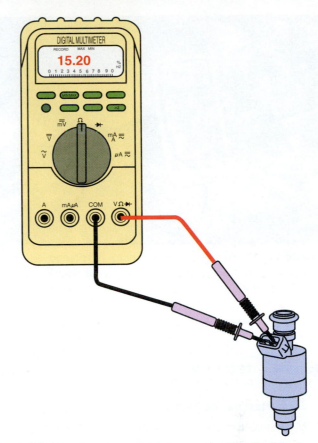

**FIGURE 22–11** An ohmmeter is connected to the injector electrical terminals to read the coil resistance.

**NOTE: Some engines require specific procedures to gain access to the injectors. Always follow the manufacturers' recommended procedures.**

With an ohmmeter, measure the resistance across the injector terminals. Be sure to use the low-ohms feature of the digital ohmmeter to read in tenths (0.1) of an ohm. ● **SEE FIGURES 22–11 AND 22–12.** Check service information for the resistance specification of the injectors. Measure the resistance of all of the injectors. Replace any injector that does not fall within the resistance range of the specification. The resistance of the injectors should be measured twice—once when the engine (and injectors) are cold and once after the engine has reached normal operating temperature. If any injector resistance is not equal to specifications, make certain that the terminals of the injector are electrically sound, and perform other tests to confirm an injector problem before replacement.

# MEASURING RESISTANCE OF GROUPED INJECTORS

Many vehicles are equipped with a port fuel-injection system that "fires" two or more injectors at a time. For example, a V-6 may group all three injectors on one bank to pulse on at the same

FIGURE 22–12 To measure fuel-injector resistance, a technician constructed a short wiring harness with a double banana plug that fits into the V and COM terminals of the meter and an injector connector at the other end. This setup makes checking resistance of fuel injectors quick and easy.

(a)

(b)

FIGURE 22–13 (a) The meter is connected to read one group of three 12-ohm injectors. The result should be 4 ohms and this reading is a little low indicating that at least one injector is shorted (low resistance). (b) This meter is connected to the other group of three injectors and indicates that most, if not all three, injectors are shorted. The technician replaced all six injectors and the engine ran great.

## TECH TIP

### Equal Resistance Test

All fuel injectors should measure the specified resistance. However the specification often indicates the temperature of the injectors be at room temperature and of course will vary according to the temperature. Rather than waiting for all of the injectors to achieve room temperature, measure the resistance and check that they are all within 0.4 ohm of each other. To determine the difference, record the resistance of each injector and then subtract the lowest resistance reading from the highest resistance reading to get the difference. If more than 0.4 ohm then further testing will be needed to verify defective injector(s).

time. Then the other three injectors will be pulsed on. This sequence alternates. To measure the resistance of these injectors, it is often easiest to measure each group of three that is wired in parallel. The resistance of three injectors wired in parallel is one-third of the resistance of each individual injector. For example,

**Injector resistance = 12 ohms (Ω)**

**Three injectors in parallel = 4 ohms (Ω)**

A V-6 has two groups of three injectors. Therefore, both groups should measure the same resistance. If both groups measure 4 ohms, then it is likely that all six injectors are okay. However, if one group measures only 2.9 ohms and the other group measures 4 ohms, then it is likely that one or more fuel injectors are defective (shorted). This means that the technician now has reasonable cause to remove the intake manifold to get access to each injector for further testing. ● SEE FIGURE 22–13.

## MEASURING RESISTANCE OF INDIVIDUAL INJECTORS

While there are many ways to check injectors, the first test is to measure the resistance of the coil inside and compare it to factory specifications. ● SEE FIGURE 22–14. If the injectors are not accessible, check service information for the location of the electrical connector for the injectors. Unplug the connector and measure the resistance of each injector at the injector side of the connector. Use service information to determine the wire colors for the power side and the pulse side of each injector.

**FIGURE 22-14** If an injector has the specified resistance, this does not mean that it is okay. This injector had the specified resistance yet it did not deliver the correct amount of fuel because it was clogged.

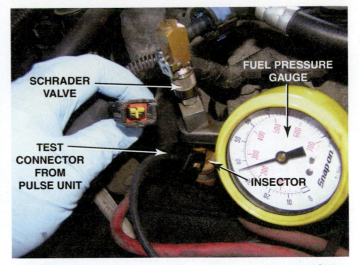

**FIGURE 22-15** After connecting a pressure gauge, unplug the electrical connector from the injector and attach the test lead from the pulse unit to the injector.

## PRESSURE-DROP BALANCE TEST

The pressure balance test involves using an electrical timing device to pulse the fuel injectors on for a given amount of time, usually 500 ms or 0.5 second, and observing the drop in pressure that accompanies the pulse. If the *fuel flow* through each injector is equal, the drop in pressure in the system will be equal. Most manufacturers recommend that the pressures be within about 1.5 PSI (10 kPa) of each other for satisfactory engine performance. This test method not only tests the electrical functioning of the injector (for definite time and current pulse), but also tests for mechanical defects that could affect fuel flow amounts.

The purpose of running this injector balance test is to determine which injector is restricted, inoperative, or delivering fuel differently than the other injectors. Replacing a complete set of injectors can be expensive. The basic tools needed are:

- Accurate pressure gauge with pressure relief
- Injector pulser with time control
- Necessary injector connection adapters
- Safe receptacle for catching and disposing of any fuel released

**STEP 1** Attach the pressure gauge to the fuel delivery rail on the supply side. Make sure the connections are safe and leakproof.

**STEP 2** Attach the injector pulser to the first injector to be tested.

**STEP 3** Turn the ignition key to the on position to prime the fuel rail. Note the static fuel-pressure reading.

**STEP 4** Activate the pulser for the timed firing pulses.

**STEP 5** Note and record the new static rail pressure after the injector has been pulsed. ● **SEE FIGURE 22-15.**

**STEP 6** Reenergize the fuel pump and repeat this procedure for all of the engine injectors.

**STEP 7** Compare the two pressure readings and compute the pressure drop for each injector. Compare the pressure drops of the injectors to each other. Any variation in pressure drops will indicate an uneven fuel delivery rate between the injectors.

For example:

| Injector | 1 | 2 | 3 | | 4 | 5 | 6 |
|---|---|---|---|---|---|---|---|
| Initial pressure | 40 | 40 | 40 | | 40 | 40 | 40 |
| Second pressure | 30 | 30 | 35 | | 30 | 20 | 30 |
| Pressure drop | 10 | 10 | 5 | | 10 | 20 | 10 |
| Possible problem | OK | OK | Restriction | | OK | Leak | OK |

## INJECTOR VOLTAGE-DROP TESTS

Another test of injectors involves pulsing the injector and measuring the voltage drop across the windings as current is flowing. A typical voltage-drop tester is shown in ● **FIGURE 22-16.** The tester, which is recommended for use by General Motors Corporation, pulses the injector while a digital multimeter is connected to the unit, which will display the voltage drop as the current flows through the winding.

**CAUTION: Do not test an injector using a pulse-type tester more than one time without starting the engine to help avoid a hydrostatic lock caused by the flow of fuel into the cylinder during the pulse test.**

FIGURE 22–16 An injector tester being used to check the voltage drop through the injector while the tester is sending current through the injectors. This test is used to check the coil inside the injector. This same tester can be used to check for equal pressure drop of each injector by pulsing the injector on for 500 ms.

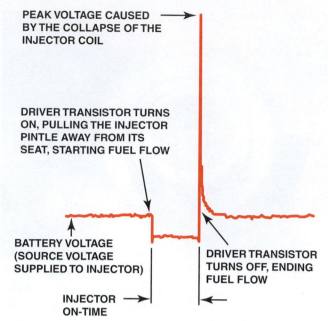

PEAK VOLTAGE CAUSED BY THE COLLAPSE OF THE INJECTOR COIL

DRIVER TRANSISTOR TURNS ON, PULLING THE INJECTOR PINTLE AWAY FROM ITS SEAT, STARTING FUEL FLOW

BATTERY VOLTAGE (SOURCE VOLTAGE SUPPLIED TO INJECTOR)

DRIVER TRANSISTOR TURNS OFF, ENDING FUEL FLOW

INJECTOR ON-TIME

FIGURE 22–18 The injector on-time is called the pulse width. *(Courtesy of Fluke Corporation)*

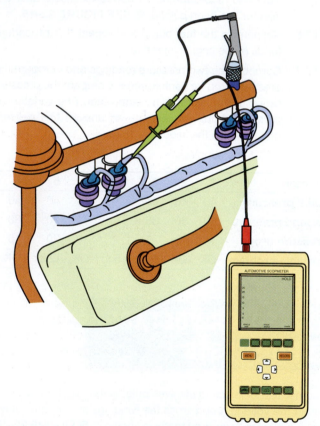

FIGURE 22–17 A digital storage oscilloscope can be easily connected to an injector by carefully back probing the electrical connector.

Record the highest voltage drop observed on the meter display during the test. Repeat the voltage-drop test for all of the injectors. The voltage drop across each injector should be within 0.1 volt of each other. If an injector has a higher-than-normal voltage drop, the injector windings have higher-than-normal resistance.

# SCOPE-TESTING FUEL INJECTORS

A scope (analog or digital storage) can be connected into each injector circuit. There are three types of injector drive circuits and each type of circuit has its own characteristic pattern. ● **SEE FIGURE 22–17** for an example of how to connect a scope to read a fuel-injector waveform.

**SATURATED SWITCH TYPE** In a saturated switch-type injector-driven circuit, voltage (usually a full 12 volts) is applied to the injector. The ground for the injector is provided by the vehicle computer. When the ground connection is completed, current flows through the injector windings. Due to the resistance and inductive reactance of the coil itself, it requires a fraction of a second (about 3 milliseconds or 0.003 seconds) for the coil to reach **saturation** or maximum current flow. Most saturated switch-type fuel injectors have 12 to 16 ohms of resistance. This resistance, as well as the computer switching circuit, control and limit the current flow through the injector. A voltage spike occurs when the computer shuts off (opens the injector ground-side circuit) the injectors. ● **SEE FIGURE 22–18.**

**PEAK-AND-HOLD TYPE** A **peak-and-hold** type is typically used for TBI and some port low-resistance injectors. Full battery voltage is applied to the injector and the ground side is controlled through the computer. The computer provides a high initial current flow (about 4 amperes) to flow through the injector windings to open the injector core. Then the computer reduces the current to a lower level (about 1 ampere). The hold current

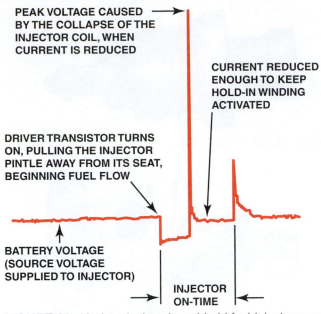

FIGURE 22–19 A typical peak-and-hold fuel-injector waveform. Most fuel injectors that measure less than 6 ohms will usually display a similar waveform.

PEAK VOLTAGE CAUSED BY THE COLLAPSE OF THE INJECTOR COIL, WHEN CURRENT IS REDUCED

CURRENT REDUCED ENOUGH TO KEEP HOLD-IN WINDING ACTIVATED

DRIVER TRANSISTOR TURNS ON, PULLING THE INJECTOR PINTLE AWAY FROM ITS SEAT, BEGINNING FUEL FLOW

BATTERY VOLTAGE (SOURCE VOLTAGE SUPPLIED TO INJECTOR)

INJECTOR ON-TIME

**? FREQUENTLY ASKED QUESTION**

**If Three of Six Injectors Are Defective, Should I Also Replace the Other Three?**

This is a good question. Many service technicians "recommend" that the three good injectors also be replaced along with the other three that tested as being defective. The reasons given by these technicians include:

- All six injectors have been operating under the same fuel, engine, and weather conditions.
- The labor required to replace all six is just about the same as replacing only the three defective injectors.
- Replacing all six at the same time helps ensure that all of the injectors are flowing the same amount of fuel so that the engine is operating most efficiently.

With these ideas in mind, the customer should be informed and offered the choice. Complete sets of injectors such as those in ● FIGURE 22–20 can be purchased at a reasonable cost.

FIGURE 22–20 A set of six reconditioned injectors. The sixth injector is barely visible at the far right.

is enough to keep the injector open, yet conserves energy and reduces the heat buildup that would occur if the full current flow remains on as long as the injector is commanded on. Typical peak-and-hold-type injector resistance ranges from 2 to 4 ohms.

The scope pattern of a typical peak-and-hold-type injector shows the initial closing of the ground circuit, then a voltage spike as the current flow is reduced. Another voltage spike occurs when the lower level current is turned off (opened) by the computer. ● SEE FIGURE 22–19.

**PULSE-WIDTH MODULATED TYPE** A pulse-width modulated type of injector drive circuit uses lower-resistance coil injectors. Battery voltage is available at the positive terminal of the injector and the computer provides a variable-duration connection to ground on the negative side of the injector.

The computer can vary the time intervals that the injector is grounded for very precise fuel control.

Each time the injector circuit is turned off (ground circuit opened), a small voltage spike occurs. It is normal to see multiple voltage spikes on a scope connected to a pulse-width modulated type of fuel injector.

## IDLE AIR SPEED CONTROL DIAGNOSIS

On an engine equipped with fuel injection (TBI or port injection), the idle speed is controlled by increasing or decreasing the amount of air bypassing the throttle plate. Again, an electronic stepper motor or pulse-width modulated solenoid is used to maintain the correct idle speed. This control is often called the **idle air control (IAC)**. ● SEE FIGURES 22–21 THROUGH 22–23.

When the engine stops, most IAC units will retract outward to get ready for the next engine start. When the engine starts, the engine speed is high to provide for proper operation when the engine is cold. Then, as the engine gets warmer, the computer reduces engine idle speed gradually by reducing the number of counts or steps commanded by the IAC.

When the engine is warm and restarted, the idle speed should momentarily increase, then decrease to normal idle speed. This increase and then decrease in engine speed is often called an engine-flare. If the engine speed does not flare, then the IAC may not be working (it may be stuck in one position).

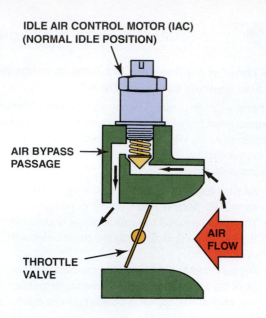

IDLE AIR CONTROL MOTOR (IAC)
(NORMAL IDLE POSITION)

AIR BYPASS
PASSAGE

AIR
FLOW

THROTTLE
VALVE

(FULLY EXTENDED POSITION)

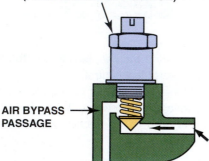

AIR BYPASS
PASSAGE

**FIGURE 22–21** An IAC controls idle speed by controlling the amount of air that passes around the throttle plate. More airflow results in a higher idle speed.

**FIGURE 22–22** A typical IAC.

**FIGURE 22–23** Some IAC units are purchased with the housing as shown. Carbon buildup in these passages can cause a rough or unstable idling or stalling.

> **REAL WORLD FIX**
>
> **There Is No Substitute for a Thorough Visual Inspection**
>
> An intermittent "check engine" light and a random-misfire diagnostic trouble code (DTC) P0300 was being diagnosed. A scan tool did not provide any help because all systems seemed to be functioning normally. Finally, the technician removed the engine cover and discovered a mouse nest. ● **SEE FIGURE 22–24.**

# FUEL-INJECTION SERVICE

After many years of fuel-injection service, some service technicians still misunderstand the process of proper fuel-system handling. Much has been said over the years with regard to when and how to perform injector cleaning. Some manufacturers have suggested methods of cleaning while others have issued bulletins to prohibit any cleaning at all.

All engines using fuel injection do require some type of fuel-system maintenance. Normal wear and tear with underhood temperatures and changes in gasoline quality contribute to the buildup of olefin wax, dirt, water, and many other additives. Unique to each engine is an idle air-control design that also may contribute different levels of carbon deposits.

Fuel-injection system service should include the following operations:

1.  **Check fuel-pump operating pressure and volume.** The missing link here is volume. Most working technicians

assume that if the pressure is correct, the volume is also okay. Hook up a fuel-pressure tester to the fuel rail inlet to quickly test the fuel pressure with the engine running. At the same time, test the volume of the pump by sending fuel into the holding tank. (One ounce per second is the usual specification.) ● **SEE FIGURE 22–25.** A two-line system tester is the recommended procedure to use and is attached to the fuel inlet and the return on the fuel rail. The vehicle onboard system is looped and returns fuel to the tank.

2.  **Test the fuel-pressure regulator for operation and leakage.** At this time, the fuel-pressure regulator would be tested for operational pressure and proper regulation, including leakage. Below are some points to consider.

    ■  Good pressure does not mean proper volume. For example, a clogged filter may test okay on pressure but the restriction may not allow proper volume under load. ● **SEE FIGURE 22–26.**

(a)

(b)

**FIGURE 22–24** (a) Nothing looks unusual when the hood is first opened. (b) When the cover is removed from the top of the engine, a mouse or some other animal nest is visible. The animal had already eaten through a couple of injector wires. At least the cause of the intermittent misfire was discovered.

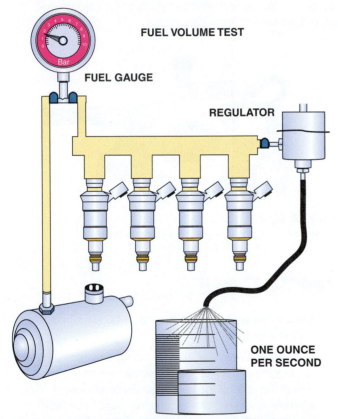

**FIGURE 22–25** Checking fuel-pump volume using a hose from the outlet of the fuel-pressure regulator into a calibrated container.

- It is a good idea to use the vehicle's own gasoline to service the system versus a can of shop gasoline that has been sitting around for some time.
- Pressure regulators do fail and a lot more do not properly shut off fuel, causing higher-than-normal pump wear and shorter service life.

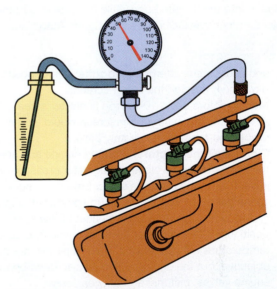

**FIGURE 22–26** Testing fuel-pump volume using a fuel-pressure gauge with a bleed hose inserted into a suitable container. The engine is running during this test.

3. **Flush the entire fuel rail and upper fuel-injector screens including the fuel-pressure regulator.** Raise the input pressure to a point above regulator setting to allow a constant flow of fuel through the inlet pressure side of the system, through the fuel rail, and out the open fuel-pressure regulator. In most cases the applied pressure is 75 to 90 PSI (517 to 620 kPa), but will be maintained by the presence of a regulator. At this point, cleaning chemical is added to the fuel at a 5:1 mixture and allowed to flow through the system for 15 to 30 minutes. ● SEE FIGURE 22–27. Results are best on a hot engine with the fuel supply looped and the engine not running. Below are some points to consider.
   - This flush is the fix most vehicles need first. The difference is that the deposits are removed to a remote tank

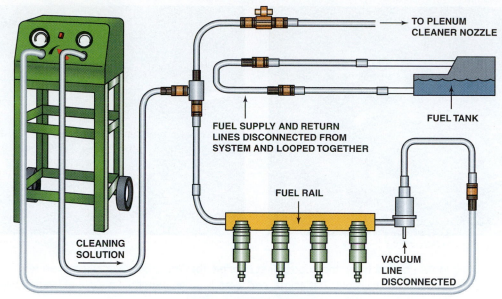

**FIGURE 22–27** A typical two-line cleaning machine hookup, showing an extension hose that can be used to squirt a cleaning solution into the throttle body while the engine is running on the cleaning solution and gasoline mixture. Typical two-line fuel-injector machines include Carbon Clean, Auto Care, Injector Test, DeCarbon, or Motor-Vac.

and filter versus attempting to soften the deposits and blow them through the upper screens.

- Most injectors use a 10-micron final filter screen. A 25% restriction in the upper screen would increase the injector on-time approximately 25%.
- **Clean the fuel injectors.** Start the engine and adjust the output pressure closer to regulator pressure or lower than in the previous steps. Lower pressure will cause the pulse width to open up somewhat longer and allow the injectors to be cleaned. Slow speed (idle) position will take a longer time frame and operating temperature will be reached. Clean injectors are the objective, but the chemical should also decarbon the engine valves, pistons, and oxygen sensor.

4. **Decarbon the engine assembly.** On most vehicles, the injector spray will help the decarboning process. On others, you may need to enhance the operation with external addition of a mixture through the PCV hose, throttle plates, or idle air controls.

5. **Clean the throttle plate and idle air control passages.** Doing this service alone on most late-model engines will show a manifold vacuum increase of up to 2 in. Hg. Stop the engine and clean the areas as needed, then use a handheld fuel injector connected in parallel with the pressure hose, along with a pulser to allow cleaning of the throttle plates with the same chemical as injectors are running on. ● **SEE FIGURE 22–28.** This works well as air is drawn into IAC passages on a running engine and will clean the passages without IAC removal.

6. **Relearn the onboard computer.** Some vehicles may have been running in such a poor state of operation that the onboard computer may need to be relearned. Consult service

**FIGURE 22–28** To thoroughly clean a throttle body, it is sometimes best to remove it from the vehicle.

🔧 **TECH TIP**

**Check the Injectors at the "Bends and the Ends"**

Injectors that are most likely to become restricted due to clogging of the filter basket screen are the injectors at the ends of the rail especially on returnless systems where dirt can accumulate. Also the injectors that are located at the bends of the fuel rail are also subject to possible clogging due to the dirt being deposited where the fuel makes a turn in the rail.

information for the suggested relearn procedures for each particular vehicle.

This service usually takes approximately one hour for the vehicle to run out of fuel and the entire service to be performed. The good thing is that the technician may do other services while this

### Be Sure to Clean the Fuel Rail

Whenever you service the fuel injectors, or if you suspect that there may be a fuel-injector problem, remove the entire fuel rail assembly and check the passages for contamination. Always thoroughly clean the rail when replacing fuel injectors.

is being performed. Some technicians may install a set of plugs or change the fuel filter while the engine is flushing. This service should restore the fuel system to original operations.

**Fuel-Injection Symptom Chart**

| Symptom | Possible Causes |
|---------|-----------------|
| **Hard cold starts** | • Low fuel pressure |
| | • Leaking fuel injectors |
| | • Contaminated fuel |
| | • Low-volatility fuel |
| | • Dirty throttle plate |
| **Garage stalls** | • Low fuel pressure |
| | • Insufficient fuel volume |
| | • Restricted fuel injector |
| | • Contaminated fuel |
| | • Low-volatility fuel |
| **Poor cold performance** | • Low fuel pressure |
| | • Insufficient fuel volume |
| | • Contaminated fuel |
| | • Low-volatility fuel |
| **Tip-in hesitation** (hesitation just as the accelerator pedal is depressed) | • Low fuel pressure |
| | • Insufficient fuel volume |
| | • Intake valve deposits |
| | • Contaminated fuel |
| | • Low-volatility fuel |

# FUEL-SYSTEM SCAN TOOL DIAGNOSTICS

**FUEL TRIM VALUES**     Diagnosing a faulty fuel system can be a difficult task. However, it can be made easier by utilizing the information available via the serial data stream. By observing the long-term fuel trim and the short-term fuel trim, we can determine how the fuel system is performing. Short-term fuel trim and long-term fuel trim can help us to zero in on specific areas of trouble. Readings should be taken at idle and at 3000 RPM. Use the following chart as a guide.

| Condition | Long-Term Fuel Trim at Idle | Long-Term Fuel Trim at 3000 RPM |
|-----------|-----------------------------|----------------------------------|
| **System normal** | 0% ± 10% | 0% ± 10% |
| **Vacuum leak** | HIGH | OK |
| **Fuel flow problem** | OK | HIGH |
| **Low fuel pressure** | HIGH | HIGH |
| **High fuel pressure** | *OK or LOW | *OK or LOW |

*High fuel pressure will affect trim at idle, at 3000 RPM, or both.

**IAC COUNTS**     A scan tool can be used to check the counts or steps needed to control the idle speed. With the engine at normal operating temperature, the following IAC position as displayed on a scan tool will help with fuel system diagnosis.

**Normal-** Normal idle air control counts should be 25-35 counts or percentage.

**Lower-than-normal-** If the IAC counts or percent age is less than 5 then there could be a vacuum leak (speed density system ) or false air on some mass air flow engines.

**Higher-than-normal-** If the counts or percentage is higher than 50 , then this could be due to an excessive drag on the engine or a dirty throttle body or throttle plate.

**1** The tools needed to diagnose a circuit containing a relay include a digital multimeter (DMM), a fused jumper wire, and an assortment of wiring terminals.

**2** Start the diagnosis by locating the relay center. It is under the hood on this General Motors vehicle, so access is easy. Not all vehicles are this easy.

**3** The chart under the cover for the relay center indicates the location of the relay that controls the electric fuel pump.

**4** Locate the fuel-pump relay and remove by using a puller if necessary. Try to avoid rocking or twisting the relay to prevent causing damage to the relay terminals or the relay itself.

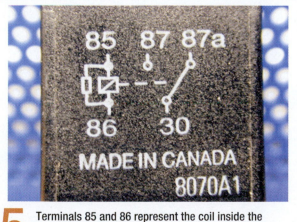

**5** Terminals 85 and 86 represent the coil inside the relay. Terminal 30 is the power terminal, 87a is the normally closed contact, and 87 is the normally open contact.

**6** The terminals are also labeled on most relays.

**7** To help make good electrical contact with the terminals without doing any harm, select the proper-size terminal from the terminal assortment.

**8** Insert the terminals into the relay socket in 30 and 87.

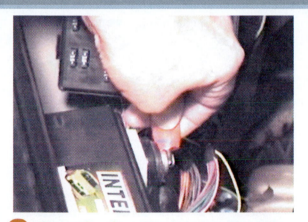

**9** To check for voltage at terminal 30, use a test light or a voltmeter. Start by connecting the alligator clip of the test light to the positive (+) terminal of the battery.

**10** Touch the test light to the negative (−) terminal of the battery or a good engine ground to check the test light.

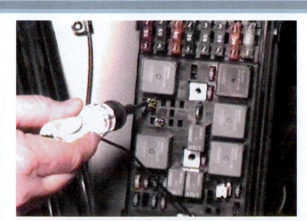

**11** Connect the ground lead of the test light to a good ground and check for voltage at terminal 30 of the relay. The ignition may have to be in the on (run) position.

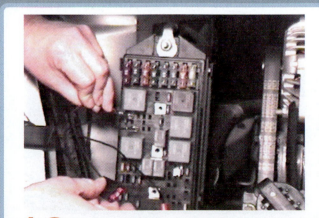

**12** To check to see if the electric fuel pump can be operated from the relay contacts, use a fused jumper wire and touch the relay contacts that correspond to terminals 30 and 87 of the relay.

CONTINUED ▶

**13** Connect the leads of the meter to contacts 30 and 87 of the relay socket. The reading of 4.7 amperes is okay because the specification is 4 to 8 amperes.

**14** Set the meter to read ohms (Ω) and measure the resistance of the relay coil. The usual reading for most relays is between 60 and 100 ohms.

**15** Measure between terminal 30 and 87a. Terminal 87a is the normally closed contact, and there should be little, if any, resistance between these two terminals, as shown.

**16** To test the normally open contacts, connect one meter lead to terminal 30 and the other lead to terminal 87. The ohmmeter should show an open circuit by displaying OL.

**17** Connect a fused jumper wire to supply 12 volts to terminal 86 and a ground to terminal 85 of the relay. If the relay clicks, then the relay coil is able to move the armature (movable arm) of the relay.

**18** After testing, be sure to reinstall the relay and the relay cover.

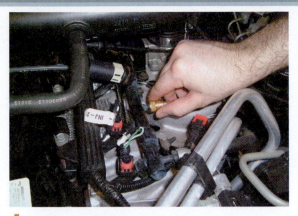

**1** Start the fuel injector cleaning process by bringing the vehicle's engine up to operating temperature. Shut off the engine, remove the cap from the fuel rail test port, and install the appropriate adapter.

**2** The vehicle's fuel pump is disabled by removing its relay or fuse. In some cases, it may be necessary to disconnect the fuel pump at the tank if the relay or fuse powers more than just the pump.

**3** Turn the outlet valve of the canister to the OFF or CLOSED position.

**4** Remove the fuel injector cleaning canister's top and regulator assembly. Note that there is an O-ring seal located here that must be in place for the canister's top to seal properly.

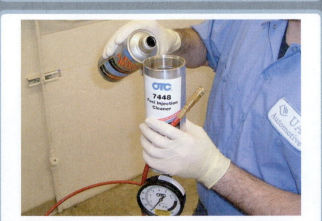

**5** Pour the injection system cleaning fluid into the open canister. Rubber gloves are highly recommended for this step as the fluid is toxic.

**6** Replace the canister's top (making sure it is tight) and connect its hose to the fuel rail adapter. Be sure that the hose is routed away from exhaust manifolds and other hazards.

CONTINUED ▶

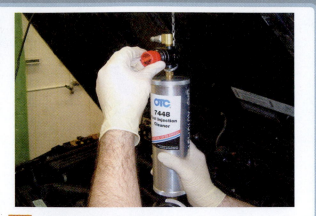

**7** Hang the canister from the vehicle's hood and adjust the air pressure regulator to full OPEN position (CCW).

**8** Connect shop air to the canister and adjust the air pressure regulator to the desired setting. Canister pressure can be read directly from the gauge.

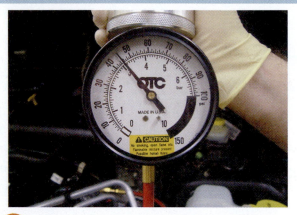

**9** Canister pressure should be adjusted to 5 PSI below system fuel pressure. An alternative for return-type systems is to block the fuel return line to the tank.

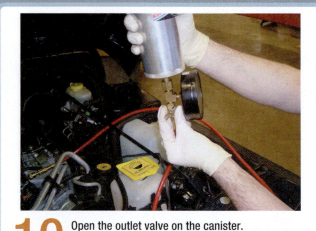

**10** Open the outlet valve on the canister.

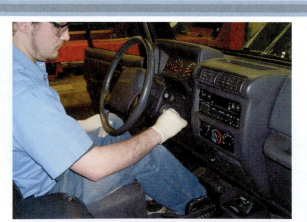

**11** Start the vehicle's engine and let run at 1000–1500 RPM. The engine is now running on fuel injector cleaning fluid provided by the canister.

**12** Continue the process until the canister is empty and the engine stalls. Remove the cleaning equipment, enable the vehicle's fuel pump, and run the engine to check for leaks.

1. A typical fuel-injection system fuel pressure should not drop more than 20 PSI in 20 minutes.

2. A noid light can be used to check for the presence of an injector pulse.

3. Injectors can be tested for resistance and should be within 0.3 to 0.4 ohms of each other.

4. Different designs of injectors have a different scope waveform depending on how the computer pulses the injector on and off.

5. An idle air control unit controls idle speed and can be tested for proper operation using a scan tool.

## REVIEW QUESTIONS

1. List the ways fuel injectors can be tested.
2. List the steps necessary to test a fuel-pressure regulator.
3. Describe why it may be necessary to clean the throttle plate of a port fuel-injected engine.

## CHAPTER QUIZ

1. Most port fuel-injected engines operate on how much fuel pressure?
   a. 3 to 5 PSI (21 to 35 kPa)
   b. 9 to 13 PSI (62 to 90 kPa)
   c. 35 to 45 PSI (240 to 310 kPa)
   d. 55 to 65 PSI (380 to 450 kPa)

2. Fuel injectors can be tested using _____.
   a. An ohmmeter
   b. A stethoscope
   c. A scope
   d. All of the above

3. Throttle-body fuel-injection systems use what type of injector driver?
   a. Peak and hold
   b. Saturated switch
   c. Pulse-width modulated
   d. Pulsed

4. Port fuel-injection systems generally use what type of injector driver?
   a. Peak and hold
   b. Saturated switch
   c. Pulse-width modulated
   d. Pulsed

5. The vacuum hose from the fuel-pressure regulator was removed from the regulator and gasoline dripped out of the hose. Technician A says that is normal and that everything is okay. Technician B says that one or more of the injectors may be defective, causing the fuel to get into the hose. Which technician is correct?
   a. Technician A only
   b. Technician B only
   c. Both Technicians A and B
   d. Neither Technician A nor B

6. The fuel pressure drops rapidly when the engine is turned off. Technician A says that one or more injectors could be leaking. Technician B says that a defective check valve in the fuel pump could be the cause. Which technician is correct?
   a. Technician A only
   b. Technician B only
   c. Both Technicians A and B
   d. Neither Technician A nor B

7. In a typical port fuel-injection system, which injectors are most subject to becoming restricted?
   a. Any of them equally
   b. The injectors at the end of the rail on a returnless system
   c. The injectors at the bends in the rail
   d. Either b or c

8. What component pulses the fuel injector on most vehicles?
   a. Powertrain control module (PCM)
   b. Ignition module
   c. Crankshaft sensor
   d. Both b and c

9. Fuel-injection service is being discussed. Technician A says that the throttle plate(s) should be cleaned. Technician B says that the fuel rail should be cleaned. Which technician is correct?
   a. Technician A only
   b. Technician B only
   c. Both Technicians A and B
   d. Neither Technician A nor B

10. If the throttle plate needs to be cleaned, what symptoms will be present regarding the operation of the engine?
    a. Stalls
    b. Rough idle
    c. Hesitation on acceleration
    d. All of the above

# chapter 23

# VEHICLE EMISSION STANDARDS AND TESTING

**OBJECTIVES:** After studying Chapter 23, the reader will be able to: • Prepare for ASE A8 certification test content area "D" (Emissions Control Systems Diagnosis and Repair) and ASE L1 certification test content area "F" (I/M Failure Diagnosis). • Discuss emission standards. • Identify the reasons why excessive amounts of HC, CO, and $NO_X$ exhaust emissions are created. • Describe how to baseline a vehicle after an exhaust emission failure. • List acceptable levels of HC, CO, $CO_2$, and $O_2$ with and without a catalytic converter. • List four possible causes for high readings for HC, CO, and $NO_X$.

**KEY TERMS:** Acceleration simulation mode (ASM) 307 • ASM 25/25 test 307 • ASM 50/15 test 307 • Clean Air Act Amendments (CAAA) 304 • Federal Test Procedure (FTP) 306 • I/M 240 test 308 • Lean indicator 311 • Non-methane hydrocarbon (NMHC) 309 • Ozone 311 • Rich indicator 310 • Sealed Housing for Evaporative Determination (SHED) test 306 • Smog 311 • State Implementation Plan (SIP) 306

## EMISSION STANDARDS IN THE UNITED STATES

In the United States, emissions standards are managed by the Environmental Protection Agency (EPA) as well as some U.S. state governments. Some of the strictest standards in the world are formulated in California by the California Air Resources Board (CARB).

**TIER 1 AND TIER 2** Federal emission standards are set by the **Clean Air Act Amendments (CAAA)** of 1990 grouped by tier. All vehicles sold in the United States must meet Tier 1 standards that went into effect in 1994 and are the least stringent. Additional Tier 2 standards have been optional since 2001, and was fully phased in by 2009. The current Tier 1 standards are different between automobiles and light trucks (SUVs, pickup trucks, and minivans), but Tier 2 standards will be the same for both types of vehicles.

There are several ratings that can be given to vehicles, and a certain percentage of a manufacturer's vehicles must meet different levels in order for the company to sell its products in affected regions. Beyond Tier 1, and in order by stringency, are the following levels:

- **TLEV Transitional Low-Emission Vehicle.** More stringent for HC than Tier 1.
- **LEV:** (also known as: **LEV I**) **Low-Emission Vehicle,** an intermediate California standard about twice as stringent as Tier 1 for HC and $NO_X$.

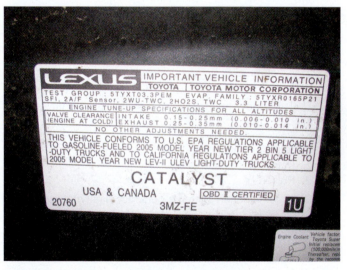

**FIGURE 23–1** The underhood decal showing that this Lexus RX-330 meets both national (Tier 2; BIN 5) and California LEV-II (ULEV) regulation standards.

- **ULEV** (also known as **ULEV I**): **Ultra-Low-Emission Vehicle.** A stronger California standard emphasizing very low HC emissions.
- **ULEV II: Ultra-Low-Emission Vehicle.** A cleaner-than-average vehicle certified under the Phase II LEV standard. Hydrocarbon and carbon monoxide emissions levels are nearly 50% lower than those of a LEV II-certified vehicle.
  ● **SEE FIGURE 23–1.**
- **SULEV: Super-Ultra-Low-Emission Vehicle.** A California standard even tighter than ULEV, including much

lower HC and $NO_x$ emissions; roughly equivalent to Tier 2 Bin 2 vehicles.

- **ZEV: Zero-Emission Vehicle.** A California standard prohibiting any tailpipe emissions. The ZEV category is largely restricted to electric vehicles and hydrogen-fueled vehicles. In these cases, any emissions that are created are produced at another site, such as a power plant or hydrogen reforming center, unless such sites run on renewable energy.

  **NOTE: A battery-powered electric vehicle charged from the power grid will still be up to 10 times cleaner than even the cleanest gasoline vehicles over their respective lifetimes.**

- **PZEV: Partial Zero-Emission Vehicle.** Compliant with the SULEV standard; additionally has near-zero evaporative emissions and a 15-year/150,000-mile warranty on its emission control equipment.

Tier 2 standards are even more stringent. Tier 2 variations are appended with "II," such as LEV II or SULEV II. Other categories have also been created:

- **ILEV: Inherently Low-Emission Vehicle** - a vehicle certified to meet the transitional low-emission vehicle standards established by the California Air Resources Board (CARB)

- **AT-PZEV: Advanced Technology Partial Zero-Emission Vehicle.** If a vehicle meets the PZEV standards and is using high-technology features, such as an electric motor or high-pressure gaseous fuel tanks for compressed natural gas, it qualifies as an AT-PZEV. Hybrid electric vehicles such as the Toyota Prius can qualify, as can internal combustion engine vehicles that run on natural gas (CNG), such as the Honda Civic GX. These vehicles are classified as "partial" ZEV because they receive partial credit for the number of ZEV vehicles that automakers would otherwise be required to sell in California.

- **NLEV: National Low-Emission Vehicle.** All vehicles nationwide must meet this standard, which started in 2001.

### FEDERAL EPA BIN NUMBER
The higher the tier number, the newer the regulation; the lower the bin number, the cleaner the vehicle. The Toyota Prius is a very clean Bin 3, while the Hummer H2 is a dirty Bin 11. ● **SEE CHARTS 23–1, 23–2, AND 23–3.**

### SMOG EMISSION INFORMATION
New vehicles are equipped with a sticker that shows the relative level of smog-causing emissions created by the vehicle compared to others on the market. Smog-causing emissions include unburned hydrocarbons (HC) and oxides of nitrogen ($NO_x$). ● **SEE FIGURE 23–2.**

### CALIFORNIA STANDARDS
The pre-2004 California Air Resources Board (CARB) standards as a whole were known as LEV I. Within that, there were four possible ratings: Tier 1, TLEV, LEV, and ULEV. The newest CARB rating system (since January 1, 2004) is known as LEV II. Within that rating system there are three primary ratings: LEV, ULEV, and SULEV. States other than California are given the option to use the federal EPA standards, or they can adopt California's standards.

| CERTIFICATION LEVEL | NMOG (G/MI) | CO (G/MI) | NO$_x$ (G/MI) |
|---|---|---|---|
| Bin 1 | 0.0 | 0.0 | 0.0 |
| Bin 2 | 0.010 | 2.1 | 0.02 |
| Bin 3 | 0.055 | 2.1 | 0.03 |
| Bin 4 | 0.070 | 2.1 | 0.04 |
| Bin 5 | 0.090 | 4.2 | 0.07 |
| Bin 6 | 0.090 | 4.2 | 0.10 |
| Bin 7 | 0.090 | 4.2 | 0.15 |
| Bin 8a | 0.125 | 4.2 | 0.20 |
| Bin 8b | 0.156 | 4.2 | 0.20 |
| Bin 9a | 0.090 | 4.2 | 0.30 |
| Bin 9b | 0.130 | 4.2 | 0.30 |
| Bin 9c | 0.180 | 4.2 | 0.30 |
| Bin 10a | 0.156 | 4.2 | 0.60 |
| Bin 10b | 0.230 | 6.4 | 0.60 |
| Bin 10c | 0.230 | 6.4 | 0.60 |
| Bin 11 | 0.230 | 7.3 | 0.90 |

**CHART 23–1**

EPA Tier 2—120,000-Mile Tailpipe Emission Limits. NMOG stands for non-methane organic gases which is a measure of all gases except those often created naturally by animals. After January 2007, the highest allowable Bin is 7.
*Source:* Data compiled from the Environmental Protection Agency (EPA).

NOTE: The bin number is determined by the type and weight of the vehicle.

| U.S. EPA VEHICLE INFORMATION PROGRAM (THE HIGHER THE SCORE, THE LOWER THE EMISSIONS) | |
|---|---|
| SELECTED EMISSIONS STANDARDS | SCORE |
| Bin 1 and ZEV | 10 |
| PZEV | 9.5 |
| Bin 2 | 9 |
| Bin 3 | 8 |
| Bin 4 | 7 |
| Bin 5 and LEV II cars | 6 |
| Bin 6 | 5 |
| Bin 7 | 4 |
| Bin 8 | 3 |
| Bin 9a and LEV I cars | 2 |
| Bin 9b | 2 |
| Bin 10a | 1 |
| Bin 10b and Tier 1 cars | 1 |
| Bin 11 | 0 |

**CHART 23–2**

Air Pollution Score
*Source:* Courtesy of the Environmental Protection Agency (EPA).

| MINIMUM FUEL ECONOMY (MPG) COMBINED CITY-HIGHWAY LABEL VALUE | | | | | |
|---|---|---|---|---|---|
| SCORE | GASOLINE | DIESEL | E-85 | LPG | CNG* |
| 10 | 44 | 50 | 31 | 28 | 33 |
| 9 | 36 | 41 | 26 | 23 | 27 |
| 8 | 30 | 35 | 22 | 20 | 23 |
| 7 | 26 | 30 | 19 | 17 | 20 |
| 6 | 23 | 27 | 17 | 15 | 18 |
| 5 | 21 | 24 | 15 | 14 | 16 |
| 4 | 19 | 22 | 14 | 12 | 14 |
| 3 | 17 | 20 | 12 | 11 | 13 |
| 2 | 16 | 18 | — | — | 12 |
| 1 | 15 | 17 | 11 | 10 | 11 |
| 0 | 14 | 16 | 10 | 9 | 10 |

**CHART 23–3**

Greenhouse Gas Score
*Source:* Courtesy of the Environmental Protection Agency (EPA).
*CNG assumes a gallon equivalent of 121.5 cubic feet.

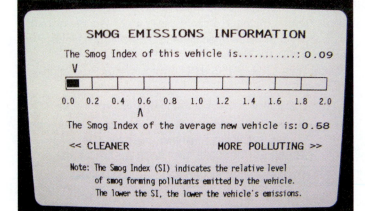

**FIGURE 23–2** This label on a Toyota Camry hybrid shows the relative smog-producing emissions, but this does not include carbon dioxide ($CO_2$), which may increase global warming.

# EUROPEAN STANDARDS

Europe has its own set of standards that vehicles must meet, which includes the following tiers:

- Euro I (1992–1995)
- Euro II (1995–1999)
- Euro III (1999–2005)
- Euro IV (2005–2008)
- Euro V (2008+)

Vehicle emission standards and technological advancements have successfully reduced pollution from cars and trucks by about 90% since the 1970s. Unfortunately, there currently are more vehicles on the road and they are being driven more miles each year, partially offsetting the environmental benefits of individual vehicle emissions reductions.

# EXHAUST ANALYSIS TESTING

The Clean Air Act Amendments require enhanced Inspection and Maintenance (I/M) programs in areas of the country that have the worst air quality and the Northeast Ozone Transport region. The states must submit to the EPA a **State Implementation Plan (SIP)** for their programs. Each enhanced I/M program is required to include as a minimum the following items:

- Computerized emission analyzers
- Visual inspection of emission control items
- Minimum waiver limit (to be increased based on the inflation index)
- Remote on-road testing of one-half of 1% of the vehicle population
- Registration denial for vehicles not passing an I/M test
- Denial of waiver for vehicles that are under warranty or that have been tampered with
- Annual inspections
- OBD-II systems check for 1996 and newer vehicles

**FEDERAL TEST PROCEDURE (FTP)** The **Federal Test Procedure (FTP)** is the test used to certify all new vehicles before they can be sold. Once a vehicle meets these standards, it is certified by the EPA for sale in the United States. The FTP test procedure is a loaded-mode test lasting for a total duration of 505 seconds and is designed to simulate an urban driving trip. A cold start-up representing a morning start and a hot start after a soak period is part of the test. In addition to this drive cycle, a vehicle must undergo evaporative testing. Evaporative emissions are determined using the **Sealed Housing for Evaporative Determination (SHED)** test, which measures the evaporative emissions from the vehicle after a heat-up period representing a vehicle sitting in the sun. In addition, the vehicle is driven and then tested during the hot soak period.

**NOTE: A SHED is constructed entirely of stainless steel. The walls, floors, and ceiling, plus the door, are all constructed of stainless steel because it does not absorb hydrocarbons, which could offset test results.**

The FTP is a much more stringent test of vehicle emissions than is any test type that uses equipment that measures percentages of exhaust gases. The federal emission standards for each model year vehicle are the same for that model regardless of what size engine the vehicle is equipped with. This is why larger V-8 engines often are equipped with more emission control devices than smaller four- and six-cylinder engines.

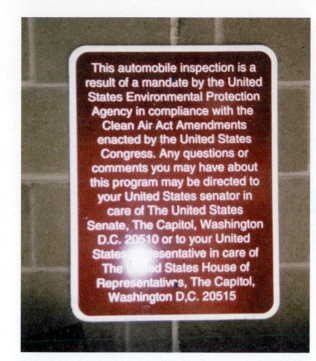

FIGURE 23–3 Photo of a sign taken at an emissions test facility.

FIGURE 23–4 A vehicle being tested during an enhanced emission test.

## I/M TEST PROGRAMS

There are a variety of I/M testing programs that have been implemented by the various states. These programs may be centralized testing programs or decentralized testing programs. Each state is free to develop a testing program suitable to their needs as long as they can demonstrate to the EPA that their plan will achieve the attainment levels set by the EPA. This approach has led to a variety of different testing programs. ● SEE FIGURE 23–3.

## VISUAL TAMPERING CHECKS

Visual tampering checks may be part of an I/M testing program and usually include checking for the following items:

- Catalytic converter
- Fuel tank inlet restrictor
- Exhaust gas recirculation (EGR)
- Evaporative emission system
- Air-injection reaction system (AIR)
- Positive crankcase ventilation (PCV)

If any of these systems are missing, not connected, or tampered with, the vehicle will fail the emissions test and will have to be repaired/replaced by the vehicle owner before the vehicle can pass the emission test. Any cost associated with repairing or replacing these components may not be used toward the waiver amount required for the vehicle to receive a waiver.

## ONE-SPEED AND TWO-SPEED IDLE TEST

The one-speed and two-speed idle test measures the exhaust emissions from the tailpipe of the vehicle at idle and/or at 2500 RPM. This uses stand-alone exhaust gas sampling equipment that measures the emissions in percentages. Each state chooses the standards that the vehicle has to meet in order to pass the test. The advantage to using this type of testing is that the equipment is relatively cheap and allows states to have decentralized testing programs because many facilities can afford the necessary equipment required to perform this test.

## LOADED MODE TEST

The loaded mode test uses a dynamometer that places a "single weight" load on the vehicle. The load applied to the vehicle varies with the speed of the vehicle. Typically, a four-cylinder vehicle speed would be 24 mph, a six-cylinder vehicle speed would be 30 mph, and an eight-cylinder vehicle speed would be 34 mph. Conventional stand-alone sampling equipment is used to measure HC and CO emissions. This type of test is classified as a Basic I/M test by the EPA. ● SEE FIGURE 23–4.

## ACCELERATION SIMULATION MODE (ASM)

The ASM-type of test uses a dynamometer that applies a heavy load on the vehicle at a steady-state speed. The load applied to the vehicle is based on the acceleration rate on the second simulated hill of the FTP. This acceleration rate is 3.3 mph/sec/sec (read as 3.3 mph per second per second, which is the unit of acceleration). There are different ASM tests used by different states.

The ASM 50/15 test places a load of 50% on the vehicle at a steady 15 mph. This load represents 50% of the horsepower required to simulate the FTP acceleration rate of 3.3 mph/sec. This type of test produces relatively high levels of $NO_x$ emissions; therefore, it is useful in detecting vehicles that are emitting excessive $NO_x$.

The ASM 25/25 test places a 25% load on the vehicle while it is driven at a steady 25 mph. This represents 25% of the load required to simulate the FTP acceleration rate of 3.3 mph/sec. Because this applies a smaller load on the vehicle at a higher speed, it will produce a higher level of HC and CO emissions than the ASM 50/15. $NO_x$ emissions will tend to be lower with this type of test.

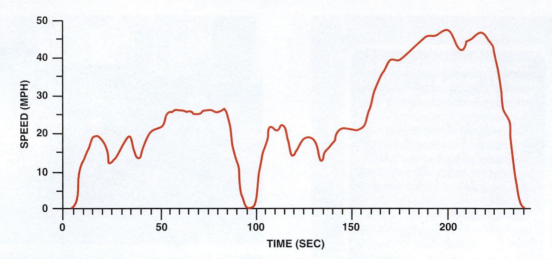

**FIGURE 23-5** Trace showing the Inspection/Maintenance 240 test. The test duplicates an urban test loop around Los Angeles, California. The first "hump" in the curve represents the vehicle being accelerated to about 20 mph, then driving up a small hill to about 30 mph and coming to a stop at 94 seconds. Then, the vehicle accelerates while climbing a hill and speeding up to about 50 mph during this second phase of the test.

**I/M 240 TEST** The **I/M 240** test is the EPA's enhanced test. It is actually a portion of the 505-second FTP test used by the manufacturers to certify their new vehicles. The "240" stands for 240 seconds of drive time on a dynamometer. This is a loaded-mode transient test that uses constant volume sampling equipment to measure the exhaust emissions in mass just as is done during the FTP. The I/M 240 test simulates the first two hills of the FTP drive cycle. ● **FIGURE 23-5** shows the I/M 240 drive trace.

**OBD-II TESTING** In 1999, the EPA requested that states adopt OBD-II systems testing for 1996 and newer vehicles. The OBD-II system is designed to illuminate the MIL light and store trouble codes any time a malfunction exists that would cause the vehicle emissions to exceed 1 1/2 times the FTP limits. If the OBD-II system is working correctly, the system should be able to detect a vehicle failure that would cause emissions to increase to an unacceptable level. The EPA has determined that the OBD-II system should detect emission failures of a vehicle even before that vehicle would fail an emissions test of the type that most states are employing. Furthermore, the EPA has determined that, as the population of OBD-II-equipped vehicles increases and the population of older non-OBD-II-equipped vehicles decreases, tailpipe testing will no longer be necessary.

The OBD-II testing program consists of a computer that can scan the vehicle OBD-II system using the DLC connector. The technician first performs a visual check of the vehicle MIL light to determine if it is working correctly. Next, the computer is connected to the vehicle's DLC connector. The computer will scan the vehicle OBD-II system and determine if there are any codes stored that are commanding the MIL light on. In addition, it will scan the status of the readiness monitors and determine if they have all run and passed. If the readiness monitors have all run and passed, it indicates that the OBD-II system has tested all the components of the emission control system. An OBD-II vehicle would fail this OBD-II test if:

- The MIL light does not come on with the key on, engine off
- The MIL is commanded on
- A number (varies by state) of the readiness monitors have not been run

If none of these conditions are present, the vehicle will pass the emissions test.

**REMOTE SENSING** The EPA requires that, in high-enhanced areas, states perform on-the-road testing of vehicle emissions. The state must sample 0.5% of the vehicle population base in high-enhanced areas. This may be accomplished by using a remote sensing device. This type of sensing may be done through equipment that projects an infrared light through the exhaust stream of a passing vehicle. The reflected beam can then be analyzed to determine the pollutant levels coming from the vehicle. If a vehicle fails this type of test, the vehicle owner will receive notification in the mail that he or she must take the vehicle to a test facility to have the emissions tested.

**RANDOM ROADSIDE TESTING** Some states may implement random roadside testing that would usually involve visual checks of the emission control devices to detect tampering. Obviously, this method is not very popular as it can lead to traffic tie-ups and delays on the part of commuters.

Exhaust analysis is an excellent tool to use for the diagnosis of engine performance concerns. In areas of the country that require exhaust testing to be able to get license plates, exhaust analysis must be able to:

- Establish a baseline for failure diagnosis and service.
- Identify areas of engine performance that are and are not functioning correctly.
- Determine that the service and repair of the vehicle have been accomplished and are complete.

**FIGURE 23–6** A partial stream sampling exhaust probe being used to measure exhaust gases in parts per million (PPM) or percent (%).

# EXHAUST ANALYSIS AND COMBUSTION EFFICIENCY

A popular method of engine analysis, as well as emission testing, involves the use of five-gas exhaust analysis equipment.
● SEE FIGURE 23–6. The five gases analyzed and their significance include:

### HYDROCARBONS
Hydrocarbons (HC) are unburned gasoline and are measured in parts per million (ppm). A correctly operating engine should burn (oxidize) almost all the gasoline; therefore, very little unburned gasoline should be present in the exhaust. Acceptable levels of HC are 50 PPM or less. High levels of HC could be due to excessive oil consumption caused by weak piston rings or worn valve guides. The most common cause of excessive HC emissions is a fault in the ignition system. Items that should be checked include:

- Spark plugs
- Spark plug wires
- Distributor cap and rotor (if the vehicle is so equipped)
- Ignition timing (if possible)
- Ignition coil

### CARBON MONOXIDE
Carbon monoxide (CO) is unstable and will easily combine with any oxygen to form stable carbon dioxide ($CO_2$). The fact that CO combines with oxygen is the reason that CO is a poisonous gas (in the lungs, it combines with oxygen to form $CO_2$ and deprives the brain of oxygen). CO levels of a properly operating engine should be less than 0.5%. High levels of CO can be caused by

clogged or restricted crankcase ventilation devices such as the PCV valve, hose(s), and tubes. Other items that might cause excessive CO include:

- Clogged air filter
- Incorrect idle speed
- Too-high fuel-pump pressure
- Any other items that can cause a rich condition

### CARBON DIOXIDE ($CO_2$)
Carbon dioxide ($CO_2$) is the result of oxygen in the engine combining with the carbon of the gasoline. An acceptable level of $CO_2$ is between 12% and 15%. A high reading indicates an efficiently operating engine. If the $CO_2$ level is low, the mixture may be either too rich or too lean.

### OXYGEN
The next gas is oxygen ($O_2$). There is about 21% oxygen in the atmosphere, and most of this oxygen should be "used up" during the combustion process to oxidize all the hydrogen and carbon (hydrocarbons) in the gasoline. Levels of $O_2$ should be very low (about 0.5%). High levels of $O_2$, especially at idle, could be due to an exhaust system leak.

**NOTE: Adding 10% alcohol to gasoline provides additional oxygen to the fuel and will result in lower levels of CO and higher levels of $O_2$ in the exhaust.**

### OXIDES OF NITROGEN ($NO_x$)
An oxide of nitrogen (NO) is a colorless, tasteless, and odorless gas when it leaves the engine, but as soon as it reaches the atmosphere and mixes with more oxygen, nitrogen oxides ($NO_2$) are formed. $NO_2$ is reddish-brown and has an acid and pungent smell. NO and $NO_2$ are grouped together and referred to as $NO_x$, where x represents any number of oxygen atoms. $NO_x$, the symbol used to represent all oxides of nitrogen, is the fifth gas commonly tested using a five-gas analyzer. The exhaust gas recirculation (EGR) system is the major controlling device limiting the formation of $NO_x$.

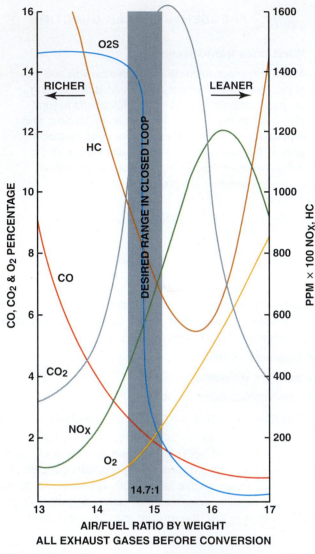

**FIGURE 23–7** Exhaust emissions are very complex. When the air–fuel mixture becomes richer, some exhaust emissions are reduced, while others increase.

Acceptable exhaust emissions include:

|  | Without Catalytic Converter | With Catalytic Converter |
|---|---|---|
| HC | 300 PPM or less | 30 to 50 PPM or less |
| CO | 3% or less | 0.3% to 0.5% or less |
| $O_2$ | 0% to 2% | 0% to 2% |
| $CO_2$ | 12% to 15% or higher | 12% to 15% or higher |
| $NO_x$ | Less than 100 PPM at idle and less than 1,000 PPM at WOT | Less than 100 PPM at idle and less than 1,000 PPM at WOT |

● **SEE FIGURE 23–7.**

## HC TOO HIGH

High hydrocarbon exhaust emissions are usually caused by an engine misfire. What burns the fuel in an engine? The ignition system ignites a spark at the spark plug to ignite the proper mixture inside the combustion chamber. If a spark plug does not ignite the mixture, the resulting unburned fuel is pushed out of the cylinder on the exhaust stroke by the piston through the exhaust valves and into the exhaust system. Therefore, if any of the following ignition components or adjustments are not correct, excessive HC emission is likely.

1. Defective or worn spark plugs
2. Defective or loose spark plug wires
3. Defective distributor cap and/or rotor
4. Incorrect ignition timing (either too far advanced or too far retarded)
5. A lean air–fuel mixture can also cause a misfire. This condition is referred to as a lean misfire. A lean air-fuel mixture can be caused by low fuel pump pressure, a clogged fuel filter or a restricted fuel injector.

**NOTE: To make discussion easier in future reference to these items, this list of ignition components and checks can be referred to simply as "spark stuff."**

## CO TOO HIGH

Excessive carbon monoxide is an indication of too rich an air–fuel mixture. CO is the **rich indicator.** The higher the CO reading, the richer the air–fuel mixture. High concentrations of CO indicate that not enough oxygen was available for the amount of fuel. Common causes of high CO include:

- Too-high fuel-pump pressure
- Defective fuel-pressure regulator

**CO Equals O$_2$**

If the exhaust is rich, CO emissions will be higher than normal. If the exhaust is lean, O$_2$ emissions will be higher than normal. Therefore, if the CO reading is the same as the O$_2$ reading, then the engine is operating correctly. For example, if both CO and O$_2$ are 0.5% and the engine develops a vacuum leak, the O$_2$ will rise. If a fuel-pressure regulator were to malfunction, the resulting richer air–fuel mixture would increase CO emissions. Therefore, if both the rich indicator (CO) and the lean indicator (O$_2$) are equal, the engine is operating correctly.

■ Clogged air filter or PCV valve

**NOTE: One technician remembers "CO" as meaning "clogged oxygen" and always looks for restricted airflow into the engine whenever high CO levels are detected.**

■ Defective injectors

# MEASURING OXYGEN (O$_2$) AND CARBON DIOXIDE (CO$_2$)

Two gas exhaust analyzers (HC and CO) work well, but both HC and CO are consumed (converted) inside the catalytic converter. The amount of leftover oxygen coming out of the tailpipe is an indication of leanness. The higher the O$_2$ level, the leaner the exhaust. Oxygen therefore is the **lean indicator.** Acceptable levels of O$_2$ are 0% to 2%.

**NOTE: A hole in the exhaust system can draw outside air (oxygen) into the exhaust system. Therefore, to be assured of an accurate reading, carefully check the exhaust system for leaks. Using a smoke machine is an easy method to locate leaks in the exhaust system.**

Carbon dioxide (CO$_2$) is a measure of efficiency. The higher the level of CO$_2$ in the exhaust stream, the more efficiently the engine is operating. Levels of 12% to 15% are considered to be acceptable. Because CO$_2$ levels peak at an air–fuel mixture of 14.7:1, a lower level of CO$_2$ indicates either a too-rich or a too-lean condition. The CO$_2$ measurement by itself does not indicate which condition is present. For example:

CO$_2$ = 8% (This means efficiency is low and the air–fuel mixture is not correct.)

Look at O$_2$ and CO levels.

A high O$_2$ indicates lean and a high CO indicates rich.

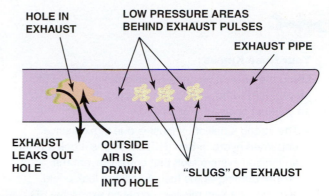

**FIGURE 23–8** A hole in the exhaust system can cause outside air (containing oxygen) to be drawn into the exhaust system. This extra oxygen can be confusing to a service technician because the extra O$_2$ in the exhaust stream could be misinterpreted as a too-lean air–fuel mixture.

**How to Find a Leak in the Exhaust System**

A hole in the exhaust system can dilute the exhaust gases with additional oxygen (O$_2$). ● SEE FIGURE 23–8.

This additional O$_2$ in the exhaust can lead the service technician to believe that the air–fuel mixture is too lean. To help identify an exhaust leak, perform an exhaust analysis at idle and at 2500 RPM (fast idle) and compare with the following:

• If the O$_2$ is high at idle and at 2500 RPM, the mixture is lean at both idle and at 2500 RPM.

• If the O$_2$ is low at idle and high at 2500 RPM, this usually means that the vehicle is equipped with a working AIR pump.

• If the O$_2$ is high at idle, but okay at 2500 RPM, a hole in the exhaust or a small vacuum leak that is "covered up" at higher speed is indicated.

# PHOTOCHEMICAL SMOG FORMATION

Oxides of nitrogen are formed by high temperature—over 2500°F (1370°C)—and/or pressures inside the combustion chamber. Oxides of nitrogen contribute to the formation of photochemical **smog** when sunlight reacts chemically with NO$_X$ and unburned hydrocarbons (HC). Smog is a term derived by combining the words *smoke* and *fog*. Ground-level ozone is a constituent of smog. **Ozone** is an enriched oxygen molecule with three atoms of oxygen (O$_3$) instead of the normal two atoms of oxygen (O$_2$).

Ozone in the upper atmosphere is beneficial because it blocks out harmful ultraviolet rays that contribute to skin cancer. However, at ground level, this ozone (smog) is an irritant to the respiratory system.

### Your Nose Knows

Using the nose, a technician can often identify a major problem without having to connect the vehicle to an exhaust analyzer. For example,

- The strong smell of exhaust is due to excessive unburned hydrocarbon (HC) emissions. Look for an ignition system fault that could prevent the proper burning of the fuel. A vacuum leak could also cause a lean misfire and cause excessive HC exhaust emissions.
- If your eyes start to burn or water, suspect excessive oxides of nitrogen ($NO_x$) emissions. The oxides of nitrogen combine with the moisture in the eyes to form a mild solution of nitric acid. The acid formation causes the eyes to burn and water. Excessive $NO_x$ exhaust emissions can be caused by:
  - A vacuum leak causing higher-than-normal combustion chamber temperatures
  - Overadvanced ignition timing causing higher-than-normal combustion chamber temperatures
  - Lack of proper amount of exhaust gas recirculation (EGR) (This is usually noticed above idle on most vehicles.)
- Dizzy feeling or headache. This is commonly caused by excessive carbon monoxide (CO) exhaust emissions. Get into fresh air as soon as possible. A probable cause of high levels of CO is an excessively rich air–fuel mixture.

## TESTING FOR OXIDES OF NITROGEN

Because the formation of $NO_x$ occurs mostly under load, the most efficient method to test for $NO_x$ is to use a portable exhaust analyzer that can be carried in the vehicle while the vehicle is being driven under a variety of conditions.

**SPECIFICATIONS FOR $NO_x$** From experience, a maximum reading of 1,000 parts per million (PPM) of $NO_x$ under loaded driving conditions will generally mean that the vehicle will pass an enhanced I/M roller test. A reading of over 100 PPM at idle should be considered excessive.

### Check for Dog Food?

A commonly experienced problem in many parts of the country involves squirrels or other animals placing dog food into the air intake ducts of vehicles. Dog food is often found packed tight in the ducts against the air filter. An air intake restriction reduces engine power and vehicle performance.

### The Case of the Retarded Exhaust Camshaft

A Toyota equipped with a double overhead camshaft (DOHC) inline six-cylinder engine failed the state-mandated enhanced exhaust emission test for $NO_x$. The engine ran perfectly without spark knocking (ping), which is usually a major reason for excessive $NO_x$ emissions. The technician checked the following:

- The ignition timing, which was found to be set to specifications (if too far advanced, can cause excessive $NO_x$)
- The cylinders, which were decarbonized using top engine cleaner
- The EGR valve, which was inspected and the EGR passages cleaned

After all the items were completed, the vehicle was returned to the inspection station where the vehicle again failed for excessive $NO_x$ emissions (better, but still over the maximum allowable limit).

After additional hours of troubleshooting, the technician decided to go back to basics and start over again. A check of the vehicle history with the owner indicated that the only previous work performed on the engine was a replacement timing belt over a year before. The technician discovered that the exhaust cam timing was retarded two teeth, resulting in late closing of the exhaust valve. The proper exhaust valve timing resulted in a slight amount of exhaust being retained in the cylinder. This extra exhaust was added to the amount supplied by the EGR valve and helped reduce $NO_x$ emissions. After repositioning the timing belt, the vehicle passed the emissions test well within the limits.

## Exhaust Gas Summary Chart

| Gas | Cause and Correction |
|---|---|
| High HC | Engine misfire or incomplete burning of fuel caused by:<br>1. Ignition system fault<br>2. Lean misfire<br>3. Too low an engine temperature (thermostat) |
| High CO | Rich condition caused by:<br>1. Leaking fuel injectors or fuel-pressure regulator<br>2. Clogged air filter or PCV system<br>3. Excessive fuel pressure |
| High HC and CO | Excessively rich condition caused by:<br>1. All items included under high CO<br>2. Fouled spark plugs causing a misfire to occur<br>3. Possible nonoperating catalytic converter |
| High $NO_x$ | Excessive combustion chamber temperature:<br>1. Nonoperating EGR valve<br>2. Clogged EGR passages<br>3. Engine operating temperature too high due to cooling system restriction, worn water pump impeller, or other faults in the cooling system<br>4. Lean air–fuel mixture<br>5. High compression caused by excessive carbon buildup in the cylinders |

### REAL WORLD FIX

**O2S Shows Rich, but Pulse Width Is Low**

A service technician was attempting to solve a driveability problem. The computer did not indicate any diagnostic trouble codes (DTCs). A check of the oxygen sensor voltage indicated a higher-than-normal reading almost all the time. The pulse width to the port injectors was lower than normal. The lower-than-normal pulse width indicates that the computer is attempting to reduce fuel flow into the engine by decreasing the amount of on-time for all the injectors.

What could cause a rich mixture if the injectors were being commanded to deliver a lean mixture? Finally the technician shut off the engine and took a careful look at the entire fuel-injection system. Although the vacuum hose was removed from the fuel-pressure regulator, fuel was found dripping from the vacuum hose. The problem was a defective fuel-pressure regulator that allowed an uncontrolled amount of fuel to be drawn by the intake manifold vacuum into the cylinders. While the computer tried to reduce fuel by reducing the pulse width signal to the injectors, the extra fuel being drawn directly from the fuel rail caused the engine to operate with too rich an air–fuel mixture.

## SUMMARY

1. Excessive hydrocarbon (HC) exhaust emissions are created by a lack of proper combustion such as a fault in the ignition system, too lean an air–fuel mixture, or too-cold engine operation.

2. Excessive carbon monoxide (CO) exhaust emissions are usually created by a rich air–fuel mixture.

3. Excessive oxides of nitrogen ($NO_x$) exhaust emissions are usually created by excessive heat or pressure in the combustion chamber or a lack of the proper amount of exhaust gas recirculation (EGR).

4. Carbon dioxide ($CO_2$) levels indicate efficiency. The higher the $CO_2$, the more efficient the engine operation.

5. Oxygen ($O_2$) indicates leanness. The higher the $O_2$, the leaner the air–fuel mixture.

6. A vehicle should be driven about 20 miles, especially during cold weather, to allow the engine to be fully warm before an enhanced emissions test.

## REVIEW QUESTIONS

1. List the five exhaust gases and their maximum allowable readings for a fuel-injected vehicle equipped with a catalytic converter.

2. List two causes of a rich exhaust.

3. List two causes of a lean exhaust.

4. List those items that should be checked if a vehicle fails an exhaust test for excessive $NO_x$ emissions.

1. Technician A says that high HC emission levels are often caused by a fault in the ignition system. Technician B says that high $CO_2$ emissions are usually caused by a richer-than-normal air–fuel mixture. Which technician is correct?
   a. Technician A only
   b. Technician B only
   c. Both Technicians A and B
   d. Neither Technician A nor B

2. HC and CO are high and $CO_2$ and $O_2$ are low. This could be caused by a _____.
   a. Rich mixture
   b. Lean mixture
   c. Defective ignition component
   d. Clogged EGR passage

3. Which gas is generally considered to be the rich indicator? (The higher the level of this gas, the richer the air–fuel mixture.)
   a. HC             c. $CO_2$
   b. CO             d. $O_2$

4. Which gas is generally considered to be the lean indicator? (The higher the level of this gas, the leaner the air–fuel mixture.)
   a. HC             c. $CO_2$
   b. CO             d. $O_2$

5. Which exhaust gas indicates efficiency? (The higher the level of this gas, the more efficient the engine operates.)
   a. HC             c. $CO_2$
   b. CO             d. $O_2$

6. All of the gases are measured in percentages except _____.
   a. HC             c. $CO_2$
   b. CO             d. $O_2$

7. After the following exhaust emissions were measured, how was the engine operating?
   HC = 766 PPM   $CO_2$ = 8.2%   CO = 4.6%   $O_2$ = 0.1%
   a. Too rich
   b. Too lean

8. Technician A says that carbon inside the engine can cause excessive $NO_x$ to form. Technician B says that excessive $NO_x$ could be caused by a cooling system fault causing the engine to operate too hot. Which technician is correct?
   a. Technician A only
   b. Technician B only
   c. Both Technicians A and B
   d. Neither Technician A nor B

9. A clogged EGR passage could cause excessive _____ exhaust emissions.
   a. HC             c. $NO_x$
   b. CO             d. $CO_2$

10. An ignition fault could cause excessive _____ exhaust emissions.
    a. HC             c. $NO_x$
    b. CO             d. $CO_2$

# chapter 24

# EMISSION CONTROL DEVICES OPERATION AND DIAGNOSIS

**OBJECTIVES:** After studying Chapter 24, the reader will be able to: • Prepare for the ASE Engine Performance (A8) certification test content area "D" (Emission Control Systems). • Describe the purpose and function of the exhaust gas recirculation (EGR) system. • Explain methods for diagnosing and testing for faults in the exhaust gas recirculation system. • Describe the purpose and function of the positive crankcase ventilation (PCV) and the secondary air-injection (SAI) reaction systems. • Explain methods for diagnosing and testing faults in the PCV and SAI systems. • Describe the purpose and function of the catalytic converter. • Explain the method for diagnosing and testing the catalytic converter. • Describe the purpose and function of the evaporative emission control system. • Discuss how the evaporative emission control system is tested under OBD-II regulations. • Explain methods for diagnosing and testing faults in the evaporative emission control system.

**KEY TERMS:** • Adsorption 334 • AIR 325 • Blowby 322 • Canister purge (CANP) 336 • Catalyst 328 • Catalytic converter 328 • Cerium 329 • Check valves 326 • Digital EGR 318 • DPFE sensor 319 • EGR 316 • EVP 318 • EVRV 320 • Fuel tank pressure (FTP) 339 • HO2S 329 • Inert 316 • Infrared thermometer (pyrometer) 331 • Leak detection pump (LDP) 337 • Light-off temperature 329 • Linear EGR 318 • LOC 329 • Mini converter 329 • Negative backpressure 317 • NOx 316 • OSC 329 • Palladium 329 • PCV 322 • PFE 318 • Platinum 329 • Positive backpressure 317 • Preconverter 329 • Pup converter 329 • Rhodium 329 • SAI 325 • Smog 315 • Smog pump 325 • Tap test 330 • Thermactor pump 325 • TWC 325 • Washcoat 328

## INTRODUCTION

Most of the major advances in engines are a direct result of the need to improve fuel economy and reduce exhaust emissions. The engine changes needed to meet the latest emission standards include:

- More efficient combustion chambers
- Low friction engine components such as low tension piston rings, roller camshaft followers (rockers), and roller lifters
- More precise ignition timing with coil-on-plug ignition systems, which have the ability to change ignition timing on individual cylinders as needed to achieve the highest possible efficiency
- Closer engine tolerances to reduce unburned fuel emissions and to improve power output
- Variable valve timing systems used to increase engine power and reduce exhaust emissions

It has been said that engine changes are due to the need to reduce three things.

1. Emissions
2. Emissions
3. Emissions

## SMOG

**DEFINITION AND TERMINOLOGY** The common term used to describe air pollution is **smog,** a word that combines two words: *smoke* and *fog*. Smog is formed in the atmosphere when sunlight combines with unburned fuel (hydrocarbon, or HC) and oxides of nitrogen (NOx) produced during the combustion process inside the cylinders of an engine. Carbon monoxide (CO) is a poisonous gas. Smog is ozone ($O_3$), a strong irritant to the lungs and eyes. Ozone is located two places.

1. Upper-atmospheric ozone is desirable because it blocks out harmful ultraviolet rays from the sun.
2. Ground-level ozone is considered to be unhealthy smog.

Emissions that are controlled include:

- **HC (unburned hydrocarbons).** Excessive HC emissions (unburned fuel) are controlled by the evaporative system (charcoal canister), the positive crankcase ventilation (PCV) system, the secondary air-injection (SAI) system, and the catalytic converter.
- **CO (carbon monoxide).** Excessive CO emissions are controlled by the positive crankcase ventilation (PCV) system, the secondary air-injection (SAI) system, and the catalytic converter.

**FIGURE 24-1** Notice the red-brown haze which is often over many major cities. This haze is the result of oxides or nitrogen in the atmosphere.

- **NOx (oxides of nitrogen).** Excessive NOx emissions are controlled by the exhaust gas recirculation (EGR) system and the catalytic converter. An oxide of nitrogen (NO) is a colorless, tasteless, and odorless gas when it leaves the engine, but as soon as it reaches the atmosphere and mixes with more oxygen, nitrogen oxides ($NO_2$) are formed, which appear as red-brown emissions. ● SEE FIGURE 24-1.

## EXHAUST GAS RECIRCULATION SYSTEMS

**INTRODUCTION** Exhaust gas recirculation (EGR) is an emission control system that lowers the amount of **nitrogen oxides (NOx)** formed during combustion. In the presence of sunlight, NOx reacts with hydrocarbons in the atmosphere to form ozone ($O_3$) or photochemical smog, an air pollutant.

**NOx FORMATION** Nitrogen ($N_2$) and oxygen ($O_2$) molecules are separated into individual atoms of nitrogen and oxygen during the combustion process. These molecules then bond to form NOx (NO, $NO_2$). When combustion flame front temperatures exceed 2,500°F (1,370°C), NOx is formed inside the cylinders which is then discharged into the atmosphere from the tailpipe.

**CONTROLLING NOx** To handle the NOx generated above 2,500°F (1,370°C), the most efficient method to meet NOx emissions without significantly affecting engine performance, fuel economy, and other exhaust emissions is to use exhaust gas recirculation (EGR). The EGR system routes small quantities,

usually between 6% and 10%, of exhaust gas into the intake manifold.

Here, the exhaust gas mixes with and takes the place of some of the intake charge. This leaves less room for the intake charge to enter the combustion chamber. The recirculated exhaust gas is **inert** (chemically inactive) and does not enter into the combustion process. The result is a lower peak combustion temperature. When the combustion temperature is lowered, the production of oxides of nitrogen is reduced.

The EGR system has some means of interconnecting the exhaust and intake manifolds. ● SEE FIGURES 24-2 AND 24-3.

The EGR valve controls the flow of exhaust gases through the interconnecting passages.

- On V-type engines, the intake manifold crossover is used as a source of exhaust gas for the EGR system. A cast passage connects the exhaust crossover to the EGR valve. The exhaust gas is sent from the EGR valve to openings in the manifold.

- On inline-type engines, an external tube is generally used to carry exhaust gas to the EGR valve. This tube is often designed to be long so that the exhaust gas is cooled before it enters the EGR valve.

**EGR SYSTEM OPERATION** Since small amounts of exhaust are all that is needed to lower peak combustion temperatures, the orifice that the exhaust passes through is small.

EGR is usually *not* required during the following conditions because the combustion temperatures are low.

- Idle speed
- When the engine is cold
- At wide-open throttle (WOT) (Not allowing EGR allows the engine to provide extra power when demanded. While the NOx formation is high during these times, the overall effect of not using EGR during wide-open throttle conditions is minor.)

The level of NOx emission changes according to engine speed, temperature, and load. EGR is not used at wide-open throttle (WOT) because it would reduce engine performance and the engine does not operate under these conditions for a long period of time.

**EGR BENEFITS** In addition to lowering NOx levels, the EGR system also helps control detonation. Detonation, also called spark knock or ping, occurs when high pressure and heat cause the air-fuel mixture to ignite. This uncontrolled combustion can severely damage the engine.

Using the EGR system allows for greater ignition timing advance and for the advance to occur sooner without detonation problems, which increases power and efficiency.

**POSITIVE AND NEGATIVE BACKPRESSURE EGR VALVES** Some vacuum-operated EGR valves used on older engines are designed with a small valve inside that

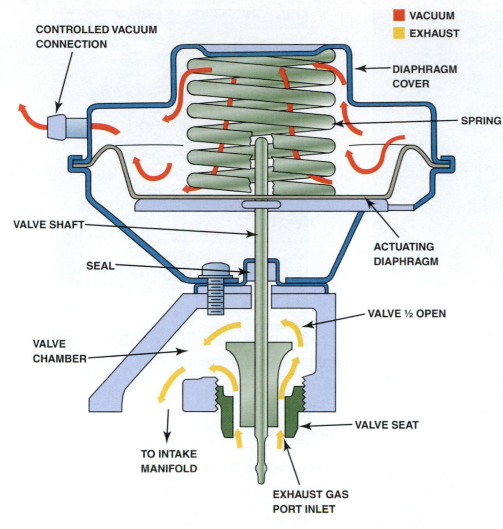

**VACUUM**

**EXHAUST**

CONTROLLED VACUUM CONNECTION

DIAPHRAGM COVER

SPRING

VALVE SHAFT

ACTUATING DIAPHRAGM

SEAL

VALVE ½ OPEN

VALVE CHAMBER

VALVE SEAT

TO INTAKE MANIFOLD

EXHAUST GAS PORT INLET

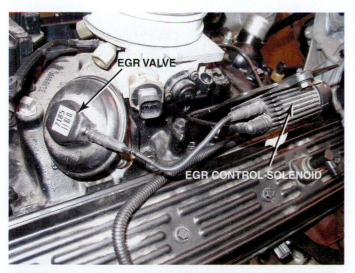

EGR VALVE

EGR CONTROL SOLENOID

**FIGURE 24–3** A vacuum-operated EGR valve. The vacuum to the EGR valve is computer controlled by the EGR valve control solenoid.

bleeds off any applied vacuum and prevents the valve from opening.

- **Positive backpressure.** These types of EGR valves require a positive backpressure in the exhaust system. At low engine speeds and light engine loads, the EGR system is not needed, and the backpressure in it is also low. Without sufficient backpressure, the EGR valve does not open even though vacuum may be present at the EGR valve.

- **Negative backpressure.** On each exhaust stroke, the engine emits an exhaust "pulse." Each pulse represents a positive pressure. Behind each pulse is a small area of low pressure. Some EGR valves react to this low-pressure area by closing a small internal valve, which allows the EGR valve to be opened by vacuum.

The following conditions must occur before a backpressure-type vacuum-controlled EGR will operate.

1. Vacuum must be applied to the EGR valve itself. The vacuum source can be ported vacuum (above the throttle plate) or manifold vacuum (below the throttle plate) and by the computer through a solenoid valve.

2. Exhaust backpressure must be present to close an internal valve inside the EGR to allow the vacuum to move the diaphragm.

**FIGURE 24–4** An EGR valve position sensor on top of an EGR valve.

**FIGURE 24–5** Digital EGR valve.

**NOTE: Installing a high-performance exhaust system could prevent a backpressure vacuum-operated EGR valve from opening. If this occurs, excessive combustion chamber temperature leads to severe spark knock, piston damage, or a blown head gasket.**

### COMPUTER-CONTROLLED EGR SYSTEMS
Many computer-controlled EGR systems have one or more solenoids controlling the EGR vacuum. The computer controls a solenoid to shut off vacuum to the EGR valve at cold engine temperatures, idle speed, and wide-open throttle operation. If two solenoids are used, one acts as an off-on control of supply vacuum, while the second solenoid vents vacuum when EGR flow is not desired or needs to be reduced. The second solenoid is used to control a vacuum air bleed, allowing atmospheric pressure in to modulate EGR flow according to vehicle operating conditions.

### EGR VALVE POSITION SENSORS
Most computer-controlled EGR systems use a sensor to indicate EGR operation. Onboard diagnostics generation-II (OBD-II) EGR system monitors require an EGR sensor to verify that the valve opened. A linear potentiometer on the top of the EGR valve stem indicates valve position for the computer. This is called an **EGR valve position (EVP)** sensor. Some later-model Ford EGR systems, however, use a feedback signal provided by an EGR exhaust backpressure sensor that converts the exhaust backpressure to a voltage signal. This sensor is called a **pressure feedback EGR (PFE)** sensor.

On some EGR systems, the top of the valve contains a vacuum regulator and EGR pintle-position sensor in one assembly sealed inside a nonremovable plastic cover. The pintle-position sensor provides a voltage output to the PCM, which increases as the duty cycle increases, allowing the PCM to monitor valve operation. ● **SEE FIGURE 24–4.**

### DIGITAL EGR VALVES
GM introduced a **digital EGR** valve design on some engines. Unlike vacuum-operated EGR valves, the digital EGR valve consists of three solenoids controlled by the powertrain control module (PCM). Each solenoid controls a different size orifice in the base—small, medium, and large. The PCM controls the ground circuit of each of the solenoids individually. It can produce any of seven different flow rates, using the solenoids to open the three valves in different combinations. The digital EGR valve offers precise control, and using a swivel pintle design helps prevent carbon deposit problems. ● **SEE FIGURE 24–5.**

### LINEAR EGR
Most General Motors and many other vehicles use a **linear EGR** that contains a pulse-width modulated solenoid to precisely regulate exhaust gas flow and a feedback potentiometer that signals the computer regarding the actual position of the valve. ● **SEE FIGURES 24–6 AND 24–7.**

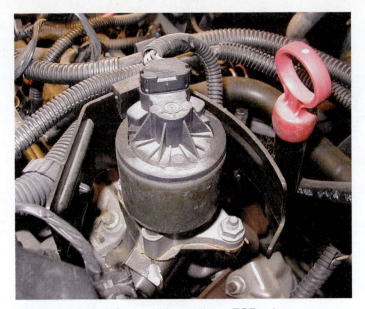

**FIGURE 24–6** A General Motors linear EGR valve.

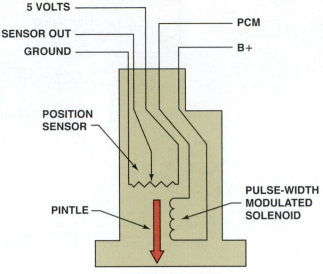

**FIGURE 24–7** The EGR valve pintle is pulse-width modulated and a three-wire potentiometer provides pintle-position information back to the PCM.

## OBD-II EGR MONITORING STRATEGIES

**PURPOSE AND FUNCTION** In 1996, the U.S. EPA began requiring OBD-II systems in all passenger cars and most light-duty trucks. These systems include emissions system monitors that alert the driver and the technician if an emissions system is malfunctioning. The OBD-II system performs this test by opening and closing the EGR valve. The PCM monitors an EGR function sensor for a change in signal voltage. If the EGR system fails, a diagnostic trouble code (DTC) is set. If the system fails two consecutive times, the malfunction indicator light (MIL) is lit.

**MONITORING STRATEGIES** EGR monitoring strategies include the following:

- Some vehicle manufacturers, such as Chrysler, monitor the difference in the exhaust oxygen sensor's voltage activity as the EGR valve opens and closes. Oxygen in the exhaust decreases when the EGR valve is open and increases when the EGR valve is closed. The PCM sets a DTC if the sensor signal does not change.

- Most Fords use an EGR monitor test sensor called a **delta pressure feedback EGR (DPFE) sensor.** This sensor measures the pressure differential between two sides of a metered orifice positioned just below the EGR valve's exhaust side. Pressure between the orifice and the EGR valve decreases when the EGR opens because it becomes exposed to the lower pressure in the intake. The DPFE sensor recognizes this pressure drop, compares it to the relatively higher pressure on the exhaust side of the orifice, and signals the value of the pressure difference to the PCM. ● **SEE FIGURE 24–8.**

- Many vehicle manufacturers use the manifold absolute pressure (MAP) sensor as the EGR monitor on some applications. After meeting the enable criteria (operating condition requirements), the EGR monitor is run. The PCM monitors the MAP sensor while it commands the EGR valve to open. The MAP sensor signal should change in response to the sudden change in manifold pressure or the fuel trim changes created by a change in the oxygen sensor voltage. If the signal value falls outside the acceptable value in the look-up table, a DTC sets. If the EGR fails on two consecutive trips, the PCM lights the MIL. ● **SEE FIGURE 24–9.**

## DIAGNOSING A DEFECTIVE EGR SYSTEM

**SYMPTOMS** If the EGR valve is not opening or the flow of the exhaust gas is restricted, then the following symptoms are likely.

- Detonation (spark knock or ping) during acceleration or during cruise (steady-speed driving)
- Excessive oxides of nitrogen (NOx) exhaust emissions

If the EGR valve is stuck open or partially open, then the following symptoms are likely.

- Rough idle or frequent stalling
- Poor performance/low power, especially at low engine speed

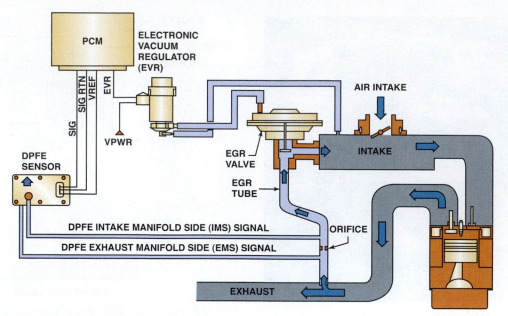

**FIGURE 24–8** A DPFE sensor and related components.

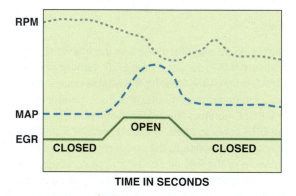

**FIGURE 24–9** An OBD-II active test. The PCM opens the EGR valve and then monitors the MAP sensor and/or engine speed (RPM) to verify that it meets acceptable values.

## TECH TIP

### Watch Out for Carbon Balls!

Exhaust gas recirculation (EGR) valves can get stuck partially open by a chunk of carbon. The EGR valve or solenoid will test as defective. When the valve (or solenoid) is removed, small chunks or balls of carbon often fall into the exhaust manifold passage. When the replacement valve is installed, the carbon balls can be drawn into the new valve again, causing the engine to idle roughly or stall.

To help prevent this problem, start the engine with the EGR valve or solenoid removed. Any balls or chunks of carbon will be blown out of the passage by the exhaust. Stop the engine and install the replacement EGR valve or solenoid.

## REAL WORLD FIX

### The Blazer Story

The owner of a Chevrolet Blazer equipped with a 4.3 liter V-6 engine complained that the engine would stumble and hesitate at times. Everything seemed to be functioning correctly, except that the service technician discovered a weak vacuum going to the EGR valve at idle. This vehicle was equipped with an EGR valve-control solenoid, called an **electronic vacuum regulator valve (EVRV)** by General Motors Corporation. The computer pulses the solenoid to control the vacuum that regulates the operation of the EGR valve. The technician checked the service manual for details on how the system worked. The technician discovered that vacuum should be present at the EGR valve only when the gear selector indicates a drive gear (drive, low, reverse). Because the technician discovered the vacuum at the solenoid to be leaking, the solenoid was obviously defective and required replacement. After replacement of the solenoid (EVRV), the hesitation problem was solved.

**NOTE: The technician also discovered in the service manual that blower-type exhaust hoses should not be connected to the tailpipe on any vehicle while performing an inspection of the EGR system. The vacuum created by the system could cause false EGR valve operation to occur.**

## EGR TESTING PROCEDURES

The first step in almost any diagnosis is to perform a thorough visual inspection. To check for proper operation of a vacuum-operated EGR valve, follow these steps.

**STEP 1** **Check the vacuum diaphragm of the EGR valve to see if it can hold vacuum.** Because many EGR valves require exhaust backpressure to function correctly, the engine should be running at a fast idle during this test. Always follow the specified testing procedures.

**STEP 2** **Apply vacuum from a hand-operated vacuum pump and check for proper operation.** The valve itself should move when vacuum is applied, and the engine operation should be affected. The EGR valve should be able to hold the vacuum that was applied. If the vacuum drops off, then the valve is likely to be defective.

**STEP 3** **Monitor engine vacuum drop.** Connect a vacuum gauge to an intake manifold vacuum source and monitor the engine vacuum at idle (should be 17 to 21 in. Hg at sea level). Raise the speed of the engine to 2500 RPM and note the vacuum reading (should be 17 to 21 in. Hg or higher).

Activate the EGR valve using a scan tool or vacuum pump, if vacuum controlled, and observe the vacuum gauge. The results are as follows:

- The vacuum should drop 6 to 8 in. Hg.
- If the vacuum drops less than 6 to 8 in. Hg, the valve or the EGR passages are clogged.

**Results**

- If the EGR valve is able to hold vacuum, but the engine is not affected when the valve is opened, then the exhaust passage(s) must be checked for restriction.

**FIGURE 24–10** Removing the EGR passage plugs from the intake manifold on a Honda.

See the Tech Tip, "The Snake Trick." If the EGR valve will not hold vacuum, the valve itself is likely to be defective and require replacement.

## EGR-RELATED OBD-II DIAGNOSTIC TROUBLE CODES

| Diagnostic Trouble Code | Description | Possible Causes |
|---|---|---|
| P0400 | Exhaust gas recirculation flow problems | • EGR valve<br>• EGR valve hose or electrical connection<br>• Defective PCM |
| P0401 | Exhaust gas recirculation flow insufficient | • EGR valve<br>• Clogged EGR ports or passages |
| P0402 | Exhaust gas recirculation flow excessive | • Stuck-open EGR valve<br>• Vacuum hose(s) misrouted<br>• Electrical wiring shorted |

## CRANKCASE VENTILATION

**PURPOSE AND FUNCTION** The problem of crankcase ventilation has existed since the beginning of the automobile, because no piston ring, new or old, can provide a perfect seal between the piston and the cylinder wall. When an engine is running, the pressure of combustion forces the piston downward. This same pressure also forces gases and unburned

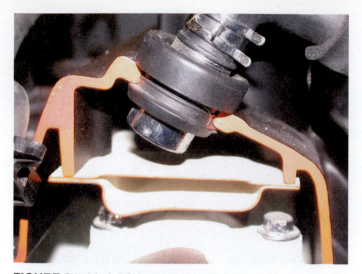

FIGURE 24–11 A PCV valve in a cutaway valve cover, showing the baffles that prevent liquid oil from being drawn into the intake manifold.

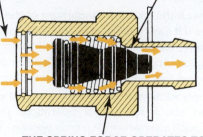

THIS END OF THE PCV VALVE IS SUBJECT TO CRANKCASE PRESSURE THAT TENDS TO CLOSE THE VALVE.

THIS END IS SUBJECT TO INTAKE MANIFOLD VACUUM THAT TENDS TO CLOSE THE VALVE.

THE SPRING FORCE OPERATES TO OPEN THE VALVE TO MANIFOLD VACUUM AND CRANKCASE PRESSURE.

FIGURE 24–12 Spring force, crankcase pressure, and intake manifold vacuum work together to regulate the flow rate through the PCV valve.

fuel from the combustion chamber, past the piston rings, and into the crankcase. **Blowby** is the term used to describe when combustion gases are forced past the piston rings and into the crankcase.

These combustion by-products, particularly unburned hydrocarbons (HC) caused by blowby, must be ventilated from the crankcase. However, the crankcase cannot be vented directly to the atmosphere, because the hydrocarbon vapors add to air pollution. **Positive crankcase ventilation (PCV)** systems were developed to ventilate the crankcase and recirculate the vapors to the engine's induction system so they can be burned in the cylinders. PCV systems help reduce HC and CO emissions.

All systems use the following:

1. PCV valve, calibrated orifice, or orifice and separator
2. PCV inlet air filter plus all connecting hoses

● SEE FIGURE 24–11.

An oil/vapor or oil/water separator is used in some systems instead of a valve or orifice, particularly with turbocharged and fuel-injected engines. The oil/vapor separator lets oil condense and drain back into the crankcase. The oil/water separator accumulates moisture and prevents it from freezing during cold engine starts.

The air for the PCV system is drawn after the air cleaner filter, which acts as a PCV filter.

NOTE: Some older designs drew from the dirty side of the air cleaner, where a separate crankcase ventilation filter was used.

### PCV VALVES
The PCV valve in most systems is a one-way valve containing a spring-operated plunger that controls valve flow rate. ● SEE FIGURE 24–12.

Flow rate is established for each engine and a valve for a different engine should not be substituted. The flow rate is

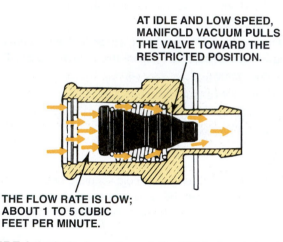

AT IDLE AND LOW SPEED, MANIFOLD VACUUM PULLS THE VALVE TOWARD THE RESTRICTED POSITION.

THE FLOW RATE IS LOW; ABOUT 1 TO 5 CUBIC FEET PER MINUTE.

FIGURE 24–13 Air flows through the PCV valve during idle, cruising, and light-load conditions.

determined by the size of the plunger and the holes inside the valve. PCV valves usually are located in the valve cover or intake manifold.

The PCV valve regulates airflow through the crankcase under all driving conditions and speeds. When manifold vacuum is high (at idle, cruising, and light-load operation), the PCV valve restricts the airflow to maintain a balanced air-fuel ratio. ● SEE FIGURE 24–13.

It also prevents high intake manifold vacuum from pulling oil out of the crankcase and into the intake manifold. Under high speed or heavy loads, the valve opens and allows maximum airflow. ● SEE FIGURE 24–14.

If the engine backfires, the valve will close instantly to prevent a crankcase explosion. ● SEE FIGURE 24–15.

### ORIFICE-CONTROLLED SYSTEMS
The closed PCV system used on some 4-cylinder engines contains a calibrated orifice instead of a PCV valve. The orifice may be

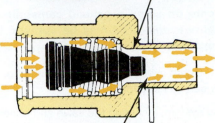

AT HIGHER SPEED OR IN A HEAVY
LOAD CONDITION, MANIFOLD
VACUUM DROPS. THE SPRING MOVES
THE VALVE OPEN.

FLOW THROUGH THE VALVE INCREASES—
FROM 3 TO 6 CUBIC FEET PER MINUTE.

**FIGURE 24–14** Air flows through the PCV valve during acceleration and when the engine is under a heavy load.

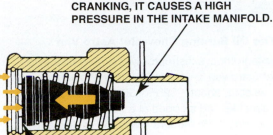

IF THE ENGINE BACKFIRES DURING
CRANKING, IT CAUSES A HIGH
PRESSURE IN THE INTAKE MANIFOLD.

PRESSURE CAUSES THE VALVE TO BACK-SEAT
AND SEAL OFF THE INLET. THIS KEEPS THE
BACKFIRE OUT OF THE CRANKCASE.

**FIGURE 24–15** PCV valve operation in the event of a backfire.

 **REAL WORLD FIX**

### The Whistling Engine

An older vehicle was being diagnosed for a whistling sound whenever the engine was running, especially at idle. It was finally discovered that the breather in the valve cover was plugged and caused high vacuum in the crankcase. The engine was sucking air from what was likely the rear main seal lip, making the "whistle" noise. After replacing the breather and PCV, the noise stopped.

**TECH TIP**

### Check for Oil Leaks with the Engine Off

The owner of an older vehicle equipped with a V-6 engine complained to his technician that he smelled burning oil, but only *after* shutting off the engine. The technician found that the rocker cover gaskets were leaking. But why did the owner only notice the smell of hot oil when the engine was shut off? Because of the positive crankcase ventilation (PCV) system, engine vacuum tends to draw oil away from gasket surfaces. But when the engine stops, engine vacuum disappears and the oil remaining in the upper regions of the engine will tend to flow down and out through any opening. Therefore, a good technician should check an engine for oil leaks not only with the engine running but also shortly after shutdown.

located in the valve cover or intake manifold, or in a hose connected between the valve cover, air cleaner, and intake manifold.

While most orifice flow control systems work the same as a PCV valve system, they may not use fresh air scavenging of the crankcase. Crankcase vapors are drawn into the intake manifold in calibrated amounts depending on manifold pressure and the orifice size. If vapor availability is low, as during idle, air is drawn in with the vapors. During off-idle operation, excess vapors are sent to the air cleaner.

At idle, PCV flow is controlled by a 0.05 in. (1.3 mm) orifice. As the engine moves off idle, ported vacuum pulls a spring-loaded valve off of its seat, allowing PCV flow to pass through a 0.09 in. (2.3 mm) orifice.

### SEPARATOR SYSTEMS
Turbocharged and many fuel-injected engines use an oil/vapor or oil/water separator and a calibrated orifice instead of a PCV valve. In the most common applications, the air intake throttle body acts as the source for crankcase ventilation vacuum and a calibrated orifice acts as the metering device.

## PCV SYSTEM DIAGNOSIS

### SYMPTOMS
If the PCV valve or orifice is not clogged, intake air flows freely and the PCV system functions properly. Engine design includes the air and vapor flow as a calibrated part of the air-fuel mixture. In fact, some engines receive as much as 30% of the idle air through the PCV system. For this reason, a flow problem in the PCV system results in driveability problems.

A blocked or plugged PCV system can cause:

- Rough or unstable idle
- Excessive oil consumption
- Oil in the air filter housing
- Oil leaks due to excessive crankcase pressure

Before expensive engine repairs are attempted, check the condition of the PCV system.

**The Oil Burning Chevrolet Astro Van**

An automotive instructor was driving a Chevrolet Astro van to Fairbanks, Alaska, in January. It was cold, about −32°F (−36°C). As he pulled into Fairbanks and stopped at a traffic light, he smelled burning oil. He thought it was the vehicle ahead of him as it was an older vehicle and did not look like it was in good condition. However, when he stopped at the hotel he still smelled burning oil. He looked under the van and discovered a large pool of oil. After checking the oil and finding very little left, he called a local shop and was told to bring it in. The technician looked over the situation and said, "You need to put some cardboard across the grill to stop the PCV valve from freezing up." Apparently the PCV valve froze, which then caused the normal blowby gases to force several quarts out the dipstick tube. After he installed the cardboard, he did not have any further problems.

**CAUTION: Do not cover the radiator when driving unless under severe cold conditions and carefully watch the coolant temperature to avoid overheating the engine.**

### PCV SYSTEM PERFORMANCE CHECK

A properly operating positive crankcase ventilation system should be able to draw vapors from the crankcase and into the intake manifold. If the pipes, hoses, and PCV valve itself are not restricted, vacuum is applied to the crankcase. A slight vacuum is created in the crankcase (usually less than 1 in. Hg if measured at the dipstick) and is also applied to other areas of the engine. Oil drainback holes provide a path for oil to drain back into the oil pan. These holes also allow crankcase vacuum to be applied under the rocker covers and in the valley area of most V-type engines. There are several methods that can be used to test a PCV system.

### RATTLE TEST

The rattle test is performed by simply removing the PCV valve and shaking it in your hand.

- If the PCV valve does *not* rattle, it is definitely defective and must be replaced.
- If the PCV valve *does* rattle, it does not necessarily mean that the PCV valve is good. All PCV valves contain springs that can become weaker with age and with heating and cooling cycles. Replace any PCV valve with the *exact* replacement according to the vehicle manufacturer's recommended intervals, usually every three years or 36,000 miles (60,000 km).

### THE 3 × 5 CARD TEST

Remove the oil-fill cap (where oil is added to the engine) and start the engine.

**NOTE: Use care on some overhead camshaft engines. With the engine running, oil may be sprayed from the open oil-fill opening.**

Hold a 3 × 5 card over the opening (a dollar bill or any other piece of paper can be used for this test).

- If the PCV system, including the valve and hoses, is functioning correctly, the card should be held down on the oil-fill opening by the slight vacuum inside the crankcase.
- If the card will not stay, carefully inspect the PCV valve, hose(s), and manifold vacuum port for carbon buildup (restriction). Clean or replace as necessary.

**NOTE: On some 4-cylinder engines, the 3 × 5 card may vibrate on the oil-fill opening when the engine is running at idle speed. This is normal because of the time intervals between intake strokes on a 4-cylinder engine.**

### SNAP-BACK TEST

The proper operation of the PCV valve can be checked by placing a finger over the inlet hole in the valve when the engine is running and removing the finger rapidly. Repeat several times. The valve should "snap back." If the valve does not snap back, replace the valve.

### CRANKCASE VACUUM TEST

Sometimes the PCV system can be checked by testing for a weak vacuum at the oil dipstick tube using an inches-of-water manometer or gauge, as follows:

**STEP 1** Remove the oil-fill cap or vent PCV opening and cover the opening.

**STEP 2** Remove the oil dipstick (oil level indicator).

**STEP 3** Connect a water manometer or gauge to the dipstick tube.

**STEP 4** Start the engine and observe the gauge at idle and at 2500 RPM.

● **SEE FIGURE 24–16.**

The gauge should show some vacuum, especially at 2500 RPM. If not, carefully inspect the PCV system for blockages or other faults.

### PCV MONITOR

Starting with 2004 and newer vehicles, all vehicle PCMs monitor the PCV system for proper operation as part of the OBD-II system. The PCV monitor will fail if the PCM detects an opening between the crankcase and the PCV valve or between the PCV valve and the intake manifold. ● **SEE FIGURE 24–17.**

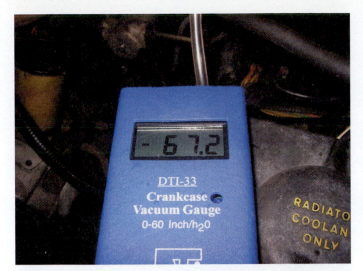

**FIGURE 24–16** Using a gauge that measures vacuum in units of inches of water to test the vacuum at the dipstick tube, being sure that the PCV system is capable of drawing a vacuum on the crankcase. Note that 28 in. of water equals 1 PSI, or about 2 in. of mercury (in. Hg) of vacuum.

**FIGURE 24–17** Most PCV valves used on newer vehicles are secured with fasteners, which makes it more difficult to disconnect and therefore less likely to increase emissions. (Halderman photo)

 **FREQUENTLY ASKED QUESTION**

**Why Are There Wires at the PCV Valve?**

Ford uses an electric heater to prevent ice from forming inside the PCV valve causing blockage. Water is a by-product of combustion and resulting moisture can freeze when the outside air temperature is low. General Motors and others clip a heater hose to the PCV hose to provide the heat needed to prevent an ice blockage.

## PCV-RELATED DIAGNOSTIC TROUBLE CODE

| Diagnostic Trouble Code | Description | Possible Causes |
|---|---|---|
| P0101 | MAF or airflow circuit range problem | • Defective PCV valve, hose/connections, or MAF circuit fault |
| P0505 | Idle control system problem | • Defective PCV valve or hose/connections |

## SECONDARY AIR-INJECTION SYSTEM

**PURPOSE AND FUNCTION** The **secondary air-injection (SAI)** system provides the air necessary for the oxidizing process either at the exhaust manifold or inside the catalytic converter.

**NOTE: This system is commonly called AIR, meaning air-injection reaction. Therefore, an AIR pump does pump air.**

**PARTS AND OPERATION** The SAI pump, also called an AIR pump, a **smog pump,** or a **thermactor pump,** is mounted at the front of the engine and can be driven by a belt from the crankshaft pulley. It pulls fresh air in through an external filter and pumps the air under slight pressure to each exhaust port through connecting hoses or a manifold. The typical SAI system includes the following components.

- A belt-driven pump with inlet air filter (older models) (● **SEE FIGURE 24–18.**)
- An electronic air pump (newer models)
- One or more air distribution manifolds and nozzles
- One or more exhaust check valves
- Connecting hoses for air distribution
- Air management valves and solenoids on all newer applications

With the introduction of NOx reduction converters (also called dual-bed, **three-way converters,** or **TWC**), the output of the SAI pump is sent to the center of the converter where the extra air can help oxidize unburned hydrocarbons (HC), carbon monoxide (CO) into water vapor ($H_2O$), and carbon dioxide ($CO_2$).

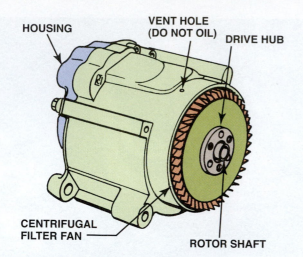

FIGURE 24–18 A typical belt-driven AIR pump. Air enters through the revolving fins behind the drive pulley. The fins act as an air filter because dirt is heavier than air and therefore the dirt is deflected off of the fins at the same time air is being drawn into the pump.

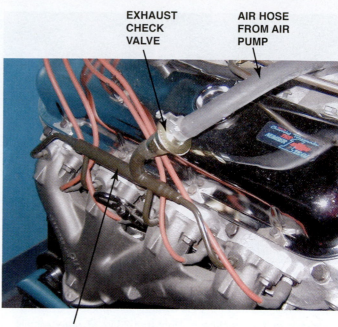

FIGURE 24–19 The external air manifold and exhaust check valve on a restored muscle car engine.

The computer controls the airflow from the pump by switching on and off various solenoid valves.

### AIR DISTRIBUTION MANIFOLDS AND NOZZLES

The secondary air-injection system sends air from the pump to a nozzle installed near each exhaust port in the cylinder head. This provides equal air injection for the exhaust from each cylinder and makes it available at a point in the system where exhaust gases are the hottest.

Air is delivered to the exhaust system in one of two ways.

1. An external air manifold, or manifolds, distributes the air through injection tubes with stainless steel nozzles. The nozzles are threaded into the cylinder heads or exhaust manifolds close to each exhaust valve. This method is used primarily with smaller engines.

2. An internal air manifold distributes the air to the exhaust ports near each exhaust valve through passages cast in the cylinder head or the exhaust manifold. This method is used mainly with larger engines.

### EXHAUST CHECK VALVES

All air-injection systems use one or more one-way check valves to protect the air pump and other components from reverse exhaust flow. A **check valve** contains a spring-type metallic disc or reed that closes under exhaust backpressure. Check valves are located between the air manifold and the switching valve(s). If exhaust pressure exceeds injection pressure, or if the air pump fails, the check valve spring closes the valve to prevent reverse exhaust flow. ● SEE FIGURE 24–19.

**NOTE: These check valves commonly fail, resulting in excessive exhaust emissions (CO especially). When the check valve fails, hot exhaust can travel up to and destroy the switching valve(s) and air pump itself.**

### BELT-DRIVEN AIR PUMPS

The belt-driven air pump uses a centrifugal filter just behind the drive pulley. As the pump rotates, underhood air is drawn into the pump and slightly compressed. The system uses either vacuum- or solenoid-controlled diverter valves to air directed to the following:

- Exhaust manifold when the engine is cold to help oxidize carbon monoxide (CO) and unburned hydrocarbons (HC) into carbon dioxide ($CO_2$) and water vapor ($H_2O$)
- Catalytic converter on many models to help provide the extra oxygen needed for the efficient conversion of CO and HC into $CO_2$ and $H_2O$
- Air cleaner during deceleration or wide-open throttle (WOT) engine operation
  ● SEE FIGURE 24–20.

### ELECTRIC MOTOR-DRIVEN AIR PUMPS

The electric motor-driven air pump is generally used only during cold engine operation and is computer controlled. The secondary air-injection (SAI) system helps reduce hydrocarbon (HC) and carbon monoxide (CO). It also helps to warm the three-way catalytic converters quickly on engine start-up so conversion of exhaust gases may occur sooner.

- The SAI pump solenoids are controlled by the PCM. The PCM turns on the SAI pump by providing the ground to complete the circuit which energizes the SAI pump solenoid relay. When air to the exhaust ports is desired, the PCM energizes the relay in order to turn on the solenoid and the SAI pump. ● SEE FIGURE 24–21.

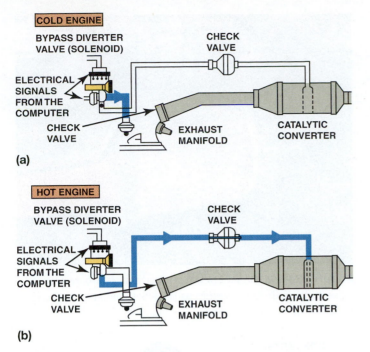

**(a)**

**(b)**

**FIGURE 24–20** (a) When the engine is cold and before the oxygen sensor is hot enough to achieve closed loop, the airflow from the air pump is directed to the exhaust manifold(s) through the one-way check valves which keep the exhaust gases from entering the switching solenoids and the pump itself. (b) When the engine achieves closed loop, the air is directed to the catalytic converter.

- The PCM turns on the SAI pump during start-up any time the engine coolant temperature is above 32°F (0°C). A typical electric SAI pump operates for a maximum of four minutes, or until the system enters closed-loop operation.

# SECONDARY AIR-INJECTION SYSTEM DIAGNOSIS

**SYMPTOMS**   The air pump system should be inspected if an exhaust emissions test failure occurs. In severe cases, the exhaust will enter the air cleaner assembly, resulting in a horribly running engine because the extra exhaust displaces the oxygen needed for proper combustion. With the engine running, check for normal operation. ● **SEE CHART 24–1.**

**VISUAL INSPECTION**   Carefully inspect all secondary air-injection (SAI) systems, including:

- Any hoses or pipes that have holes and leak air or exhaust, which require replacement

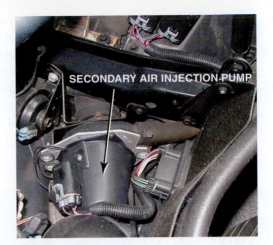

**FIGURE 24–21** A typical electric motor-driven SAI pump. This unit is on a Chevrolet Corvette and only works when the engine is cold.

| ENGINE OPERATION | NORMAL OPERATION OF A TYPICAL SAI SYSTEM |
|---|---|
| Cold engine (open-loop operation) | Air is diverted to the exhaust manifold(s) or cylinder head. |
| Warm engine (closed-loop operation) | Air is diverted to the catalytic converter. |
| Deceleration | Air is diverted to the air cleaner assembly. |
| Wide-open throttle | Air is diverted to the air cleaner assembly. |

**CHART 24–1**

Typical SAI system operation showing the location of the airflow from the pump.

- Check valve(s), when a pump has become inoperative
- Exhaust gases that may have gotten past the check valve and damaged the pump (Look for signs of overheated areas upstream from the check valves. In severe cases, the exhaust can enter the air cleaner assembly and destroy the air filter and greatly reduce engine power.)
- Drive belt on an engine-driven pump, for wear and proper tension (If the belt is worn or damaged, check that the AIR pump rotates.)

**FOUR-GAS EXHAUST ANALYSIS**   An SAI system can be easily tested using an exhaust gas analyzer and the following steps.

**STEP 1**   Start the engine and allow it to run until normal operating temperature is achieved.

**STEP 2**   Connect the analyzer probe to the tailpipe and observe the exhaust readings for hydrocarbons (HC) and carbon monoxide (CO).

**STEP 3** Using the appropriate pinch-off pliers, shut off the air-flow from the SAI system. Observe the HC and CO readings. If the SAI system is working correctly, the HC and CO should increase when the SAI system is shut off.

**STEP 4** Record the $O_2$ reading with the SAI system still inoperative. Unclamp the pliers and watch the $O_2$ readings. If the system is functioning correctly, the $O_2$ level should increase by 1% to 4%.

## SAI-RELATED DIAGNOSTIC TROUBLE CODE

| Diagnostic Trouble Code | Description | Possible Causes |
|---|---|---|
| P0410 | SAI solenoid circuit fault | • Defective SAI solenoid<br>• Loose or corroded electrical connections<br>• Loose, missing, or defective rubber hose(s) |

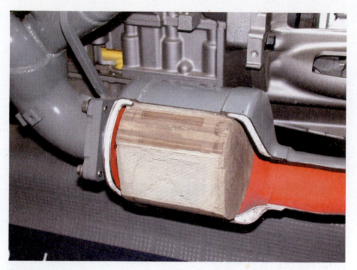

**FIGURE 24–22** Most catalytic converters are located as close to the exhaust manifold as possible, as seen in this display of a Chevrolet Corvette.

## CATALYTIC CONVERTERS

**PURPOSE AND FUNCTION** A **catalytic converter** is an after treatment device used to reduce exhaust emissions outside of the engine. The catalytic converter uses a **catalyst,** which is a chemical that helps start a chemical reaction but does not enter into the chemical reaction.

- The catalyst materials on the surface of the material inside the converter help create a chemical reaction.
- The chemical reaction changes harmful exhaust emissions into nonharmful exhaust emissions.
- The converter, therefore, converts harmful exhaust gases into water vapor ($H_2O$) and carbon dioxide ($CO_2$).

This device is installed in the exhaust system between the exhaust manifold and the muffler, and usually is positioned beneath the passenger compartment. The location of the converter is important, since as much of the exhaust heat as possible must be retained for effective operation. The nearer it is to the engine, the better. ● **SEE FIGURE 24–22.**

**CATALYTIC CONVERTER CONSTRUCTION** Most catalytic converters are constructed of a ceramic material in a honeycomb shape with square openings for the exhaust gases.

- There are approximately 400 openings per square inch (62 openings per square centimeter) and the wall thickness is about 0.006 in. (1.5 mm).

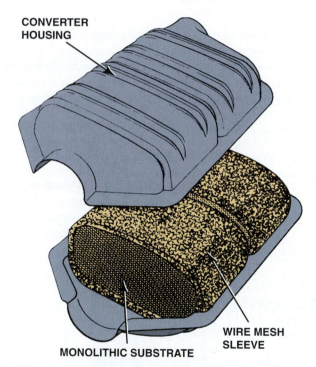

CONVERTER HOUSING

WIRE MESH SLEEVE

MONOLITHIC SUBSTRATE

**FIGURE 24–23** A typical catalytic converter with a monolithic substrate.

- The substrate is then coated with a porous aluminum material called the **washcoat,** which makes the surface rough.
- The catalytic materials are then applied on top of the washcoat. The substrate is contained within a round or oval shell made by welding together two stamped pieces of stainless steel. ● **SEE FIGURE 24–23.**

The ceramic substrate in monolithic converters is not restrictive; however, the converter can be physically broken if exposed to shock or severe jolts. Monolithic converters can be serviced only as a unit.

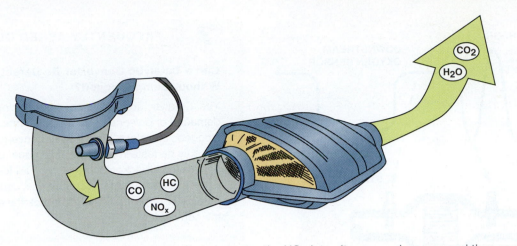

**FIGURE 24–24** The three-way catalytic converter first separates the NOx into nitrogen and oxygen and then converts the HC and CO into harmless water ($H_2O$) and carbon dioxide ($CO_2$).

An exhaust pipe is connected to the manifold or header to carry gases through a catalytic converter and then to the muffler or silencer. V-type engines can use dual converters or route the exhaust into one catalytic converter by using a Y-exhaust pipe.

### CATALYTIC CONVERTER OPERATION

The converter substrate contains small amounts of **rhodium, palladium,** and **platinum.** These elements act as catalysts, which, as mentioned, start a chemical reaction without becoming part of, or being consumed in, the process. In a three-way catalytic converter (TWC), all three exhaust emissions (NOx, HC, and CO) are converted to carbon dioxide ($CO_2$) and water ($H_2O$). As the exhaust gas passes through the catalyst, oxides of nitrogen (NOx) are chemically reduced (that is, nitrogen and oxygen are separated) in the first section of the catalytic converter. In the second section of the catalytic converter, most of the hydrocarbons and carbon monoxide remaining in the exhaust gas are oxidized to form harmless carbon dioxide ($CO_2$) and water vapor ($H_2O$). ● **SEE FIGURE 24–24.**

Since the early 1990s, many converters also contain **cerium,** an element that can store oxygen. The purpose of the cerium is to provide oxygen to the oxidation bed of the converter when the exhaust is rich and lacks enough oxygen for proper oxidation. When the exhaust is lean, the cerium absorbs the extra oxygen. For the most efficient operation, the converter should have a 14.7:1 air-fuel ratio but can use a mixture that varies slightly.

- A rich exhaust is required for reduction—stripping the oxygen ($O_2$) from the nitrogen in NOx.
- A lean exhaust is required to provide the oxygen necessary to oxidize HC and CO (combining oxygen with HC and CO to form $H_2O$ and $CO_2$).

If the catalytic converter is not functioning correctly, check that the air-fuel mixture being supplied to the engine is correct and that the ignition system is free of defects.

### CONVERTER LIGHT-OFF TEMPERATURE

The catalytic converter does not work when cold, and it must be heated to its **light-off temperature** of close to 500°F (260°C) before it starts working at 50% effectiveness. When fully effective, the converter reaches a temperature range of 900°F to 1,600°F (482°C to 871°C). In spite of the intense heat, however, catalytic reactions do not generate a flame associated with a simple burning reaction. Because of the extreme heat (almost as hot as combustion chamber temperatures), a converter remains hot long after the engine is shut off. Most vehicles use a series of heat shields to protect the passenger compartment and other parts of the chassis from excessive heat. Vehicles have been known to start fires because of the hot converter causing tall grass or dry leaves beneath the just-parked vehicle to ignite, especially if the engine is idling. This is most likely to occur if the heat shields have been removed from the converter.

### CONVERTER USAGE

A catalytic converter must be located as close as possible to the exhaust manifold to work effectively. The farther back the converter is positioned in the exhaust system, the more the exhaust gases cool before they reach the converter. Since positioning in the exhaust system affects the oxidation process, cars that use only an oxidation converter generally locate it underneath the front of the passenger compartment.

Some vehicles have used a small, quick heating oxidation converter called a **preconverter,** a **pup converter,** or a **mini converter** that connects directly to the exhaust manifold outlet. These have a small catalyst surface area close to the engine that heats up rapidly to start the oxidation process more quickly during cold engine warm-up. For this reason, they were often called **light-off converters (LOCs).** The larger main converter, under the passenger compartment, completes the oxidation reaction started in the LOC.

### OBD-II CATALYTIC CONVERTER PERFORMANCE

With OBD-II equipped vehicles, catalytic converter performance is monitored by a **heated oxygen sensor (HO₂S),** both before and after the converter. The converters used on these vehicles have what is known as **oxygen storage capacity (OSC).** This OSC is due mostly to the cerium coating in the catalyst rather than the precious metals used. When the three-way converter (TWC) is operating as it should, the postconverter HO₂S is far less

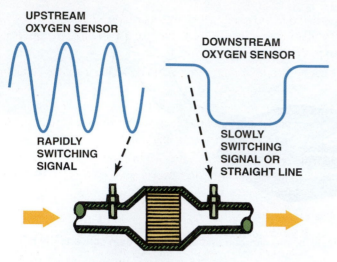

UPSTREAM OXYGEN SENSOR

DOWNSTREAM OXYGEN SENSOR

RAPIDLY SWITCHING SIGNAL

SLOWLY SWITCHING SIGNAL OR STRAIGHT LINE

CATALYTIC CONVERTER

**FIGURE 24–25** The OBD-II catalytic converter monitor compares the signals of the upstream and downstream HO2S to determine converter efficiency.

active than the preconverter sensor. The converter stores, then releases, the oxygen during normal reduction and oxidation of the exhaust gases, smoothing out the variations in $O_2$ being released.

Where a cycling sensor voltage output is expected before the converter, because of the converter action, the postconverter $HO_2S$ should read a steady signal without much fluctuation. ● **SEE FIGURE 24–25.**

### CONVERTER-DAMAGING CONDITIONS

Since converters have no moving parts, they require no periodic service. Under federal law, catalyst effectiveness is warranted for 80,000 miles or eight years.

The three main causes of premature converter failure are as follows:

- **Contamination.** Substances that can destroy the converter include exhaust that contains excess engine oil, antifreeze, sulfur (from poor fuel), and various other chemical substances.

- **Excessive temperatures.** Although a converter operates at high temperature, it can be destroyed by excessive temperatures. This most often occurs either when too much unburned fuel enters the converter, or with excessively lean mixtures. Excessive temperatures may be caused by long idling periods on some vehicles, since more heat develops at those times than when driving at normal highway speeds. Severe high temperatures can cause the converter to melt down, leading to the internal parts breaking apart and either clogging the converter or moving downstream to plug the muffler. In either case, the restricted exhaust flow severely reduces engine power.

- **Improper air-fuel mixtures.** Rich mixtures or raw fuel in the exhaust can be caused by engine misfiring, or an excessively rich air-fuel mixture resulting from a defective

**?** FREQUENTLY ASKED QUESTION

**Can a Catalytic Converter Be Defective Without Being Clogged?**

Yes. Catalytic converters can fail by being chemically damaged or poisoned without being mechanically clogged. Therefore, the catalytic converter should not only be tested for physical damage (clogging) by performing a backpressure or vacuum test and a rattle test, but also for temperature rise, usually with a pyrometer or propane test, to check the efficiency of the converter.

coolant temp sensor or defective fuel injectors. Lean mixtures are commonly caused by intake manifold leaks. When either of these circumstances occurs, the converter can become a catalytic furnace, causing the previously described damage.

To avoid excessive catalyst temperatures and the possibility of fuel vapors reaching the converter, follow these rules.

1. Do not use fuel additives or cleaners that are not converter safe.

2. Do not crank an engine for more than 40 seconds when it is flooded or misfiring.

3. Do not turn off the ignition switch when the vehicle is in motion.

4. Do not disconnect a spark plug wire for more than 30 seconds.

5. Repair engine problems such as dieseling, misfiring, or stumbling as soon as possible.

## DIAGNOSING CATALYTIC CONVERTERS

**THE TAP TEST** The simple **tap test** involves tapping (not pounding) on the catalytic converter using a rubber mallet. If the substrate inside the converter is broken, the converter will rattle when hit. If the converter rattles, a replacement converter is required.

**TESTING BACKPRESSURE WITH A PRESSURE GAUGE** Exhaust system backpressure can be measured directly by installing a pressure gauge in an exhaust opening. This can be accomplished in one of the following ways.

1. To test backpressure, remove the inside of an old, discarded oxygen sensor and thread in an adapter to convert it to a vacuum or pressure gauge.

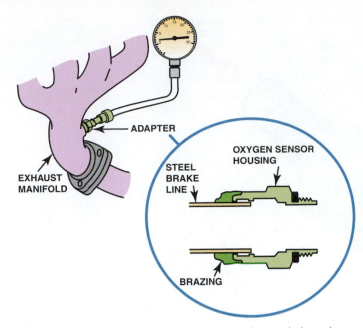

**FIGURE 24–26** A back pressure tool can be made by using an oxygen sensor housing and epoxy or braze to hold the tube to the housing.

**NOTE: An adapter can be easily made by inserting a metal tube or pipe into an old oxygen sensor housing. A short section of brake line works great. The pipe can be brazed to the oxygen sensor housing or it can be glued with epoxy. An 18 mm compression gauge adapter can also be adapted to fit into the oxygen sensor opening.** ● **SEE FIGURE 24–26.**

2. To test the exhaust backpressure at the exhaust gas recirculation (EGR) valve, remove the EGR valve and fabricate a plate equipped with a fitting for a pressure gauge.

3. To test at the secondary air-injection (SAI) check valve, remove the check valve from the exhaust tubes leading to the exhaust manifold. Use a rubber cone with a tube inside to seal against the exhaust tube. Connect the tube to a pressure gauge.

At idle, the maximum backpressure should be less than 1.5 PSI (10 kPa), and it should be less than 2.5 PSI (15 kPa) at 2500 RPM. Pressure readings higher than these indicate that the exhaust system is restricted and further testing will be needed to determine the location of the restriction.

### TESTING FOR BACKPRESSURE USING A VACUUM GAUGE
An exhaust restriction can be tested indirectly by checking the intake manifold vacuum with the engine operating at a fast idle speed (about 2500 RPM). If the exhaust is restricted, some exhaust can pass and the effect may not be noticeable when the engine is at idle speed. However, when the engine is operating at a higher speed, the exhaust gases can build up behind the restriction and eventually will be unable to leave the combustion chamber. When some of the exhaust is left behind at the end of the exhaust stroke, the resulting pressure in the combustion chamber reduces engine vacuum. To test for an exhaust restriction using a vacuum gauge, perform the following steps.

**STEP 1** Attach a vacuum gauge to an intake manifold vacuum source.

**STEP 2** Start the engine. Record the engine manifold vacuum reading. The engine vacuum should read 17 to 21 in. Hg when the engine is at idle speed.

**STEP 3** Increase the engine speed to 2500 RPM and hold that speed for 60 seconds while looking at the vacuum gauge.

**Results**

- If the vacuum reading is equal to or higher than the vacuum reading when the engine was at idle speed, the exhaust system is *not* restricted.

- If the vacuum reading is lower than the vacuum reading when the engine was at idle speed, then the exhaust is restricted. Further testing will be needed to determine the location of the restriction.

### TESTING A CATALYTIC CONVERTER FOR TEMPERATURE RISE
A properly working catalytic converter should be able to reduce NOx exhaust emissions into nitrogen (N) and oxygen ($O_2$) and oxidize unburned hydrocarbon (HC) and carbon monoxide (CO) into harmless carbon dioxide ($CO_2$) and water vapor ($H_2O$). During these chemical processes, the catalytic converter should increase in temperature at least 10% if the converter is working properly. To test the converter, operate the engine at 2500 RPM for at least two minutes to fully warm up the converter. Measure the inlet and the outlet temperatures using an **infrared thermometer (pyrometer),** as shown in ● **FIGURE 24–27.**

**NOTE: If the engine is extremely efficient, the converter may not have any excessive unburned hydrocarbons or carbon monoxide to convert! In this case, a spark plug wire could be grounded out using a vacuum hose and a test light to create some unburned hydrocarbon in the exhaust. Do not ground out a cylinder for longer than 10 seconds or the excessive amount of unburned hydrocarbon could overheat and damage the converter.**

### CATALYTIC CONVERTER EFFICIENCY TESTS
The efficiency of a catalytic converter can be determined using an exhaust gas analyzer.

- **Oxygen level test.** With the engine warm and in closed loop, check the oxygen ($O_2$) and carbon monoxide (CO) levels. A good converter should be able to oxidize the extra hydrocarbons caused by the rapid acceleration.

  - If $O_2$ is zero, go to the snap-throttle test.

  - If $O_2$ is greater than zero, check the CO level.

  - If CO is greater than zero, the converter is *not* functioning correctly.

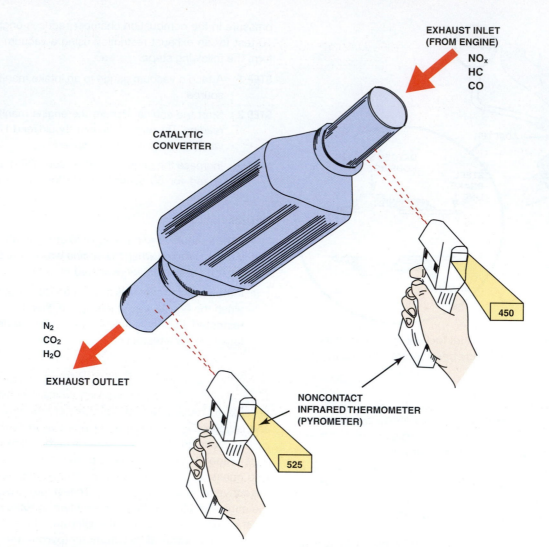

EXHAUST INLET
(FROM ENGINE)

$NO_x$
HC
CO

CATALYTIC
CONVERTER

$N_2$
$CO_2$
$H_2O$

EXHAUST OUTLET

450

NONCONTACT
INFRARED THERMOMETER
(PYROMETER)

525

**FIGURE 24–27** The temperature of the outlet should be at least 10% hotter than the temperature of the inlet. If a converter is not working, the inlet temperature will be hotter than the outlet temperature.

■ **Snap-throttle test.** With the engine warm and in closed loop, snap the throttle to wide open (WOT) in park or neutral and observe the oxygen reading.

■ The $O_2$ reading should not exceed 1.2%; if it does, the converter is *not* working.

■ If the $O_2$ rises to 1.2%, the converter may have low efficiency.

■ If the $O_2$ remains below 1.2%, then the converter is okay.

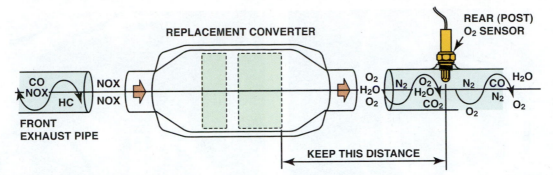

FIGURE 24–28 Whenever replacing a catalytic converter with a universal unit, first measure the distance between the rear brick and the center of the rear oxygen sensor. Be sure that the replacement unit is installed to the same dimension.

## CATALYTIC CONVERTER REPLACEMENT GUIDELINES

Because a catalytic converter is a major exhaust gas emission control device, the Environmental Protection Agency (EPA) has strict guidelines for its replacement, including:

- If a converter is replaced on a vehicle with less than 80,000 miles or eight years, depending on the year of the vehicle, an original equipment catalytic converter *must* be used as a replacement.
- The replacement converter must be of the same design as the original. If the original had an air pump fitting, so must the replacement.
- The old converter must be kept for possible inspection by the authorities for 60 days.

- A form must be completed and signed by both the vehicle owner and a representative from the service facility. This form must state the cause of the converter failure and must remain on file for two years.

## CATALYTIC CONVERTER-RELATED DIAGNOSTIC TROUBLE CODE

| Diagnostic Trouble Code | Description | Possible Causes |
|---|---|---|
| P0422 | Catalytic converter efficiency failure | 1. Engine mechanical fault<br>2. Exhaust leaks<br>3. Fuel contaminants, such as engine oil, coolant, or sulfur |

## EVAPORATIVE EMISSION CONTROL SYSTEM

**PURPOSE AND FUNCTION** The purpose of the evaporative (EVAP) emission control system is to trap and hold gasoline vapors, also called volatile organic compounds, or VOCs. The evaporative control system includes the charcoal canister, hoses, and valves. These vapors are routed into a charcoal canister, then into the intake airflow where they are burned in the engine instead of being released into the atmosphere.

**COMMON COMPONENTS** The fuel tank filler caps used on vehicles with modern EVAP systems are a special design. Most EVAP fuel tank filler caps have pressure-vacuum relief built into them. When pressure or vacuum exceeds a calibrated value, the valve opens. Once the pressure or vacuum has been relieved, the valve closes. If a sealed cap is used on an EVAP system that

FIGURE 24–29 A capless system from a Ford Flex does not use a replaceable cap; instead, it has a spring-loaded closure.

FIGURE 24–30 A charcoal canister can be located under the hood or underneath the vehicle.

### FREQUENTLY ASKED QUESTION

**When Filling My Fuel Tank, Why Should I Stop When the Pump Clicks Off?**

Every fuel tank has an upper volume chamber that allows for expansion of the fuel when hot. The volume of the chamber is between 10% and 20% of the volume of the tank. For example, if a fuel tank had a capacity of 20 gallons, the expansion chamber volume would be from 2 to 4 gallons. A hose is attached at the top of the chamber and vented to the charcoal canister. If extra fuel is forced into this expansion volume, liquid gasoline can be drawn into the charcoal canister. This liquid fuel can saturate the canister and create an overly rich air-fuel mixture when the canister purge valve is opened during normal vehicle operation. This extra-rich air-fuel mixture can cause the vehicle to fail an exhaust emissions test, reduce fuel economy, and possibly damage the catalytic converter. To avoid problems, simply add fuel to the next dime's worth after the nozzle clicks off. This will ensure that the tank is full, yet not overfilled.

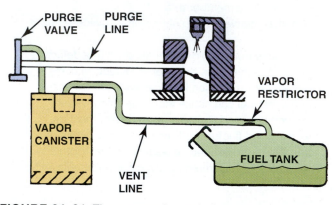

FIGURE 24–31 The evaporative emission control system includes all of the lines, hoses, and valves, plus the charcoal canister.

requires a pressure-vacuum relief design, a vacuum lock may develop in the fuel system, or the fuel tank may be damaged by fuel expansion or contraction. ● **SEE FIGURE 24–29.**

## EVAPORATIVE CONTROL SYSTEM OPERATION

The canister is located under the hood or underneath the vehicle, and is filled with activated charcoal granules that can hold up to one-third of their own weight in fuel vapors. ● **SEE FIGURE 24–30.**

**NOTE: Some vehicles with large or dual fuel tanks may have dual canisters.**

Activated charcoal is an effective vapor trap because of its great surface area. Each gram of activated charcoal has a surface area of 1,100 m² (more than a quarter acre). Typical canisters hold either 300 or 625 grams of charcoal *with a surface area equivalent to 80 or 165 football fields.* By a process called **adsorption,** the fuel vapor molecules adhere to the carbon surface. This attaching force is not strong, so the system purges the vapor molecules quite simply by sending a fresh airflow through the charcoal.

- **Vapor purging.** During engine operation, stored vapors are drawn from the canister into the engine through a hose connected to the throttle body or the air cleaner. This "purging" process mixes HC vapors from the canister with the existing air-fuel charge. ● **SEE FIGURES 24–31 AND 24–32.**

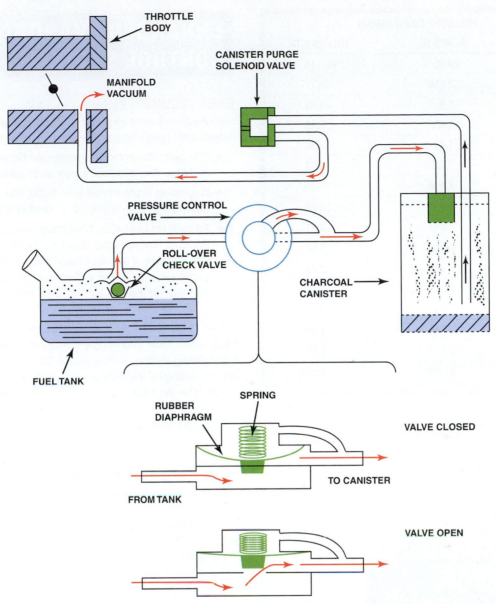

**FIGURE 24–32** A typical evaporative emission control system. Note that when the computer turns on the canister purge sole-noid valve, manifold vacuum draws any stored vapors from the canister into the engine. Manifold vacuum also is applied to the pressure control valve. When this valve opens, fumes from the fuel tank are drawn into the charcoal canister and eventually into the engine. When the solenoid valve is turned off (or the engine stops and there is no manifold vacuum), the pressure control valve is spring-loaded shut to keep vapors inside the fuel tank from escaping to the atmosphere.

■ **Computer-controlled purge.** The PCM controls when the canister purges on most engines. This is done by an electric vacuum solenoid, and one or more purge valves. Under normal conditions, most engine control systems permit purging only during closed-loop operation at cruising speeds. During other engine operation conditions, such as open-loop mode, idle, deceleration, or wide-open throttle, the PCM prevents canister purging.

Pressures can build inside the fuel system and are usually measured in units of inches of water (in. $H_2O$) (28 in. of water equals 1 PSI). Some scan tools display other units of measure for the EVAP system that make understanding the system difficult. ● **SEE CHART 24–2** for the conversion among PSI, in. Hg., and in. $H_2O$.

Pressure buildup in the EVAP system can be caused by:

■ Fuel evaporation rates (volatility)
■ Gas tank size (fuel surface area and volume)
■ Fuel level (liquid versus vapor)
■ Fuel slosh (driving conditions)
■ Hot temperatures (ambient, in-tank, close to the tank)
■ Returned fuel from the rail

| PRESSURE CONVERSIONS | | |
|---|---|---|
| PSI | INCHES HG | INCHES H$_2$O |
| 14.7 | 29.93 | 407.19 |
| 1.0 | 2.036 | 27.7 |
| 0.9 | 1.8 | 24.93 |
| 0.8 | 1.63 | 22.16 |
| 0.7 | 1.43 | 19.39 |
| 0.6 | 1.22 | 16.62 |
| 0.5 | 1.018 | 13.85 |
| 0.4 | 0.814 | 11.08 |
| 0.3 | 0.611 | 8.31 |
| 0.2 | 0.407 | 5.54 |
| 0.1 | 0.204 | 2.77 |
| 0.09 | 0.183 | 2.49 |
| 0.08 | 0.163 | 2.22 |
| 0.07 | 0.143 | 1.94 |
| 0.06 | 0.122 | 1.66 |
| 0.05 | 0.102 | 1.385 |

**CHART 24–2**

NOTE: Pressure conversions.
1 PSI = 28 in. H$_2$O
1/4 PSI = 7 in. H$_2$O

# NONENHANCED EVAPORATIVE CONTROL SYSTEMS

Prior to 1996, evaporative systems were referred to as nonenhanced evaporative (EVAP) control systems. This term refers to evaporative systems that had limited diagnostic capabilities. While they are often PCM controlled, their diagnostic capability is usually limited to their ability to detect if purge has occurred. Many systems have a diagnostic switch that could sense if purge is occurring and set a code if no purge is detected. This system does not check for leaks. On some vehicles, the PCM also has the capability of monitoring the integrity of the purge solenoid and circuit. These systems' limitations are their ability to check the integrity of the evaporative system on the vehicle. They could not detect leaks or missing or loose gas caps that could lead to excessive evaporative emissions from the vehicle. Nonenhanced evaporative systems use either a canister purge solenoid or a vapor management valve to control purge vapor.

# ENHANCED EVAPORATIVE CONTROL SYSTEM

**BACKGROUND** Beginning in 1996, with OBD-II vehicles, manufacturers were required to install systems that are able to detect both purge flow and evaporative system leakage.

- The systems on models produced between 1996 and 2000 must be able to detect a leak as small as 0.04 in. diameter.
- Beginning in the model year 2000, the enhanced systems started a phase-in of 0.02 in. diameter leak detection.
- All vehicles built after 1995 have enhanced evaporative systems that have the ability to detect purge flow and system leakage. If either of these two functions fails, the system is required to set a diagnostic trouble code (DTC) and turn on the MIL light to warn the driver of the failure.

**CANISTER VENT VALVE** The canister vent valve is a *normally open* valve and is only closed when commanded by the PCM during testing of the system. The vent valve is only closed during testing by the PCM as part of the mandated OBD-II standards. The vent solenoid is located under the vehicle in most cases and is exposed to the environment, making this valve subject to rust and corrosion.

**CANISTER PURGE VALVE** The purge valve, also called the **canister purge (CANP)** solenoid is *normally closed* and is pulsed open by the PCM during purging. The purge valve is connected to the intake manifold vacuum and this line is used to draw gasoline vapors from the charcoal canister into the engine when the purge valve is commanded open. Most purge valves are pulsed on and off to better control the amount of fumes being drawn into the intake manifold.

🔧 **TECH TIP**

**Problems After Refueling? Check the Purge Valve.**

The purge valve is normally closed and open only when the PCM is commanding the system to purge. If the purge solenoid were to become stuck in the open position, gasoline fumes would be allowed to flow directly from the gas tank to the intake manifold. When refueling, this would result in a lot of fumes being forced into the intake manifold; and as a result, would cause a hard-to-start condition after refueling. This would also result in a rich exhaust (likely black) when first starting the engine after refueling. Although the purge solenoid is usually located under the hood of most vehicles and less subject to rust and corrosion, as with the vent valve, it can still fail.

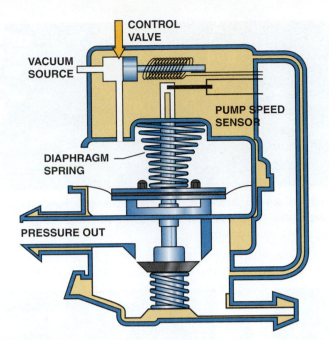

**FIGURE 24–33** A leak detection pump (LDP) used on some Chrysler vehicles to pressurize (slightly) the fuel system to check for leaks.

**FIGURE 24–34** A restricted fuel fill pipe shown on a vehicle with the interior removed.

## LEAK DETECTION PUMP SYSTEM

**PURPOSE AND FUNCTION** Many vehicles use a **leak detection pump (LDP)** as part of the evaporative control system diagnosis equipment. ● **SEE FIGURE 24–33.**

**OPERATION** The system works to test for leaks as follows:

- The purge solenoid is normally closed.
- The vent valve in the LDP is normally open. Filtered fresh air is drawn through the LDP to the canister.
- The LDP uses a spring attached to a diaphragm to apply pressure (7.5 in. $H_2O$) to the fuel tank.
- The PCM monitors the LDP switch that is triggered if the pressure drops in the fuel tank.
- The time between LDP solenoid off and LDP switch close is called the pump period. This time period is inversely proportional to the size of the leak. The shorter the pump period, the larger the leak. The longer the pump period, the smaller the leak.

  EVAP large leak (greater than 0.08 in.): less than 0.9 second

  EVAP medium leak (0.04 to 0.08 in.): 0.9 to 1.2 seconds

  EVAP small leak (0.02 to 0.04 in.): 1.2 to 6 seconds

## ONBOARD REFUELING VAPOR RECOVERY

**PURPOSE AND FUNCTION** The onboard refueling vapor recovery (ORVR) system was first introduced on some 1998 vehicles. Previously designed EVAP systems allowed fuel vapor to escape to the atmosphere during refueling.

**OPERATION** The primary feature of most ORVR systems is the restricted tank filler tube, which is about 1 in. (25 mm) in diameter. This reduced size filler tube creates an aspiration effect, which tends to draw outside air into the filler tube. During refueling, the fuel tank is vented to the charcoal canister, which captures the gas fumes; and with air flowing into the filler tube, no vapors can escape to the atmosphere. ● **SEE FIGURE 24–34.**

## STATE INSPECTION EVAP TESTS

In some states, a periodic inspection and test of the fuel system are mandated along with a dynamometer test. The emissions inspection includes tests on the vehicle before and during the dynamometer test. Before the running test, the fuel tank and cap, fuel lines, canister, and other fuel system components must be inspected and tested to ensure that they are not leaking gasoline vapors into the atmosphere.

- First, the fuel tank cap is tested to ensure that it is sealing properly and holds pressure within specs.
- Next, the cap is installed on the vehicle, and using a special adapter, the EVAP system is pressurized to approximately 0.5 PSI and monitored for two minutes.
- Pressure in the tank and lines should not drop below approximately 0.3 PSI.

If the cap or system leaks, hydrocarbon emissions are likely being released, and the vehicle fails the test. If the system leaks, an ultrasonic leak detector may be used to find the leak.

Finally, with the engine warmed up and running at a moderate speed, the canister purge line is tested for adequate flow using a special flow meter inserted into the system. In one example, if the flow from the canister to the intake system when the system is activated is at least 1 liter per minute, then the vehicle passes the canister purge test.

# DIAGNOSING THE EVAP SYSTEM

**SYMPTOMS** Before vehicle emissions testing began in many parts of the country, little service work was done on the evaporative emission system. Common engine-performance problems that can be caused by a fault in this system include:

- **Poor fuel economy.** A leak in a vacuum-valve diaphragm can result in engine vacuum drawing in a constant flow of gasoline vapors from the fuel tank. This usually results in a drop in fuel economy of 2 to 4 miles per gallon (mpg). Use a hand-operated vacuum pump to check that the vacuum diaphragm can hold vacuum.
- **Poor performance.** A vacuum leak in the manifold or ported vacuum section of vacuum hose in the system can cause the engine to run rough. Age, heat, and time all contribute to the deterioration of rubber hoses.

Enhanced exhaust emissions (I/M-240) testing tests the evaporative emission system. A leak in the system is tested by pressurizing the entire fuel system to a level below 1 lb/in.$^2$ or 1 PSI (about 14 in. $H_2O$). The system is typically pressurized with nitrogen, a nonflammable gas that makes up 78% of our atmosphere. The pressure in the system is then shut off and monitored. If the pressure drops below a set standard, then the vehicle fails the test. This test determines if there is a leak in the system.

**HINT: To help pass the evaporative section of an enhanced emissions test, arrive at the test site with less than one-half tank of fuel. This means that the rest of the**

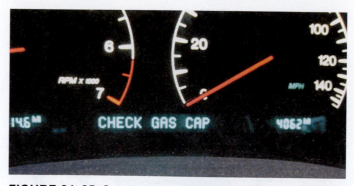

**FIGURE 24–35** Some vehicles will display a message if an evaporative control system leak is detected that could be the result of a loose gas cap.

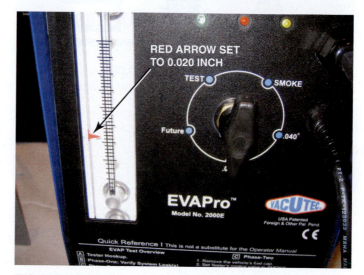

**FIGURE 24–36** To test for a leak, this tester was set to the 0.02 in. hole and turned on. The ball rose in the scale on the left and the red arrow was moved to that location. When testing the system for leaks, if the ball rises higher than the arrow, then the leak is larger than 0.02 in. If the ball does not rise to the level of the arrow, the leak is smaller than 0.02 in.

**volume of the fuel tank is filled with air. It takes longer for the pressure to drop from a small leak when the volume of the air is greater compared to when the tank is full and the volume of air remaining in the tank is small.**

**LOCATING LEAKS IN THE SYSTEM** Leaks in the evaporative emission control system will cause the malfunction check gas cap indication lamp to light on some vehicles. ● **SEE FIGURE 24–35.**

A leak will also cause a gas smell, which would be most noticeable if the vehicle were parked in an enclosed garage. The first step is to determine if there is a leak in the system by setting the EVAP tester to rate the system, either a 0.04 in. or a 0.02 in. hole size leak. ● **SEE FIGURE 24–36.**

**FIGURE 24–37** This unit is applying smoke to the fuel tank through an adapter and the leak was easily found to be the gas cap seal.

**FIGURE 24–38** An emission tester that uses nitrogen to pressurize the fuel system.

After it has been determined that a leak exists and that it is larger than specified, then there are two methods that can be used to check for leaks in the evaporative system.

- **Smoke machine testing.** The most efficient method of leak detection is to introduce smoke under low pressure from a machine specifically designed for this purpose. ● **SEE FIGURE 24–37.**
- **Nitrogen gas pressurization.** This method uses nitrogen gas under a very low pressure (lower than 1 PSI) in the fuel system. The service technician then listens for the escaping air, using amplified headphones. ● **SEE FIGURE 24–38.**

## EVAPORATIVE SYSTEM MONITOR

**OBD-II REQUIREMENTS** OBD-II computer programs not only detect faults, but also *periodically test various systems* and alert the driver before emissions-related components are harmed by system faults.

- Serious faults cause a blinking malfunction indicator lamp (MIL) or even an engine shutdown.
- Less serious faults may simply store a code but not illuminate the MIL.

The OBD-II requirements did not affect fuel system design. However, one new component, a fuel evaporative canister purge line pressure sensor, was added for monitoring purge line pressure during tests. The OBD-II requirements state that vehicle fuel systems are to be routinely tested *while underway* by the PCM.

All OBD-II vehicles perform a canister purge system pressure test, as commanded by the PCM. While the vehicle is being driven, the vapor line between the canister and the purge valve is monitored for pressure changes.

- When the canister purge solenoid is open, the line should be under a vacuum since vapors must be drawn from the canister into the intake system. However, when the purge solenoid is closed, there should be no vacuum in the line. The pressure sensor detects if a vacuum is present, and the information is compared to the command given to the solenoid.
- If, during the canister purge cycle, no vacuum exists in the canister purge line, a code is set indicating a possible fault, which could be caused by an inoperative or clogged solenoid or a blocked or leaking canister purge fuel line. Likewise, if vacuum exists when no command for purge is given, a stuck solenoid is evident, and a code is set. The EVAP system monitor tests for purge volume and leaks.

A typical EVAP monitor first closes off the system to atmospheric pressure and opens the purge valve during cruise operation. A **fuel tank pressure (FTP)** sensor then monitors the rate with which vacuum increases in the system. The monitor uses this information to determine the purge volume flow rate. To test for leaks, the EVAP monitor closes the purge valve, creating a completely closed system. The fuel tank pressure sensor then monitors the leak-down rate. If the rate exceeds PCM-stored values, a leak greater than or equal to the OBD-II standard of 0.04 in. (1 mm) or 0.02 in. (0.5 mm) exists. After two consecutive failed trips testing either purge volume or the presence of a leak, the PCM lights the MIL and sets a DTC.

The fuel tank pressure sensor is similar to the MAP sensor, and instead of monitoring intake manifold absolute pressure, it is used to monitor fuel tank pressure. ● **SEE FIGURE 24–39.**

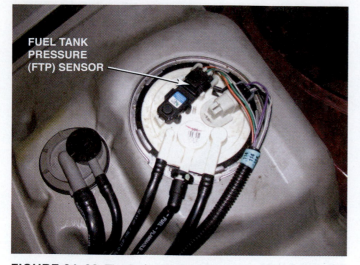

**FIGURE 24–39** The fuel tank pressure sensor (black unit with three wires) looks like a MAP sensor and is usually located on top of the fuel pump module (white unit).

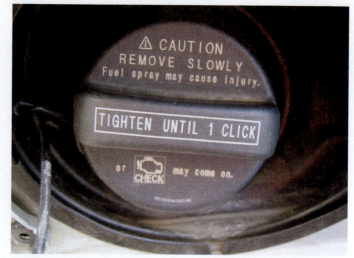

**FIGURE 24–40** This Toyota cap has a warning. The check engine light will come on if not tightened until one click.

**ENGINE-OFF NATURAL VACUUM** System integrity (leakage) can also be checked after the engine is shut off. The premise is that a warm evaporative system will cool down after the engine is shut off and the vehicle is stable. A slight vacuum will be created in the gas tank during this cooling period. If a specific level of vacuum is reached and maintained, the system is said to have integrity (no leakage).

## TYPICAL EVAP MONITOR

The PCM will run the EVAP monitor when the following enable criteria are met.

- Cold start
- Barometric pressure (BARO) greater than 70 kPa (20.7 in. Hg or 10.2 PSI)
- Intake air temperature (IAT) between 39°F and 86°F at engine start-up

- Engine coolant temperature (ECT) between 39°F and 86°F at engine start-up
- ECT and IAT within 39°F of each other at engine start-up
- Fuel level within 15% to 85%
- Throttle position (TP) sensor between 9% and 35%

**RUNNING THE EVAP MONITOR** There are three tests that are performed during a typical EVAP monitor. A DTC is assigned to each test.

1. **Weak vacuum test (P0440—large leak).** This test identifies gross leaks. During the monitor, the vent solenoid is closed and the purge solenoid is duty cycled. The fuel tank pressure (FTP) should indicate a vacuum of approximately 6 to 10 in. $H_2O$.

2. **Small leak test (P0442—small leak).** After the large leak test passes, the PCM checks for a small leak by keeping the vent solenoid closed and closing the purge solenoid. The system is now sealed. The PCM measures the change in FTP voltage over time.

3. **Excess vacuum test (P0446).** This test checks for vent path restrictions. With the vent solenoid open and purge commanded, the PCM should not see excessive vacuum in the EVAP system. Typical EVAP system vacuum with the vent solenoid open is about 5 to 6 in. $H_2O$.

**FIGURE 24–41** The fuel level must be between 15% and 85% before the EVAP monitor will run on most vehicles.

| Diagnostic Trouble Code | Description | Possible Causes |
|---|---|---|
| P0440 | Evaporative system fault | • Loose gas cap<br>• Defective EVAP vent<br>• Cracked charcoal canister<br>• EVAP vent or purge vapor line problems |
| P0442 | Small leak detected | • Loose gas cap<br>• Defective EVAP vent or purge solenoid<br>• EVAP vent or purge line problems |
| P0446 | EVAP canister vent blocked | • EVAP vent or purge solenoid electrical problems<br>• Restricted EVAP canister vent line |

## SUMMARY

1. Recirculating 6% to 10% inert exhaust gases back into the intake system by the EGR system reduces peak temperature inside the combustion chamber and reduces NOx exhaust emissions.

2. EGR is usually not needed at idle, at wide-open throttle, or when the engine is cold.

3. Many EGR systems use a feedback potentiometer to signal the PCM the position of the EGR valve pintle.

4. OBD-II requires that the flow rate be tested and then is achieved by opening the EGR valve and observing the reaction of the MAP sensor.

5. Positive crankcase ventilation (PCV) systems use a valve or a fixed orifice to control and direct the fumes from the crankcase back into the intake system.

6. A PCV valve regulates the flow of fumes depending on engine vacuum and seals the crankcase vent in the event of a backfire.

7. As much as 30% of the air needed by the engine at idle speed flows through the PCV system.

8. The secondary air-injection (SAI) system forces air at low pressure into the exhaust to reduce CO and HC exhaust emissions.

9. A catalytic converter is an aftertreatment device that reduces exhaust emissions outside of the engine. A catalyst is an element that starts a chemical reaction but is not consumed in the process.

10. The catalyst material used in a catalytic converter includes rhodium, palladium, and platinum.

11. The OBD-II system monitor compares the relative activity of a rear oxygen sensor to the precatalytic oxygen sensor to determine catalytic converter efficiency.

12. The purpose of the evaporative (EVAP) emission control system is to reduce the release of volatile organic compounds (VOCs) into the atmosphere.

13. A carbon (charcoal) canister is used to trap and hold gasoline vapors until they can be purged and run into the engine to be burned.

14. OBD-II regulation requires that the evaporative emission control system be checked for leakage and proper purge flow rates.

15. External leaks can best be located by pressurizing the fuel system with low-pressure smoke.

1. How does the use of exhaust gas recirculation reduce NOx exhaust emission?

2. How does the DPFE sensor work?

3. What exhaust emissions does the PCV valve and SAI system control?

4. How does a catalytic converter reduce NOx to nitrogen and oxygen?

5. How does the computer monitor catalytic converter performance?

## CHAPTER QUIZ

1. Two technicians are discussing clogged EGR passages. Technician A says clogged EGR passages can cause excessive NOx exhaust emission. Technician B says that clogged EGR passages can cause the engine to ping (spark knock or detonation). Which technician is correct?
   a. Technician A only
   b. Technician B only
   c. Both Technicians A and B
   d. Neither Technician A nor B

2. An EGR valve that is partially stuck open would *most likely* cause what condition?
   a. Rough idle/stalling
   b. Excessive NOx exhaust emissions
   c. Ping (spark knock or detonation)
   d. Missing at highway speed

3. How much air flows through the PCV system when the engine is at idle speed?
   a. 1% to 3%
   b. 5% to 10%
   c. 10% to 20%
   d. Up to 30%

4. Technician A says that if a PCV valve rattles, then it is okay and does not need to be replaced. Technician B says that if a PCV valve does not rattle, it should be replaced. Which technician is correct?
   a. Technician A only
   b. Technician B only
   c. Both Technicians A and B
   d. Neither Technician A nor B

5. The switching valves on the AIR pump have failed several times. Technician A says that a defective exhaust check valve could be the cause. Technician B says that a leaking exhaust system at the muffler could be the cause. Which technician is correct?
   a. Technician A only
   b. Technician B only
   c. Both Technicians A and B
   d. Neither Technician A nor B

6. Two technicians are discussing testing a catalytic converter. Technician A says that a vacuum gauge can be used and observed to see if the vacuum drops with the engine at 2500 RPM for 60 seconds. Technician B says that a pressure gauge can be used to check for backpressure. Which technician is correct?
   a. Technician A only
   b. Technician B only
   c. Both Technicians A and B
   d. Neither Technician A nor B

7. At about what temperature does oxygen combine with the nitrogen in the air to form NOx?
   a. 500°F (260°C)
   b. 750°F (400°C)
   c. 1,500°F (815°C)
   d. 2,500°F (1,370°C)

8. A P0401 is being discussed. Technician A says that a stuck-closed EGR valve could be the cause. Technician B says that clogged EGR ports could be the cause. Which technician is correct?
   a. Technician A only
   b. Technician B only
   c. Both Technicians A and B
   d. Neither Technician A nor B

9. Which EVAP valve(s) is(are) normally closed?
   a. Canister purge valve
   b. Canister vent valve
   c. Both canister purge and canister vent valves
   d. Neither canister purge nor canister vent valve

10. Before an evaporative emission monitor will run, the fuel level must be where?
    a. At least 75% full
    b. Over 25%
    c. Between 15% and 85%
    d. The level of the fuel in the tank is not needed to run the monitor test

# chapter 25

# ENGINE CONDITION DIAGNOSIS

**OBJECTIVES:** After studying Chapter 25, the reader will be able to: • Prepare for ASE Engine Performance (A8) certification test content area "A" (General Engine Diagnosis). • List the visual checks to determine engine condition. • Discuss engine noise and its relation to engine condition. • Describe how to perform dry, wet, and running compression tests. • Explain how to perform a cylinder leakage test. • Discuss vacuum testing to determine engine condition. • Describe how to test for excessive exhaust system back pressure.

**KEY TERMS:** Back pressure 356 • Compression test 350 • Cranking vacuum test 353 • Cylinder leakage test 352 • Dynamic compression test 351 • Idle vacuum test 353 • In. Hg 353 • Paper test 349 • Power balance test 353 • Restricted exhaust 356 • Running compression test 351 • Vacuum test 353 • Wet compression test 351

## TYPICAL ENGINE-RELATED COMPLAINTS

If there is an engine operation problem, then the cause could be any one of many items, including the engine itself. The condition of the engine should be tested when the operation of the engine is not satisfactory.

Many driveability problems are *not* caused by engine mechanical problems. A thorough inspection and testing of the ignition and fuel systems should be performed before testing for mechanical engine problems.

Typical engine mechanical-related complaints include the following:

- Excessive oil consumption
- Engine misfiring
- Loss of power
- Smoke from the engine or exhaust
- Engine noise

## ENGINE SMOKE DIAGNOSIS

The color of engine exhaust smoke can indicate what engine problem might exist. ● SEE CHART 25–1.

**FIGURE 25–1** A binder clip being used to keep a fender cover from falling.

🔧 **TECH TIP**

**The Binder Clip Trick**

It is important to use fender covers when working on an engine. The problem is few covers remain in place and they often become more of a hindrance than a help. A binder clip, available at most office supply stores, can be used to hold fender covers to the lip of the fender of most vehicles. When clipped over the lip, the cover is securely attached and cannot be pulled loose. This method works with cloth and vinyl covers. ● SEE FIGURE 25–1.

| TYPICAL EXHAUST SMOKE COLOR | POSSIBLE CAUSES |
|---|---|
| Blue | Blue exhaust indicates that the engine is burning oil. Oil is getting into the combustion chamber either past the piston rings or past the valve stem seals. Blue smoke only after start-up is usually due to defective valve stem seals. ● SEE FIGURE 25–2. |
| Black | Black exhaust smoke is due to excessive fuel being burned in the combustion chamber. Typical causes include a defective or misadjusted throttle body, leaking fuel injector, or excessive fuel pump pressure. |
| White (steam) | White smoke or steam from the exhaust is normal during cold weather and represents condensed steam. Every engine creates about 1 gallon of water for each gallon of gasoline burned. If the steam from the exhaust is excessive, then water (coolant) is getting into the combustion chamber. Typical causes include a defective cylinder head gasket, a cracked cylinder head, or in severe cases a cracked block. ● SEE FIGURE 25–3.<br><br>NOTE: **White smoke can also be created when automatic transmission fluid (ATF) is burned. A common source of ATF getting into the engine is through a defective vacuum modulator valve on older automatic transmissions.** |

**CHART 25–1**

The color of exhaust and possible causes.

FIGURE 25–2 Blowby gases coming out of the crankcase vent hose. Excessive amounts of combustion gases flow past the piston rings and into the crankcase.

CRANKCASE VENT HOSE

FIGURE 25–3 White steam is usually an indication of a blown (defective) cylinder head gasket that allows engine coolant to flow into the combustion chamber where it is turned to steam.

## VISUAL CHECKS

The first and most important "test" that can be performed is a careful visual inspection.

**OIL LEVEL AND CONDITION**    The first area for visual inspection is oil level and condition.

1. Oil should be to the proper level.
2. Oil condition
   a. Using a match or lighter, try to light the oil on the dipstick; if the oil flames up, gasoline is present in the engine oil.
   b. Drip some of the engine oil from the dipstick onto the hot exhaust manifold. If the oil bubbles or boils, there is coolant (water) in the oil.
   c. Check for grittiness by rubbing the oil between your fingers.

**What's Leaking?**

The color of the leaking fluids observed under a vehicle can help the technician determine and correct the cause. Some leaks, such as condensate (water) from the air-conditioning system, are normal, whereas a brake fluid leak is very dangerous. The following are colors of common leaks:

| Sooty black | Engine oil |
|---|---|
| Yellow, green, blue, or orange | Antifreeze (coolant) |
| Red | Automatic transmission fluid |
| Murky brown | Brake or power steering fluid or very neglected antifreeze (coolant) |
| Clear | Air-conditioning condensate (water) (normal) |

**FIGURE 25–4** What looks like an oil pan gasket leak can be a rocker cover gasket leak. Always look up and look for the highest place you see oil leaking; that should be repaired first.

**COOLANT LEVEL AND CONDITION** Most mechanical engine problems are caused by overheating. The proper operation of the cooling system is critical to the life of any engine.

**NOTE: Check the coolant level in the radiator only if the radiator is cool. If the radiator is hot and the radiator cap is removed, the drop in pressure above the coolant will cause the coolant to boil immediately and can cause severe burns when the coolant explosively expands upward and outward from the radiator opening.**

1. The coolant level in the coolant recovery container should be within the limits indicated on the overflow bottle. If this level is too low or the coolant recovery container is empty, then check the level of coolant in the radiator (only when cool) and also check the operation of the pressure cap.

2. The coolant should be checked with a hydrometer or refractometer for boiling and freezing temperature. This test indicates if the concentration of the antifreeze is sufficient for proper protection.

3. Pressure-test the cooling system and look for leakage. Coolant leakage can often be seen around hoses or cooling system components because it will often cause the following:
   a. Grayish white stain
   b. Rusty stain
   c. Dye stains from antifreeze (greenish or yellowish depending on the type of coolant)

4. Check for cool areas of the radiator indicating clogged sections.

5. Check operation and condition of the fan clutch, electric fan, and coolant pump drive belt.

**FIGURE 25–5** The transmission and flexplate (flywheel) were removed to check the exact location of this oil leak. The rear main seal and/or the oil pan gasket could be the cause of this leak.

**OIL LEAKS** Oil leaks can lead to severe engine damage if the resulting low oil level is not corrected. Besides causing an oily mess where the vehicle is parked, the oil leak can cause blue smoke to occur under the hood as leaking oil drips on the exhaust system. *Finding* the location of the oil leak can often be difficult. ● **SEE FIGURES 25–4 AND 25–5.**

FIGURE 25–6 Using a black light to spot leaks after adding dye to the oil. Always use dye designed for use in engine oil and for best results change the oil before testing because the dye works best with clean oil.

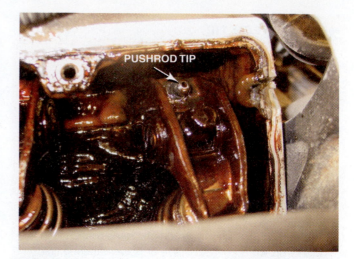

FIGURE 25–7 A noisy valve was discovered to be a pushrod that punched through a rocker arm on this General Motors 3100 V-6 engine.

To help find the source of oil leaks, follow these steps.

**STEP 1** Clean the engine or area around the suspected oil leak. Use a high-powered hot water spray to wash the engine. While the engine is running, spray the entire engine and the engine compartment. Avoid letting the water come into direct contact with the air inlet and ignition distributor or ignition coil(s).

**NOTE: If the engine starts to run rough or stalls when the engine gets wet, then the secondary ignition wires (spark plug wires) or distributor cap may be defective or have weak insulation. Be certain to wipe all wires and the distributor cap dry with a soft, dry cloth if the engine stalls.**

An alternative method is to spray a degreaser on the engine, then start and run the engine until warm. Engine heat helps the degreaser penetrate the grease and dirt. Use a water hose to rinse off the engine and engine compartment.

**STEP 2** If the oil leak is not visible or oil seems to be coming from "everywhere," use a white talcum powder. The leaking oil will show as a dark area on the white powder. See the Tech Tip, "The Foot Powder Spray Trick."

**STEP 3** Fluorescent dye can be added to the engine oil. Add about 1/2 oz (15 cc) of dye per 5 quarts of engine oil. Start the engine and allow it to run about 10 minutes to thoroughly mix the dye throughout the engine. A black light can then be shown around every suspected oil leak location. The black light will easily show all oil leak locations because the dye will show as a bright yellow-green area. ● SEE FIGURE 25–6.

**NOTE: Fluorescent dye works best with clean oil.**

# ENGINE NOISE DIAGNOSIS

An engine knocking noise is often difficult to diagnose. Use a mechanical or electronic stethoscope to listen for engine-related noises, or a short length of rubber hose or a long screwdriver. Items that may cause engine noise include:

- **Valves clicking.** This can happen because of lack of oil to the lifters. The noise is most noticeable at idle when the oil pressure is the lowest. It can also be due to a fault in the valve train. ● SEE FIGURE 25–7.
- **Torque converter.** The attaching bolts or nuts may be loose on the flex plate and cause a deep knocking noise

**FIGURE 25–8** An accessory belt tensioner. Most tensioners have a mark that indicates normal operating location. If the belt has stretched, this indicator mark will be outside of the normal range. Anything wrong with the belt or tensioner can cause noise.

that is often thought to be main or rod bearing related. This noise is most noticeable at idle or when there is no load on the engine.

- **Cracked flex plate.** The noise of a cracked flex plate is often mistaken for a rod or main bearing noise.

- **Loose or defective drive belts or tensioners.** If an accessory drive belt is loose or defective, the flopping noise often sounds similar to a bearing knock. ● **SEE FIGURE 25–8.**

- **Piston pin knock.** This knocking noise is usually not affected by load on the cylinder. If the clearance is too great, a double knock noise is heard when the engine idles. If grounding out cylinders one at a time does not change the sound, then a defective piston pin could be the cause.

- **Piston slap.** A piston slap is usually caused by an undersized or improperly shaped piston or oversized cylinder bore. A piston slap is most noticeable when the engine is cold and tends to decrease or stop making noise as the piston expands during engine operation.

- **Timing chain noise.** An excessively loose timing chain can cause a severe knocking noise when the chain hits the timing chain cover. This noise can often sound like a rod bearing knock.

- **Rod bearing noise.** The noise from a defective rod bearing is usually load sensitive and changes in intensity as the load on the engine increases and decreases. A rod bearing failure can often be detected by grounding out the spark plugs one cylinder at a time. If the knocking noise decreases or is eliminated when a particular cylinder is grounded (disabled), then the grounded cylinder is the one from which the noise is originating.

- **Main bearing knock.** A main bearing knock often cannot be isolated to a particular cylinder. The sound can vary in intensity and may disappear at times depending on engine load.

Regardless of the type of loud knocking noise, after the external causes of the knocking noise have been eliminated, the engine should be disassembled and carefully inspected to determine the exact cause.

● **SEE CHART 25–2** for examples of noises and possible causes.

| TYPICAL NOISES | POSSIBLE CAUSES |
|---|---|
| **Clicking noise,** like the clicking of a ballpoint pen | 1. Loose spark plug<br>2. Loose accessory mount (for air-conditioning compressor, alternator, power steering pump, etc.)<br>3. Loose rocker arm<br>4. Worn rocker arm pedestal<br>5. Fuel pump (broken mechanical fuel pump return spring)<br>6. Worn camshaft<br>7. Exhaust leak (● SEE FIGURE 25–9.)<br>8. Spark plug wire arcing |
| **Clacking noise,** like tapping on metal | 1. Worn piston pin<br>2. Broken piston<br>3. Excessive valve clearance<br>4. Timing chain hitting cover<br>5. Valve lifter |
| **Knock,** like knocking on a door | 1. Rod bearing(s)<br>2. Main bearing(s)<br>3. Thrust bearing(s)<br>4. Loose torque converter<br>5. Cracked flex plate (drive plate) |
| **Rattle,** like a baby rattle | 1. Manifold heat control valve<br>2. Broken harmonic balancer<br>3. Loose accessory mounts<br>4. Loose accessory drive belt or tensioner |
| **Clatter,** like rolling marbles | 1. Rod bearings<br>2. Piston pin<br>3. Loose timing chain |
| **Whine,** like an electric motor running | 1. Alternator bearing<br>2. Drive belt<br>3. Power steering (low fluid level or bad pump)<br>4. Belt noise (accessory or timing) |
| **Clunk,** like a door closing | 1. Engine mount<br>2. Drive axle shaft U-joint or constant velocity (CV) joint |

**CHART 25–2**

Typical engine-related noises and possible causes.

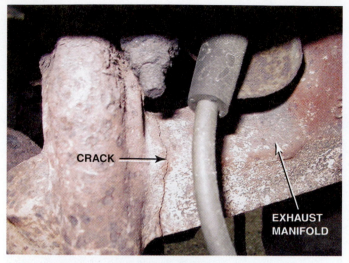

FIGURE 25–9 A cracked exhaust manifold can make a clicking sound that is often difficult to find.

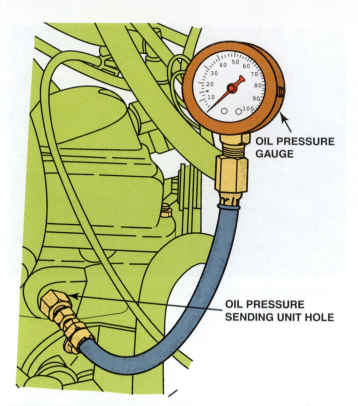

FIGURE 25–10 To measure engine oil pressure, remove the oil pressure sending (sender) unit usually located near the oil filter. Screw the pressure gauge into the oil pressure sending unit hole.

### Engine Noise and Cost

A light ticking noise often heard at one-half engine speed and associated with valve train noise is a less serious problem than many deep knocking noises. Generally, the deeper the sound of the engine noise, the more the owner will have to pay for repairs. A light "tick tick tick," though often not cheap, is usually far less expensive than a deep "knock knock knock" from the engine.

# OIL PRESSURE TESTING

Proper oil pressure is very important for the operation of any engine. *Low oil pressure can cause engine wear, and engine wear can cause low oil pressure.*

If main, thrust, cam, or rod bearings are worn, oil pressure is reduced because of oil leakage around the bearings. Oil pressure testing is usually performed using the following steps.

**STEP 1**  Operate the engine until normal operating temperature is achieved.

**STEP 2**  With the engine off, remove the oil pressure sending unit or sender, usually located near the oil filter. Thread an oil pressure gauge into the threaded hole. ● **SEE FIGURE 25–10.**

**NOTE: An oil pressure gauge can be made from another gauge, such as an old air-conditioning gauge and a flexible brake hose. The threads are often the same as those used for the oil pressure sending unit.**

**STEP 3**  Start the engine and observe the gauge. Record the oil pressure at idle and at 2,500 RPM.

Most vehicle manufacturers recommend a minimum oil pressure of 10 PSI per 1,000 RPM. Therefore, at 2,500 RPM, the oil pressure should be at least 25 PSI. Always compare your test results with the manufacturer's recommended oil pressure.

Besides engine bearing wear, other possible causes for low oil pressure include:

- Low oil level
- Diluted oil
- Stuck oil pressure relief valve

**OIL PRESSURE WARNING LAMP**  The red oil pressure warning lamp in the dash usually lights when the oil pressure is less than 4 to 7 PSI, depending on vehicle and engine. The oil light should not be on during driving. If the oil warning lamp is on, stop the engine immediately. Always confirm oil pressure with a reliable mechanical gauge before performing engine repairs. The sending unit or circuit may be defective.

### Keep It Simple

Engine testing is done to find the cause of an engine problem. All the simple things should be tested first. A loose spark plug can make the engine perform as if it had a burned valve. Simple items that may cause serious problems include the following:

### Oil burning

- Low oil level
- Clogged PCV valve or system, causing blowby and oil to be blown into the air cleaner
- Clogged drainback passages in the cylinder head
- Dirty oil that has not been changed for a long time (Change the oil and drive for about 1,000 miles [1,600 km] and change the oil and filter again.)

### Noises

- Carbon on top of the piston(s), which can sound like a bad rod bearing (often called a carbon knock)
- Loose torque converter-to-flex plate bolts (or nuts), causing a loud knocking noise

NOTE: **Often this problem will cause noise only at idle; the noise tends to disappear during driving or when the engine is under load.**

- A loose and/or defective drive belt, which may cause a rod or main bearing knocking noise (A loose or broken mount for the alternator, power steering pump, or air-conditioning compressor can also cause a knocking noise.)

### The Paper Test

A soundly running engine should produce even and steady exhaust at the tailpipe. You can test this with the **paper test.** Hold a piece of paper or a 3 X 5 card (even a dollar bill works) within 1 in. (2.5 cm) of the tailpipe with the engine running at idle. The paper should blow out evenly without "puffing." If the paper is drawn *toward* the tailpipe at times, the exhaust valves in one or more cylinders could be burned. Other reasons why the paper might be sucked toward the tailpipe include the following:

1. The engine could be misfiring because of a lean condition that could occur normally when the engine is cold.
2. Pulsing of the paper toward the tailpipe could also be caused by a hole in the exhaust system. If exhaust escapes through a hole in the exhaust system, air could be drawn in during the intervals between the exhaust puffs from the tailpipe to the hole in the exhaust, causing the paper to be drawn toward the tailpipe.
3. Ignition fault may occur, causing misfire. ● **SEE FIGURE 25–11.**

# RELATIVE COMPRESSION TESTING

**PURPOSE** Performing a compression test on all cylinders can be a challenge on many vehicles. The normal mechanical method involves removing all of the spark plugs and then testing each cylinder for proper compression by cranking the engine. Due to the location of the spark plugs and the complexity of the underhood area, performing a relative compression test can be real time saver. Many scan tools can perform a relative compression tests by looking at cranking RPM variations.

**USING A SCOPE** Many digital storage oscilloscopes (DSOs) are capable of sensing the engine's relative compression by monitoring the drop in voltage that occurs at the battery every time a cylinder is on the compression stroke during

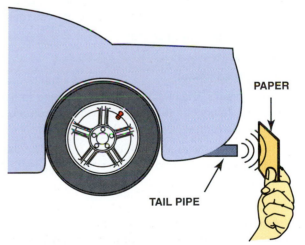

**FIGURE 25–11** The paper test involves holding a piece of paper near the tailpipe of an idling engine. A good engine should produce even, outward puffs of exhaust. If the paper is sucked in toward the tailpipe, a burned valve is a possibility.

cranking. If the voltage at that cylinder drops less than other cylinders, then the cylinder has a lower compression. Follow the instructions of the scope or tester when performing a relative compression test, including ways that allow the display to be synchronized to cylinder number 1. ● **SEE FIGURE 25–12.**

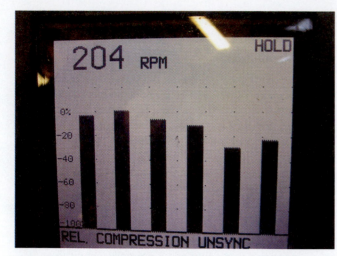

FIGURE 25–12 This relative compression test display indicates that this 6-cylinder engine has two strong cylinders (the two on the far left), two cylinders that are down about 10% from the best cylinder (middle two), and two cylinders that are about 30% weaker than the best cylinders.

FIGURE 25–13 It often requires an assistant to perform a compression test: One person watches the first puff reading on the gauge and the other person cranks the engine.

## COMPRESSION TEST

**CRANKING COMPRESSION TEST** An engine **compression test** is one of the fundamental engine diagnostic tests that can be performed. For smooth engine operation, all cylinders must have equal compression. An engine can lose compression when air leaks through one or more of three routes.

- Intake or exhaust valve or seat
- Piston rings (or piston, if there is a hole)
- Cylinder head gasket

For best results, the engine should be warmed to normal operating temperature before testing. An accurate compression test should be performed as follows:

**STEP 1** Carefully remove all spark plugs. This allows the engine to be cranked to an even speed. Be sure to label all spark plug wires.

> **CAUTION: Disable the ignition system by disconnecting the primary leads from the ignition coil or module or by grounding the coil wire after removing it from the center of the distributor cap. Also disable the fuel-injection system to prevent the squirting of fuel into the cylinder.**

**STEP 2** Block open the throttle at the linkage. This permits the maximum amount of air to be drawn into the engine. This step also ensures consistent compression test results.

**STEP 3** Thread a compression gauge into one spark plug hole and crank the engine. Continue cranking the engine through *four* compression strokes. Each compression stroke makes a puffing sound and causes the gauge needle to pulse.

**NOTE: Note the reading on the compression gauge after the first puff.**

This reading should be at least one-half the final reading. For example, if the final, highest reading is 150 PSI, then the reading after the first puff should be at least one-half of the final reading or higher than 75 PSI in this example. A low first-puff reading indicates possible weak piston rings or a leaking valve or valve seat. Release the pressure on the gauge and repeat for the other cylinders. ● **SEE FIGURE 25–13.**

**STEP 4** Record the highest readings and compare the results. Most vehicle manufacturers specify the minimum compression reading and the maximum allowable variation among cylinders. Most manufacturers specify a maximum difference of 20% between the highest reading and the lowest reading. For example:

| | |
|---|---|
| If the high reading is | 150 PSI |
| Subtract 20% | −30 PSI |
| Lowest allowable compression is | 120 PSI |

**NOTE: To make the math quick and easy, think of 10% of 150, which is 15 (move the decimal point to the left one place). Now double it: 15 × 2 = 30. This represents 20%.**

**NOTE: During cranking, the oil pump cannot maintain normal oil pressure. Extended engine cranking, such as that which occurs during a compression test, can cause hydraulic lifters to collapse. When the engine starts, loud valve clicking noises may be heard. This should be considered normal after performing a compression test, and the noise should stop after the vehicle has been driven a short distance.**

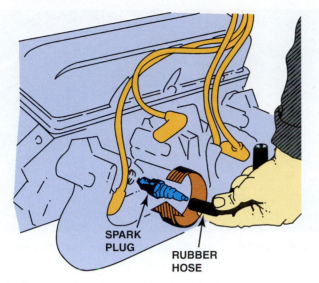

FIGURE 25–14 Use a vacuum or fuel line hose over the spark plug to install it without danger of cross-threading the cylinder head.

SPARK PLUG

RUBBER HOSE

FIGURE 25–15 A leaking valve will cause a lower-than-normal compression reading.

**The Hose Trick**

Installing spark plugs can be made easier by using a rubber hose on the end of the spark plug. The hose can be a vacuum hose, fuel line, or even an old spark plug wire boot. ● **SEE FIGURE 25–14.**

The hose makes it easy to start the threads of the spark plug into the cylinder head. After starting the threads, continue to thread the spark plug for several turns. Using the hose eliminates the chance of cross-threading the plug. This is especially important when installing spark plugs in aluminum cylinder heads.

**WET COMPRESSION TEST** If the compression test reading indicates low compression on one or more cylinders, add three squirts of oil to the cylinder and retest. This is called a **wet compression test,** because oil is used to help seal around the piston rings.

**Caution: Do not use more oil than three squirts from a hand-operated oil squirt can. Too much oil can cause a hydrostatic lock, which can damage or break pistons or connecting rods or even crack a cylinder head.**

Perform the compression test again and observe the results. If the first-puff readings greatly improve and the readings are much higher than without the oil, the cause of the low compression is worn or defective piston rings. If the compression readings increase only slightly (or not at all), then the cause

of the low compression is usually defective valves. ● **SEE FIGURE 25–15.**

**NOTE: During both the dry and wet compression tests, be sure that the battery and starting system are capable of cranking the engine at normal cranking speed.**

**RUNNING (DYNAMIC) COMPRESSION TEST** A compression test is commonly used to help determine engine condition and is usually performed with the engine cranking.

What is the RPM of a cranking engine? An engine idles at about 600 to 900 RPM, and the starter motor obviously cannot crank the engine as fast as the engine idles. Most manufacturing specifications require the engine to crank at 80 to 250 cranking RPM. Therefore, a check of the engine's compression at cranking speed determines the condition of an engine that does not run at such low speeds. A **running compression test,** also called a **dynamic compression test,** is used to test the engine for valve train–related faults that do not show up during a cranking compression test. A running compression test is performed with the engine running rather than during engine cranking as is done in a regular compression test.

But what should be the compression of a running engine? Some would think that the compression would be substantially higher, because the valve overlap of the cam is more effective at higher engine speeds that would tend to increase the compression. Actually, the compression pressure of a running engine is much *lower* than cranking compression pressure. This results from the volumetric efficiency. The engine is revolving faster, so there is less *time* for air to enter the combustion chamber. With less air to compress, the compression pressure is lower. Typically, the higher the engine RPM is, the lower the running compression. For most engines, the value ranges are as follows:

- Compression during cranking: 125 to 160 PSI
- Compression at idle: 60 to 90 PSI
- Compression at 2,000 RPM: 30 to 60 PSI

As with cranking compression, the running compression of all cylinders should be equal. Therefore, a problem is not likely to be detected by single compression values, but by *variations* in running compression values among the cylinders. Engine faults that are often detected by performing a running compression test include:

- Broken valve springs
- Worn valve guides
- Bent pushrods
- Worn cam lobes

To perform a running compression test, take the following steps.

**STEP 1** Remove just one spark plug at a time.

**STEP 2** With one spark plug removed from the engine, use a jumper wire to *ground* the spark plug wire to a good engine ground. This prevents possible ignition coil damage.

**STEP 3** Start the engine, push the pressure release on the gauge, and read the compression. Increase the engine speed to about 2,000 RPM and push the pressure release on the gauge again. Read the gauge and record the reading.

**STEP 4** Stop the engine, install the spark plug, reattach the spark plug wire, and repeat the test for each of the remaining cylinders.

**Results:** Just like the cranking compression test, the running compression test can inform a technician of the *relative* compression of all the cylinders.

## CYLINDER LEAKAGE TEST

One of the best tests that can be used to determine engine condition is the **cylinder leakage test.** This test involves injecting air under pressure into the cylinders one at a time. The amount and location of any escaping air helps the technician determine the condition of the engine. The air is injected into the cylinder through a cylinder leakage gauge installed in the spark plug hole. ● **SEE FIGURE 25–16.**

**STEP 1** For best results, the engine should be at normal operating temperature (upper radiator hose hot and pressurized).

**STEP 2** The cylinder being tested must be at top dead center (TDC) of the compression stroke. ● **SEE FIGURE 25–17.**

**NOTE: The greatest amount of wear occurs at the top of the cylinder because of the heat generated near the top of the cylinders. The piston ring flex also adds to the wear at the top of the cylinder.**

**FIGURE 25–16** A typical handheld cylinder leakage tester.

**FIGURE 25–17** A whistle stop used to find top dead center. Remove the spark plug and install the whistle stop, then rotate the engine by hand. When the whistle stops making a sound, the piston is at the top.

**STEP 3** Connect tester to shop air not over 100 PSI.

**STEP 4** Calibrate the cylinder leakage unit as per manufacturer's instructions.

**STEP 5** Inject air into the cylinders one at a time, rotating the engine as necessitated by firing order to test each cylinder at TDC on the compression stroke.

**STEP 6** Evaluate the results:
Less than 10% leakage: good
Less than 20% leakage: acceptable
Less than 30% leakage: poor
More than 30% leakage: definite problem

**NOTE: If leakage seems unacceptably high, repeat the test, being certain that it is being performed correctly and that the cylinder being tested is at TDC on the compression stroke.**

**STEP 7** Check the source of air leakage.
  a. If air is heard escaping from the oil filler cap, the *piston rings* are worn or broken.
  b. If air is observed bubbling out of the radiator, there is a possible blown *head gasket* or cracked *cylinder head*.
  c. If air is heard coming from the throttle body, there is a defective intake valve(s).
  d. If air is heard coming from the tailpipe, there is a defective *exhaust valve(s)*.

# CYLINDER POWER BALANCE TEST

## PURPOSE
Most large engine analyzers and scan tools have a cylinder power balance feature. The purpose of a cylinder **power balance test** is to determine if all cylinders are contributing power equally. This is determined by shorting out one cylinder at a time. If the engine speed (RPM) does not drop as much for one cylinder as for other cylinders of the same engine, then the shorted cylinder must be weaker than the other cylinders. For example:

| Cylinder Number | Drop When Ignition Is Shorted (RPM) |
|---|---|
| 1 | 75 |
| 2 | 70 |
| 3 | 15 |
| 4 | 65 |
| 5 | 75 |
| 6 | 70 |

Cylinder 3 is the weak cylinder.

**NOTE: Most automotive test equipment uses automatic means for testing cylinder balance. Be certain to correctly identify the offending cylinder. Cylinder 3 as identified by the equipment may be the third cylinder in the firing order instead of the actual cylinder number 3.**

## POWER BALANCE TEST PROCEDURE
When point-type ignition was used on all vehicles, the common method for determining which, if any, cylinder was weak, was to remove a spark plug wire from one spark plug at a time while watching a tachometer and a vacuum gauge. This method is not recommended on any vehicle with any type of electronic ignition. If any of the spark plug wires are removed from a spark plug with the engine running, the ignition coil tries to supply increasing levels of voltage and attempts to jump the increasing gap as the plug wires are removed. This high voltage could easily track the ignition coil, damage the ignition module, or both.

The acceptable method of canceling cylinders, which will work on all types of ignition systems, including waste spark, is to *ground* the secondary current for each cylinder. The cylinder with the least RPM drop is the cylinder not producing its share of power. ● **SEE FIGURE 25–18.**

# VACUUM TESTS

## PURPOSE
Vacuum is pressure below atmospheric pressure and is measured in **inches** (or millimeters) **of mercury (Hg)**. An engine in good mechanical condition will run with high manifold vacuum. Manifold vacuum is developed by the pistons as they move down on the intake stroke to draw the fuel and

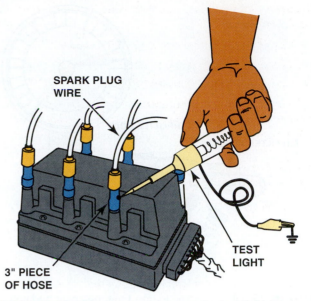

SPARK PLUG WIRE

3" PIECE OF HOSE

TEST LIGHT

**FIGURE 25–18** Using vacuum hose and a test light to ground one cylinder at a time on a waste-spark type of ignition system. This works on all types of ignition systems and provides a method for grounding out one cylinder at a time without fear of damaging any component.

air charge from the throttle body and intake manifold. Air to refill the manifold flows past the throttle plate into the manifold. Vacuum will increase anytime the engine turns faster or has better cylinder sealing while the throttle plate remains in a fixed position. Manifold vacuum will decrease when the engine turns more slowly or when the cylinders no longer do an efficient job of pumping. **Vacuum tests** include testing the engine for **cranking vacuum, idle vacuum,** and vacuum at 2,500 RPM.

## CRANKING VACUUM TEST
Measuring the amount of manifold vacuum during cranking is a quick and easy test to determine if the piston rings and valves are properly sealing. The engine should be warm and the throttle closed. The idle air control passage also should be blocked on port fuel-injected engines, because the open passage would be similar to a partially open throttle and therefore reduce the amount of cranking vacuum.

**STEP 1** Disable the ignition or fuel injection.

**STEP 2** Connect the vacuum gauge to a manifold vacuum source.

**STEP 3** Crank the engine while observing the vacuum gauge.

Cranking vacuum should be higher than 2.5 inches of mercury (in. Hg). (Normal cranking vacuum is 3 to 6 in. Hg.) If it is lower than 2.5 in. Hg, then the following could be the cause.

- Too slow a cranking speed
- Worn piston rings
- Leaking valves
- Excessive amounts of air bypassing the throttle plate (This could give a false low vacuum reading. Common sources include a throttle plate partially open or a high-performance camshaft with excessive overlap.)

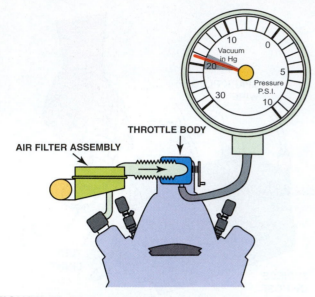

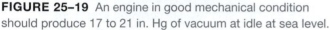

**FIGURE 25–19** An engine in good mechanical condition should produce 17 to 21 in. Hg of vacuum at idle at sea level.

## IDLE VACUUM TEST
An engine in proper condition should idle with a steady vacuum between 17 and 21 in. Hg. ● **SEE FIGURE 25–19.**

**NOTE: Engine vacuum readings vary with altitude. A reduction of 1 in. Hg per 1,000 ft (300 m) of altitude should be subtracted from the expected values if testing a vehicle above 1,000 ft (300 m). For example, a vehicle in good operating condition would have an idle vacuum of 12 to 16 in. Hg in Denver, Colorado (elevation 5,100 ft). The same vehicle would read 17 to 21 in. Hg at sea level.**

## LOW AND STEADY VACUUM
If the vacuum is lower than normal, yet the gauge reading is steady, the most common causes include:

- Retarded ignition timing
- Vacuum leaks
- Retarded cam timing (Check the timing chain for excessive slack or the timing belt for proper installation. ● **SEE FIGURE 25–20.)**

## FLUCTUATING VACUUM
If the needle drops, then returns to a normal reading, then drops again, and again returns, this indicates a sticking valve. A common cause of sticking valves is lack of lubrication of the valve stems. ● **SEE FIGURES 25–21 THROUGH 25–29.**

**NOTE: A common trick that some technicians use is to squirt automatic transmission fluid (ATF) down the throttle body or into the air inlet of a warm engine. Often the idle quality improves and normal vacuum gauge readings are restored. The use of ATF creates excessive exhaust smoke for a short time, however, but it should not harm oxygen sensors or catalytic converters.**

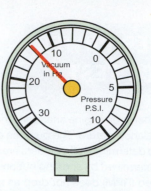

**FIGURE 25–20** A steady but low reading could indicate retarded valve or ignition timing.

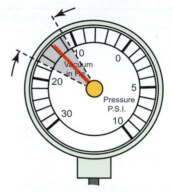

**FIGURE 25–21** A gauge reading with the needle fluctuating 3 to 9 in. Hg below normal often indicates a vacuum leak in the intake system.

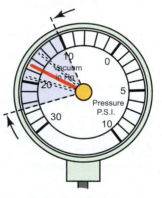

**FIGURE 25–22** A leaking head gasket can cause the needle to vibrate as it moves through a range from below to above normal.

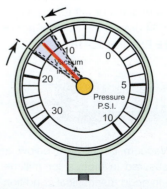

**FIGURE 25–23** An oscillating needle 1 or 2 in. Hg below normal could indicate an incorrect air-fuel mixture (either too rich or too lean).

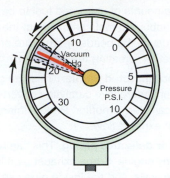

**FIGURE 25–24** A rapidly vibrating needle at idle that becomes steady as engine speed is increased indicates worn valve guides.

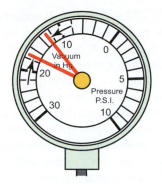

**FIGURE 25–25** If the needle drops 1 or 2 in. Hg from the normal reading, one of the engine valves is burned or not seating properly.

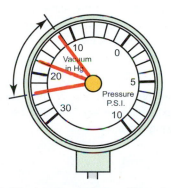

**FIGURE 25–26** Weak valve springs will produce a normal reading at idle, but as engine speed increases, the needle will fluctuate rapidly between 12 and 24 in. Hg.

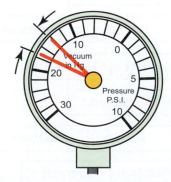

**FIGURE 25–27** A steady needle reading that drops 2 or 3 in. Hg when the engine speed is increased slightly above idle indicates that the ignition timing is retarded.

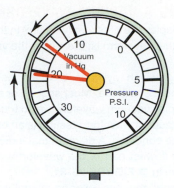

**FIGURE 25–28** A steady needle reading that rises 2 or 3 in. Hg when the engine speed is increased slightly above idle indicates that the ignition timing is advanced.

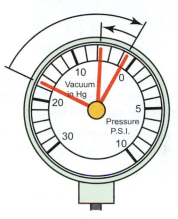

**FIGURE 25–29** A needle that drops to near zero when the engine is accelerated rapidly and then rises slightly to a reading below normal indicates an exhaust restriction.

If the vacuum gauge fluctuates above and below a center point, burned valves or weak valve springs may be indicated. If the fluctuation is slow and steady, unequal fuel mixture could be the cause.

## VACUUM WAVEFORMS

**PRINCIPLES**   A digital storage oscilloscope can be used to create a vacuum waveform if a vacuum transducer is attached to an intake manifold vacuum source. A transducer is a device that converts pressure, vacuum, temperature, or other input signals into an electrical signal that will vary with changes in input levels. Transducers allow meters and scopes to accurately measure other things besides electricity. Vacuum created during cranking is the direct result of cylinder sealing and therefore indicates the engine condition. Vacuum waveform is not affected by any of the following:

- Ignition timing or faults in the ignition system
- Fuel injector faults
- Fuel delivery faults

## INTERPRETING A VACUUM WAVEFORM

A vacuum waveform will display the pressure (vacuum) in the intake manifold. The lower the waveform is, the higher the vacuum. ● **SEE FIGURE 25–30.**

Determining which cylinder is which using a vacuum waveform can be a challenge. Most scopes or testers that are equipped to display vacuum waveforms also trigger off of cylinder number 1. Vacuum waveform testing is an excellent way to determine engine condition. A diagram that indicates where the highest vacuum (lowest part of the waveform) will be for each cylinder is shown in ● **FIGURE 25–31.**

Always follow the oscilloscope manufacturer's recommended procedures as found in the instruction manual.

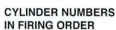

## EXHAUST RESTRICTION TEST

**PURPOSE** If the exhaust system is restricted, the engine will be low on power yet will operate smoothly. Common causes of **restricted exhaust** include the following:

- **Clogged catalytic converter.** Always check the ignition and fuel-injection systems for faults that could cause

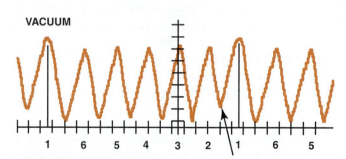

excessive amounts of unburned fuel to be exhausted. Excessive unburned fuel can overheat the catalytic converter and cause the beads or structure of the converter to fuse together, creating the restriction.

- **Clogged or restricted muffler.** This can cause low power. Often a defective catalytic converter will shed particles that can clog a muffler. Broken internal baffles can also restrict exhaust flow.

- **Damaged or defective piping.** This can reduce the power of any engine. Some exhaust pipe is constructed with double walls, and the inside pipe can collapse and form a restriction that is not visible on the outside of the exhaust pipe.

## USING A VACUUM GAUGE

A vacuum gauge can be used to measure manifold vacuum at a high idle (2,000 to 2,500 RPM). If the exhaust system is restricted, pressure increases in the exhaust system. This pressure is called **back pressure.** Manifold vacuum will drop gradually if the engine is kept at a constant speed if the exhaust is restricted.

The reason the vacuum will drop is that all exhaust leaving the engine at the higher engine speed cannot get through the restriction. After a short time (within one minute), the exhaust tends to "pile up" above the restriction and eventually remains in the cylinder of the engine at the end of the exhaust stroke. Therefore, at the beginning of the intake stroke, when the piston traveling downward should be lowering the pressure (raising the vacuum) in the intake manifold, the extra exhaust in the cylinder *lowers* the normal vacuum. If the exhaust restriction is severe enough, the vehicle can become undriveable because cylinder filling cannot occur except at idle.

## USING A PRESSURE GAUGE

Exhaust system back pressure can be measured directly by installing a pressure gauge into an exhaust opening. This can be accomplished in one of the following ways.

**FIGURE 25–30** Notice that the cylinder number 2 vacuum waveform does not go down as low as the others. This indicates that the cylinder is not sealing.

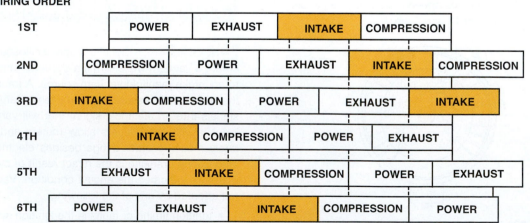

**FIGURE 25–31** The relationship among cylinders showing where the intake stroke occurs in relation to other cylinders.

FIGURE 25–32 A technician-made adapter used to test exhaust system back pressure.

FIGURE 25–33 A tester that uses a blue liquid to check for exhaust gases in the exhaust, which would indicate a head gasket leak problem.

- **With an oxygen sensor.** Use a back pressure gauge and adapter or remove the inside of a discarded oxygen sensor and thread in an adapter to convert to a vacuum or pressure gauge.

  **NOTE: An adapter can be easily made by inserting a metal tube or pipe. A short section of brake line works well, too. The pipe can be brazed to the oxygen sensor housing or it can be glued in with epoxy. An 18 mm compression gauge adapter can also be adapted to fit into the oxygen sensor opening.** ● SEE FIGURE 25–32.

- **With the exhaust gas recirculation (EGR) valve.** Remove the EGR valve and fabricate a plate to connect to a pressure gauge.

- **With the air-injection reaction (AIR) check valve.** Remove the check valve from the exhaust tubes leading down to the exhaust manifold. Use a rubber cone with a tube inside to seal against the exhaust tube. Connect the tube to a pressure gauge.

At idle, the maximum back pressure should be less than 1.5 PSI (10 kPa), and it should be less than 2.5 PSI (15 kPa) at 2,500 RPM.

## DIAGNOSING HEAD GASKET FAILURE

The following items can be used to help diagnose a head gasket failure.

- **Exhaust gas analyzer.** With the radiator cap removed, place the probe from the exhaust analyzer above the radiator filler neck. If the hydrocarbon (HC) reading increases, the exhaust (unburned fuel) is getting into the coolant from the combustion chamber.

- **Chemical test.** A chemical tester using blue liquid is also available. The liquid turns yellow if combustion gases are present in the coolant. ● SEE FIGURE 25–33.

- **Bubbles in the coolant.** Remove the coolant pump belt to prevent pump operation. Remove the radiator cap and start the engine. If bubbles appear in the coolant before it begins to boil, a defective head gasket or cracked cylinder head is indicated.

- **Excessive exhaust steam.** If excessive water or steam is observed coming from the tailpipe, this means that coolant is getting into the combustion chamber from a defective head gasket or a cracked head. If there is leakage between cylinders, the engine usually misfires and a power balance test and/or compression test can be used to confirm the problem.

- **Install a pressure gauge to the radiator.** If a head gasket failure is suspected, then an increase in cooling system pressure will often be detected before the coolant temperature becomes hot enough to boil.

If any of the preceding indicators of head gasket failure occur, remove the cylinder head(s) and check all of the following:

1. Head gasket
2. Sealing surfaces, for warpage
3. Castings, for cracks

# COMPRESSION TEST

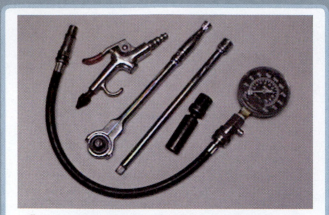

**1** The tools and equipment needed to perform a compression test include a compression gauge, an air nozzle, and the socket ratchets and extensions that may be necessary to remove the spark plugs from the engine.

**2** To prevent ignition and fuel-injection operation while the engine is being cranked, remove both the fuel-injection fuse and the ignition fuse. If the fuses cannot be removed, disconnect the wiring connectors for the injectors and the ignition system.

**3** Block open the throttle (and choke, if the engine is equipped with a carburetor). Here a screwdriver is being used to wedge the throttle linkage open. Keeping the throttle open ensures that enough air will be drawn into the engine so that the compression test results will be accurate.

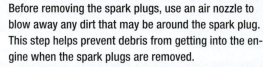

**4** Before removing the spark plugs, use an air nozzle to blow away any dirt that may be around the spark plug. This step helps prevent debris from getting into the engine when the spark plugs are removed.

**5** Remove all of the spark plugs. Be sure to mark the spark plug wires so that they can be reinstalled onto the correct spark plugs after the compression test has been performed.

**6** Select the proper adapter for the compression gauge. The threads on the adapter should match those on the spark plug.

**7** If necessary, connect a battery charger to the battery before starting the compression test. It is important that consistent cranking speed be available for each cylinder being tested.

**8** Make a note of the reading on the gauge after the first "puff," which indicates the first compression stroke that occurred on that cylinder as the engine was being rotated. If the first puff reading is low and the reading gradually increases with each puff, weak or worn piston rings may be indicated.

**9** After the engine has been cranked for four "puffs," stop cranking the engine and observe the compression gauge.

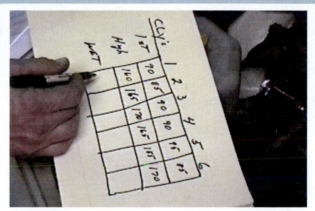

**10** Record the first puff and this final reading for each cylinder. The final readings should all be within 20% of each other.

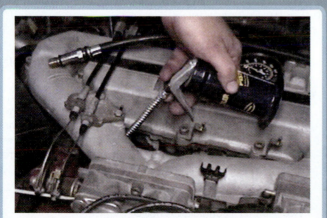

**11** If a cylinder(s) is lower than most of the others, use an oil can and squirt three squirts of engine oil into the cylinder and repeat the compression test. This is called performing a wet compression test.

**12** If the gauge reading is now much higher than the first test results, then the cause of the low compression is due to worn or defective piston rings. The oil in the cylinder temporarily seals the rings which causes the higher reading.

## SUMMARY

1. The first step in diagnosing engine condition is to perform a thorough visual inspection, including a check of oil and coolant levels and condition.

2. Oil leaks can be found by using a white powder or a fluorescent dye and a black light.

3. Many engine-related problems make a characteristic noise.

4. A compression test can be used to test the condition of valves and piston rings.

5. A cylinder leakage test fills the cylinder with compressed air, and the gauge indicates the percentage of leakage.

6. A cylinder balance test indicates whether all cylinders are working normally.

7. Testing engine vacuum is another procedure that can help the service technician determine engine condition.

## REVIEW QUESTIONS

1. Describe four visual checks that should be performed on an engine if a mechanical malfunction is suspected.

2. List three simple items that could cause excessive oil consumption.

3. List three simple items that could cause engine noises.

4. Describe how to perform a compression test and how to determine what is wrong with an engine based on a compression test result.

5. Describe the cylinder leakage test.

6. Describe how a vacuum gauge would indicate if the valves were sticking in their guides.

7. Describe the test procedure for determining if the exhaust system is restricted (clogged) using a vacuum gauge.

## CHAPTER QUIZ

1. Technician A says that the paper test could detect a burned valve. Technician B says that a grayish white stain on the engine could be a coolant leak. Which technician is correct?
   a. Technician A only
   b. Technician B only
   c. Both Technicians A and B
   d. Neither Technician A nor B

2. Two technicians are discussing oil leaks. Technician A says that an oil leak can be found using a fluorescent dye in the oil with a black light to check for leaks. Technician B says that a white spray powder can be used to locate oil leaks. Which technician is correct?
   a. Technician A only
   b. Technician B only
   c. Both Technicians A and B
   d. Neither Technician A nor B

3. Which of the following is the *least likely* to cause an engine noise?
   a. Carbon on the pistons
   b. Cracked exhaust manifold
   c. Loose accessory drive belt
   d. Vacuum leak

4. A smoothly operating engine depends on _____.
   a. High compression on most cylinders
   b. Equal compression between cylinders
   c. Cylinder compression levels above 100 PSI (700 kPa) and within 70 PSI (500 kPa) of each other
   d. Compression levels below 100 PSI (700 kPa) on most cylinders

5. A good reading for a cylinder leakage test would be _____.
   a. Within 20% between cylinders
   b. All cylinders below 20% leakage
   c. All cylinders above 20% leakage
   d. All cylinders above 70% leakage and within 7% of each other

6. Technician A says that during a power balance test, the cylinder that causes the biggest RPM drop is the weak cylinder. Technician B says that if one spark plug wire is grounded out and the engine speed does not drop, a weak or dead cylinder is indicated. Which technician is correct?
   a. Technician A only
   b. Technician B only
   c. Both Technicians A and B
   d. Neither Technician A nor B

7. *Cranking* vacuum should be _____.
   a. 2.5 in. Hg or higher
   b. Over 25 in. Hg
   c. 17 to 21 in. Hg
   d. 6 to 16 in. Hg

8. Technician A says that a relative compression test can find cylinders that have lower compression compared to the other cylinders in the same engine. Technician B says that a vacuum waveform can detect an ignition or fuel injector problem. Which technician is correct?
   a. Technician A only
   b. Technician B only
   c. Both Technicians A and B
   d. Neither Technician A nor B

9. When should a wet compression test be performed?
   a. Before a dry compression test
   b. After a cylinder fails a dry compression test
   c. When the engine is cold
   d. When a defective head gasket is suspected

10. A running compression test is used to locate what type of engine problems?
    a. Piston or connecting rod faults
    b. Valve train–related faults
    c. Leaking intake manifold gasket faults
    d. Excessive exhaust system back pressure

**OBJECTIVES: After studying Chapter 26, the reader will be able to:** • Prepare for ASE certification test content area "A" (General Engine Diagnosis) • Diagnose and replace the thermostat. • Diagnose and replace the water pump. • Diagnose and replace an intake manifold gasket • Determine and verify correct cam timing • Replace a timing a belt • Describe how to adjust valves • Explain hybrid engine precautions

**KEY TERMS:** EREV 365 • Fretting 363 • HEV 365 • Idle stop 365 • Skewed 362

## THERMOSTAT REPLACEMENT

**FAILURE PATTERNS** All thermostat valves move during operation to maintain the desired coolant temperature. Thermostats can fail in the following ways:

- **Stuck Open**—If a thermostat fails open or partially open, the operating temperature of the engine will be less than normal. ● **SEE FIGURE 26–1.**

- **Stuck Closed**—If the thermostat fails closed or almost closed, the engine will likely overheat.

- **Stuck Partially Open**—This will cause the engine to warm up slowly if at all. This condition can cause the powertrain control module (PCM) to set a P0128 diagnostic trouble code (DTC) which means that the engine coolant temperature does not reach the specified temperature.

- **Skewed**—A **skewed** thermostat works, but not within the correct temperature range. Therefore, the engine could overheat or operate cooler than normal or even do both.

**REPLACEMENT PROCEDURE** Before replacing the thermostat, double-check that the cooling system problem is not due to another fault, such as being low on coolant or an inoperative cooling fan. Check service information for the specified procedure to follow to replace the thermostat. Most recommended procedures include the following steps:

**STEP 1** Allow the engine to cool for several hours so the engine and the coolant should be at room temperature.

**STEP 2** Drain the coolant into a suitable container. Most vehicle manufacturers recommend that new coolant be used and the old coolant disposed of properly or recycled.

**FIGURE 26–1** A stuck-open thermostat. This caused the vehicle to set a diagnostic trouble code P0128 (coolant temperature below thermostat regulating temperature).

**STEP 3** Remove any necessary components to get access to the thermostat.

**STEP 4** Remove the thermostat housing and thermostat.

**STEP 5** Replace the thermostat housing gasket and thermostat. Torque all fasteners to specifications.

**STEP 6** Refill the cooling system with the specified coolant and bleed any trapped air from the system.

**STEP 7** Pressurize the cooling system to verify that there are no leaks around the thermostat housing.

**STEP 8** Run the engine until it reaches normal operating temperature and check for leaks.

**STEP 9** Verify that the engine is reaching correct operating temperature.

**FIGURE 26–2** Use caution if using a steel scraper to remove a gasket from aluminum parts. It is best to use a wood or plastic scraper.

**FIGURE 26–3** An intake manifold gasket that failed and allowed coolant to be drawn into the cylinder(s).

## WATER PUMP REPLACEMENT

**NEED FOR REPLACEMENT** A water pump will require replacement if any of the following conditions are present:

- Leaking coolant from the weep hole
- Bearing noisy or loose
- Lack of proper coolant flow caused by worn or slipping impeller blades

**REPLACEMENT GUIDELINES** After diagnosis has been confirmed that the water pump requires replacement, check service information for the exact procedure to follow. The steps usually include the following:

**STEP 1** Allow the engine to cool to room temperature.

**STEP 2** Drain the coolant and dispose of properly or recycle.

**STEP 3** Remove engine components to gain access to the water pump as specified in service information.

**STEP 4** Remove the water pump assembly.

> **NOTE: Always compare the replacement pump with the original to be sure that they are the same.**

**STEP 5** Clean the gasket surfaces and install the new water pump using a new gasket or seal as needed. ● **SEE FIGURE 26–2.** Torque all fasteners to factory specifications.

**STEP 6** Install removed engine components.

**STEP 7** Fill the cooling system with the specified coolant.

**STEP 8** Run the engine, check for leaks, and verify proper operation.

## INTAKE MANIFOLD GASKET INSPECTION

**CAUSES OF FAILURE** Many V-type engines leak oil, coolant, or experience an air (vacuum) leak caused by a leaking intake manifold gasket. This failure can be contributed to one or more of the following:

1. Expansion/contraction rate difference between the cast-iron head and the aluminum intake manifold can cause the intake manifold gasket to be damaged by the relative motion of the head and intake manifold. This type of failure is called **fretting.**

2. Plastic (Nylon 6.6) gasket deterioration caused by the coolant. ● **SEE FIGURE 26–3.**

**DIAGNOSIS OF LEAKING INTAKE MANIFOLD GASKET** Because intake manifold gaskets are used to seal oil, air, and coolant in most causes, determining that the intake manifold gasket is the root cause can be a challenge. To diagnose a possible leaking intake manifold gasket, perform the following tests:

**Visual inspection**—Check for evidence of oil or coolant between the intake manifold and the cylinder heads.

**Coolant level**—Check the coolant level and determine if the level has been dropping. A leaking intake manifold gasket can cause coolant to leak and then evaporate, leaving no evidence of the leak.

**Air (vacuum) leak**—If there is a stored diagnostic trouble code (DTC) for a lean exhaust (P0171, P0172, or P0174), a leaking intake manifold gasket could be the cause. Use propane to check if the engine changes when dispensed around the intake manifold gasket. If the engine changes in speed or sound, then this test verifies that an air leak is present.

**FIGURE 26–4** The lower intake manifold, attaches to the cylinder heads.

**FIGURE 26–5** The upper intake manifold, often called a plenum, attaches to the lower intake manifold.

## INTAKE MANIFOLD GASKET REPLACEMENT

When replacing the intake manifold gasket, always check service information for the exact procedure to follow. The steps usually include the following:

**STEP 1** Be sure the engine has been off for about an hour and then drain the coolant into a suitable container, if required.

**STEP 2** Remove covers and other specified parts needed to get access to the retaining bolts.

**STEP 3** To help ensure that the manifold does not warp when removed, loosen all fasteners in the reverse order of the tightening sequence. This means that the bolts

**FIGURE 26–6** Many aftermarket replacement intake manifolds have a different appearance from the original manifold.

should be loosened starting at the ends and working toward the center.

**STEP 4** Remove the upper intake manifold, if equipped, and inspect for faults. ● **SEE FIGURES 26–4 AND 26–5.**

**STEP 5** Remove the lower intake manifold, using the same bolt removal procedure of starting at the ends and working toward the center.

**STEP 6** Thoroughly clean the area and replace the intake manifold if needed. Check that the correct replacement manifold is being used, and even the current part could look different from the original. ● **SEE FIGURE 26–6.**

**STEP 7** Install the intake manifold using new gaskets as specified. Some designs use gaskets that are reusable. Replace as needed.

**STEP 8** Torque all fasteners to factory specifications and in the proper sequences. The tightening sequences usually start at the center and work outward to the ends.

**CAUTION: Double-check the torque specifications and be sure to use the correct values. Many intake manifolds use fasteners that are torqued to values expressed in pound-inches and not pound-feet.**

**STEP 9** Reinstall all parts needed to allow the engine to start and run, including refilling the coolant if needed.

**STEP 10** Start the engine and check for leaks and proper engine operation.

**STEP 11** Reset or relearn the idle if specified, using a scan tool.

**STEP 12** Install all of the remaining parts and perform a test drive to verify proper operation and no leaks.

**STEP 13** Check and replace the air filter if needed.

**STEP 14** Change the engine oil if the intake manifold leak could have caused coolant to leak into the engine, which would contaminate the oil.

**FIGURE 26–7** A single overhead camshaft engine with a timing belt that also rotates the water pump.

aligned according to the specified marks. ● **SEE FIGURE 26–7.**

**STEP 4** Loosen or remove the tensioner as needed to remove the timing belt.

**STEP 5** Replace the timing belt and any other recommended items. Components that some vehicle manufacturers recommend replacing in addition to the timing belt include:
- Tensioner assembly
- Water pump
- Camshaft oil seal(s)
- Front crankshaft seal

**STEP 6** Check (verify) that the camshaft timing is correct by rotating the engine several revolutions.

**STEP 7** Install enough components to allow the engine to start to verify proper operation. Check for any leaks, especially if seals have been replaced.

**STEP 8** Complete the reassembly of the engine and perform a test drive before returning the vehicle to the customer.

## TIMING BELT REPLACEMENT

**NEED FOR REPLACEMENT** Timing belts have a limited service and a specified replacement interval ranging from 60,000 miles (97,000 km) to about 100,000 miles (161,000 km). Timing belts are required to be replaced if any of the following conditions occur:

- Meets or exceeds the vehicle manufacturer's recommended timing belt replacement interval.
- The timing belt has been contaminated with coolant or engine oil.
- The timing belt has failed (missing belt teeth or broken).

**TIMING BELT REPLACEMENT GUIDELINES** Before replacing the timing belt, check service information for the recommended procedure to follow. Most timing belt replacement procedures include the following steps:

**STEP 1** Allow the engine to cool before starting to remove components to help eliminate the possibility of personal injury or warpage of the parts.

**STEP 2** Remove all necessary components to gain access to the timing belt and timing marks.

**STEP 3** If the timing belt is not broken, rotate the engine until the camshaft and crankshaft timing marks are

## HYBRID ENGINE PRECAUTIONS

**HYBRID VEHICLE ENGINE OPERATION** Gasoline engines used in **hybrid electric vehicles (HEVs)** and in **extended range electric vehicles (EREVs)** can be a hazard to be around under some conditions. These vehicles are designed to stop the gasoline engines unless needed. This feature is called **idle stop.** This means that the engine is not running, but could start at any time if the computer detects the need to charge the hybrid batteries or other issue that requires the gasoline engine to start and run.

**PRECAUTIONS** Always check service information for the exact procedures to follow when working around or under the hood of a hybrid electric vehicle. These precautions could include:

- Before working under the hood or around the engine, be sure that the ignition is off and the key is out of the ignition.
- Check that the "Ready" light is off. ● **SEE FIGURE 26–8.**
- Do not touch any circuits that have orange electrical wires or conduit. The orange color indicates dangerous high-voltage wires, which could cause serious injury or death if touched.
- Always use high-voltage linesman's gloves whenever depowering the high-voltage system.

**HYBRID ENGINE SERVICE** The gasoline engine in most hybrid electric vehicles specifies low viscosity engine oil as a

**FIGURE 26–8** A Toyota/Lexus hybrid electric vehicle has a ready light. If the ready light is on, the engine can start at anytime without warning.

**FIGURE 26–9** Always use the viscosity of oil as specified on the oil fill cap.

way to achieve maximum fuel economy. ● **SEE FIGURE 26–9.** The viscosity required is often:

- SAE 0W-20
- SAE 5W-20

Many shops do not keep this viscosity in stock so preparations need to be made to get and use the specified engine oil.

In addition to engine oil, some hybrid electric vehicles such as the Honda Insight (1999–2004) require special spark plugs. Check service information for the specified service procedures and parts needed if a hybrid electric vehicle is being serviced.

**1** Before starting the process of adjusting the valves, look up the specifications and exact procedures. The technician is checking this information from a computer CD-ROM-based information system.

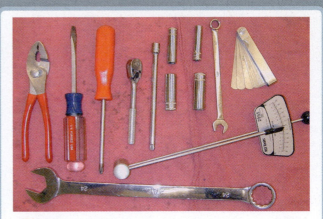

**2** The tools necessary to adjust the valves on an engine with adjustable rocker arms include basic hand tools, feeler gauge, and a torque wrench.

**3** An overall view of the four-cylinder engine that is due for a scheduled valve adjustment according to the vehicle manufacturer's recommendations.

**4** Start the valve adjustment procedure by first disconnecting and labeling, if necessary, all vacuum lines that need to be removed to gain access to the valve cover.

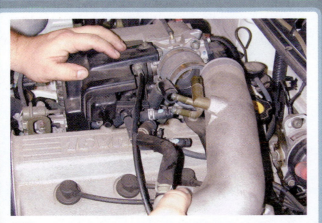

**5** The air intake tube is being removed from the throttle body.

**6** With all vacuum lines and the intake tube removed, the valve cover can be removed after removing all retaining bolts.

CONTINUED ▶

# VALVE ADJUSTMENT (CONTINUED)

**7** Notice how clean the engine appears. This is a testament of proper maintenance and regular oil changes by the owner.

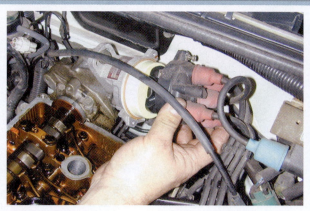

**8** To help locate how far the engine is being rotated, the technician is removing the distributor cap to be able to observe the position of the rotor.

TIMING MARK

**9** The engine is rotated until the timing marks on the front of the crankshaft line up with zero degrees—top dead center (TDC)—with both valves closed on #1 cylinder.

**10** With the rocker arms contacting the base circle of the cam, insert a feeler gauge of the specified thickness between the camshaft and the rocker arm. There should be a slight drag on the feeler gauge.

**11** If the valve clearance (lash) is not correct, loosen the retaining nut and turn the valve adjusting screw with a screwdriver to achieve the proper clearance.

**12** After adjusting the valves that are closed, rotate the engine one full rotation until the engine timing marks again align.

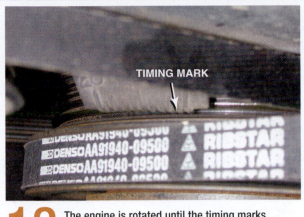

**13** The engine is rotated until the timing marks again align indicating that the companion cylinder will now be in position for valve clearance measurement.

**14** On some engines, it is necessary to watch the direction the rotor is pointing to help determine how far to rotate the engine. Always follow the vehicle manufacturer's recommended procedure.

**15** The technician is using a feeler gauge that is one-thousandth of an inch thinner and another one-thousandth of an inch thicker than the specified clearance as a double-check that the clearance is correct.

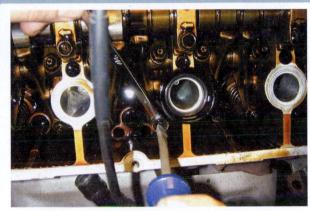

**16** Adjusting a valve takes both hands—one to hold the wrench to loosen and tighten the lock nut and one to turn the adjusting screw. Always double-check the clearance after an adjustment is made.

**17** After all valves have been properly measured and adjusted as necessary, start the reassembly process by replacing all gaskets and seals as specified by the vehicle manufacturer.

**18** Reinstall the valve cover being careful to not pinch a wire or vacuum hose between the cover and the cylinder head.

CONTINUED ▶

**19** Use a torque wrench and torque the valve cover retaining bolts to factory specifications.

**20** Reinstall the distributor cap.

**21** Reinstall the spark plug wires and all brackets that were removed to gain access to the valve cover.

**22** Reconnect all vacuum and air hoses and tubes. Replace any vacuum hoses that are brittle or swollen with new ones.

**23** Be sure that the clamps are properly installed. Start the engine and check for proper operation.

**24** Double-check for any oil or vacuum leaks after starting the engine.

## SUMMARY

1. Thermostats can fail in the following ways:
   - Stuck open
   - Stuck closed
   - Stuck partially open
   - Skewed

2. A water pump should be replaced if any of the following conditions are present:
   - Leaking from the weep hole
   - Noisy bearing
   - Loose bearing
   - Lack of normal circulation due to worn impeller blades

3. A leaking intake manifold gasket can cause coolant to get into the oil or oil into the coolant, as well as other faults, such as a poor running engine.

4. When a timing belt is replaced, most vehicle manufacturers also recommend that the following items be replaced:
   - Tensioner assembly
   - Water pump
   - Camshaft seal(s)
   - Front crankshaft seal

5. When working on a Toyota/Lexus hybrid electric vehicle (HEV), be sure that the key is off and out of the ignition and the READY light is off.

## REVIEW QUESTIONS

1. How can a thermostat fail?

2. How can a water pump fail requiring replacement?

3. What will happen to the engine if the intake manifold gasket fails?

4. Why must timing belts be replaced?

5. Why is it important that the READY light be out on the dash before working under the hood of a hybrid electric vehicle?

## CHAPTER QUIZ

1. A thermostat can fail in which way?
   a. Stuck open
   b. Stuck closed
   c. Stuck partially open
   d. Any of the above

2. A skewed thermostat means it is _____
   a. Working, but not at the correct temperature
   b. Not working
   c. Missing the thermo wax in the heat sensor
   d. Contaminated with coolant

3. Coolant drained from the cooling system when replacing a thermostat or water pump should be _____
   a. Reused
   b. Disposed of properly or recycled
   c. Filtered and reinstalled after the repair
   d. Poured down a toilet

4. A water pump can fail to provide the proper amount of flow of coolant through the cooling system if what has happened?
   a. The coolant is leaking from the weep hole
   b. The bearing is noisy
   c. The impeller blades are worn or slipping on the shaft
   d. A bearing failure has caused the shaft to become loose

5. Intake manifold gaskets on a V-type engine can fail due to what factor?
   a. Fretting
   b. Coolant damage
   c. Relative movement between the intake manifold and the cylinder head
   d. All of the above

6. A defective thermostat can cause the Powertrain Control Module to set what diagnostic trouble code (DTC)?
   a. P0171
   b. P0172
   c. P0128
   d. P0300

7. A replacement plastic intake manifold may have a different design or appearance from the original factory-installed part.
   a. True
   b. False

8. The torque specifications for many plastic intake manifolds are in what unit?
   a. Pound-inches
   b. Pound-feet
   c. Ft-lbs per minute
   d. Lb-ft per second

9. When replacing a timing belt, many experts and vehicle manufacturers recommend that what other part(s) should be replaced?
   a. Tensioner assembly
   b. Water pump
   c. Camshaft oil seal(s)
   d. All of the above

10. Hybrid electric vehicles usually require special engine oil of what viscosity?
    a. SAE 5W-30
    b. SAE 10W-30
    c. SAE 0W-20
    d. SAE 5W-40

# chapter 27

# SYMPTOM-BASED DIAGNOSIS

**OBJECTIVES:** After studying Chapter 27, the reader will be able to: • Prepare for ASE Engine Performance (A8) certification test content area "A" (General Engine Diagnosis) and ASE Advanced Level (L1) certification test content area "A" (General Powertrain Diagnosis). • List the possible causes of an engine performance problem based on its symptoms. • List the possible causes of a rich air-fuel mixture. • List the possible causes of a lean air-fuel mixture. • Describe what symptoms may occur if a particular sensor is defective. • List the possible causes of excessive HC, CO, and $NO_x$ exhaust emissions.

**KEY TERMS:** Backfire 378 • Detonation 375 • Dieseling 378 • Fuel economy 377 • Hesitation 372 • Lean misfire 383 • Misfire 380 • Ping 375 • Rough (unstable) idle 374 • Run-on 378 • Sag 372 • Spark knock 375 • Stall 374 • Stumble 373 • Surges 380 • Symptom 381

About 80% of problems can be solved using a systematic approach. However for the remaining 20%, it is the skill and experience of the service technician that will help narrow the problem to the root cause.

This chapter is different from the previous chapters in this textbook, as it will be devoted to providing:

- Lists for common causes of problems based on their symptoms
- Lists of symptoms that a particular component could cause if it were defective
- Typical causes of a too rich or too lean condition that are included to help find those exhaust emission testing failures

This chapter is similar to having an experienced service technician next to you while you are working on a problem that seems difficult to solve. Enjoy.

## ENGINE HESITATES, SAGS, OR STUMBLES DURING ACCELERATION

**Hesitation** means a delay in the operation of the engine when the accelerator pedal is depressed. Sometimes hesitation is described as **sag** or "lack of response" as the accelerator is pushed down.

The most common cause of hesitation is a too lean air-fuel mixture being delivered to the engine during the time the accelerator is depressed. When the accelerator pedal is depressed, additional air can quickly flow into the engine. Gasoline is

**? FREQUENTLY ASKED QUESTION**

**What Is the Best Way to Find the Cause of Intermittent Problems?**

Intermittent driveability problems are usually difficult to find. Most experts recommend the following procedures that have successfully been used to locate those hard-to-find faults.

1. With the engine running or the component operating, start wiggling the wires, connectors, and hoses. Watch for any change in the operation of the engine or components being moved.
2. Use a water spray bottle that has a little salt added and spray all the electrical wiring and wiring connections. The small amount of salt in the water helps make the water more electrically conductive. Watch for any change in the operation of the engine or component while spraying.
3. Unplug all the electrical connectors and look for rust or corrosion. If possible, use a male metal terminal of the correct size and try mating it with the female terminal, checking to see if the terminal may be too loose to make proper contact. This test is called the "pull test."

heavier than air and cannot flow as fast into the engine as the air. As a result, the engine normally would hesitate until the correct amount of gasoline flow matches the increased amount of air entering the engine. Fuel systems are designed to compensate for this lag or hesitation by providing an additional shot

**FIGURE 27–1** Valve deposits on the intake valves can cause hesitation during acceleration, especially if the engine is cold.

IDLE AIR CONTROL (IAC)    MASS AIRFLOW (MAF) SENSOR

THROTTLE POSITION (TP) SENSOR

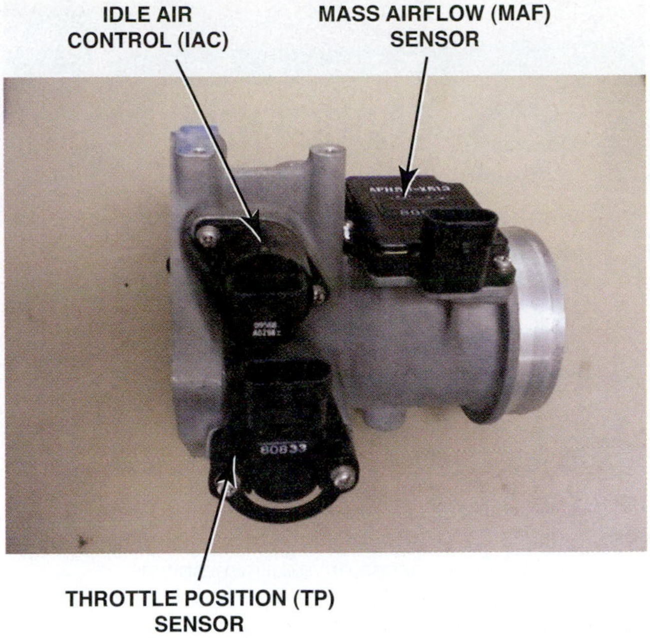

**FIGURE 27–2** Typical throttle-position (TP) sensor.

or squirt of fuel into the intake manifold or cylinder just as the accelerator pedal is depressed.

- Carbon buildup on the backside of the intake valves absorbs gasoline vapors and can cause a hesitation, especially when the engine is cold. ● **SEE FIGURE 27–1.**
- A throttle-position (TP) sensor is used on electronic fuel-injection systems to signal the computer to provide an extra pulse to the fuel injector(s) just as the accelerator pedal is depressed to prevent a hesitation (● **SEE FIGURE 27–2).**

| Possible Cause | Reason |
|---|---|
| Throttle-position (TP) sensor | • The TP sensor voltage should be within the specified range at idle. If too high or too low, the computer may not provide a strong enough extra pulse to prevent a hesitation.<br>• An open or short in the TP sensor can result in hesitation because the computer would not be receiving correct information regarding the position of the throttle. |
| Throttle-plate deposit buildup (port fuel-injected engines) | • An air flow restriction at the throttle plates creates not only less air reaching the engine but also swirling air due to the deposits. This swirling or uneven air flow can cause an uneven air-fuel mixture being supplied to the engine, causing poor idle quality and a sag or hesitation during acceleration. |

| | |
|---|---|
| Manifold absolute pressure (MAP) sensor fault | • The MAP sensor detects changes in engine load and signals to the computer to increase the amount of fuel needed for proper operation. Check the vacuum hose and the sensor itself for proper operation. |
| Check the throttle linkage for binding | • A kinked throttle cable or cruise (speed) control cable can cause the accelerator pedal to bind. |
| Contaminated fuel | • Fuel contaminated with excessive amounts of alcohol or water can cause a hesitation or sag during acceleration. |

**NOTE: To easily check for the presence of alcohol in gasoline, simply get a sample of the fuel and place it in a clean container. Add some water and shake. If no alcohol is in the gasoline, the water will settle to the bottom and be clear. If there is alcohol in the gasoline, the alcohol will absorb the water. The alcohol-water combination will settle to the bottom of the container, but will be cloudy rather than clear. ● SEE FIGURE 27–3.**

| | |
|---|---|
| Clogged, shorted, or leaking fuel injectors | Any injector problem that results in less than an ideal amount of fuel being delivered to the cylinders can result in a hesitation, a sag, or **stumble** during acceleration. |
| Spark plugs or spark plug wires | Any fault in the ignition system such as a defective spark plug wire or cracked spark plug can cause hesitation, a sag, or stumble during acceleration. At higher engine speeds, a defective spark plug wire is not as noticeable as it is at lower speeds, especially in vehicles equipped with a V-8 engine. |

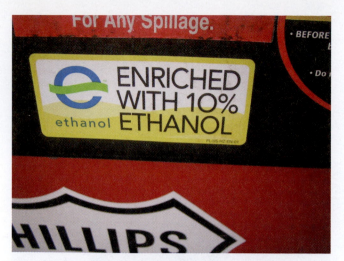

**FIGURE 27–3** Many areas of the country use gasoline that is blended with up to 10% ethanol (ethyl alcohol). Sometimes too much alcohol can cause driveability problems.

**FIGURE 27–4** The deposits on the back (engine) side of the throttle plate can cause rough idle or stalling due to lack of proper air flow into the engine.

| Possible Cause | Reason |
|---|---|
| EGR valve operation | • Hesitation, a sag, or stumble can occur if the EGR valve opens too soon or is stuck partially open. |
| False air | • A loose or cracked intake hose between the MAF sensor and the throttle plate can be the cause. |

## ROUGH IDLE OR STALLING

**Rough** (or **unstable**) **idle** is a common occurrence because many different systems have a direct effect on idle quality. If the engine **stalls** (stops running), most customers are very concerned because it can be a safety-related malfunction. For the engine to idle correctly, each cylinder has to have the same (or nearly the same) compression, air-fuel mixture, ignition timing, and quality of spark.

| Possible Cause | Reason |
|---|---|
| Vacuum leak | • A vacuum leak (also called an air leak) allows extra air to enter the intake manifold or an individual cylinder, thereby leaning the air-fuel mixture to one or more cylinders. Because the cylinder(s) is not receiving the *same* air-fuel mixture, the engine will not run smoothly and a rough idle can result.<br>• In some cases, a vacuum leak can cause a higher-than-normal idle speed or even cause the engine to stall. |
| Dirty throttle plate(s) (port fuel-injected engines) | • Dirty throttle plates can restrict the amount of air entering the engine. ● SEE **FIGURE 27–4.** This is especially noticeable when the engine is idling. Often, the idle air control valve can offset the effect of the dirty throttle by increasing the amount of air that bypasses the throttle plate. Although this may restore the proper idle speed, idle quality may still be poor.<br>• In severe cases, dirty throttle plates can cause stalling, especially when coasting to a stop. |
| Clogged, shorted, or leaking fuel injectors | • A clogged or inoperative fuel injector causes the cylinder or cylinders affected to be leaner than usual. Because all cylinders are not receiving the same amount of fuel, the engine will run roughly and may even stall.<br>• If an injector is leaking and not shutting off when power is removed from the injector, the injector will cause excessive amounts of fuel to be drawn into the affected cylinder or cylinders.<br>• If an injector is electrically shorted, excessive current will flow through the windings of the injector coil. Two situations can occur: (1) The shorted injector may operate, but will draw current from another injector that shares the same injector driver inside the computer. In this case, the injector that is shorted will work okay, but the "good" injector will not work. (2) The shorted injector may work depending on how badly the injector is shorted and how the injector driver circuit inside the computer controls (limits) the current flow through the injector. |

| | |
|---|---|
| Ignition system fault | • Defective spark plug wires can cause a rough running or idling engine, and in severe cases can cause the engine to stall. |
| | • Dirty, cracked, unevenly gapped, or excessively worn spark plugs can cause poor engine operation, a rough idle, or even stalling. |
| | • Weak ignition may result from a shorted ignition coil, defective ignition module (igniter), or defective pickup coil or crankshaft position sensor. |
| Exhaust gas recirculation (EGR) valve stuck open | • An open EGR valve allows inert exhaust gases to be mixed with the proper air-fuel mixture. The exhaust gases cannot burn and the EGR being open at idle is likely to cause a rough idle or stalling. |
| | • At higher engine speeds, exhaust gases can be introduced into the cylinder as is normally done; therefore, the engine runs okay above idle speed. |
| Positive crankcase ventilation (PCV) systems fault | • About 20% of the air going into the engine at idle comes from the PCV system. |
| | • Check that a replacement PCV valve may not be correctly calibrated for the engine (wrong PCV valve application during a previous service). |
| | • All vacuum hoses should be carefully inspected for cracks. |
| | • All vacuum passages should be carefully inspected for obstructions such as carbon buildup in manifold ports where the PCV hose attaches to the manifold. |
| Secondary air injection system malfunction | • Inspect the one-way check valves. A hole in a check valve can cause exhaust gases to flow into the air pump system and into the intake manifold, greatly affecting the air-fuel mixture. |
| Idle air control (IAC) problems | • If the IAC is stuck, the valve cannot provide the correct idle speed. Usually, this results in too high an idle speed, but it can result in a too low idle speed, causing the engine to idle roughly and, in severe cases, even stall. |
| | • Restricted IAC passages can limit the amount of air going into the engine at idle. |
| Manifold absolute pressure (MAP) or mass airflow (MAF) sensor fault | • A MAP sensor vacuum hose, either split open or collapsed, can greatly affect the operation of the MAP sensor. An incorrect MAP sensor signal to the computer can cause the computer to supply either a too rich or too lean command. |
| | • A defective MAP or MAF sensor can also cause a rough idle or stalling. |

| | |
|---|---|
| Malfunction or misadjusted park-neutral switch | • The computer will not command the proper air-fuel mixture if the gear selection is in drive or reverse, yet the computer "thinks" that the gear selector is still in park or neutral. |
| | • The idle speed is affected by the park-neutral switch and the engine may idle roughly or even stall. |

## SPARK KNOCK (PING OR DETONATION)

**Spark knock** (also called **detonation** or **ping**) is most noticeable during acceleration. Spark knock is usually due to excessively lean air-fuel mixtures or excessively hot engine operation. The noise or knock is a result of a secondary rapid burning of the last 3 to 5% of the gases inside the combustion chamber. When this secondary flame front hits the primary spark-ignited flame front, two situations occur:

1. Temperature greatly increases at the instant the two flame fronts collide.

2. Pressure greatly increases at the same time due to the temperature rise.

These two factors combine to cause the piston to "ring" like a bell, creating the characteristic sound of spark knock.

| Possible Cause | Reason |
|---|---|
| Vacuum leak | Causes a leaner-than-normal air-fuel mixture. |
| Defective EGR valve/system | Exhaust gas recirculation (EGR) system uses inert gases to slow the burning process. If not enough exhaust gas is recirculated spark knock can occur. |
| Low coolant level | Could cause the engine to operate too hot. |
| Contaminated $O_2$ sensor | Causes the computer to deliver a too lean air-fuel mixture. |
| Electric cooling fan inoperative | Can cause the engine to operate at too high a temperature. |
| Too low fuel pressure | Can cause the engine to operate with a too lean air-fuel mixture. |
| Too advanced ignition timing | Causes excessive pressure buildup in the combustion chamber. |
| Knock sensor or system is not operating | If the knock sensor (KS) system is not operating, the ignition timing will not be retarded when spark knock is detected. |
| Park-neutral switch | The computer is not seeing a drive gear and the EGR is not commanded on if the vehicle is not in a drive gear (drive or reverse). |

| Possible Cause | Reason |
|---|---|
| Defective valve stem seals | • Causes excessive carbon buildup inside the combustion chamber, creating higher-than-normal compression.<br>• Defective valve stem seals are sources of carbon that can glow, which could be an ignition source that ignites the air-fuel mixture before the spark plug fires, causing preignition. |
| Engine mechanical faults | Incorrect engine parts such as pistons, camshaft, or cylinder heads that can cause excessive compression. |
| PROM | An updated PROM (programmable read-only memory) may have been released that changes the ignition timing or air-fuel mixture to solve a spark knock concern. |

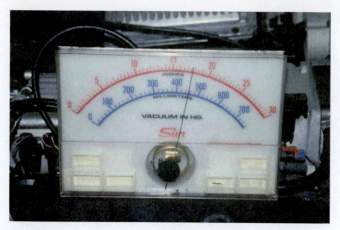

**FIGURE 27–5** A vacuum gauge is an excellent and low-cost tool to use to make sure that the engine is functioning normally.

# ENGINE CRANKS OKAY, BUT IS HARD TO START

In order for engines to start, the correct air fuel ratio must be delivered to the cylinders and a strong spark must be present to ignite the mixture. Worn engine parts can also cause an engine to not have enough compression or to have the valves open and close at the proper time and duration.

| Possible Cause | Reason |
|---|---|
| Weak spark to the spark plugs | A weak spark caused by faults in the ignition coil(s), secondary spark plug wires, or distributor cap or rotor (if so equipped) can prevent the air-fuel mixture from igniting when the cylinder is under compression when the engine is being cranked. |
| Low fuel pressure | Low fuel pressure due to a weak fuel pump or defective fuel-pressure regulator can cause a lack of fuel being supplied to the engine. A defective check valve in the fuel pump can also cause the fuel pressure to drop to zero and can cause a long cranking period to occur before starting. |
| Contaminated or stale gasoline | Gasoline with excessive amounts of alcohol can cause hard starting, especially in cold weather. Stale gasoline is gasoline that has been stored for a long time (several months) and the light ends have evaporated, leaving the heavier portions of the gasoline that are hard to ignite. |
| Leaking, clogged, or inoperative fuel injectors | • If a fuel injector were to stick open, an excessive amount of fuel would fill the cylinder, causing the spark plug(s) to foul and make starting difficult.<br>• If an injector were clogged or inoperative, a lack of fuel would cause the cylinder to be too lean, and hard starting (or no starting) may occur. |
| Low cranking vacuum | • Low cranking vacuum (lower than 2.5 in. Hg) can result from an idle air control (IAC) being stuck open or from an excessively worn engine.<br>• Another cause of low cranking vacuum is the installation of a high-performance camshaft with too much duration. ● SEE FIGURE 27–5. |
| Excessively advanced or retarded ignition timing | • Excessively advanced ignition timing causes the spark to occur too soon while the piston(s) is coming up at the end of the compression stroke. This overadvanced timing usually causes the engine to crank slowly and unevenly.<br>• Excessively retarded ignition timing causes the spark to occur near or after the piston reaches top dead center (TDC). This causes the engine to have to crank a long time before starting. |
| Excessively advanced or retarded valve timing | • Incorrect valve timing can occur due to wear (stretching) of the timing chain.<br>• Incorrect installation of a replacement timing chain or timing belt may have occurred. Look for evidence of a previous timing belt or chain repair or replacement. |

**FIGURE 27–6** This meter indicates a cranking voltage of 10.32 volts, which is within specifications (above 9.6 volts during cranking).

## ENGINE DOES NOT CRANK OR CRANKS SLOWLY

The starter motor is designed to crank the engine between 80 and 250 revolutions per minute (RPM) to permit proper intake of a combustible air-fuel mixture to start. If the engine does not crank, then the fault is in the cranking circuit, which consists of the following components:

- Battery
- Starter motor
- Starter solenoid
- Ignition switch
- Park-neutral or clutch safety switch
- Cables, wires, and connectors

A fault in any of these components can cause slow cranking or no cranking of the engine when the ignition switch is turned to the Start position.

| Possible Cause | Reason |
| --- | --- |
| Weak or discharged battery | The battery should be at least 75% charged with at least 12.4 volts for proper operation of the starter. ● SEE FIGURE 27–6. |
| Loose or dirty battery connections at the battery | Loose or corroded connections can cause an excessive voltage drop, resulting in lower voltage across the starter motor. |
| Defective or misadjusted park-neutral safety switch | The safety switch (either park-neutral with an automatic transmission or the clutch with a manual transmission) may cause an open circuit to the starter solenoid. With no voltage to the solenoid, a no-crank condition occurs. |
| Defective or misadjusted ignition switch | A defective or misadjusted ignition switch may cause an open circuit to the starter solenoid. With no voltage to the solenoid, a no-crank condition is noticed. |
| Blown fuse or fusible link | Most circuits are protected by a fuse and a fusible link. If either is blown or defective, no voltage can reach the starter solenoid; therefore, no cranking of the engine is possible. |

## POOR FUEL ECONOMY

Poor **fuel economy** means lower-than-usual miles per gallon (or liters per 100 kilometers in the metric system) as determined by an actual road test. The test procedure should include the following steps:

1. Fill the fuel tank (DO NOT overfill) and record the mileage (for example, 52,168 miles).
2. Drive the vehicle normally for 100 to 200 miles or more.
3. Fill the tank again. Record the gallons of fuel used and the ending mileage (for example, 10.6 gallons and 52,406 miles).
4. Calculate the miles per gallon:

$$52,406 - 52,168 = 238 \text{ miles}$$
$$238 \text{ miles} \div 10.6 \text{ gallons of fuel} = 22.4 \text{ MPG}$$

Fuel efficiency is determined by many factors including:

- Proper air-fuel mixture
- Proper ignition timing
- Proper gear ratio (this ensures as low a piston speed as practical while cruising in high gear)
- Mechanically sound engine including proper valve timing components
- Engine operating at its most efficient coolant temperature
- Proper operation of the exhaust emissions and fuel evaporative control systems
- Whether the vehicle has been operating with the A/C or defrost on all the time (This can reduce fuel economy.)

| Possible Cause | Reason |
| --- | --- |
| The engine is not operating at the proper coolant temperature | • A defective or stuck-open thermostat can cause the engine to operate less efficiently. Using a lower-than-specified temperature thermostat can also reduce fuel economy. The temperature of the thermostat represents the opening temperature, and the thermostat is fully open 20°F higher than the opening temperature. For example: (1) a 180°F thermostat starts to open at 180°F and is fully open at 200°F. (2) A 195°F thermostat opens at 195°F and is fully open at 215°F. ● SEE FIGURE 27–7 for an example of a stuck-open thermostat. |

**FIGURE 27-7** This stuck-open thermostat caused the engine to fail to reach normal operating temperature. As a result, the fuel economy was much lower than normal and it failed a state vehicle exhaust emission test due to excessive hydrocarbons (HC).

| Possible Cause | Reason |
|---|---|
| | • Inoperative torque converter clutch (lockup torque converter). When a vehicle equipped with an automatic transmission/transaxle with a lockup converter reaches cruising speed, the torque converter clutch is applied, reducing the normal slippage that occurs inside a torque converter. When the torque converter clutch applies, the engine speed drops 150 to 250 RPM and increases fuel economy. Use a scan tool or tachometer to monitor the engine speed (RPM). The engine speed should drop as soon as the computer commands the torque converter clutch to apply. |
| | • Check the evaporative emission control system for proper operation. A hole in the vacuum diaphragm can cause liquid gasoline to be drawn from the fuel tank directly into the engine, greatly reducing fuel economy. Use a hand-operated vacuum pump to check all charcoal canister vacuum diaphragms. |
| | • Check the following engine-related systems: (1) ignition timing, (2) vacuum leaks, (3) dirty (clogged) air filter or air intake, and (4) exhaust system for restrictions. |

## DIESELING OR RUN-ON

**Dieseling** or **run-on** is a term used to describe the engine continuing to run after the ignition is turned off. A diesel engine operates by ignition of the fuel by heat of compression without the need for a spark to occur. Therefore, if the engine continues to run, an ignition source and fuel must be available. The ignition source is usually hot carbon deposits inside the combustion chamber.

| Possible Cause | Reason |
|---|---|
| Leaking injectors | For the engine to continue to run with the key off, a source of fuel is necessary. An injector(s) that is leaking can provide the fuel, and the carbon deposit inside the combustion chamber can provide the ignition source. |
| Defective fuel-pressure regulator | A hole in the rubber diaphragm can provide a source of fuel after the ignition is turned off. |

## BACKFIRE

A **backfire** is the burning of fuel in the intake manifold or in the exhaust system. It is accompanied by a loud popping noise.

| Possible Cause | Reason |
|---|---|
| Vacuum leak | A vacuum leak causes a leaner-than-normal air-fuel mixture. A lean mixture burns hotter and slower than the correct mixture. This slow burning mixture can continue burning throughout the exhaust stroke and can ignite the incoming air-fuel mixture when the intake valve opens at the end of the exhaust stroke. This burning of the intake charge in the intake manifold causes a backfire. |
| Low fuel pressure | Causes a leaner-than-normal air-fuel mixture. |
| Clogged or inoperative fuel injector | Causes a leaner-than-normal air-fuel mixture. |
| • **Incorrect ignition timing**<br>• **Crossed spark plug wire** | If the ignition timing is incorrect, either too advanced or retarded, the spark will not occur when it should. Due to the time it takes for |

- **Crossfire between two cylinders side-by-side**
- **Cracked or carbon-tracked distributor cap**
- **Defective or worn spark plugs**
- **Worn camshaft**
- **Fault in the valve train that could prevent proper valve opening and closing**

the air-fuel mixture to burn (about 3 ms), it may cause the mixture to be burning in the exhaust system or into the intake manifold when the intake valve opens at the end of the exhaust stroke.

If the valves do not open fully and close fully at the proper time, a backfire can occur. If the intake valve does not open as far as it should, a leaner-than-normal air-fuel mixture will be in the cylinder when the spark plug fires. This can cause the fuel to still be burning when the intake valve opens at the end of the exhaust stroke. A leaking valve can cause the burning air-fuel mixture to escape and can cause a backfire.

Exhaust gas recirculation (EGR) valve open all the time or defective EGR valve gasket

Exhaust gases are inert and do not react chemically with the air-fuel mixture. The purpose and function of the EGR system are to slow down the rate of burning of the air-fuel mixture by introducing a metered amount of exhaust gas into the cylinders. Too much EGR can drastically slow the burning of the fuel. This slowing down of the burning of the air-fuel mixture can cause the burning of the fuel to continue as the intake valve opens at the end of the exhaust stroke, which causes a backfire.

Air pump fault such as a defective switching valve

Air pump operation injects extra air into the exhaust manifold or catalytic converter, depending on engine temperature and other factors. To prevent a backfire, the air pump output should be directed to the atmosphere or air cleaner during deceleration when the intake manifold vacuum is high.

Hole in the exhaust

An exhaust leak can cause excessive noise, which could be interpreted by the owner as a backfire.

# LACK OF POWER

A lack of power may also be noticeable as *sluggish* or *spongy* performance. This means that the engine delivers less-than-expected power and the vehicle speed does not increase as desired when the accelerator pedal is depressed.

| Possible Cause | Reason |
|---|---|
| Retarded ignition timing | If the spark occurs later than normal, a decrease in power is the result. For example, the ignition timing is retarded if the spark occurs at 2 degrees before top dead center (BTDC) rather than at the specification of 10 degrees BTDC. |
| Retarded camshaft timing | A stretched timing chain or incorrect installation of a timing chain or belt can cause low power at low engine speeds. When the engine speed increases, however, the engine will perform correctly because the air-fuel mixture is better able to get into and out of the engine at a higher speed if the camshaft timing is retarded. |
| Exhaust system restriction | A restricted exhaust system can cause low power because some of the burned exhaust is still in the cylinder at the end of the exhaust stroke. This causes a less-than-ideal air-fuel mixture to be drawn into the cylinder on the next intake stroke. Check the following for possible restriction: |

- Exhaust system for collapsed or damaged sections.
- Inspect and pound on the catalytic converter(s) and muffler(s) by hand to check for possible broken internal baffles.
- Use a fitting that takes the place of the oxygen sensor and measure the amount of back pressure with the engine running using a pressure/ vacuum gauge. Most vehicle manufacturers specify a reading of less than 2.5 PSI at 2500 engine RPM.

| | |
|---|---|
| Weak ignition coil or worn spark plugs | The ignition output of the coil should be capable of providing a high enough voltage to fire a spark tester that has a minimum required voltage of 25,000 volts (25 kV). A weak coil or an excessively worn spark plug can prevent the proper burning of the air-fuel mixture inside the cylinder. If the air-fuel mixture is not ignited, a lack of power results. |

| Possible Cause | Reason |
|---|---|
| Restricted fuel filter, low fuel pump pressure, or contaminated gasoline | A lack of clean fuel at the proper pressure can cause the engine to produce less-than-normal power. A lack of fuel causes a lean air-fuel mixture that can also cause spark knock (ping or detonation), backfire, hesitation, and related problems. |
| Excessive knock sensor activity | If an engine knock is detected, the computer retards the ignition timing to reduce or eliminate the spark knock. When the ignition timing is retarded, the engine produces less-than-normal power. Excessive spark knock activity can result from one or more of the following:<br><br>• Too low octane-rated gasoline<br><br>• Too lean air-fuel mixture<br><br>• Excessive carbon buildup inside the combustion chamber<br><br>• Engine mechanical or accessory drive belt faults causing a vibration or noise that is being sensed by the knock sensor as being caused by spark knock. |
| Engine mechanical faults | If the engine has a worn camshaft or low compression, it cannot produce normal power. |
| Accelerator pedal not opening the throttle all the way | If the mechanical linkage is out of adjustment or the interior carpet or mat prevents the throttle from opening all the way, a loss of power will be noticed. Have an assistant check that the throttle opens all the way when the accelerator pedal is depressed from inside the vehicle. |

## SURGES

A **surge** is a change in engine power under steady throttle conditions. A driver may feel a surge as if the vehicle was speeding up and slowing down with no change in the accelerator pedal. A lean air-fuel mixture is the most common cause of this condition.

| Possible Cause | Reason |
|---|---|
| Lean air-fuel mixture | • A false rich condition caused by a contaminated oxygen sensor could cause the computer to reduce the amount of fuel delivered to the cylinders.<br><br>• A restricted fuel line or fuel filter can cause a lean condition. |

| Excessive exhaust gas recirculation | A defective EGR valve or solenoid can cause an excessive amount of exhaust gas to enter the combustion chamber, resulting in a less-than-efficient mixture. |
|---|---|
| Weak spark | A weak ignition coil, worn spark plugs, or defective spark plug wires can cause an ignition misfire, resulting in a lack of power that could be intermittent and cause a surge. |
| A clogged or defective fuel injector | Proper engine operation depends on each cylinder receiving the same amount of clean fuel at the proper pressure. |

## CUTS OUT OR MISFIRES

When an engine **misfires,** it jerks or pulsates and is usually more noticeable when the engine is accelerated. Because the engine is not running smoothly, the cause of the misfire is usually due to faults in one or more cylinders, either with a lack of spark, fuel, or compression.

| Possible Cause | Reason |
|---|---|
| Spark plugs and/or spark plug wires | Any fault in the secondary ignition system results in uneven firing of the cylinders, causing the engine to miss or cut out. |
| Engine mechanical faults such as:<br><br>• **Worn camshaft**<br><br>• **Bent pushrod**<br><br>• **Broken valve spring**<br><br>• **Lack of compression** | Any malfunction in the valve train would cause an uneven firing of the cylinders. |

## RICH EXHAUST

A rich exhaust can be determined by a variety of methods, including:

- High CO exhaust readings (over 0.5%)
- Exhaust smell
- Poor fuel economy
- High O2S readings (consistently over 700 mV)
- More than −20% long term fuel trim (LTFT).
- Black exhaust smoke

Although the oxygen sensor should provide a rich signal (O2S high) to the computer and the computer should restore proper operation, many faults in the engine management system can cause the engine to operate too rich, including:

1. Oxygen sensor skewed low or defective
2. False lean signals to the oxygen sensor caused by:
   - Ignition misfire (defective spark plug wires or fouled plugs)
   - Exhaust leak upstream of O2S such as a cracked exhaust manifold or leaking crossover pipe connections
3. Defective fuel-pressure regulator—a hole in the diaphragm can allow gasoline to flow from the fuel line directly into the intake manifold

# LEAN EXHAUST

A lean exhaust can be determined by a variety of methods including:

- High $O_2$ exhaust readings (over 2%).
- Engine hesitates, bucks, jerks, or backfires through the air inlet.
- Low O2S reading (consistently less than 200 mV).
- High block lean numbers (more than 150 or more than a +20% long-term fuel-trim correction factor).

Although the oxygen sensor should provide a lean signal (O2S low) to the computer and the computer should restore proper operation, many faults in the engine management system can cause the engine to operate too lean, including:

1. Oxygen sensor skewed high or defective
2. False rich signal from O2S caused by silicon-contaminated or coated oxygen sensor
3. Large intake manifold or vacuum hose leak
4. Broken intake valve spring causing large internal vacuum (air) leak
5. Low fuel-pump pressure
6. Low voltage to the injectors
7. Poor computer ground causing improper opening of the injectors

TECH TIP

**The Lighter Fluid Trick**

A vacuum (air) leak is often difficult to find. A common technique is to use lighter fluid and carefully squirt along the intake manifold gasket and other possible sources of a leak. The small nozzle of the lighter fluid container makes it easy to find even a small leak. For hard-to-reach areas, attach a straw to the nozzle of the container to direct the lighter fluid. Propane also can be used effectively to locate vacuum leaks.

# SYMPTOMS OF A DEFECTIVE COMPONENT

It is a good idea to know what **symptoms** a particular part or component will cause if defective. In this section, a component part or sensor is listed with typical symptoms the part or sensor could cause if defective.

NOTE: Many symptoms are similar for more than one component part or sensor. This section should *not* be used for diagnosis of an engine performance problem.

| Engine Part or Sensor | Problem if Defective |
|---|---|
| Ignition coil | • No start or hard to start<br>• Misfire under load<br>• Intermittent missing/stalling<br>• Cuts out at high engine speeds |
| Manifold absolute pressure (MAP) sensor | • A MAP sensor is used to measure atmospheric pressure (altitude) when the ignition key is first turned on and to signal engine vacuum, which is a measure of engine load, to the computer.<br>• Light load—less fuel, more ignition timing is possible.<br>• Heavy load—more fuel, less ignition timing is possible.<br>• Therefore, a fault in the MAP sensor can have a major effect on the air-fuel mixture supplied to the engine.<br>• Some characteristic symptoms include:<br>Rough idle and stalling<br>Poor fuel economy<br>Hesitates on acceleration<br>Failed exhaust emissions tests for excessive HC and CO |
| Oxygen sensor | • Poor fuel economy, rough running, stalling, and excessive exhaust emissions (high HC and CO likely) can occur. |

NOTE: The engine will usually operate correctly at or near wide-open throttle (WOT) because the computer ignores the oxygen sensor during these conditions and simply supplies the engine with a rich mixture needed for maximum acceleration.

| | |
|---|---|
| | • Oxygen sensors usually fail low, meaning that the computer gases appear leaner than they actually are and, therefore, the computer will command a richer-than-needed amount of fuel. This is another reason why a defective oxygen sensor is not noticed during rapid acceleration. |
| Spark plug wires | • Engine misfire (especially in wet weather)<br>• Loss of power |

| Engine Part or Sensor | Problem if Defective |
|---|---|

**Caution: If a spark plug wire is defective, high voltage can cause a carbon track in the distributor cap or rotor (if equipped) or cause the ignition coil to become tracked (ruining the coil and requiring replacement).**

| Engine Part or Sensor | Problem if Defective |
|---|---|
| Throttle-position (TP) sensor | • The TP sensor signals the computer regarding not only the position of the throttle, but also the rate of change (speed) at which the throttle is being depressed or released. The TP sensor is an important input device for the torque converter clutch (TCC). The TP voltage has to be greater than a certain percentage (usually about 10%) and less than a certain percentage (usually about 80%). |

CORRODED TERMINAL

**FIGURE 27–8** This corroded coil terminal on a waste spark-type ignition system caused a random misfire DTC to set (P0300) and it affected both cylinders and not just the one than had the corroded terminal.

# EXCESSIVE CO EXHAUST EMISSIONS

The chemical abbreviation CO stands for carbon monoxide, which is formed during the combustion process inside the engine by combining the carbon (C) from the gasoline (HC) and the oxygen (O) from the air. An efficient engine should produce very little CO if there is enough oxygen in the cylinder to create $CO_2$. However, if the air-fuel mixture is too rich, an excessive amount of CO emissions will be created. Therefore, CO is called the *rich indicator* exhaust gas.

| Possible Cause | Reason |
|---|---|
| Clogged or restricted positive crankcase ventilation (PCV) system including the valve itself, the rubber hose, or the manifold vacuum port | Because about 20% of the air needed comes from the PCV system, a restriction in the system reduces the amount of air and increases the amount of CO produced by the engine. |
| Defective fuel-pressure regulator | A fuel-pressure regulator uses a spring-loaded rubber diaphragm to control fuel pressure. The strength of the spring determines the fuel pressure. On most port fuel-injected engines, a vacuum hose from the intake manifold attaches above the rubber diaphragm which changes the fuel pressure in relation to manifold vacuum. A hole in the rubber diaphragm can draw fuel from the fuel rail directly into the intake manifold. This extra fuel can cause the engine to run too rich and produce excessive CO exhaust emissions. |
| Too high fuel pressure | A restricted fuel return line or defective regulator can cause excessive fuel pressure. This excessive fuel pressure often results in excessively rich air-fuel mixture and excessive CO emissions. |
| Degraded catalytic converter | A degraded catalytic converter can cause the vehicle to fail an emission test for excessive CO emissions. |

# EXCESSIVE HC EXHAUST EMISSIONS

The chemical abbreviation for hydrocarbons (gasoline) is HC. Excessive HC exhaust emissions mean that the gasoline is not being properly burned inside the engine. Because the ignition system is used to ignite the air-fuel mixture, any malfunction in this system can result in higher-than-normal HC exhaust emissions.

| Possible Cause | Reason |
|---|---|
| Ignition system faults | Allows unburned fuel to exit the engine. The entire ignition system should be inspected and tested, including: <br> • Spark plugs. <br> • Spark plug wires. <br> • Distributor cap and rotor (if so equipped). ● **SEE FIGURE 27–8.** <br> • Ignition timing. |

| | |
|---|---|
| Excessively lean air-fuel mixture | A very lean air-fuel mixture is often too lean to ignite. As a result, this unburned fuel is pushed out of the engine during the exhaust stroke. This is called a **lean misfire.** |
| Thermostat inoperative (stuck open) or opening temperature too low | An engine operating colder than normal causes a greater-than-normal amount of fuel to condense on the cylinder walls. Because liquid fuel cannot burn without oxygen, this layer of unburned fuel (HC) is pushed out the exhaust system by the piston on the exhaust stroke. Using the specified-temperature thermostat reduces the amount of this quenched fuel, reduces HC emissions, and improves fuel economy. |
| Degraded catalytic converter | A degraded catalytic converter can cause a vehicle to fail an emission test for excessive HC emissions. |

**FIGURE 27–9** This badly eroded water (coolant) pump caused the engine to overheat.

# EXCESSIVE NO$_x$ EXHAUST EMISSIONS

The chemical abbreviation for oxides of nitrogen is NO$_x$. Both nitrogen (N) and oxygen (O$_2$) are normally part of our atmosphere. It requires heat and/or pressure to combine them to form oxides of nitrogen. Excessive NO$_x$ emissions, therefore, mean that the engine combustion chamber temperatures are too high or the chamber has excessive compression.

| Possible Cause | Reason |
|---|---|
| Inoperative or restricted flow EGR valve | The purpose and function of the exhaust gas recirculation system are to introduce inert burned exhaust gases into the combustion chamber to reduce the peak temperatures to reduce NO$_x$ emissions. |
| Cooling system fault such as low coolant level, clogged radiator, restricted air flow through the radiator | Any fault in the cooling system can cause an increase in engine operating temperatures, and therefore cause the engine to create excessive NO$_x$ emissions. ● **SEE FIGURE 27–9.** |
| Too far advanced ignition timing | Advanced ignition timing causes the spark to occur too soon while the piston is coming up on the compression stroke. As a result, the temperature and pressures inside the combustion chamber are increased, which increases the formation of NO$_x$. |
| Too low octane-rated fuel | Using a gasoline with an octane rating lower than specified by the vehicle manufacturer can cause the engine to spark knock (ping). Spark knock or ping is caused by a secondary explosion inside the combustion chamber, which causes a rapid pressure and temperature rise to occur. Therefore, if an engine is spark knocking (pinging), it is also emitting an excessive amount of NO$_x$. |
| Degraded catalytic converter | A degraded catalytic converter can cause a vehicle to fail an emission test for excessive NO$_x$ emissions. |

## SUMMARY

1. A lean air-fuel mixture is the usual cause of hesitation or stumble during acceleration.

2. A vacuum leak and lean air-fuel mixture can cause a rough idle or stalling.

3. Spark knock (ping or detonation) is often caused by a too lean air-fuel mixture, or if the engine operating temperature is too high.

4. A hard-start problem is often due to a lack of fuel.

5. A slowly cranking engine is usually due to low battery voltage. A no-crank condition is usually due to an open circuit in the cranking circuit.

6. Poor fuel economy is usually due to an excessively rich air-fuel mixture.

7. A lean air-fuel mixture is usually due to a vacuum leak.

8. A rich air-fuel mixture can be caused by a defective oxygen sensor or the engine getting fuel from another source not controlled by the computer or fuel system.

1. List five engine performance faults that can occur if a vacuum (air) leak occurs.

2. What symptom(s) may occur if the EGR valve is inoperative (never opens)?

3. List four items that can cause excessive CO exhaust emissions.

4. List four items that can cause excessive HC exhaust emissions.

5. List four items that can cause excessive $NO_x$ exhaust emissions.

## CHAPTER QUIZ

1. Technician A says that a partially stuck-open EGR valve can cause ping (spark knock) during wide-open throttle engine operation. Technician B says that the partially stuck-open EGR valve could cause the engine to stall while operating at idle speed. Which technician is correct?
   a. Technician A only
   b. Technician B only
   c. Both Technicians A and B
   d. Neither Technician A nor B

2. Technician A says that a too rich air-fuel mixture can be caused by a defective fuel-pressure regulator. Technician B says that a defective pressure regulator can cause a too lean air-fuel mixture. Which technician is correct?
   a. Technician A only
   b. Technician B only
   c. Both Technicians A and B
   d. Neither Technician A nor B

3. Technician A says that excessive $NO_x$ exhaust emissions can be due to a defective PCV valve. Technician B says that a too lean air-fuel mixture can cause excessive $NO_x$ exhaust emissions. Which technician is correct?
   a. Technician A only
   b. Technician B only
   c. Both Technicians A and B
   d. Neither Technician A nor B

4. Technician A says a defective TP sensor can cause the engine to hesitate during acceleration. Technician B says that dirty throttle plate(s) on a port-injected engine could cause a hesitation during acceleration. Which technician is correct?
   a. Technician A only
   b. Technician B only
   c. Both Technicians A and B
   d. Neither Technician A nor B

5. Technician A says that defective spark plug wires can cause the engine to misfire. Technician B says a fouled spark plug can cause the engine to misfire. Which technician is correct?
   a. Technician A only
   b. Technician B only
   c. Both Technicians A and B
   d. Neither Technician A nor B

6. Technician A says a rough idle on a fuel-injected engine can be caused by dirty throttle plates. Technician B says the wrong PCV valve could cause the engine to idle roughly. Which technician is correct?
   a. Technician A only
   b. Technician B only
   c. Both Technicians A and B
   d. Neither Technician A nor B

7. Technician A says that spark knock (ping or detonation) can be caused by a lean air-fuel mixture. Technician B says an inoperative cooling fan could cause the engine to spark knock. Which technician is correct?
   a. Technician A only
   b. Technician B only
   c. Both Technicians A and B
   d. Neither Technician A nor B

8. Technician A says that a stretched (worn) timing chain can cause the engine to lack power at slow speeds. Technician B says a clogged exhaust system can cause the engine to lack power at high speeds. Which technician is correct?
   a. Technician A only
   b. Technician B only
   c. Both Technicians A and B
   d. Neither Technician A nor B

9. Technician A says that poor fuel economy can be caused by a defective thermostat. Technician B says a defective evaporative charcoal canister can cause poor or reduced fuel economy. Which technician is correct?
   a. Technician A only
   b. Technician B only
   c. Both Technicians A and B
   d. Neither Technician A nor B

10. Technician A says a rich exhaust could be caused by a hole in the rubber diaphragm of the fuel-pressure regulator on a port-injected engine. Technician B says that a defective spark plug wire can cause the engine computer to supply a too rich air-fuel mixture. Which technician is correct?
    a. Technician A only
    b. Technician B only
    c. Both Technicians A and B
    d. Neither Technician A nor B

For every task in Engine Performance the following safety requirement must be strictly enforced:

Comply with personal and environmental safety practices associated with clothing; eye protection; hand tools; power equipment; proper ventilation; and the handling, storage, and disposal of chemicals/materials in accordance with local, state, and federal safety and environmental regulations.

## ENGINE PERFORMANCE (A8)

| TASK | TEXTBOOK PAGE NO. | WORKTEXT PAGE NO. |
|---|---|---|
| **A. GENERAL ENGINE DIAGNOSIS** | | |
| 1. Complete work order to include customer information, vehicle identifying information, customer concern, related service history, cause, and correction. (P-1) | 1–2 | 1 |
| 2. Identify and interpret engine performance concern; determine necessary action. (P-1) | 1–5 | 6, 111, 112 |
| 3. Research applicable vehicle and service information, such as engine management system operation, vehicle service history, service precautions, and technical service bulletins. (P-1) | 5 | 40, 41, 52 53, 87, 90, 91, 98 |
| 4. Locate and interpret vehicle and major component identification numbers. (P-1) | 8 | 3, 4, 7, 54 |
| 5. Inspect engine assembly for fuel, oil, coolant, and other leaks; determine necessary action. (P-2) | 2–4 | 113 |
| 6. Diagnose abnormal engine noise or vibration concerns; determine necessary action. (P-3) | 2–4 | 114 |
| 7. Diagnose abnormal exhaust color, odor, and sound; determine necessary action. (P-2) | 2–4 | 115 |
| 8. Perform engine absolute (vacuum/boost) manifold pressure tests; determine necessary action. (P-1) | 353–356 | 116 |
| 9. Perform cylinder power balance test; determine necessary action. (P-2) | 353 | 117, 118 |
| 10. Perform cylinder cranking and running compression tests; determine necessary action. (P-1) | 350–351 | 119 |
| 11. Perform cylinder leakage test; determine necessary action. (P-1) | 352 | 120 |
| 12. Diagnose engine mechanical, electrical, electronic, fuel, and ignition concerns; determine necessary action. (P-1) | 118–138, 350–357 | 121 |
| 13. Prepare 4 or 5 gas analyzer; inspect and prepare vehicle for test, and obtain exhaust readings; interpret readings, and determine necessary action. (P-3) | 309–313 | 99 |
| 14. Verify engine operating temperature; determine necessary action. (P-1) | 166 | 122 |
| 15. Perform cooling system pressure tests; check coolant condition; inspect and test radiator, pressure cap, coolant recovery tank, and hoses; perform necessary action. (P-1) | - | 123 |
| 16. Verify correct camshaft timing. (P-1) | 365 | 131 |

| TASK | TEXTBOOK PAGE NO. | WORKTEXT PAGE NO. |
|---|---|---|
| **B. COMPUTERIZED ENGINE CONTROLS DIAGNOSIS AND REPAIR** | | |
| 1. Retrieve and record diagnostic trouble codes, OBD monitor status, and freeze frame data; clear codes when applicable. (P-1) | 8–14 | 16, 92 |
| 2. Diagnose the causes of emissions or driveability concerns with stored or active diagnostic trouble codes; obtain, graph, and interpret scan tool data. (P-1) | 8–14 | 2, 8, 9, 10 |
| 3. Diagnose emissions or driveability concerns without stored diagnostic trouble codes; determine necessary action. (P-1) | 6 | 80, 93, 100, 101 |
| 4. Check for module communication (including CAN/BUS systems) errors using a scan tool. (P-2) | 31–34 | 5 |
| 5. Inspect and test computerized engine control system sensors, powertrain/engine control module (PCM/ECM), actuators, and circuits using a graphing multimeter (GMM)/digital storage oscilloscope (DSO); perform necessary action. (P-1) | 33, 73–78 | 24, 55–79 |
| 6. Access and use service information to perform step-by-step diagnosis. (P-1) | 5 | 11 |
| 7. Diagnose driveability and emissions problems resulting from malfunctions of interrelated systems (cruise control, security alarms, suspension controls, traction controls, A/C, automatic transmissions, non-OEM-installed accessories, or similar systems); determine necessary action. (P-3) | 1–6 | 12 |
| 8. Perform active tests of actuators using a scan tool; determine necessary action. (P-1) | 281, 293 | 13 |
| 9. Describe the importance of running all OBDII monitors for repair verification. (P-1) | 47 | 14, 15, 17 |
| **C. IGNITION SYSTEM DIAGNOSIS AND REPAIR** | | |
| 1. Diagnose ignition system related problems such as no-starting, hard starting, engine misfire, poor driveability, spark knock, power loss, poor mileage, and emissions concerns; determine necessary action. (P-1) | 118–138 | 43, 44 |
| 2. Inspect and test ignition primary and secondary circuit wiring and solid state components; test ignition coil(s); perform necessary action. (P-1) | 119–124 | 45, 46, 47, 48 |
| 3. Inspect and test crankshaft and camshaft position sensor(s); perform necessary action. (P-1) | 131–132 | 49–50 |
| 4. Inspect, test, and/or replace ignition control module, powertrain/engine control module; reprogram as necessary. (P-2) | 120–122 | 51 |
| **D. FUEL, AIR INDUCTION, AND EXHAUST SYSTEMS DIAGNOSIS AND REPAIR** | | |
| 1. Diagnose hot or cold no-starting, hard starting, poor driveability, incorrect idle speed, poor idle, flooding, hesitation, surging, engine misfire, power loss, stalling, poor mileage, dieseling, and emissions problems; determine necessary action. (P-1) | 284–297 | 94 |
| 2. Check fuel for contaminants and quality; determine necessary action. (P-2) | 147–148, 162 | 55 |
| 3. Inspect and test fuel pumps and pump control systems for pressure, regulation, and volume; perform necessary action. (P-1) | 243–251 | 81–85 |
| 4. Replace fuel filters. (P-2) | 243 | 86 |
| 5. Inspect throttle body, air induction system, intake manifold and gaskets for vacuum leaks and/or unmetered air. (P-2) | 294–297 | 89 |
| 6. Inspect and test fuel injectors. (P-1) | 289–293 | 95–97 |
| 7. Verify idle control operation. (P-1) | 293–294 | 88 |
| 8. Inspect the integrity of the exhaust manifold, exhaust pipes, muffler(s), catalytic converter(s), resonator(s), tail pipe(s), and heat shield(s); perform necessary action. (P-1) | 330–333 | 124 |
| 9. Perform exhaust system back-pressure test; determine necessary action. (P-1) | 331 | 102 |
| 10. Test the operation of turbocharger/supercharger systems; determine necessary action. (P-3) | – | 125 |

| TASK | TEXTBOOK PAGE NO. | WORKTEXT PAGE NO. |
|---|---|---|
| **E. EMISSIONS CONTROL SYSTEMS DIAGNOSIS AND REPAIR** | | |
| 1. Diagnose oil leaks, emissions, and driveability concerns caused by the positive crankcase ventilation (PCV) system; determine necessary action. (P-2) | 323 | 103 |
| 2. Inspect, test, and service positive crankcase ventilation (PCV) filter/breather cap, valve, tubes, orifices, and hoses; perform necessary action. (P-2) | 323–324 | 103 |
| 3. Diagnose emissions and driveability concerns caused by the exhaust gas recirculation (EGR) system; determine necessary action. (P-1) | 321 | 104 |
| 4. Inspect, test, service, and replace components of the EGR system, including EGR tubing, exhaust passages, vacuum/pressure controls, filters, and hoses; perform necessary action. (P-1) | 320–321 | 105 |
| 5. Inspect and test electrical/electronic sensors, controls, and wiring of exhaust gas recirculation (EGR) systems; perform necessary action. (P-2) | 318 | 106 |
| 6. Diagnose emissions and driveability concerns caused by the secondary air injection and catalytic converter systems; determine necessary action. (P-2) | 327–328, 330–333 | 107 |
| 7. Inspect and test mechanical components of secondary air injection systems; perform necessary action. (P-3) | 326 | 108 |
| 8. Inspect and test electrical/electronically-operated components and circuits of air injection systems; perform necessary action. (P-3) | 326–327 | 108 |
| 9. Inspect and test catalytic converter efficiency. (P-1) | 331 | 107 |
| 10. Diagnose emissions and driveability concerns caused by the evaporative emissions control system; determine necessary action. (P-1) | 338–341 | 109 |
| 11. Inspect and test components and hoses of the evaporative emissions control system; perform necessary action. (P-1) | 338–341 | 110 |
| 12. Interpret diagnostic trouble codes (DTCs) and scan tool data related to the emissions control systems; determine necessary action. (P-1) | 341 | 110 |
| **F. ENGINE RELATED SERVICE** | | |
| 1. Adjust valves on engines with mechanical or hydraulic lifters. (P-1) | 367–370 | 133 |
| 2. Remove and replace timing belt; verify correct camshaft timing. (P-1) | 365 | 134 |
| 3. Remove and replace thermostat and gasket/seal. (P-1) | 362 | 135 |
| 4. Inspect and test mechanical/electrical fans, fan clutch, fan shroud/ducting, air dams, and fan control devices; perform necessary action. (P-1) | – | 126 |
| 5. Perform common fastener and thread repairs, to include: remove broken bolt, restore internal and external threads, and repair internal threads with a threaded insert. (P-1) | – | 127 |
| 6. Perform engine oil and filter change. (P-1) | – | 128 |
| 7. Identify hybrid vehicle internal combustion engine service precautions. (P-3) | – | 129 |

# ENGLISH GLOSSARY

**AC Coupling**   A signal that passes the AC signal component to the meter, but blocks the DC component. Useful to observe an AC signal that is normally riding on a DC signal; for example, charging ripple.

**AC/DC Clamp-On DMM**   A type of meter that has a clamp that is placed around the wire to measure current.

**Accumulator**   A temporary location for fluid under pressure.

**Actuator**   An electromechanical device that performs mechanical movement as commanded by a controller.

**AFV**   Alternative fuel vehicle.

**Air-Fuel Ratio**   The ratio of air to fuel in an intake charge as measured by weight.

**AKI**   Anti-knock index. The octane rating posted on a gas pump, which is the average of the RON and MON octane ratings.

**Alternator**   An electric generator that produces alternating current; also called an AC generator.

**Analog-to-digital (AD) converter**   An electronic circuit that converts analog signals into digital signals that can then be used by a computer.

**Anhydrous Ethanol**   Ethanol that has no water content.

**ASM**   Acceleration simulation mode.

**ASTM**   American Society for Testing Materials.

**B20**   A blend of 20% biodiesel with 80% petroleum diesel.

**Back Pressure**   The exhaust system's resistance to flow. Measured in pounds per square inch (PSI).

**Baffle**   A plate or shield used to direct the flow of a liquid or gas.

**BARO Sensor**   A sensor used to measure barometric pressure.

**Battery**   A chemical device that produces a voltage created by two dissimilar metals submerged in an electrolyte.

**Battery Electrical Drain Test**   A test to determine if a component or circuit is draining the battery.

**Bias Voltage**   In electrical terms, bias is the voltage applied to a device or component to establish the reference point for operation.

**Binary**   A computer system that uses a series of zeros and ones to represent to information.

**Biodiesel**   A renewable fuel manufactured from vegetable oils, animal fats, or recycled restaurant grease.

**Biomass**   Nonedible farm products, such as corn stalks, cereal straws, and plant wastes from industrial processes, such as sawdust and paper pulp used in making ethanol.

**Blowby Gases**   Combustion gases that leak past the piston rings into the crankcase during the compression and combustion strokes of the engine.

**BNC Connector**   Coaxial-type input connector. Named for its inventor, Neil Councilman.

**BTU**   British thermal unit. A measure of heat energy. One BTU of heat will raise the temperature of one pound of water one Fahrenheit degree.

**California Air Resources Board**   A state of California agency which regulates the air quality standards for the state.

**Catalytic Converter**   An emission control device located in the exhaust system that changes HC and CO into harmless $H_2O$ and $CO_2$. If a three-way catalyst $NO_x$ is also divided into harmless separate nitrogen ($N_2$) and Oxygen ($O_2$).

**Catalytic Cracking**   Breaking hydrocarbon chains using heat in the presence of a catalyst.

**CCM**   Comprehensive Component Monitor.

**Cellulose Ethanol**   Ethanol produced from biomass feedstock such as agricultural and industrial plant wastes.

**Cetane Rating**   A diesel fuel rating that indicates how easily the fuel can be ignited.

**Charging Circuit**   Electrical components and connections necessary to keep a battery fully charged.

**CID**   Component Identification.

**Clock Generator**   A crystal that determines the speed of computer circuits.

**Closed Loop Operation**   A phase of computer-controlled engine operation in which oxygen sensor feedback is used to calculate air/fuel mixture.

**CNG**   Compressed natural gas.

**Coil-On-Plug Ignition System**   An ignition system without a distributor, where each spark plug is integrated with an ignition coil.

**Companion cylinder**   The cylinder that fires at the same time in a waste-spark-type ignition system.

**Cold Cranking Amperes**   The rating of a battery's ability to provide battery voltage during cold-weather operation. CCA is the number of amperes that a battery can supply at 0°F (−18°C) for 30 seconds and still maintain a voltage of 1.2 V per cell (7.2 V for a 12-V battery).

**Continuity Light**   A test light that has a battery and lights if there is continuity (electrical connection) between the two points that are connected to the tester.

**Controller**   A term that is usually used to refer to a computer or an electronic control unit (ECU).

**Controller Area Network**   A type of serial data transmission.

**CPU**   Central Processor Unit.

**Cranking Amperes**   A battery rating tested at 32°F (0°C).

**Cranking Circuit**   Electrical components and connections required to crank the engine to start. Includes starter motor, starter solenoid/relay, battery, neutral safety switch, ignition control switch, and connecting wires and cables.

**Cross Counts**   Cross counts are the number of times an oxygen sensor changes voltage from high to low (from low to high voltage is not counted) in 1 second (or 1.25 second, depending on scan tool and computer speed).

**CRT**   Cathode Ray Tube.

**DC Coupling**   A signal transmission that passes both AC and DC signal components to the meter. (See also AC coupling.)

**DDS**   Demand Delivery System.

**Detonation**   A violent explosion in the combustion chamber created by uncontrolled burning of the air-fuel mixture; often causes a loud, audible knock. Also known as spark knock or ping.

**DI**   Distributor Ignition.

**Diesohol**   Standard #2 diesel fuel combined with up to 15% ethanol.

**Digital**   A method of display that uses numbers instead of a needle or similar device.

**DIS**   Distributorless ignition system; also called direct-fire ignition system.

**Distillation**   The process of purification through evaporation and then condensation of the desired liquid.

**Distillation Curve**   A graph that plots the temperatures at which the various fractions of a fuel evaporate.

**Division**   A specific segment of a waveform, as defined by the grid on the display.

**DMM**   Digital multimeter. A digital multimeter is capable of measuring electrical current, resistance, and voltage.

**DSO**   Digital Storage Oscilloscope.

**Duty Cycle**   Refers to the percentage of on-time of the signal during one complete cycle.

**DVOM**   Digital volt-ohm-milliammeter.

**Dwell**   The amount of time, recorded on a dwell meter in degrees, that voltage passes through a closed switch.

**E10**   A fuel blend of 10% ethanol and 90% gasoline.

**E85**   A fuel blend of 85% ethanol and 15% gasoline.

**EAC**   Electronic Air Control.

**ECA**   Electronic Control Module. The name used by Ford to describe the computer used to control spark and fuel on older model vehicles.

**ECM**   Electronic control module on a vehicle.

**ECT**   Engine coolant temperature.

**ECU**   Electronic control unit on a vehicle.

**E-Diesel**   Standard #2 diesel fuel combined with up to 15% ethanol. Also known as diesohol.

**EEPROM**   Electronically erasable programmable read-only memory.

**Electromagnetic Induction**   The generation of a current in a conductor that is moved through a magnetic field. Electromagnetic induction was discovered in 1831 by Michael Faraday.

**Electromagnetic Interference**   An undesirable electronic signal. It is caused by a magnetic field building up and collapsing, creating unwanted electrical interference on a nearby circuit.

**Electronic Ignition**   General term used to describe any of various types of ignition systems that use electronic instead of mechanical components, such as contact points.

**Electronic Returnless Fuel System**   A fuel delivery system that does not return fuel to the tank.

**Electronic Spark Timing**   The computer controls spark timing advance.

**Engine Mapping**   A computer program that uses engine test data to determine the best fuel-air ratio and spark advance to use at each speed of the engine for best performance.

**ETBE**   An octane enhancer for gasoline. It is also a fuel oxygenate that is manufactured by reacting isobutylene with ethanol. The resulting either is high octane and low volatility. ETBE can be added to gasoline up to a level of approximately 13 percent.

**Ethanol**   An octane enhancer added, at a rate of up to 10 percent, to gasoline; will increase the octane rating of the fuel by 2.5 to 3.0. Ethanol is a fuel oxygenate.

**EWMA Monitor**   Exponentially Weighted Moving Average Monitor.

**Exhaust Gas Recirculation**   The process of passing a small, measured amount of exhaust gas back into the engine to reduce combustion temperatures and formation of $NO_x$ (oxides of nitrogen).

**External Trigger**   When using an oscilloscope connecting when the scope is to be triggered or started is connected to another circuit when the one being measured.

**FFV**   Flex-fuel vehicle. Flex-fuel vehicles are capable of running on straight gasoline or gasoline/ethanol blends.

**Firing Order**   The order that the spark is distributed to the correct spark plug at the right time.

**Fischer-Tropsch**   A refining process that converts coal, natural gas, or other petroleum products into synthetic motor fuels.

**Flare Nut Wrench**   A type of wrench used to remove brake lines.

**Freeze Frame**   A snapshot of information.

**Frequency**   The number of times a waveform repeats in one second, measured in Hertz (Hz), frequency band.

**FTD**   Fischer-Tropsch diesel process. See Fischer-Tropsch.

**FTP**   Federal Test Procedure.

**Fuel Compensation Sensor**   A sensor used in flex-fuel vehicles that provides information to the PCM on the ethanol content and temperature of the fuel as it is flowing through the fuel delivery system.

**Fuel Trim**   A computer function that adjusts fuel delivery during closed-loop operation to bring the air-fuel mixture to as close to 14.7:1 as possible.

**Gasoline**   Refined petroleum product that is used primarily in a gasoline engine.

**Gasoline Direct Injection**   A fuel injection system design in which gasoline is injected directly into the combustion chamber.

**Generic OBD II**   See Global OBD II.

**Global OBD II**   Is the standardized format of on-board diagnostics that is the same for all vehicles, following SAE standard J1962. Global OBD II was designed for engineers and when OBD II was first introduced, it was not intended to be used by service technicians.

**GMM**   Graphing Multimeter.

**Grain Alcohol**   See Ethanol.

**Graticule**   The series of squares on the face of a scope. Usually 8 by 10 on a screen.

**GTL**   Gas-to-liquid. A refining process in which natural gas is converted into liquid fuel.

**Hall-Effect Switch**   A semiconductor moving relative to a magnetic field, creating a variable voltage output. Used to determine position. A type of electromagnetic sensor used in electronic ignition and other systems. Named for Edwin H. Hall, who discovered the Hall effect in 1879.

**Hertz**   A unit of measurement of frequency. One Hertz is one cycle per second, abbreviated Hz. Named for Heinrich R. Hertz, a 19th-century German physicist.

**High Energy Ignition**   The brand name for the electronic ignition used in General Motors vehicles.

**High Impedance Meter**   A digital meter that has at least 10 million ohms of internal resistance as measure between the test leads with the meter set to read volts.

**HSD**   High side driver.

**Hybrid Electric Vehicle**   Describes any vehicle that uses more than one source of propulsion, such as internal combustion engine (ICE) and electric motor(s).

**Hydrocracking**   A refinery process that converts hydrocarbons with a high boiling point into ones with low boiling points.

**IAC**   Idle air control.

**IEC**   International Electrotechnical Commission.

**Ignition Coil**   An electrical device consists of two separate coils of wire: a primary and a secondary winding. The purpose of an ignition is to produce a high-voltage (20,000 to 40,000 V), low-amperage (about 80 mA) current necessary for spark ignition.

**Ignition Off Draw**   A Chrysler term used to describe battery electrical drain or parasitic draw.

**Ignition Timing**   The exact point of ignition in relation to piston position.

**Impeller**   The mechanism in a water pump that rotates to produce coolant flow.

**Inches of Mercury**   A measurement of vacuum; pressure below atmospheric pressure.

**Inductive Ammeter**   A type of ammeter that is used a Hall Effect senor in a clamp that is used around a conductor carrying a current.

**Inductive Reactance**   An opposing current created in a conductor whenever there is a charging current flow in a conductor.

**Input Conditioning**   What the computer does to the input signals to make them useful; usually includes an analog to digital converter and other electronic circuits that eliminate electrical noise.

**Ion-Sensing Ignition**   An electronic ignition system that uses the spark plug as a sensor to determine camshaft position, misfire, and knock.

**ISC**   Idle speed control.

**KAM**   Keep alive memory.

**Kilo**   Means 1000; abbreviated k or K.

**Knock Sensor**   A sensor that can detect engine spark knock.

**Lambda Sensor**   Oxygen sensor or $O_2$ sensor. Lambda is the Greek letter that represents ratio, as in air-fuel ratio.

**LED Test Light**   Uses an LED instead of a standard automotive bulb for a visual indication of voltage.

**Load Test**   A type of battery test where an electrical load is applied to the battery and the voltage is monitored to determine the condition of a battery.

**Logic Probe**   A type of tester that can detect either power or ground. Most testers can detect voltage but most of the others cannot detect if a ground is present without further testing.

**LPG**   Liquefied petroleum gas. Another term for propane.

**LSD**   Low side driver.

**M85**   Internal combustion engine fuel containing 85% methanol and 15% gasoline.

**Malfunction Indicator Lamp**   This amber dash board warning light may be labeled check engine or service engine soon.

**Manifold Absolute Pressure**   Sensor used to measure the pressure inside the intake manifold compared to a perfect vacuum.

**MCA**   Marine cranking amps. A battery specification.

**Mechanical Returnless Fuel System**   A returnless fuel delivery system design that uses a mechanical pressure regulator located in the fuel tank.

**Mega**   Million. Used when writing larger numbers or measuring large amount of resistance.

**Meter Accuracy**   The accuracy of a meter measured in percent.

**Meter Resolution**   The specification of meter that indicates how small or fine a measurement the meter can detect and display.

**Methanol**   Typically manufactured from natural gas. Methanol content, including co-solvents, in unleaded gasoline is limited by law to 5 percent.

**Methyl Alcohol**   See Methanol.

**Micro**   One-millionth of a volt or ampere.

**MID**   Monitor Identification.

**Milli**   One thousandth of a volt or ampere.

**MTBE**   Methyl tertiary butyl ether. MTBE is an oxygenated fuel that is used as a gasoline additive to enhance its burning characteristics being phased out due to ground water contamination concerns.

**MTHF**   Methyltetrahydrofuron. A component of P-series nonpetroleum-based fuels.

**Multiplexing**   A process of sending multiple signals of information at the same time over a signal wire.

**Mutual Induction**   The generation of an electric current due to a changing magnetic field of an adjacent coil.

**Network**   A communications system used to link multiple computers or modules.

**Neutral Safety Switch**   A switch connected in series in the starter control circuit that allows operation of the starter motor to occur only when the gear selection is in neutral (N) or park (P).

**NGV**   Natural gas vehicle.

**NMHC**   Non-methane hydrocarbon.

**Nonvolatile RAM**   Computer memory capability that is not lost when power is removed.

**NTC**   Usually used in reference to a temperature sensor (coolant or air temperature). As the temperature increases, the resistance of the sensor decreases.

**OBD**   Onboard diagnosis.

**Octane Rating**   The measurement of a gasoline's ability to resist engine knock. The higher the octane rating, the less prone the gasoline is to cause engine knock (detonation).

**Open Circuit**   Any circuit that is not complete and in which no current flows.

**Open Loop Operation**   A phase of computer-controlled engine operation where air/fuel mixture is calculated in the absence of oxygen sensor signals. During open loop, calculations are based primarily on throttle position, engine RPM, and engine coolant temperature.

**Organic**   A term used to describe anything that was alive at one time.

**ORVR**   Onboard refueling vapor recovery.

**Oscilloscope**   A visual display of electrical waves on a fluorescent screen or cathode ray tube.

**Oxygenated Fuels**   Fuels such as ETBE or MTBE that contain extra oxygen molecules to promote cleaner burning. Oxygenated fuels are used as gasoline additives to reduce CO emissions.

**Ozone**   Oxygen rich ($O_3$) gas created by sunlight reaction with unburned hydrocarbons (HC) and oxides of nitrogen ($NO_x$); also called smog.

**Parameter Identification**   The information found in the vehicle datastream as viewed on a scan tool.

**PCV**   Positive crankcase ventilation.

**Petrodiesel**   Another term for petroleum diesel, which is ordinary diesel fuel refined from crude oil.

**Petroleum**   Another term for crude oil. The literal meaning of petroleum is "rock oil."

**PID**   Parameter Identification.

**Ping**   Secondary rapid burning of the last 3 to 5% of the air-fuel mixture in the combustion chamber causes a second flame front that collides with the first flame front causing a knock noise. Also called detonation or spark knock.

**Polarity**   The condition of being positive or negative in relation to a magnetic pole.

**Powertrain Control Module**  The on-board computer that controls both the engine management and transmission functions of the vehicle.

**Pressure Differential**  A difference in pressure from one brake circuit to another.

**Pressure Vent Valve**  A valve located in the fuel tank to prevent over-pressure due to the thermal expansion of the fuel.

**PROM**  Programmable read-only memory.

**Propane**  See LPG.

**Pulse Generator**  An electromagnetic unit that generates a voltage signal used to trigger the ignition control module that controls (turns on and off) the primary ignition current of an electronic ignition system.

**Pulse Train**  A DC voltage that turns on and off in a series of pulses.

**Pulse Width**  The amount of "on" time of an electronic fuel injector.

**PWM**  Pulse-width modulation. The control of a device by varying the on-time of the current flowing through the device.

**RAM**  A nonpermanent type of computer memory used to store and retrieve information.

**Read Only Memory**  A permanent type of computer memory programmed by the computer manufacturer to store the operating instructions and parameters of the computer.

**Reserve Capacity**  The number of minutes a battery can produce 25 A and still maintain a battery voltage of 1.75 V per cell (10.5 V for a 12 V battery).

**RFG**  Reformulated gasoline. RFG has oxygenated additives and is refined to reduce both the lightest and heaviest hydrocarbon content from gasoline in order to promote cleaner burning.

**RMS**  Root mean square.

**Roller Cell**  Vane pump.

**RVP**  Reid vapor pressure. A measure of the volatility at exactly 100 degrees F.

**Saturation**  The point of maximum magnetic field strength of a coil.

**Self-Induction**  The generation of an electric current in the wires of a coil created when the current if first connected or disconnected.

**Sequential Fuel Injection**  A fuel injection system in which injectors are pulsed individually in sequence with the firing order.

**Serial Data**  Data that is transmitted by a series of rapidly changing voltage signals.

**SHED Test**  Sealed housing for evaporative determination test.

**SIDI**  Spark ignition direct injection.

**SIP**  State implementation plan.

**Slip Ring End**  The end of a generator (alternator) that has the brushes and the slip rings.

**Smog**  The term used to describe a combination of smoke and fog. Formed by $NO_x$ and HC with sunlight.

**Society of Automotive Engineers**  A professional organization made up of automotive engineers and designers that establishes standards and conducts testing for many automotive-related functions.

**Spark Knock**  Secondary rapid burning of the last 3 to 5% of the air-fuel mixture in the combustion chamber. Causes a second flame front that collides with the first flame front causing a knock noise.

**Splice Pack**  A central point where many serial data lines jam together, often abbreviated SP.

**State of Charge**  The degree or the amount that a battery is charged. A fully charged battery would be 100% charged.

**Surface Charge**  A "false" charge that exists on the battery plates when a vehicle is first turned off.

**Switchgrass**  A feedstock for ethanol production that requires very little energy or fertilizer to cultivate.

**Syn-Gas**  Synthesis gas generated by a reaction between coal and steam. Syn-gas is made up of mostly hydrogen and carbon monoxide and is used to make methanol. Syn-gas is also known as town gas.

**Synthetic Fuel**  Fuels generated through synthetic processes such as Fischer-Tropsch.

**TAME**  Tertiary amyl methyl ether. TAME is an oxygenating fuel and is used as a gasoline additive similar to ETBE or MTBE.

**TBI**  Throttle body injection.

**TEL**  Tetra ethyl lead. TEL was used as an antiknock additive in gasoline, but has been phased out in favor of more benign additives such as ethanol.

**Terminating Resistor**  Resistors placed at the end of a high-speed serial data circuit to help reduce electromagnetic interference.

**Test Light**  A light used to test for voltage. Contains a light bulb with a ground wire at one end and a pointed tip at the other end.

**Throttle Position Sensor**  Signals the computer as to the position of the throttle.

**TID**  Task Identification.

**Time Base**  The setting of the amount of time per division when adjusting a scope.

**Transistor**  A semiconductor device that can operate as an amplifier or an electrical switch.

**Trigger Level**  The voltage level that a waveform must reach to start display.

**Trigger Slope**  The voltage direction that a waveform must have to start display. A positive slope requires the voltage to be increasing as it crosses the trigger level; a negative slope requires the voltage to be decreasing.

**UCG**  Underground coal gasification.

**ULSD**  Ultra-Low-Sulfur Diesel. Diesel fuel with a maximum sulfur content of 15 parts per million.

**Vacuum**  Any pressure less than atmospheric pressure (14.7 PSI).

**Vapor Lock**  A lean condition caused by vaporized fuel in the fuel system.

**V-FFV**  Virtual Flexible Fuel Vehicle. This fuel system design does not use a fuel compensation sensor and instead uses the vehicle's oxygen sensor to adjust for different fuel compositions.

**Volatile**  Volatile RAM memory is lost whenever the ignition is turned off.

**Volatile Organic Compound**  These compounds include gases emitted from paints, solvents, glass, and many other products.

**Volatility**  A measurement of the tendency of a liquid to change to vapor. Volatility is measured using RVP, or Reid Vapor Pressure.

**Voltage Drop**  Voltage loss across a wire, connector, or any other conductor. Voltage drop equals resistance in ohms times current in amperes (Ohm's law).

**Volumetric Efficiency**  The ratio between the amount of air-fuel mixture that actually enters the cylinder and the amount that could enter under ideal conditions expressed in percent.

**Wood Alcohol**  See Methanol.

**WWFC**  World Wide Fuel Charter. A fuel quality standard developed by vehicle and engine manufacturers in 2002.

# SPANISH GLOSSARY

**Acoplamiento de corriente alterna**   Una señal que permite el paso del componente de corriente alterna de la señal en su trayecto al medidor, pero que bloquea el componente de corriente directa. Sirve para observar una señal de corriente alterna que típicamente viaja sobre una señal de corriente directa; por ejemplo, una ola cargante.

**Acoplamiento de corriente directa**   Una señal que transmite tanto el componente de corriente alterna como el componente de corriente directa al medidor. *Véase también* Acoplamiento de corriente alterna.

**Actuador**   Un aparato electromecánico que realiza movimientos mecánicos dirigidos por un controlador.

**Acumulador**   Un depósito o recipiente temporal para fluidos bajo presión.

**AFV**   Siglas en inglés de vehículos de combustibles alternativos.

**Alcohol de grano**   *Véase* Etanol.

**Alcohol de madera**   *Véase* Metanol.

**Alcohol metilo**   *Véase* Metanol.

**Alternador**   Un generador eléctrico que produce corriente alterna. También se lo conoce como un generador de corriente alterna.

**Amperaje de arranque en frío**   Valuación de la habilidad de una batería de producir un voltaje en tiempo frío. El número de amperes que una batería puede proporcionar a una temperatura de -18°C (0°F) durante 30 segundos mientras que mantiene un nivel de voltaje de 1.2 V por celda (7.2 V para una batería de 12 V).

**Amperímetro inductivo**   Un tipo de amperímetro que utiliza un sensor de efecto Hall en una tenaza que se usa para envolver un conductor que transporta una corriente.

**Anchura de pulso**   Duración del tiempo de encendido de un inyector de combustible electrónico.

**ASM**   Siglas en inglés para modo de simulación de aceleración.

**ASTM**   Siglas en inglés de la Sociedad Americana para Materiales de Prueba.

**Auto inducción**   La generación de una corriente eléctrica en los alambres de una bobina cuando una corriente comienza o deja de fluir a través de éstos.

**B20**   Una mezcla de 20% de biodiésel con 80% de petrodiésel.

**Batería**   Un dispositivo químico que produce un voltaje por medio de dos metales disímiles sumergidos en un electrolito.

**Biodiésel**   Un combustible renovable producido a partir de aceites vegetales, grasas animales o grasa de restaurante reciclada.

**Biomasa**   Productos agrícolas no comestibles, tales como tallos de maíz y pajas de cereal, y deshechos botánicos de procesos industriales, tales como el aserrín y la pulpa de papel utilizadas en la elaboración del etanol.

**Bobina del encendido**   Aparato eléctrico que consta de dos bobinas distintas de alambre: un bobinado primario y uno secundario. El objetivo de un encendido es producir una corriente de alto voltaje (entre 20,000 y 40,000 V) y bajo amperaje (cerca de 80 mA) necesaria para producir el encendido de la chispa.

**Bomba de paleta oscilante**   Bomba de paleta.

**Caída de tensión**   Pérdida de voltaje a través de un alambre, conector o cualquier otro conductor cuando fluye una corriente a través de un circuito. La caída de tensión equivale a la resistencia en ohmios multiplicado por la corriente en amperios (la Ley de Ohm).

**Capacidad de Arranque**   Una calificación de batería que se prueba a 32°F (0°C).

**Capacidad de reserva**   El número de minutos que una batería puede producir 25 amperios y aún así mantener un voltaje de 1.75 voltios por celda (10.5 V para una batería de 12 V).

**Carga de superficie**   Un carga "falsa" que existe en las placas de una batería cuando un vehículo acaba de ser apagado.

**CCM**   Siglas en inglés para monitor de componente integral.

**Ciclo de duración**   Porcentaje de tiempo en el que una señal se mantiene encendida en un ciclo completo.

**CID**   Siglas en inglés para identificación de componente.

**Circuito abierto**   Cualquier circuito que no está cerrado y en el cual no fluye la corriente.

**Circuito de carga**   Los componentes eléctricos y las conexiones necesarias para mantener una batería completamente cargada.

**Circuito de mando**   Los componentes eléctricos y conexiones que se requieren para arrancar el motor. Dicho circuito incluye el motor de arranque, el solenoide/relevador del motor de arranque, la batería, el interruptor de seguridad neutral, el interruptor de control de encendido y las conexiones y cables correspondientes.

**CNG**   Siglas en inglés para gas natural comprimido.

**Combustibles oxigenados**   Combustibles tales como el *ETBE* o el *MTBE* que contienen moléculas de oxígeno adicionales para promover un quemado más limpio. Los combustibles oxigenados se usan como aditivos de la gasolina para reducir las emisiones de monóxido de carbono.

**Combustibles sintéticos**   Combustibles creados a través de procesos sintéticos tales como el proceso Fischer-Tropsch.

**Compensador de gasolina**   Una función de la computadora vehicular que ajusta la provisión de combustible durante la fase de operación de ciclo cerrado para que la mezcla aire/combustible se aproxime lo más posible a una proporción de 14.7:1.

**Compuesto orgánico volátil**   Estos compuestos incluyen los gases emitidos por pinturas, disolventes, vidrio y muchos otros productos.

**Conector BNC**   Un mini conector de entrada estándar de tipo coaxial. Nombrado por sus inventores Paul Neill y Carl Concelman.

**Consumo de corriente en apagado**   Un termino utilizado por la compañía *Chrysler* para describir el fenómeno de descarga parasítica de la batería.

**Conteo o frecuencia de cambio de voltaje**   El número de veces que un sensor de oxígeno cambia su voltaje de alto a bajo (el alza de voltaje no cuenta en el conteo) en un segundo (o 1.25 segundos, dependiendo de la velocidad de la computadora o sonda que se utiliza).

**Contrapresión**   La resistencia al flujo del sistema de escape que se mide en libras por pulgada cuadrada (*PSI*).

**Controlador**   Un término utilizado para referirse a una computadora vehicular o unidad de control electrónico (*ECU* por sus siglas en inglés).

**Convertidor catalítico**   Un mecanismo de control de emisiones ubicado en el sistema de escape que convierte el HC y el CO en $H_2O$ y $CO_2$ inocuos. En un catalizador de tres vías, el $NO_x$ también se divide en nitrógeno ($N_2$) y oxígeno ($O_2$).

**Convertidor de análogo a digital (*ADC* por sus siglas en inglés)**   Un circuito electrónico que convierte señales análogas en señales digitales que pueden ser usadas por una computadora.

**CPU** Siglas en inglés para unidad de procesamiento central.

**Cristal oscilante** Un cristal que determina la velocidad de los circuitos electrónicos.

**CRT** Siglas en inglés para tubo de rayo catódico.

**Cuadrícula** Conjunto de cuadrados en la cara de un osciloscopio. Generalmente hay 8 por 10 en una pantalla.

**Curva de destilación** Una gráfica que grafica las temperaturas a las cuales se evaporan las diferentes fracciones de un combustible.

**DDS** Siglas en inglés para sistema de provisión por demanda.

**Desintegración catalítica** La desintegración de cadenas de hidrocarburos utilizando el calor en presencia de un catalizador.

**Destilación** Es el proceso de purificación a través de la evaporación y luego condensación del líquido deseado.

**Detonación** Una explosión violenta en la cámara de combustión creada por una incineración incontrolada de la mezcla aire y combustible; generalmente causa un golpeteo fuerte y audible. También conocido como golpeteo o ping.

**DI** Siglas en inglés de sistema de encendido con distribuidor.

**Diesohol** Combustible diésel estándar #2 combinado con hasta un 15% de etanol. *Véase también E-Diésel*.

**Diferencial de presión** Una diferencia en la presión de un circuito de frenos a otro.

**Digital** Un método de visualización que utiliza números en vez de recurrir a una aguja o un aparato parecido.

**DIS** Siglas en inglés para sistema de encendido sin distribuidor. También llamado sistema de ignición estática.

**Disparo externo** Un modo de disparo de un osciloscopio en el cual el inicio del despliegue en pantalla del mismo es activado a través de un circuito externo al que está siendo medido.

**División** Un segmento específico de una onda, según es definido por la cuadrícula de la pantalla.

**DMM** Siglas en inglés para multímetro digital. Un multímetro digital tiene la capacidad de medir la corriente eléctrica, la resistencia y el voltaje.

**DSO** Siglas en inglés para osciloscopio de almacenamiento digital.

**DVOM** Siglas en inglés para un miliamperímetro digital de voltios ohmios.

**E10** Una mezcla de combustible compuesta de 10% etanol y 90% gasolina.

**E85** Una mezcla de combustible compuesta de 85% etanol y 15% gasolina.

**EAC** Siglas en inglés para control electrónico de aire.

**ECA** Siglas en inglés para módulo de control electrónico. El nombre utilizado por *Ford* para describir la computadora utilizada para controlar el abastecimiento de combustible y el encendido en los modelos de vehículos más antiguos.

**ECM** Siglas en inglés para módulo de control electrónico en un vehículo.

**ECT** Siglas en inglés para temperatura del refrigerante del motor.

**ECU** Siglas en inglés para unidad de control electrónico en un vehículo.

**E-Diésel** Diésel estándar #2 que contiene hasta un 15% de etanol. También conocido como diesohol.

**EEPROM** Siglas en inglés para memoria de sólo lectura electrónicamente borrable y programable.

**Eficiencia volumétrica** La relación entre la cantidad de mezcla aire/combustible que en realidad ingresa al cilindro y la cantidad que potencialmente podría ingresar si se diesen las condiciones ideales y que es expresado en un porcentaje.

**El cilindro del compañero** El cilindro que despide al mismo tiempo en un sistema de ignición de tipo de chispa residual.

**Encendido sensor de iones** Sistema electrónico de encendido que utiliza la bujía como sensor para determinar la posición del árbol de levas, el fallo de encendido y el golpeteo.

**Ensamblaje de empalme** Un término utilizado para describir la interconexión de muchas líneas de data en serie. A menudo se abrevia SP.

**Esmog** Contaminación del aire formada por NOx y HC con incidencia de la luz solar. Una combinación de los términos en inglés para "humo" y "niebla."

**Estado de carga** Nivel, cantidad o porcentaje de carga de una batería. Una batería completamente cargada está 100% cargada.

**Etanol** Aditivo para mejorar el octanaje, añadido a la gasolina a razón de hasta por ciento. El etanol aumentará el octanaje del combustible por un factor de 2.5 a 3.0. El etanol es un combustible oxigenado.

**Etanol anhidro** Etanol que no tiene agua.

**Etanol de celulosa** Etanol producido a partir de cargas de alimentación de biomasa tales como residuos vegetales agrícolas e indústriales.

**ETBE** Etil terbutil éter. El ETBE es un combustible oxigenado producido haciendo reaccionar isobutileno con etanol. El éter que resulta tiene un alto contenido de octano y baja volatilidad. El ETBE puede utilizarse como un aditivo de la gasolina hasta un nivel de aproximadamente 13%.

**Extremo del anillo de deslizamiento** El extremo de un generador (alternador) que contiene escobillas y anillos de deslizamiento.

**FFV** Siglas en inglés de vehículos de combustible flexible. Los vehículos de combustible flexible son capaces de moverse con gasolina pura o con mezclas de gasolina y etanol.

**Fidelidad de medición** El porcentaje de exactitud de un medidor.

**Frecuencia** El número de veces que se repite una onda en un segundo, medido en Hercio (Hz), frecuencia de banda.

**FTD** Siglas en inglés para el proceso Fischer-Tropsch de refinación de diésel. *Véase* Proceso Fischer-Tropsch.

**FTP** Siglas en inglés para Procedimiento Federal de Evaluaciones.

**Gases de fuga** Gases producto de la combustión que se escurren más allá de los aros del pistón y se introducen al cárter del cigüeñal durante los golpes de compresión y combustión del motor.

**Gasolina** Producto de petróleo refinado que es utilizado principalmente como combustible vehicular.

**Generador de pulsos** Una unidad electromagnética que genera una señal de voltaje utilizada para disparar el modulo de control de encendido que controla (enciende y apaga) la corriente primaria de encendido de un sistema de ignición o encendido electrónico.

**GMM** Siglas en inglés para multímetro gráfico.

**Golpeteo** Quemado rápido secundario de los últimos 3% a 5% de la mezcla de aire/combustible en la cámara de combustión que causa un segundo frente de llama que choca con el primer frente de flama causando un ruido de golpeteo. También llamado detonación o ping.

**HEI** Siglas en inglés para la marca de encendido de alta energía utilizada en los vehículos de *General Motors*.

**Hercio** Unidad de medida de la frecuencia. Un Hercio es un ciclo por segundo y se abrevia Hz. Nombrado por Heinrich R. Hertz, un físico alemán del siglo 19.

**Hidrocraqueo** Proceso de refinamiento que convierte los hidrocarburos con alto punto de ebullición en otros con bajo punto de ebullición.

**HSD** Siglas en inglés de circuito manejador (*driver*) controlable por el lado de alta tensión (*high side*).

**IAC** Siglas en inglés para control de aire de ralentí.

**IEC** Siglas en inglés la Comisión Electrotécnica Internacional.

**Imagen congelada** Un muestreo instantáneo de información.

**Impulsor (propulsor)** El mecanismo en una bomba de agua que rota para producir la circulación del elemento refrigerante.

**Índice antidetonante (AKI por sus siglas en inglés)** El octanaje que se exhibe en las gasolineras.

**Índice de cetano (cetanaje)** Medida que indica cuán fácil un combustible diésel puede encenderse en combustión.

**Índice de octano** Medida de las características antidetonantes de una gasolina. Cuanto más alto es el octanaje menos proclividad tiene la gasolina de causar golpeteo del motor (detonación).

**Inducción electromagnética** La generación de una corriente en un conductor que se pasa a través de un campo magnético. La inducción electromagnética fue descubierta en 1831 por Michael Faraday.

**Inducción mutua** La generación de una corriente eléctrica debido a un campo magnético cambiante de un bobinado adyacente.

**Intercambio en serie de datos** Datos transmitidos en serie por medio de señales de voltaje altamente variable.

**Interferencia electromagnética** Una señal electrónica indeseada, causada por la expansión y colapso de un campo magnético, lo cual genera interferencia eléctrica no deseada en un circuito eléctrico cercano.

**Interruptor de efecto Hall** Un semiconductor moviéndose en relación a un campo magnético, creando así una salida de voltaje variable. Utilizado para determinar una posición. Un tipo de sensor electromagnético utilizado en el encendido electrónico y otros sistemas. Llamado así en honor a Edwin H. Hall, el descubridor del efecto Hall en 1879.

**Interruptor de seguridad neutral** Un interruptor eléctrico conectado en serie en el circuito de control de arranque que permite la operación del motor de arranque sólo si el selector de engranaje está en neutro (N) o estacionado (P).

**Inyección directa de gasolina** Diseño del sistema de inyección de combustible en el cual se inyecta la gasolina directamente a la cámara de combustión.

**ISC** Siglas en inglés para control de velocidad de marcha mínima.

**Junta de recursos atmosféricos de California (CARB por sus siglas en inglés)** Agencia gubernamental del estado de California que regula los estándares de calidad de aire para el estado.

**KAM** Siglas en inglés para memoria siempre activa.

**Kilo** Significa 1,000; se abrevia "k" o "K".

**Lámpara indicadora de mal funcionamiento** Luz de advertencia en el tablero que puede estar rotulada con *check engine* (revisar motor) o *service engine soon* (mantenimiento del motor necesario).

**Llave para tuercas cónicas** Un tipo de llave utilizada para retirar líneas de frenos.

**LPG** Siglas en inglés de gas licuado de petróleo. Otro término para propano.

**LSD** Siglas en inglés de circuito manejador (*driver*) controlable por el lado de baja tensión (*low side*).

**Luz de prueba de continuidad** Una luz de prueba que contiene una batería y que se enciende si detecta la presencia de la continuidad (conexión eléctrica) entre los dos polos que están conectados al probador.

**Luz de prueba** Una luz utilizada para comprobar la presencia de voltaje. Contiene un foco conectado, en un extremo, a un cable puesto a tierra y a un puntal en el otro extremo.

**Luz de prueba tipo LED** Una luz de prueba que utiliza un diodo emisor de luz (*LED* por sus siglas en inglés) en lugar de un foco automotriz para proveer una indicación visual del voltaje.

**M85** Un combustible de motor de combustión interna que contiene 85% metanol y 15 % de gasolina.

**Mapeo de motor** Un programa de computadora que utiliza la información de las pruebas de motor para determinar la mejor relación aire/combustible y la velocidad apropiada de avance de chispa para el desempeño ideal del motor.

**MCA** Siglas en inglés para amperios de arranque en aplicaciones marinas. Un indicador para batería.

**Medidor de alta impedancia** Un medidor digital que tiene al menos 10 millones de ohmios de resistencia interna al medirse entre las sondas de prueba con el medidor configurado en el modo de lectura de voltios.

**Mega** Millón. Termino utilizado para referirse a números muy grandes o para la medición de una gran cantidad de resistencia eléctrica.

**Metanol** Alcohol típicamente elaborado a base de gas natural. El contenido de metanol, incluyendo cosolventes, en la gasolina sin plomo está limitado por ley al cinco por ciento (5%).

**Metiltetrahidrofurano (MeTHF)** Un componente de los combustibles de serie P que no son a base de petróleo.

**Micro** Una millonésima parte de un voltio o un amperio.

**MID** Siglas en inglés de identificación de monitor.

**Mijo** Una planta o carga de alimentación usada en la producción de etanol que requiere muy poca energía o fertilizante para su cultivo.

**Mili** Una milésima parte de un voltio o un amperio.

**Módulo de control del tren de fuerza** La computadora de manejo del motor que controla el motor y las funciones de la transmisión.

**Monitor tipo EWMA** Un monitor de promedio móvil ponderado exponencialmente.

**MTBE** Siglas en inglés de metilterbutil éter. El MTBE es un combustible oxigenado que se usa como aditivo en la gasolina para mejorar sus características de combustión. El mismo está siendo eliminado debido a preocupaciones con contaminación de agua subterránea.

**Multímetro digital de corriente alterna y directa con sujetador** Un tipo de medidor que tiene una tenaza, o clip, que se sujeta al cable para medir la corriente.

**Multiplexación** Un proceso de enviar múltiples señales de información a la misma vez utilizando un solo cable.

**NGV** Siglas en inglés para vehículo a gas natural.

**Nivel de disparo** El nivel de voltaje al cual debe llegar una onda para activar la visualización en la pantalla.

**NMHC** Siglas en inglés para hidrocarburos no metánicos.

**NTC** Siglas en inglés para coeficiente de temperatura negativa. Usualmente utilizado en referencia a los sensores de temperatura (de refrigerante o de temperatura ambiente). A medida que la temperatura aumenta, la resistencia del sensor disminuye.

**OBD** Siglas en inglés para diagnóstico a bordo.

**Obstrucción por vapor** Combustible vaporizado, usualmente en las líneas de combustible, que previene o aplaza la provisión del combustible a los cilindros.

**Operación de circuito abierto** Fase de la operación computarizada del motor en la cual la mezcla de aire y combustible se calcula en la ausencia de las señales del sensor de oxígeno. Durante esta fase, los cálculos se basan principalmente en la posición del acelerador, las RPM del motor y la temperatura del refrigerante del motor.

**Operación de circuito cerrado**    Una fase en la operación computarizada del motor en la cual los datos del sensor de oxígeno se utilizan para calcular nivel de la mezcla aire/ combustible.

**Orden de encendido**    La orden para que la chispa sea distribuida a la bujía correcta y en el momento preciso.

**Orgánico**    Un termino que se utiliza para describir algo que alguna vez haya gozado de vida.

**ORVR**    Siglas en inglés para sistemas de diagnóstico a bordo y recuperación de vapores.

**Osciloscopio**    Un medidor que muestra una visualización de los niveles de voltaje en una pantalla.

**Ozono**    $(O_3)$ Gas rico en oxígeno formado por la combinación de hidrocarburos (HC) sin quemar y óxidos de nitrógeno ($NO_x$) en la presencia de la luz solar. También llamado niebla tóxica (esmog).

**Parámetro de identificación**    La información que se encuentra en el flujo de datos vehiculares y que se visualiza en un instrumento de medición electrónico.

**PCV**    Siglas en inglés para válvula de ventilación positiva del cárter.

**Pendiente de disparo**    Dirección de voltaje que una onda debe tener para comenzar visualización en la pantalla. Una pendiente positiva requiere que el voltaje aumente mientras cruza el nivel del disparado; una pendiente negativa requiere que el voltaje disminuya.

**Petrodiésel**    Otro término para el diésel de petróleo, que es el combustible diésel ordinario refinado del crudo de petróleo.

**Petróleo**    Otro termino para el crudo de petróleo. El significado literal de petróleo es "aceite de piedra".

**PID**    Siglas en inglés para identificación de parámetro.

**Ping**    Quemado rápido secundario de los últimos 3% a 5% de la mezcla de aire/combustible en la cámara de combustión que causa un segundo frente de llama que choca con el primer frente de flama causando un ruido de golpeteo.

**Polaridad**    La condición positiva o negativa en relación con un polo magnético.

**Procesamiento de datos o información**    Los cambios que una computadora ejecuta sobre las señales de entrada a fin de convertirlas en información útil. Estos procesos usualmente requieren un convertidor de análogo a digital y otros circuitos electrónicos que eliminan la interferencia.

**Proceso Fischer-Tropsch**    Un proceso de refinación mediante el cual se convierte el carbón, gas natural u otros productos del petróleo a combustibles sintéticos para motores.

**PROM**    Siglas en inglés para memoria programable de sólo lectura.

**Propano**    *Véase LPG.*

**Prueba de capacidad de carga**    Un tipo de prueba de la batería donde se aplica una carga eléctrica a la batería y se monitorea el voltaje para determinar el estado de la batería.

**Prueba de fuga eléctrica de la batería**    Una prueba para determinar si un componente o circuito está causando que la batería se agote.

**Prueba SHED**    Prueba para determinar las emisiones por evaporación en vehículos a motor, mediante la recolección de éstas en una cabina sellada.

**Pulgadas de mercurio**    Unidad de medida utilizada para medir un vacío o presión por debajo de la presión atmosférica.

**PWM**    Siglas en inglés para modulación del ancho de pulso. Operación de un aparato variando el tiempo de encendido de la corriente que fluye por el aparato.

**RAM**    Siglas en inglés para memoria de acceso aleatorio. Una memoria electrónica de tipo temporal utilizada para propósitos de almacenamiento y recuperación de la información.

**RAM de memoria no volátil**    La cualidad de una memoria electrónica que no se pierde cuando se corta el flujo de energía a la computadora. *Véase también ROM.*

**Reactancia inductiva**    Una corriente opuesta que se genera en un conductor de electricidad cuando existe una corriente que fluye por dicho conductor.

**Recirculación de los gases de escape (*EGR* por sus siglas en inglés)**    Un proceso en el que se pasa una cantidad pequeña y medida del gas de escape al motor para reducir las temperaturas de combustión y la formación de $NO_x$ (óxidos de nitrógeno).

**Red**    Un sistema de comunicaciones utilizado para conectar múltiples computadoras o módulos entre sí.

**Red de control de área**    Un tipo de transmisión de datos en serie.

**Relación aire/combustible**    La relación entre aire y combustible en una entrada de combustible determinada por el peso.

**Resistor terminal**    Un resistor colocado en el extremo de un circuito de transmisión de datos en serie de alta velocidad a fin de reducir la interferencia electromagnética.

**Resolución del medidor**    Las especificaciones de un medidor que indican a qué grado de precisión puede detectar y mostrar una medida el medidor.

**RFG**    Siglas en inglés de gasolina reformulada. La gasolina reformulada tiene aditivos oxigenados y ha sido refinada con el propósito de reducir tanto el contenido de los hidrocarburos más pesados como el de los más livianos de la gasolina a fin de promover una combustión más limpia de la misma.

**RMS**    Siglas en inglés para la media cuadrática. También se conoce como valor eficaz.

**ROM**    Siglas en inglés para memoria de sólo lectura. Una memoria electrónica de tipo permanente programada por el fabricante de computadoras para almacenar los comandos operativos y los parámetros guía de la computadora.

**RVP**    Siglas en inglés para presión de vapor Reid. Una medida de la volatilidad a exactamente 38 grados centígrados (100 grados Fahrenheit).

**Saturación**    El punto en que el nivel de fuerza de un campo magnético alcanza el máximo.

**Sensor BARO**    Un sensor utilizado para medir la presión barométrica.

**Sensor de compensación del combustible**    Un sensor utilizado en vehículos de combustible flexible que proporciona información al módulo de control del tren de fuerza acerca del contenido de etanol y la temperatura del combustible a medida que éste pasa a través del sistema de distribución del combustible.

**Sensor de golpeteo**    Sensor que puede detectar el golpeteo de chispa del motor.

**Sensor de posición de la mariposa/válvula de admisión**    El sensor que proporciona información de datos sobre la posición de la placa de la mariposa.

**Sensor detector de presión absoluta de admisión**    Un sensor utilizado para medir la presión dentro del múltiple de admisión en comparación con un vacío perfecto.

**SIDI** Siglas en inglés de inyección directa por encendido de chispa.

**Sincronización electrónica de chispa** El control del avance de la sincronización de chispa que se lleva a cabo por medio de la computadora.

**SIP** Siglas en inglés para Plan de implementación estatal.

**Sistema binario** Un sistema de computadora que usa una serie compuesta de ceros y unos para representar la información.

**Sistema de encendido de bobina en bujía** Un sistema de encendido sin distribuidor (estático) en el cual cada bujía de encendido está integrada con un bobinado de encendido.

**Sistema de encendido electrónico** Es el término general usado para describir cualquiera de los múltiples tipos de sistema de ignición o encendido que utilizan componentes electrónicos en lugar de mecánicos, tales como puntos de encendido o de contacto.

**Sistema de inyección secuencial de combustible** Un sistema de inyección de combustible en el cual se pulsan los inyectores individuales en sucesión.

**Sistema electrónico de combustible sin retorno** Un sistema de provisión de combustible que no devuelve el combustible al tanque.

**Sistema mecánico de combustible sin retorno** Un diseño de sistema de provisión de combustible que no devuelve el combustible al tanque, que utiliza un regulador de presión mecánico localizado en el tanque de combustible.

**Sistema OBD II genérico** *Véase* Sistema OBD II global.

**Sistema OBD II global (Versión 2 de Diagnósticos a bordo global)** El formato estándar de diagnósticos a bordo para todos los vehículos y que sigue el estándar SAE J1962. El OBD II global fue diseñado por ingenieros y cuando se introdujo al mercado por primera vez no fue con la intención de ser utilizado por técnicos de servicio automotriz.

**Sociedad de Ingenieros Automotrices (*SAE* por sus siglas en inglés)** Una organización profesional compuesta de ingenieros y diseñadores automotrices que propone y fija estándares para la industria automotriz y lleva a cabo pruebas en relación a diversas funciones automovilísticas.

**Sonda lambda** Un sensor de oxigeno o de $O_2$. La letra lambda es la letra griega que representa proporción, es decir la relación aire/combustible.

**Sonda lógica** Un tipo de medidor que puede detectar tanto la presencia de energía eléctrica como una conexión a tierra. La mayoría de los medidores pueden detectar un voltaje pero la mayoría no puede detectar la presencia de una conexión a tierra sin la necesidad de llevar a cabo pruebas adicionales.

**Syn gas** Gas sintético creado como resultado de una reacción química entre el vapor de agua y el carbón. El gas sintético está principalmente compuesto de hidrogeno y monóxido de carbono y se utiliza para crear metanol. El syn gas también es conocido como gas artificial.

**Tabique deflector** Una placa o pantalla utilizada para dirigir el flujo de un líquido o de un gas.

**TAME** Siglas en inglés de ter-amil metil eter. Un combustible oxigenado que es utilizado como un aditivo de la gasolina similar al *ETBE* o *MTBE*.

**TBI** Siglas en inglés para inyección de cuerpo de la mariposa/válvula de admisión.

**Tecnología gas a líquido (*GTL* por sus siglas en inglés)** Un proceso de refinación mediante el cual el gas natural se convierte en líquido.

**TEL** Siglas en inglés de plomo tetra etílico El *TEL* fue utilizado como un aditivo antidetonante en la gasolina, pero fue remplazado por aditivos más benignos tales como el etanol.

**Tensión de polarización** En términos eléctricos, una tensión de polarización es un voltaje que se aplica a un aparato o componente para establecer un punto de referencia para su operación.

**TID** Siglas en inglés para identificación de trabajo.

**Tiempo base/unidad de tiempo** La cantidad fija de tiempo por división cuando se regula un osciloscopio.

**Tiempo de encendido** Punto exacto del encendido con relación a la posición del pistón.

**Tiempo de permanencia** Cantidad de tiempo, registrado en grados por un medidor de tiempo de permanencia, que un voltaje pasa por un interruptor cerrado.

**Transistor** Dispositivo semiconductor que puede funcionar como un interruptor eléctrico o un amplificador.

**Tren de pulsos** Voltaje de corriente directa que se enciende y apaga en una serie de pulsos.

**UCG** Siglas en inglés para gasificación subterránea de carbón.

**ULSD** Siglas en ingles de diésel de contenido sulfúrico ultra bajo. Combustible diésel con un contenido de sulfuro máximo de 15 partes por millón.

**Unidad térmica británica (*British Thermal Unit* o BTU)** Una unidad de medida de calor. Un BTU de calor aumentará la temperatura de una libra de agua por un grado Fahrenheit.

**Vacío** Cualquier presión menor a la presión atmosférica (14.7 psi a nivel de mar).

**Válvula de puerto de ventilación a presión** Una válvula ubicada en el tanque de combustible para prevenir una sobrepresión debido a la expansión térmica del combustible.

**Vehículo eléctrico híbrido** Describe cualquier vehículo que utiliza más de un modo de propulsión, tal como un motor de combustión interna y un motor eléctrico.

**V-FFV** Siglas en inglés de Vehiculo de combustible flexible virtual. Este diseño de sistema de combustible no utiliza un sensor de compensación del combustible y a cambio usa el sensor de oxígeno del vehículo para compensar por las diferentes composiciones del combustible.

**Volátil** La memoria RAM volátil se pierde cuando se apaga el encendido.

**Volatilidad** Una medida de la tendencia de un líquido para pasar al estado gaseoso. La volatilidad se mide usando la presión de vapor Reid o RVP.

**WWFC** Siglas en inglés para Convenio mundial de combustibles. Un estándar de calidad de combustible desarrollado por fabricantes de motores y vehículos en el año 2002.

# INDEX